A QUEER HISTORY OF NEWFOUNDLAND

RHEA ROLLMANN

Published in Canada by Engen Books, Chapel Arm, NL.

Library and Archives Canada Cataloguing in Publication information is available upon request.

Print: 978-1-77478-144-9
eBook: 978-1-77478-145-6

Distributed by:
Engen Books
www.engenbooks.com
submissions@engenbooks.com

First mass market paperback printing: October 2023

Cover Design: Ellen Curtis

Cover Photo Credits:
Top Row, Left-Right: 1,2, 3, 5 - Derrick Bishop, 4 - Aimee Finlay, 6 - Kris Elder
Middle Row, Left-Right: 7 - Susan Rose, 8 - Kris Elder, 9-11 - Derrick Bishop, 12 - Gerald Hannon
Bottom Row, Left-Right:13, 14, 17, 18 - Derrick Bishop, 15 - Aimee Finlay, 16 - Susan Rose

We are grateful for help and funding from the City of St. John's, the Canada Council of the Arts, and ArtsNL during this project.

A QUEER HISTORY OF NEWFOUNDLAND

RHEA ROLLMANN

Dedicated to the memory of:

Jeanie Sheppard
Felicia Faye
Liam Hustins
Alexandria Tucker
Julie Berman

and all those who led the way

CONTENTS

INTRODUCTION

In 2007 I accidentally wound up as an organizer for St. John's Pride. I was working with the Students' Union at Memorial University, and decided we ought to have a Pride Week on campus. I was not yet out as trans, and wasn't really part of the queer community per se, although as a young partygoing NLer I was inevitably involved to some degree in all of the city's communities, as one often is in St. John's.

I had heard under-the-breath rumours from queer activists on campus that there were tensions between "campus queers" and "downtown [non-student] queers" so I decided I ought to find out who was organizing St. John's Pride and try to establish a friendly relationship, so the two Prides could proceed in as friendly and non-competitive a manner as possible. After making inquiries, I discovered that in fact there was no real plan for St. John's Pride (this was before the founding of St. John's Pride Inc.). So my close friend Stel Magalios (Campaigns Director at the Students' Union) and I wound up setting up a committee that would effectively organize the city's Pride Week. It was open - anybody who was interested could be on it - and our meetings were advertised publicly for anyone who wanted to show up.

It was a surprisingly fun and mostly harmonious experience (a rarity for Pride organizing, I have learned). We lacked any formal structure, so decision-making was consensus-based and very ad hoc. I managed to find the organizer of the previous year's Pride; he dropped by my house with a bag full of leftover t-shirts, a bit of cash wrapped in rubber bands, and some glitter sticks. "Good luck!" he said as he handed it to me with evident glee.

There were already one-off events being planned locally; the gay bar was going to have a dance night; a local queer-owned tour company was going to have a gay harbour cruise (several of our organizing meetings were held on the boat). Our ad hoc committee gave the entire week some structure and brought everyone together.

It was chaotic and fun. I recall driving downtown to the flag-raising ceremony at City Hall (which we had organized) and discovering en route that we were expected to provide the flag (we had none). Fortunately during the panicked drive to City Hall we passed a downtown business establishment that was flying a rainbow flag, and we clambered up the front of the building and absconded with it (we returned it later, naturally).

City Hall accidentally approved an open bar for the Pride Week reception (on the City's tab), a beautiful mistake that would go down in queer history. What began as an awkward and stilted formal ceremony morphed into the sexiest dance party ever witnessed at City Hall (a disco ball appeared from who-knows-where at one point, and most dancers were in varying states of undress by the end of it).

The Pride March was an unexpected delight. I remember showing up half an hour before the scheduled start time and panicking because no one was there. True-to-Newfoundland-form, during the last ten minutes literally hundreds of people showed up seemingly out of nowhere, and we had the city's biggest march yet. Myself and Stel had walked the march route previously to figure out the best route, but we had not marched it with hundreds of people behind us; the actual march felt a bit like driving a car for the first time. A police escort showed up to lead the march, but in the chaos of it all we accidentally forced the cop car off the road and trapped it down an alleyway, where it remained stuck until the march was over (it was an accident, honest!).

It was during that week that I first began grappling with the gaps in NL queer history. As I was preparing speaking notes and media materials, I wanted to find out when Pride Week had first been celebrated in NL. No one seemed to know; which is to say, everyone I asked had a different answer. So in an effort to ascertain the truth I spent a glorious day in the Centre for Newfoundland Studies at Memorial University, and that's when I discovered the queer archives located there (which I discuss in Chapter 8). I became absorbed; mesmerized. I had never imagined what a rich queer history existed in this province. The material I pored over raised as many questions as it provided answers.

I determined at that point to return to those archives one day. I remember thinking to myself 'This would make a great book!' and dreamed of one day writing it.

This is that book.

I returned to those archives at various points over the years, especially as I started working as a journalist and wrote articles engaging with the province's queer history. But that dream of putting it all together in a book someday never went away. Every visit to the archives fuelled it with greater and greater intensity.

When the COVID pandemic hit in 2020, I like many others found myself wondering what to do with myself as lockdowns set in and remote work became the norm. It was a frightening time, and I decided I needed a focus, something to give me purpose while the rest of my daily life seemed to be falling apart. So I decided to write that book I had always dreamed of.

Over three years later, here we are. My approach to the book has shifted tremendously over the past few years of working on it. Initially my plan was simply to take what I could find in the archives, put it in a loose order and present it as a narrative. I thought the book would be mostly archival based.

But the more I studied the archives, the more I realized their limitations. Archival material is tremendously helpful, but is of limited value without the people who lived through the period and shaped it. Their perspectives help bring the archives to life, and help the documents make sense. There were news stories that contradicted each other; journalists from the period made plenty of errors. There were euphemisms and things clearly omitted from the record. How was I to make sense of the gaps, the awkward silences, the many spots where media archives were conflicted or even just plain wrong about what had happened in the past?

I began hunting down some of the past activists whose names appeared in the archives, and reaching out to them. I started doing interviews. As a journalist, this was familiar and even comforting territory for me. One interview would often lead to two, three, ten more, as interviewees put me in contact with other folks from the period. The richness of the stories that emerged was astonishing. I began to look at the archives - and the entire period - in a whole new light.

So what initially I had thought would be a straightforward work of archival history, started to become more of a community oral history.

I have, at this stage, done over 120 interviews with members of the queer community from the years covered in this book. I have interviewed some people multiple times; some of the interviews have been group sessions that came to resemble activist reunions (I'm delighted to say that this work even rekindled some former, decades-old friendships between activists). That, combined with the archival work I have also done - at the CNS, The Rooms, with the ArQuives in Toronto, and elsewhere - forms the basis of this book.

As the book progressed, I found I had to make some difficult decisions. In retrospect, I don't know what I was thinking in proposing to cover an entire century of queer history in one book. Sometimes one can take on ridiculously audacious tasks without realizing how audacious they are, and then by the time one realizes, they're already mostly done. I suppose I am grateful for my ignorance in that respect, but it led to tough decisions as I tried to give the book final form.

As I acquired a publisher and a deadline, I had to make tough calls. The more interviews I did, the more suggestions of other people I should talk to I was given. I couldn't very well interview every queer person in NL, but began to feel the pressure that I ought to do so. My list of prospective interviewees to contact became insurmountable, and I realized I would never be able to get to them all if I intended to get the book submitted on time (in fact, the book is over a year behind schedule, and I still haven't gotten to them all). I do feel a sense of regret for many of the interviews I was unable to get to, because I know there are many more incredible stories to be told than I have been able to tell in these pages. As I was introduced to queer folks - especially queer elders - whom I had never heard of before, I encountered incredible stories from these people and realized there are undoubtedly many more people out there I do not know who also have incredible stories to tell. I'm sure with more time I could have discovered and included some of these.

But I had a publisher (albeit a very flexible and forgiving one) and a deadline, and realized I would never be able to talk to everyone and fit everything in. My hope therefore is that what I have been able to put together in this book - fully acknowledging its incomplete and partial nature - will serve as a foundation for future work, both from myself and others. I hope there may one day be an updated and expanded version of this book which will include even more of these important stories. I hope that some of those people I haven't yet had the chance to interview - and others whom I don't even know and have never met - will come forward and share their stories with me for that future work. I hope to be able to tell those additional stories one day. I am sorry for all the people and stories that did not make it into this book, and I know that if you lived here during the period covered by this book, you might feel a bit jilted that you are not a part of it. You're right to feel that way – I think everyone who lived here during that period has an important part of that history to contribute. So if you're reading this and feeling that way, I do apologize for omitting you and your contribution to this history; and I would love to be in contact to document your stories for future work.

The original draft of this book was over 1000 pages long. You can imagine how many stories and how much material I had to omit during the editing process.

Style and Method

I have always been torn between my duelling identities of journalist and academic, and struggled with the appropriate balance to achieve in this book. At one point I had stacks of theoretical, academic queer studies by my bedside, and considered putting an intellectual sheen on this work by doing some theoretical analyses (I saw so many unexplored opportunities for this with NL queer historical content). But in the end, I mostly opted for a journalistic approach. NL's queer history is a vibrant story that needs to be told, and I wanted to tell that story. I wanted to get the basic facts and information out there, and to provide it in an accessible form that everyone can read. There is still plenty of room for those intellectual studies to come.

Because of the limitations of archival and media records, much of this history is told through the form of storytelling. The reason I share large excerpts of individual lives is not just because I find them interesting and important, but because I hope readers will be able to develop an understanding of what it was like to live during those times, by witnessing the times through the first-hand experiences of those whose stories I share.

I struggled with what to call this book. "The Queer History of Newfoundland" was the title I used in my pitch to publishers and funding agencies because it sounded good. But I was intellectually uncomfortable with it. First of all - what about Labrador? And secondly, it seemed audacious to call it "The

Queer History of Newfoundland" given how much of that history I knew would not be able to fit into the book. Myself and my publisher debated a variety of other prospective titles that I felt were more honest.

But as the book took shape over these past few years, I came back to the original title. Only it wasn't "*The* Queer History of Newfoundland"; it was "*A* Queer History of Newfoundland." That one little word – just a letter – is an important distinction, and was an important part of me coming to accept what my role in documenting this history is. There are many, many queer histories to be told, in and about Newfoundland (and Labrador). This is just one. I hope those other queer histories will also be told one day.

The book does focus almost exclusively on the island of Newfoundland. There are of course Labradorians in it, and some mention of Labrador. But I didn't want to make just a token gesture to Labrador in order to claim that I had done it; I felt Labradorians deserve more than that. So I kept the title limited to Newfoundland, to reflect that that is what the book focuses on. Labrador has its own rich and vibrant queer history, and I knew that to tell it I would need to go there, spend time there, immerse myself in the place and its people just as I had done here in Newfoundland. Knowing that I would not have the time or capacity to do that for this book, the title reflects its island focus. I hope that Labrador's queer history will also be told one day, by myself or others.

Chronologically, I focus only on the twentieth century. Granted, I do skirt around the edges a bit — I discuss the 19th century lives of some characters who died in the early 20th century; and I trace the lives of some 1990s-era activists into the present century. But for all intents and purposes my focus is the 20th century. I chose this cut-off point for a few reasons. With the advent of the Internet, the range and style of archival records becomes more complex. Queer activism flourished dramatically in the first two decades of the twenty-first century, and to document all of this more recent history — archived extensively via the Internet – would have taken a tremendous amount of additional time and work. Also, the turn of the century provided a timely cut-off point in that the long-running campaign to achieve human rights protections around sexual orientation — a campaign first started in the early 1970s – finally succeeded with a legislative amendment at the end of 1997. This book in many ways is a story of that struggle (with various side-trips along the way) and so it provided a neat end-point to the book.

Trans activism really kicked into high gear in the last couple of years of the century, and so I trace that movement a bit farther. My initial hope was to connect the early emergence of gender-affirming care in the province in the late 1990s (as chronicled in this book) with the present state of affairs for trans folks, and explicate the many twists and turns gender-affirming care has taken in this province in the past two decades. And while I was able to collect the rough materials and interviews to accomplish this, I realized once again that it was a more complex story that would require a lot more time, space and research to tell properly. So I end this portion of the book in 1999 (I continue to work on the broader history of local trans activism and gender-affirming care on my own and hope to publish it in some fashion some day). Another decision this approach led to was my choice not to chronicle the fight for same-sex marriage rights. It was already well underway in the late 1990s, and continued into the new century. I initially began documenting that struggle, but realized it would take too much time and space to do justice to it, and so I decided to save that incredible story for another day as well.

This book contains a lot of oral history, gathered through first-hand interviews with activists and members of the community. The people I interviewed were in some cases quite up-front about the haziness of their memories, given that we were discussing events that took place up to fifty years ago (or more). Other interviewees were very confident in their memories, but the stories they told contradicted other accounts. Wherever possible, I tried to do independent verification of elements of their stories – through media archives, cross-checking with other interviewees, etc – and sometimes I went back and forth with interviewees, clarifying elements, drilling down on hazy points so as to try to ferret out the veracity of events and chronologies. But in many cases, there was simply no way to independently corroborate the accounts I was given. I am satisfied that the majority of what I was told was accurate; however, it is always possible that stories and accounts may have been mis-remembered, embellished, or subject to other errors. Such is the nature of oral history, and I would flag this as a caveat to readers. Nevertheless, I am satisfied that the overwhelming majority of what I was told – especially insofar as it represents peoples' personal, first-hand, subjective experiences of these years – is broadly accurate.

When it comes to terminology used, for the most part I defer to my interviewees when I am quoting them. They deploy a variety of terms for related concepts – gay, queer, LGBT, etc. For reasons I explain below, I prefer the term 'queer' in most contexts, but when I am quoting people or discussing those quotes I use the language chosen by the interviewees. One exception comes to discussion of trans and non-binary identities. In most cases, when I am discussing trans individuals – or even quoting from the archival record – I use the present name and pronouns of the individual in question (even if that requires changing the pronouns in published material or in quotes from interviews). An exception is those cases where the trans or non-binary individual specifically requested me to do otherwise.

What is queer history?

The term 'queer' provoked differing reactions among folks I spoke with. A few folks, especially those from older generations, were still disinclined toward the term, preferring the nomenclature "LGBTQ+" or variants thereof.

Some older participants very flatly stated that they still refer to everything as "gay" while recognizing that includes lesbian, trans, and other identities (for others, it was considered unacceptable to collapse all the other identities under the single term 'gay'). Suffice it to say that there was no universal consensus on what term is preferable; there never has been.

And yet, 'queer' remained not only the broadest and most inclusive term (by way of its own generative vagueness) but also the preferred term of the majority of participants in this history. There is today a sort of poorly articulated effort - mostly by bigots - to denounce the term 'queer' and pretend that it provokes widespread offence, or that it's a recent term. Those claims are historically inaccurate. While there has always been critique of every term and nomenclature, one of my interviewees[1] put it best, recalling similar debates in the early 1990s:

"Myself and my buddy did up posters that we put up around town about reclaiming the word queer and why that was a thing. I see discourse now about people reclaiming queer, and I'm like: Oh honey. Honey. I was late to that party, and that was 1993. Like come on."

So what is queer? When I was in graduate school at York University in Toronto I took a fascinating course in Queer History from the esteemed queer historian Marc Stein, and his syllabus provided what I think is still one of the most succinct definitions of the term and the variety of possibilities it encompasses:

"Queer theory emerged in the early 1990s, developing in dialogue with bisexual, gay, intersex, lesbian, queer, transgender, and transsexual political formations and with scholarship in what was then generally called "gay and lesbian studies." One of the original motivations of queer theory was to reclaim, re-appropriate, and re-signify the term "queer," which had often been wielded as a weapon of hostility and violence but which had a different set of meanings within queer cultures. Since the early 1990s, queer theory has come to have multiple meanings. Some use the term "queer" to encompass bisexual, gay, intersex, lesbian, queer, transgender, transsexual, and a variety of other sexed, gendered, and sexualized phenomena. "Queer" is also used to refer to radical, dissident, subversive, and transgressive possibilities in the realms of sex, gender, and sexuality, which implies that conservative lesbian, gay, bi, and trans formations are nonqueer and that non-normative heterosexual formations might be queer. For scholars focused on intersections of sex, gender, and sexuality with other categories of power and difference – including ability, class, race, and religion – the term "queer" can be used to challenge multiple social, cultural, and political hierarchies. "Queer" can also refer to poststructural conceptions of sex, gender, and sexuality that are anti-essentialist, antiidentitarian, and anti-minoritarian. In this latter sense queer theory deconstructs the dominant order and destabilizes the definitions and classifications that sustain that order, including classifications such as "heterosexuality"

---

[1] Chris St. Croix

and "homosexuality." Each of these uses of "queer" has also generated opposition..." (Stein, 2009, 1).

If you find that a bit difficult to wrap your head around, consider this approach, which is how I described the term before I went to grad school and started speaking like the above quote. I used to say that 'queer' was similar to the term 'punk' - not just in being a reclaimed identity, but particularly in being a subversive one. The term is oppositional, defiant, and deliberately difficult to define. What does it mean to call something 'punk'? It refers broadly to an attitude, a sensibility, an orientation, but it is also eminently subjective and subject to change. Something that might have been 'punk' twenty years ago may no longer be considered 'punk.' Something that's 'punk rock' in one context might not be in another context. If punk refers to defiance against power and authority, then the fact that power and authority is constantly shifting means that the definition of punk is constantly shifting too. It's slippery, constantly morphing to avoid being appropriated by the very same cultural elements it seeks to challenge. Queer is a very similar beast, at least for me. So yes, on a superficial level the term is a useful stand-in for "2SLGBTQIA+" and its kin. But it is also so much more than that.

The book's title itself has multiple readings. It is "A Queer History of Newfoundland" not only in the sense that it provides a history of queer community and activism in Newfoundland. I also strive to provide what is in a sense a history of Newfoundland (in the twentieth century) as seen through a queer lens. The histories we are often provided of Newfoundland – in school, in media narratives, in books – are those seen through the lens of rich and powerful white men. Here, then, is a history of Newfoundland – from its early years as a Dominion, through the Depression, through the vibrant 1960s and '70s and beyond – as seen through the lens of its queer community. I have tried to pay attention to painting a picture of the times - as experienced by queer people - in addition to chronicling the activism and community-building that went on. History is experienced differently by different people. Here, then, is how our twentieth century history was experienced by queers.

This history was challenging to write. Aside from the technical challenges of working with the interviews and archives, much of it hit close to home. There is pain, sadness, and death in these pages. There are large sections of the book that still bring me to tears every time I read them. Given how many times I have had to read over sections during the editing process, I have shed many, many tears. The sections dealing with trans histories and individuals in particular were very personal, and I explore some of the challenges of working with them in Chapter 8.

"A death, however tragic, is only a very small part of a life," writes Emily Berry in an article for *The Guardian* (Berry 2023). She's discussing Sylvia Plath, and the manner in which "the circumstances around her death have been described, fictionalised, analysed – sometimes sensitively, more often voyeuristically – in biographies, memoirs, films and literature." A similar thing could be said of trans and queer deaths, particularly suicides. Berry praises Plath's biographer Heather Clark for how she "sought to make the poet's life, not her death, the driving force of her book." I employ a similar method here, trying to present the richness and vibrancy of queer and trans lives. While it is important for us to acknowledge the often violent nature of their deaths and fight to change the circumstances which render this a still common reality today, their deaths were only a small part of their lives, and it is their lives that we should seek to know, honour and celebrate.

But there is also tremendous queer and trans joy in this book. And I hope it is that which will linger in the reader's mind – a sense of how rich, joyful and wonderful it is to be queer; how special and important queer identity is; and the many varied forms it has taken here in Newfoundland and Labrador.

Doing queer archival work

There are various common themes or tropes that emerge when it comes to how our queer history is re/presented. I wish to engage with some of these here.

There is, first of all, the notion that being queer in NL is a recent thing. This is total nonsense, as I hope this book helps demonstrate. There have always been queers in NL: sexual and gender non-conformists who today would fall all along the spectrum of identities which includes gay, lesbian, bi, trans, Two Spirit, and more. The notion that queerness is a recent thing, or a "mainland" thing, is one of those tropes used by oppressive institutions (like the powerful churches) to try to marginalize and 'other' those identities which challenge their social and political hegemony. Early AIDS activists encountered this from government: "there are none of *those* people here" was a common refrain from government officials. Sexual orientation protections were resisted by the provincial government in the 1970s with the excuse that they were unnecessary because neither homosexuals nor homophobia existed in Newfoundland. Two decades later, government officials were making the same - completely untrue - arguments.

This notion has even been absorbed, to some degree, by some queer people themselves. When I reached out to older activists for interviews and told them I was writing a book on NL's queer history, the response of some of them was literally "oh that'll be a short book!" This, despite the evidence of rich queer culture stretching back into the early part of the twentieth century and beyond.

This, then, is the first myth to be busted: NL's queer history is in fact deep, rich, long and complex. It has been affected by mainland connections, yes, but it has had an equally powerful impact on mainland queer identities and activism too, as we shall see.

And let's also dispel the notion that queer research in NL is a recent thing. It's not either. Ever since queer activists began organizing, they've been documenting and archiving this process. Librarian-activists began archiving their movement in collections at Memorial University as far back as the 1970s. There are literally crates upon crates of feminist and queer archives in the various city archives. And there's been a plethora of scholarly archival and research work done as well. Lynn Hartery (2001), Sharp Dopler (1996), and Brenda Ponic all conducted graduate research in these areas in the 1990s, and many more have come to fill their ranks in the years since.

A second trope or theme that emerges when we think about the province's queer history, is the notion of Newfoundland exceptionalism: the idea that things were (and are) somehow different here. As an island culture this notion emerges frequently in all spheres. One of the manifestations of this exceptionalism is the idea that homophobia didn't exist here (either because homosexuals didn't exist here, or because NLers are by nature nicer and kinder and more accepting than people on the mainland). These misleading ideas are perpetuated by the frequently-encountered upbeat, progressivist strain of NL queer history which acknowledges NL's rich and deep queer history but tends to ignore the darker sides of it. There are a plethora of social media groups that promote a constant stream of images, posters and archival snippets from the past which convey the impression that NL's queer history was vibrant, active and full of fun and life – and so it was! But they downplay – intentionally or unintentionally – the dark side: the homophobia; the violence; the racism; the bigotry of institutions and communities. There were instances of transphobia within queer spaces for many years, and this is often ignored. Even some academics perpetuate this false sense of positivity, by indulging in social media engagement that is stacked toward the positive and by failing to provide a more complete context for what they share. Yes, there were positive moments, spaces, and projects throughout NL queer history. But there was also tremendous violence and harm visited upon queers. It's important to recognize the nuanced nature of this history, and how our present has been shaped by both the darkness and the light.

This book strives to push back against both of the above tendencies. Our history is long and deep and complex. It is full of darkness as well as light. It's important to acknowledge this in order to fully understand it, and to understand each other.

How do we do queer history?

This is a question I wrestled with. As I struggled to chart my own path through this work, and witnessed others doing the same, I came to some interesting and sometimes uncomfortable realizations.

In a capitalist world, any academic or intellectual undertaking is also a hustle. Queer history is no different. Queer research is a hustle. Academics, both queer and straight, strive to build careers the way academics do, by amassing grants and publications and forming initiatives that bring in revenue and secure them jobs. In this day and age many of them make their livelihoods off of queer history (as they do other forms of history). There is nothing wrong with this in a sense; everyone needs to make a living. And these histories are ones that ought to be told, studied, and learned from.

And yet, there is also a form of subtle (and sometimes not-to-subtle) violence packed up in this. Picture the aspiring queer historian: armed with a SSHRC grant,[2] driving out to the outport to interview a queer elder. That elder lives in a rundown shack. They never completed university because they were drummed out because of their queer nonconformity or their activism. Or perhaps they did complete university; perhaps they had a job as a professor when they were outed or fell afoul of social mores and didn't have their contract renewed. Perhaps they were an activist, waging a fiery fight for change until they succumbed to the inevitable infighting that occurs within activist organizations, or lost their job when government de-funded their precariously funded organization. They struggle with mental health issues from the trauma and oppression they experienced over the course of their life. They're poor, without a pension, without a source of income, without family, living on welfare cheques. They cannot afford therapy, counselling, or even proper health care.

The academic drives into the community in their newly leased car, interviews the elder, takes their story, writes it up in a publication, wins an award, gets a promotion, gets a raise. The elder whose story they took experiences a double form of oppression: oppressed first historically (when they initially lost their job, experienced their trauma) by a homophobic society, and now exploited a second time by the academic who mines their story for material for their own benefit. The academic benefits from the queer elder, but what does the queer elder get? Some minor satisfaction, perhaps, knowing that their name might live on in an obscure journal article somewhere. The brief and passing satisfaction of conversation with another human being who has somewhat of an understanding of what they went through. And yet these two realities are worlds apart. The academic benefits from the work that queer elder did years earlier to create the space in which the academic can now freely thrive and live their best life, both as a queer person and as an academic. And they benefit yet again by being the one to tell the story of that queer elder's suffering, getting to stick it in their book or document for their queer research initiative. To get another grant, another line on their CV.

I don't know what the solution is to this dilemma. During the course of my research, I've encountered so many poor, traumatized, hurting queer el-

---

[2] Social Science and Humanities Research Council – the primary federal agency funding academic research in the humanities and social sciences in Canada.

ders (and many not-so-elderly, too). Their stories are important to document, and their lives are important to know and to celebrate. But they deserve more than that. To be treated merely as research subjects and cast off; to have their stories fund the jobs and research initiatives that keep young white academics employed without any compensation for the queer elder living in poverty - this is all a profound injustice. I am probably guilty of this myself. I know other queer researchers are too, some more than others. We must grapple with this, honestly and openly, and find a better way of doing what we do - one which shares the risks, honours, and rewards of this type of work.

As a journalist who works in independent media, I am often asked what distinguishes a person-on-the-street who's recording a news event on their cellphone, from a professional 'journalist'. This is a complex debate, but one of the answers I give is that a journalist always works within a transparent ethical framework. I think queer researchers must do the same. Here, then, are some of the elements of my own ethical framework as I undertake this work.

Queer people are experts in their own lives. This should go without saying, but it often does need saying. It needs saying especially to government bureaucrats and to academics. Queer people don't need to be 'mentored' in how to research their lives and they shouldn't have to hire consultants or 'experts' to present their needs to government. Yet bureaucrats and academics alike tend to ignore the learned wisdom and lived experience of queer individuals and communities and insist that queer knowledge-building and knowledge-sharing must conform to their standardized norms and ways of doing things. Queer people must resist this. We must speak for ourselves, learn and develop new ways of building and sharing knowledge rooted in an awareness of the oppression we ourselves have historically experienced.

Historical research needs to be critical research. Okay that sounds smart but I'm not even entirely sure what it means. What I think it means for me is a few things, or rather it's a statement that responds to a few things. I discovered early on that there were a lot of contradictions in the research I was doing. Different people, talking about the same event, tell the story very differently – sometimes in contradictory ways. Sometimes they disagree on facts. Sometimes even news articles disagree on facts. Journalists can make mistakes too, and when we uncritically accept what we encounter in the historical record, we risk replicating those mistakes. I learned to take everything I read, or was told, with a grain of salt. Rather than accept simply one narrative that I encountered, I asked other folks to share with me their version of the same story. What do you do when two people are equally convinced that a historical incident happened in two very different ways? Sometimes you can identify straightforward errors of dates or lack of understanding on someone's part. But sometimes you simply cannot easily reconcile these accounts. In which case you must accept that history is complicated. There is clearly a reason why something is remembered in different ways by different people. Sometimes that reason – the reason they remember an event in a certain way – is what's really important and interesting. So yes, let's be critical and fact-check and seek multiple sources of verification for the things we study. But let's also sometimes be willing to accept that multiple interpretations or understandings of events can exist. History is complex.

And it's nuanced. *It's important to contextualize what we learn.* When I see people randomly posting excerpts of articles or ephemera from the 1960s or '70s or '80s I am often critical of it (and yes, I sometimes do it too, because I get that it's fun and sometimes you just want to share something really neat). But it can undermine the broader task of historical and cultural understanding, because when it's presented without context, people can often derive the wrong lessons from it, or miss the important lessons that could be derived from it.

For instance, I've seen folks sometimes posting random photos on social media of queer people together taken a hundred years ago. On the one hand, I appreciate this because yes, it helps to normalize queerness and pushes back against the false narrative that queerness didn't exist in the past. But on the other hand, it deprives those queer people of a voice. It instrumentalizes and objectifies them for the benefit of the contemporary user (often an academic). My work aims to give the queer subjects I work with a voice. I quote anonymously where I am asked. But I also strive to ensure that the queer people I work with are able to speak in their own words, and own their words. I went to a great deal of painstaking work trying to make sure people sharing sensitive or personal stories consented to how their words were presented. Queer subjects have so often had their voices and words either silenced or appropriated, and both are forms of violence. I believe it's important to acknowledge ownership of queer subjects over our words, actions, and histories, while also acknowledging that ownership over these collective histories is shared with the broader queer community. Navigating a balance which respects the rights of both individual and community is challenging, but a challenge worth accepting. It speaks to the heart of what queer research is and should be.

Queer history is one of oppression and resistance. Queer research must acknowledge, respect and participate in that struggle. Queer liberation has been brought about in solidarity with other movements. *Queer research must act in solidarity too.* When I see people forming queer research associations or initiatives, I am compelled to ask: how is the work you are doing a form of resistance against other forms of oppression? Against racism, capitalism, sexism, colonialism? How does it centre critical race theory, critical disability studies, abolition work? How does it engage in working class solidarity? The answers to these questions reveal a great deal about the quality, depth and motivation of queer researchers and initiatives. And it influences and shapes the material they produce.

Queer people must retain control over how their – our – queer history is presented and told. Here too I struggle with my obligations as a journalist, versus my obligations as a human being and member of the queer community. I do believe there are some stories and realities that become the property of the wider community; they are subject to shared ownership or stewardship, if you will. But I also believe that people deserve power, agency and control over their own stories. Drawing on the growing and rich body of thinking around Indigenous archival work - in which there are many parallels and lessons to be drawn - I also think that queer people deserve a 'right of response' to the presentation of archival material about their – our – lives.

How does one achieve this in a practical, tangible, applied way? I worked with many of my interviewees to ensure they were comfortable with how their stories were told, and this often entailed rewriting large sections, and changing or omitting how I presented portions of the material. I sought to achieve a balance between my own sense of what constitutes good scholarship and journalism, and what my interviewees felt properly reflected their experiences. This was difficult work; it was tedious and it contributed to the book being over a year behind schedule. But it's important to undertake this commitment when doing work of this nature. I don't presume that I made all the right calls, or that I even achieved the high aspirational ethical standards that I set for myself - and so I apologize in advance for any mistakes I have made or portions of this book which make contributors feel uncomfortable. I have tried my best, and hope the final work reflects that.

Summing it up: What can we say about NL's queer history?

If there is any generalized statement that can be made about how queerness manifested in this place, it ought to be a recognition of the diversity of experiences that comprises NL's queer history. The sprawling, decentralized nature of population growth and the isolated nature of rural communities meant that every community developed its own features when it came to engaging with queerness. There were some commonalities, but also tremendous difference and variety. Some communities exhibited surprising degrees of tolerance and acceptance for the period. Others inflicted horrific trauma and violence against queer people (and others who exhibited forms of difference).

It is a truism that many of us who are from NL talk about "the way things are" in this province in an authoritative manner which suggests there are certain experiences and behaviours common to everyone here. We tend to generalize from our own experiences, and assume that what we experienced growing up here was the same for everyone. It was not. We must resist such generalizations. Being queer in NL was extremely different for different people.

There is a long-running myth that Newfoundland is a conservative Christian society rooted in 'traditional values.' Like most myths, it obscures the reality. Regardless of what may have been preached at the pulpit, sex outside of marriage was common (regardless of whether one was straight or queer), as was homosexuality and gender-non-normative behaviour."

"Everybody was screwing everybody all the time," said one of my interviewees,[3] referring in this case to Deer Lake, a town of almost 5000 on the island's west coast. As a child growing up and observing the behaviour of adults in the community, it was the double standard that bothered him: the facade of religious virtue which masked people's true behaviour. "What bothered me [most] was the betrayal, the dishonesty," he said.

Likewise, homosexuality was common but people and communities developed varying ways of incorporating it. Several of my interviewees recounted how common it was for boys and young men in rural communities to develop intimate and sexual relationships, yet not all of those young men considered themselves gay. Such behaviour was sometimes ignored or accepted among youth, with the expectation that the boys would 'grow out of it.' One interviewee[4] recounted how a same-sex teenaged sexual partner one day told him it was time for their sexual relationship to end:

"[H]e said to me that he wanted to stop doing this, because he was now becoming a man and men didn't do this. I remember saying to him: 'Well I don't want to stop!' And he said: 'That's because you're a queer.'"

This quote is important: it reflects the distinction some men drew between having sex with men, and being gay or queer. For some – including adults – same-sex sexual behaviour was considered different from being gay, or queer (which were considered identities). "Buddies helping buddies" is how this behaviour was frequently described to me. In a province in which men often wound up in each other's company for long periods - during the seal fishery, in logging camps, on fishing expeditions – it was not uncommon for normally heterosexual men to engage in same-sex activity; there were no women around. Many of these men would be married to women, and have children at home. These men sometimes drew a distinction between purely physical sexual relationships (which they did not believe meant they were gay) and emotional or romantic relationships.

The distinction recurs in other ways later in the twentieth century. As queer activist groups emerged in the 1970s, one thing they grappled with was the question of who was part of the queer community. Joining a queer activist group was in a sense a first step toward coming out – it meant acknowledging one's queer identity, even if only within the privacy of the organization (the early groups were assiduous about privacy and confidentiality, since many of their members remained closeted in their daily lives). But many men who had sex with men didn't even take that step. They would be married to women, sometimes with families, yet regularly have sex with men 'on the side' without telling their wives (some did tell their wives, and even found acceptance for

---

[3] Barry Nichols

[4] John Guiney Yallop

this behaviour within their marriage). Some out queer activists were very critical of this behaviour, and felt it was not fair to the men's families to maintain
this secrecy. This critique became even more pronounced with the spread of
AIDS. In 1987 the Gay Association In Newfoundland (GAIN) estimated that
half the calls they received on their phone support line - including calls from
Labrador – were from gay men who were married and kept their gay sexual
relationships secret from their wives. GAIN representatives pointed out this
was one of the ways in which homophobia was fueling a public health crisis
(Whelan 1997) - had the social taboos against homosexuality and risks to queer
peoples' livelihoods not existed, they might have been more open about their
sexual partners and relationships. And when dozens of men were arrested during the Village Mall scandal of the early 1990s and publicly shamed, it's noteworthy that no queer activists or groups appear to have taken up their cause.
I spoke about this with activists from the period, who attributed it to a variety
of reasons. For some, the fear of being associated with pedophilia – the police
launched the investigation following a complaint from the family of a minor –
deterred them from engaging with the issue. For others, it just didn't occur to
them to get involved because they didn't consider the men to be members of
the queer community. They were predominantly closeted men, many of whom
had straight families.

"How many of those men were gay? I don't know," said one community
member I interviewed.[5] "There are men who simply have sex with men on
occasion. They swear up and down that they are not bisexual and that they
are not gay. And who am I to challenge that person's self-identification?… It's
always been a struggle for me, because as a member of the queer community,
what duty or allegiance do I owe, and to who?"

It should be noted that these dynamics were all very different for women.
One interviewee[6] - who was in fact removed from her community as a young
child and threatened with institutionalization after being found in a physically
intimate situation with another girl – asserted that she would have been treated
very differently if she had been a boy found in that situation.

The upshot of all this is that queerness was everywhere in this province,
and different communities, institutions, families and individuals all developed
differing ways of responding to it. As we now know, homosexuality and queer
and trans identities are a natural part of the human experience; but in NL, like
elsewhere, this natural behaviour came up against the lingering and tenacious
presence of legal and religious strictures and social taboos – themselves stemming from complex social and historical roots – denouncing and forbidding it.
This tension between normal behaviour (queerness) and artificial homo/trans-
phobic social mores (rooted in whiteness, colonialism, and hegemonic political

---

[5] Tom Mills

[6] Dallas Noftall

structures of control and domination) is what led to the violent enactment of homophobia.

Thus violence and discrimination was a common response to queerness. The provincial government's failure to enact legislative protections around sexual orientation until the end of the century contributed immensely to the suffering faced by many queer individuals, and, in fact, lent a tacit approval to the discriminatory behaviour perpetrated throughout the province. As Gays and Lesbians Together (GALT - formed in 1990) activist Gary Kinsman put it in a 1991 interview with CBC: "[Provincial government officials] weren't just saying no to a piece of human rights legislation. They were actually in many ways saying yes to discrimination against lesbians and gay men. They weren't saying that in so many words but that's the implication. That the type of discrimination and violence that goes on will continue and the government is basically giving a green light to it" (CBC 1991).

The Christian churches also deserve a tremendous amount of blame for their conduct. While there were numerous instances of tolerant, inclusive, supportive and even queer priests, nuns and other religious personnel – and their supportive role had a huge impact on many individual lives – as an institution the churches contributed very directly to the spread of homophobia. The churches deserve blame for the deaths of countless queer individuals in the province, both those driven to suicide by the discrimination they experienced as well as the hundreds who died from AIDS while the churches fought against modern sexual health education and safe sex.

Homophobia even had an economic impact on the province. Several of the queer activists I spoke with from the 1980s referred to the "queer brain drain" which the province experienced prior to the advent of human rights protections. While many queer people stayed (or were unable to leave for various reasons), many others left in pursuit of more accepting and tolerant environments elsewhere. At one point in the early 1990s, according to activists, Newfoundlanders and Labradorians comprised the second largest number of deaths at Casey House, a hospital in Toronto specializing in HIV treatment (Dwyer 1992). This was a sad testament not only to the ongoing NL queer diaspora but also to the fact that so many NLers were either unwilling or unwelcome to return home, even at the end of their lives.

It's not surprising – given the variety of responses to queerness in communities throughout the province – that NL's queer liberation movement arose in St. John's. St. John's was the capital and largest city: a place which attracted all those experiencing discrimination elsewhere in the province, or those simply desiring a bigger and more diverse place. It was in St. John's that a critical mass of queers were able to connect with each other, share the diversity of their experiences, develop a mutual awareness of the discrimination they were experiencing, and begin to have conversations about why and how to fight for their rights.

One of the complex aspects of the province's queer history was engagement between queers from this province and newly arrived queers from outside the province. For many years homophobic priests and politicians would characterize queerness as something that was not innately present in NL but brought in from elsewhere – the trope of infection from the outside. As we will see, this was patently untrue - queerness has always been part of Newfoundland and Labrador's history and peoples. But it is true that engagement between NL and the wider world had an impact on the emerging struggle. It helped NLers realize that queers elsewhere around the world were also calling out the discrimination they experienced and were rising up against it. NLers learned about these struggles from books, magazines and newspapers. Newly arrived queers shared ideas, experiences and tactics first-hand. But the process was a two-way street: queers from NL also had an enormous impact on the emerging queer rights movement outside of the province. This came both in the form of ex-patriate NLers who moved away and got involved in activism elsewhere, but also in the form of national organizing initiatives. Lesbians from this province, for instance, played a key role in putting queer rights on the agenda of national feminist and women's organizations, as we will see. And national queer publications, such as *The Body Politic*, kept a close eye on NL's queer rights movement, and kept activists in the rest of the country up to speed on developments here.

It's wrong to say that NL queer activism was primarily shaped by outside influence. It's also wrong to apply blanket generalizations on how queerness was experienced here. As always, there are multiple, complex and messy truths comprising the reality of our history. Hopefully this book will help to offer an entry point into understanding some of this history, in all of its complexity, pain, and beauty.

A final word on lessons to be learned. At the time of publication there is a resurgence in homophobic and transphobic hate in many parts of the world, echoes of which have appeared in this province as well. In determining how to respond to hatred and violence, it is useful to draw on the lessons of the past. Much of the rhetoric deployed by contemporary bigots and hatemongers is rehashed almost directly from the period explored in this book. If anything, this book ought to serve as a reminder that homophobic/transphobic bigots are not simply conservative-minded people exercising their right to a different opinion; they are dangerous hate-mongers who must be confronted and stopped. This book offers many stirring examples of solidarity and cooperation from the twentieth century which will hopefully inspire those struggles in the present day and future. Let's close this introduction with an apt reflection from Joey Shulman, a Jewish Newfoundlander who was swept up in the Toronto Bathhouse Raids in 1981.

"We need to learn from our past. No matter how comfortable we get as gay people, there are always people like Hitler, people like McCarthy in the 1950s

US, people like the RCMP fruit machine, the Bathhouse Raids. The Bathhouse Raids happened at a time when we felt so fucking liberated!... It's important for younger people to know that this was a real attempt to stop us from finding and having and sharing love. And that shouldn't be allowed."

Outline of the book

The book proceeds for the most part chronologically.

Chapter One - Historical Hints - chronicles some of the examples of queer presence in the early decades of the twentieth century. I explore this mostly through the lives of some of the better-known queer actors present in NL during this period: Charles Danielle, Margaret Campbell Macpherson, Robert Bond, Bob Bartlett, Edith Watson and Victoria Hayward, Violet Cherrington and Mabel Baudains, Harold Horwood. Mary Ellicott Arnold and Mabel Reed are another couple whose story I examine in this chapter. They documented their years in Newfoundland in remarkable depth, and to the best of my knowledge, the Newfoundland portion of their story has never been told, so I provide an extended telling of that story. It also coincides with a tumultuous period in Newfoundland history: the poverty of the Great Depression which led to suspension of self-government and the establishment of the Commission of Government in NL. Arnold and Reed's activism and writing offers an invaluable snapshot of this formative period in Newfoundland history.

The Indoor Guy and the Outdoor Guy - links together this early period with the more recent modern era. I look at other expressions of queer identity in the early twentieth century, as well as queer presence in the fishery. However, the bulk of that chapter offers a series of brief biographical sketches of queer NLers. It is my hope that by offering these snapshots of queer lives, readers will begin to gain an understanding both of what it was like growing up queer in this period, as well as the immense diversity of experiences and reactions this provoked. Some queers led seemingly charmed lives; others suffered tremendous homophobia. We look at a few life stories that reflect this complexity.

Chapter Two - Community Organizing: The Early Years - begins telling the history of NL's formal queer community organizations and the work they undertook. I proceed chronologically with the Community Homophile Association of Newfoundland (CHAN - formed in 1974); Gay Association In Newfoundland (GAIN - formed in 1981); Gays And Lesbians Together (GALT - formed in 1990) - and conclude with a reflection on the history of Pride Week organizing in St. John's.

Chapter Three - Lesbian Organizing - there is a tremendous history and energy associated with lesbian organizing in this province, not least of which included two organizations: Gay Organization of Women in Newfoundland (GOWN) and Newfoundland Amazon Network (NAN). However, lesbian organizing has also been deeply interwoven with feminist organizing in this province – to the point of the two movements being inseparable, really – and so I struggled with how to articulate and present all of this. After trying unsuccessfully to weave it into other chapters, I eventually decided lesbian organizing needed a chapter of its own. The chapter opens with a history of the modern women's movement in NL. I am not by any means the first woman to explore this history, and there are some other excellent sources on this period out there (I would give a special nod to the 1999 collection Pursuing Equality, edited by Linda Kealey, and especially the chapter "Change Within and Without: The Modern Women's Movement in Newfoundland and Labrador" by Sharon Pope and Jane Burnham). However, a considerable portion of the history I present has never – to my knowledge – been published. I deliberately avoid dwelling on portions of this history that have already been written about in depth, and instead try to explore angles that have been less explored. Much of this draws on interviews with women who were involved in this history, and several of those interviews are the first to my knowledge conducted on the topic. So the history is original in several respects. I also explore the historical tensions surrounding lesbians in the women's movement, and the manner in which both the women's movement as well as lesbian activism shaped the broader queer rights movement in this province.

Chapter Four - Organizing at Memorial University - takes a focused look at the role of MUNL in the province's queer history. The university played a significant role as a space where a lot of activism began, and I explore the emergence of queer presence and activism on campus. I also explore the role of *The Muse* student newspaper, which was catalytic both in documenting queer history as well as playing a central role in that ongoing history. The controversy surrounding the 1991 Lesbian and Gay Supplement published by *The Muse* is also explored in depth.

Chapter Five – Homophobia - in this chapter I explore a variety of instances of institutionalized homophobia in the province. I look at homophobic violence and 'queer-bashing.' I look at how homophobia manifested in response to the Mount Cashel sexual abuse revelations as well as the Royal Newfoundland Constabulary arrests of men having sex in the Village Mall washrooms. I look at homophobia in media institutions like the CBC, and in provincial politics.

Chapter Six - Fighting and Winning Human Rights - deals in a focused way with the struggle for legislative human rights protections around sexual orientation in this province. It's comprised of three sections. In the first, I look at early campaign and lobby efforts for human rights protections in the 1970s, '80s and early '90s. In the second, I look at the catalytic case of Brian Nolan, who filed several complaints including a human rights complaint against the Royal Newfoundland Constabulary in 1993. And finally, I look at the campaign for a human rights amendment in the wake of the Supreme Court ruling in Nolan's case, which eventually led to the recognition of human rights protections.

Along the way, I explore the establishment of Newfoundland Gays And Lesbians for Equality (NGALE) in 1993 and the further development of NAN, and the key role these two groups played in achieving human rights protections.

Chapter Seven - AIDS Changes Everything - looks at AIDS activism in the 1980s and '90s in NL, examined from a variety of angles.

Chapter Nine - Trans Visibility, Trans Activism - looks at the experience of transgender people in this province. Of course, the experience of trans folks is woven throughout this book, but just as in the case of lesbian activism, I felt the experience of trans people deserved its own special focus in its own chapter as well. Due to the paucity of documentation on the earliest decades of trans activism and community-building (itself a product of the period's transphobia) I explore much of that early period through the lives of several trans people who lived through them. As in the opening chapters of this book, my hope is that by reading trans lives the reader will gain a sense of the diversity of experiences trans people had in this province. I also seek to remember, celebrate and honour the remarkable lives lived by these trans people, and to help ensure their memory is never forgotten. The chapter opens with a reflection – produced in collaboration with scholar/activist/artist Daze Jefferies - on the challenges of doing queer and trans historical research. The chapter concludes by looking at the early development of a service path to gender-affirming health care in this province.

Chapter Ten - Gay Bars and Social Spaces - looks primarily at the development of the 'gay bar scene' in St. John's. This topic could easily encompass a book of its own, and so I present a cursory view of the key bars, along with vignettes and memories from patrons remembering the period and the establishments. I also look at the role the bar scene played in activism and community-building.

Chapter Eleven - Pushing Boundaries in the Arts - offers a cursory look at some of the ways in which the arts contributed to the fight against homophobia, and offers a few snapshots of the lives of some of the important artists involved in this work. There are so many more I could have included; my aim again was to remember some of the iterations of activism and community-building that have not been extensively documented elsewhere (so for instance, I touch in only the briefest of ways on Tommy Sexton, who has his own biography presently in the works).

Acknowledgements

First of all, I would like to thank the many contributors who so generously shared their stories with me. I wish I could offer a little message to each one of you individually and by name right here, but this would add another fifty pages to the book and my editor would kill me. Suffice it to say that this book would not have been possible without you. Many of you are identified by name in the book; some of you requested to be quoted anonymously; others requested not to be quoted at all, but provided invaluable background or contextual information. Each and every one of you has touched me, and changed me, in profound ways. I have learned so much from you. I think of each of you often. Thank you for sharing so much of your time, experiences, and insights with me - and with our readers.

Thank you to my publisher - Engen Books, and especially Matthew Le-Drew - who has been unswervingly supportive and encouraging of this project. Thank you for help in pursuing funding, in understanding the complex nature of this work, and in flexibility around deadlines, size, and other myriad details. I feel so lucky to have decided to go with Engen Books which is a wonderful publisher. Thank you as well to non-fiction editor Lisa M Daly for superb assistance and collaboration in the final editing process.

As I took time off work for this project, suffered equipment breakdowns, and engaged with archives both locally as well as farther afield, I discovered that it often takes money to do research. With the help of my publisher, I was able to obtain much-needed grants from the Canada Council for the Arts, ArtsNL, and the City of St. John's, and I am very thankful for those.

Thank you to the many archivists and researchers who helped me over the course of the past few years, and in particular the incredible staff at Memorial University's Centre for Newfoundland Studies and Archives and Special Collections; also The Rooms archives; the ArQuives in Toronto; the Newfoundland and Labrador Provincial Resource Library Archives at the Arts & Culture Centre; and the City of St. John's archives; all of whom helped me repeatedly and in myriad ways. Thank you to the hard-working staff at the Information Management division (archives) of the Supreme Court of NL, for going to tremendous lengths to help me track down long-buried historical and archival material (and for letting me into that cool vault in the basement! Also I appreciated the leather cowboy hat). Thank you to Michael Connors at NTV News for the same. Thank you to my parents, for having supported and helped in so many ways to guide me onto the intellectual path.

Thank you to my fellow queer researchers with whom I have engaged throughout this project – our mutual chats and sharing kept me invigorated and excited about this project, and helped me to think in more expansive ways about the work I was doing. Daze Jefferies and Andrew Sampson have also been working on research in this area and our shared discussions and pooling of information have been a tremendous source of insights and encouragement, but also provided companionship and emotional solace in having fellow researchers to share these struggles with. Thank you also to Sarah Worthman for our lively chats on queer history.

Gary Kinsman is both a scholar I have looked up to intellectually since my undergraduate days, but also one of the activists who features within these very pages. Thank you tremendously for your foundational scholarship, your activism past and present, the knowledge and memories and experiences you've shared, and the intellectual insights you've sparked during our discussions and correspondence.

Significant draft sections of this book were reviewed in advance by Gary Kinsman and Lexx Ambrose, and I thank you both tremendously for your feedback and insights.

A special thanks to Aimee Finlay, Kelly Thornber, Kris Elder and Sharron Sheppard, not just for the information you shared but also for the trust you placed in me, and the personal support you provided as I worked through this sometimes difficult material.

Thank you to Elizabeth Whitten for your wise insights and suggestions, dear friendship and the shared joy of writing.

This book is a celebration of queer community and family, and I could not have accomplished it without mine. Thank you to Brit Byrnes for your support, encouragement, love and friendship over these years, as well as your powerful everyday activism and insights on this work. Thank you to Tania Heath and Lexx Ambrose for coming into my life when I needed it the most; for friendship, love, healing, inspiration and so much more, as well as perceptive insights and help with this work. The creativity, care and joy you all bring to this world makes everything else possible.

And finally, thank you to all the queer and trans souls – both here and elsewhere; both now and then – who make our community so beautiful and our history so rich. Stay vibrant and magickal always.

CHAPTER ONE: EARLY BEGINNINGS

There have always been queers in Newfoundland and Labrador.

"There was two older men that, when I was young, lived in the community," recalled Wally Upward, of his childhood in the 1950s in Green Bay.

"They weren't related, but they lived there together for decades and decades and decades. One guy was the indoor guy, did all the cooking and housework. The other guy was outdoors, went fishing and got wood and that kind of stuff. And they lived together until they both died. They died actually within a few months of each other. I never heard once in my life not one disparaging word against them. And it took me years to actually figure out, these two were gay. People invited them to Christmas and church socials, they were a part of the community. But not a word was said, and it took me years and years later to actually realize, you know what? They were queer. Yeah, in Green Bay. It was just – it was what it was."

Similar accounts were recalled by others I spoke with: same-sex couples, sometimes living on the outskirts of the community, yet undeniably *part* of the community. In a province where, until recently, isolated communities could be worlds unto themselves, responses to same-sex couples varied widely. Not all communities were as accepting as Upward's. Not everyone had the social capital or skills that were often required to achieve acceptance in their community. Yet for every boatload of queers who fled to Toronto or Montreal or Vancouver in the face of discrimination, there were others who remained, fashioned a life and were sometimes accepted, to varying degrees, by their community.

Accepted — but not acknowledged. Their acceptance was often predicated on silence; on a tacit refusal to discuss queer relationships, sexualities or identities. Queer community members during those early decades were not guaranteed rights or dignity on an equal basis with straight or cisgender members. They could not show love or even self-expression in the way their cis and straight neighbours could. The fight for human rights protections, and the right to publicly live one's sexual orientation or gender identity as loudly as straight and cis people did, developed into a fierce struggle as the twentieth century unfolded.

Newfoundlanders and Labradorians fought this struggle from both inside and outside the province. During the same period when Upward was a child in Green Bay, Paul Hearn was growing up in a large Catholic family in Petty Harbour. After moving to St. John's and studying at Memorial University for a few years, he left the province and moved to Toronto in 1976. There he came out, and dove into queer activism in Canada's largest city. He played an important role in organizing the early Pride Weeks in that city; Toronto Pride's 1987 slogan 'Rightfully Proud' has been attributed to him. That was the year sexual orientation protections were added to Ontario's human rights code; over 15,000 attended that year's Toronto Pride parade.

For Hearn and his friends, activism was inseparable from everyday life. Hearn had a bank account with TD Bank, which didn't provide same-sex partner benefits until 1994. So he and his friends used to write "Gay Money!" on their bills before depositing them, hoping the bank would get the message. They did: "They realized we had money and then they wanted us," he told his niece Kayla Hearn before he died, recalling those heady days of activism (TD Bank now boasts of having been the first bank in North America to provide same-sex spousal benefits).

But as Toronto Pride became increasingly corporate, Hearn didn't approve of the direction it was taking and so he stepped back from the organization.

"He always watched it but he didn't feel the need to participate in it any more because he felt a little disconnected when it became a big corporate event, he didn't like that," recalled Kayla. "He always liked the Dyke March for that reason, because it was more true to his roots.

"He got involved just by being him. He didn't view it as activism. For him, it was just 'This is my life and this is what I've got to do for it.'"

Paul Hearn eventually came out to his family back in Newfoundland during the early 1980s.

"And then my grandmother did the whole Catholic prayer thing, with rosaries and whatever," explained Kayla. "But he just said: 'This is not going to change, this is who I am.' And then she was chill with it. I've always admired that about my family because in a small Catholic town that's not always the way it turns out. But it became a normal thing in our family, which made it easier for me to come out."

Kayla's uncle played a role in that too. In 2008 — on National Coming Out Day, by coincidence — Kayla and Paul attended a family wedding. During the break between the ceremony and reception, they got to chatting.

"He said, 'You know Kayla, you should live the gay lifestyle - it's fabulous!'" recounted Kayla.

"I mean, he's not wrong. So then I said: 'You do know I'm gay, right?' And he said: 'Oh yes, I just needed you to say it.' Then my mom came downstairs and said: 'What are you two talking about?' I said: 'Nothing!' But she went: 'I knows what you're talking about!' I said: 'It's fine, I don't want to talk about it.' Then we were at the wedding reception later and my dad's twin sister comes over to me and she says: 'I heard you got some news!' I looked over at my mom, and she's just shrugging her shoulders. So I was like: 'Oh my god.' And then - no joke - the band started playing 'Somewhere Over the Rainbow'

and Paul slides over and he goes: 'Kayla, it's our song!' And I go: 'Okay, now I'm out to everybody.' But I'm happy he did that, that he accidentally pushed me towards that."

Paul Hearn — who married his partner John in 2008 — died in 2020. His story forms part of the quilted fabric of vibrant NL queer lives that stretches right across Canada and beyond.

"The Greatest Thing in the World"

Hints of Newfoundland and Labrador's queer history stretch back much farther. They are hinted at in earlier expressions of queer pride, as reflected in Upward's account. Or in the compassionate arguments of Reverend William James Lockyer from Trinity, NL. In the early decades of the twentieth century Reverend Lockyer wrote a periodic column for *The Evening Telegram* newspaper, in which he covered news and happenings from the Trinity Bay area. In his column for April 19, 1924, he includes a startling reflection titled "Love - The Greatest Thing In The World." It's written in praise of "the actions of virile men, whose love for each other was of the Jonathan-and-David-type." This was a common euphemism for homosexuality. Although Rev. Lockyer doesn't make explicit reference to homosexuality, he does explain that "David, in his efforts to do full justice to Jonathan's love for him, referred to it as a love, 'passing the love of women'" (Lockyer 1924).

While the phrase has been used as an allusion for homosexuality since medieval times, it should come as no surprise that some scholars dispute the homoerotic dimensions of this bond. Oscar Wilde referenced the phrase in the 1895 trial which led to his conviction for gross indecency, although in that case he attempted to downplay the erotic elements of that love for obvious reasons. I believe that given the context and Reverend Lockyer's obvious care in presenting his view, he's fully aware of the controversial nature of his proposal, and that this reinforces the likelihood he had a more erotic form of love in mind.

"We hesitate to-day to refer to the love of one man for another, as though such love were effeminate," writes Lockyer. "[A]nd yet, history is full of instances of such love" (Ibid.).

"Every settlement, and village in our country has produced men whose actions towards each other indicated the existence of such a mutual love; though in the large majority of instances it has been known only to the men themselves, or to their immediate friends" (Ibid.).

Lockyer goes on to make a passionate argument in support of normalizing and accepting such a form of love. He refers to the recently concluded First World War, observing that the "war spirit" caused greater calamity than this type of love has ever caused. He offers an example from the Trinity area, citing the love of two men he calls George Smith and Charles Brown (pseudonyms).

He says these two men lived sixty years earlier (in the 1860s) and he knew them personally.

They "were friends from boyhood. That friendship deepened and increased with years, till by the time they had become young men, their feelings towards each other could be fully expressed only by one word, viz., 'love.' They spent all their spare time together, and they were often referred to as 'lovers'" (Ibid.).

Lockyer tells of an incident one year when Brown had to go off to the seal fishery without Smith, and Smith had dreams about his partner's ordeals which later proved to be true. Brown eventually returned safely and attested to the accuracy of his partner's dreams. Lockyer credited this to "the electricity of a mutual love on the part of two men - 'passing the love of women'" (Ibid.).

This remarkable account was published in a full-page spread in *The Evening Telegram*, one of Newfoundland's largest newspapers in 1924. Was Rev. Lockyer merely referring to a platonic love, or something deeper? We know little about the good reverend, and do not know the identities of the two other men he refers to. But it's more than likely he was making an early case for respecting same sex relationships, in his ardent desire to defend and praise "the love of one man for another."

Not all of the early queer references to NL were equally positive. The April 4, 1952, issue of *The Western Star* reports on what might be the first instance of a gay panic defense being used by a NLer. Alexander Williams, a 25-year-old seaman from the Goulds, was convicted of murdering Dong Yew Yin, a 20-year-old Chinese man. The two were both employed aboard the Canadian Pacific Steamships vessel *Princess Joan*. The Crown argued that Yin had been murdered in Williams' cabin during a journey from Vancouver to Victoria in January of that year, and that Williams had thrown his body into the ocean. The court "reviewed testimony which suggested that [Dong] was a homosexual and a statement allegedly made by Williams to police that Dong had made improper advances to him and that he had struck and killed him in anger." True to homophobic form, the charge of murder was reduced to manslaughter by the jury (*The Western Star* 1952).

Queer Historical Visages

Those unfamiliar with the queer contours of Newfoundland and Labrador's heritage might be surprised at some of the characters whose sexuality assumed queer dimensions. This doesn't necessarily mean they were what we would today call gay, lesbian, or trans, but they certainly deviated from the ciscentric, heteronormative roles of the period.

This book initially contained a large section exploring some of these characters, but for reasons of space – and what I felt was the importance of prioritizing an in-depth history of NL's modern queer liberation struggle – most of that content had to be removed during final editing. Hopefully a brief glimpse at the lives of two of these characters will suffice for this edition. But before proceeding, let's talk about why. Certainly these individuals' lives are interesting in and of themselves. But it's also important to dispel the notion that queer identities in NL are a recent thing. Nothing could be farther from the truth. Since there were first people in NL, there were people exploring all aspects of human sexuality and gender. We don't have historical records of Indigenous queerness the way we have biographical data on the characters below, but Indigenous oral traditions attest to the complexity and playfulness of gender and sexual identities long before Europeans arrived to wreak havoc and genocide.

From the earliest documented records of European settlers, we find challenges to the gender and sexual norms imposed by European authorities. One of the earliest mentions of same-sex activity in historian Paul O'Neill's 1975 opus *The Oldest City: The Story of St. John's, Newfoundland*, dates back to the late 1700s. O'Neill references the case of a soldier stationed at Fort Townshend who was accused of sodomy with another soldier.

"[T]estimony showed that the men slept three to a bunk," writes O'Neill. "[T]he defendant, who claimed he was asleep and dreaming of a beautiful girl, was hanged a few days later for his "unnatural crime"" (O'Neill 1975).

O'Neill flags other documented instances of sodomy charges in St. John's, including one in 1807 and one in 1833. There's no record of the outcome in the 1807 case, but in the latter case the accused - Richard Roleston - was hanged.

Underscoring the queer presence throughout the province's early history reminds us it is nothing new. When I was an elementary school child, I remember a teacher warning us that homosexuality was something that came from Toronto. Nothing could be farther from the truth; in fact insofar as St. John's is an older city than Toronto, there was probably a queer presence here long before Toronto or any other Canadian metropolis existed.

NL's history is full of examples.

Perhaps the most well-known is Charles Henry Danielle, an American dancer and dressmaker who is believed to have wound up in Newfoundland sometime in the 1860s. He developed a life-long love-hate relationship with the island, coming and going over the years. He launched a number of business enterprises in St. John's – restaurants, costume rentals and event sites – and became known for the extravagant fancy-dress balls and galas he put off, which were said to rival those of London. He was perhaps best known for Octagon Castle, a grandiose edifice constructed outside of the city which operated as a hotel and event site. Reporters and wealthy socialites from all over North America came to experience the extravagant palace, and local organizations held their annual parties and events there. When he died in 1902, Danielle's funeral was attended by thousands, and his casket carried by four former prime ministers (Harrington 1992, Sweet 2019).

Rumours have swirled for years about the good Professor's homosexuality, but the most fascinating account is to be found in a correspondence[7] which took place not long after his death, between Frederick Brazil - a young Newfoundlander who had been Danielle's "manservant" and designated heir, and Charles Waugh, an American who knew Danielle in his younger years.

"He was a great lover of men," wrote Waugh, who struggled to reconcile his disapproval of homosexuality with his admiration for Danielle. "He used to hug and kiss them and want to sleep with them. I did not like this. But there was much about him that I did like."

"He in early life was always infatuated with men - never women - and these men would work on his soft side to get all the money they could and then drop him - and he gave freely," writes Waugh in another letter to Brazil. "They bled him."

Danielle would have been fabulously wealthy if not for all the money he spent on his boyfriends, Waugh said. Waugh mentions one of them - a dentist named Dr. Harry Burnett - "whom he took to Newfoundland and introduced to the public, and spent his money like water on him, and then Burnett turned against him."

Waugh writes more about this in another letter: "Dr. Harry Burnett was a dentist and Charles worshipped him. He was good looking and Charles' money was paid out for him like water. Charles afterwards told me that for all his kindness Burnett treated him like a thief. Charles got him up there [to Newfoundland] and introduced him and wrote out a fine lecture for him, and afterwards Burnett made lots of money...all of Charles' friends went back on him sooner or later."

He mentions others, including a Charlie Clark: "as handsome as any woman - in fact he had a woman's face and form and was really a beautiful man. My wife knew him and she said so too."

Waugh wrestled over his feelings toward Danielle, trying to contextualize his homosexuality (of which he disapproved, in line with the prevailing bigotry of the period) against his other qualities.

"With all of his glaring faults, did he have more of them than most of us? We are all imperfect, but in different ways. Our faults are different. For that reason I exercise the broadest charity towards all my fellow men."

...

"[F]aults aside, I have always considered Prof. Danielle a remarkable man - superior to nearly all other men. His ability, executiveness, his creative genius and art was sublime. His tender heart and charity to the poor was conspicuous throughout his life. Taken all in all we shall not see his like again," he wrote.

There is also Margaret Campbell Macpherson, one of the finest painters ever to emerge from Newfoundland. Part of the Macpherson clan of merchant elites, she was born in 1860 and attended school at the Wesleyan Academy in

---

[7] Located in the Charles H. Danielle fonds in the Provincial Resource Library, Arts & Culture Centre.

St. John's, where she first showed artistic promise. She went on to study in Edinburgh, Scotland and Neuchatel, Switzerland. When the Scottish Society of Artists decided to begin admitting women as members, she was one of the first. She switched from signing her work "Maggie Macpherson" to "M. Campbell Macpherson"; it's speculated this was to avoid being classified as a "lady artist." Indeed, discussion of her work in newspapers and art journals sometimes referred to the artist simply as "Campbell Macpherson" and assumed this was a man (Art Gallery of Nova Scotia 2006).

By 1889 she was sharing studio space with another female artist, Josephine (Jo) Hoxie Bartlett, who may initially have been one of her students. Their relationship became romantic, and they would spend the remainder of their lives together. While eventually settling in Paris, Macpherson made periodic trips home to Newfoundland and her work became a permanent fixture in local exhibitions. In 1896 an exhibition of her work was held which was described by the St. John's Daily News as "the first ever held in Newfoundland in which all the paintings were the work of a native artist holding a leading place among the famous painters of the day." During the time of that visit of hers to St. John's, an interesting item ran in the Evening Herald newspaper, informing readers that "a well-known city lady, who is an artist of no mean repute" was sighted on Lemarchant Road "boldly appearing on her wheel in the latest approved style of bloomers. She has determined to brave criticism, and, with a courage few would expect, intends to adopt this rational dress in future." Could this "bold" - and possibly gender-bending - artist have been Macpherson?

Throughout the early years of the twentieth century Macpherson played a prominent role in the Parisian salon scene. Did she also meet and mingle with the famous lesbian modernists of that same era, who made Paris the centre of the literary world? It's tempting to imagine. In 1931, at the age of 66, Macpherson died at her home in Versailles. Her partner Jo Bartlett lived on in their home in Versailles until the outbreak of the Second World War. As the Germans advanced Bartlett fled to England, and died there in a nursing home in June 1944 (Ibid.).

Sir Robert Bond, the first Prime Minister of the Dominion of Newfoundland, is another individual around whom rumours swirl. First elected to the House of Assembly in 1882, he became Premier when Newfoundland was still a colony, and then Prime Minister when it assumed Dominion status in 1907. He left politics in 1914, and died in 1927. He never married, which doubtless fuelled some of the rumours around his sexuality. On February 27, 1902 The Daily News published a letter of complaint from Beatrice Bonstelle, titled "The Burning Question: Bachelor Bond Gets a Straight Tip".

"Look out for me! I am boiling over with wrath!" bristled the bitter Bonstelle. The source of her anger was Bond's upcoming trip to London for the coronation of King Edward VII. As Premier, Bond was invited to the coronation along with his wife. Only he had no wife.

"The invitation was issued last December, giving Sir Robert ample time to choose his fair one," complained Bonstelle in her letter to the editor. "I say it is a disgrace; and I can hear the twenty thousand young marriageable women of Newfoundland re-echo my sentiments...because of a fad of Sir Robert Bond's none of us can go. It is time for us women to protest against such an outrage... Think of the disgrace, the contempt, the people of England will hold for us fair daughters of Terra Nova, when they find that none of us were thought worthy of accompanying our Premier to the coronation...It would be serving him right if we women mobbed Sir Robert and debarred him from witnessing the coronation ceremonies...let me tell Mr. Bond that if he goes to London without a wife he need not return."

The tongue-in-cheek letter was doubtless humorous in intent, singling out Bond's bachelor-hood as a public concern. But it should also be remembered that humour is a common method of reinforcing social norms, and for The Daily News to publish a public castigation of Bond's disinclination to marry cast a public spotlight on his personal life.

Bond's purported gay sexuality has become a fixture of oral lore, although I was unable to find any concrete evidence to lend objective credence to the rumours. It may, by contrast, be that he was what today would be referred to as asexual or aromantic. Indeed, a suggestive bit of evidence to lend weight to that idea is to be found in a letter he wrote to his niece Roberta when she was attending medical school. Her father George — Robert's brother — had expressed concern that Roberta seemed troubled and was losing weight (a perhaps not uncommon situation for those attending medical school! - especially in an era when women were still widely excluded from that field). Robert duly wrote to his niece, and expressed his concern as an uncle: "I hear that you have got very thin. What is the trouble? It is very evident to me from your letter that something is giving you worry, and causing you to lose flesh. Come, out with it and I will see if I can prescribe a cure for your disease. I hope it is not a love affair, for in that disease I have unfortunately had no experience."

Although drawn to politics, Bond remained a very private person, and enjoyed his solitary pursuits: reading, hunting, romping through the barrens. Perhaps romantic sexuality was something that simply never interested him.

In her biography *Unchained Man*, Caitlan Hanrahan speculates that NL's famed Arctic explorer Robert 'Bob' Bartlett may have been gay. He never married and was most comfortable in masculine company. Hanrahan cites an intriguing correspondence with an American named LeRoy Baker Gulotta, with whom Bartlett roomed in 1920 in New York City, and maintained an affectionate correspondence (Hanrahan 2018).

Hanrahan observes that oral lore in his hometown of Brigus suggests he was gay, but the most intriguing evidence came from a discussion she had in March 2008 with renowned Newfoundland historian Paul O'Neill. O'Neill told her that the politician Peter Cashin, who had known Bartlett personally, had firmly asserted to him (O'Neill) that Bartlett was indeed "a homosexual." Some scholars have criticized this speculation; we will likely never know for certain (Ibid.).

Edith Watson and Victoria Hayward were an American lesbian couple who played an important role in documenting Newfoundland history - especially the lives of women - in the early twentieth century. Born in 1861, Edith grew up in Connecticut, and developed a talent for painting. She was also a restless, inveterate traveller, and in either 1891 or 1892 made her first journey to Newfoundland. Although she would travel widely throughout Canada, the US and the Caribbean, Newfoundland seems to have taken a special place in her heart, and she fitted it into her travels almost every year for nearly four decades. In the 1890s she also began shifting from watercolour to photography, and was soon referred to in Newfoundland as "the camera artist." In the spring of 1911, while back in the US, she met Victoria Hayward, a journalist and teacher. Later that year Victoria came to visit her, and by the following year when they travelled together to Bermuda (Hayward's birthplace) they were inseparable. For the next 32 years they would live, work and travel together (Rooney 2017).

During their journeys to Newfoundland (which included expeditions to Labrador) the couple would room with local families in the small outport communities, photographing the residents and their lives. The two lesbian adventurers clearly relished their forays through rural wilderness, and perhaps their greatest contribution lies in the vast photographic archive they produced during their dozens of visits, which offers an unparalleled record of outport people and lives during the period. They were especially interested in the lives of women, and documented women's daily work (carrying water, curing fish) in precise detail. The couple remained together until Edith's death in 1943. Hayward then relocated to their cottage and died in a nursing home in 1956. Frances Rooney deserves tremendous credit for her ambitious work salvaging their memory and reconstructing their story, which can be followed in greater detail in her book *Working the Rock: Newfoundland and Labrador in the photographs of Edith S. Watson, 1890-1930* (Ibid.).

A number of very interesting lesbian couples emerge from the fog in the early years of the twentieth century in Newfoundland. The inimitably named Violet Cherrington and her partner Mabel Mary Baudains was another such couple, and they played a pivotal role in the field of education in early twentieth century Newfoundland.

Mabel Mary Baudains was born in 1876 in Jersey in the Channel Islands. She arrived in Canada in the early 1900s, where she obtained employment as Matron at Havergal College.

Teaching was one of the few fields at the time open to single women seeking employment. As Whitehead (2008) observes, "Newfoundland was no different from other British dominations such as Canada and Australia, where the creation of state school systems in the 19th century had resulted in predominantly female teaching workforces and confirmed educational administration as a male domain."

Havergal was a boarding school for girls located in Toronto. Founded in 1894, it is still operating, and has counted among its alumni the likes of journalist Linda Frum, actress Margot Kidder, and graphic novelist Mariko Tamaki. The school was dramatized in the 1993 novel *The Wives of Bath* by Susan Swan, another alumna. The novel features gender-non-conforming characters and complex lesbian relationships, and was inspired by the author's own experiences at the school. The book drew both controversy (in 2003 a Canadian Border Security Agency officer seized a copy at the border and deemed it obscene) as well as praise (it was nominated for Ontario's Trillium Award and the Guardian Fiction Prize). In 2001 it was adapted into the feature film *Lost and Delirious*.

It was at Havergal that Mabel and Violet met and fell in love. Mabel arrived in 1915; Violet in 1918. They were together at Havergal for close to four years. Then in 1922 Violet was recruited to the position of Principal of Bishop Spencer College, a school for girls run by the Anglican Church in St. John's. The school also included a residence located on Forest Road, which was for girls coming from outport communities to attend the school. Violet swiftly convinced her employer that it was time to expand and modernize this residence. Then she hired Mabel to join her in St. John's and assume the position of Superintendent of the new residence, for which a house was purchased at 55 Rennie's Mill Road (Peavy 2012).

Mabel and Violet lived there along with their students until Mabel's retirement in 1939, at which point the two women moved into their own home at 75 Barnes Road. Violet, who suffered from severe arthritis which worsened over the years, did not retire until 1952, and died in 1956. Mabel died five years later on October 21, 1961 (Ibid.).

Harold Horwood is probably best known as one of NL's most famous authors, and he packed a lot into his 82 years. He first came to public prominence as a fiery union organizer in the 1940s, working for groups as varied as the General Workers' Union, the Newfoundland Federation of Labour, and the Canadian Congress of Labour. As a politician and early ally of Joseph R. Smallwood, he played a key role in the campaign to bring Newfoundland into confederation with Canada. He represented Labrador in the new province's House of Assembly from 1949-51. He later broke with Smallwood and the relationship became for a time bitter and antagonistic. Horwood moved into journalism, working with the Evening Telegram as journalist, editor and columnist until 1970. During that time he also broke ground as a literary author, penning several novels. His first, *Tomorrow Will Be Sunday*, was published with Doubleday Books in 1966 and centred on life in the Newfoundland outports. It's been noted for its explicit portrayal of homosexuality, among other themes (Bartlett 2007).

Horwood was quite open about his bisexuality, and addressed the matter frankly in his autobiographical writings. Although he had a long-term relationship with a freelance journalist named Marguerite, and later married Cornelia 'Corky' Lindesmith (they had two children), he had intimate relationships with men as well.

"My first romantic relationships, in my middle and late teens, were with boys of my own age, or somewhat younger," he wrote in a memoir essay provided to the Canadian Encyclopedia. "I sometimes walked home with a girl, and talked with her on levels of surprising intimacy, but the deep emotional relationships were with boys." He recalls "boating among the islands of Mundy Pond" as a young child, and gazing at "older boys swimming there nude as young Greeks" (Ibid.).

For many years he lived in a small cabin in Beachy Cove, from which he and his partner operated a free school called Animal Farm. His writings from the period describe the very 1960s atmosphere of the time, full of drugs and experimentation and free love between all genders.

Horwood rarely hid his convictions, and during his years of acrimony with Premier Smallwood the latter sought to use this against him. Horwood's political rift with Smallwood was a bitter one, and Horwood attacked the Smallwood government in scathing newspaper columns published in The Evening Telegram. In retaliation, Smallwood had Horwood followed by police officers in the early 1950s, in the hopes of catching him engaging in then-illegal homosexual acts. The matter is addressed in the National Film Board documentary *The Author of These Words* (1982), directed by William D. MacGillivray. In that film the two men - reunited again in their senior years, politics now behind them both - reflect on their rift.

"It was the first time in my career as premier and as leader of the Liberal party where I was really attacked. I was really damaged," says Smallwood.

"I felt that you had to be damaged at this time," reflects Horwood. "I honestly felt that it was a public duty to damage you because I felt that you had too much power, that the Opposition was too weak...The one thing I really felt bad about in my life was feeling that I had to do this thing during the years I was working at the Telegram. I'm not blaming them, it was something that I felt I had to do."

"There were times...where I could have hired someone to assassinate you. There were times when I hated you," responds Smallwood. Horwood then offers further reflections on the experience, and his identity.

"It was after I had made my break with Smallwood and the Liberal party in New-foundland, and I was being followed around by secret police. The Newfoundland authorities had put people on my trail in the hope of getting something on me. Specifically in the hope of finding out that I was a homosexual and prosecuting me on a homosexual charge. Which since I wasn't, and which since I wasn't committing any kind of homosexual acts, then or previously or subsequently, they never did get the goods on me. But

this kind of thing - the possibility of being framed as a homosexual - was very very active in my case back in the 1950s, early 1950s. And I wrote Tomorrow Will Be Sunday under this sort of threat hanging over me. I had all these kids surrounding me that I was trying to do things with and do things for, and the danger was that I would myself be framed on a charge of homosexuality and all these kids would suffer too. I was facing the situation where I could have cut off all these relationships and become an ordinary sort of straight person, or else I try to walk down the middle and tread very carefully.

"In the human condition there's a lot of choice in sexual relationships. And I honestly believe in bisexuality. I honestly believe that people can have relationships with their own sex that are coloured with sexuality. And relationships with the other sex that are coloured also with sexuality, with or without the complete sexual thing. And I think you have a lot of choices. I think I'm a true bisexual. And I hate to say this because in most people it's a cover-up. And in my case it isn't. I have never had a homosexual relationship that went all the way, to use the 1940s expression. I never have. But I could have. I very well could have."

In what remains of this section, let's take a closer look at another fascinating lesbian couple who had an impact on rural Newfoundland in the late 1930s.

Mary Ellicott Arnold and Mabel Reed, revolutionaries[8]

"[D]oes the common man in the United States possess the same potentialities as the men of Newfoundland and Nova Scotia?

Courage and endurance.

Intelligence and wisdom adequate to deal with the problems of our day and age.

Technical skill and ability to be used not only in the interest of a few,

Kindness and consideration for the welfare of others, not for the few but for all men and women,

Ability to work together for a common aim.

And that aim: not welfare and profits for a few, but slowly and steadily, the building of a better world.

Mary Ellicott Arnold (1876-1968) and Mabel Reed (1876-1962) were two Americans prominently involved in the North American 'Cooperative' movement.

They were also life partners at a time when lesbianism was still deeply frowned upon. But they had little time to worry about the bigotry of the homophobe: their lives were dedicated to building a better world through the Cooperative movement, a progressive movement that originated around the time of the Industrial Revolution in England, and rapidly spread around the

---

[8] This narrative was compiled from the correspondence and personal narratives contained in the Mary Ellicott Arnold Papers, found in the Archives and Special Collections, Queen Elizabeth II Library, Memorial University.

world. Cooperative organizers often worked closely with labour and other left-leaning social movements; one of their most tangible iterations which remain important today are credit unions.

Arnold and Reed first met at the age of six, when their mothers stopped for a brief chat on the streets of Somerville, New Jersey. "If I remember correctly, I do not think that either of us was favourably impressed with the other," Arnold commented wryly in her unpublished memoirs many years later.

But impressions change. By the age of twelve they were good friends, staying at each other's homes.

"When we were twenty or so, we decided to farm the Reeds' fifty five acres (then considered far from a seemly occupation for young ladies) and took a short course in agriculture at Cornell University. From then on everything we have done has been done together," wrote Arnold in her memoirs.

The couple spent five years farming Reeds' family lands, then abandoned that for the social activism that proved their true forte. They started as housing activists for the poor in New York City. Then they accepted a position with the Bureau of Indian Affairs, working on the Hoopa Valley Indian Reservation in California. They despised the racist approach of the Bureau, and instead eagerly adopted the cultural practices of the Indigenous community in which they lived, forming close friendships with local women. After a period of time they returned north, diving back into Cooperative movement work in Maine and along the Atlantic coast into Canada.

They were skilled and sought-after organizers. In 1937, they were living in Cape Breton, Nova Scotia, working to establish housing cooperatives in the region's mining communities. On the night of Saturday, October 23, Arnold and Reed received an unexpected visit.

"Our house as usual had been in a turmoil when Gerald and Gussie Mac-Donald boiled in, left their car outside on the road and told us that we were being kidnapped for a Conference in Newfoundland," Reed wrote in a letter to her sister. "In less time than it takes to tell it, we were off and away."

It was the beginning of a three-year love affair for the both of them with Newfoundland.

The MacDonalds and Arnold and Reid drove to the ferry at North Sydney. The stewards quickly took a shine to the women, and argued with each other over which was the best stateroom to assign them for the ferry-ride. After crossing over from Nova Scotia, they took the train to Stephenville Crossing (part of the French Shore, a region colonized by France and where French was still widely spoken). Arnold documented the Conference with breathtaking immediacy.

"In Stephenville and Port au Port we heard the French language. School children snatched at their caps and said "Allo!" as we passed. Little houses stood in small rocky pastures. In the distance are the hills of Newfoundland and glimpses of the Bay. Everyone greets us and we are asked whether we want

to come in and sit down. "Oh yes, they know all about Cooperation. They are in a study club and they are going to have a credit union. Yes, Mr Richardson and Mr McEochren have told them about Cooperation. You have to study and work hard and stick together even if things don't go so good at first. Do we have Cooperation in the United States? And are we coming again next year? There is going to be lots of Cooperation by that time."

The meeting opened with the roughly one hundred delegates belting out, in lieu of an anthem, a stirring rendition of The Ryans and the Pittmans: "We'll rant and we'll roar like true Newfoundlanders!" Protestant and Catholic church leaders alike joined in, lending their mutual support to the cooperative movement in a rare display of interdenominational solidarity.

As the conference began, speakers from towns and villages along the coast described setting up study clubs in small communities - "the study club is a university that every man and woman can attend," described a delegate from the Codroy Valley, which had 23 study clubs and a brand new credit union. Eleven study clubs had been set up in Cape St. George in merely two months. Port au Port had set up five study clubs over the past year, and had set up their own credit union as well. In Stephenville ten study clubs were operating, and they were well on the way to establishing a credit union. The next day organizers discussed how to go about establishing community libraries.

"We are attempting something unique in the history of this country," proclaimed one speaker. "We have got to lay aside our selfish ideas and work for the common good."

"The cooperative way is the only way of solving our problems," declared another.

As the Depression era's dire poverty gripped Newfoundland – exacerbated by the country's war debt, and a shameful history of underdevelopment – NL'ers in rural communities were organizing proletarian responses to the crisis with a remarkable sense of energy. They were forming study clubs, credit unions, community libraries, and other grassroots initiatives.

The speeches at the conference reflected a growing idealism in stark contrast to the Depression-era poverty around them. The juxtaposition of these two realities was remarkable. Newfoundland had always been poor, but during the Depression it was mired in a state of unprecedented misery. Just getting to the Conference had been a challenge, as a Mr. Benoit from Cape St. George described. "[The road] is pretty bad. Father Green and I started Sunday. We had a rig. But an accident was looking for a place to happen. The wheels came off. We thought we wouldn't get to the Conference. But we borrowed a truck from a neighbour. Then there was another accident. The seat came off. Father Green sat on the floor in the back and I stood up and drove. Then the truck gave out and someone brought Father Green to the Conference and I walked."

Yet the conference revealed rural communities across the island taking matters into their own hands, forming study clubs to educate themselves and credit unions to pool their resources and support their communities. By the end of the Conference, the hundreds of delegates and townspeople were fast friends.

"The station at Stephenville Crossing is crowded for the delegates from the Codroy Valley and the Visitors from Nova Scotia are taking the train for home. Everyone has come to see them off. It is a very different crowd from that on Sunday. It is one big family on its way home from a fine time and we rant and roar at the top of our lungs, dashing to the platform to wave goodbye to the delegates as the different home stations come along. As the numbers fall the intimacy mounts. Promises are exchanged to "stop and see me if you are in my town." It is dusk before the last delegate drops off the lighted train into the dark."

Arnold and Reed were deeply moved by this introduction to Newfoundland, and they stayed in touch with those they met at the Conference. Two years later, the couple accepted an offer to bring their Cooperative experience to Newfoundland full-time. For months, Arnold recounted in a letter to a friend, the organizers they'd met in Newfoundland had been urging the couple to join them there. "The problem [there] is a desperate one. The country is bankrupt and the major part of the population are on the dole. Mr. Gorvin[9] has been sent over from England with a pretty free hand and he is very favourable to Cooperation. It is a very difficult problem and I don't know how much can be done but...a group of young fellows are tackling it from different centers along the coast...Inshore fishing is dead. The fish have gone. There is no arable land on the coast. The people are starving on a dole of six cents a day per person."

Newfoundland was at that time under Commission of Government. As Arnold described it: "The hard facts were that, following their own financial collapse in 1933, the people in Newfoundland surrendered their political freedom, sold their birthright of self government for a mess of pottage, and were governed by a Royal Commission from England."

The former self-governing Dominion had indeed reverted back to the status of Colony, and was now governed by a Commission appointed by the British government. One of the Commissioners — John Gorvin, Commissioner of Natural Resources, Agriculture and Rural Reconstruction — had launched an ambitious program of land settlement. The goal was to convert thousands of unemployed fishermen on the south coast of the island into subsistence farmers. The plan - which was ultimately stymied by the outbreak of World War II - initially targeted five thousand fishermen in nine communities. It was an ambitious plan. But as Anderson noted wryly: "Don't forget that Newfoundland was a dictatorship in 1939-1940 under exceptionally able and dedicated leadership...And under a dictatorship, you can move fast."

Gorvin was eager to draw on the couple's expertise and to set them to work

---

[9] One of the Commissioners in the Commission of Government that now governed the former Dominion

in the outports. They were surprised to find the Commissioners so open to the left-leaning ideas toward which other governments sometimes looked askance. But Newfoundland's situation was desperate, and the Commissioners recognized that it required desperate measures.

"It is curious to be in a place where the Government attitude is so very favourable to Cooperation," wrote Reed. "On the other hand the poverty is the most desperate I have ever seen and what can be done is a very grave question."

Gorvin felt their Cooperative organizing had an important place in rural reconstruction.

"The introduction of cooperative ideas and ideals would play an important part in the struggle of the people to win their way back to self-respect and independence," wrote Arnold.

The lesbian couple arrived in St. John's and set about meeting with government to figure out what their precise role could be. As Arnold and Gorvin met one day to chat about their potential role in rural reconstruction, it occurred to them that it would be helpful if the Commissioner of Finance, John Hubert Penson, were on board. Gorvin spontaneously called Penson up and made an appointment for him to meet Arnold at 8:30pm at the Newfoundland Hotel. Arnold and Reed went to Nonia to buy some clothes — they'd met the nurses running that cooperative at a dinner the previous evening — and Arnold found herself a real "humdinger" of a rust-coloured homespun suit with a high-necked gray sweater. "It is a whiz and I am very much taken with myself and spend long minutes before the glass," she wrote to a friend. Arnold's meeting with Penson that night was a success.

"He promptly took me to his house to spend the evening and lamented the fact that I wouldn't stay in St. John's and house both masses and classes for him," she wrote. "I only hope he doesn't think better of his words in the cold light of morning."

The couple were making headway in selling Commission on their Cooperative ideas. But Newfoundland at the time was in many ways a world unto itself. As Arnold observed early on, "Nova Scotia is so far away in feeling it might be India for all it lies across the Cabot Straight."

She reiterated the point in a letter to another friend. "Nova Scotia has become very far away, even farther than New York. Our world centers around the Colonial Building of which Mr. Gorvin is the bulls eye."

But the couple loved their new home.

"Mary and I are much enamoured of St. John's," wrote Reed to a friend. "It reminds me of Edinborough. I think the 'Coves' and the stairways to Duckworth St are charming. I have spent my time pricing household gear or climbing Signal Hill while Mary has gone dutifully to the Colonial House with the result that the Commissioner has made her a high official of some kind, she doesn't seem to know just what."

Reed's own position was equally vague: "According to [government] I am Secretary-Manager of the Placentia Bay Regional Special Area Corporation. But so far I have been unable to find anyone who knows what that involves…it appears I am a banker, and the Lord help those for whom I bank…under any conditions it ought to give us a marvellous chance to see the wheels go round and our tails are in the air."

The official appointments came through in January of the following year - after they'd already been at work for six months - but retroactive to August 11, 1939. Arnold was officially appointed to the position of Housing Expert in the Department of Rural Reconstruction, along with her "assistant" Mabel Reed. They were collectively granted a $300 per month remuneration.

Things were off to a good start as the couple made excited plans for their journey to the outports. "I doubt whether all this will last but never mind, it is a gay life while it does," Arnold wrote.

They made for Marystown, from which they would undertake initial operations. Their sojourn in the outports however got off to a difficult start.

"Just before our house in Maryland was ready for occupancy Mabel and I were invited to a "Time" by some of the settlers. A 'time' in Newfoundland is a very giddy affair, dancing, story telling and FOOD, the food part especially important."

When they left, walking giddily, they hiked four miles through the dark to their boat. "Walking at night came easy to us. But getting in to a dory did not."

Reed tumbled into the boat and broke her right arm. Arnold managed to row them across the harbour, but the only doctor on the south coast was a three mile walk away. With the aid of two locals they carried Reed to the doctor, who set her arm. But it was a lengthy recovery, and for most of their stay in Newfoundland Reed's ability to help was limited by her injury. Arnold had to undertake all the strenuous journeys up and down the coast without her.

"This hit us both hard, as we have always done everything together," Arnold wrote.

Hardships aside, they soon came to love their outport home.

"We are very much enchanted with Marystown," wrote Reed. "It is a beautiful place with air like wine which ought to be enough in itself and when you add the chance of putting up twelve houses our spirits soar into the air and the days are not long enough."

Moving fishermen toward land settlement proved a challenge however. And the poverty was beyond anything the couple had seen previously in North America. The first day Arnold went out with a crew of men to begin building a house, she discovered most of the men had only brought a couple of crackers to eat for their lunch — it was all they had. Arnold and Reed had learned about coping with poverty from their previous assignments, and they began baking a kind of nourishing whole wheat cake using minimal ingredients which they fed to the men to build their strength. Soon local women were coming by in droves to take cooking lessons from Reed.

Pretty soon it wasn't just cooking advice the women were dispensing. The Commissioners in St. John's recognized the wisdom and practical sense of the two women they had unleashed on the south coast. When the local magistrate sought advice from St. John's, the telegrams he received in response began to have "better consult Miss Arnold" appended to them.

The two women adopted a kitten, which they named Patrick James Hodder, or Paddykitten for short.

Arnold and Reed were resourceful, coming up with ways around the problems they encountered. They had ordered considerable amounts of lumber from St. John's for house-building, but the schooner that was to bring the lumber didn't show up. So Arnold recruited some locals and began scouring the region for sawmill operations, from which they solicited whatever wood was available. During one of these expeditions, she encountered a group of men from Rock Harbour. As they all warmed themselves around a stove, she asked them to tell her about their community. They offered to show it to her in person. A week later a delegation showed up at the house with a dory to bring her and Reed over. The two women were welcomed like royalty. Arnold described the visit:

"As we drew in to the little wharf, we saw it was crowded with people. "Everyone has come down to see you," said Jim G. "That is most everyone. One fellow was took sick pretty bad. He couldn't come. It made him feel bad that he couldn't come. He thought maybe you would stop in to see him. We'll take you there if you'd like to go."

Followed by all the men, women and children in Rock Harbour we went to see the man who was sick. Still followed by every man, woman and child in Rock Harbour we went to see every house in Rock Harbour and every garden in Rock Harbour. We felt like Queen Victoria making a royal progress.

Then they took us to the house of Jim G's mother where we were to have dinner.

"We'll be back again," said all the people in Rock Harbour. "As soon as you've had dinner, we'll be back again."

Food is very, very hard come by in Rock Harbour. Where Mrs. Hodder had gotten the food for our dinner we did not know. What we ate stuck in our throats.

"Have some more," said Jim G.'s mother.

"Please have some more."

After dinner, Mrs Hodder told us about the Tidal Wave in Rock Harbour. We have told you about that in another story.

When we came to go, Mrs. Hodder went out for a minute and came back with something in her hand. It was a very lovely little silver spoon. It was beautifully made and must have been a hundred years old.

"This is for you," said Mrs. Hodder.

"But you mustn't give it to us," we pleaded. "You mustn't give it to us. That spoon is very old and very valuable. And it is exceptionally beautiful. Please keep it for your

children and your grandchildren."

"Please take it," said Mrs. Hodder. "I wish you to have it. Please take it."

Storm clouds were gathering as we walked back to the little wharf. The crowd was silent as we got into the dory and Jim G. picked up the oars.

"Come again," they all shouted as the sail filled. "It ain't so far from where you are to Rock Harbour."

"Come back again."

Detailed accounts such as this cover much of their time in Newfoundland: meetings with fisherman, efforts to teach them to build houses, reflections about the fishery, struggles to find ingredients to bake bread. Reed's broken arm kept the usually prolific writer from documenting her own experiences, but Arnold kept up the effort for both of them. She documented songs, and everyday conversations with neighbours. She recorded a riveting first-person account of the 1929 tidal wave that hit the coast. In Reed's writings everyday experiences -- putting up a roof on a house — become epic, heroic tales of class consciousness.

Arnold was struck by the sense of hopelessness that pervaded parts of the outports. She felt it was imperative to instill a sense of pride back into Newfoundlanders. She and Reed oversaw the construction of a demonstration house in Maryland, to which visitors were given tours as an example of what the cooperative movement could accomplish. On every wall, and every piece of locally made furniture - from shingles and rugs to chairs and tables - they affixed signs: "This was made by a Newfoundlander".

"The effect on the people who came to see the house was even greater than we anticipated," she wrote.

Arnold was fascinated above all by the people. She wrote a detailed account of a young man she met in Marystown whom she dubbed "Pretty Boy" (she never learned his real name).

"Pretty Boy must have been nineteen or twenty. He wore some kind of uniform and looked as though he had come out of a bandbox. His uniform was speckless. He had beautiful shiny boots. He was good-looking and obviously aware of it.

And that was all there was to Pretty Boy. Just a good-looking outside. That was all.

We never spoke to Pretty Boy and he never spoke to us, on our trips to Marystown.

We didn't like Pretty Boy and we didn't want to know him. Pretty Boy typified for us the class that Levi [a local songwriter] called, "those cruel, rogue merchants", the class that was responsible for the desperate straits in which Newfoundland found itself in 1939."

Then one day Arnold found herself on a train with Pretty Boy. The train had a near miss with a mountainous snow drift they all thought would be the end of them, but they survived and made it to the next station. Shaken by the near-death ordeal - "[W]e were not the same people we had been before we struck the drift" - Arnold and the others waited for the next train to St. John's.

Equally moved by the experience, Pretty Boy suddenly came over and poured out his soul to her.

"He told me all about himself. What he thought and what he felt. Especially he told me about the trip he had just made to the outports.

I don't know why Pretty Boy had been sent to the outports. But he told me that when he got there he found an epidemic. In every house, in every cabin, lay the sick, unable to move from their beds. In all the settlement, Pretty Boy was the only one on his feet. He went from house to house with food. He cleaned the rooms and washed the sick and emptied slops. He cut and gathered what wood he could find and made fires and tried to keep out the deadly cold.

Then slowly a few of the sick struggled to their feet and could give him some help. Then others began to recover and the worst was over, and Pretty Boy was on his way home.

I have never forgotten those hours with Pretty Boy on the main line while we waited for the train...Was he a different person because of what he had been through? I do not know.

But of all the people I knew in Newfoundland, Pretty Boy is someone I shall never forget.

And he is someone I am proud, I am very proud, to have known."

Arnold's optimism was irrepressible. She wrote in glowing terms of the fishermen-cum-farmers-cum-carpenters with whom she worked.

"Everyone is very much pleased with himself," she wrote. "'Maybe the houses don't look so good now,' say the carpenters who two months before were fishermen. 'But just wait until they all get painted and we get the spruces cut down and there's a garden.'"

"This has been the peach of a job," she wrote to another friend. "We like the men very much. They have neither the intelligence or the ability of the miners [in Nova Scotia] but they move you more."

Arnold's detailed chronicles offer a perceptive insight into the times. Her observations spanned the gamut. Why was Newfoundland's government so corrupt? she wondered. She concluded that in England, the bureaucracy was in charge of most decisions and kept things honest, overruling unscrupulous politicians. "In Newfoundland decisions were made by ministers and not by civil servants," she observed.

They documented their observations in personal journals as well as a rich correspondence they carried on with friends and comrades around the world, despite their remote location (they often went weeks without seeing the mail-boat, to their chagrin). "Aren't you thankful the Lord keeps us several hundred miles away so I can't make passes at you?" Arnold wrote playfully to her friend Ruth. "Imagine all the things I would think up for you to do."

Arnold and Reed had intentions to stay in Newfoundland, and continue their work. They loved the place, and the people. They felt real progress was being made toward organizing the Cooperative movement, and improving rural lives. And they had been welcomed with open arms by the poverty-stricken Newfoundlanders among whom they lived. So why did they leave after only a year?

"At times there seemed to be a very warm feeling of friendship between ourselves and the Newfoundlanders with whom we worked," Arnold wrote. "And then we would feel the undercurrent."

Jimmy Johnson was one of the first local residents they met, and they became close friends. They had never felt anything but warmth and support from him. They traveled with him by sled from community to community, dug their way through snow-clogged roads and spent long nights up past midnight talking excitedly about plans for growing the Cooperative movement.

So neither Arnold nor Reed anticipated the conversation they had with him when they all wound up in St. John's one night. As usual, they stayed up late talking about local and global events. Then they told Jimmy that they'd been asked to stay on and continue their work.

"How do you feel about it, Jimmy, should we stay or go?" Arnold asked him. She probably expected an enthusiastic yes. She described his eventual response.

"Jimmy was silent.

He was silent for so long that we were a bit startled.

He didn't look at us when, finally, he said:

"Do you want my honest opinion?"

"Of course we do," we replied.

"Then, for God's sake, go back to your own country," said Jimmy, "and let us Newfoundlanders handle our own country our own way."

"Maybe our standards are not up to yours in England or in America. But that is our affair."

"I don't mean this unkindly," he went on. "I know we are friends and that you mean well. But you people from England and from the United States get under our skins.

This is our country, not yours.

Why don't you go back to your own country where you belong."

We didn't sleep much that night. We had grown to care a good deal for Newfoundland. And for what would happen to Newfoundland.

But the more we thought about it, the more we thought that Jimmy was right.

The new approach to land settlements was working out. In some places they were already getting results. If the land settlement managers wanted to carry on, the way was clear ahead.

If they did not want to carry on, as Jimmy said, it was their country and their affair.

We did not tell Mr. Gorvin what Jimmy had said, when we told him we were going back to the United States. Leaving him with so much to be done, hit us hard.

Mr. Gorvin didn't say anything except something about the support we had given him. But it was enough to give us another sleepless night.

But Jimmy was right. Newfoundland was their country. They could make or break it as they might choose.

It was up to them."

It was a sad end to a joyous and hard-working year. The cruel, xenophobic nationalism of Jimmy Johnson was one that has often risen its head in Newfoundland; indeed, we will see it appear again before the end of this book.

But as always, Arnold and Reed bolstered their spirits by focusing on the positive. When they left Canada to return to the US, after three years in Nova Scotia and Newfoundland, wrote Arnold, "We brought something with us. That something was a belief in the common man."

"The 'cruel, rogue merchants' on the south coast of Newfoundland might be selfish, maybe cruel, and indifferent to the welfare of the fishermen. But in all the little bays and harbours of Newfoundland's long coastline, Newfoundland fishermen were not indifferent to the welfare of other men.

If you were a fisherman, maybe you could just manage to sign your name and write a letter of sorts.

But you could learn.

House building, for most of the fishermen we knew, was a new trade. But with only a minimum of instruction and help, Newfoundland fishermen mastered a new trade, stuck to it, bad weather or good, patiently and steadily, and did a creditable job.

Cost accounting was an entirely new experience to the men from Rock Harbor but none of the people we had known back in the United States took to it more readily or came out with better results.

Helping each other in a tight place was part of the way of life of a Newfoundland fisherman…

Newfoundland fishermen had what it takes.

They had courage and endurance.

They had intelligence and technical skill.

They had kindness and consideration for other men.

With a bit of trial and error, they could learn to work together in a new way of life.

What more do you want if you would build a new life for yourself.

Or build a better world?

Queering the fisheries

While all genders played an equally important role in the prosecution of the fishery, fishing vessels themselves were a predominantly male space, and are often associated with normative expressions of masculinity. It's a space ripe for queering.

The Portuguese White Fleet plays an iconic role in Newfoundland's history. For centuries, Portuguese fleets fished, alongside those of other nations, off the Grand Banks of Newfoundland. Those white-hulled vessels of the Portuguese fleet became iconic in the twentieth century. During much of Portugal's Second Republic (a period of right-wing military rule spanning roughly 1926-1974) the country's authoritarian leadership resisted innovation in a variety of fields, including the fishery. Consequently, Portugal's aging and old-fashioned White Fleet (including handliners and dories) remained in use long after other nations had modernized their fleets using more destructive factory trawler technologies. The Portuguese White Fleet provided a striking visual display when the vessels entered St. John's Harbour en masse to shelter from approaching storms or re-supply for the long journey home at the end of their annual fishery. At the end of the season (which spanned roughly May to October), the fleet would sail into St. John's Harbour for a few days of hard-earned rest, shopping and carousing before returning home to Portugal (Andrieux 2013).

Relationships between Portugal and NL flourished during this period. In 1955, when the Roman Catholic Cathedral in St. John's became a Basilica, a statue of the Lady of Fatima was donated to the City of St. John's by the Portuguese fishermen for installation in the Basilica. The entire White Fleet sailed into St. John's Harbour for the occasion, and their crews — roughly 4000 fishermen — marched from the waterfront to the Basilica in a parade, carrying the statue and chanting in Latin. The statue of Gaspar Corte-Real, a Portuguese explorer and slave-trader which has stood in front of the Confederation Building for decades, was donated in 1965 and dedicated by the Portuguese ambassador to Canada; its plaque also commemorates the fishing relationship between the two countries. There is also a small parkette celebrating the bilateral relationship near the harbourfront in downtown St. John's.

That relationship became increasingly strained from the late 1950s onward, and when Portugal began modernizing its fleet (as fish stocks plummeted due to overfishing, the antiquated Portuguese fishing techniques meant they were plagued by low catches sooner than other fishing fleets) the threat they posed to fish stocks came under the same criticism as the fleets of other nations. In 1974 a tumultuous series of events marked the end of the White Fleet. By then, comprised of only three remaining ships, the fleet left Portugal a mere two days before the Carnation Revolution that toppled the military regime in that country and ushered in a period of political turmoil before Portugal eventually settled into a sort of democracy. The Portuguese on the Grand Banks were excited to learn about events back home, and wanted to participate in the revolutionary action. So, upon learning of the revolution, the fishers sailed their vessels to the French island of St. Pierre and announced they were on strike in solidarity with the revolutionaries back home. Nervous French officials, together with the boats' captains, eventually tricked or strong-armed most of the sailors back on board and they returned to the Grand Banks. However, one of the vessels caught fire and sank shortly thereafter, and so the remaining two boats put in at St. John's to off-load the rescued crew. There, the fishers went on strike once more, demanding better wages (in fact, most of them were paid with a percentage of the catch, so wages at all were an improvement). The captains offered them pay increases, but the crews didn't trust them. An official with the fishermen's union flew to St. John's from Portugal to negotiate. J.P. Andrieux, in his pictorial history *The White Fleet*, describes the situation:

"The fishermen had posted signs in the windows of the fishermen's centre on Water Street in St. John's, which translated to 'Up with democracy; down with fascism.' The union representative, who had been a fisherman himself until the formation of the union after the overthrow of the previous regime, was not happy, and said that the fishermen were making impossible demands. 'All they understood was strike, strike, strike'" (Andrieux 2013).

Eventually the vessels were ordered to leave Newfoundland. One of the remaining two boats caught fire just outside of the harbour and sank. The crew was rescued and returned to St. John's, from whence they were flown back to Portugal. On July 24, 1974, the final surviving boat of the White Fleet left St. John's harbour, never to return.

For the gay community, the White Fleet played an iconic role as well. Many of the Portuguese sailors were gay, or at least bisexual, and queer hookups were common when the Fleet sailed in to town. Ron Knowling remembered the excitement of his friends on those occasions.

"The Portuguese sailors would come off the White Fleet and I don't know if it's because they were Latin, but they'd be as happy to hook up with a guy as with a girl," he recalled. Others remember them too.

"I don't know what was going on, I don't know whether it was bisexual stuff or whether they identified as gay, but definitely there were lots of gay men in St. John's who had relations with Portuguese sailors - seamen, fishermen," recalled Karl Wells.

Larry Kelly remembers them as well. "They would play ball on the waterfront. Soccer – or football as they called it. They had lots of spectators."

"And they played music," added Wells. "They all played accordions. Life downtown, the life of the harbour, was so enriched by those people. It broke my heart when we banned them. Our relationship with the Portuguese went back hundreds of years."

Gay men who lived through the final years of the White Fleet remember the Portuguese sailors making a beeline for the same bars frequented by gay men as soon as they got off their boats. Wells remembers them filling up the Fogo-a-Gogo, and Brian Caines remembers them packing into the Waterfront before that. Both these bars were centres of downtown gay life in the 1970s.

"The Waterfront is where the Portuguese sailors would often go," explained Caines. "And they would get sexual satisfaction, some of them. They didn't speak English – their English was very basic. You'd buy them beer or whatever. I think they were quite lonely."

"The White Fleet was popular amongst very closeted gay men," explained John Bragg. The likelihood of anyone finding out about sexual escapades with the returning sailors - who would only be in town for a few days, and mostly didn't speak English — was low. And the prospect of thousands of new young men, in a city of barely a quarter million, was undoubtedly an attraction as well. But sometimes communication could be tough. Bragg recalls one personal adventure from 1973, during the Fleet's final years.

"I drove a friend's car – it was a lime green Comet with a white and green houndstooth roof. It glowed in the dark! [My friend] and I picked up these two Portuguese sailors, and took them in this car to the Southside Hills. I'd never been up there in my life. We went to a gravel pit in the Southside Hills. After sex one of the sailors said: "Jiggy jiggy five dollar." I said to [my friend]: 'What the fuck is he talking about?' But he knew the expression from somewhere. They wanted money for this service they thought they had given us!" (Bragg, 2021).

Snapshots of queer lives

In the pre-Internet era, NL was more isolated than it is today but queer people and communities in the province maintained vibrant connections with the wider world. They travelled widely, they wrote letters and a fledgling queer press kept different parts of the country in communication with each other. In 1996, Michael Riordan published *Out Our Way: Gay and Lesbian Life in the Country*. The book is worth a read, both for the rich diversity of queer lives it chronicles, as well as the pleasure of Riordan's bucolic prose. He travelled across Canada, meeting and documenting queer lives. In Newfoundland, he met and documented the stories of several individuals. Jim Genge, a Glovertown resident who grew up there in the 1950s and 1960s, was one of many rural NLers who engaged with wider queer community via correspondence. "Philip" (a pseudonym) was a Torontonian hired to teach at Grenfell College, while "Morrissey" (also a pseudonym) was a teenaged resident of a small west coast town. In small-town Ontario Riordan finds an ex-pat Newfoundlander running a guest house (and now art gallery) with his partner. Nearly a quarter century later Joey Shulman (the ex-pat) is still going strong, and makes his own appearance later in this book. Riordan's work shone an important light on the vibrant presence of queer life, not just in Canada's big cities, but in every rural corner of the country, this province included (Riordan 1996).

While some queer NLers - like Upward - had positive childhoods growing up in small communities, for others the experience was tremendously difficult. Barry Nichols was born in 1955 and grew up in Deer Lake.

"I hated growing up in Deer Lake," he recalled. "It was so behind in so many ways. It didn't have any core values. People talk about 'traditional val-

ues' but these places really didn't have any values. Or they were all horrible values – misogyny and sexism. In Deer Lake everybody was screwing everybody all the time. Parents were...all screwing each other. It was traumatizing for the kids because you feel betrayed. I was just amazed by it, growing up in a small place. I think what bothered me more than anything else was the sense of betrayal, the dishonesty. It just felt so dishonest and so horrible. But it was totally conservative as well...it just made me cringe. It felt like, this is hopeless and you can't even change it (Nichols, 2021)."*

But change it they did. What follows are a few other accounts of queer lives: a snapshot of the diversity that comprises NL queer history.

Walt Chaisson: From Codroy Valley to the Toronto bathhouses

The Codroy Valley is farming country.

When Walt Chaisson went back to visit his family on the west coast of Newfoundland in the 2010s, he was astonished how much had changed. Pride celebrations were happening in Corner Brook, Bay St. George, Stephenville Crossing. Kids he remembered as homophobic bullies had grown up and now, as adults, identified as allies.

"Some of the toughest guys that I went to school with have gay kids, have trans kids, and they're open about it. To my face! Even the ones that don't have LGBTQ kids, they're supporting it, they're all 'Rah rah rah, long live gay rights!' It's incredible."

Chaisson was born in the small community of Searston in 1965. Searston is one of the several tiny communities that make up the Codroy Valley. Chaisson was born into a family of six children. His father was a farmer.

"I knew from a very early age that I was different," he recalled. "Just knew it, gut instinct. But I couldn't vocalize exactly what it was."

As he grew up, he realized he was attracted to other men. He also realized this was information he couldn't safely share with those around him.

"Growing up on a farm, with a father who's very vocal about queers and fairies and fruits, you knew you couldn't act either bit soft. As a gay kid, you know what you shouldn't do in public. So you don't do certain things, you don't talk about certain things. You make sure that you hold yourself a certain way. You make sure that you try to do sports. I couldn't, but I practiced basketball and stuff at home.

"It was always about looking over your shoulder, making sure you didn't do anything wrong. Did I say anything wrong? Do I look a certain way? I remember being teased about the way I looked. My lips were redder back then, and I was told that I was a fruit because my lips were red. This was when I was seven or eight. I remember crying, I remember praying to God – like a good little Catholic boy – 'please make me normal, please make me normal. Please

make me normal.' And growing up, going to school, and just making sure that you did nothing to draw attention (Chaisson, 2021)."

"The elementary school years were brutal. I hated them beyond belief. [I was] picked on, bullied continuously…You're trying to blend in, but by doing that you're actually calling more attention to yourself."

As a young child, Chaisson had an experience that underscored for him the dangers of enacting gender in ways that violated expected norms. He was brought to St. John's to have an operation done on his leg. After the operation, he spent several weeks at the rehab centre at the Janeway Children's Hospital, recovering. There, he met an older child – a teenager of fourteen or fifteen years, as he recalls – who he now realizes was a transgender girl.

"[The patient] was dressing in girls' clothes on the ward, and they had a huge issue with it – the nurses and staff. It was very looked down upon."

On Regatta Day, inmates and staff at the Penitentiary put off an annual carnival for children at the rehab centre, and Chaisson remembers winning a prize, which turned out to be a plastic fairy necklace and lipstick package. The child he believes to be trans came over and begged him for the prize, asking if she could have the lipstick. Sure thing, said Chaisson, and handed it over.

"I can remember seeing the people in the hospital bristling, just shaking their heads, so angry with her. Just not understanding, not accepting, not having any time for it. They were like – 'this is not right. We're not doing this.'"

In high school, Chaisson joined the drama club, which gave him a bit of leeway to act differently. But his overall memory of school years was that of a constant struggle to avoid being perceived as different, and the bullying it would elicit if he was.

Chaisson graduated high school in Grade 11, when he was sixteen years old. The nearby city of Corner Brook housed Sir Wilfred Grenfell College, which is a campus of Memorial University. At the time, students could only take their first two years of an undergraduate degree at Grenfell. But this enabled him to move out of his parents' home, and into a student residence in Corner Brook. At the time, the city had a population of about 25,000.

"That was a whole different ball game," he recalls. "That's where I looked, but I didn't touch. The first year was horrible for me, because I was quiet, and shy, and just really introverted. It was rough. I was going through a whole bunch of stuff in my head, about 'Am I really gay? If so, how do I live – literally how do I live – how do I do this?' Corner Brook was still very small, and I had relatives there. So that first year I was just really overwhelmed."

In his second year, Chaisson picked up cigarette smoking in order to meet people socially. He also started doing drugs, and these activities helped him develop a social circle. He was able to pursue male bonding experiences without being suspected or accused of being gay.

In his third year, he moved to St. John's to continue undergraduate studies. "Oh god, all the doors came off then," he recalls.

At this point he began having sexual experiences with other men. But he had also been seeking sexual experiences with women, since he knew this was the conventional form of relationship that was expected of him. The same year he started sleeping with men, he also began dating a woman whom he would eventually marry.

"We had a very healthy, very active sex life," he recalls. "Even though in my head I didn't consider myself straight, I considered myself gay."

Chaisson continued pursuing hook-ups with other men, but was terrified of being caught.

"I remember in university, meeting up with this guy from the Phys Ed department. He was so nice, so awesome, and I saw him one night at a dance in a club. I walked by and he grabbed my shoulder. I remember this terror, this feeling of 'Oh my god, someone's going to know!' And so I pulled away. It was probably one of my biggest regrets, because he was so nice, and he had reached out to me - and of course he had to be very careful too. So even though I had accepted that I was gay at that point, I was still thinking: 'You cannot let anyone know! You cannot!'

"This was the early 1980s. To be a fag was probably the worst thing that you could be — especially in university. You were nothing — you were less than nothing. It wasn't accepted. It was very down-low, very cloistered, very closeted. There were no gay bars, no gay clubs, there were no gay organizations on campus, nothing.[10] *So you had nothing. You had no refuge. I cannot remember seeing anyone promoting the fact that they were gay. No one actively saying 'This is who I am, I'm queer, leave me the fuck alone' kind of thing. There were no resources. There was nothing promoting any kind of LGBT community acceptance in university during the 1980s when I was there. Nothing. It was really kind of isolating and that's why I felt that I had to be very closeted and have these brief encounters in washrooms and showers and wherever you could get them"* (Ibid.).

The one glimmer of openness Chaisson remembers happened one day as he passed the university's Interfaith Society office. There he saw a student sitting with a rainbow flag pinned to his coat.

"I immediately thought - I gotta stay away from that organization. There was a gay guy there, so I couldn't go near that. He might have seen me somewhere."

After graduating in 1988, Chaisson managed to get into a program at Memorial University's Harlow Campus in the UK, and so he spent a summer in Europe.

"I was amazed at the difference. The acceptance, the feeling of 'who cares?' The difference that sexual orientation didn't seem to matter. It was liberating."

Chaisson wound up in a relationship with a British man during those sum-

---

[10] In fact there were, but the fact he was unaware of them attests to the low profile they kept.

mer months at Harlow.

"I met this guy in a bathroom — old habits die hard I suppose - and we started seeing each other on the down-low, because I was with this group of Canadian people, and no one knew that I was gay. But it was incredible. It actually changed me, because after that I became much more confident in who I was. But when I came back to Newfoundland I fell right back into the old way of doing things, because there was still no safety net - there was nothing here" (Ibid.).

Chaisson wound up marrying the woman he'd been seeing, and together they moved back to the Codroy Valley. He got a job teaching at his old high school, and they remained there for three years.

"It was a safety net for me because I knew how to behave in that location. I didn't have to learn any of the norms of what I could do or what I couldn't do in another town. I knew that this is the way it has to be - you can't do this, you can't do that, you have to join this committee, you have to be in the Knights of Columbus, you have to read in church, you have to do all that kind of crap correctly in order to cover your tail... When someone would say to me that they didn't have any time for gay people, I would reply 'I don't care as long as they don't come around me.' That was my response. That was considered an acceptable response for a heterosexual guy to have, so that was the line I always used, in the Valley or in university.

"So I pushed all my sexuality down for three years in that community" (Ibid.).

The first two years went smoothly. The third year did not.

"Unbeknownst to me, the kids at the high school always chose a different teacher to pick on each year. That third year was my year, apparently. They tried to burn my house down — on Hallowe'en we had pumpkins out on the doorstep and they threw gasoline on them and tried to burn us out. Then they made all kinds of threatening phone calls about raping my wife and killing me and all kinds of stuff. Small-town Newfoundland, right? We got a phone tap, and they traced the line back to whoever was making the calls. And it happened to be some of the godchildren of the principal. So we went to court - it was a police matter at that point - the cops took them to court with me, but they were all [juveniles]. Then – conveniently – my job became redundant. So we said: 'We're done.' We packed everything into the back of a car and headed to Toronto." (Ibid.).

When Chaisson and his wife arrived in Toronto, he remained in the closet for the first few years. But in a city of that size it became easier to have secret hookups with men, which he also pursued. He eventually made friends with another closeted gay man who was married.

"He was so normal and he was very conservative in his thinking and in his politics. No one would think it was possible that he could be gay, so therefore by association I couldn't be gay either. It was a way of covering my ass."

It was considered normal for two married men to be friends and spend time together, so they would often purport to go into the city to watch sports games, and head to the gay bathhouses instead. It was at the bathhouses that Chaisson first began to confront his relationship with his sexuality.

"I met two guys who totally changed my life. Those two guys said to me: 'You have to be who you are. You have to make choices. It's tough, but you have to make choices and be who you are. You can choose to be happy, or you can choose to be unhappy for the rest of your life.'"

The two men told him that if he wanted to come out, and needed a place to stay after telling his wife, he was welcome to stay with them.

"It was like, wow. My entire life changed on a dime. Overnight. I had a place to stay, I had someone to help me. I found the guidance, I found the mentorship that I had been lacking all my life. I never once had had any kind of male role model that I could lean on. Ever. But then these guys were there, and suddenly – boom. I had someone I could stay with, I had someone I could rely on" (Ibid.).

Things happened very quickly after that. Chaisson told his wife that he was gay. She didn't take the news well, and he moved out. He was teaching at a Catholic school, and she contacted the school board to tell them he was gay. He realized he needed to act quickly and proactively, and so he came out to his employer and colleagues. His union supported him, and he was able to keep his job.

The year was 2000, and the gay rights movement was in full swing.

"Everything started coming into place. The whole birth of [gay rights] protections was when I was taking my baby steps as a fully identified gay man, and that made me feel very much empowered. It was something I had never had before. Because you couldn't speak up for gay rights when you were in Newfoundland, in the 1970s, 1980s, even 1990s. 'Cocksuckers' were meant to be beaten up, and the worst insult you could possibly have is that you were called a 'fruit' or a 'fag.' You didn't have the same rights, you weren't allowed an opinion. You were a non-status person. You had no one to come to your rescue and say 'That's not right.' I was lucky that I didn't get beaten up, and I didn't get bashed. But there was an overwhelming sense of being abandoned and disowned. There was no room for any kind of different opinions. There was no margin for error. Unless you wanted to be shunned and disowned growing up, which I didn't" (Ibid.).

Once Chaisson came out, he became openly involved in queer activism. He continued working at a Catholic school board until his retirement, but he openly identified as gay and became provincial LGBTQ representative on his union's diversity and inclusion committee. He wrote articles about his experience as a queer teacher in a Catholic school, and mentored other young gay teachers in the system.

"I would tell them: 'for the love of Christ stop saying that if you're gay you're lucky to have a job. You know what - they're lucky to have you. So stop saying that.' It's getting better. It's not perfect, and never will be. But you keep kicking and you keep fighting."

Chaisson met his partner Jack at The Barn, a dance club on Church Street in downtown Toronto. The two danced together, and then made out on the patio. Later that night as Chaisson was going to the washroom, he saw Jack again.

"He just kind of winks at me and slaps his ass, and gave me a wink that I thought was the funniest thing I'd ever seen in my life. I started peeing all over the wall because I was laughing so hard. I was like, 'This is incredible. He's so funny, and kind of cute.' So I said fuck it - I told him 'I'm going to the spa next door, if you want to meet me I'll see you there.' So I go over, and I'm in my room, and I stick my head out the door and lo and behold here's Jack coming down the hallway" (Ibid.).

Before leaving that night Jack asked for Chaisson's phone number. Neither of them had anything to write on, so Chaisson told him his number and said if he was able to remember it, then he could give him a call sometime. Jack phoned at 8:30am the next morning to ask him out for coffee.

"I met him on a Friday, we got together on a Saturday, and we've been together ever since," says Chaisson with a smile. They were married on July 23, 2011.

Chaisson was making a summer visit home to Newfoundland several years ago when his sister – then a city councillor – invited him to take part in Corner Brook's first Pride Parade. It was a small parade, but he remembers it fondly.

"About twenty of us walked up the road with a boombox. We went to that park by the old movie theatre, right in the centre of town, close to where they have the Corner Brook sign now. That was amazing. It was really kind of cool to be part of that.

"I remembering being in Corner Brook for that first Pride, and thinking: 'I'm gay, this is awesome.' It boggles my mind. I often wonder what it would have been like to grow up now. I think I would have been a totally different person. My generation had something to struggle against. But when we gathered for that first Corner Brook Pride, I realized that wow — this has been worth the struggle" (Ibid.).

Rick Boland: From Corner Brook to Stonewall

1969 is a year etched into popular consciousness. It was the year the first humans landed on the moon. It was the year of the Woodstock Music Festival. It was the year of the iconic Stonewall Riots in New York City.

And in early 1969, in Curling – a rural community on the west coast of Newfoundland - Rick Boland was a teenager looking for love.

He thought he'd found it, in the form of a high school classmate. They were sexual partners, at any rate. But when Boland brought up the subject of love, it elicited an angry, scornful reaction from the other boy.

"He was not interested in that," Boland recalled half a century later. "He said it was only queers that fell in love with each other."

The other boy was adamant the sexual acts they engaged in didn't make them gay. "What we were doing was fine, it was just buddies helping buddies," he told Boland. As long as romance didn't enter the picture, they weren't gay.

Boland wanted romance. He wanted a relationship. He finally concluded that in order to find another man he could be openly romantic with, he would have to come out publicly as gay.

And so, in that west coast community in 1969, Rick Boland decided to come out.

The decision didn't come easily. Homosexuality had only been decriminalized that same year, and the social stigma surrounding it would take decades to erode. Boland struggled with his sexual identity. He knew what he liked, but he also knew that the social institutions around him – media, schools, and of course the all-powerful Catholic church – told him it was wrong for him to feel attracted to men. There were no other role models to look to; Boland would become one of the first Newfoundlanders to be open about his sexuality. But coming to that decision was a torturous process.

First he consulted one of the teachers at his school. He attended Regina High School in nearby Corner Brook, which was the Catholic regional high school. It was run by the Irish Christian Brothers. He told one of the Brothers, whom he considered a mentor, about the feelings he was having.

The Brother told him: "This doesn't make you any less of a person. It doesn't make you a bad person. But you have to be very careful in your life."

There was also an older priest, in his nineties, attached to the school as a chaplain. It was to this priest that Boland next confessed he felt an attraction to other boys.

"Basically [the priest] said to me: 'You're a child of God. You know what sin is, and I don't think this is a sin. I don't think God meant to have you on the periphery because of who you love.' And this from a 95-year-old priest! I thought that was amazing."

The social stigma was pervasive, and he still feared there was something wrong with him. He made an appointment to see a psychiatrist at Western Memorial Hospital in Corner Brook. The psychiatrist he wound up seeing was a young American, a draft-dodger who had moved to Newfoundland.

"He said: 'Look, there's nothing wrong with you. You shouldn't be going to see a psychiatrist. If every teenager who was in love and got jilted came to see me, I'd have no time for people who are really sick.' He suggested that I might have some hard times because of [being gay], but I should persevere. He said there was certainly nothing deviant – that was the word at the time – there was nothing deviant about me, and what was going on with me was something that was really important and society would catch up to me sooner or later.

That was the best advice I could possibly have had. It was self-affirming and just so clear, not couched in any dogma" (Boland 2021).

It's remarkable that at a time when other Newfoundlanders faced the threat of losing their jobs, homes and families; and in some cases were institutionalized in mental hospitals for being queer, young Rick Boland encountered positive reinforcement almost everywhere he turned.

When he did encounter would-be bullies, he relied on a quick wit to fend them off.

"I was a saucy little fucker and if somebody said I was a fairy or a queer or whatnot, what I'd say is: 'Oh so you're interested, are you?' And that'd take them aback and they'd back off."

"Most people didn't really want to hear about it. People were afraid of it, I think. They were afraid of knowing, for the most part. Nobody was willing to [come out] in Corner Brook. If you were gay you moved to Montreal or Vancouver."

While Boland wasn't afraid of the repercussions to himself, what he regrets today is not realizing how his identity would impact his family. 'He didn't get that from me!' was his father's reaction to rumours about his sexuality. His mother was fine with it, and his grandmother simply added a prayer "for Ricky and his affliction" to her nightly devotionals. But his siblings faced the brunt of it, in the form of taunting and bullying at school.

Boland eventually approached an older man he suspected – by his behaviour and manner of dress – to be gay, and finally found the sort of support he'd been seeking.

"I sort of followed him around town, and finally one day as I was stalking him he turned around to me and said: 'What's wrong with you?' I said: 'Well, I'm gay, and I think you're gay, and I need to talk to somebody who's gay.' And he laughed, and he said: 'Oh well, yes, let's get together.'"

"So I was out, and I was out in Corner Brook, a mill town where everybody knew everybody's business."

Boland didn't stay in Corner Brook for long. And although he was out, he hadn't yet acquired the zeal for activism that would drive him in later years. That inspiration would come, in part, from an encounter with a Black trans woman named Delores.

The fall of 1969 found Boland hitchhiking his way through Canada and the US. It was a time of social flux, he recalls. People were fired up with new ideas, and eager to share their perspectives with others in a way he found more intense and personal than today.

"It was a time of great education," he recalls. "I met people on the road who were just ordinary people – today they might be called hippies – who were much more willing to [share] than people are today. They had thought about these ideas. Back then everybody wanted to tell you their idea about how the world was, and how it was evolving."

Boland met Delores in Boston. The child of civil rights activists, she was a drag performer who lived in New York City. But she introduced herself to Boland as an 'epicurean'.

"She said she was an Epicurean in the old Greek sense of epicurean, which was that in life we have to experience and to taste. Anything that you encounter in life has to be examined, and [because] we have free will, whatever made you happy was what was right for you. If you didn't feel well enough to talk about who you were, to experience what you felt, then there was no point in living. It meant that you were the arbiter of your fate, not somebody else or some god who had been dead for many millennia" (Ibid.).

Boland was taken with Delores, and the two became fast friends. She insisted he accompany her back to New York City, and even bought his bus ticket. They talked the entire bus ride there, eagerly exchanging ideas.

The Stonewall riots had happened just weeks earlier, and Delores told him about the dramatic events. She and her circle of queer friends had been at the heart of the riots. When they got to New York, Boland accepted her invitation to crash at Delores' apartment, and he stayed there for the next few weeks, sleeping on her couch. Every evening the apartment became a hub of activity.

"Her apartment was filled with drag queens who would take two hours preparing to go out, and chatting about what had happened [at Stonewall]. There was a great disgust of the police because many of the girls felt that they had been betrayed. They were friends with a number of the police who had raided the club, and who were quite familiar with the club and the girls and guys that went there. [The police] were known as sort of friendly, and [the women] had never thought there was going to be any hate or anything.

"Delores was very good friends with a couple of police officers. She had been thrown in jail on a number of occasions in the race riots... she felt that there were many allies in the police force and that [the Stonewall raids] shouldn't have happened. She felt that the whole crackdown on LGBT culture was a vindictive thing, that it was a political move" (Ibid.).

Boland, swept up in this maelstrom of ideas and activism, initially imagined himself falling in love and settling down in New York, but the more he got to know the city, the more he decided it was too big for his liking. He returned to Newfoundland and enrolled at Memorial University in St. John's. But his experience among the Black drag queens and trans women of Stonewall changed him forever.

"They were much more aware of what was going on in terms of their sexuality, and they were more militant. So when I got to university I was really pumped up to be a kind of activist, as much of an activist as you could be in St. John's."

Karl Wells and Larry Kelly: A Love Story

Karl Wells was born in 1953, in Buchans. His father was the cook in the town's hotel. When Wells was only two years old the family relocated to St. John's. His father opened a grocery store – Wells' Groceteria - at the top of Golf Avenue, in the centre city near Buckmaster's Circle (back then it was considered the city's west end). Karl grew up above the grocery store.

"I've known since I was a child that I was different," he reflects. "I remember when I was very young, hearing my mother talk about homosexuality, and it was in a negative way. Somehow, even though I was only ten years old, I knew that she was talking about me, in the sense that I knew I was one of those people. It was a bit scary.

"As I grew older my attraction for others of my gender became obvious. So when I was thirteen or fourteen, another boy of the same age, in the same grade, basically seduced me. And then I realized: this is who I am. And there's nothing I can do about it. I knew I was in a minority – but I also realized that at the end of the day there was nothing I could do about it, this was just who I am" (Wells 2021).

Wells came out to his family in 1976.

"When I told my mother, she began to weep and get very upset, but eventually she said that she had always had a feeling that I might be [gay]. And I never ever spoke to my father about it. I guess I wasn't brave enough or something. But I knew that he wouldn't have a problem with it, because my father had had a gay friend. My father was killed in a car crash not long after I came out, but my mother told me that it didn't bother him one bit.

"Eventually I connected with some other people who were gay and who would talk to me about being gay in a clandestine kind of way. Eventually we figured out that you could go downtown and there were clubs, and you could cruise Water Street and get picked up or pick up somebody. I never really cruised very much, I didn't really like anonymous hook-ups. So I went to gay bars.

"The first bar I remember where gay people went was the Fogo-a-Gogo, on Baird's Cove. It's where Boca's Restaurant is now, in that building. Soon afterwards Friends opened. That's where Larry and I met. The first time I laid eyes on Larry I thought he was straight, I didn't think he was gay. Here's this guy – this macho guy – leaning up against the cigarette machine with a beard and looking at me. I thought he wanted to beat me up or something!

("I just wanted to handcuff him" – interjects Larry with a laugh).

"It was a very, very pleasant surprise when I found out he was gay and was actually interested in me! A mutual friend of ours happened to bump into me, and I said: 'Do you know that guy over there by the cigarette machine?' He said: 'Oh yeah. Do you want to meet him?' I said: 'Well, yeah, if he's gay.' So he introduced us. And the rest is history. We have not been apart a day since.

That was in 1980.

"Prior to meeting Larry I was in a gay relationship. I wasn't single very long because I guess I've always wanted to be part of a couple, I wanted to have a partner, long-term. And so I became partners with a guy and we were together about three years. I thought we were having a monogamous relationship until one day I found out that he was having the occasional session of anonymous sex outside our relationship. And that's when I told him it was over. Because I was not interested in being in a relationship that was anything but monogamous. He wanted to continue living together and I said: 'Well we can continue to live together but I am not going to be your lover any more. But if you want to continue as roommates then fine.' So we did, up until I met Larry.

"When I met Larry, I didn't realize he was married. He was married - to a woman. I had always – I've changed my opinion since – but at that time I had always believed that gay people who got married [to women] were not being true to themselves. I had a gay friend who got married simply because it would help him get promotions in the company that he worked for. I mean, why would you do that? Why would you do that to another human being? Pretend that you're something you're not?" (Ibid.).*

Larry Kelly was born in Gander. He spent his pre-school years in Gambo, and at the age of seven his family moved to Glenwood, in central Newfoundland. He came from a large Catholic family – eight siblings - and went to school in Gander.

"I didn't know anybody who was gay growing up," Larry said. "And I didn't identify as being gay although I knew I was different from my siblings. At school I do recall having attractions toward other guys... but I didn't identify as being gay. And I got married when I was really young, to a woman. I was nineteen, and I think I was putting pressure on myself to either hide or suppress what was really going on. So that marriage didn't last. It lasted for four years, or less. Thankfully there were no children involved. But I did stray from that marriage and meet a couple of guys during that time, when I started realizing [that I was gay]. All I can remember is fear and self-loathing and anxiety and all those kinds of feelings.*

"Then I was walking home one evening and it hit me. It was kind of overwhelming, and I realized: I am gay. It was like there was a switch and there was no going back, no turning back. So that's when I started moving forward in that direction.*

"When I first realized I was gay and I knew the marriage was going to break down, I went to see a priest here in St. John's. I used to go to church then. But I didn't get a warm reception. I got told: 'You're in for it! It's a very dark road you're going down, and yadda yadda yadda.' It was not helpful at all. The first priest I went to see gave me that spiel, and then later on after I had moved out, this older priest also told me off. I never went back to the Catholic Church.*

Ever. Except to go to my father's funeral.

"When the marriage split up and my family became aware, they were outraged. Outraged. The first thing my mother wanted to do – and she did – was
she made an appointment with the bishop in Grand Falls. She said: 'You have
to go see the bishop.' And my dad's first reaction was: 'I don't want to see him
again.' That only lasted a brief period of time, that initial reaction; my dad
was fine after that. But I had brothers who just wanted to kill Karl, because
they blamed him.

"My mom came around eventually. It took a long time for them to come
around and invite Karl into their house in Glenwood. Ten years, probably. And
it came after an ultimatum: either you accept this, or you don't see me. I'm
done. I can't do it any more (Kelly 2021).

"Well, it worked out, but I remember those early days. I lived in fear all
the time, it seemed. I'd go to a bar but I was fearful that somebody would see
me from work. I was fearful of the police if I drove downtown. I didn't cruise
either, but even if I was going into Friends [bar] or something, I'd have to run
in under cover. That went on for years, that fear."

When Karl and Larry met, it was love at first sight. But the fact Larry was
married nearly derailed their relationship.

"Back then I would see lots of gay guys in marriages with women," explained Karl. "The term was 'a beard.' He has a beard. The woman was his
beard, right? I just hated it. I hated it. Because I decided long ago that I was
never going to pretend to be anything other than what I am, come hell or high
water. So when I found out Larry was gay, I was like – oh gee. But then when I
found out he was married, I was just like: 'Sorry. I can't do this. I just cannot
do this. I can't get involved in this.'

"But I had fallen in love with him. So I remember saying to him: we cannot live together or be together unless you get divorced. Which is what he did"
(Wells 2021).

"It was a couple of tumultuous years!" remarked Larry. "It was difficult
because we were struggling around all of this, and I didn't have any family support. Any friends that I had had as part of a married couple, they were gone. I
hadn't been part of the gay community, so I didn't really have any gay friends,
either, only people that [Karl] knew. I did have two boyfriends before Karl but
they were very brief. And they both died of AIDS. Well one died of suicide, he had
AIDS but he took his own life" (Kelly 2021).

"When AIDS came along, a lot of our friends died," explained Karl. "Our
contemporaries. A lot of our friends died. And right around the time AIDS was
hitting, a lot of our friends moved to Toronto. And then they started dying up
there. So everything changed. Our lives would have turned out much differently - we'd have many, many more gay friends than we do now if AIDS hadn't
hit."

"And they were brilliant. And they were funny. And they were full of life," reflected Larry.

"The only thing that saved myself and Larry was the fact that we were in a monogamous relationship," said Karl. "There's absolutely no doubt in my mind that I would not be here talking to you today if we had not been together. This relationship saved our lives. No doubt about it."

Larry had been working at the General Hospital in St. John's, and then the Health Sciences Centre. In 1982 he went back to school to study nursing. After that he got a job at the Miller Centre, where he eventually became program director for rehabilitation and palliative care services. He worked there his entire life, and it was a workplace he remembers as being inclusive and respectful.

Karl went on to a storied career with CBC. He experienced a great deal of homophobia in his work environment, and his story is explored further in Chapter 5.

In 2010, Karl and Larry were married. Same-sex marriage had been legal for several years before they decided to tie the knot.

"We didn't get married right away, because we thought: 'We've been together decades, why get married?' reflected Karl. "Then ultimately we just wanted to do it."

"It felt right," adds Larry with a warm smile, placing his hand over Karl's.

"I think we both wanted to make a public commitment and have friends and family there," said Karl. "Even though sadly I honestly don't know if certain members of our families really think our marriage is as legitimate as a straight marriage."

"That's their problem," responds Larry. "We were the first same-sex couple to be married at Gower Street United Church.

"And I think now is the best time in my life, really," he says, looking over at Karl with a shy smile. "As we grow older."

Lori Seay: Bay Girl

Lori Seay is from Dunville. Born in 1971, she comes from a younger generation than the preceding men. "I'm a bay girl!" she exclaims with pride, although she now lives on Canada's other west coast (Galiano Island, British Columbia). Her father was an American military officer who remained in the province after marrying a Newfoundlander who refused to leave. He worked at the US military base in Argentia, and the family lived on base until Lori was a teenager. By then, she knew without a doubt she was lesbian.

"There were loads of dykes around," she recalls of her childhood on the US base. "There were gorgeous butch dykes in uniform everywhere and I was swooning."

Homosexuality was a recurring subtext on the base and in her childhood. Her father, she says, would today be considered an ally — he thought homophobia was ridiculous, and was disgusted at the waste of time, energy and resources the US military put into trying to catch queer soldiers. Some of the officers who worked with her father were gay. One was a "giant farm boy" from the southern US named Tom.

"He was gay, and one day my dad said 'I think you and Tom should be friends.' I was in university by that point, so I was like: 'I know what that means. That means Tom's gay and Tom needs help.' So I took Tom to the gay bar in St. John's and it was the last time I saw him — the men were on him like locusts because he was so beautiful" (Seay 2022).

The gay bar in St. John's — at that time the main venue was Solomons on Water Street — was however a dangerous environment for soldiers and other military employees.

"Military police would follow them, and go to the gay bar and try to catch gay people. It happened — there were at least two dishonourable discharges. [...] It was really, really unsafe. The military had people undercover at the gay bar, and they'd have eyes on everyone. I grew up in that kind of dread watching these respected military people lose their livelihoods because they went to a gay bar" (Ibid.).

Lori wasn't in the military, and when she eventually came out as an adult her parents were open-minded and supportive of her sexuality. But that didn't make growing up in a small, mostly Catholic community any easier.

"It was terrifying. I grew up in this very, deeply heterosexist environment and nobody was out in my hometown. Nobody. There was a cautionary tale about this guy who was a fag and [when he came out] he was estranged from his family, cut off so to speak. Everybody heard this story of the terrible things that had happened to him because he came out. So it was this super intense environment, and I was terrified" (Ibid.).

Fortunately, Lori wasn't entirely alone. As a child she thought she was - "I was convinced I was the only gay woman in the world." But in kindergarten she became close friends with a boy who also lived in the community, and he discovered at a young age that he was gay as well.

"He was gayer than a bag of daisies," said Lori. *"So we had each other. It made a big difference. I was smart, and so was he. We were like: 'Okay, we need to not let people know.' We talked to each other; we were out to each other. We were talking to each other about the fact we had same-sex attractions probably by Grade 6. So we had this incredible peer support, which I think for us made a huge difference"* (Ibid.).

Life changed dramatically for Lori when she moved to St. John's to attend Memorial University.

"I moved to St. John's mostly to escape my tiny Catholic deeply homophobic town. University was just a bonus," she said. *"Coming from Placentia Bay, moving to St. John's was like moving to Manhattan. Very quickly I found my people. University was full of dykes! I found other queer kids in residence. And*

I was living in a Catholic residence!

"It was hysterical because I was the only one who had a really good ro- mantic life because no boys were allowed upstairs on the residential floor, it was women only upstairs. So I could have my girlfriends sleep over, and it re- ally pissed off the straight girls on my floor. It was great. I told them – 'This is the only upside to being a dyke in Newfoundland b'ys" (Ibid.).

In the pre-internet era, university was an intensely social environment.

"The queer and artsy kids all hung out together in the Thomson Student Centre. The Student Centre was where we lived. You'd see the same people all the time and get to know them. So you only needed to meet one gay person. I met these very glamorous gay boys, one of them had a phone in his car – in 1989! – which was like right out of a John Waters movie. He was from Mount Pearl and had a white convertible. I was like – 'What are you? I'm from the bay, this is something I've never seen before!' Those boys just scooped me up because I loved to dance and loved to be on the go.

"I began to meet women through my courses. I started dating a woman I met in a course. And then I met other queers through her. It doesn't take long in St. John's to know everybody" (Ibid.).

For a time, Lori dated a woman who worked at the iconic downtown health food store called Mary Jane's, and this offered her a brief glimpse at what life was like for a different generation of lesbians.

"[We met] these very established older dykes. So once my girlfriend and I got invited to this very nice house out in Middle Cove, Tors Cove, somewhere like that. I was so young, I was nineteen, and I showed up and it was this sea of women who were in their forties. They were all partnered up, and they had homes, and some of them had kids, and I was like - what! I didn't know this was possible, right? It was pretty shocking to me to see these older dykes. And there was such a sense of [solidarity]. They would hire young queers, and if anyone was moving, everybody would make sure - 'Oh, there's a dyke house on this street,' or 'So-and-so owns a rental on that place.' There was a real sense of the older queers looking out for us stupid, young, hopeless children that we were" (Ibid.).

After a stint in the university residence, Lori decided to move out. Through the lesbian networks she had formed, she learned of an apartment available at a "dyke-house" downtown.

"[This house on] Gower Street was known at that time as a dyke-house," she said. *"It had been owned by dykes forever. The women who owned it…only rented to dykes and they kept the rent really affordable.*

"We were part of this super vibrant queer scene…it was a great exciting time. We were this little tribe of people. Everyone knew everyone, and we all kind of lived out of each other's back pockets. The queer scene was very famil- ial. People took care of each other" (Ibid.).

As HIV infections mounted, Lori threw herself into volunteer work with the AIDS Committee, as did most of her friends. She still hadn't come out to her parents, but her mother took pre-emptive action.

"We were eating Chinese food in my apartment on Pleasant Street, a terrible third floor walk-up. My mother came for a visit and we were eating Chinese take-out from Magic Wok. And she just dropped it in like a bomb. I guess she's a mother of five and she knows how to do this stuff. We're eating chow mien and she goes: 'So like are you gay or wha?' Out of nowhere! No lead-off. I was just like: 'Would it make a difference how I answer this?' And she said: 'No, don't care. I just wondered.' So I was like: 'Yup! Super-gay!' That was it. Full-stop. Amazing" (Ibid.).

Lori suspects perhaps some of her parents' open-mindedness came from the fact their own marriage was not the norm for Newfoundland. As an American, her father was a Southern Baptist, and her mother a Catholic. She feels the fact they were a 'mixed-marriage' gave them an insight into what it was like to feel othered.

Lori is now married herself. Her wife Rolyn is from British Columbia, and moved to St. John's in 1999 to do a firefighting program at the Marine Institute. They met at the Duke of Duckworth, an iconic pub in downtown St. John's.

"She walked in with one of the managers of Mary Jane's - all roads lead to Mary Jane's - the manager walked in with this stunning, six-foot tall butch, and I was like, 'Get outta my way! Hi, I'm Lori.' And that was it. We were off to the races."

When her partner finished her firefighting course a few months later, the lovestruck couple moved to BC together, where they have lived ever since.

Lori looks back on her life in Newfoundland as one of contrasts. In St. John's, surrounded by queer community, her memories are joyful. But whenever she returned to her hometown in Placentia Bay, the small Catholic town's deep-seated homophobia became starkly apparent.

"I was very lucky, but my parents have suffered. Me and my wife came home for Christmas the first year I moved away [to British Columbia]. My mom is Catholic in a big way and wanted us to go to midnight mass. So we went to midnight mass. Every eye in that church was on us. I'm not exaggerating.

"Mom and dad were sitting on either side of us, proud as peacocks, and I had this revelation. The problem that people have with us is not that I'm gay, but it's that my parents are okay with it. I think that really bothered people. My parents have never talked about it, but I know that it was hard on them in lots of ways" (Ibid.).

Brenda Ponic: The politics of place

Brenda Ponic was originally from a small farming community near Windsor, Ontario. Her working-class family did not approve of her attending university, but she saved up $8500 and enrolled at Trent University in 1982. Her family stopped speaking to her when she made her decision and left. But that didn't stop her.

"I was overwhelmed, and excited," she recalled. But once at university, she soon realized the class divide she had hoped to surmount existed there as well.

"I had never known anybody other than my schoolteachers who had gone to university. There was a class divide. I was like, what the hell is this world? So I dropped out of university.

"I got politicized about my own identities... As part of that I came out as a lesbian, or bisexual, and that was political too. Nobody supported me about that, but it was a process of discovery of myself and politicization around the difficulties that I'd had. And about trying to do stuff about that on all sorts of fronts — as a woman, as a queer person. It took me a long time - seven or eight years - to finish my BA, but I think that as a queer, the developmental things that you experience are delayed because you're having to figure out a lot more" (Ponic 2022).

Before going back to finish her BA, she got involved with the rape crisis movement in Ontario. "We invented it, really," she reflects.

Eventually, politicized, experienced and with a firmer understanding of the class politics which existed in the academy, she returned to university. She became an award-winning editor of the student newspaper, which under her leadership provided extensive coverage of local labour politics, and even investigated Ku Klux Klan operations in the area. Eventually she graduated, and was accepted into a Masters program in Toronto.

Then, in 1990, the course of her life changed when she met a Newfoundlander. It wound up being just a summer affair, but it brought her to Newfoundland.

"I just showed up on the Rock. I didn't have any money. I didn't have any family. The [partner] wasn't interested, not for very long. But for me Newfoundland was like the geography of my soul. I love Newfoundland. I love it geographically, but there's also a sense of comfort I have that has to do with the culture, with the lack of pretension, with all sorts of stuff. So I was like: I'm staying" (Ibid.).

Activism was what she knew, and she soon started spending time at the St. John's Status of Women Centre. It didn't take long for her to become immersed in the circuit of house parties, downtown bar-hopping, and theatre-going at the LSPU Hall.

The job of Coordinator at the Women's Centre opened up, and she was hired.

After a stint running the Women's Centre, she decided to return to school, and was accepted into a Masters program in Sociology at Memorial. The ground breaking occupation of the federal Secretary of State's office (explored in Chapter 3) had happened just before she arrived, and she decided to focus her graduate research on social movements as a way of exploring and documenting that occupation. She was almost finished her graduate work, when something happened that derailed everything.

One day her thesis supervisor asked her to come in for a meeting. The memory is still vivid as she describes it.

"She said: 'Brenda sit down.' And then she said that she had been approached by a delegation from the community who believed that I was a CSIS[11] agent who had come to Newfoundland to infiltrate the queer and feminist communities after the occupation of the Secretary of State [office]. I laughed, and I sort of said: 'What?' But she was very serious, and she said: 'No, this is a very serious accusation.' And I just said: 'Well you'd think I'd have more money if I was a CSIS agent!' But it was apparently really serious. She wouldn't tell me who was in that delegation. And for me, it was like, these were my friends! Like, who was it? People I had slept with? I don't know! But it was apparently a large delegation that had come.

"That accusation devastated me. It made me completely unstable. I was so busy, and I had a lot of friends, and now I didn't know who to trust. [My supervisor] was so serious about it. And I said: 'I am not a CSIS agent! Nor have I ever been!' But it was so devastating for me that it made me leave Newfoundland. I ended up not finishing that Masters, and I had been so fucking close. I also decided activism was not for me. I couldn't emotionally bear it" (Ibid.).

Ponic moved to Boston, and then back to Ontario, where she started over and built a successful career as a therapist. She's reflected a great deal on the events that drove her out of Newfoundland, and her equanimity is more than one might expect. Yet there is also a sense of lingering hurt beneath these stoic reflections. She's considered multiple possibilities. She was openly polyamorous, and knew that some members of the lesbian community judged her for that. She was openly lesbian, and some members of the feminist community judged her for that. But what she kept returning to was the fact she was a 'come-from-away.'

"In retrospect, you know, I think I did have the privilege of being a mainlander. I did come into that community and got accorded all those privileges in terms of a job, and a voice, and all those things. Perhaps people felt jealous of that. At the time there were far fewer come-from-aways or mainlanders there. And I did arrive at a prime time, right after the occupation. And I did immediately infiltrate all the queer and feminist community stuff. And then I did a thesis where I asked all these people about all sorts of stuff. So I can see where it might have all come

---

[11] Canadian Security Intelligence Service (Canada's version of the American CIA).

together in that way.

"But it's so hard, because it felt like I had given my heart and soul to activism, and to this community, and to these friends, and I lost all that. There were very few people I kept in contact with. It was not something I could talk about. And I still don't know who it was. My supervisor knew I was almost done that thesis, and knew I didn't hand it in, and never talked with me about the impact of that conversation. [My supervisor] was a mainlander and an activist, and I think she felt that she needed to be accountable to her community in order to keep her trust from people there. So for me, what happened to me was a statement about the time, and about the layers of fear within the gay and lesbian and feminist communities. I don't know if people thought it was a small thing, but I don't think they did. She said they had had many meetings about it. But I have empathy for that, and I see the layers of how it could have happened. Sure, I probably did shitty things, I probably was cocky or something, I don't know. But I know that I'm not an asshole, and I know that I could have been talked to, and I know that they knew me better than that. To me it said a lot about activism and politics. It was like - wow, this is so unsafe" (Ibid.).

"Part of what hurts me the most is it feels like it was my queer community who did it."

John Guiney Yallop: The Poet of Admirals' Cove

John Guiney Yallop was born in 1959. He grew up in Admiral's Cove, a community of 120 people on Newfoundland's southern shore. Today it's part of Cape Broyle. He has vivid memories of the then-booming fishery which dominated the town during his childhood.

"It was a very active fishing community, a very active wharf," he recalled. *"The men would go out fishing... there was a lot of activity when the men brought their fish in in the boats. There were stages where they would fillet the fish, and people would be there buying the fish for the fish plants. It was a pretty active place. And it was a smelly place. On the beach, there was lots of blubber - whale oil - there were a lot of gulls around, because the leftovers of the fish were thrown into the water so the gulls would eat them.*

"It's a very different place now because the fishing ended in the 1990s, when the cod moratorium started. After that the stages just kind of fell apart. And because it wasn't maintained, the wharf also fell apart. Eventually it was all removed. Today when you go to Admirals' Cove beach, it's just a beach. There's no evidence there that it was ever a fishing community" (Guiney Yallop 2022).

Then simply John Guiney, he grew up in a family of seven children. Their family was poor, and lived in a small house. He shared a bed with an older sister and younger brother. His father worked at the fish plant, and his mother worked there as well in the summertime. The entire community was Catholic.

"I remember the first time I saw a non-Catholic — an Anglican — it was in high school," he recalls. But John's distinction was of a different sort.

"Growing up, I guess I knew I was gay. I knew I was different. I knew I liked boys. I was…six years old when I was aware of my difference. I'm not sure I could call it sexuality at the time, but I knew I wanted to be with a boy."

He remembers when the community had its first telephones installed, and when televisions arrived as well. He was attracted to the muscular men on the television shows. As a child, local girls would let him join them in playing house, and together they'd pretend they were waiting for their husbands to return home from fishing.

As he entered adolescence and early teenage years, he went camping with other boys and they sometimes engaged in sexual play with each other. "We never talked about it afterwards," he said.

In his early teenage years, he developed a fixation on Bobby Sherman, a popular singer at the time. He acquired magazines and cut out articles and images of Sherman, putting together scrapbooks. His brother had a hockey player on his wall; John had pictures of Bobby Sherman. One day he found his older brother ruminating on the pictures. "[My brother] says: 'Look he's got a picture of Bobby Sherman's ass, he's a queer!' I didn't know what a queer was, but I guessed you're not supposed to be it. But I didn't care, I loved Bobby Sherman."

When John was in Grade 8, his family's house burned down in an accidental fire. Everyone in the house escaped safely. He had been at a hockey game in St. John's – there was no nearby arena so Southern Shore hockey teams would travel by bus to St. John's to play each other. His father met the bus on the crossroads outside of town, to inform John and his siblings of what had happened.

His family was poor and had no insurance. Their house burned down right after Christmas, leaving them with nothing. The family was spread among nearby relatives; John stayed with an uncle. The morning after the fire, the realization hit him that he no longer had anything besides the clothes he'd been wearing the day before. It was his scrapbooks of Bobby Sherman that he missed the most.

The close-knit community chipped in to help. "People collected money for us to rebuild our house. Some people gave two dollars, some gave five dollars. Other people went around up along the shore collecting money for the Guiney family that had lost their house. People gave us a lot… I had more clothes than I'd ever had before, because people gave us so many clothes. It was really quite amazing. Students brought in things as well, my classmates brought in things from their family, my teachers gave us things."

After a few weeks, the family was back together again in a rented house under one roof. That year John was off to high school, and things changed rapidly.

"I sometimes describe high school as a nightmare," he said. "I hated high school. I'm sure I had good times, but I don't remember them very well. I hated high school because I was really aware that I was gay."

In Grade 11, John's religion teacher brought a copy of *Time Magazine* to class. The cover read: "I Am A Homosexual." It was a feature article on Leonard Matlovich, a former US soldier who came out as gay in 1974 and became a high-profile activist (*Time Magazine* 1975).

"The teacher passed around this copy of **Time Magazine**. *I remember just looking at it very quickly because I didn't want people thinking that I was interested in it. But there were a few other pictures in there as well about people in relationships. There were gay people and they had relationships and they were happy. The teacher said the article must have been written by a homosexual because it was so positive - remember, this is a Catholic school. But I just remember thinking: 'My goodness — this is who I am.' It was actually terrifying in some ways"* (Guiney Yallop 2022).

"People called me queer…they called me a girl actually. I probably got that more often. Somehow that was considered a major insult."

He continued engaging in sexual play with other boys his age in the community.

"I remember one time, one of the guys I was having sex with - we had sex sometimes in a tent, or we'd go for walks by ourselves at night, up behind the church, and feel each other - I wanted to do it again one time and he said to me that he wanted to stop doing this, because he was now becoming a man and men didn't do this. I remember saying to him: 'Well I don't want to stop!' And he said: 'That's because you're a queer.' And I felt really sad. But I wasn't going to let him see how sad I was.

"He really hurt me. It really hurt. And I think this is when I realized that this is how some relationships were going to go. That because of who I am, some relationships will end. Especially if I tell them who I am. There was this awareness" (Ibid.).

John always had a spiritual bent, and after high school he entered a seminary with the intent of becoming a Catholic priest. At the time, seminarians from the southern shore of the island were still sent directly to Ireland for their training, part of a long-standing tradition of which John would be one of the last. It didn't work out, and so he returned to Newfoundland after one year, and enrolled at Memorial University instead.

He maintained his involvement with the Catholic community. At the time there was a vibrant queer rights movement within the Catholic Church called 'Dignity' and John wanted to start up a branch in this province. He got the impression there had been informal attempts to start one previously, but nothing had come to fruition. So, while he was living in the Catholic student residence on campus, St. John's College, he approached the chaplain. The chaplain reacted positively to his proposal, but said that such undertakings required the supervision of a chaplain and he was too busy with other duties to take on the role. So John sent out a letter to all the parish priests in the province, announcing he was starting a Dignity chapter for gay and lesbian parishioners, and asking whether anyone would be willing to serve as their chaplain.

"I just got one response, and he was basically scolding me, saying that this was against the Catholic Church. This priest basically lectured me... he was a bit of a pompous intellectual."

John also put an ad in the chapel bulletin, announcing the intended formation of the new Dignity chapter and seeking interested members. His residence chaplain advised John not to put his name on the announcement, but to keep it anonymous due to the risk of backlash.

"I said that if my name is not on it, the message to people would be that we need to be invisible, we need to be silent. And that's the opposite of what this organization is supposed to do. So I said: 'I'm aware of the potential consequences, that I might be harassed, but I'm also aware that I can fight those things.' I was 21, I don't know where I got the balls to do that" (Ibid.).

John doesn't remember any backlash. There was a little bit of interest, and he organized one meeting of the fledgling group. It was attended by a few older men. They all knew each other, and it felt a bit cliquish, he recalls. He was disappointed there didn't seem to be any interest from younger people his age, and no women either. He also recognized he was drifting away from Catholicism, and realized that if he was losing his faith in the church, it didn't make much sense for him to try to lead a Dignity group.

Before putting out the ad for the Dignity group, John also came out to his parents. He came out first to a younger sister, and she insisted he tell their parents.

"I went home that weekend, and I told Mom. I was crying, and she said: 'Stop crying, just talk to Dad when he comes home.' When I talked to Dad I was also crying – it was a hyper emotional time, coming out to your parents. I was also in love with someone at the time. I said: 'I'm in love. I don't want to be a priest because I'm in love. And I'm in love with a man'... I told my parents I'm in love with this guy, I don't want to be a priest because I'm in love with someone and he's leaving and so I can't be with him. And my father just said: 'You'll find someone else.' I was speechless, dumbfounded. I thought: 'Did you hear what I just said? I said I'm in love with a man!' I really thought he didn't hear me! But then I was like – wow that's really great! I couldn't care less who knew I was gay after that. It was an affirmation I had never experienced before. I knew I was safe, with my father and mother. It was life-changing, really" (Ibid.).

John's parents accepted and embraced him, but the wider world was not yet so enlightened. Just weeks after completing his undergraduate degree at Memorial in 1982, John got a "dream job" in Nova Scotia working for Canada

World Youth. The hiring process was gruelling: multiple interviews, group interviews, live workshop assessments. He excelled at them all and was hired as a supervisor for overseas youth placements.

"And then six weeks after I was hired, I was fired because I was an out gay man," he recounted grimly.

John tried to fight the firing, but without anti-discrimination protections around sexual orientation, his prospects were slim.

"Their position was that I wouldn't be able to [do my job] because I would be going to Sri Lanka where homosexuality wasn't approved. Their feeling was that I wouldn't be able to conceal my sexuality. I argued with them, I said I can [conceal it]. They thought I was too obvious. They referred to me as 'gentlemanly' – as 'a very soft person.' I mean, those are good qualities in a man! I said I didn't plan on being out in Sri Lanka, I told them I wasn't going there to have sex, I was going there to supervise" (Ibid.).

John wanted to escalate his fight to the national level, but his co-workers told him he had no grounds to do so given the lack of sexual orientation protections and clauses in their contract which allowed termination for very broad 'suitability' reasons. The organization offered him three months' severance and transportation home, and he reluctantly agreed. He didn't want to go home to Newfoundland, so he asked instead for transportation to Toronto.

"I left Newfoundland for this job and felt like I would be going backward – I didn't want to go back to Newfoundland. I wanted to keep going."

John arrived in Toronto, and there he became roommates with Paul Hearn, the Newfoundlander introduced earlier in this chapter. They'd previously met through a mutual friend, and had maintained a correspondence.

"I stayed with him, and he showed me around Toronto. I fell in love with Paul. He was an out gay man in Toronto. And he was very attractive – he was a big man, he was a beautiful man and we became friends for life. It was Paul who got me through that period of being fired.

"He was wonderful. He knew that I was attracted to him. But that attraction evolved and we became just very close friends. He was a great friend. A lot of people will say that about him. He was a very loyal friend. You could really depend on him. A wonderful person. He was such an out, gay, proud man" (Ibid.).

Within a year, Paul moved in with his partner, and John eventually moved out on his own. He immersed himself in Toronto queer life. The summer after his arrival, he went home to Newfoundland for a visit, and reflected on how much his life had changed in such a short time.

"I went back home during Toronto Pride Week. I went back for a week or two. I remember the feeling of looking at Pride Day from Admirals' Cove, and I think I was so overwhelmed by gay life in Toronto that I needed to get away from it in order to look at it. I actually went back to Newfoundland so I wouldn't be around Toronto for Pride Day – it was almost like sensory over-

load" (Ibid.).

John stayed in Toronto for the following year's Pride Week. That year, while attending a Pride dance, John met Gary Yallop.

"They used to have these big Pride dances in Toronto at the Masonic Temple. We saw each other, smiled and chatted. We recognized each other from a community meeting a few weeks earlier. And then we danced together that night. And we've been together ever since."

In 1986, John brought his partner Gary home to Newfoundland to meet his parents. It was March break, and they arrived just after a massive snowstorm. "It was really incredible, almost like Snowmageddon. I had grown up in Newfoundland but had never seen so much snow in my life. It was an interesting time to introduce a Torontonian to rural Newfoundland."

John was nervous about the encounter. Although his parents had been accepting when he came out to them, he wasn't sure how they would react upon meeting his partner.

"I actually had it in mind that if they didn't welcome him, then they'd never see me again," he reflects. Fortunately, it didn't come to that.

"My parents adored Gary. They loved him. I said: 'Gary's my partner' and they welcomed him from day one. My father always called Gary on his birthday until the day my father died. And my mother kept in touch with him until she developed Alzheimers. She actually remembered Gary longer than she remembered me, because Gary was a gardener and she loved flowers. She remembered Gary but didn't know who I was. It was sad but lovely at the same time" (Ibid.).

The small, close-knit community of Admiral's Cove appeared to accept Gary as well, from his first visit in 1986 onward.

"They had a dart club in the community that went on during the winter. That was usually when Gary and I would come, during March break. Gary would play darts with the guys. All the men and women would play darts, drinking Dominion or Black Horse beer, and he was just part of the group. I have pictures of him playing darts. Maybe it was because my father was well-respected in the community, so when my father accepted him, then that was it. But they welcomed Gary. It was unexpected. I don't think they were surprised that I was gay. I think they were probably happy that I found someone that I was happy with" (Ibid.).

After eighteen years together, John Guiney and Gary Yallop married. They wed on the anniversary of their first dance - Pride Day, June 29, 2004. It was the month same-sex marriage was legalized in Ontario. They were the first legal same-sex marriage at the Unitarian Congregation in Toronto. They put their last names together, forming Guiney Yallop. Less than a year after their marriage, they adopted a daughter, Brittany, and a few months later flew to Newfoundland to introduce Brittany to her new extended family. Their daughter got to meet John's mother – then in late-stage Alzheimers – shortly before she died.

"We thought she'd be afraid because my mother was old and in a home and had Alzheimers dementia, but [our daughter] was five years old and she was fearless. She just walked in, and touched her hair. She was really unafraid of my mother. She fed her, touched her hair, she was very physical which was lovely to see."

John went on to become an elementary school teacher in Ontario. As an out gay educator, he took part in the struggle for sexual orientation rights, keenly aware that a lack of those protections had cost him his job in Nova Scotia.

"Once [human rights legislation] was passed, I realized: 'This changes the landscape now. I actually have protection.'" So he continued to participate in the fight for queer rights, demanding same-sex partner benefits for Gary.

"One of the biggest fights I had was with my union, my teachers' union, because they were pretty conservative. They didn't actually want to do it. I remember giving this really passionate speech one time. I said: 'My partner's there - whenever you have strikes or picket lines, he's been there by my side, supporting me. He's been there at lots of union protests, and you've always counted his head then. He matters then. But when it comes to including him on my benefit package, you're saying he doesn't count. You're not supporting me. That's a double standard.' And after that they voted in favour [of same-sex partner benefits]" (Ibid.).

John eventually went on to work with the teachers' union. He acquired a Masters degree, as well as a PhD. He also became a published poet, a field in which he remains active today. In 2008 – twenty-four years after being fired for being gay in Nova Scotia – he returned to that province, taking up a job as a professor at Acadia University. In 2021 he retired, and John, Gary, and their daughter moved home to Newfoundland.

What still stands out for John is the way his family and community accepted Gary. "It wasn't just tolerance — but acceptance. I don't think Gary was just tolerated by the community and by my father, he was really accepted. And celebrated. My father would call him for his birthday. They never lived to see us married but I'm sure they would have celebrated that as well."

Robert Petite: Priest and activist

Robert Petite was born in 1946 in the small fishing village of Belleoram, in Fortune Bay. He has vivid memories of his childhood there.

"I remember going to Christmas times[12] — the Fishermen's Lodge would have a time, the Orange Lodge would have a time. It was amazing. It was a party for everybody. Not only were the adults there, the kids were there too. One of my memories of those days was all the adults dancing – they danced

---

[12] Traditional Newfoundland parties were referred to as 'times.'

in a group – and all the kids asleep on the chairs around the edge of the hall. The kids would eventually get tired and fall asleep on the chairs. It was a very integrated community experience where there were elderly people, middle-aged people, young people, and little children, all together enjoying this party.

"There was a stage, and there would be three Christmas trees on it. To me as a child they looked absolutely huge. They may not have been, but to me they looked huge, and they were decorated with toys. When you came in the door as a kid, you got a ticket. And every kid received a toy from that tree. So I have a lot of wonderful memories" (Petite 2022).

Other memories were not as pleasant. Petite grew up in a poor family, with two siblings; a brother and sister. Their father was a schooner captain, who spent extended periods either at sea, or away looking for work.

"He disappeared for several years, which made it very difficult for my mother. My brother had to leave school to support us financially. He left school and worked in the fish plant to support us. He was sixteen when he left school.

"It was a difficult time. When the bottom dropped out of the fishing industry in Newfoundland, schooners were used for hauling coal. So that was part of my father's work. And then he went south to get work – way south, somewhere in South America. He was away for a long time. It was a difficult time for my family, and my brother had to leave school to make sure we could eat. That made a lasting impact on me.

"My mother was a deeply strong-willed woman, and I owe a lot of my energy to the kind of person she was. She's the person I identify with, and when she died, I was devastated. But she had a very difficult time in the outports of Newfoundland. She was left alone – my dad disappeared for several years – she had to look after three kids, she had to deal with gossip, all kinds of stuff. I remember the day she said to me: 'Bob my son, we're getting the hell out of here.' And we left" (Ibid.).

They moved to St. John's, where they moved in with his aunt who lived in the Battery. That's the iconic harbour front community commonly featured in provincial tourism photos. At the time it was a poor but close-knit neighbourhood; effectively a town unto itself. Today the old-fashioned houses perched precariously along the cliffside compete for space with garish, out-sized mansions; most of the families that used to reside here have been pushed out by gentrification.

Petite and his family lived there for a year.

"I had to walk several miles to get to school. I had a hard time adjusting to the city. I was so homesick for the outport that I had a hard time adjusting. I would have nightmares, and I would cry, I just missed it so much. I'd hear an accordion play and I would cry."

Petite's father eventually returned, and landed a job in Halifax as a tugboat captain. The entire family then relocated to Nova Scotia.

"That's when life really began. I would not be a priest today had we stayed in the outports. I would not have gotten an education had we stayed in the outports. Much as [life in the outports] has informed who I am, it was not my future. I grew up in a very poor family and no one had had an education. But I ended up going to the University of King's College [in Halifax]. It was an extraordinary environment, and an environment that I had never known in my life before. It was like being at Oxford" (Ibid.).

The church played an important role in Petite's childhood in Belleoram – it was the centre of the community – and continued to do so as he grew to adulthood.

"I actually don't have any memory of not wanting to be a priest. It was always, always, always there. I was called to be a priest."

After completing his undergraduate studies at King's, he enrolled in a seminary at Trinity College in Toronto. He himself was nowhere near to coming out at the time, but it was there he first grew aware of a larger gay community.

"There was lots of evidence of gay men in ministry, but there was also a need to be closeted. There were two spheres that gay folks lived in in the late 1960s and 1970s. There were times when you were closeted with people – especially while you were in the process [of becoming a priest] with your bishop and committees and faculty. And then you had this underground group of people that you connected with. I wasn't part of that because I wasn't out by then, although I was certainly grappling with it. There certainly were other people at seminary who I knew to be gay and who were struggling. But there was no room for anyone to be out. There was no room to be an out gay person. People might make an assumption that somebody was gay, but that person never owned it publicly. And as long as they were discreet about it they were left alone" (Ibid.).

Petite would eventually violate that unspoken policy, and pay a price. It took him time before he was prepared to come out. He married a woman, and they had children together. He was hired as chaplain at Dalhousie University, and then became the parish priest in Antigonish, Nova Scotia. It was during this time that he began to accept his sexuality, and came out to a few people as gay.

"It was very unsettling for me. I thought: well I really wasn't the priest I thought I was. I wasn't the father I thought I was. I wasn't the husband I thought I was. It really threw me into somewhat of a chaos."

Petite decided he ought to resign as a priest, and in 1979 he wrote to the bishop of his diocese, explaining that he was gay and needed to resign his priesthood.

"We had a conversation, and [the bishop] said: 'You certainly are not [resigning]!' He was a very supportive person of me. I was in trial and tribulation at the time."

The bishop said he had a parish in Halifax that required a priest. He suggested Petite move there, and that he might be more comfortable and find better support in a larger centre where he had gay friends. Petite agreed to give it a try.

"I agreed to come for nine months, and I ended up staying for nine years."

Petite became the priest at St. George's Round Church in Halifax, a beautiful Neo-Palladian wooden building built in 1800 that he remembers with great fondness. The congregation there soon won his heart as well.

"It had a small congregation, pretty much all of whom were Newfoundlanders. It was really an expatriate place where a lot of Newfoundlanders went to church when they came to the mainland. In fact the former rector there, who had retired, was also a Newfoundlander."

Petite quickly took to the congregation and to the community, which included several queer individuals, some of them Newfoundlanders. Over the years he would become deeply involved in AIDS outreach work (his role in this regard is discussed in Chapter 7). He also became involved in the broader struggle for queer rights; he participated in the very first GLBTQ march in Halifax, which was only attended by around two dozen people, he recalls.

Petite threw himself into organizing and activist work, and soon found himself outpacing even the more liberal leaders in the Anglican Church.

"I began having so many difficulties with my parish. I was in the media a lot, I was writing a lot, I was demonstrating a lot, I was doing AIDS ministry. And my parish got really frightened. People got very concerned. I certainly would want to own some strategic errors on my part during those days. But it was a difficult time because of AIDS and also because people were still very closeted and had a fair bit of internalized homophobia going on. So there was a response to the work I was doing in the parish that really wasn't very supportive. Many people were supportive, but many others were not, for various reasons" (Ibid.).

As part of his AIDS education and outreach work, Petite spent time at Rumours, Halifax's legendary queer nightclub.

"Rumours was where the gay community gathered," he recalls. "And I was certainly at Rumours for both personal and professional reasons. I went to Rumours as a 40-year-old gay man who wanted to be in the gay community. All my friends were in the gay community. So I was certainly at Rumours for all sorts of personal reasons. But it was also where I made contacts to help me [with work]. Rumours is a block away from my church. In fact the bishop wrote a letter to the congregation, basically giving permission for me to be at Rumours because of the kind of work I was doing in the community. At that time there were people in the parish and elsewhere complaining about me being at Rumours and at the gay bars.

"They were getting really concerned about the notoriety that the parish was getting, especially around the fact that it was getting to be known as a

gay parish. It was a wonderful parish, and I think my mistake was not really knowing how to bring the parish along with me. I was quite young, and when I look back on those days I would do some things differently. To quote Dickens – it was the best of times and it was the worst of times. Because we developed such a community and fast friendships. We were grieving the loss of people every week, every month [to AIDS]. But we endured. We did the work that we needed to do. And we had a lot of fun and joy in doing it, even though there were lots of discouragements and political machinations. But we got organized. We started involving the lesbian community in the work that we were doing. It was really the defining time in my life" (Ibid.).

As the community grew and became more active, so did the opposition to the work Petite and others were doing, especially within his parish.

"Things eventually really came to a head, there was concern about me as a gay man and working [as a priest]. In fact I wasn't publicly out, but as you can imagine I lived in a kind of glass closet. So there was a big meeting, a big huge community meeting with one of the bishops of the diocese chairing. It got very volatile. One leader in the parish punched out a member of the press – the press were at the door and had been forbidden to attend the meeting. Almost everybody in the parish attended the meeting, and wanted some explanation from me and some consideration from me about what this was all about. That meeting ended with me saying: 'Okay, I will resign.' Because they were pressing me to resign, and there were even some closeted gay people in the parish pressing me to resign as well.

"I don't know of anyone else who had to leave the ministry because they were considered to be gay. It was all about discretion. I had been the [priest] in Nova Scotia who came out [as gay]. I was gay, and I was involved in the gay community and I had a gay relationship. So that was all considered intolerable" (Ibid.).

When he submitted his resignation, Petite managed to negotiate a year's deferral, in order to save money and look for other work. He was separated from his wife and paying child support. He considered leaving the priesthood, but toward the end of his final year he landed a job in Chicago.

"I'm a bright man and a reader and I went through everything that I could get my hands on to get some understanding of myself. I never once doubted that my Christian tradition could comprehend me. That the Anglican Church with its three pillars of reason, tradition and scripture, could comprehend who I was. And maybe one day even accept it. I never gave up on that. That really helped me stay focused on being a priest.

"What I thought was the worst thing that could ever happen to me – to be required to leave a parish – turned out to be the best thing that happened to me. I came here [to Chicago] and I was able to live an out gay life, in the church. There were lots of gay clergy of my generation here – a generation of gay men who weren't going to have anything to do with this closety stuff any more. We

were going to live our lives and be open" (Ibid.).

Petite met his partner in Chicago, and they are now married. He's now re-tired, although still actively involved in his parish. He's astonished and pleased at how much the world has changed since his early days as a priest and the ho-mophobia he experienced. While he feels he may have made mistakes in some of his youthful activist exuberance, he also recognizes that in many ways it was what the time called for.

"In those early days, you had to step out. And there were two ways of step-ping out. One was to step out into the bushes at night – what I call pinstripe by day and leather by night. That's one way of stepping out. Another way of step-ping out is to be a part of the community. Make friends. Get support that way. Everybody needs community. That's one of the things that I've learned about why we need the church – people need to make connections that support them. When I was a young gay man coming out in Halifax, the gay community was my anchor. And not just gay men – there were lots of women involved too. Including lots of professional women: lawyers and teachers. We did a lot of really good work together. We made good friends and we formed a community together to support ourselves. That's what really made it possible for me to stick to my guns and keep growing" (Ibid.).

The other thing that shaped his outlook, he says, was his childhood in Bel-leoram Newfoundland. He never returned while his mother was alive – she made it clear she didn't want any of them returning to the community where she had had to deal with poverty and gossip. In his later years he would eventu-ally return, and even preached in the church he remembered from his youth.

"I don't idealize the outport at all, but I take from it lots of good things that helped me. Community was one of them. I am so deeply aware of how my life in an outport in Newfoundland shaped me. It's made me value relation-ships. It's made me value elderly people, because every house in Belleoram had an elderly widow or an elderly gentleman that they were looking after. There would be a daybed in the kitchen for an elderly person to have a nap in the afternoon.

"And I remember living in a community in which there were never any doors locked. And everybody lived in the kitchen, and everybody visited all the time, and they provided their own musical entertainment. The church was the centre of life – not just religious life, but social life, education, social work. I really look back on my time in Belleoram as a time that really shaped the deep-est values that I hold" (Ibid.).

Dallas Noftall: DJ Dallas

Dallas Noftall says she comes from "the Bible Belt of Newfoundland - Sun-nyside, Goobies, Come By Chance, that area." Born in the mid-1960s, she grew up in a religious family where she was raised Pentecostal.

"Every single room we'd walk in had a quote from the Bible with a beautiful vivid colour painting. So you were never not aware of God and Jesus. It was mostly about the love of Jesus and God, versus the wrath of God which is what I saw when I went to Catholics' houses a few times. So I grew up loving God and the Bible and Jesus, but I also knew who I was which was a huge conflict. Pretty early on I just assumed that as soon as my family knew who I was, they wouldn't want me" (Noftall 2022).

Dallas' parents divorced when she was two years old, and she was raised by her father and stepmother in Conception Bay. Then one day she was discovered with two other girls. "We were doing a little bit of show and tell, like here's my body and here's yours and what is this - we were just exploring. But this was abhorrent, to have three young girls caught doing this together. I think if I had been a boy I wouldn't have been removed from my home, but I was removed from the home because it was two girls."

She was sent to St. John's to live with her birth mother, where she received a traumatic threat. At the age of eleven, she was driven to the Girls' Training School, a government-run institution in St. John's that was used to house minors who did not have homes or had been removed from their homes.

"I was told in a clear and concise manner that were I to be having any more of these shenanigans that I would be put in the Girls' Home. My mother made that threat very real by driving me there and making me sit in the waiting room. That was a very solid threat.

"So my dad kicked me out because I got caught with the two girls, and then my mom picked me up, drove me to that girls' school – the reform school for wayward girls – and laid the threat on me before she even brought me back to her house when I was eleven.

"So for a year I laid low and said I hated lezzies. My dad called them fairies, but people in the city called them lezzies. At that point I decided I had to convince my mother and my family that I wasn't a fairy or a lezzie, and so I had to spew hatred against them. So I got a fake boyfriend and said I hated lezzies and fags and fairies" (Noftall 2022).

Then one day she encountered two girls her age walking up Long's Hill. She recognized them as two girls she'd met during a previous sojourn in St. John's a few years earlier.

"Lo and behold, do I not find two lezzies coming up the hill. It's okay to not have a puppy if you're not surrounded by puppies, but if they're there, and I'm there — uh-oh, here we go again!"

When Dallas started junior high school shortly thereafter, she discovered one of the girls was in the same school, in the class across the hall from hers. They started hanging out together. The teachers noticed, and didn't like it. Although Dallas was performing well in school, the guidance counsellor called her parents in for a meeting, and warned them that Dallas was hanging around with "undesirables."

"They wanted to 'catch me' before I got too far. At first they said they were calling to protect me, telling my mother that I needed protection, because I was softer looking and pretty and smart and feminine and these girls were a little more androgynous, and they got very concerned that I was being corrupted. They started calling my mother and warning my mother to watch me and watch who I was with, that I was going down a bad path and that my mother was risking losing me. They just didn't understand that it was my decision, my choice, and I sought out these girls because whatever we felt, we all felt it at the same time. We were growing and maturing and we knew it right away – every single one of us was gay and still is today. But those teachers called my mother and I was grounded and locked away in the basement for a whole summer" (Ibid.).

Nevertheless, she and the other young girls persisted in forging friendships and relationships despite the efforts of adults to keep them apart.

"We started seeing each other. Her best friend was a lesbian, but they didn't know they were, and they didn't talk about it, they just hung out together – two tomboys, you know. And here was me coming from the country, now I'm here in the city, and I found these two. One of them ended up finding a girlfriend – she was cute as a button – and then I found another [lesbian] who I was in army cadets with, and I told her: 'You're coming with us, we all belong together.' She was like: 'No I don't!' I mean, back then no young lesbian ever said: 'Yes I'm a lesbian, I found my people and I'm so happy.' None of us ever said that. We were so afraid of what was going to happen at home, whether we were even going to have a home, whether we'd be allowed to be together, whether we were going to be beaten by our families, chased and beaten and threatened by the community – and all of those things did happen. But at least, at the end of the day, we had each other. We always had each other" (Ibid.).

Gradually, over a period of years spanning the late 1970s and early 1980s, their small gang grew.

"We didn't understand what we were doing, we didn't have a plan, but people like us heard about us and they all just came to us. They all kept hearing about this group of wild lesbians who hung out on Patrick Street across from Peter's Pizza. People would find us because they knew where to find us and what we were.

"So I established, along with some other eager young lesbians, we established a very strong little clique. A little community of teenagers in St. John's so that we didn't have to spend our lives, our childhoods, being other than who we were. We were true to ourselves, and we kind of all found each other with the gaydar. We managed to find a group where we found support and love. We were the young ones.

"We had nothing to do but run up and down the streets all night in our groups of two, four, six, eight, ten. I didn't smoke or drink, but just about all of the others

did. Wild teenagers we were. We would dress in outlandish clothes, dress up in leather. Five or six of us would march into places all dressed in leather with chains and whips. We would march through the malls, just being like: 'We're here! We're queer!' We didn't even know we were queer, it was just a daily demonstration that we were strong in our own identities. We never hid a single thing from the world, we never hid all our boldness.

"Certainly we were not safe. At that age, if we were alone we weren't safe, not as teenage girls running around the streets of St. John's. We were not safe. We were chased, rocks were thrown at us, groups of five or six guys on Fitz-patrick Avenue would chase me regularly and throw snowballs. I would look around the corner and down the street, and if they were there I would go all the way around the block and come up the other way. I would take shortcuts to avoid wherever they were hanging out, because they would yell 'Lezzie on the loose! Lezzie on the loose!' and then they would chase me with snowballs. So we had to run a fair bit to be safe. We were unsafe from the older teenage boys if we were in smaller numbers, for sure.

"We were too young to be going out to clubs, to the bars, but that didn't stop us. We would infiltrate, we would mesh among the older people in the lineups and get in before cover and then once the place was in full mayhem we'd gather in our little group, once we wouldn't be noticed. So at age 14, 15, 16 we started going to the dances at the Grad House, the Alley Pub, Friends, Madames, the Upper Deck. There was Katz up on Duckworth as well" (Ibid.).

Dallas began going to queer bars before her girl friends, thanks to friend-ships with slightly older gay men. Dallas didn't drink herself and managed to save cash by doing a range of odd jobs — babysitting, dog-walking, delivering newspapers. "The young gay guys were mostly poor or homeless, so I would buy them drinks and they would sneak me in and sit with me all night. That's how I managed to get in at fourteen. In my youth I was truly supported by younger gay men, the cute boys. They were really beautiful. So wonderful and loving and kind. Eventually the gals joined me, once we'd made ourselves a bit of a community."

"It wasn't really safe in our homes to be gay, but we were. It wasn't safe on the streets to be gay, but we were. We had strength in numbers. They knew we were the lesbians. We were those young wild teenagers. A lot of the older people who weren't gay believed we were just wild young girls in a phase. As our families waited for our phase to run its course, we kept maturing and aging up to where we actually could start going out to the bars. It still wasn't safe, so a lot of us had little decoy boyfriends or decoy names that we would throw around our families just to keep them from stopping us being together. We all had to pretend to have boyfriends and stuff.

"There were some older lesbians who appreciated us, who saw value in us and believed in us. They had seen that we were young lesbians and they were all hiding away. They hid a lot more. We were bolder and wilder, because we

had the support of each other. I guess they had more things to protect, like their jobs. Not many of those older lesbians were out. We didn't have any real role models, no one to look up to who had a lesbian partner who was out that we could see. There was no one who we could see and say: 'Oh, we can be thirty years old and have a girlfriend! We can be forty and have a girlfriend!' It was just hard to see what our future was based on looking around us, beyond the fact that we had a lot of youthful energy and we would dance from before the bars would open until they would close. We would just dance and dance and dance and dance" (Ibid.).

Looking back on those years, Dallas remembers both the hostility of straight society, as well as the fear of older queer people in the city.

"It wasn't easy. Families didn't want gays, schools didn't want gays, churches didn't want gays, stores didn't want gays. We were quite the talk, just because we didn't conform. We didn't listen. I'm not political – these fights were just the fight for my right to be me, and fight for my friends. I've been micro-fighting for my own identity since I was ten years old. I wasn't bad, I wasn't evil, I wasn't dirty, and yet I was made to feel bad and evil and dirty at every turn by every adult that I ever knew.

"Then when I met older lesbians, I saw them not standing up for themselves. I met all these women – professors and accountants and swim instructors and this and that, and they were all in the closet. Us teenagers were so out of the closet that it got to be a thing that people would be outed if we were around them. So people didn't want to be around us publicly. They would come and meet us privately. They wouldn't be seen with us, but they would come if we were under a roof and enclosed, then they would come and hang with us. We were really seen as either pariahs, or just plain bad" (Ibid.).

In addition to the homophobia, classism also contributed to divisions many of the young lesbians experienced, even within the lesbian community and women's activist circles.

"Me, a lot of my friends, we weren't well off. We were from middle class, lower middle class families. Some girls had come from hard places, like group homes and stuff, but we all had to find somewhere to belong. It sure as heck did not seem like we belonged in the lesbian community. We didn't feel welcomed, the doors were slammed, the sneers – they were as rude to us as the straight community was. Role models? There were none. There was no one who said: 'Wow, they're bold, they're courageous, this is the future, these are young lesbians, let's include them, let's invite them, let's coach them, let's mentor them, let's welcome them – at least let's not be hostile to them!'" (Ibid.).

There were some exceptions, Dallas recalls. She remembers in particular a handful of the lesbians involved with the St. John's Status of Women Centre – Sandy Pottle, Susan Rose, Beth Decker – who did gradually form bonds with the younger women.

"They were kind and soft and they kind of giggled at us, giggled at our youth and our spirit, but they were absolutely beautiful women. Phenomenal advocates, tireless and relentless and solid and brilliant."

However, they were the exception; many of the Women's Centre activists and older lesbians in the city didn't want anything to do with the younger, more out youth. The lack of any space or community resources for queer youth was especially felt by the younger, poorer lesbians in the city like Dallas and her friends.

"There was absolutely no resource for young lesbians and we had to wait until we could go to a club at nineteen. That was the only place where we knew we could possibly find other lesbians. So we started going there early on. The [older lesbians] didn't like that – we wore black leather, we were sexually active and not ashamed of anything. They were really not kind. It was tough. I can imagine how alone someone would have felt. Someone who's 14, 15, 16 and didn't have a group, who had a family that was against them, their neighbourhood was against them, their school was against them. And then to try and find other actual lesbians and have them turn their backs on you and slam the door, that was kind of hard. When your own people don't want you" (Ibid.).

Dallas feels she also experienced exclusion because she didn't fit in with the image many of the older lesbians cultivated.

"I think I threatened those women. I was young, very pretty, very feminine, and I didn't look like them. They wore jeans, sweatshirts, a lot of them had the wallet in the back pocket, they almost all had extremely short, army-style haircuts – not all of them, but this was a lot of what [lesbians] looked like and what you had to look like to be a lesbian. So this was quite a culture shock. I didn't know there were people in other parts of the world and country who were like me until I found the older lesbians, and then they weren't quite like me – they shunned me because I didn't fit in with any of them. Nobody looked like me. Nobody had long hair, long fingernails, wore lipstick. They all belonged to ball teams and wore jeans, sweatshirts and short hair. I didn't look like them" (Ibid.).

Dallas now recognizes that the older lesbians had their own struggles and experiences which shaped their outlooks and behaviour, and that many of them were trying to improve things in their own often quiet ways. But she still feels bitter at the tangible harms experienced by herself and other queer youth because of the lack of proudly out role models or community supports.

"We were all looking for some kind of guidance. We were looking for strong, powerful role models. And [the lesbians we met] were a bunch of pissants. They didn't do anything for their community. They might have done it through writing and books and secret back ways that we couldn't see, but there was absolutely no parade we could join, there was nowhere that we could feel we belonged, there was nothing for us as the next generation. They felt no desire or urgency to usher us in and lay the groundwork or break ceilings. They did nothing at all for the young gays that were coming up. They taught us that

hiding away was what they did, and they told us to go away and hide away too. But we wouldn't.

"When I moved to Toronto, and I heard the chant: 'We're here! We're queer!' I thought, oh my god! Oh my god – here they are! They're here, and they're queer! So I went from Newfoundland where I was shunned for being feminine, and for being out, and for being wild, for not hiding and not settling down – I came here to Toronto and within a few short months I had a stage and they put me on it and they said: 'Here — you've found your people'" (Ibid.).

That happened in 1986. Dallas made a trip to Toronto in December 1985 to visit Newfoundland friends there for Christmas. Her friends lived in the gay village.

"It was the most gay, most wonderful street in the world as far as I knew. I had brought my shoes with me in a bag just in case we went out somewhere – I'm from Newfoundland so I had my skidoo boots on, right? But in Toronto I didn't have to wear those boots – I could wear my shoes to the sidewalk, jump in a cab and be at the bar in two minutes. It was amazing. So I said: 'I'm coming back here!'" (Ibid.).

Dallas was doing a training course in travel and tourism at a college in St. John's at the time. She returned and finished the course in June 1986, and then took the bus, boat and train back to Toronto.

"I started going out dancing every single day and every single night – dancing, dancing, dancing. I've never really cared for the drinking and drugs and stuff, I just wanted to dance and dance and dance."

Her enthusiasm caught the attention of the owners of the clubs she frequented in Toronto. One night, the owners of a bar she was at – a lesbian club called Chez Moi – approached her and said one of the DJs for that weekend had hurt herself and cancelled. Would she like to DJ?

"I said: 'Oh my god I've never touched a stereo in my life!' So they said: 'Fine, we'll start you downstairs.'"

She DJ'ed for the first time on a Friday night, in the smaller downstairs portion of the club. "It was fun and scary," she recalls. But on Saturday, the DJ at the larger upstairs portion of the bar fell out of the DJ booth and broke her shoulder. The owners dashed downstairs, grabbed Dallas and told her to take over the main DJ booth.

"I said: 'Oh my god – upstairs?' Upstairs at Chez Moi was the biggest happening – a hot, sexy, fantastic dance floor but everybody was welcome. It was like Friends and the Upper Deck and Madames, but it was here in another city, and everyone was welcome. This was where I saw trans people, and this was where I saw femmes and dykes and gay-bois. As soon as I came to Toronto I started seeing trans people" (Ibid.).

Dallas' crash course in deejaying was a success, and she went on to deejay for many years at several of the hottest queer clubs in Toronto. As DJ Dallas, she's been the subject of newspaper and magazine features, and a sought-after deejay and promoter for queer events in that city and beyond. She's also built a career as a businesswoman, but continues her deejay work with focus and intention. For her it's an important part of building community, and her commitment to that has been shaped by the sense of exclusion she experienced growing up.

"Today we look and we see such a wealth of creativity and diversity and colours and faces and expressions, but for so many years we weren't even valid. We didn't count in a census, we didn't have rights, we were jailed. So a big part of my approach is that I'm just inclusive, for everyone. If you're an asshole, don't come to my events. But we are LGBTQI2S+ — we are gay, we are queer, we are Two Spirit, we are trans. We are family" (Ibid.).

Derrick Bishop – NGALE Organizer

Derrick Bishop was born in St. Johns in 1954. He grew up in the centre city area, on Hamel Street just off Empire Avenue; today the area is part of what's referred to as Rabbittown. It was at Junior High School — he attended MacPherson Junior High, on Newtown Road — that he started becoming aware of the importance people attached to sexuality.

"I was very confused — I knew I wasn't attracted to females but was attracted to other males. I just thought it would pass. But at that age you started hearing about sex, and people would talk about other people who were different. At that time we didn't use the word 'gay', they used 'queer.' There were all these weird little idiosyncrasies people used to say — like if you went to school on a Thursday wearing green socks you were labelled queer. I don't know why. So you had to be very careful. I was very diligent that on Thursdays I didn't wear green socks.

"Then I went on to high school at Prince of Wales Collegiate and I definitely knew at that time that I was gay. And I didn't want to be gay. I didn't know anybody else who was. There were people I suspected might be. But I just didn't seem to fit in with anybody at that point.

"At that time, back in the 1970s, sex was never mentioned in the schools. I think the closest thing to sex that came up was when a Grade 11 teacher quoted the Apostle Paul, who said 'it is better to marry than to burn.' And the teacher asked: 'What does Paul mean by that?' Nobody else could answer the question, so I said: 'Well obviously it's better to get married than to have lust and desire — in order to satisfy your desire you have to get married.' And the teacher gave me five cents for answering the question. He threw me a nickel" (Bishop 2021)

Derrick grew up in a very religious family — his relatives were all either Anglican or United. It was while he was struggling with his sexuality in high school that he encountered the Mormon Church. Despite, or maybe because of, his struggle to come to terms with his sexuality, something about the more conservative strictures of Mormonism attracted him.

"I thought that maybe if I followed them and I was very devout, God would change me. This was the focus of my entire being when I was seventeen, eighteen years old — that God would change me and I would be 'healed.'"

His conversion to Mormonism upset his family, and he didn't feel he could be open with them about his motives. He stayed with the Mormon Church for several years, and became a schoolteacher on the west coast of the province.

"But I realized that I wasn't changing. I still had these desires that I wanted to get rid of. So I thought that maybe if I went on a mission for the Church, then maybe God would change me."

In fact, he reflects, that's exactly what happened, although not in the way he expected. He went on a missionary undertaking in Washington State in the late 1970s, and was paired up with another Mormon. They went door to door, and one day the door was answered by a young Black teenager. The teenager said his parents weren't home, and when Derrick tried to schedule a return visit, his companion grew irritated. There was, Derrick explained, a great deal of institutionalized racism within the Mormon Church at the time — the church would not ordain Black men as clergy, although that was later changed — and after their visit his companion complained to him that they should not be applying such effort to proselytize among Black households.

"And something about that just struck me like a bolt of lightning," Derrick explained. "I realized — that's wrong. I cannot accept that. And if this is wrong, then maybe all the other things about the church are wrong as well. I realized that I believed very deeply that God is a respecter of persons, and if I believed that God didn't have a problem with a person because they're Black, then maybe God also doesn't have a problem with a person who was gay, or lesbian. That was really an awakening for me."

Derrick quit his missionary position, and returned to Newfoundland. He left the Mormon Church, and returned to the United Church. He decided to enrol in a nursing program at Memorial University. That was in 1979.

"By that point I was out to myself, but I certainly didn't feel ready to come out to other people. Then in one of my courses I ran into a person that I felt was obviously gay. I sat next to that person in class one day, and after class I started a conversation with the person and we became friends. And we discussed this coming out business. He was definitely out and didn't hide it at all. This person really helped me along, and introduced me to other gay people at the university. So I spent a lot of time at the Thomson Student Centre — when I probably should have been studying — with other people who identified as gay or lesbian. I felt comfortable coming out to them, and then they had friends who were straight and so I started coming out to them as well. I started going to Friends, the gay bar in St. John's, and from there I basically felt very free and accepted."

It took him a while longer to come out to his family. His father had died when he was seven years old, but he hesitated in telling the rest of his family. Finally, after entering into a relationship, he decided to tell his mother.

"That's when the shit hit the fan," he recalled. "It was not at all accepted. That caused me a lot of stress. But I recognized that it caused my family stress as well. My parents were older when I was born, and came from a generation when these things were not acceptable. They didn't know anybody who was gay or lesbian — they probably did but didn't know it — and they didn't have any experience with this. So it didn't go over very well" (Ibid.).

Derrick trained as a nurse, and looked after his own elderly mother when she became too infirm to look after herself. She eventually died at home.

"I always felt that our relationship had been greatly impacted by my coming out, and not in a good way," he reflected. "I always felt that our relationship had been greatly damaged by my coming out. But about a week before she died, I arranged to have a communion for her, with one of our clergy at the Anglican Cathedral... after that, after everyone else was out of the room, my mother, who hadn't spoken for several weeks, she called me by name, and she said: 'I love you.' And I realized that what she meant by that, was that she was accepting me" (Ibid.).

Derrick worked as a nurse for the next several years, and while he continued his involvement in the queer community it wasn't until the 1990s that he took on an active leadership role. It was a scandal in the Catholic Church that drove him to get involved.

In October 1996, Monsignor Dermot O'Keefe, of the Parish of Saints Peter and Paul in Bay Bulls, gave a sermon in which he called on parishioners to oppose proposed changes adding sexual orientation protections to the provincial Human Rights Code. He called homosexuality a "disorder" that "must be controlled and conquered with God's supernatural help," and said it was "the root cause of AIDS." He published equally homophobic content in the church bulletin. He described discrimination faced by gays and lesbians as "rightful discrimination" and defended the right to refuse gays and lesbians housing and employment as teachers. He also accused UNICEF of conducting abortions and distributing contraceptives (Murphy 1996; Barron 1996).

Jerry Vink, Executive Director of the provincial Human Rights Association at the time, denounced these comments as "borderline hate literature." Gerard Yetman, then Executive Director of the AIDS Committee of NL (ACNL), warned the comments risked undoing all the hard education and outreach work AIDS activists had done in the region (Barron 1996).

Derrick heard about all this from a gay friend, who was a teacher and had obtained a copy of the offensive church bulletin.

"I asked my friend: 'Well why don't you do something about it?' And he said: 'Well I'm a teacher. If I say anything about it, then I would be coming out to my employer and I would lose my job.'

"But this angered me so much that I felt I had to do something about it,"

continued Derrick. *"So I got on the radio — on CBC's On The Go program. I called up CBC and told them what had been written in this church bulletin. They asked me if I would do an interview on the radio. And I realized — well if I do that I'm definitely coming out to the whole community now, aren't I? But I was so angered by what had been written, that I said yes"* (Bishop 2021)

He recorded an interview with CBC. After his comments aired, he was contacted by people who were grateful to him for speaking out.

"There were a lot of people angry at what had happened in that particular parish," he said. "After the radio interview one person from that area approached me at work and said she had been in church the day this happened, and she had been very, very angry — very disturbed by what he said. People supported me and said 'I don't accept this [homophobic] attitude at all.'"

When Derrick later heard the story air on the radio, it also included an interview with Brian Hodder, chairperson for the community organization NGALE. Derrick was impressed by what he heard and decided to start attending NGALE meetings. His involvement deepened, and within a short time he became chairperson of the organization, a position he held for several years. There he played an important role in the fight for provincial human rights protections around sexual orientation, and later in the fight for same-sex marriage rights both at the legislative level as well as within the Anglican Church. It still astonishes him to reflect on how much has changed in his own lifetime.

"Once the ball started rolling, it just happened. It was like lightning speed. I mean I know it was a long struggle — it started back in the 1960s, the 1970s, with the Stonewall protests and the gay liberation movement. It was years later that these changes happened. But once they started, it seemed as if it happened very quickly. You had inclusion in the human rights legislation, same-sex marriage, all these things that happened within a decade.

"It was a struggle. I'm glad I lived in this time, but I sometimes wish that these things had been in place before I had to deal with it. Because it could be very hard, and at times very frightening" (Ibid.).

CHAPTER TWO: COMMUNITY ORGANIZING: THE EARLY YEARS

As the previous snapshots demonstrate, queer life in the latter half of the twentieth century remained precarious. While some individuals were fortunate to encounter acceptance, others faced the loss of jobs, family, friends and other personal hardships. Many left the province.

This was the state of affairs which began to fuel organized activism. The queer movement in this province was part and parcel of a national movement and would be deeply influenced by activists and ideas from elsewhere in Canada and the US. Newfoundland and Labrador was an equal partner in this movement from the earliest days.

It's difficult to pinpoint the exact origins of queer activism in Canada — there were queer publications as far back as 1918 — but many point to the groundbreaking work of Jim Egan, a Toronto-based activist who began writing letters to newspapers effectively calling for gay rights as far back as 1949, the year Newfoundland and Labrador joined Canada. Momentum intensified with the launch of *GAY* — Canada's first explicitly gay magazine — in March 1964, and the establishment of Canada's first explicitly queer community organization — Association for Social Knowledge (ASK) — in Vancouver the following month. Throughout the 1960s, more and more mainstream magazines and newspapers began publishing articles on homosexuality, some of them even positive in tone. Increased visibility and growing advocacy paid off: in 1967 the federal Liberal government signalled its intention to decriminalize homosexuality. This process came to fruition by 1969. That inspired a new wave of furious queer organizing, with gay or 'homophile' organizations popping up in Ontario, Quebec, and British Columbia in 1970. Gender affirming surgeries for trans people were also being performed in Canada by that year, if not earlier. In August 1971 the first formal gay rights protest — the 'We Demand Rally' — took place on Parliament Hill in Ottawa, and in November 1971 a national queer magazine called *The Body Politic* launched (McLeod 1996). *The Body Politic* would play an important role documenting, and in some ways catalyzing, queer organizing in Newfoundland.

And in 1974, Newfoundland and Labrador joined the ranks of other provinces with organized queer activist movements.

***

When high school teacher Ann Escott took her recess break that pivotal day in May 1974, it was a routine morning. Escott worked at Bishops College, where she taught physical education and biology. Mid-way through the morning she joined other teachers in the staff-room for recess. The women preparing lunch for the students turned on the radio, to a popular phone-in radio program that aired daily on CJON. None of this was unusual. But what Escott heard next caused her jaw to drop.

The host of the program was interviewing a man named Norman Hay, who was a member of Gay Ottawa. Hay was visiting St. John's, and had reached out to CJON offering to talk about his work with Gay Ottawa. They invited him in, and put him on the air. When Escott tuned in, Hay was chatting about his work, and said he was perplexed as to why he could find no sign of organized gay community in St. John's. 'Where are all the Newfoundland gays?' he demanded, in a tone of bemused frustration.

Escott was floored. The visitor from the mainland was out and proud – a far cry from most Newfoundland queers at the time. Escott was a teacher – if she was outed as gay she could be fired for it, thanks to clauses in her contract (colloquially referred to as 'morality' clauses).

"So I was sitting there, sort of zombie-like, pretending not to pay attention but paying very close attention," she explained.

She remembers the broadcast quite vividly.

"I thought he was incredibly brave, because some of the people phoning in were just horrible. Others were quite supportive. I was just elated. I couldn't believe someone was actually doing this."

As soon as she could, Escott slipped off to find a telephone. She phoned her girlfriend at the time, Sandy Pottle.

"I said: 'There's someone on the radio and they want to get a group together! Has anybody gotten his information?'"

This was long before the Internet, but the informal queer phone tree was already in operation. Pottle replied that another friend had just reached out and gotten his contact information (apparently at least a dozen gay people had phoned CJON looking for his contact information). There was going to be a meeting with him the following night.

"It was so wonderful," recalled Escott, of the day she heard Hay on the radio. "It's hard to explain – it was wonderful but terrifying. It was a mix of emotions. It was like – oh my god, there are other people out there who are doing this, and on the radio! And maybe we actually can do something and not be murdered or killed."

That morning's program set off a powerful buzz in the city's still largely underground queer community. Those who heard it discussed the remarkable interview, and decided that if mainlanders could get on the radio and openly ask – 'Where are all the Newfoundland gays?' – it was time for the Newfoundland gays to get organized.

What came of that interview, and the phone conversations which followed, was the first meeting of the Community Homophile Association of Newfoundland (CHAN). Escott and her friends called a few other friends they knew to be gay or lesbian, and arranged a meeting at the apartment of Margaret Chan, a mutual friend. A dozen community members — seven women and five men – attended that inaugural meeting. So did Norman Hay, the man who sparked this mobilization. Hay, who died of cancer in 1988, was an active member of Gay Ottawa, and an architect. He'd had been one of the site designers for Expo '67 in Montreal, and later worked on Expo '86 in Vancouver, among other projects (Bebout 2003). Hay was a former lover of Alan Jarvis, iconoclastic former director of Canada's National Gallery in the 1950s, who was described by British art historian Sir Kenneth Clark as "the best-looking man I've ever seen" (Ord 1998). Others were similarly smitten: Montreal artist Jacques de Tonnancour called Jarvis "a walking work of art," while novelist Robertson Davies fictionalized this "male beauty" in his 1985 novel *What's Bred in the Bone* (Adams 2009). Hay himself was working on a biography of Jarvis when he died.

In addition to his work with Gay Ottawa, Hay was also deeply involved with *The Body Politic*, Canada's queer monthly/bi-monthly magazine which ran from 1971-1987 (later succeeded by its younger sibling Xtra). The magazine played a pivotal role in queer organizing in Canada, and provided important coverage of early organizing initiatives in Newfoundland and Labrador. In 1982, the magazine was charged with obscenity over some of its articles, including a piece titled "Lust With a Very Proper Stranger," about fist-fucking (Xtra #82, April 1982). This article was attributed to Angus MacKenzie (1982), but that was a pseudonym. When the paper's editors refused to divulge the name of the author – "We are all Angus MacKenzie" they responded defiantly when asked – the entire nine-person editorial collective was charged. The ensuing case became an important test of freedom of the press in Canada, and well-known defence lawyer Clayton Ruby took up the paper's defense. The paper won both the initial case and a subsequent appeal. Much later, Hay admitted to being the author of the controversial article (Bebout 2003).

"He was an older man but very sweet and supportive of the movement's work, yet I never saw him as particularly political," reflected Ed Jackson, a founding member of the Body Politic collective.

Uncertainty still surrounds the precise purpose of Hay's visit to Newfoundland. Was he on holiday? Did he travel to Canada's eastern-most province with the express aim of kickstarting queer activism there? When he met with the local activists, he told them he was in Newfoundland on a work-related meeting, or conference. But he also gave them a false name at first, and told them he was an archivist. As Escott pointed out, it was common back then for members of the queer community to invent fake identities and back stories as a method of self-protection.

"In those days we had a lot of people who showed up and used false names – sometimes for years. They created these false stories about themselves, as a cover. That was reasonable at the time. The name [Hay] gave us apparently was not the name that he went by. [The fake name] was also the name he'd used on the radio."

Hay left a profound impression on the local activists. Nearly fifty years later, Escott remembers him tramping into Chan's apartment in Hillview Terrace.

"He was a big guy, wore a sort of leather big-brimmed hat. Not quite a cowboy hat, but almost. And he carried a big leather courier bag, instead of a briefcase. All that seemed really just beyond cool at that time. He was very much a people person, and he was really keen to encourage us to do something, to start something. He offered to help. He encouraged us to do whatever we could and he would try to help us out in any way he could, in terms of emotional support and that kind of thing. He was very encouraging" (Escott 2021)

At his funeral, activist Rick Bebout said of Hay that despite a hard life he reminded "a bunch of lucky if too sober gay kids of something we knew but had to be reminded of: that life is not awful. It's a joy, a joy to be celebrated" (Bebout 2003).

A similar sentiment prevailed that night in St. John's as Escott and her friends determined to form a group that would celebrate the joy of queer life and love in Newfoundland and Labrador. The group formed that night in 1974 — CHAN — would become the province's first formal queer organization.

Early meetings of the group were held on Thursday nights at an apartment in Hillview Terrace where Escott lived with her partner, Pottle. As the organization grew, for a time the group booked meeting space at the Press Club, an institution then located in the Arts & Culture Centre. But soon CHAN established headquarters of a different sort, in a location which became an important fixture of early queer community in the city.

In 1974, a young graduate student named Michael Calcott moved to St. John's. Originally from Stratford Ontario, Calcott came to St. John's to pursue a Master's degree in English at Memorial University. He was married when he arrived, and his wife accompanied him. They were both socially active, and she quickly became involved in local feminist organizing. He had been questioning his sexuality for some time however, and when his wife became ill and was hospitalized, he needed support. He'd heard about CHAN on campus, and reached out to the group. He started attending meetings, and eventually came out after becoming attracted to a man he met there. He and his wife separated, although she remained a close supporter and ally of the fledgling organization.

Calcott and his wife had been living in a house at 122 Waterford Bridge Road, along with a boarder named John Bragg (who was also a member of CHAN). After Calcott and his wife separated, he needed roommates in order to keep the spot. It was a fair-sized house, and so he reached out to CHAN to see if anyone in the group would share the house with him. Escott and Pottle took him up on the offer. Calcott and his new partner, Escott and Pottle, and Bragg all became roommates.

St. John's has not — yet — had a queer community centre of its own. But the house at 122 Waterford Bridge Road in the mid 1970s was probably the closest thing the city has had. With five CHAN members living in the house, it became a de facto headquarters for the group. They set up the spare room as a small community library – "mostly gay men's porn" recalls Escott — and began operating a phone support line from the house as well. Meetings were held at the house, along with numerous parties and social events. Visiting queers, not just from St. John's but outside the city as well, knew they could stay at the house if they needed, and guests were frequently put up in any space available.

"We had the only purely gay house in the city," explained Calcott. "Everyone else was either with parents or living with a partner who might not be out. We were available. People knew there would usually be somebody around, so people dropped in all the time. It was a real community centre."

"The house on Waterford Bridge Road was very important in the gay movement," said Roberta Buchanan, a retired English professor with Memorial University who recalled spending many a delightful evening there. "It became a kind of centre. It was a place where people could go and be in a safe environment."

The house, part of a duplex, was owned by two elderly sisters — the Walshes — who lived next door. The two sisters had a routine of going to bed early, then waking up at one in the morning. They would have a cup of tea, sing some hymns, and then go back to bed for the remainder of the night. "A Mother's Love's a Blessing" was one hymn that all former residents of the house remembered hearing frequently through the paper-thin walls at night.

For all their hymn-singing, the elderly sisters were quietly supportive of the queer activism going on in their house. They got to know all the queers who became regulars there. Pottle got in the habit of driving the sisters to Mass every Sunday at Corpus Christi Church down the road, and she'd wait outside in the car to drive them home again.

"They were lovely," said Escott. "We'd say to them: 'Now we're going to have a party on such and such a night, I hope the noise doesn't disturb you.' And the sisters, those dollies, would turn off the lights and wait by the windows, upstairs. Then they'd say to us the next morning: 'You had a lot of women at your party!' and giggle. People would come in drag of course" (Escott 2021).

"They loved it when we had parties," said Calcott. "They'd listen in and they thought it was a riot."

With 122 Waterford Bridge Road as their base, CHAN began to grow rapidly. The group published a small ad in *The Evening Telegram*. At first the unobtrusive ad simply read "Gay? Looking for friends? Contact CHAN" and Pottle recalls that they received numerous responses from members of the Chinese community, thinking it was a Chinese social organization starting up and Chan was the organizer's name. Gradually, between postal mail and the phone line they began building a network of queer connections throughout the province.

"Between the phone and the mail, we contacted over a thousand people across the island," recalled Escott. None of the organizers recall any contacts from Labrador during the initial years, but connections proliferated across the island portion of the province. "All across the island. Up and down. Anybody who was coming to town, we'd let them know when there was a party or a social happening, so if they could possibly come to town – or if they came to town on a vacation or something – we'd give them a number to look them up, or we'd go meet them" (Ibid.).

"It was about bringing people together, socializing," recalled Calcott.

CHAN member Lynn Murphy remembers the parties well.

"They were amazing," she recalled. "Wild would be another word for it. It was a wilder time back then than it is these days. We didn't have the same fears, of disease for instance. Everybody had a sense of what a freedom it suddenly was to meet other [gay] people, to see other people! We hadn't had that before. Oh, it was joyful."

One of the strengths of that early organizing dynamic was CHAN's ability to seamlessly blend work and pleasure. People who showed up at the house would be drafted into organizing work — putting together mail-outs, or typing newsletter articles. Monthly meetings were laid-back affairs, yet a lot got done.

"There would be a talk, then a business meeting, then there'd be a party with wine and stuff to eat, and probably everyone would bring a bottle of wine or something," recalled Buchanan. "That was wonderful, because gay people could meet each other."

Sometimes the meetings would run for an hour or two, sometimes merely fifteen minutes. The social party that followed each meeting would sometimes run for a couple of hours; sometimes it would run all night.

It was that social aspect which initially attracted Buchanan. She was one of Calcott's professors, and he invited her to join the group.

"I joined more for the social thing," she said. "To them, if you were friends you became part of their tribe. You went everywhere, they took you everywhere with them."

Increasingly secure in their growing strength in numbers, members had a great deal of fun.

"We'd all dress up in various outfits – whatever tickled our fancy in the evening – and we'd often go off to the Arts and Culture Centre dressed in bizarre outfits, just to shock," recalled Pottle. "Some of our group was quite shocking. John Bragg always dressed in bright orange and was quite flamboyant. [Others] were very effeminately dragged up. We had a lot of fun. I don't think we really cared [about public reactions]. We were more just entertaining each other. If we shocked people that was great. But our intent was to have fun with the

people we were with. And if we shocked people that would probably have been desirable too. But we were just having a good time" (Pottle 2022).

They did eventually receive some hate mail, but nothing that gave them pause in their work. While everyone recognized the need for political action, the primary focus of organizers at that early stage was social. The first step in building community — building a movement — was bringing people together. Calcott and Escott did some interviews on CBC Radio during those early years, but protests or marches were not yet on the radar.

"Jeezus no, everyone was too closeted," explained Escott. "At that point, certainly in all the schools and most other places in Newfoundland, if you were gay you could be fired. The schools and many other places were run by the assorted churches, and so you had to sign a morals clause when you got employed. So you kept a low profile."

Calcott remembers the atmosphere of fear that surrounded queer identity in those years. Although no one I spoke with knew anyone who was actually fired for being gay, the knowledge that it *could* happen — and the fear of being outed — sufficed as a mechanism to intimidate many from coming out publicly.

"You can imagine how different it was then," recalled Calcott. "People were afraid. Afraid of their family knowing, afraid of other people knowing. It was a community thing. There was a lot of that [fear]."

"A lot of people worked in family businesses," explained Escott. "In Newfoundland, if you got a job it was often because you knew someone or someone knew someone who would put in a good word for you."

In a society where employment was often acquired through nepotism, being outed could be a death knell for job prospects. Us-and-them divisions were rife in Newfoundland during this period: Catholics versus Protestants, townies versus baymen. Coming out as gay was to invite a further form of discrimination and division on top of these others.

CHAN did send a letter to government[13] during its first two years, according to organizers I interviewed. They highlighted the need for human rights protections for gay people, especially teachers. There is no surviving record of this correspondence, but Escott remembers the reply they received.

"The reply came back, after some time, saying that first – there were no gay teachers. And second, if one should sadly occur, they would be immediately dismissed."

Activists interviewed by Tom Warner for his 2002 book *Never Going Back: A History of Queer Activism in Canada*, also recall submitting a brief to government on the need for human rights protections (it's unclear whether this is the same outreach recalled by the activists I interviewed). According to the activists Warner interviewed, the response was "cold" and "scathing." One of the

---

[13] Organizers' memories differed as to precisely which department this letter was directed toward.

activists told Warner that a response came from the provincial health minister at the time: "He answered our letter saying that it was a sickness and we should never have rights... It was a very negative reaction" (Warner 1993).

Joan Dewling was one of the early members of CHAN, which she came into contact with in a roundabout way. She was born in St. John's and grew up in what is today Pippy Park. Her family's house was expropriated by the City of St. John's for the park in the 1960s, and they moved to Pine Bud Avenue, near Memorial University. When she was sixteen, her father died. Her mother was an instructor at the School of Nursing and took in a boarder, a young woman from Ohio who was a student at the School. Unbeknownst to her daughter, this young American woman was lesbian. The 19-year-old Dewling had had the same boyfriend since the age of 13; they went through cycles of breaking up and getting back together.

"During this period of time we were really going through a [difficult] period, we were breaking up all the time, and then in comes this woman," recalls Dewling. CHAN had just been formed – she recalls hearing about it in the news, as well as gossip at the university.

"And then one day this woman who was staying with us, handed me a letter to deliver for her. I went to school with it and then I looked at the letter and it was for CHAN! So I didn't go looking for CHAN — CHAN found me. Anyway, we got closer and closer. I had never thought about being gay, but in retrospect of course things started to fit together, and so then we started having this affair.

"She decided she had to tell my mother, and my mother blew her stack. And so she threw me out. That's when I met CHAN" (Dewling 2022).

Ann Escott and Sandy Pottle and a team of CHAN volunteers showed up in a Volkswagen van and helped move the young couple into a new apartment they found on Longs Hill, in the city's downtown.

"It was all very traumatic though," recalled Dewling. Things had escalated following her outing, and before she was kicked out.

"I remember one day coming home, [my mother] was really drunk and flipping out that I couldn't possibly be gay. I said: 'Look, you're drinking, let's talk.' I was trying to be really calm, because I learned that it's better to be calm than be reactive. But anyway, she said: 'Oh so you think I'm drunk?' So then she called the police and they came – paddy wagon and all – and she talked to them for about an hour. After that for a while I had a police tail. The police would report to her everywhere I went and everything I did.[14]

"My father had been a high-ranking Mason – when he died he was district grand master – and that was a period of time when the Masons had some sway. And a lot of the police were Masons. [My girlfriend] was from Ohio, and they had Pringles potato chips at that time in the United States but we didn't have

---

[14] Dewling also notes however that "after eight years and three disownments, [her mother] finally became and remained a very staunch supporter of gay rights."

them in Canada. So she had a box of Pringles sent from the United States to our house, and my mother called the Constabulary to say that it must be a drug shipment. So the police came and took away the Pringles. I'll always remember us walking into the police station to pick them up. It was hilarious in retrospect. But it was a pretty rough time, it was pretty hard. I was trying to find my feet, and we were thrown into this relationship, and I was thinking 'What have I done?' But that's how I met CHAN. They were really supportive, and really there for everyone. I wasn't politically active because I was still too confused, but I did go to all the meetings, and all the socials, and I always found they were really kind.

"Primarily what they did that I think impressed me the most was their outreach. I know some people said that the activists in Halifax were far more political. And I went to Halifax at one point and I do remember there was a bar that was set up by their organization and it was really well controlled – you had to be signed in and all that kind of thing. Whereas we really weren't that well organized in Newfoundland. But Nova Scotia is attached to the mainland, and it has twice the population in half the space. Whereas the isolation in Newfoundland was really paramount. That's what CHAN focused on and did so well, was huge outreach. I know they went all over the place and met people and that built a really strong community. It was so important" (Ibid.).

For the province's gays and lesbians, CHAN's formation had a catalytic effect. For the first time, NLers seeking queer community had a place to turn, and were able to connect with other queers.

"Before us, before our group, I'd say about 90 percent of people who realized they were gay immediately – or as soon as they could – moved away," said Escott. "You didn't want to stay here. You didn't want to be around your family or anybody you knew [if you came out]. You went to either Montreal or Toronto. Some of us came back, but for most it was – 'Oh god, I'm gay, I gotta get out of here.' This was across all genders, all socio-economic levels."

Thanks to CHAN, gay and lesbian NLers finally found community, and forged connections that would last a lifetime.

"After I found the gay group, I saw less and less of my straight friends," reflected Bragg. "I'd found a new family."[15]

---

[15] Bragg was born in Bonavista in 1952 and lived in Port Union before moving to St. John's in 1969 to attend Memorial. He then worked in the biochemistry department as a research technician for a couple of years, during which time he got involved with CHAN. The group not only had an impact on his life as a gay man, but shaped his future career as well. Calcott was a voracious chef, and Bragg wound up catching his enthusiasm. They had a copy of Julia Childe's *The Art of French Cooking* in the house on Waterford Bridge Road, and proceeded to cook their way through the book. After Bragg eventually left Newfoundland, he wound up in Calgary in 1982 where he managed to convince an upscale restaurant to hire him as a chef based purely on his enthusiasm and self-training at the CHAN house. Thus began a professional career in food services that would span 35 years.

CHAN's work was noticed by organizers on the mainland, who kept the national scene apprised of the group's progress. *The Body Politic* editorial collective, based in Toronto, kept a close eye on developments in Canada's most easterly queer enclave, allowing readers across the country to share in the excitement. "The pressing task which faced the new group was the creation of a viable gay community, a foundation for further progress," wrote Ken Popert, chronicling CHAN's early days for the publication. "CHAN went to work, using the press, radio, and even washroom walls to draw Newfoundland gays together" (Popert 1976).

It worked. By 1976, Popert reported, the group had around four hundred members, two thirds of them women. Membership was spread across the vast and sparsely populated province, so one of CHAN's aims was to facilitate the formation of smaller regional chapters wherever possible. Less than two years after its founding, reported *The Body Politic*, there were initiatives underway to form groups in Harbour Grace, Corner Brook, Conception Bay, and at Memorial University. The core group in St. John's published a newsletter titled *About Face*, which was mailed out across the province.

Surviving issues offer a lively snapshot of members' lives at the time. In the Fall 1975 issue, a recipe for Tuna Noodle Bake shares a page with discussion about a recent shortage of KY Jelly on the island. Meanwhile in the same issue, Independent Liberal MHA Steve Neary vies with an unnamed judge for CHAN's "Homophobe of the Month Award" in a column which illustrates the breadth of ignorance and homophobia at the time.

The judge in question "presided over the trial of a car thief who said he stole the car because he was upset by homosexual advances the owner made toward him. The owner admitted he is gay but denied making advances (he has since left St. John's). The thief was convicted but given a suspended sentence by the magistrate on account of the anguish he had suffered, presumably due to his name being linked to gays" (About Face 1975).

It was Neary who was singled out by CHAN for the ad hoc award, for comments he made to CBC Corner Brook "to the effect that he was glad the gays had an organisation so that they would not be lurking around parks, seducing unwary passers-by. He went on to say that we were sick and parents should be vigilant lest their child should be stricken by this dread disease" (Ibid.).

The newsletter chronicles the organization's vibrant social life. Donations were collected for local Christmas charities. A Hallowe'en house party, featuring a drag and strip show, was attended by more than 35 members. 'Josephine' and 'Laverne' were awarded the "Ms. CHAN 1975" award for their performances; best costume went to "The Lady in Red." CHAN held an "April Fool's Affair" dance in April 1976 that was attended by 75 people from across the island, and put off an anniversary gala with a buffet supper in May of that year to celebrate its second anniversary, with over 100 in attendance. The barrage of social events continued that summer with a July Jean Jamboree and drag sensation Laverne's Birthday Party in August. CHAN also organized smaller-scale activities for interested members: a weekly bowling team, swimming sessions, card nights and movies.

For all its growing activity, confidentiality was still a pressing concern. The lack of human rights protections meant members could be in danger of losing their jobs, and even their housing, if they were outed. So CHAN was careful to safeguard the privacy of members and volunteers. This assiduous confidentiality rankled more radical activists, including some of the mainland writers for *The Body Politic*.

"The impact of the group is reduced by the reluctance of all but a few to be identified publicly," wrote Popert. "This cautious attitude is perhaps understandable in a province where jobs are scarce and unemployment hovers at fifteen percent. But in St. John's, as elsewhere, the question has to be constantly posed: how much closetry is necessary, and how much is irrational? The future of every gay community can be read in its answer to this question" (Popert 1976).

Still, Popert expressed pride in the group's successes. "In just two years CHAN has produced a profound change in the quality of gay life in St. John's. It has been able to do this because its members are the kind of people out of whom the gay movement is fashioned and on whom the gay movement depends: proud and courageous gay women and men who stand up and fight for their rights" (Ibid.).

Wish Leonard was a university student, and later worked at MUN. He remembers how his own involvement with the group came about, and the almost cloak-and-dagger secrecy which prevailed at the time.

"My friend Gordon – my best friend forever, who died as a result of AIDS in the early '90s – and I went to a small bar near the War Memorial just below Duckworth Street in St. John's. Although small, it had two floors. Our table was just above a table below us on the lower floor. Overhearing the conversation below us, we knew these were gay guys. Although I didn't smoke, Gordon insisted I break the ice by asking for a smoke. I did, and they gave me two. So then I actually had to smoke it – yuck! But now that we were 'buddies' one of the guys asked if we were gay. 'Hmm...yes!' I replied. So I was told about an upcoming meeting at a house on a downtown street, in the coming week.

"We both went to that address on the night noted, but the woman who answered the door said there was no event happening. I explained that we were told about it by a couple of men at the bar we'd been at. Fortunately, another lady came down the stairs and said: 'Let them in.' So, we were ushered in and there were about five other people present. A few more came later. In attendance was a lawyer, who was surprised to find his sister there too! They had not known about each other. Since I was sporting a long woollen scarf that night, he kept calling me 'Isadora.' All of this was terribly exciting for me, and I was hooked. That's how it all started" (Leonard 2021).

Leonard would later become treasurer for the organization. He remembers opening a bank account for the group at a CIBC branch located on campus. "This drew the attention of the bank personnel, who came out from their work areas to see a gay person!" he recalled.

"We all kept everything pretty hidden," recalled Dewling. "You didn't tell people. I think I felt more for the men. It was always easier, it seemed, for women. Although whenever a straight man came around all of the sudden we'd be vulnerable because I didn't think we were given much credibility."

One of the things that bothered Dewling, and others I spoke with, was the tendency of some gay men to deliberately maintain relationships with women as a way of avoiding scrutiny over their sexuality. It was a form of self-protection, but one that was criticized by many within the community.

"It used to bug me that some of the men would talk about going to Signal Hill and necking with their girlfriends and hoping the police would catch them so that they would leave them alone [thinking they were straight] because they were really gay. That bothered me. It wasn't everybody, but I did hear people talk about that. It was contrary to everything else that was happening" (Dewling 2022).

By 1976, the group was growing too large for meetings to feasibly be held at members' houses. Between 35 and 50 people were routinely showing up for bi-weekly – and for a time weekly – meetings. CHAN by now had sufficient resources to rent offices, and leased a space on the third floor of 127A Queens Road in downtown St. John's, which they dubbed 'The Clubhouse.' The space was used for group meetings and smaller social events, including a regular women's night. A general drop-in night was held on Mondays at 8:30pm, while organizing meetings took place every second Thursday at 8:30pm. A membership structure was also developed, with 'supporter cards' entitling members to free issues of the newsletter and discounts at CHAN events.

CHAN, growing in confidence as well as size, also began operating more publicly. A poster campaign was developed to promote the group, and when CJON hosted a call-in radio talk show on the subject of homosexuality (hosted by iconic NL broadcaster Bas Jamieson), CHAN members phoned in and participated directly. "The opinions expressed by the callers and the moderator were much more favourable than those of past shows on the subject," reported Wish Leonard in the *About Face* newsletter.

CHAN knew there were plenty of queers struggling in the smaller rural outport communities, and not all of them were able to make it into St. John's. So sometimes they undertook outreach into those communities, going to meet with folks who had reached out. One such outreach mission is described by Roger Johnson in the following section of this chapter. Joan Dewling remembered another expedition to Catalina, a small community of less than a thousand people on the Bonavista Peninsula.

"I remember going to Catalina," she said. "This young man had reached out to CHAN and he had a place in Catalina and I remember all of us going there for a weekend. It was all pretty amazing to me. There were all these [gay] men, and they were married, and some of their wives were really supportive… I was always impressed by how much love there was."

CHAN's energy was remarkable, and the group took on fights at the provincial, national, and even international level. In 1977, nine women who had been stationed at Argentia in Newfoundland were dismissed from the Canadian Forces under Administrative Order 19-20, which forbade homosexuals from serving in the military (this incident is discussed further in Chapter 5). CHAN tried to get in contact with the women, but efforts to reach them were unsuccessful. Nevertheless, the issue made it into the news and radio talk shows, and so CHAN reached out to CJON and negotiated for two of its members – Larry McCarthy and Sheila Robinson – to appear on popular radio talk show "Hotline." Homosexuality had been the topic of the show on at least two previous occasions, yet on neither occasion were any of the hosts or guests actually queer themselves. "This is the first time local gay people will have aired their opinion on this talk show," wrote Wish Leonard[16] in a report to *The Body Politic*. It was probably the first time "local gay people" had spoken publicly on their own behalf on any broadcast in the province.

Leonard explained that in the wake of the incident at Argentia, CHAN had decided to pursue a strategy of "going public" in order to increase public awareness of gay issues and perspectives, as well as the fact that the local community was full of gay people.

As the group became more networked and confident, CHAN also began connecting with activists elsewhere in the country. On June 4, 1975, public hearings were held at the Hotel Newfoundland on changes to Canada's Immigration Act. A member of CHAN attended the hearings, and said that CHAN endorsed a brief from Gay Ottawa calling on the government to remove the ban on gay immigrants and visitors to Canada (the federal government eliminated this ban in 1978).

Also that year, the National Gay Rights Coalition (NGRC) was formed during the third annual National Gay Rights Conference that took place in Ottawa from June 28-July 1, 1975, and was attended by over 200 delegates from around the country (the group was renamed National Lesbian and Gay Rights Coalition in 1978). CHAN was represented – after a fashion – as well.

Robin Metcalfe was a young Nova Scotia resident whose father was a Newfoundlander. He'd spent time living in Newfoundland as a child, and his older sister, Margot, attended Memorial University in St. John's in the early 1970s. She was deeply involved in feminist activism, and Robin came out to her as gay shortly before visiting her for Christmas break in 1974. She excitedly organized a party, inviting as many gay people as she knew. Robin — who would go on to

---

[16] Leonard notes that not all the articles attributed to him in The Body Politic were actually written by him; some were a mistaken attribution.

become one of Canada's foremost queer activists in subsequent decades – also attended a CHAN meeting in St. John's, the first gay organization he ever took part in.

He was living in Halifax at the time of the National Gay Rights Conference (NGRC) in 1975, and was doing activist work with Gay Alliance for Equality (GAE) in that city. He showed up at the Conference only to discover there were no credentials or placards for GAE. There were, however, credentials and placards for CHAN – which the organizers for some reason had expected to show up – and so he stepped in as the CHAN rep for the Conference, carrying their placard at the iconic protest rally which took place on Parliament Hill.

"Although CHAN did not have a big voice at the conference, at least gays from across the country now know of CHAN, what it is and where it is," wrote an anonymous contributor to its *About Face* newsletter (About Face Vol. 1 No. 4). The NGRC was active until 1980, and in April 1976, CHAN voted to become members of the coalition.

In 1976, eager to learn more first-hand about the flurry of organizing going on in Atlantic Canada, *The Body Politic* collective members and NGRC organizers Ken Popert and his partner, Brian Mossop, conducted a brief Atlantic tour. They flew in to Halifax, met with organizers, then rented a car and drove to Newfoundland as well as Prince Edward Island. In St. John's, they met with CHAN members and also arranged an appearance on CBC, featuring Popert, Mossop, and two CHAN organizers discussing the NGRC and its work. Two CHAN delegates attended the NGRC conference that took place in Toronto later that year.

CHAN also directed its attention farther afield, engaging in a fraught ongoing public debate in the United States, where well-known singer and right-wing activist, Anita Bryant, was railing against gay rights initiatives in that country. CHAN submitted a letter to a Miami newspaper supporting queer activists fighting for their rights in that city (About Face 1977).

CHAN's Corner Brook branch was also growing. The group was by now comprised of fifteen members and was able to rent its own post office box in that city.

Unfortunately, all this momentum was short-lived. In November 1976, CHAN held elections but was unable to fill three of the group's executive positions. Attendance at meetings had also dropped precipitously by the end of the year. But the group rallied and in early 1977 managed to fill its vacant executive.

By the end of 1977, however, things were looking precarious again. In fall 1977, Leonard reported to *The Body Politic* that "participation in the group has been sporadic and finances tenuous." They were looking forward to the start of the new academic year at Memorial University, in the hopes it would bring new campus-based activists to the fold. Meanwhile, finances were hurting: CHAN had to give up its offices and returned to meeting in members' homes.

Some of the early members attribute some of the group's waning fortunes to the rise of a new phenomenon: gay bars, or at least gay-friendly ones. Prior to the proliferation of a gay bar scene in the city, CHAN events were among the few places to find queer community. Once the gay bars began to flourish, Buchanan says, people were less prone to stick around in intimate house environments or attend hybrid meetings/socials — many of them wanted to go cruising and partying in the clubs. This sentiment was echoed by others. The need for queer social contact is what had drawn many of the less political-minded members to those weekly meetings, which guaranteed a good party once the work was done. CHAN organizers skillfully tapped into that dynamic, gently drawing in the broad membership into other forms of activism. Now that folks could go out directly to the bars, some were less compelled to participate in other forms of community organizing.

By the beginning of the 1980s, CHAN was no more. Writing a state-of-the-gay-scene article for *The Body Politic* in July/August 1981, Lynn Murphy dated the demise of CHAN to 1979. Her summary was tinged with bitterness, even anger. From an active membership of 300 in its early years, CHAN had been "destroyed" by "a dead feeling in the hearts of a handful of supporters," she wrote. "No one was interested." CHAN's organizers had tried desperately to keep interest alive in its final months, she said (Murphy 1981).

"[CHAN's executive] tried the political angle and wrote to the Human Rights Association to discover their feelings on homosexuals and lesbians, hoping this would stir up emotions. Even a negative reply bothered no one but the writers. They tried the social angle and held dances, but only a few attended, mostly those interested in cheap alcohol and an easy good time; they were not interested in CHAN" (Ibid.).

Murphy attributed the collapse of CHAN to a failure by Newfoundland's queer community to understand the importance of representation. She said this stemmed from two sources:

"First, if you take a group of people who as a whole are the object of prejudice and add just a little more prejudice, that segment probably will not complain. They are accustomed to discrimination; a defeatist attitude has already been established. Secondly, gays in Newfoundland don't think they are being discriminated against: because no one knows they are there, no acts take place against them. They do not know that that they should not have to hide. They have learned to accept the fear of discovery and think they should live with it" (Ibid.).

She ended on what was not so much a hopeful note, but a call to action. Already a new cohort of organizers were meeting and planning to follow in CHAN's footsteps, she said. A handful of people were preparing to "resurrect the idea of a gay organization for Newfoundland." But it would take work, she cautioned.

"A new organization will have to work on the pride of these people. Make

them refuse to live with prejudice and show them that a person who must hide is being discriminated against. The budding gay movement in Newfoundland will not have to face much opposition; it will be confronted with something more deadly [apathy]. Opposition may inspire people, apathy deadens them. The distance to be traveled by a gay movement in this quiet province is staggering. First people must be made to feel pain, brutal as it may seem. Then they must be convinced to fight... The next few years should be interesting" (Ibid.).

Saving Lives

CHAN remained in operation for less than a decade, but its work was pivotal. It created the template for queer activism in the province, and many of the activists who formed subsequent groups traced their inspiration back to CHAN. CHAN networked and brought queer people from across the province together for the first time. It brought queer activists onto the provincial mediascape, on news programs and radio phone-in shows. It played a pivotal role in shaping the city's queer bar scene (this will be explored further in Chapter 10). It brought queer activism in this province to the attention of national queer activists, and connected our province to a vital and growing national and international movement. CHAN's members offered proactive, empathetic support to queers from one end of the province to the other: in person, by mail and by telephone.

We'll never know exactly how many lives were saved by CHAN and its outreach efforts. One of those lives was Roger Johnson. Johnson was a native of Prince Edward Island, who came out at a precocious age. "Prince Edward Island was not a very friendly place for a gay boy," he recalled wryly, and so he left home in 1968 at the age of fifteen, sneaking aboard the ferry to New Brunswick because he didn't have money for a ticket.

Johnson hitchhiked across the country several times as a youth, working odd jobs and seeking adventure. He travelled west, hitchhiked to Alberta, and then into the Northwest Territories. He eventually worked his way back east, and lived in Toronto for a while. The Maritimes beckoned once more, and he briefly returned to PEI, where he got a job working for an industrial finance company in Charlottetown. In 1974 the company transferred him to Gander, Newfoundland.

It was his first time in the province, and he was miserable.

"I'm in Gander, it's in the dead of winter, there are snowbanks twenty feet high everywhere, and I was living in a windowless basement apartment working for a finance company, trying to repossess dump trucks in blizzards," he recalled. Worst of all, he couldn't find any sign of gay community in the town.

"I was very unhappy, I was very depressed, and self-medicating with copious quantities of alcohol. I was super depressed. I was suicidal, and then I saw this newspaper ad."

The ad was an innocuous, small box buried in the *Evening Telegram*'s television guide insert. It was an ad for CHAN, and it listed their support phone number.

As his depression got the better of him, he drove out onto the Trans-Canada Highway one night in the pouring rain. He recalls lying down on the highway, hoping to get run over. But then he remembered the ad, which he had kept. He rose, found a pay phone at a nearby gas station, and called the number.

John Bragg still remembers the call – Johnson's suicidal state of mind rattled him, and without any formal training he supported the man as best he could.

"I answered the phone one night and there was a guy on the other end who was actually quite distraught," Bragg recalled, nearly a half century later. "He had been in the middle of the Trans-Canada with an umbrella over his head in the pouring rain. In Gander. He was very alone, and had that sense of 'oh my god I'm the only queer person in the world'.

"None of us was really equipped to deal with such a situation. We were all volunteers and just trying to do the right thing and the good thing to help people come out. I remember being distraught after the phone call" (Bragg 2021)

Bragg urged Johnson to come to St. John's, where he said they could talk in person and he could meet other gay people. Bragg told him he was welcome to stay at the house on Waterford Bridge Road.

Johnson followed their suggestion, and made the six-hour bus ride from Gander to St. John's as soon as he was able. Michael Calcott and his partner met Johnson when he got off the bus at the Newfoundland Hotel. By fluke, the night he arrived was also the night of one of CHAN's legendary parties. Before he knew it, recalled Johnson, "I found myself in somebody's living room with twenty gay men and everyone's listening to music and smoking and drinking and having a wonderful time, and I thought – well this is paradise!"

That was Johnson's first ever visit to St. John's, but he soon became a regular at the house on Waterford Bridge Road.

"It was just a riotous place to be around, just full of gay people and lesbians," he recalled. "There was always a crowd of people around, and Michael [Calcott] used to cook a lot so there was always fabulous food and great parties."

The clever thing about it was that the social atmosphere reinforced organizing efforts. Before he knew it, simply by hanging around the house Johnson found himself drafted into helping with CHAN's newsletter production, writing articles and helping with layout and distribution.

Johnson eventually quit his job with the finance company and left the province. He moved to Nova Scotia to pursue his dream of becoming a cosmetologist. But the time he'd spent with the gays and lesbians of St. John's – thanks to CHAN – lingered in his memory, and drew him back. After completing his training course in Nova Scotia, he returned to the province – this time to St.

John's – and opened a hair salon in Bowring's department store.

CHAN, and the queer community centred on 122 Waterford Bridge Road, was still going strong.

"Michael Calcott had a talent for just getting a bunch of people together that would start talking nonstop. One time about sixty people showed up – and this was a small house, the front door was open and people spilled out onto the lawn."

He met personalities from CBC, from the arts community, from the university. He met gay teachers, gay lawyers, even gay clergy. He entered into a short-lived relationship with a young man from a rural community near Carbonear, who took him to visit his home town. This man's parents were aware that their son was gay, and were quietly supportive of him. They devotedly fed Johnson: fish'n'brewis, moose, ham. At midnight a brace of rabbits came out of the oven for a midnight snack.

Now that he'd made connections through CHAN, he witnessed first-hand how hard the group worked to maintain social supports for its members. During his sojourn in Newfoundland, Johnson was at one point assigned to Long Harbour, where he spent "one horrible winter." The group organized a visit to bolster the isolated man's feelings: they filled up a Volkswagen van with members and drove out to Long Harbour. There they went skinny-dipping in a pond, and proceeded to host an elegant dinner party at his house, with fifty pounds of crab legs. Again, the group provided vital support at a tough time.

Johnson – who is now retired and living in Ottawa with his husband – made friendships that would last more than forty years. Many of those friendships are still going strong. But none of it would have happened without the CHAN support line. In fact, without it, he might not even have survived his first year in Newfoundland.

"*I know that now it seems kind of old-fashioned, that people would advertise a queer group, a support group, in a newspaper," he reflected. "That's so old-fashioned, isn't it? But you have to remember – think of the times. No one had Internet. No one had a cellphone. Long distance was expensive. There were very few ways to communicate discreetly. Those newspaper ads were life-savers. And not just for me, but I'm sure for hundreds of other Newfoundlanders who were isolated in small towns. Towns where religious things were going on, and all sorts of persecution. It meant a lot. You may not think it means a lot, but at the right time, it means a life*" (Johnson 2021).

Gay Association In Newfoundland (GAIN)

There are few buildings in downtown St. John's as iconic as the LSPU Hall on Victoria Street.

From 1789 until 1817 the location served as the site for the first Congregational church in Newfoundland. Destroyed in a fire in 1817, other faith-based meeting halls were erected in its place (and also tended to be destroyed by fires). During the nineteenth century, what is today Victoria Street was called Meeting House Lane, in recognition of the use of the site. In 1912 the location passed into the hands of the Long Shoremen's Protective Union (LSPU), who wanted it in part because it provided a ready vantage of the harbour, and of any ships that sailed in. The LSPU allowed local residents and community groups to make frequent use of the building for social events and meetings. Fire continued to enjoy the site as well: in 1922 the building was rebuilt following yet another conflagration (Heritage NL 2022).

In 1975, with the once-mighty LSPU in decline, an unlikely hippie came knocking at the door. Christopher Brookes was the artistic director of a small theatre company called The Mummer's Troupe.

"We were considered to be what some would call political theatre," he reflected. "But I would say we were socially relevant theatre. We would go into a community, often invited by the regional development association, or a union, or whatever it might be, and we would make a play about the community as a vehicle for community development."

"We went everywhere," he recalled. From Grand Falls to Buchans, they toured the island. They were invited to Nain, Makkovik, and Hopedale by the Labrador Inuit Association. Brookes recalls spending a few months in Labrador in the dead of winter.

"What we would do is we would go around and talk to people and sometimes record them, get to know people and talk about different issues in the community. Then we would go into the rehearsal hall and improvise scenes based on what we learned. Our process was always to go into a community and live there for a couple of months and make a play" (Brookes 2022).

In the summer of 1975, a local branch of the Community Planning Association of Canada invited the Troupe to make a piece about the east end of St. John's.

"There were some urban renewal issues going on and they wanted a piece that would focus on that," Brookes explained. The Troupe had up to that point focused on rural communities and hadn't done any plays about St. John's or other urban areas. Brookes, who was living in Petty Harbour-Maddox Cove at the time, hit the streets of St. John's, scouting around in the downtown east end for a location where they might be able to rehearse and put something together.

"That's when I wandered by the LSPU Hall, which I'd never really noticed before," he said.

He approached the union which still owned and operated the Hall – they were by that point the oldest surviving union in the province – and asked whether the Troupe might be able to use it.

"They were really welcoming," he said. "They were really great. Maybe it

was because we had done a couple of plays about labour issues, I don't know.
But they were terrific, I must say... I don't know what they thought of us but
it was great for us to have longshore union members occasionally wandering
through our rehearsals. It kept us from getting too arty-farty" (Ibid.).

The play they put together that summer was a hit, and the Troupe decided to do another play around labour issues, this one about the International
Woodworkers of America (IWA) strike in 1959. They put it off in the fall of 1975
and the two-week run sold out instantly. Unfortunately, the Hall, now a vibrant centre of public activity once more, became a victim of its own success. At
the end of the first week city fire inspectors showed up to check the place out.

"The inspectors said that the Hall was a fire trap and shouldn't be used for
public assembly. So that was that. The longshoremen weren't very happy about
it. I wasn't either," Brookes said.

Now faced with the prospect of expensive safety upgrades, the union –
which no longer needed the Hall for the strategic reasons they'd acquired it in
1912 – decided it would be easier to simply sell the building. There was avid
interest; the Bank of Montreal (which at that point had a branch next door, in
what is presently the Anna Templeton Centre) wanted to acquire the Hall to
tear it down and replace it with a parking lot. The LSPU weren't enthusiastic
about their building, with all of its history, being demolished, so they inquired
whether the Mummers' Troupe might be interested in buying the building.
Mummers Troupe administrator Lynne Lunde learned about a federal program which at the time assisted performing arts companies to purchase studio
space. With the help of the federal program and a great deal of fundraising, the
Mummers' Troupe purchased the LSPU Hall for $40,000.

Thus began the Hall's long association with the arts community. The artists
now running the Hall were also open to providing the space to other local community groups who needed a place to meet and organize. The city's growing
community of queer activists included many who were involved in the city's
vibrant arts scene, and so the LSPU Hall became one of the spaces in which
queer organizing started to happen. It was one of the few public spaces that
was open to, and supportive of, queer organizing at the time.

So it was that on November 5, 1981, a meeting was held at the LSPU Hall
in downtown St. John's. The purpose of the meeting was to establish a new gay
and lesbian organization to fill the void left when CHAN dissolved.

The initial meeting was attended by several individuals "in professions
of intellectual and academic status," reported Wendi Smallwood, a Memorial University student who interviewed GAIN's new executive for *The Muse*
campus newspaper (Smallwood 1982). The group lacked a name – at first it
was simply called "Gay Association," and later "Gay Association of St. John's."
The group would eventually broaden its ambit, settling on "Gay Association in
Newfoundland," or GAIN.

Three women and two men were elected to form an executive at that first meeting, and three primary goals were laid out:

"i) to have an information package printed in order to inform various organizations and institutions of their presence and other details pertaining to the rights and support of the homosexual, ii) to provide counselling services for their members and other individuals who have questions and problems with their homosexuality, and iii) to organize social events so as to provide a meeting ground for homosexuals" (Ibid.).

Paramount to all of this, the organizers emphasized, was the need to fundraise.

Smallwood interviewed the group's steering committee, and the article conveys the shock she felt upon learning about the discrimination gays and lesbians faced in St. John's. They told her it was common for gay people to be pelted with beer bottles downtown, or jumped and dragged into downtown alleys where they would be beaten up. Most were afraid to report such attacks or take legal action, she was told. She didn't hide her shock at learning all of this in her starkly opinionated report.

"In the career world the homosexual who is in contact with children or young adults is a definite no-no! Why? Fear of sexual assault upon society's innocent! Of course they don't consider the heterosexual male who has all those young spry chickadees at his disposal. Sexual abuse is sexual abuse no matter what type!" she wrote (Ibid.).

Attendees showed an early awareness of demands that would later become central to the movement – fighting for same-sex partner benefits, for instance. Organizers also pointed out that many local gays and lesbians refused to attend meetings like the one happening that night, due to fear of being outed.

"It's organizations like these that will draw the discriminated together and as one they can fight for the Human Rights of not just the homosexual but for all mankind," wrote Smallwood in the aspirational conclusion to her article (Ibid.).

Beth Lacey and Lynn Murphy were among the founding members of GAIN. Another early organizer with GAIN was Wally Upward. Upward was originally from Harry's Harbour in Green Bay, Newfoundland. Harry's Harbour was a small village which today has a population of just over 70. When Upward was a child it was larger, with a population of almost 200 (there were, however, more hens than people recorded in the census the decade he was born).

Ever since he was a child, Upward had a profound curiosity about the world. Harry's Harbour was frequently used by vessels traveling between Newfoundland and the Caribbean, and he explained that stowaways were a not uncommon occurrence. He recalled one incident that was well remembered in the community when he was growing up:

"In the 1920s a young Black man from Jamaica – I think his name was Clyde – ended up on a schooner that arrived in Harry's Harbour in the fall. He had nothing when he arrived. So the community got together, they got him

clothes, he lived with an old fisherman family and they paid his school fees until a ship came in the summer and he came to St. John's. Nobody knows what happened to him after. He was only fourteen or so. But the community just took him on. Even though I know there's racism, there's also been compassion in remote communities for a long time" (Upward 2021).

As a child and teenager Upward spent a lot of time letter-writing from Harry's Harbour, seeking information about the world. In response to one of his letters he recalls receiving an information package from the Communist Party of China, containing a copy of Mao Tse Tung's little red book, which became an object of widespread interest in Harry's Harbour when it showed up; it was studied and discussed by many of the residents.

At the age of 19, Upward left his hometown and spent eight years traveling the world as a sailor, working on boats. He would remain an inveterate traveller all his life; working on the boats took him to places as far afield as Russia, Portugal, Germany and Poland.

"I wanted to see mountains. I wanted to see historic places. I wanted to walk in the Coliseum and climb the mountain in Pompeii," he reflected fifty years later.

Central America was a particularly exciting place for a young Newfoundlander in the 1970s, he recalls. He saw volcanoes in Nicaragua (one erupted as he was hiking it, sending him fleeing the ensuing forest fires), and was in Guatemala when an insurrection broke out there. He promptly fled that country to neighbouring Honduras, only to find himself in the middle of a military coup. He returned to Guatemala, and after crossing a small river in the jungle, discovered that he was in El Salvador.

"That was the harshest place I've been," he recalls. "People were being executed when I was there, bodies were in the streets. The university was shot up, dozens of university students were found decapitated and tortured. The university was full of bullet holes and burnt-out cars, there were gunmen and tanks everywhere. And so many militias – you didn't know who the fuck was who!" (Ibid.).

In 1980 he finally settled, after a fashion, in St. John's, where he got a job as a nursing assistant at the General Hospital. He came out publicly as gay in 1985, when he spoke on GAIN's behalf at a meeting of the House of Commons Sub-committee on Equality Rights[17] and was interviewed extensively by media afterward. Visibility came at a cost: he recalls one of the Progressive Conservative cabinet ministers at the time going on the radio and denouncing him as "a self-appointed social reformist and a threat to the community."

"I heard that and I was like 'What?'" he recalled. "Now the self-appointed social reformist I will admit to being guilty of. But I don't think I'm a threat to society!"

Looking back on those years, Upward is quick to point out that he had a

---

[17] It met August 26, 1985, at the Holiday Inn in St. John's.

positive relationship with most politicians, something he attributes to his out-going character. When interviewed by the *Sunday Express* in March 1989, he at-tested to the flourishing gay community with which GAIN was connected. He estimated there to be 5000 gays and lesbians in the capital city, and described the downtown neighbourhoods of Bond Street, Gower Street and Prescott Street as "just like a gay ghetto" (Lynk 1989).

GAIN rapidly caught the attention of mainland activists as well, receiv-ing a nod in the April 1982 edition of *The Body Politic*. The unattributed article "Rural Outreach: 'What? Gay people here?'" celebrated the resurgence of NL activism:

"The newest group in the Maritimes is the Gay Association in Newfound-land (GAIN), a revival of another organization [CHAN] which died three years ago. Organizer Beth Lacey is determined to make it work. Various fundraising events, including a flea market, a skating party, a bridge party and a dance are all planned. GAIN has had hassles getting advertisements in two provincial papers, but secured one which prompted about 40 letters. The group is assem-bling a mailing list and maintaining a pen pal relationship with people all over the province. 'Some people have never been able to contact anyone,' Lacey says. 'We're really going to try to stay here'" (The Body Politic 1982).

Records suggest there was a disagreement, or "split" as some put it, early on in GAIN's existence between those who wanted the organization to be pri-marily a social group, and those who wanted it to play more of a political and activist role. Those who wanted it to be primarily social were nervous about the prospect of political activism and the heightened visibility this would bring both to GAIN as well as the local queer community generally. At one point, members recall a vote being taken, with the outcome being that GAIN would be primarily social and not political. This drove some members to leave. Evi-dently this decision didn't hold sway for long, as GAIN was politically active and increasingly visible throughout the majority of its nearly decade-long ex-istence (ArQuives 1993).

In the days before the Internet – and even now – phone support lines were crucial to providing information, comfort and support to queer and question-ing individuals throughout the province. The phone lines were staffed by vol-unteers, often without any training or support beyond the desire to help, and they undoubtedly saved many lives, as described in the previous section.

CHAN's phone line was one of the most important services it provided in the 1970s. Organizations in other provinces also concentrated their efforts on phone lines. The first Atlantic Lesbian and Gay Phone Line Conference was held in Halifax from June 17-19, 1983, under the name 'Connexions'. Partici-pants came from three provinces and included representatives from Frederic-ton Lesbians and Gays (FLAG), Gay Association in Newfoundland (GAIN), the Gay Alliance for Equality, and others.

In 1983, GAIN had an influx of new members and began the year with

renewed energy. Tree Walsh was elected president, and the group's social committee published an active calendar of events. The group also launched a new
newsletter: *Gain Foresight*. Initially the newsletter was produced almost single-
handedly by Upward.

GAIN worked to provide an active social life for the queer community.
It organized dances at the Grad House. It sponsored a softball team. Upward
recalls the organization hosting picnics in Bannerman Park that regularly attracted 30-40 people.

"There were house parties, and people would get together and go on little
trips, like a weekend hiking trip to somewhere outside of town. There was
sports things as well — hiking and biking groups."

On December 15, 1984, the group held a Christmas party which, according
to their newsletter, was deemed "a great success." They provided music, a case
of champagne, and gave away a turkey and a ham as door prizes. The St. John's
Status of Women Centre provided meeting space to the growing organization.

In the early 1980s, controversy had erupted over the book – popular in the
queer community – titled *The Joy of Gay Sex*. In early 1983, the book had been
banned from entry into Canada. In September 1984, Progressive Conservatives
led by Brian Mulroney defeated the Liberals in a federal election, and well-
known Newfoundland politician John Crosbie was named Minister of Justice
in Mulroney's first cabinet. GAIN promptly took advantage of this connection
and wrote to Crosbie, requesting the ban be rescinded. Crosbie responded that
he was forwarding their request to Elmer McKay, Minister of National Revenue, whose department had authority over such matters. McKay wrote back to
indicate that, following a federal ruling which declared the rules under which
it was banned to be invalid, the Customs regulations had been revised earlier
that same year. As a consequence, the book had been removed from lists of
prohibited publications, and it was still under review by Customs officials "to
determine its classification."

GAIN's political activism at the federal level continued. In 1985, the Federal Parliamentary Committee of Equality Rights had produced a report titled
"Equality For All," which among other things called on the federal Human
Rights Code to be amended to include sexual orientation as a prohibited
ground of discrimination. It also called for an end to discrimination against
gays and lesbians in the Canadian Armed Forces and the RCMP, and an end to
inequalities in the age of consent for sexual activities. The federal Liberals had
endorsed the report and its recommendations. While the Progressive Conservative (PC) government mulled over its response to the report (which it had to
provide by February 21), on January 7, 1986, GAIN wrote to each of the seven
NL Members of Parliament urging them to support the report and its recommendations. Only three responded. PC MP John Crosbie answered cryptically
that "the questions that you ask will be answered (before Feb 21) but I cannot
indicate to you what the answers will be." PC MP James McGrath's assistant re-

sponded that McGrath was away from Ottawa but the letter would be brought to his attention upon his return. PC MP Captain Morrissey Johnson responded that he would support the [pro-gay] recommendations.

GAIN set itself a broad ambit, and in 1985, the organization joined the IGA (International Gay Association – eventually to become ILGA, or International Gay and Lesbian Association). Upward and three other members travelled to Toronto for the IGA Convention which was being held in Canada that year.

The AIDS crisis erupted not long after GAIN's formation, and GAIN would come to play a key role in early AIDS activism and education. While NL's experience of the AIDS crisis will be explored in a later chapter, it's worth noting that long before any of the provincial AIDS organizations came into existence, GAIN was organizing meetings and reaching out to government and medical officials. In 1988, local physician Dr. Ian Bowmer gave a speech at Memorial's medical school at which he credited GAIN's activism during this period, saying that in the face of government inaction GAIN had done the most to educate the public and save lives (Hillier 1988).

Upward, the on-again off-again president of GAIN, also took a lead role as an AIDS outreach worker and educator. He would later be employed by the AIDS Committee of NL in that capacity after it formed in 1989. Because of the overlap of activists, the line was often blurred between GAIN's work and that of groups like the AIDS Committee of NL (ACNL) and the NL AIDS Association. As AIDS became an over-arching priority, it also became the focus of GAIN's activism.

This may have been part of the reason for GAIN's eventual dissolution. Upward was hired by the ACNL and became focused on outreach work for that organization. Other former GAIN activists were also spending much of their time working for the ACNL and its predecessor organizations. As the AIDS crisis came to dominate volunteers' time and energies, those activists doing double duty – like Upward – found it harder and harder to keep their feet in both organizations. By the end of the eighties, GAIN had effectively ceased to exist.

The gap in queer political organizing outside of the AIDS crisis wouldn't last long. Already a new and younger generation of activists – more militant in their approach, fuelled by a sense of anger at both homophobic repression as well as government inaction in the face of AIDS – were preparing to hit the scene both locally and nationally.

GALT

By 1990, the need for a new LGBTQ community organization was evident. Efforts by the NL Human Rights Association to expand provincial human rights legislation had borne fruit in several areas, particularly women's rights, but the provincial Liberal government was adamantly refusing to move forward on sexual orientation rights. Justice Minister Paul Dicks had a notorious reputation in the queer community for publicly rejecting the existence of homophobia in Newfoundland and Labrador: it simply wasn't a problem that needed addressing, he argued. When pressed, he responded with veiled insinuations about homosexuals posing a threat to young people [Dicks 1990 - see Chapter 6 for further details].

By 1990, MUN student Padraic Brake had heard enough of this nonsense. He organized a meeting on September 27, 1990, at the St. John's Status of Women Centre, to form an organization that would do something about it. The meeting was advertised by posters in downtown queer-friendly clubs and on campus. But mostly the news was spread by word of mouth, he told *The Muse* reporter Dawn Mitchell, who covered the inaugural meeting (Mitchell 1990).

What came of that initial meeting was the founding of one of NL's shortest-lived but feistiest queer activist groups: Gays and Lesbians Together, or GALT. The group only held together for barely three years, but during this short timespan it catalyzed some of the fiercest activism the province had yet seen.

The inaugural meeting confirmed for Brake that the time was ripe for queer community activism. Fifteen people showed up, but Brake expressed surprise that even that many came given the hostile environment. Most of the meeting was spent discussing the group's future goals. While AIDS-related work had come to dominate the attention of older activists, progress on other queer issues had languished. Attendees expressed the need for a support group to help those who were coming out or questioning their sexuality. Others flagged the need for political activism. Amending the provincial human rights code was cited as a key goal, as well as raising public awareness about homophobia and heterosexism, especially among community and professional organizations. Organizers were urged to set up a phone support line, although it was pointed out that would require money, of which the group had none.

But political activism emerged as one of the top priorities, and Brake was glad to see it.

"We have a provincial government that willingly refuses to accept that we exist in our society by refusing to amend the Human Rights Code to include sexual orientation," he told **The Muse.** *"I am unwilling to sit back and allow [Justice Minister] Paul Dicks to tell us there is no need for protection [under the Code] at this time. Again and again the lesbian and gay community has told the provincial government that we're being discriminated against in the workplace, in our apartments, and in public places"* (Ibid.).

A follow-up meeting was set for two weeks later. The St. John's Status of Women Council offered their space for any organizing needs the group had.

"It demonstrates the interrelationship of our struggles," Brake said, noting that few other community organizations were as willing as the Women's Centre to offer space and support to the fledgling group (Ibid.).

Sharp Dopler also attended the founding meeting, and wound up as vice-president.

"Our meetings were pretty casual," they recalled, looking back on those years. "We weren't quite sure what the fuck we were doing. But we figured it was better to be doing it together until we figured it out. We asked ourselves: What are we going to do with this group? Well, we're gonna shake some shit up."

Gary Kinsman had been living in St. John's for almost a year by that point. Originally from Ontario, he finished his PhD in 1988 and took a term contract teaching sociology at Acadia University. The following year he took a contract with Memorial, and moved to St. John's in September 1989. When he decided to stay for a second year, his partner Patrick Barnholden joined him in the fall of 1990.

The two became intensely active in the local queer community, and were among GALT's outspoken cadre of core volunteers. Kinsman and Barnholden had seen that surveys were a useful organizing strategy that had been used in other provinces, and so they modified one that had been used in New Brunswick ("removing its essentialist assumptions" noted Kinsman), and conducted a survey of the province's queer community. To lobby effectively they needed information, and the wide-ranging survey afforded an opportunity to hear first-hand about the experiences of queer residents from across the province. Drawing on the information they gathered from the survey, they prepared a formal brief which they submitted to the provincial government, to bolster their case for a human rights amendment.

GALT's primary orientation was political, but they didn't only focus on the provincial government. They also set their sights on homophobia in the city's downtown. One of their targets was the popular George Street pub Trapper John's.

"Trapper John's had made an announcement that anyone who requested a Madonna song would be shown the door because it was clear that they were queer," recalled Dopler. So on October 8, 1990, GALT decided to take over the venue.

"We weren't sure if we were going to get killed or not," reflected Dopler. GALT mustered between twenty or thirty activists for what was called a "march against homophobia." The group gathered at the nearby gay-friendly bar Private Eyes, on Water Street. Then they marched en masse down Water Street, onto George Street, and into Trapper John's. The group "took over" the bar – media had been notified and were there to watch – "and we went and we requested every fucking Madonna song that we could think of," said Dopler. "We had made a pact with one another that we were all going to dance together on the dance floor, that nobody was going to get up and dance by themselves."

The protest also included a 'Kiss-In.'

"I don't know if this part was formal, but when we went down there we all made out for one hot minute before we decided we didn't want to die and got the fuck out of there," recalled one attendee[18] with a laugh.

This was one of the group's first actions, and it sent a clear message to the community about how serious they were.

GALT activists were serious about their work, but knew how to have fun too. Barnholden recalls putting off safe-sex workshops with gay men, where proper condom use was demonstrated. He remembers a young man who showed up to one of the workshops and demonstrated a unique ability: he put the condom over his head and under his nose, and then inflated the entire thing by breathing out through his nose. The condom expanded over the young man's head – "It looked like Marg Simpson's hair," recalled Barnholden. "It was amazing."

Brenda Ponic was one of the GALT stalwarts, and said she tried valiantly to get a telephone support line set up. They eventually succeeded.

"I remember gathering the research about the vulnerability of queer youth and isolation in rural communities, and the vulnerability and suicide rates. I did the preparatory work around that, and spoke about it. We put together a model and tried to get funding for it. We tried to get endorsements from politicians in order to support it. That was one of the things we were trying hardest for, a provincial hotline" (Ponic 2022).

Kinsman remembers them organizing a reading group as well.

As far back as CHAN in the 1970s, activists had talked about the importance of getting sexual orientation protections into the provincial human rights code. Quebec was the first province to amend its human rights code to include sexual orientation protections in 1977. Ontario followed suit in 1986, and Manitoba in 1987. Nova Scotia had introduced a human rights amendment in May 1991. Campaigns were underway in the other provinces, as well as one at the federal level. In December 1990, GALT decided it was time to concentrate its efforts on developing a formal campaign in Newfoundland and Labrador.

The academics in GALT knew how important it was to have data to support their demands. They launched their provincial survey on February 1, 1991, and by March 1 they had collected 97 responses. They analyzed the data and incorporated it into a brief titled "Here to Stay: Lesbians and Gays in Newfoundland and Labrador Fighting For Our Rights." A preliminary version of the brief was publicly released at a press conference on March 17. New Democratic Member of Parliament Svend Robinson, an out gay man, was brought in from British Columbia to speak at the event. GALT released the final report on June 22, 1991.

The data offered an important snapshot of the experience of gays and lesbians in the province. 87 percent reported experiencing some form of homophobic discrimination. 68 percent had been called homophobic slurs. 35 percent had been threatened with some form of physical violence, and 30 percent had

---

[18] They requested anonymity.

been chased or followed as a form of homophobic harassment. 20 percent reported experiencing discrimination at the hands of the police. 19 percent had been physically assaulted in homophobic attacks, and 10 percent had been raped or sexually assaulted because they were perceived to be gay or lesbian (GALT 1991).

The report laid bare the homophobia that was still pervasive in the province:

"People have been beaten up for being lesbian or gay near a downtown St. John's club frequented by gays and lesbians. Gays who have been beaten up in downtown St. John's have found the police completely uncooperative and unhelpful. There have also been attacks on the MUN campus in St. John's including a violent incident in a residence in 1990 and an assault on at least one heterosexual man who was thought to be gay" (Ibid.).

The report outlined respondents' experiences being spit on and having objects thrown at them if they were perceived to be gay. "Several respondents reported that the 'police did not take seriously' reports of anti-gay violence." 22 percent of respondents reported discrimination in employment, including firing or being ostracized in the workplace. One respondent reported being "told a co-worker was fired because he was gay and told others should keep quiet" (Ibid.).

One case was cited of a lesbian couple being evicted from their apartment after they were outed; others reported eviction attempts and harassment from neighbours. Trapper Johns wasn't the only bar cited for homophobia: gay patrons also reported being kicked out of Erin's Pub and the Cotton Club. "In a 1991 incident at a club frequented by gays in St. John's the police over-reacted to a distress call using unnecessary force against several people, forcing people out of the club, and denying the distressed man's lover access to the ambulance" (Ibid.).

There were other forms of police discrimination cited in the report:

"[G]ays and lesbians often will not report violence against them to the police and when they do the police will often not listen or take it seriously. One respondent did not report the violence he/she experienced to the police because she/he 'felt at the time they wouldn't truly care. It seemed more trouble than it was worth.' Another reported that 'many people in the legal system are very homophobic'... Even if a gay man or lesbian wishes to press charges against someone who has assaulted them many fear a court trial because it could attract media attention and make them even more susceptible to abuse" (Ibid.).

The report also said organizers of an anti-homophobia demonstration in the summer of 1990 had been refused airtime on VOCM Radio's community line to announce their event.

In addition to being unable to access spousal or partner benefits, "Many open lesbians and gays have been excluded from our families of origin," the report stated. "Many of us continue to face hostility, discrimination and being cut off from our families of origin. 32% reported discrimination from members of their families. One respondent reported that 'my partner has had threats made on him by my family. They blame him for my orientation'" (Ibid.).

45 percent of respondents reported experiencing homophobic harassment, threats and assaults in the K-12 school system. 12 percent reported experiencing homophobic harassment at university.

GALT also played a key role in the controversy surrounding *The Muse's* publication of a 1991 Lesbian and Gay Supplement. That remarkable episode is explored at length in Chapter 4. As discussed in that chapter, GALT members were not only involved in the production of the Supplement, but also offered a ferocious defense of *The Muse* in the controversial days that followed its publication. And in 1991, GALT activists also helped win the first official recognition of Pride Week in the province (discussed later in this chapter).

Because GALT employed a more radical, loud, in-your-face activism than had been practiced by its predecessors CHAN and GAIN – GALT's activism was sometimes more in line with that practised by other more radical North American groups like ACT UP and AIDS Action Now – they sometimes came under criticism from older local queer activists who disliked their radicalism. And because some of the visible and outspoken GALT activists, including Kinsman, Barnholden, and Ponic, were originally from mainland Canada, the group would sometimes be criticized for its mainland connections. For their part, some mainland GALT activists felt sensitive to this critique. This was another form of the xenophobia experienced by Arnold and Reed in the 1940s and by Ponic later that decade (see Chapter 1). This critique completely ignored the fact that GALT was in fact founded by young NLers, many of whom were sick and tired of the slow pace of progress. A younger generation of activists felt less bound by the "closetry" for which CHAN was gently rebuked by Popert in the 1970s. This dynamic is explored further in Chapter 4, in the context of the controversy surrounding *The Muse's* Lesbian and Gay Supplement.

In many ways the cross-exchange of experiences and strategies was what gave queer activism its strength. It worked both ways – in Chapter 3, there are examples provided of how NL lesbians were at the forefront of helping to foment queer activism within national, mainland feminist groups. And NL-born members, like Barry Nichols, observed that outside perspectives helped break through the insularity of an island identity, especially for those who had grown up in rural, repressive environments. He had previously avoided involvement in activism, because it seemed too much energy with too few results. But the exception, he felt, was GALT.

"When I met Patrick [Barnholden] and Gary [Kinsman] I was very much motivated by the both of them. I've always connected with people from outside, because I like the richness of their process and how they're engaged and how they see things, which is different from the way we've all been forced to see. So it helps open things up. Gary and Patrick were fearless that way, com-

pared to us. You know what it was like here – we were all cowering, and being gay on top of that it's like you're double cowering. That makes it hard to get on your feet. You have to make the choice to stand up" (Nichols 2021).

During its brief existence, GALT's in-your-face activism drew unprecedented public awareness to the problem of homophobia in the province. But by the end of 1992 its fierce activism had come to an end, largely due to the departure of key members from the province. Kinsman and Barnholden left Newfoundland in the summer of 1992; Kinsman had been offered a position at Acadia University in Nova Scotia. Ponic was working on her Masters thesis, and left following the events described in Chapter 1. Dopler continued to play a leadership role, and made sure the City of St. John's recognized Gay Pride Week for a second year in 1992. But they too would soon leave Newfoundland to pursue further educational opportunities in Ontario. As the ranks of its fiery organizers thinned, GALT faded away, and by the end of 1992 the organization had effectively ceased to exist.

Pride Week

While Pride Week has been celebrated in an official capacity almost continuously for at least 30 years in the capital city, the 1991 Pride was not the first in St. John's. There had been previous Pride Week celebrations, with gaps across intervening years. The earliest record of an organized Pride Week dates back to 1983. GAIN held a 'Lesbian and Gay Pride Week' in St. John's that year which sounds tremendously similar to the festivals held today – it included a softball game at Kelly's Brook Field, film screenings, a beer bash, a BBQ, bowling, card nights, and a beach party and bonfire. GAIN's president at the time was Tree Walsh (The Body Politic 1983).

Most Pride gatherings in the 1980s were privately held in peoples' homes, if they happened at all. The October 9, 1987, issue of GAIN's newsletter notes that "we have had small private events over the years" and encourages members to organize for a public march in 1988, but nothing appears to have come of it. The first publicly (government) acknowledged Pride Week took place in 1991. A group of GALT members, including Kinsman and Barnholden, put together a committee to organize Pride. At the time, several Canadian municipalities refused to acknowledge Pride Week, and both Kinsman and Barnholden had experience fighting these decisions in Toronto. In that city, Mayor Art Eggleton – who held office from 1980-1991 – unrepentantly refused to acknowledge Pride, sparking large protests. Eventually in 1991, Toronto City Council voted to acknowledge Pride Week in defiance of the recalcitrant mayor; then-Councillor (and future federal NDP leader) Jack Layton read the proclamation at the first flag-raising that year (Pride Toronto 2022).

Barnholden contacted Toronto Pride and obtained the wording for the City of Toronto Pride Week declaration. He substituted the name of the city and submitted that declaration to the City of St. John's, requesting they acknowledge Pride Week. Shannie Duff was mayor at the time, and one day Barnholden answered the telephone to find Mayor Duff on the other line. He braced himself for an argument, especially when she said she wanted to make some changes to the proposed declaration. It turned out the changes were purely grammatical in nature; she had no opposition to accepting the substance of the proclamation as it was written, and issuing a public declaration for Pride Week in St. John's.

Then-Mayor Duff later acknowledged that the issue was personal for her. Her son had come out as gay in the early 1980s. At that time, there was virtually no guidance or education for parents with queer children.

"I don't think we handled it that well at the time," she reflected. "When I grew up it was almost a no-no thing. There were snide remarks and dropped wrists and that kind of thing, but there was never really any open discussion. And even though there were people that you knew were gay, it was clandestine and negative. If you were in the arts there was kind of an acceptance of creative people being a little different, but in other spheres it wasn't. And of course coming from a strongly Catholic background it was even worse because it was considered hellfire and brimstone.

"I was so terrified when I found out [my son] was gay, terrified that he would be beaten up or kicked out of medical school, or that something would happen to him that was negative. It panicked me... I almost felt like I was in a deep mourning state.

"But I would have to say that my son was my teacher. He had infinite patience. He was determined that we were going to understand. He gave me books to read and really had the patience to maintain our family relationship, for which I am profoundly grateful, because we're very close right now. But it took a fair bit of education and patience and really good handling of the situation by our son, who cared enough about our relationship to take the time to bring us around" (Duff 2022).

After the initial shock at his coming out, Duff worked hard to be a supportive mother and ally. She spoke at conferences and events about the experience of finding out her child was gay, and even participated in Pride parades elsewhere.

"I had [before 1991] been to New York where [my son] lived and walked in a gay pride parade with him, with a lovely little placard that said 'My son is gay and that's okay'," she recalled. "So I knew about gay pride parades and the reasons for them... by the time there was a request [for the City of St. John's to acknowledge Pride Week] I was in a position to have an understanding of it. And there were other people on Council who I think had a sensitivity to it, and wanted to normalize things and recognize Pride Week and be part of the breaking down of all these stereotypes that were very harmful to gay people. So I didn't face a lot of opposition. Some raised eyebrows and dropped wrists, but

basically most of Council was in favour of raising the gay pride flag and having the city seen as in favour of breaking down some of those barriers" (Ibid.).

Barnholden recalls the busy opening day of that year's Pride Week. The committee organized an evening film screening at the LSPU Hall, and he spent the afternoon with other organizers preparing the Hall for the event. They were very nervous about the event, and worried no one would show up. The declaration at City Hall was that same evening, so he and Brenda Ponic left the LSPU Hall shortly before doors opened, to dash up to City Hall for the proclamation. Then they raced back to the LSPU Hall, where they were slated to speak at the beginning of the film screening. They arrived just in time, burst into the Hall and dashed to the stage. It was at that point that Barnholden looked out at the audience for the first time, and discovered to his astonishment they had a full house – over 200 people.

"It was phenomenally successful," he recalls. "I mean who knew more than 200 people in St. John's were going to come out to a queer film showing? But there they were. It was so cool. I remember being on stage introducing it, and feeling like I was floating above the stage. I was so happy about it."

St. John's continued recognizing Pride Weeks in the capital city – once GALT ceased to exist they were organized by ACNL volunteers, and later by NGALE and NAN – and Pride '95 featured an important innovation: the first ever Pride March. It's important to note this was not called a 'Pride Parade', but rather was presented as a "March for Freedom."

That year, Deputy Mayor Andy Wells spoke at the Pride Proclamation event on Monday June 12, designating Pride Week as June 19-25, 1995. Beth Lacey spoke at the event on behalf of NAN, and Brian Hodder on behalf of NGALE.

"NAN and NGALE have joined forces to help us celebrate," proclaimed the June 1995 NAN newsletter. The schedule of events reveals how much more public and accepted queer organizing had become. NAN hosted a pre-Pride Dance at the Loft in Haymarket Square on Saturday, June 17. Monday, June 19, featured a news conference. On Tuesday, June 20, there was a 'Nature Walk' beginning at the Memorial Stadium (now Memorial Dominion grocery store). On Wednesday, June 21, there was a bowling event at Plaza Bowl, and on Thursday, June 22, NAN hosted a film night at the Grad House on Military Road. The evening of Friday, June 23, featured more events at the Grad House: a potluck, talent night, and Pride Dance. On the afternoon of Saturday, June 24, members of the community were encouraged to come to the offices of the AIDS Committee for a sign-making event in advance of the Pride March.

And at 2pm on Sunday, June 25, the province's first-ever March for Freedom was held. The event opened with a rally in front of City Hall featuring a number of speakers, including Brian Hodder (NGALE) and Beth Lacey (NAN). No politicians spoke, but provincial New Democratic Party (NDP) leader Jack Harris sent a letter of support. Ministers from the United and Anglican churches attended as well. Then participants marched along Queens Road to the Grad House. "Make Our Voices Heard!" proclaimed ads for the event. The March culminated in a barbecue at the Grad House. Over 100 people marched in that first ever Pride March.

"It was a protest," emphasized Michael Riehl, one of the organizers. "It was a March for Freedom."

"That was the first Pride March," recalls Beth Lacey, who was there on behalf of NAN. "It was wild. There I was, up front with a megaphone and my mullet, yelling: 'We're here, we're queer, get used to it!'"

At the Pride March the following year – June 24, 1996 — again over 100 people showed up. Speakers included Michael Riehl (NGALE), Joyce Hancock (PACSW) and Jack Harris (NDP).

Michael Riehl was one of the NGALE activists who took a lead role in organizing Pride Week once that organization took over the task. NGALE's budget was minimal, and the ACNL continued to provide support in the form of office space and telephones. After Zone 216 opened and became the city's primary queer bar, Riehl would spend weekends staffing a table by the coat check, selling ribbons and other paraphernalia to fund Pride Week.

Riehl enjoyed the work he put into organizing Pride Weeks, but remembers how difficult it still was in the 1990s for many in the city's queer community to participate.

"When we did our little Pride March down Duckworth Street, and down to Water Street, the funny thing was how many of the gay boys and girls were standing on the street just watching. Not clapping, not looking, sunglasses on. Of course you couldn't even wave at them – you were trying to respect them, right? But it was one of those things. There were a lot of people who wanted to be there, but they couldn't. But then they would show up at the club later, which was fine."

Organizers recall one Pride Week in the late 1990s, when some participants showed up in drag as well as leather fetish wear. This was normal in most cities, but still a rare sight in St. John's.

"There were drag queens and leather dudes, and it was scandalous," recalled Mikiki. "It was the thing that the news media got ahold of and then there were articles in the paper, photos in the paper that were pretty much exclusively of the drag queens and the leather guys."

"The news reporter totally focused on the guy in leather and the person in drag," Riehl said. "Hardly anything else. So I contacted the reporter and I had an honest conversation with him. I said: 'Looking at your piece, it's not balanced. The population thinks we're freakish as it is, and all you're showing is the drag queen and the leather guy. You didn't focus on the rest of us – the teachers, the doctors, the plumbers, the electricians. You didn't focus on any of that.' The reporter apologized, they said: 'Good point - it won't happen again.'"

Mikiki went on to begin organizing drag races for the annual pride parades, an initiative for which they are still widely remembered.

"I started doing drag at the first time at age 16," they explain. "For me it was always about activism and about politics. I had learned from magazines like Gay Times about the hilarity that activism could be, and it was there that I saw this very alternative version of what being a drag queen meant. I wasn't doing impersonation drag, I wasn't doing female illusion, even at the beginning. I was 17 and about to turn 18 when the drag race started [at St. John's Pride] in 1996. This was obviously very pre-Rupaul. Before Rupaul's drag race even started I did drag race performances every year for a decade... One of the reasons I started doing the drag race was because there were no youth events but there were also no trans events yet during Pride (Mikiki 2023).

Attendance at Pride events would wax and wane in the ensuing years, but when former Mayor Duff looks back on the early years, she's still astonished at how much changed so quickly.

"There has been light-years of change in public attitudes," she reflects. "I'm proud of my city and I think there's a lot of goodwill and tolerance now in the city which wasn't always there. It says something about the people of St. John's, and the people who were leaders in bringing about change. I think about the important role of the activists, and all those people who were out there trying to effect change" (Duff 2022).

CHAPTER THREE: LESBIAN ORGANIZING

The history of queer organizing and the history of feminist organizing in this province are deeply intertwined. There were times when feminist spaces in the province were open and welcoming to lesbians, and times when they were not. It was not a linear progression: there were leaps forward and backward slides. At times, it was the feminist movement which provided the resources, space and energy for queer organizing to move forward. At other times, it was the province's lesbians who kept the feminist dream alive. This section explores these complex, interwoven threads.

"Lesbianism threatens the social structure that depends upon... institutions that preserve inequality," wrote RM Kennedy, in a 1989 article for *The Muse* titled "Lesbianism: A Political Alternative to the Male Power Structure." While today, Kennedy, a published academic, looks back cringingly at the content he produced as a student journalist, the statement aptly underscores the vibrant aspirations of lesbian activism in the latter half of the twentieth century.

The following chapters focus on lesbian organizing during those years. First let's set the stage with a look back at the broader rise of the modern second-wave feminist movement in Newfoundland and Labrador. This movement — begun in the quiet corners of mainstream social and political institutions, over kitchen tables and in living-room consciousness raising groups — would give rise to today's feminist institutions like the Status of Women Councils. These institutions have grappled with their roles and responsibilities in the fight for queer rights in the province. So let us first examine the roots of these organizations, and the disparate seeds from which their movement was born.

In the 1960s, there were a variety of organizations in Newfoundland and Labrador working to improve the situation of women in the province. These groups were awkwardly located somewhere between what's often referred to as 'first-wave' and 'second-wave' feminism. 'First-wave feminism,' rooted in the early twentieth century struggle to extend political and economic equality to women (voting rights, property ownership, employment), was an ongoing project in NL as the 1970s dawned. Women in NL could not serve on juries until 1972, had a lower minimum wage than men until 1972, and the legal identity and property rights of married women remained a fraught battleground until the late 1980s (Clement 2012; Bouzane 1990). NL groups pushing for reform on these fronts in the 1960s included such organizations as the Business and Professional Women's Association (BPWA), the Women's Institutes (formerly known in NL as the Jubilee Guilds), the Local Council of Women, the Newfoundland Home Economics Association, the Canadian Federation of University Women (CFUW), and the Young Women's Christian Association (YWCA), among others.

It was not uncommon for these groups to be referred to – sometimes jokingly, sometimes scathingly – as feminist or radical by male politicians and media pundits. In fact, they were not necessarily either. Groups like the Women's Institutes (prior to 1968 known in NL as the Jubilee Guilds, with roots going back to 1935) conducted philanthropic initiatives and promoted the role of women in public life, however were increasingly at odds with a rising feminist consciousness that sought to challenge and overthrow patriarchal institutional structures. In 1977, for instance, the Women's Institutes adopted a resolution affirming that "as an organization a top priority must be to encourage and preserve the strengthening of the family unit" (Evening Telegram 1977). This was a stark contrast to newer feminist groups driven by a younger membership[19] who were distributing divorce kits and arranging transportation off the island for women seeking abortions.

Similarly, the Business and Professional Women's Association was part of an international federation of women's associations ardently rooted in the defense and promotion of free market capitalism. When the NL branch was chartered in 1951, *The Evening Telegram* reassured readers that BPWA national president Allie Aherne was "a very feminine, dresden china-type lady, with a very soft and fluent voice." Women were not trying to compete with men, she reassured the paper, nor would they be aggressive in their demands. They wanted to work "in partnership" with men (Evening Telegram 1951).

Nor were they socialists, emphasized an early guest speaker to the St. John's BPWA. Nazia L. Dane, a businesswoman from Toronto, told the St. John's audience that what women sought were simply their "Three R's" – their rights, responsibilities, and rewards.

"Miss Dane warned that rights of all free people must be jealously guarded against encroaching socialism," *The Evening Telegram* reassured readers (Evening Telegram 1953).

While the BPWA framed its demands for equal pay for equal work within the context of the existing political-economic structure, other women's groups were beginning to move toward the more radical, left-leaning and identity-based activism that would come to be associated with 'second-wave' feminism. Two such organizations were the CFUW and the YWCA.

YWCA St. John's

As the 1970s dawned, the YWCA's membership grew rapidly. Women

---

[19] Such as A Woman's Place and the Newfoundland Status of Women Council.

were becoming increasingly restive and looking for an outlet for their energies and activism, and the YWCA seemed a logical place for many of these budding feminists. This inevitably set the stage for conflict between a younger wave of progressive women and older generations of long-term members. The range of programs offered by the St. John's YWCA – filled beyond capacity by the early 1970s – reflect these contrasting interests. New programs like "Women and the Law," "Women and Communications," and workshops on "Better Boards and Committees" and "Robert's Rules" competed for resources with existing programs like "Modelling and Charm" and "Flower Arranging."

The YWCA has its roots as a service organization analogous to its male counterpart, the YMCA. However, in the late 1960s and early 1970s the YWCA took a hard left-wing turn which led to conflict within some of its branches, including the one in St. John's. The ensuing schism was tied in with a variety of ongoing internal debates within the YWCA, but in many respects, it boiled down to differing attitudes toward feminism. This division became particularly pronounced in St. John's and would have important implications for the modern feminist movement in this province.[20]

One ongoing debate had to do with the future of the YWCA itself, which was dealing with somewhat of an identity crisis. At a national level the YWCA was wrestling with a decision over whether to amalgamate the two gendered divisions of the organization. As far back as 1953, the topic of amalgamation had cropped up within the YWCA, and it returned with increasing frequency over the years at both the national and local levels. The YMCA had already started accepting women as members, and by 1974 about half of the 1300 YMCA members in St. John's were women, including two YMCA St. John's Board members.

The YWCA was split over the issue; many members wanted to remain women-only. They were afraid women would lose their voice if they amalgamated with the YMCA. Many of those women saw the YWCA as a prospective feminist organization, and argued that the YMCA was not nearly as progressive when it came to social justice activism. They pointed out that men still dominated in YMCA leadership positions throughout the country. They began criticizing what they felt was an effort by older, wealthier women within the YWCA to push the organization toward amalgamation.

At the same time, the YWCA had taken a hard turn toward left-wing social activism. YWCA Canada adopted a broad-ranging "Social Action Platform" in 1971 which was a remarkable (for the time) recognition of second-wave feminist principles rooted in identity politics. It called on members to engage in activism with a particular attention toward increasing diversity in the organization and

---

[20] The following summation of events within the YWCA St. John's is drawn from a distillation of documents contained within the Dorothy Inglis collection at Memorial University's QEII Library, Archives and Special Collections unit. These contain YWCA publications, reports, meeting minutes, and personal correspondence.

enhancing its accessibility by many of society's marginalized groups. It called on members to adopt a "diversity of tactics" in their activism, including political lobbying and "direct" mobilization "to where the action is." It called on the organization's leadership – staff and board members – to be more responsive to grassroots membership.

In local branches throughout the country, the Social Action Platform spurred the establishment of Social Action Committees, which took on the responsibility for carrying out this broad-ranging activism (local YWCA branches were loosely affiliated with the national organization but retained a great deal of autonomy). In April 1972, the St. John's YWCA endorsed the Social Action Platform and struck its own Social Action Committee (SAC). The YWCA St. John's Social Action Committee became a potent force for change, gathering together and cultivating a cohort of feminist activists who would later go on to form more radical organizations in the province, including the NL Status of Women Council. This cadre of activists included such individuals as Iris Kirby, Frances Ennis, Shirley Goundrey, Bonnie Leyton, and Dorothy Inglis, among others.

The YWCA St. John's Annual Report for 1973 reveals the variety of community projects the SAC was working on that year: an initiative to develop a children's museum on Signal Hill; work with the Prices Review Board around the impact of inflation and grocery prices; solidarity work with Chilean activists. There was outreach to residents of the Gros Morne Park area to provide advocacy support over disputes around the park development. The SAC organized a series of seven widely advertised, public voters' forums for municipal elections which took place that year in St. John's. The SAC joined the Canadian Association in Support of the Native People and participated in activism against a hydro development in Quebec that would negatively impacts thousands of Indigenous community residents. It protested the Vietnam War, and it protested the Little Miss Downtown beauty pageant in St. John's. It endorsed calls for more community input into the controversial Atlantic Place development in downtown St. John's.

Less progressive-minded YWCA board members were unsettled by all this vigorous public activism. Their concerns were further fueled by a proposal within the St. John's YWCA to establish a 'Women's Issues Committee.' Its terms of reference were drawn up by YWCA members in April 1973, but the Board hesitated for several months before accepting them.

While the YWCA St. John's board hesitated over the notion of a Women's Issues Committee, the SAC was also undertaking feminist activism of its own. It played a key role in helping to put off a weekend-long women's film festival at Memorial University from July 6-8, 1973. Run by a Toronto-based group called Women and Film, the festival was well remembered by early activists in both the local feminist and queer communities (some of the Toronto activists were lesbian). The Toronto group put together a women's film series which toured the country – a radical undertaking at that time – and the SAC invited them to St. John's and offered material and logistical support. The fledgling Newfoundland Status of Women Council also provided a great deal of logistical support. The tour, which spanned a week or more in other spots, only occupied a weekend in St. John's. Participants however remember it as a life-changing, round-the-clock extravaganza. Brian Caines, one of the early CHAN organizers, recalled it as one of his stand-out memories from the period.

It was all films by women – documentaries and stuff like that. In Toronto it took place over about two weeks, but at MUN it was just a weekend. It started Friday night and went until Sunday evening. I went to every one of the films! It was films from all over the world – documentaries, short films, movies. The first time I saw an Agnes Varda film was there, it was one of the movies that were shown. I watched every one of them. My arse was staunched at the end of it! (Caines 2022).

Ruth Pierson, one of the local organizers, described a similarly physically exhausting experience in her report in the Newfoundland Status of Women Council (NSWC) newsletter:

Late Sunday evening, having just been stirred to righteous indignation at the cruel injustice of patriarchy in pre-revolutionary Russia, our eyes red-rimmed and glazed from 3 days of movie watching, the Gertrude Stein refrain "When This You See, Remember Me" still echoing in one corner of the brain, those of us who had been fortunate enough to take in most of the Women and Film Festival staggered out of [the screening room], sorry that the movie marathon was over, wondering whether we would be able to cope with return to unedited reality...(NSWC 1973C).

There had been a panel discussion, an art exhibition, and more as part of the proceedings. Pierson said that the three Toronto-based women[21] running the festival – which was funded through the federal Opportunities For Youth program – repeatedly told them that the St. John's event "was the best on the eastern tour" (NSWC Newsletter 1973).

Jane Goundrey, whose mother, Shirley, was one of the founders of the NSWC and also worked with the YWCA, was a teenager at the time but vividly remembers that project as well, and the impression left upon her by the team of young feminists from Toronto.

It was very memorable for me," she recalled. "These were young women who were on a mission. They were feminist! And to have a group of young women who were not only not questioning [feminism] – but they were committed to it! And they were so vibrant. It was very inspiring. They made such an impression on a whole community of young women that summer (Goundrey 2022).

All this activism was becoming too much for less progressive members of the YWCA. Tensions flared between progressives on the SAC and more tradi-

---

[21] Organizers included Marni Jackson, later an award-winning journalist, Jill Frayne, author and filmmaker, and filmmaker Sheila Paige

tional-minded YWCA members. The more conservative members, who predominated the organization's executive, tried to assert control over the younger radicals. They began demanding the SAC get approval from the executive before undertaking initiatives; the SAC resisted this. Not long after, the SAC voted to provide "support financially and otherwise" to the Canadian Coalition for the Repeal of the Abortion Law. Abortion was still a highly controversial touchstone issue among women's organizations, and SAC records indicate trepidation about how the YWCA executive would react to this.

When executive board elections were delayed in 1973, SAC activists cried foul. A general meeting and election were eventually held in early 1974, at which the YWCA St. John's President stated "that the past year has been one of disharmony mainly due to issues regarding Social Action, Amalgamation and the Feminist movement." A progressive slate of candidates put forward by the SAC was largely defeated, leading several SAC members and supporters to organize a petition challenging the legality of the meeting and elections. The YWCA executive responded by announcing it was shutting down the SAC.

The SAC "dissidents" (as they were now being called) announced they were holding a new general meeting and election. The YWCA executive declared it illegal. Both groups ran notices in *The Evening Telegram* – the dissidents urging members to attend, the executive warning that the meeting was illegal (there is a wry humour in the newspaper running content from both groups condemning each other).

The "dissident" meeting took place at the Hotel Newfoundland in March 1974, and got off to a rough start when it was discovered one of the attendees was secretly tape recording the meeting (the tape was destroyed and the tape recorder ejected from the meeting). A motion of non-confidence in the YWCA St. John's Board was passed, along with a call for new elections. The "dissidents" began formally calling themselves The Group of Concerned YWCA Members, and began media outreach as well.

The struggle was taking a toll on the membership. Resignations from the organization mounted, especially among younger progressives, who wanted to see more activism, not less. Some resignation letters blamed the executive's "opposition to… Social Action and Women's Issues." A feeling that the more conservative executive was also pushing amalgamation with the YMCA fueled some resignations.

Jane Goundrey remembers the strife and infighting taking its toll on her mother, Shirley, and the others involved in the SAC.

I remember there was some discord. My mom would have meetings at our house, and I do remember overhearing discord both in the meetings and then afterwards when she would be talking to my dad. From my young perspective it seemed that it was basically the right-wingers against the left-wingers (Goundrey 2022).

As the controversy grew and received coverage in local newspapers, YWCA

Canada dispatched two officers to St. John's to try to sort out the conflict. They submitted a report, which recommended that the Social Action Committee be brought back and that it also encompass "Status of Women" under its mandate.

Dorothy Inglis – a well-respected academic and columnist and one of the progressives who had managed to get elected to the Board – fought for the re-establishment of the SAC, and also for a reconciliation between the two sides. Each side obtained legal opinions arguing they were in the right; both sides also recognized that a court battle would be detrimental to the organization, no matter who won. Although officially disbanded, the SAC continued to meet and organize local events. Eventually the progressives on the Board convinced the Board to recognize that "the dissident group" had legitimate rights and concerns, and to compromise.

The conflict was more than just political drama; it revealed in stark clarity the tensions emerging in NL between traditional first-wave feminists and a younger generation of more radical, identity-based activists. The dispute was, in many ways, one between differing interpretations of feminism, and its role within the YWCA. During one of the Board debates over the Women's Issues Committee, one Board member had challenged "the term Women's Issues as possibly implying 'Women's Liberation' movement" (YWCA St. John's 1974A). Today the term might be considered passe but in the 1970s it had a very different power.

Sharon Gray, who was later involved with the NSWC, recalled the attitude of the time:

'Women's Liberation' became sort of a nasty thing, where you were 'one of those women's libbers. I think that women's lib and being a lesbian sort of became synonymous for a while. And that was more like an insult than anything. It was like: 'What's the worst thing I can say to you? It's that you're not really a woman at all, you're a lesbian' (Gray 2023).

The January-February 1974 issue of the NSWC newsletter also reflects this concern in a lead editorial. The author – NSWC President Sally Davis – opines:

Are we WOMEN'S LIBBERS? We are attacked as WOMEN'S LIBERS which seems to mean to our attackers that we are out to break up marriages; to encourage women to become divorced; to teach women to be man haters; to disallow the wearing of bras and lipstick – ad nauseam... We do acknowledge that some women in the movement as they begin to feel liberated react superficially, or may over-react. They may go through a stage of feeling that the enemy is men, not society (which is hard on men as well as women). Over-reacting, or being militant, is sometimes the only tactic left in order to bring an issue to the attention of those who control government, but it must be carefully planned. Otherwise we might find ourselves out front but with no followers (NSWC 1974).

While the SAC had been re-instated following the visit of YWCA Canada mediators, and a new committee struck to resolve differences within the organization, the amalgamation issue still loomed, and in it many of the progressives saw a back-handed effort to tamp down the feminist activism they were pushing within the YWCA. According to a hand-written letter found in the archive addressed to one member at the time, the YWCA:

Has, to its credit, taken public stands on controversial issues... But I believe now that the [executive] want amalgamation because they see in that difficult union an end to social action and women's issues and I think they are right. Amalgamation would dilute and end any effective work in these areas of human concern.

Both factions continued dueling. A vote was taken by the YWCA St. John's at which a majority voted against amalgamation; the executive then disputed whether they were bound by it. The arguments spilled over, once again, into local newspapers, both between factions of the YWCA as well as between the YWCA and YMCA.

Although there's no record of the topic arising locally, the YWCA during this period was becoming one of the spaces in which lesbians were emerging with a new and assertive visibility. The May 10, 1974, national YWCA newsletter (*YW Resource*) described a national Women's Conference held earlier that year at the University of Waterloo, which included a Saturday evening performance by the Women's Theatre Collective. Patrice Merrin, a national staffer, wrote:

Their thought-provoking presentation added 'fire' to the weekend. During the presentation and following it, a number of views were expressed about women's sexuality, and a positive viewpoint on homosexuality was expressed. Women participating in the conference were also fortunate to exchange views with women who were happily living in homosexual relationships and finding it very fulfilling. This session, through much soul-searching and self-examination, brought many women to a far more enlightened and accurate picture of homosexuality (YW Resource 1974).

The purpose of exploring this early 1970s conflict within the local YWCA is to emphasize the new and more assertive feminist identity that was emerging in this province at that time. The "dissidents" during the YWCA conflict were those who took the Social Action Platform to heart and fought to promote a louder, more in-your-face activism, including direct action tactics, as a way of fighting a broad range of social justice struggles affecting not just women but also other oppressed and marginalized identity groups. The ranks of these young dissidents included many names now recognized as leaders in the modern NL feminist movement. They began their work, logically enough, within the confines of an existing long-running women's organization. Their demands for change and their bold activism generated strife between the more progressive activists and an older generation of more conservative-minded women. During the course of those years of conflict, new organizations were also emerging to pick up the banner of a more radical feminism, and several of the YWCA activists – including lesbian activists – would subsequently transition their activism to one new group in particular: the Newfoundland Status of Women Council. Indeed, as the amalgamation debate flared amid ongoing (and often intergenerational) struggles over the place of feminist activism in the YWCA, several of the 'dissident' members drifted away from the latter organization to invest their energy into the newer, more overtly feminist NSWC. But let's not get ahead of ourselves. Let's return to the end of the 1960s, as the tensions within the YWCA were just beginning to foment.

Canadian Federation of University Women (CFUW)

At that same time, another organization playing a key role in local as well as national feminist activism was the Canadian Federation of University Women, which in the 1960s was led nationally by a fiery activist named Laura Sabia. The CFUW's roots lie with the International Federation of University Women (IFUW), a group which came about after meetings between representatives of the American Association of University Women and the British Federation of University Women in 1918. This led to a 1920 conference attended by delegates from fifteen nations. Canada, having formed its own Canadian Federation of University Women (modelled after the American and British associations) in 1919, was one of the eight national associations granted voting rights at the inaugural IFUW meeting (CFUW 2023).

The organization, both national and international iterations, was concerned with the situation facing women on a broad level – especially with the rise of fascism and global militarism in the 1930s – and very specifically with job prospects, working conditions, and employment access for female university graduates and women academics. During the ensuing decades, the CFUW would become a leading advocacy force for women not just in academia but in the broader community as well. This especially became the case in the early 1950s post-WWII period; a St. John's branch was founded in 1945, and a Grand Falls branch in 1957. The CFUW's Status of Women committee began encouraging women to run for public office, and the 1952 triennial convention was focused around the theme "Women and the State." The CFUW had set its sights firmly on the need for systemic change at the political level. In the 1950s, the CFUW also began working closely with the Elizabeth Fry Society to support reforms around women and the law. They pushed for legislative reform to grant women stronger property rights, and also pushed for greater women's representation on government bodies. These trends accelerated in the 1960s, with the CFUW intensifying its lobbying into a broad-based call for women's equality in Canada (Ibid.).

In 1962, CFUW Vice-President (Ontario) Laura Sabia went to New York to attend the United Nations Commission on the Status of Women. The work being undertaken there inspired her, and when she was elected CFUW National President in 1964, she determined to use the organization to push for similar action at the Canadian level. She knew the CFUW could only achieve so much on its own, and so in 1966 she reached out to dozens of national women's organizations, 32 of which eventually joined together in a coalition. They met in Toronto and formed a Committee for the Equality of Women, with Sabia as national chair (it would later be renamed the Ad Hoc Committee on the Status of Women). Canadian women activists had never been so united before (Ibid.).

Sabia adopted a conservative dress and style but had a reputation as a firebrand. An article in the national YWCA newsletter described one of her speeches at a national conference as:

Dramatic, powerful, electrifying... She exhorted women to be active, to be political. She spoke with great strength about the need of the YWCA to remain a unified women's organization. She encouraged women to stand behind the fight to repeal abortion from the Criminal Code, and to ensure equal pay for work of equal value. Laura 'makes no bones about it' when she says that we should attack our M.P.'s – that's political pressure! (YW Resource 1974).

The Liberals were in federal government at the time, led by Prime Minister Lester B. Pearson. Sabia and her coalition worked closely with women in the Liberal government, setting as their target the establishment of a Royal Commission on the Status of Women. They delivered this request to the Prime Minister, who initially resisted. Former *Chatelaine* editor, Dorothy Anderson, writing in Canadian Woman Studies, described what happened next:

When they were turned down by Prime Minister Lester Pearson, [Sabia] was asked by a Globe and Mail reporter what she intended to do. 'I think I'll march to Ottawa with three million women!' she replied, but was horrified the next day to see the headline. But the strategy worked. Three days later the government gave in. She often chuckled, 'I doubt if I could have persuaded even three women to march on Ottawa' (Anderson 1997).

Royal Commission on the Status of Women

As a result of this activism, the Royal Commission on the Status of Women in Canada was set up by the federal government and chaired by journalist Florence Bird. It spent six months traveling the country, holding public hearings and receiving submissions. Over 468 briefs were submitted as well as more than 1000 letters. It tabled a 488-page report on December 7, 1970, along with 167 recommendations. The report led to a number of changes at the national level, while individual provinces also undertook the initiative to review and consider changes under their provincial purviews.

It wasn't just the Royal Commission's final report which was important. During its tenure, the Commission traveled the country, meeting with women and women's organizations. This consultation process itself became a form of collective national consciousness raising, firing up feminist activism across the nation.

When the Commission visited St. John's, a few local groups made formal presentations: the Canadian Federation of University Women (St. John's Club), the Association of Registered Nurses of Newfoundland, the Business and Professional Women's Club (St. John's Branch), the Council of Associations of University Student Personnel Services, and the Newfoundland Home Economics Association, along with Doris Janes, a CBC reporter in Corner Brook. The CFUW (Grand Falls Branch) also sent in a written submission.[22]

The 167 recommendations presented in the Commission's final report spanned the gamut of women's lives, from workplace concerns to abortion and birth control access. With the report tabled, feminists and allies prepared themselves for the next stage of the fight: making sure the Royal Commission's recommendations were acted upon. The responsibility for this would lie with both federal and provincial governments.

Newfoundland and Labrador was the first province to take action in response to the Royal Commission's report. On April 15, 1971, the NL government struck a Special Committee to review and respond to the Royal Commission's 167 Recommendations. The Committee, reporting to the Minister of Labour, consisted of eleven women and was chaired by Dorothy Wyatt. Wyatt was a prominent feminist activist, city councillor, and future mayor of the City of St. John's – she would also become an early advocate of queer rights. The structure of the Committee reflected its emphasis on the status of working women: the members were hand-picked to represent a broad range of vocations, as well as ages and geographic regions of the province. It also reflected class biases deeply rooted in the province's history. Many of the women came from backgrounds of wealth, power and privilege. The entire process was deeply technocratic: each woman would indicate their approval or disapproval of each of the 167 recommendations, rank them in order of priority, and indicate if and how they ought to be implemented in Newfoundland and Labrador. As "Chairman" Wyatt was responsible for tabulating the results and compiling the final report. There was no expectation for the Committee to even meet with each other, although they were permitted to do so if they felt it was necessary. Rather than engage in broad consultations, the provincial government intended to rely on the experience and opinion of these eleven women.

That Committee submitted its report to the NL government on November

---

[22] The following discussion of the Royal Commission, its impact on NL, and the NL response to the report, is drawn from a distillation of documents contained within the St. John's Status of Women Council archives located in the Provincial Archives at The Rooms in St. John's.

16, 1971.

Far from being a radical or even a feminist undertaking, the Report of the [NL] Special Committee reflected the class and status locations of its members. While many of them were active in varieties of liberal feminist activism, they also included family members of local politicians and media personalities; writers; women active in various churches; educated women whose experience was rooted in upper to middle class liberal society. While some of the Royal Commission's recommendations had been profoundly progressive and left-leaning, the hand-picked NL Committee members sought to temper their application in this province from a more centrist, even right-leaning position. Recommendations that questioned the centrality of capitalism and private enterprise were shot down by the Special Committee. While the Report did recommend enforcement of an equal minimum wage, for both women and men, and unemployment insurance benefits for "maids and homemakers," it also rejected maternity leave as "discriminatory... those who were not producing families were subsidizing those who were." Use of gender quotas to pursue equality were anathema to the Committee: "Private enterprise should have some choice in selection of staff... Employer who pays the bill should have some choice." The Report also opined, "No extras for women – discrimination towards men." As well as, "Women with dependent children should not be in Armed Forces."

The Royal Commission had recommended the establishment of a Household Workers Bureau. The NL Special Committee shot it down – "area of private enterprise."

Discriminatory textbooks? Not good, but not their responsibility to correct either. "The Committee felt that a revision in the text books should portray women in diversified roles but tossed the challenge to women to produce this desired result and prepare acceptable texts themselves."

On the topic of 'Family life' education, it was not to happen on the Special Committee's watch: "Family life education is a family responsibility." The Special Committee did permit, cryptically, for some in-school family life education provided by "medical and nursing personnel and homemakers and not left to the imagination of the unimaginative." The need for birth control education had by now permeated Newfoundland and Labrador – a very Catholic province characterized by large families many of whom were struggling in poverty – and the Committee did feel "that it was necessary to have birth control information available to all. Parents are reluctant to discuss this information with their adolescents... The fault lies with Church, State and inertia of the medical profession."

The Special Committee was averse to easing divorce laws: "We recommend that 18-24 months separation be required as minimum. It is felt that turbulence could affect rationality in this area."

As for public daycare? Again, a hard no: "Day Care Centres should be an area of private enterprise... day care centres are never a substitute for mother and father care homes. We do not want a whole generation of stereotype children as products of daycare centres."

The Special Committee's biggest rejection was reserved for one of the Royal Commission's most controversial recommendations: abortion on demand. "The Newfoundland Committee objected to this recommendation. The Committee was divided in terms of approval or disapproval but the comments were significantly contra abortion," wrote Wyatt in summary.

This is not to say the Special Committee was entirely regressive: there was some diversity of perspective and disagreement on issues, for instance abortion. Yet in the main, the committee's recommendations sought to temper the slightly more radical flavour of the Royal Commission report. Many of the positions expressed in the Special Committee's report would today be considered deeply conservative, even far right. The brand of 'feminism' endorsed by the Special Committee can perhaps best be summed up by its recommendation that: "Individual initiative should be encouraged" (Special Committee 1971).

At least some NL feminists at the time were unimpressed with the Special Committee. There is an original copy of their report in the St. John's Status of Women archives in The Rooms, St. John's. It's not clear whose personal copy it was, but the Report is scribbled up with exclamation marks, underlined question marks, and angry, outraged comments from the reader.

In the new year, work ramped up to find ways to implement the Royal Commission recommendations in concrete action. In April 1972, a 'Strategy for Change' conference was organized in Toronto, with the aim of furthering and implementing the Royal Commission's recommendations. Over 500 women from across the country attended the conference, and among them were at least five women from NL: Iris Kirby (then still Executive Director of the St. John's YWCA), Shirley Goundrey (a St. John's YWCA board member), Vi Hodder (president of United Church Women of Newfoundland and Labrador), Donna Todd (member of the group Voice of Women), and Leone Ferguson, a resident of Goose Bay Labrador.

Notwithstanding the somewhat reactionary flavour of the NL Special Committee's Report, its release — fuelled by the broader momentum of the more radical Royal Commission report — nevertheless provided fuel for the growing momentum of feminist activism in the province. In St. John's and elsewhere, the BPWA organized public meetings to discuss the Report. In NL, the BPWA brought Justice Doris Ogilvie, one of the Royal Commission members, to the province. Ogilvie doubled as a sort of unofficial rep for Atlantic Canada on the Royal Commission. Born in Halifax, Nova Scotia, she graduated from Mount Saint Vincent University with a degree in Secretarial Science. Not prepared to be a secretary, she went on to pursue a law degree at the University of New Brunswick; she eventually settled and served as lawyer and judge in that province.

In April 1972, Judge Ogilvie did a brief tour of Newfoundland organized by local branches of the BPWA. The meeting in Gander was covered by *The Monitor*, a provincial Catholic newspaper, and is illustrative of the participatory approach organizers took to educating the public about the Report and its recommendations. The Gander branch of the BPWA – which also published a newsletter called '*The Feminist*' – held a day-long workshop on the Royal Commission report. It was broken down into ten subject areas, and a committee of women reviewed and analyzed each of those areas and their recommendations, before reporting back to the entire body. Members of the general public were invited to participate in this process. After the workshop, a dinner took place at Hotel Gander, with the guest speaker being Justice Ogilvie herself. She discussed the Report and the work which had informed it (The Monitor 1972).

The culmination of her tour took place in St. John's. On a Saturday afternoon in April 1972, over two hundred women showed up at the Foran Room in St. John's City Hall for the meeting over which she presided.

"It was mass confusion," recalled one attendee (who requested anonymity), looking back on it with a chuckle. According to one description of the event:

It was a stirring and memorable occasion, not least because of the very broad spectrum of age groups represented in the audience. So urgent was the enthusiasm of those present that it was spontaneously decided to meet again in order to form an organization which would harness this hitherto unsuspected and untapped source of energy and forge it into an effective force in the community and ultimately in society at large (SJSWC 1972).

In fact, at the time opinion was mixed as to whether the recommendations of the Report were best achieved by existing women's organizations, or by a new group. Existing groups like the BPWA, YWCA and CFUW were already working on incorporating relevant recommendations into their own agendas, but some women – including some such as the YWCA dissidents who found themselves stifled within existing organizations – wanted a new, independent organization focused exclusively on "the status of women in the fullest meaning of the term" and one which "would demand no other qualification for membership than that one be a woman." The implication behind this demand – as suggested by some of the YWCA internal conflict – is that gatekeeping in existing women's organizations on the basis of class, religion, nationality, and other identity factors (including sexuality) continued to be a barrier to creating a universal, mass women's movement. Many of the more conservative-minded supporters of those existing organizations also supported the idea of a new group. Those who wanted a new group to pursue the Report's recommendations announced they would hold a meeting the following month. The BPWA, CFUW and YWCA agreed to support this proposal by handling logistics and publicity (Goundrey 1975).

At that May 1972 follow-up meeting, also held at City Hall, those present formed an interim steering committee of fifteen women to coordinate the creation of this new organization. They would work throughout the summer, drawing up articles of incorporation and laying the groundwork for the new group, with a view toward launching it at a public general meeting in September. It would be called the Newfoundland Status of Women Council (NSWC).

That inaugural meeting was full of enthusiasm and hope, but it was not without tension. At one point during the meeting, some women began circulating a petition to repeal abortion laws, which sparked angry outbursts from others. According to a 1975 reflection by Shirley Goundrey, this "gave rise to much emotionalism and hostility... this one issue alienated many women from the whole movement, which was unfortunate because many of these women were aware of and concerned about other issues of concern to women." Meeting facilitators calmed the incipient dispute between proponents and opponents of abortion laws, but the issue would emerge again later that year (Goundrey 1975).

On May 26, 1972, the fifteen women selected to organize this new group met to review a draft constitution, set up interest groups (labeled "ginger groups", after an old British parliamentary term referring to a focused political faction or sub-group) and make other plans. The summer of 1972 flared with energy and activism. Early meetings of the NSWC steering committee were held at the YWCA offices, and as the internal strife and debates over amalgamation intensified within the YWCA, several of the more radical members there opted to refocus their work into the nascent NSWC. While the fifteen-person steering committee prepared the foundations of what would become the NL Status of Women Council at an inaugural General Meeting to be held on September 18 (at the same time the interest groups, or ginger groups, began holding their own meetings and workshops around their respective topics), other initiatives got underway as well.

Around the same time, a group of eight young women, under the direction of feminist activists Sharon Gray and Anne Budgell, applied for federal funding under the Opportunities For Youth (OFY) program. The OFY, which was specifically for unemployed students, and its broader non-student counterpart Local Initiatives Program (LIP) were federal Liberal government programs widely criticized by right-wing policymakers and media at the time, yet in retrospect they had an unprecedentedly positive impact on community development across the country. Billed as an effort to tackle youth unemployment, the federal Liberal government invited OFY applications from young people for any community-oriented projects that interested them. Most were funded, without much scrutiny.

Its philosophy was basically – we don't have work for you, clearly, so tell us what you can do, what you want to do, how you think it would better your community, and we'll fund it if we deem it worthy. The first year [1971] there were almost 13,800 applications for LIP grants alone, and $20 million doled out. 1972's LIP program, was worth $100 million. In 1973, as it wound down, it was $85 million (Goodhand 2017).

Right-leaning policymakers, opposition parties, and media quickly lined up and opened fire on this creative and progressive initiative, singling out a handful of strange-sounding projects for ridicule while ignoring the far greater number of beneficial initiatives it was sparking. While opponents argued it was inefficient, wasteful and poorly scrutinized, in fact the applicants submitted proposals for a remarkably broad range of progressive and forward-thinking projects. And while the OFY program only lasted a few years, many of the projects it kickstarted have survived into the present. Margo Goodhand, in her history of the women's shelter movement in Canada, points out that it created the tangible foundation for countless women's shelters, women's bookstores, crisis lines, daycare centres and other feminist initiatives which launched during this period.

It seeded and nurtured social service activism in the young and creative. The greatest LIP and OFY benefactors were Canadian women and First Nations… The program appealed to university-educated women spurning the traditional jobs available to them and seeking more meaningful work, and women on welfare who saw the grants as a path to create and establish entirely new social services for women (Goodhand 2017).

Newfoundland and Labrador was no different. In St. John's, the eight young women under Gray and Budgell's supervision applied for a project calling themselves 'The Women's Bureau.' Their application was to research and publish a booklet on 'Women and the Law in Newfoundland.' It was modelled on a similar initiative undertaken in Nova Scotia by the Halifax Women's Bureau. In addition, they aspired to deal "with the nobody-knows-who's-doing-what problem" by compiling a list of all the women's organizations active in Newfoundland and Labrador along with information on what they did, to serve as a resource guide and to "save people from duplicating projects." They also began putting together a resource library, buying feminist books and subscribing to feminist magazines that were not widely available in the province. At first, the Women's Bureau operated out of the St. John's YWCA building at 55 Military Road, and later they acquired office space of their own downtown at 144 Duckworth Street (Payne 1972).

Sharon Gray was one of the young feminists who was involved in this project. "The money was well used for sure," she said. "Any little seed money we could get went on to turn into other things."

At the same time, archival records indicate a group calling itself "The New Feminists" was also building a large community resource library of feminist materials in St. John's, which was eventually donated to the Women's Centre. It's unclear whether these were the same people, or different groups.

The city was on fire with feminist activity. Much of it was uncoordinated, spontaneous, and idealistic. Soon an event would serve to unify much of this energy: the arrival of a Toronto-based feminist named Bonnie Kreps.

***

Every great movement has its pivotal founding moment. For the St. John's (then NL) Status of Women Council it was a potluck supper held at the YWCA offices on Military Road on the evening of Friday, June 9, 1972. The dinner was to welcome well-known Canadian feminist Bonnie Kreps to the province. The supper meeting was organized by the YWCA SAC, and they invited the nascent NSWC to join.

Kreps was a Dutch filmmaker born in 1937, whose parents joined the Dutch anti-Nazi resistance when she was a young child in Copenhagen. They hid dozens of Jews in their basement, and smuggled several of them to safety in Sweden. Her father was eventually arrested by the Nazis, but survived the ordeal. After the war, in 1951, the family immigrated to the United States (Ibranya-Kiss 1974; Huffman 2021). Both Bonnie and her younger sister, Anne Koedt, became deeply involved in the radical feminist movement. Anne was, with Shulamith Firestone, a co-founder of New York Radical Feminists and authored *The Myth of the Vaginal Orgasm*; she married her long-term partner Ellen Levine in 2011 (Faludi 2013). Bonnie moved to Toronto, Canada, in 1967, where she continued her activism. She co-founded a group known as The New Feminists, billed as Toronto's first radical feminist organization.[23] Kreps single-handedly wrote and presented her own submission to the Royal Commission on the Status of Women in 1968, representing no one but herself and her second-wave, radical feminist views. She would go on to forge a career as an acclaimed filmmaker. At the same time, she was busy founding Toronto's first Women's Centre (Dewar 2020).

Kreps was one of the country's most prominent radical feminists, and was invited by the YWCA SAC to come and tour Newfoundland. NSWC/YWCA SAC activists Shirley Goundrey and Jill Schooley had met Kreps at the Strategy for Change conference in Toronto in 1972 and were impressed by her "dynamism and her movie-making skills" (SJSWC 2002). When they returned, they shared their enthusiasm and the growing network of activists put plans in motion to bring Kreps to Newfoundland. Kreps was also personal friends with Mary Jane Lewis (then -Payne), a local activist and businesswoman involved with the NSWC. Kreps' two-week visit to the province proved pivotal in many respects. Twenty-three people showed up at the welcome pot-luck dinner that night at the YWCA: seven SAC organizers and sixteen other guests.

After eating, one of the attendees asked Kreps to talk about her ongoing effort to establish a Women's Centre in Toronto. Kreps was working with another Toronto-based feminist, Sherrill Cheda, and had gotten a grant from the federal government to rent a building, hire staff (including Kreps and Cheda) and undertake some programming. They'd gotten funding from a variety of sources, including the federal Office of the Secretary of State. Kreps encour-

---

[23] It's possible 'The New Feminists' mentioned in NL archival records from 1972 was a St. John's-based consciousness-raising group inspired by Kreps' visit.

aged local feminists to try a similar initiative in St. John's. She brought a copy of their proposal for the Toronto centre, which she left with the SAC. The NSWC would later adopt what it referred to as the 'Kreps-Cheda model' in its own application to the Secretary of State, essentially duplicating the Toronto proposal and changing the name and minor details wherever appropriate.

Kreps' visit was catalytic in other respects. She held a well-attended public meeting at the National Film Board office in Pleasantville where she screened one of her films. She also made several media appearances on the province's airwaves. These proved memorable; her appearance on Ron Pumphrey's "Phone Forum" (a radio program which claimed to be the most popular open line phone-in radio show in NL at the time) was discussed at length, and reported on in *The Muse*, when she spoke at Memorial University on June 7, 1972.

"Pumphrey is archetypal of the media," she told the crowd assembled at Memorial. "He is the worst that I have come across" (The Muse 1972).

Pumphrey had continually shouted at her that she was 'trying to create neuters,' and demanded to know why she didn't wear lipstick and a dress. Little apparent attention was payed to what she was trying to say. 'He wanted a fight,' [Kreps] said. 'I think he would have been happy if I'd pulled out a whip. He was looking for a stereotype, but he was disappointed. He is ignorant, a waste of time to deal with. He feeds off human problems' (Ibid.).

Thirty people showed up for her talk at the Little Theatre at Memorial University, which took the form of a conversation. Kreps "said she wanted to come here 'to talk to women and to hear their ideas' rather than simply give speeches and appear in the local media," reported *The Muse*. Kreps talked to the audience about the distinction between first-wage "suffragette" feminism and the current ('second-wave') feminist movement, which was about more than just political and economic equality. It was about social equality, about challenging and transcending traditional gender roles (Ibid.).

The audience was mostly female, but unsurprisingly, men wound up dominating some of the conversation. When Kreps criticized gendered social roles and machismo, one man in the audience loudly objected, crying out that women liberationists were trying to "emasculate" him. Kreps countered that machismo was a "distorted" version of personal growth, and other male students spoke up in support of Kreps (Ibid.).

Sharon Gray vividly remembers the impact of Kreps' visit:

It was a sensation! St. John's was a very small town – it's still a fairly small town – you had The Evening Telegram, you had Ron Pumphrey, you had The Daily News, it wasn't a big place but it had a lot of media coverage. I worked for The Telegram for a couple of years and that was the sort of thing they loved in terms of stories – somebody comes to town, has a radical point of view and you do interviews with them. Her visit was very well publicized and really attracted a lot of young women.

She was just very powerful, and energetic. She just radiated radicalism in a way that to me was very, very attractive. What she was saying – as far as I understood at the time – was that you could explore yourselves and you could take that into action but first of all you had to understand yourself and your relationships to other women. And then you could go out from that and make really good contributions to society. From her I took away the idea that personal exploration comes first, and then social action. It's no good going out and starting to demonstrate if you don't understand how you feel about it yourself (Gray 2023).

"She was galvanizing," said Jane Goundrey, whose mother Shirley worked with both the SAC and the NSWC.

Perhaps the biggest impact of Kreps' visit – besides moving forward the notion of a Women's Centre – was in its impact on individual women through the form of 'Consciousness-Raising' groups. Kreps met with small groups of women throughout St. John's and beyond. *The Muse* reported that she also held a meeting with "housewives in Dunville" (The Muse 1972).

"Several consciousness-raising groups formed as a result of her visit," reported Lynn Hartery in her graduate thesis on the history of the Rape Crisis Centre. In fact, Kreps herself organized several consciousness-raising sessions during her trip, enabling her to connect with women in smaller groups (Hartery 2001).

What were Consciousness-Raising groups? These informal gatherings took place in people's homes. Sometimes the groups became established and met regularly; other times they remained amorphous and sporadic. Groups might splinter and merge, and members might join other groups that were more to their interests. Some groups bonded tightly and continued meeting together for years. There were no hard and fast rules to Consciousness Raising, although there were some common practices. Each group adopted its own set of principles, which might be more or less formally stated. The main point was to share perspectives, and 'elevate consciousness' through the mutual sharing of experiences and ideas.

Like all things, the small-town, gossip-prone fabric of Newfoundland society put its own spin on CR. As Anne Escott recalled:

The 1960s were just over, but the sixties were later getting here than they were on the mainland. There were all these Consciousness Raising – CR – groups. Consciousness Raising groups were incredible. Everybody who was in those groups, the first thing you had to do, was swear to secrecy. [Laughs] So it was great – you'd go to someone's house after the group and you'd hear everything about everybody (Escott 2021).

In the early 1970s, Consciousness Raising groups were widespread and organic. In later years, particularly the late 1970s and 1980s, interest would wane despite the concerted efforts of some early feminists and organizations to keep them going.

In a reflection on the topic for the Women's Centre newsletter in 1972, Sharon Gray wrote:

In the heyday of the women's liberation movement many of us began to explore our feelings and new-found freedoms in consciousness-raising groups. A C-R group provides a space where women can be totally open with other women about their feelings of fear, money, power, work, marriage and other aspects of life that cause us all problems. In many ways C-R groups act as a kind of therapy, but it is within the context that many of our problems are caused by common conditioning that cast us into roles of 'daughter', 'girlfriend', 'wife', and 'mother'. In the C-R group we are none of these, we are just women with different life experiences finding out the extent to which all women suffer from similar conditioning (Gray 1972).

Looking back on that period fifty years later, Gray still emphasizes the importance of CR groups to the emergent feminist movement.

When this was all happening I was in my early 20s, and one of the things that got me really involved was when Bonnie Kreps came down. That was the first time I got really involved in it. A friend of mine said 'There's a really good speaker' and we went to it. And she was forming these consciousness raising groups. So this to me sounded like a fantastic idea.

They were supposed to be structured groups of 10 weeks and you had a topic each week starting with your perceptions of growing up female. And ending in – I think a lot of people were quite afraid of the last couple of topics because they all had to do with sexuality and orgasms and stuff. In the group I was in, there were two older – I think at that time they were in their thirties – two older-to-me women who each had six children. So in a lot of ways they were very traditional but in a lot of ways they were also extremely radical, I think they just had more life experience... So we did the whole ten weeks and then we went on for another two years, meeting periodically to see how everybody was and stuff. I'd say that some of my best friends came out of that particular group, people I've kept in touch with my whole life.

The consciousness-raising groups were absolutely instrumental. Some people didn't get that much out of them, [some people] thought they were just kind of boring. But it might have been the group. Because you were assigned groups randomly (Gray 2023).

For some, it precipitated their first discussions around issues of sexuality and lesbianism, as well.

Sexuality was talked about. It came up in our consciousness-raising group, it got into what your primary sexuality was and how you felt about it, and a couple of the women said that they didn't feel primarily heterosexual, and that was new to them, and new to other people in the group. But it was something that they were still exploring. One particular woman ended up going full gay, after she'd had two children and stuff. But I think for a lot of people it was just a time when they could see where they were and look at other possibilities that maybe a decade or a generation earlier just weren't open to being looked at.

I know that being gay is not new at all, but at the time, in our little culture

here in St. John's and Newfoundland, there just wasn't a whole lot of aware-
ness of it. People came to St. John's because they were so persecuted in their
home communities, they just had no place that they could be open at all, and
especially in Salvation Army communities – there were people that came from
them and they had absolute horror stories about how they were treated (Ibid.)

Sometimes Consciousness Raising groups would evolve into more formal
organizations. This was the case with one important group, called A Woman's
Place.[24] A Woman's Place arose when the women involved in of one of the
groups wanted to take things a step further, and find a physical location for
their consciousness-raising work.

The original members of A Woman's Place were an eclectic blend of young
radicals. They included the writer and journalist Sharon Gray, Mary Jane Lewis, after whom the iconic health food store Mary Jane's was named, and Del
Texmo, an American professor at Memorial who was active in feminist initiatives on campus as well as an active member of the local business community,
opening several local shops over the years. Janet Kelly and Lynn Sorensen were
teachers and activists concerned with education and early childhood development – they would later launch an independent, co-operative "free school" to
educate a cohort of children. It operated for a few years in a variety of venues,
ranging from feminists' basements to a former US military prison. Janet Kelly
would also open Auntie Crae's, an iconic specialty food store that would operate for many years. Other members lived in a large, radical student co-op which
had taken over a house on Monkstown Road (it was considered radical at the
time for a group of male and female students to be sharing a house together).

Vicky Hammond was another member of the group. She worked at Mary
Jane's, the independent grocery operated by Mary Jane Lewis. Mary Jane's was
originally a health food store but after a year or so evolved into one of the
province's first specialty grocery stores, stocking a variety of global products
which were common elsewhere in Canada but at that time impossible to find
in Newfoundland. The shift, recalls Hammond, was in response to members
of the local Chinese, Indian and other communities visiting the store looking
for products like rice and lentils that were difficult to find elsewhere. Mary
Jane shared her suppliers' catalogues with the community and followed their
advice on which items to order.

It was in fact Hammond's yearning for one such exotic product – sunflower
seeds – which got her involved in the feminist movement. She had tried sunflower seeds as a child – a friend of her mother's had acquired some – but they
were hard to come by in Newfoundland in the 1970s.

Hammond recalls, with a laugh, how she started working at Mary Jane's:

"So when I heard there was a health food store opening in St. John's, I

---

[24] In interviews with members, archival documents from the period, as well as documents produced by the group, it is referred to at times as "A Woman's Place" and other
times as "Women's Place"

thought ooh – they might have sunflower seeds! St. John's was about ten years behind the rest of North America, right? So I went down there and just imme-diately clicked with Mary Jane and she did have sunflower seeds, and she was looking for help. I started baking bread on Fridays and Saturdays and then she hired me and I became her employee. I was her employee for about two or three years and then intermittently after that. It was a lot of fun, especially after she started getting into the international stuff and we would be unpacking these big pallets full of stuff that we didn't even know what it was. She was such an interesting person. The last time I knew her location she was in Ecuador. She's always been a big traveller, a very adventurous woman, a very interesting one" (Hammond 2023).

Mary Jane Payne had initially come to Newfoundland in 1970 when her husband – a professor – got a job at Memorial University. Only recently mar-ried, they divorced soon after their arrival, and she reassumed her original name Mary Jane Lewis. Her dream was to open a specialty grocery, but the banks refused to give her a loan because she was a single woman. Eventually she got her former husband to co-sign the loan.

Payne told her friend Sally Davis in an interview for the NSWC newsletter that:

[The idea] came to me one evening at a party when I heard for the eight thousandth time, this time from an older couple, about the trouble people had obtaining food items which were the kind of things readily available in all cities on the mainland. Such as different spices (fresh), beans, pastas, cheeses, bread containing substance, olives, teas, and even vitamin pills (NSWC 1976).

Her shop rapidly became a beloved mainstay of the local community. Such was the demand that she had to move the shop several times to progressively larger locations. She also stocked feminist and queer magazines and newspa-pers, both locally-produced as well as titles from mainland Canada and farther abroad. She had two Siamese cats, including one named Orzo which she had named after one of the mysterious pastas she found advertised in the supply catalogues. Eventually in 1976, she handed over the shop, piled her two cats and a few belongings into a red pickup truck, and took off to drive back to the US. The store she founded would live on for many years, and could be consid-ered the progenitor of other specialty food stores which opened in the province in its wake.

Mary Jane was friends with Bonnie Kreps before she moved to Newfound-land, and later stayed with Kreps in Toronto when she visited there looking for suppliers for her new grocery. When she drove back to St. John's in her rickety old Volkswagen van, she took Kreps' young 10-year-old daughter with her for the adventure, and the younger Kreps stayed for several months and worked with her in the shop.

When Bonnie came to St. John's, she also stayed with Mary Jane for a while, and charged her with responsibility for spreading the cause of consciousness-raising groups. One of the ones she kick-started was the group which would eventually grow into the Woman's Place Collective. But all these conscious-ness-raising groups needed a place to operate out of. As Hammond explains:

[Kreps] was the spark for us, definitely. She wanted Mary Jane to spark a feminist surge here in St. John's... I was Mary Jane's sidekick, we were friends, it was not just an employer employee relationship, she was kind of a mentor to me in a lot of ways, a great friend. So Bonnie said the first thing we had to do was solicit interest and set up consciousness raising groups. So that's what we did. And that was mind-boggling and amazing. There were quite a few of us. There was more than one group, and my group was not that small... Those meetings changed my life and I'm still friends with most of those women who are still around to this day. And at some point we decided we needed a place, for all of us to meet. Because people had husbands and families and stuff. So in order for all of the groups to get together and meet as a bunch, we figured we needed a bigger place. And we also hoped to do some kind of outreach (Hammond 2023).

"It wasn't just us, there were a number of groups," said Gray. "But there was a feeling that we needed a space to come to."

The NSWC was working on getting a space – they had struck a committee to put together the application for funding for a women's centre. The commit-tee consisted of four members of the NSWC executive, and four members of "the consciousness raising groups." This process would take them longer than anticipated – it appears the initial ambitious proposal was for almost $40,000 – akin to what Kreps was requested for her Centre in Toronto – and the federal Secretary of State haggled them down to an initial start-up grant for $500 fol-lowed by another one for $3000. But even this process took several months.

Meanwhile, the office space at 144 Duckworth Street which had been used by the Women's Bureau was still available. Even after the OFY grant that fund-ed the Women's Bureau was finished, those young women together with the Woman's Place CR group decided they might as well continue using the office space as an interim Women's Centre. NSWC members concentrated their ef-forts on the funding application and dealing with the Secretary of State, while the more radical members of Woman's Place collective took the lead in orga-nizing the existing space on Duckworth Street into what became a functioning women's centre, staffed by a cadre of committed feminist volunteers. Feminists began referring to this location as the women's centre, while some of them also referred to it as 'A Woman's Place.' It wasn't quite the well-organized, well-funded and structured entity the NSWC had been hoping for, but New-foundland and Labrador had its first women's centre. It would eventually fall prey to divisions within the incipient women's movement, but during its short existence it had a profound impact on many of the province's women, includ-ing Cathy Murphy.

Cathy Murphy was a young mother living in Hillview Terrace apartments in St. John's. She was eighteen years old, married with two children. She came from a poor family, and had dropped out of high school when she became pregnant. "I was very inexperienced, undereducated, naive and opinionated," she reflected fifty years later.

It was her opinionated nature that brought her into the feminist movement. When the owners of Hillview Terrace imposed a rent increase, Murphy decided to launch a petition, and started going door-to-door collecting signatures. As she did, she was told another petition was already in circulation. She made contact with the residents behind that petition – they agreed to join efforts – and there she met Gertrude Mabey. "Gert was a teacher, an Acadian from Nova Scotia, a mother and a general activist," Murphy recalled. Gert's husband, Don, worked for MUN Extension Services — the community outreach arm of Memorial University which had a reputation for social activism. "They struggled to lead MUN into community involvement as the true focus of a university education," Murphy explained.

Maybe told Murphy that she was involved with a Consciousness-Raising group operating out of a newly formed women's centre on Duckworth Street, called A Woman's Place. Their C-R group had grown to the point where they were looking to hive it off into a second group, and she thought Murphy would be a great prospective member.

She told me I should go to Woman's Place. She told me when the next meeting of the group was, and I went down because they were trying to bring together enough women to form a second CR group.

I was curious. I was a bit nervous about it all because it was so new to me, all these things. I grew up poor, I left school early, I was an isolated mother at home with two children. So I was unlike anyone else [at Woman's Place] in my age group at the time. I was curious, willing to learn and see what people had to say. I wanted to know more.

It was life-changing for me. I learned a tremendous amount from those years. It really shaped my politics and the rest of my life (Murphy 2022).

Murphy had missed the formative meetings earlier that year, as well as Kreps' visit, but she'd been aware that things were going on.

I actually heard about [Kreps' visit] through my father, who read the newspaper. He read the news so he was making comments about it and he didn't approve of it at all. So I heard about it that way, through word of mouth. And [Kreps] caused a shake-up in town, when she was in town, because she was saying these radical things (Ibid.).

As Murphy began going to meetings at A Woman's Place, one of the things that struck her was how few of the women activists were originally from this province.

There were very few people actually from St. John's that were involved in Woman's Place. Quite a few of the women that were involved, the activists, were American. They were from the university. The treatment of women at the university was a big issue for them, so that was one of the focuses at the time

(Ibid.).

Murphy – born and bred in St. John's – had a typically nationalist attitude at the time, and wasn't impressed by the presence of so many 'come-from-away's'.

I had a typical attitude of Newfoundlanders, especially when we haven't travelled or had much exposure. You know: these people, they're come-from-aways, they don't know what they're talking about.

But what I soon found out is these people did know what they were talking about! They actually had an appreciation of the history, the architecture, and the culture of Newfoundland that people from Newfoundland didn't necessarily have at that time. They were very interested in preserving the city of St. John's, and improving it. They had seen things in other places, and they brought something of an international flavour to St. John's (Ibid.).

As the feminists of A Woman's Place solicited donations of furniture and began remodelling the new space, those involved with the newly formed NL Status of Women Council were also hard at work preparing their own organization. Whereas the Woman's Place team had taken a sort of DIY 'just do it' approach and taken over the space at 144 Duckworth St with little preparation or organizing, the NSWC was being more meticulous with its plans. The Steering Committee had begun developing articles of incorporation, and were drawing up detailed funding proposals for a centre and staff. But the fact the Woman's Place activists had just gone ahead and taken action meant there was now some duplication in these efforts. The relationship was not one of animosity: everyone knew each other and they were all driven by a shared feminist energy. Many of them were working together on other projects and initiatives. The situation did raise questions about how best to coordinate efforts to avoid needless duplication. The NSWC were preparing a funding application for a Centre; the Woman's Place activists had just gone ahead and launched one in a space that was available. While the Woman's Place team were driven by a shared radical feminist consciousness, and organized along the anti-hierarchical lines encouraged by feminist consciousness-raising, the NSWC envisioned a somewhat more structured province-wide organization. Balancing the two visions would prove challenging.

The NSWC Steering Committee worked hard all that summer of 1972. They decided to call their organization the Newfoundland Status of Women Council. The name was deliberately ambitious; its first articles of incorporation designate its geographic area served as "all of Newfoundland and Labrador." The group consulted with Margaret Cameron — one of the province's few women lawyers at the time — and she recommended they adopt that name specifically to force other incipient centres of feminist organizing to come under their umbrella. They felt that it was important to impose some structure on all this energy and activism.

"Ms. Cameron, who has agreed to act as Honorary Solicitor for the Status of Women Council, advised us to call ourselves the Newfoundland Status of Women Council. By adding 'Newfoundland' to our title, we make sure that any other group who wants to start a Status of Women Council in the province will have to affiliate with us," noted the minutes of a NSWC executive council meeting for June 22, 1972. That decision would later prove controversial, and spark a vitriolic debate amongst feminists across the province as other Status of Women Centres opened in other towns and cities in Newfoundland and Labrador. Finally in 1984, the NSWC voted to change its name to the St. John's Status of Women Council (SJSOWC). In doing so, it effectively ceded any lingering aspirations to direct the provincial women's movement from St. John's; the Centres would instead form a more egalitarian network called the Provincial Action Network on the Status of Women to coordinate their efforts.

Between June and September of 1972, the steering committee laid the groundwork for the new organization, filing articles of incorporation, developing a constitution, identifying grants and other preparatory work. The NSWC newsletter made its first appearance in July of that year – 200 people subscribed for the initial issue. It was produced jointly with Woman's Place, underscoring the collaborative approach the two groups sought to build.

The steering committee also struggled with what to do about the issue of abortion, which had caused such division at the May 1972 founding meeting. According to Shirley Goundrey:

... the committee discussed its position here very thoroughly and decided that even though supporting repeal of the abortion law meant losing the support of a lot of women, it was considered impossible for a group concerned with the status of women to ignore the right of a woman to decide whether she will give birth or not... The decision reached by the committee was that individual women could and should be responsible for the moral decision of whether to have an abortion or to carry the pregnancy to term, and that society's role was to back up this decision by providing safe, legal abortions in dignity on the one hand, and good day care and health support on the other (Goundrey 1975).

The first general meeting of the NSWC was held on September 18, 1972, with 52 charter (founding) members. An election of officers was scheduled for the next general meeting on November 16 at City Hall. The group received its first grant from the Secretary of State, basically a start-up grant for $500. The Steering Committee's proposed position on abortion was also presented to the members in attendance, and approved. Things were off to a fine start.

In February 1973, the NSWC received a $3000 grant from the Secretary of State's Women's Program. Rather than proceed with its own ambitious plans to open a Centre along the model and scale proposed by Kreps, the NSWC offered to provide these funds toward the continued operation of the Woman's Place Centre, and collaborate with the Woman's Place CR collective group to expand the Centre's operations. Their hope was that the two groups could operate the centre jointly. The exact nature of this relationship would remain unclear and ambiguous during much of its lifespan. Some volunteers recall Woman's Place as being in charge of the space and this is also reflected by the collective's later refusal to discuss use of the space with NSWC immediately before the two groups split. At times, minutes refer to Woman's Place as an autonomous collective "under the NSWC umbrella," though the meaning of this is ambiguous. The two groups shared newsletter production duties. In the beginning, the two groups agreed to alternate responsibility for the newsletter – one month it would be produced by NSWC, the next month by the Woman's Place collective. The covers and masthead even changed monthly to reflect this. This approach created some tension as the months progressed; sometimes issues turned into a form of dialogue, with the two groups criticizing each other's articles. The absence of a single editor to oversee the newsletter was criticized by some, and an effort was eventually made to amalgamate both newsletters together.

Much like the title "Status of Women Centre," which was adopted by other women's groups across the country, the name "A Woman's Place" was also adopted by several early women's centres across the country, including centres in Toronto, Kitchener-Waterloo, Halifax and Winnipeg. The groups however were completely unaffiliated and all operated independently of each other.

Despite the initial efforts by the two feminist groups in St. John's to collaborate, it didn't take long for divisions to arise within the incipient movement. According to a reflection written in 1975 by Shirley Goundrey, the differing organizational structures of both groups contributed to tensions. A Woman's Place "operated by consensus and were unstructured." The NSWC, by contrast, "was operating as a structured organization, albeit a rather loose and informal structure."

Speaking to students at Memorial University's Women's Resource Centre in 1982, Barbara Doran, representing the NSWC, presented a similar impression of the two groups' ideological differences. *The Muse* reporter Martha Muzychka reported: "'These two groups represented two factions,' said Doran, 'the NSWC as a structured group and the Women's Place as unstructured.' The two groups came in conflict over abortion and they both received a lot of bad press" (Muzychka 1982).

Murphy reflected on the group's organizing dynamic half a century later:

Woman's Place ran as a collective. That meant we had to talk through issues till we could all agree on a consensus. This process requires hours of work and some frustrating times in decision-making. It can result in better decisions sometimes and better analysis. But it is time consuming and can be painful in an atmosphere where we were all learning – different ages, personalities, values and classes.

I was likely a lot more class conscious than most. I grew up poor, prejudiced against privilege and against those who had so much. I also, at that time, thought like an Islander and was not open to people from outside NL. I gained self-esteem through the women's movement, and identity. I am sure that in my brashness I did not make it easy for those around me. Many were patient with me, fortunately. That dynamic no doubt fuelled disagreements (Murphy 2022).

Murphy also recognized differences in how the two groups operated.

"The NSWC found it necessary to have some sort of structure with designated women responsible for certain specific actions, on a continuing basis and on an ad hoc basis. [A Woman's Place] collective worked on a consensus basis and seemed to emphasize working with individual women through CR groups and generally appeared to be more radical," she explained. (Ibid.).

Lynn Hartery, in her graduate thesis on the origins of the Rape Crisis Centre, argues that the NSWC was fundamentally grounded in liberal feminism, and in its early years at least, reflected the liberal priorities of the older middle and upper class women who had spearheaded the Royal Commission and the community organizing which ensued. One outcome of this, she argues, is that early NSWC priorities were focused around economic equality for women (equality in hiring, childcare accessibility, divorce laws), and issues like violence against women were not as prominent. "Violence against women, rape and wife battering were not on their immediate agenda... As the [NSWC] focus was the implementation of the recommendations of the RCSW, it too was liberal in its mandate and goals," she writes (Hartery 2001).

The more radical feminists of A Woman's Place appear to have placed a higher emphasis on violence against women. According to activists interviewed by Hartery, "the members of [Woman's Place] collective also assisted rape victims... the members of the Women's Place collective welcomed women into their homes, considering this the best way to assist them. [They] characterised the group as more radical than the NSWC" (Ibid.).[25]

Curiously, the NSWC even took the step of publicly stating they were not an "anti-rape" centre, in response to a media article which had characterised them as such. While the members were obviously anti-rape, Hartery suggests this statement was an effort to distinguish the organization's primary goals

---

[25] In an interview, Cathy Murphy, an early Woman's Place activist, noted that although Woman's Place were vocal critics of the police on issues of sexual violence, the police later came to seek their assistance. She recounted one incident involving an elderly woman in Portugal Cove who left her abusive and alcoholic husband. The woman was all alone – this was prior to the internet or even cell phones – and had no place to go, so she wound up in a gravel pit and built a fire. "We got a call from the RCMP... the RCMP patrol car was driving along down around St. Phillips somewhere, and they saw smoke rising out of a pit that's down there. So of course they went in, they figured there was probably kids in there with a fire going or something in this pit... so they go in and they find this old woman. She's in there and she's got her cat with her, and you know there was no cell phones, she had no access to a phone or anything, so she lit the fire and she was sending up smoke signals to draw attention! So the RCMP officer calls me, and he says: 'Can you believe it? She sent up smoke signals!' I thought what the hell? So anyway she was such a nice woman, she came to us and she brought her cat, and she was with us for a little while."

from those of more radical groups: "I speculate that the NSWC did not want to appear too radical, considering that violence against women was associated with the radical feminist movement." Hartery does, however, point out that some of the activists she interviewed disagreed with her analysis of this, and argued with her that radical feminists were also part of the early NSWC cadre (Hartery 2001).

An editorial written by Vicky Hammond for the October-November 1972 issue of the newsletter reflected on the tensions that were clearly emerging between the two groups:

The first meeting I attended here was one of the original Woman's Place-NSWC meetings. It was big and energetic... There was no president and no secretary but it happened and the minutes even got written... I said then that I didn't think I could function under heavy structure and I didn't believe bureaucracy and feminism could co-exist. Now I believe more than ever that I was right and that I should have stuck to my feelings. There seems to be a great deal of interest in making the women's movement respectable. Some women don't seem entirely aware that feminism is a radical and revolutionary movement absolutely committed to effecting major changes. Why should we of all people want to maintain the status quo?... NSWC seems to be mainly concerned with society's (men's) view of women and of the NSWC structure itself. We are concerned with breaking down an archaic sexist structure.[26] We should also be working towards a generally high level of political awareness for sexism is only a part of a far larger process. I think that we should be very careful of bureaucracy and all its attendant evils and question structure at every opportunity – it is one of our biggest hassles and it seems to be causing a great deal of damage (NSWC 1972).

Hammond goes on to question whether the organization needed positions, memberships, minutes, and other bureaucratic elements: "couldn't committees and persons come and go as they're needed working together for good change?" She disputes that this is idealistic, and points as an example to the 1972 student occupation of Memorial University, where an ad hoc occupation force of hundreds of students managed to form spontaneous groups to feed, house and maintain the occupation for several days.

Reflecting on events fifty years later, Hammond recalls her feelings about the creeping bureaucratization within the women's movement. She has memories of one of the early NSWC meetings, held at the Grad House on Military Road.

I was quite dismayed by that whole meeting. To me I could kind of see our grassroots, non-hierarchical understanding of how we operated [change]. I guess as it grew maybe it needed some structure, but I didn't think so. And I also was dismayed that it had suddenly become about recognition in the larger community. Some of the stuff they were interested in was so different than

---

[26] It is unclear, but I believe Hammond is referring to Woman's Place when she says "we," drawing a distinction between the two groups.

what we had started with. They were interested in equal pay. And I mean I'm all for equal pay, but then it seemed to me to be kind of jumping the gun. I was more interested in just recruiting a lot more women and just helping women who were struggling in their lives. That's harder to articulate – and I don't think I articulated it well – but I do remember that was how I felt (Hammond 2023).

Conflict between the two collectives also arose over the intertwined issues of both class and sexuality. Gray and Burnham, in their history of this period, observe that members of the Woman's Place collective viewed NSWC members as "middle class" while members of NSWC viewed the collective as "radical" (Pope & Burnham 1999: 172-173).

One of the trigger points of these divisions and the subsequent split between the two groups involved, of all things, an argument over curtains. The more liberal, middle-class women wanted to put curtains up in their new office space, but the more working-class radicals were outraged at the idea and considered curtains too bourgeois.[27]

Gray remembered the curtain incident.

I thought it was silly, the whole thing. I couldn't see what all the fight was all about. But I could also understand from what people said – you know you get a house and the first bourgeois thing you do is you put up curtains. The more radical women said: 'Look if you need for people not to look in, just pin a bedsheet up over the window.' But part of it was that they went and made the curtains. It wasn't just that they bought curtains – it was that they thought it was important and so somebody made them and brought them in. But it was not well accepted. I think they were kind of a girly, pinky girly kind of [curtain]. But yeah it was a fight. A silly thing, but people did take offense (Gray 2023).

In their thesis research, Dopler interviewed another founding mother about the incident.

This woman remembered the conflict coming to a head over the NSWC members wanting to hang curtains at the Centre and the "radicals" who ran the Centre challenging this as middle-class and politically incorrect. Later in our discussion she stated that most of the "radicals" were probably lesbians. Lesbians recall the story very differently, remembering it distinctly as a "lesbian purge" and noting that lesbian involvement was minimal or nonexistent from that point until the early 1980s (Dopler 1996).

Murphy remembers the fight over curtains, but in her recollection, it was part of a broader disagreement over what the space should be like. "Tensions were growing over more radical feminism [versus] a more mainstream ap-

---

[27] While several of the early activists I interviewed remembered the curtain incident, some declined to comment on the record about it; I believe they feared it might make the early activists appear silly. But I believe it's important to mention since it illustrates quite starkly the growing division between liberal and more radical forms of feminism.

proach. Some of the mainstream women wanted to have a nice, brightly painted room that was intended to invite women in to explore and discuss issues and perhaps feminism." The radicals were critical about the idea of a prettified room with sofas and coffee tables.

"Curtains were discussed but never hung," Murphy said. "We would have taken them down anyway, the radicals would have taken them down. We wouldn't have allowed it. It was a real turf battle at that point."

However, she recalls walking in one day and discovering one of the rooms in question had just been painted bright yellow. Not impressed, she slapped an abortion rights sticker on the freshly painted wall.

"That was very confrontational for sure," she recalled, chuckling. She said it led to a brief period of tense, hostile silence between the two factions. Helen Porter, one of the volunteers who subsequently became an acclaimed novelist, eventually tried to reconcile the two sides. Murphy later found out Porter had been one of the ones advocating for a friendly, welcoming room (with curtains), but she said that Porter also always made an effort to understand the views of others and to find common ground between the sometimes-divergent activist ideologies. Porter was a bit of a mediator in that respect.

I had a lot of respect for Helen Porter. A few days after [the abortion sticker incident], she said to me one night – I still remember it – she said to me that night: 'You know, there's three rooms in this place. There's enough room for the kind of activism that you're into, and enough room for other things too.' That night I had the conversation with Helen Porter I felt, like I could have done better here (Murphy 2022).

In addition to class politics, sexuality lurked in the background as a simmering source of tension. Sandy Pottle, one of the early CHAN members, recalls the leadership of the Human Rights Association in those early years being very concerned that the growing feminist movement not associate itself with lesbianism.

The head of the Human Rights Association… was at the time very concerned about having anything like [lesbianism] associated with the Women's Centre. He said it was sensationalism. And this is the kind of point of view that some of the founding members of the Women's Centre had – they just did not want to be associated with that (Pottle 2022).

Marion Atkinson, another early volunteer, also had the impression that sexuality played a significant underlying role in the tensions between the NSWC and Woman's Place collectives. In a summary of her impressions, she said:

When the women's movement started out, there was a division of ideas. There was a gay group, and a not-gay group. The not-gay group were mainly middle-class wives with time on their hands, and they were rather conservative. Then bit by bit, over the next couple of years, more and more people got involved and with this mix came the gelling of the two groups. We didn't start off friendly. I was only in my early twenties, but a lot of the women there then were in their thirties and forties and fifties. They were established. So they were kind of progressive and kind of conservative at the same time. Now in retrospect it was good to have them, because they had a lot of time and income. That's because they didn't have to go to work. The rest of us had to work for a living. The Woman's Place was pro-gay. But the other older women didn't know how to handle that. But now eventually they learned. Oh yes, they learned. As the younger crowd got involved, the attitudes changed, and the older women had to change with it (Atkinson 2021).

Shirley Goundrey was one of the founding mothers of the NSWC; she died in 2006 (her obituary also lists her as a founder of Woman's Place). Her daughter Jane was a teenager during this period, and her mother often involved her in the work they were doing. Jane recalls some of the tensions of the time.

I think it probably was the first time a lot of these middle-class intelligent housewives, many of whom had felt stifled in their lives by their gender, found themselves in contact with women who were of a different sexual orientation. It was a whole learning experience for them too. I know there was a bit of: 'Oh!' 'Oh my goodness!' But in the end they did manage to include them, to their credit. I certainly remember meeting some of those women who were clearly – even to my inexperienced eyes – not going to end up being mothers and housewives (Goundrey 2022).

Jane Goundrey's family were part of the 'come-from-away' generation brought in to help establish and grow Memorial University. Her father was a Canadian economist whose work had taken the family around the world. He had worked at the United Nations in New York, and the family had also lived in Sri Lanka, Zambia, England, and a variety of other North American cities. He was recruited to chair the Economics Department at Memorial; immediately prior to that the family had been living in London, England.

"We were right in the middle of the flower power era, living in Chelsea, and then we moved to Newfoundland," explained Jane. "In the 1970s Newfoundland was a culture shock."

Jane – fresh from four years on the fashionable streets of London – was enrolled at Booth Memorial High School in St. John's.

Quite seriously, the first week I was at Booth really the only word that I clearly understood in any sentence was the F-word. And you really heard that word, in the corridors! I thought I had died and gone to hell, that's the truth. I was fourteen and in Grade 11. I didn't fit in at all.

I had come right from Chelsea, at the top of King's Road. I had a gold lamme maxi-coat which I promise you was the height of fashion in London, but I remember walking home from Booth with little boys following me on the road, laughing at me and going: 'Where did you get that coat, Miss?' People didn't have TV's. St. John's was really kind of back in the 1950s (Ibid.).

Jane's mother, Shirley, threw herself into feminist organizing work. She brought home magazines and books for Jane to read.

"We had quite the little library of feminist literature – Betty Friedan and Gloria Steinem and more."

Jane also joined one of the budding consciousness-raising groups, and began volunteering with the Woman's Place collective as well. At that time high school in the province only went up to Grade 11, and so the year after her arrival Jane started her undergraduate studies at Memorial University. She immediately joined *The Muse* student newspaper, and wound up establishing the first iteration of what would go on to become the Women's Resource Centre on campus (today it's known as Intersections: A Resource Centre for Marginalized Genders).

We had a room in the Students' Union building, and all sorts of women's literature. The Students' Union was reasonably progressive, and I knew a few of the people from being on the newspaper. So I started [the Women's Resource Centre]. We got funding from the Students' Union for a room and for a library and I staffed it. I managed to get one or two other women who also took shifts there. I have to say it wasn't well-attended. But it was advertised in the student newspaper. And I did have people come in and ask questions. I was pretty young – just sixteen.

I remember one young woman coming in, I can't remember if she was from St. John's or not, and she was struggling with the whole concept of feminism, because everyone around her thought that feminism was the work of the devil. She was starting to question that idea, but she was worried and asked me: 'Is it possible we're wrong and they're right?' I said: 'No, I don't think so.' But back then it was a novel idea that women were being societally oppressed (Ibid.).

Tensions between differing varieties of feminism cut across a range of identities: age and generational differences; sexuality; class and socio-economic status. These differences could manifest in things as simple as style of dress, which for some women could also be a potent expression of resistance and change.

"It was fun, going out dressed in those heavy boots and heavy military jackets and stuff like that," recalled Gray. "That was very liberating to be able to wear that sort of stuff because before that I'd worn heels and all the things that women are trained to do – nylons and heels and skirts.

When I started at Memorial University, in 1969, during my first year I had a math class. And the woman [instructor] still wore those black cloaks that [instructors] used to wear at Memorial. And the rule at the time was that you had to wear a dress. Women had to wear a dress. I was staying with my aunt and uncle at the time, and I stomped out of there one morning, I wore the dress but I had jeans rolled up underneath. When I got to the university I changed into jeans and I went into the math class. And this woman [instructor] raises her hand up with her long black cape and she says: 'You! You!' And I realized she was talking to me. She said: 'You! Get out! And don't ever come back here unless you have a skirt on!' So that was it for me and math. I never went back to the class. But there was a lot of that kind of attitude around (Gray 2022).

As the volunteer bases of both Woman's Place and NSWC tried to share the new centre, other points of contention emerged. Abortion remained a source of tension, although abortion rights were fervently supported by leading organizers of both collectives. The groups' newsletter ran petitions in support of repealing abortion restrictions, and physical copies of petitions were on display for signing at the Centre. A petition in support of abortion rights organized by Canadian authors June Callwood and Pierre Berton received particular uptake, and NSWC representatives took the signed petitions with them to lobby meetings with the six St. John's MHAs. NSWC member Elinor Newbauer participated in a national lobby session at Parliament in Ottawa, and was subsequently elected to the national board of the Committee Advocating Repeal of Abortion Laws (CARAL – today the group's acronym is Canadian Abortion Rights Action League). In January 1975, the NSWC further entrenched its pro-choice position when it decided to take out an official organizational membership with CARAL.

Murphy's recollection is that the earliest meetings at Woman's Place were small and not well attended. "It was more of an information collection hub than anything else," she said. While Woman's Place established and resourced CR groups, most of the members of those groups were "only loosely connected to Woman's Place. It was more a centre to share info and connect on issues."

Some of the meetings she attended there stand out in Murphy's memory. She remembers that one of the early meetings featured a lesbian activist from Toronto, although she doesn't remember the woman's name or who invited her.[28]

She worked as part of a collective in Toronto. She introduced me to the term 'gay' and spoke about why lesbians needed their own organizations separate from gay men, while also needing to join organizations to fight for rights... I remember I struggled to keep an open mind and not judge. I didn't get the personal part of being gay, however I did gain an awareness as to why it is political. For us in the women's movement at that time we talked a lot about how the personal is political, so it was not a stretch to make the connections (Murphy 2022).

The women present were moved by the lesbian activist's presentation. "Collectively we committed to ensure that the struggle to gain lesbian rights was part of our agenda," said Murphy.

Ann Escott was one of the organizers with CHAN, and as part of its outreach the group reached out to the nascent NSWC to speak to them about their own organization and the push for queer rights. Although the NSWC would later come to play an important role in the queer rights movement and would form close connections with subsequent queer organizations, its relationship

---

[28] It is possible this was one of the activists from the Toronto-based Women and Film Collective which put off the film festival at Memorial University in 1973; other activists recall them being queer-positive advocates during their visit to the province.

with CHAN would remain a distant one in those early years. As Escott recalls:

When the Women's Centre started out, there were some lesbians associated with it, but it was a fairly homophobic situation. I knew there were lesbians who were associated with it in the beginning, but things were fairly homophobic. And of course any feminist was always accused of being a lesbian in the worst sort of way, so there was really no support or encouragement on either side, for a long time (Escott 2022).

Nonetheless, Escott and Pottle did attend a meeting of the early NSWC as part of their outreach work.

We went there one night and talked to them. It was supposed to be an open meeting for anyone in the public, but there were only about four people who showed up and they were all members of the [NSWC] Board. They were somewhat nervous, so it was really a no-go. They were very polite and thanked us for coming, but we never saw or heard from them again (Ibid.).

Murphy also recalls a discussion centred on the publication *Our Bodies Our Selves*, which she feels may have incorporated a discussion of transgender identities, although she doesn't remember any specifics.

On Sunday April 15, 1973, the Women's Centre moved. A notice went out to members, acknowledging some of the confusion and concerns about the relationship between the two groups.

The Women's Place and the Newfoundland Status of Women Council are moving Sunday, April 15 to new, larger and cheery premises at 203 Water Street (third floor [above Arcade]). Our telephone will remain the same, 722-4533. We want to announce to our friends that we will occupy the premises jointly. We know that many have sometimes been confused about the relationship between The Women's Place and NSWC. We want everyone to understand that we emphatically support each other's ultimate goals – to improve the lot of women in society. And we want to make clear that our programs are autonomous and distinct; we neither ask each other for prior approval, nor do we judge or interfere with each other's activities. We do this, not because we cannot agree, but because we are convinced that the Women's Movement must have more than one approach. Our movement will succeed only if we can pursue solutions to women's disadvantaged position in society in our own ways – without conflict amongst ourselves (NSWC Newsletter: April 1973).

The notice was signed "Yours, for all Women's Equality, The Women's Place-NSWC."

By now the volunteer base of activists was growing, and space was getting cramped. The new larger space allowed Woman's Place to grow: a main office, two meeting rooms, and even a telephone. Gert Maybe began facilitating courses at the centre for women interested in videography; Liz Genge offered courses in mechanics and electrical work.

The growing movement was also becoming more confrontational. Abortion had surged to a place of prominence on the national agenda, in part because of the Royal Commission's recommendation for abortion on demand. CARAL intensified its lobbying to repeal abortion laws; anti-abortion activists, particularly with the Catholic Church, intensified legal and protest efforts against them.

One of the important roles served by the early Women's Centre was as an abortion referral and support service. Sandy Pottle, one of the early CHAN members, became a local St. John's area chapter representative for CARAL. She'd gotten involved in helping with abortion referrals as an undergraduate at Memorial University.

We used to arrange abortions for people when I was a prefect at Squires House [student residence] at Memorial. I went to Montreal once, during the FLQ crisis! I had never been out of Newfoundland in my life, and I took a young woman there to have an abortion. She was only seventeen, and I was nineteen I suppose. I had tried everywhere in St. John's to get her an abortion and that was not going to happen, so we ended up going to Montreal. She was so young, and it turned out she was past the twelve weeks – just past the fucking twelve weeks! – so we had to get her a fake ID to say she was 21 years old, and then have her appear in front of a panel of three psychiatrists in order to have them approve the abortion. The decision didn't come immediately, so we had to then come back to St. John's. Meanwhile I was missing all my classes – and I had some pretty heavy courses, I'm amazed I passed at all! Her roommate then went back with her to Montreal. But then I discovered a place in New York that was much easier. People could fly directly to New York and then bizarre things would happen – a taxicab would pick them up and there'd be code words and all sorts of bloody strange things. But you could go to New York in the morning and come back to St. John's by various routes in the afternoon and it was in fact cheaper than getting an abortion in Montreal (Pottle 2022).

In Newfoundland and Labrador, the issue came up with increasing frequency as organizations started taking official positions for or against abortion. Activists from Woman's Place/NSWC started crashing anti-abortion meetings when they heard about them. Murphy remembers one such undertaking when a local service organization (she forgets precisely which one, though it might have been Knights of Columbus) put an anti-abortion resolution on their agenda at a meeting in St. John's. Some women who were affiliated with the group and were secretly pro-choice contacted the feminists to give them a heads-up. Pro-choice activists infiltrated the meeting, and then when the topic came up, they seized the mics and began speaking loudly in support of abortion until they were removed from the building.

"We were not well received," chuckles Murphy. But it didn't deter them: they repeated the tactic a few more times.

Another collaborative effort between NSWC and Woman's Place involved winning women the right to enter the city's downtown bars and pubs. It seems inconceivable today, but in the 1970s, many downtown bars refused admission to women as a matter of policy. These bars would only provide male washrooms and used this as an excuse to deny entry to women.

Sharon Gray reminisced about the time:

I remember one bar, I was living on Mullock Street and it was just up around the corner. One night Mary Walsh dropped over to see if I wanted to go downtown to have a drink or something, and she said: 'Just for fun let's go and see if we can get a drink at this bar up the street.' So we both went in. I think we both had jackboots on – big heavy hiking boots – and we didn't look like women, we looked like we were ready for stomping. And we just came right into the bar and Mary says: 'I'll have a beer please.' The guy looks at her and he goes: 'We don't serve women here.' And I said: 'I'll have another beer on top of that!' And he said: 'You can't stay here! You've got to leave!' So we stood there and made a fuss for a while. We didn't expect to get in so we laughed and then we went on down to the Ship Inn (Gray 2022).

The activists contacted the province's fledgling Human Rights Commission, and were told that in order for them to do anything about this problem, they needed a test case. They needed a woman to be denied entry to a bar, and then file a complaint. So a group of Woman's Place activists got together and went on a pub-crawl one night through the downtown, challenging men-only bars wherever they found them.

"That was fun," recalled Gray, who also participated in the feminist pub-crawl. "I remember that. That was such fun."

"We had such a ball that night," recalled Murphy. "It was so much fun."

Murphy was not yet 21 years old – the legal drinking age – so she would not even have been allowed into the bars regardless.

But that didn't matter because we never got in any, anyway. There were people who probably didn't have much intent at hanging out at pubs anyway, but we knew the discrimination was there and we had talked to the human rights [commission] about it, and they needed a case. They needed [a test case] filed with them. So we hatched a plan and carried it out one evening and we had a ball with it. We got thrown out of six or seven places, or not allowed in – we didn't even get through the door! (Murphy 2022).

"That was one of the fun nights," recalled Murphy with a chuckle.

The complaint was filed, and out of that boisterously fun night the women of St. John's won the right to access the city's bars. The activists were having fun, but just as importantly they were making tangible change in women's lives.

Yet tensions between the radical and mainstream factions continued to rise. One day, when Murphy was staffing the centre, two women came in. They explained they were Trotskyites (a variety of Communism) from Toronto, on a cross-country tour of women's centres. They tried to recruit Murphy to the Trotskyite cause, without much success. Murphy did agree to let them leave their materials – stickers, pamphlets, posters – on the centre's information table. Later, when other volunteers came in and saw a Communist 'Workers Unite!' poster on the wall, tensions flared.

Jane Goundrey recalled the tensions that were already high around being a feminist at the time, let alone a lesbian feminist.

I can honestly say that you would not believe the push-back – the opposition – to what to me was the very self-evident concept that women were second-class citizens. There was trouble even getting that agreed upon. So I can see that the women who were trying to get that concept across would have been concerned that the gay rights people were adding an element that would just not have been acceptable to anybody. And they just didn't want to be associated with it. The phrase bra-burning was scattered widely at the time. There was verbal abuse thrown at people when they raised feminist issues.

A lot of these women were talented, middle class, fairly well educated women who had had their lives shut down by becoming mothers. That is what happened to a lot of the women in the 1970s who got feminism. They were frustrated because they had so much potential that was being shut down. I have a friend who had to take her wedding ring off and go by 'Miss' when she went back to nursing school... and then on the weekend she could put her wedding ring back on and live with her husband. Because back then when you got married, if you were a nursing student you got chucked out of the program. Flight attendants got chucked. You could not work if you were a married woman, in so many careers. You had to choose. So a lot of these women were frustrated. A friend of mine back in the 1970s was teaching with the Catholic school board in St. John's and she was fired because it was discovered that she was living with a married man.

There was so much hatred and misunderstanding and intolerance. Truly, you could have affected your career by coming out and saying you were a feminist back then. So to come out and actually be associated with a group that was working for gay rights... I do remember there was a lot of discord about how are we going to deal with this issue (Goundrey 2022).

Joan Scott was another early volunteer at the Women's Centre. She came to Newfoundland from England in 1962 when her then-husband got a job at Memorial University. She eventually did her undergraduate studies at Memorial, taught in the school system for a period, and then obtained her PhD, after which she became a professor at Memorial herself. She remembers the early years during which the Women's Centre moved offices frequently, and the back-handed debates which often arose about the role of lesbians in the movement.

It was a hot issue, because you didn't want 'them' to take over, did you?. There were fears that the lesbians were categorized as different and they might give the rest of us 'nice' women a bad name. So that was on the go, and it was actively discussed as to whether they should be kept out or not. Oh, yes. But the problem was that several of them were major pillars of the Women's Centre and it would have all fallen down if they'd left.

There was a sort of identification of [lesbians] as being somehow not respectable. The question certainly came up, it was a hot issue for a time. Eventually the Women's Centre got over it and moved on with things. They realized that these people were very valuable (Scott 2021).

By December 1973, conflict between the two groups had taken centre stage again. Looming construction work required a relocation of the Centre from 203 Water Street. NSWC took advantage of this opportunity to extricate themselves from the relationship with A Woman's Place, and for a brief period both groups would operate their own separate Women's Centres. A December 13, 1973, communique to NSWC members explained the situation:

The Committee elected at the NSWC Annual Meeting in November, was directed by the membership at our meeting December 3rd to ask for a chance to talk over with the Women's Collective the future of Women's Place. We were flatly refused this opportunity so were faced with no alternative but to take independent action and find our own quarters. However, both groups look forward to cooperating in the future on projects since we both are concerned with women's liberation.

The NSWC selected as its inaugural solo location the second floor of 142-144 Duckworth Street (above the Cod Jigger), former location of Second Story Bookstore. This was next to the original location of A Woman's Place, and the NSWC was able to absorb that former office as well, providing a larger space than ever.

A Woman's Place moved to 4 Prescott Street, where it intersects with Water Street. This location included a public storefront, with large windows facing the busy street. The activists took full advantage of this, filling up the windows with a large pro-choice abortion rights poster that could be seen by everyone on the street (confrontational though the tactic was, to the best of Murphy's recollection no one ever complained).

With the volunteer base now split between two groups, Woman's Place found it more difficult to keep the office staffed. They began to prioritize abortion rights activism. A Woman's Place was, at the time, the primary location for women seeking information or access to abortion (their posters on the street-facing window advertised this). Abortions were not at this time performed in the province, and many NL women seeking abortions went to New York City. In the pre-Internet era, with long distance telephone access prohibitively expensive, it was difficult for women to know where to go or what to do to access abortions. A Woman's Place would help with these arrangements, putting women in contact with providers in New York City, arranging appointments, arranging accommodations for the women if and as necessary. As Murphy recalls:

We continued to meet as a collective and tried to staff the office enough to receive visitors and to keep up abortion referrals... We were really too few to keep the Place going. We did plan and carry out a small project on women and film, bringing women's films to communities in and around NL and southern Labrador (Murphy 2022).

That was one of the final projects of A Woman's Place.

"We closed our doors, which were often closed anyway, a few months later," said Murphy. "Of course, for a feminist, feminism never ends so we continued to be active in the community as individuals."

While Woman's Place and NSWC had split organizationally, the split didn't appear to rupture the ability of the women to work together. Many friendships continued across both groups, and individuals continued to collaborate on the issues that concerned them. For her part, Murphy, along with Liz Genge, proceeded to design and open the province's first Transition House for women trying to leave violent situations, for which they received a one-year government grant. Murphy stated that it successfully demonstrated the urgent need for such a facility – something feminist activists had been arguing for some time. The Transition House closed after that first year, but another one would open shortly thereafter under the direction of Gerry Rogers and the NSWC.

As the NSWC parted ways with A Woman's Place, a much-needed boost to their work came when the federal government began moving toward providing operational funding to women's centres. In early 1974, Jane Taylor was hired by the Women's Programme of the Secretary of State to conduct a survey of women's centres across the country. She visited dozens of them, from BC to NL, and produced a report for the Secretary of State. Her stirring report helped inform government's decision on if and how to support the growing women's movement – a decision which was seen as part of government's obligation to follow through on the recommendations of the Royal Commission. Taylor's report cast no doubt on the vitality of feminist activism in Canada.

Let me state categorically, right at the beginning, there is a Women's Movement alive, well and struggling in Canada. There can be no other name but that for the amount of time, energy, and effort spent by so many women working towards the same goals and all moving in the same direction. Chaotic, uncontrolled, and confused though it may seem as a whole, it nevertheless has a singleness of purpose that is almost incredible when you realize that it is the product of a spontaneous, self-directed desire for change.

A concrete example of women's desire to change their status has been the formation of women's centres... The motivating force behind the formation and execution of a women's centre is the recognition of the need for a 'space' specific to the articulation of women's present and future position (Taylor 1974).

Taylor's report was a heartfelt, moving paean to the diversity of women's centres across the country. She offered a survey of the types of work they were doing, and the various organizational models they had developed. Her report is written in jargon-free, honest, empathic writing; she situates herself as a feminist activist whose life was also changed by the centres she worked with.

Centres come in all sizes, shapes, and descriptions ranging from the spacious old office, with an incredible view of the surrounding mountains through its windows, in Nelson, B.C.; to the small storefront office with even the bathroom doing double duty as a darkroom, at the Woman's Place in St. John's, Nfld (Ibid.).

Taylor did put her finger on the issue of the class divisions that threatened the incipient movement (and which had become pronounced in St. John's):

[A]lways lurking in the background whenever the subject of what sort of community do you serve came up was that monster that haunts the women's movement, the words either scathingly, sheepishly, or belligerently (though never proudly) uttered, 'THE MIDDLE-CLASS WOMAN'. Somebody is going to have to do something about her and her importance to the women's movement soon. Not me, not this time — though it's tempting (Ibid.).

Taylor warned that the predominance of "middle-class women" involved in some – though not all – women's centres risked excluding many of those women most in need of support: "the immigrant women, the [Indigenous] women, the rural women, and the just plain poor women" (Ibid.).

Taylor also addressed the issue of splits within the women's movement. She drew on the example of one city she visited, where a split at the city's first women's centre led to the establishment of two centres. It's very likely she was referring to the situation in St. John's. Much like the activists I spoke with, she sought to frame the split in optimistic terms.

One of the most successful of so-called splits has developed into two centres in one city, thereby reaching even more women. All centres should be so lucky! As far as I am concerned the more such 'splits' the better. There are definitely divergences of opinion – no movement dealing with topics as emotionally laden as the women's movement does could be without them. True, some women are turned off a particular centre but I've yet to meet a feminist who has become an anti-feminist because of a disagreement. Out of every division I've heard, something of value has evolved. If we can capitalize on our differences then we add new strength (Ibid.).

Finally, the perceptive and no-holds-barred Taylor also put her finger on one of the sources of splits which was already impacting the women's centres in St. John's:

It may at first seem strange that one of the most fundamental concepts of the women's movement, that of sisterhood, should cause problems but it is beginning to. It is not a problem of a magnitude to disastrously affect the running of a centre, but it is one that is being recognized as such. Sometimes it surfaces as a problem if and when lesbians are a known part of a centre. This brings about a recognition of the extent of women's diversity in background and experience, and pits it against the strength of the desire to regard all women as equals (Ibid.).

Taylor concluded her report with an astute observation on the erratic, non-linear course of the women's movement:

From what I've seen so far of the women's movement I would say that it is not so much a solid, steady, advancing line but rather small thrusts, some further ahead than others, some stationary, some moving laterally, and some even marking time. A lot of it is very like guerrilla warfare: isolated attacks then withdrawal (Ibid.).

After parting ways with Woman's Place, the NSWC undertook to operate a centre of its own. The now solo outfit first operated out of the 144 Duckworth Street location, but not for long. Only a month after they moved in, a fire broke out in the building. It was caused by "an overheated stove on the floor above being used to thaw frozen pipes" and although the building and office itself were saved there was extensive damage.[29] The damage necessitated another move. While the NSWC searched for a space, the damaged former office was broken into and some of their belongings stolen. The NSWC appealed to the YWCA for meeting space, but the YWCA executive declined, saying its spare rooms were needed for other purposes. Eventually the NSWC acquired use of a storefront at 64 Prescott Street. The situation there was not ideal either: the roof leaked, the pipes were frozen and neither the toilet nor heating worked. It was so cold that members had to wear gloves while using the typewriter (NSWC 1975). Additional federal funding in 1975 – International Year of the Woman – allowed the NSWC to move to better quarters at 77 Bond Street, in the former Bishop Spencer School.

The moves were taxing, and volunteers decided a more permanent location was necessary. In 1977 they took out a mortgage on a house located at 83 Military Road, directly across from the Colonial Building and Bannerman Park and more or less beside what is now Needs Convenience Store. Back then this was a convenience store called The Fountainspray, in homage to a large fountain which used to exist in front of the Colonial Building.

Drawing on generous federal programs of the time designed to encourage individuals and organizations to purchase homes and buildings, coupled with then-low housing prices in the city's downtown, 21 NSWC volunteers each contributed $100 to come up with the downpayment on the mortgage. Atkinson recalls the state of the building:

The house was a wreck, so we got a Canada Manpower grant to hire carpenters who would teach women how to do the carpentry. And we hired women to work with those carpenters, and made an apartment upstairs, to have a bit of income. So we had the Women's Centre on the main floor and basement. That was the first time we had a place of our own (Atkinson 2021).

It took several months of renovations before the house was ready to use. At the opening of the Centre on June 25, 1978, former NSWC president Shirley Goundrey – who had by then left Newfoundland – flew in from New York as special guest speaker for the launch. In her opening comments, she described

---

[29] Among the lost furniture was "a pair of drapes" – perhaps the ones that had caused such controversy the previous year?

her arrival in St. John's. Work was already underway to tidy up and renovate the newly purchased location, and her friends and fellow volunteers brought her down to the location immediately upon her arrival. "I was put to work cleaning spilled paint and taking out broken panes of glass. I had some misgivings...[but] it was a joy to see the tremendous enthusiasm of the women who came in to contribute to the repairing and cleaning during these past three days" (Goundrey 1978).

The new Women's Centre operated out of the first floor of the three-story house; the upper two floors were rented out to women. Here the Newfoundland – soon-to-be-renamed St. John's – Status of Women Centre would grow and thrive for the next two decades.

The point of providing all this history is to set the stage for the sometimes-tumultuous debates which would embroil the province's feminist movement – and already had embroiled them – over the role of lesbians within that movement. My goal has been to illustrate some of the key dynamics of the early feminist movement in this province. It was dynamic, organic, and fluid – which are positive ways of also observing that it was often chaotic and ad hoc. As with any social movement, there was no single, straightforward trajectory. It's important to resist the idea – so easy to slip into in hindsight – that a movement is sparked and then grows in a steady, linear progression. The early feminist movement was populated by a diversity of activists who often disagreed with each other. There were conservative upper class feminists; there were radical, working class feminists. There were straight women and there were lesbians. There were transgender and gender diverse people who at the time lacked the language or supportive spaces in which to grow into their own identities safely and easily; some of them would transition in later years, often after leaving a province where gender identity and expression even within queer and feminist circles was still very much rooted in a binary.

What *was* feminism? How did gender, class and sexuality fit into it? These were topics of intense discussion, debate and sometimes conflict. The traditional notion of a conservative Newfoundland existing placidly outside of 1970s radical politics in North America is quickly shattered when we come face to face with a movement where something as simple as whether or not to hang curtains could touch off conflict. Newfoundland's feminists were arguing about Trotskyism, producing fake IDs for women seeking abortion and flying them off to code-word-protected clinics in New York City; storming male-chauvinist bars that would not allow them in; and seizing the microphones at local meetings where abortion was under discussion. This is how the modern feminist movement in Newfoundland and Labrador was born: in creative, sometimes chaotic, frequently radical and often conflictual energy that nonetheless brought women and allies together in an unprecedented struggle for change.

It would be inaccurate to say this was purely a story of solidarity. Much the same way some women's organizations discriminate against trans, non-binary people and gender-diverse people today, many feminist organizations engaged in overt discrimination against lesbians during this period, and that dynamic was clearly present in the early Newfoundland feminist movement. Yet far from accepting this rejection, NL's lesbians fought back. They assumed leadership roles in the movement (many of them remaining in the closet), and their activism was such that they became "major pillars of the Women's Centre and it would have all fallen down if they'd left," as activist Joan Scott put it. They doggedly fought for rights and recognition within the feminist movement, and the movement which exists today is the result of those efforts.

The local feminist movement was greatly impacted by influence from outside of the province – in particular all the Americans and Europeans brought in to help expand Memorial University – but its activists also played key roles in shaping national and international activist movements. Influence flowed both ways. The movement progressed by fits and spurts, stumbling forward, pausing to recenter and reorient itself. Yet it was the continuity afforded by the feminist movement that would prove tremendously important to queer organizing during the later 1970s, '80s and '90s. Unlike the NSWC – which was in existence more or less continuously from its 1972 founding – the province's queer organizations were shorter-lived. The feminist movement provided a space that kept the fight for queer rights alive whenever there was a vacuum in explicitly queer organizing. And it provided the space – including the physical space – in which new queer organizations were nurtured and born. There was a great deal of overlap as the years progressed, with queer activists cultivating their activist skills through the women's centre, and vice versa.

As the feminist movement continued to grow, lesbians would come to assert even greater space and visibility within the movement.

The Rape Crisis Centre

The Rape Crisis Centre – which today operates independently as the Newfoundland and Labrador Sexual Assault Crisis and Prevention Centre – had its origins in the NSWC Women's Centre. Originally it was established as a Rape Crisis Committee, which operated out of the backroom of the Centre's house at 83 Military Road.[30] Talk about forming such a committee began following a visit by Joanie Vance, National Coordinator for the National Association for Rape Crisis Centres, to the Women's Centre in St. John's in early 1977. Opinion was mixed at the time as to whether the Women's Centre had the capacity to undertake rape crisis activities – for instance counselling and other services – but 'rape crisis' meetings began taking place among interested members be-

---

[30] Hartery states that when the mortgage on the house at 83 Military Road was taken out, a document was also drawn up guaranteeing the RCC its own room in the house (Hartery 2001).

tween April and May 1977, and an informal committee began to coalesce (Hartery 2001).

In November 1977, it was formally established as the Rape Crisis Committee (RCC), and began advertising itself in the telephone book as 'Rape Crisis Centre' (although the number was the same as the Women's Centre). In 1978, the RCC received a $1000 donation from the City of St. John's to operate a 24-hour rape crisis line. The phone line, as well as the RCC, continued to operate out of the Women's Centre. In October of 1978, a training program was developed and launched for volunteers. The Centre affiliated with the Association of Canadian Rape Crisis Centres, and in March 1982 the Atlantic Regional Rape Crisis Centres conference was hosted by the RCC at the Status of Women Centre in St. John's.

As the RCC began to grow, tensions also rose within the NSWC about what the relationship between the RCC and the NSWC ought to be. Some NSWC members were concerned about the volume of resources, time and effort being consumed by rape crisis work and some members felt political advocacy was suffering. As the RCC developed and trained its own core of volunteers, a situation resembling the NSWC-Woman's Place dynamic arose, whereby two groups with similar and overlapping yet also distinct mandates and different methods of organizing struggled to share the same physical space. Questions began to arise about whether the RCC ought to seek approval from the NSWC for its activities, or whether it had the right to operate autonomously. Neither group wanted to separate from the other – they both considered themselves part of a unified feminist movement – but they also struggled to figure out what their relationship with each other ought to be. This ambiguity would spark tensions at various points over the following decade. Various reporting and organizational relationships were experimented with, with varying outcomes, up through the 1990s when the two groups finally formally separated (Ibid.).

In her work, Hartery singles out the role of lesbians in the RCC as an important area of research, linking it to the broader significance of lesbian involvement in the NSWC and NL feminist movement as a whole:

Lesbians were heavily involved in establishing Transition House, and later Iris Kirby House, both shelters for abused women. Lesbians also played a major role in bringing the Morgentaler clinic to St. John's, making abortion more accessible to the women of Newfoundland and Labrador. In a focus group designed to discuss responses to a survey about lesbians and their lives in St. John's, one woman said that 'lesbians are the backbone of the feminist community [in St. John's]' (Ibid.).

Hartery also says that the RCC instituted formal discussions about sexuality as part of its training program for new volunteers, at a time when such discussions could sometimes prove fraught or awkward within the wider NSWC:

Part of the [RCC] training for new volunteers centred on homophobia and heterosexism to ensure volunteers could talk freely and without prejudice to a gay or lesbian caller. Discussions also revealed and challenged prejudices based on sexuality, so that the volunteers could work together. Volunteers were asked directly how they felt about lesbianism and sometimes, how it felt to be sitting next to a lesbian (Ibid.).

Reflecting on the subject, some of the former activists interviewed[31] by Hartery "said that lesbians' contribution to the RCC and the women's movement needs to be acknowledged and documented as integral part of lesbian history and lesbian work" (Ibid.).

Beginning in 1984, the RCC and SJSWC organized annual Take Back the Night marches in St. John's. These marches were already taking place in cities across North America; they spread throughout the 1970s as a way of drawing attention to and protesting the violence women experienced while walking alone at night. Several activists associate the early Take Back the Night marches with the growing visibility of lesbians in the feminist movement. The marches were a powerfully emotive space; in St. John's the marches often paused at the Supreme Court building and participants covered the building's front walls and adjacent sidewalks and buildings with feminist slogans and chalk art. Amid the spontaneous outpouring of personal and political expression, and in the presence of dozens of other women protestors, some lesbians felt more free to engage in public displays of identity or to express lesbian slogans.

"When the Take Back the Night marches started, that's when it became more obvious that there were a lot of gay women," recalled Gray. "The power of those marches was phenomenal – absolutely phenomenal."

The early history of the Rape Crisis Centre is inseparable from the woman who could effectively be referred to as its founder: Diane Duggan.

Diane Duggan was born in Halifax on June 1, 1942. Her family moved to Bell Island, NL, when she was 14 years old. She married at the age of 19 and had four children. She and her husband and children moved to Ontario, where she became involved in feminist activism through volunteering with the Women's Centre in Kitchener. She was an early abortion rights activist, and first returned to Newfoundland as a guest speaker campaigning on behalf of CARAL. In the mid-1970s, her family moved back to Newfoundland permanently (Lacey 1989).

Duggan became one of the early organizers with the Newfoundland Status of Women Council. She was a member of the Working Group on Child Sexual Abuse, a multi-agency committee established in 1985. She helped found the Rape Crisis Centre in 1977. She was the Atlantic Regional Representative with the Canadian Association of Sexual Assault Centres. She served as trustee on the Avalon Consolidated School Board since 1977, and on the Labrador School Trustees' Association from 1982-85. She was a member of the board of directors

---

[31] Some of Hartery's interviewees are named while others remain anonymous, however as her graduate thesis research was conducted in the late 1990s she had access to, and interviewed, several former activists who are no longer with us.

of Planned Parenthood NL, the provincial School Tax Authority, the St. John's Status of Women Centre, and the Canadian Mental Health Association. In 1979 she was hired as project leader for the federal Feminist Services Training Program (where she did pre-employment training and advocacy) and she had also worked as Director of Volunteer Services with Exxon House (Lacey 1989; The Evening Telegram 1989).

During those years of activism, she separated from her husband, came out as a lesbian and settled into a same-sex relationship. She became one of the most visible and loudest of the early lesbian activists (Lacey 1989).

From her earliest involvement with the NSWC she was a vocal advocate of it taking on rape crisis work, and took a lead role in the early meetings which led to the formation of the RCC. According to Hartery's history of the RCC, Duggan:

... was the face of the RCC and her name was synonymous with the Centre. She was named by other volunteers as the leader, the decision-maker, the one who took the most responsibility, the one volunteers called if they needed advice or to talk and the person members of the community called upon for information. Diane spearheaded the establishment of the RCC in 1977 and remained co-ordinator, officially or unofficially, for the next twelve years (Hartery 2001).

Hartery acknowledges that some volunteers had mixed feelings about this; while they all respected the immense outpouring of personal time and energy she threw into this work, some "criticized her apparent unwillingness to relinquish control over the Centre" (Ibid.).

In 1985, the RCC was involved in an interesting situation. In August of that year, Duggan attended an Atlantic regional conference of the Canadian Association of Sexual Assault Centres (CASAC). It was held in Prince Edward Island, under the auspices of the Charlottetown Rape Crisis Centre, and funded by the federal government. One of the speakers at the conference was Yvette Perreault, a member of the Lesbian Speakers' Bureau in Toronto.

Following the conference, one of the attendees – an employee of the Pictou County Women's Centre in Stellarton, Nova Scotia, complained to her colleagues about the "radical lesbian" nature of the event. Some of the colleagues to whom she denounced the conference were apparently lesbian themselves. At a subsequent meeting of the Women's Centre, she levelled more complaints against the Centre's "involvement with abortion counselling and lesbianism."

The women at the Pictou County Women's Centre struggled to deal with the matter internally, in the manner of feminist collectives of the day. They met with the homophobic complainant and "indicated to the worker that being truly feminist meant being totally supportive of pro-lesbian choice." The employee said that violated her personal convictions. She was subsequently asked not to return to the Centre but to complete the duration of her employment contract working from home (she had been hired on a job grant). She objected to this, claiming discrimination, and made public her accusations against "radical lesbianism" at the Centre. She submitted a report on the matter to her pastor, and the Council of Churches Nova Scotia wound up writing to the federal government to express "concern" at the situation. A series of follow-up meetings on the matter, meanwhile, led the Pictou Country Women's Centre to take a more defiant stance in opposition to homophobia. The Centre reaffirmed its inclusivity policies and committed to being even more open in its support of lesbians. According to an undated interview and article published in REAL Women Canada's newsletter, *The Interim*, the anti-lesbian employee was fired after she made her accusations public.

REAL Women Canada – a right-wing anti-feminist lobby group – seized on the case, and provided their own framing of the conference. According to a January 1986 statement from the group's BC chapter:

During the conference, it became apparent that the whole thrust of the meeting was to build a strong political movement for 'radical lesbian feminists.' (Title taken from the literature handed out.) During the discussions, it was also made clear that radical lesbians must be at the very core of the Women's Centres in Canada (supported by the Secretary of State) in order to control areas of hiring, facilitating the infiltration of others into their movement... it was firmly believed by those in attendance at the conference that Women's Centres must be restricted to lesbians or at least by radical feminists who supported lesbianism... In short, the central theme of the conference was a 'revolution, infiltration and conversion' to the lesbian movement (REAL Women Canada 1986).

Duggan, writing on behalf of CASAC Atlantic region in an undated letter, provided an explanation to her colleagues at the St. John's Status of Women Centre and elsewhere in a letter written on behalf of the RCC seeking their support. She provided a carefully worded explanation of what had transpired. She explained that for many attendees it was the first time they had discussed sexual assault in that sort of a context, and the result was "a highly charged, emotional, exciting and consciousness-raising weekend."

Among the issues discussed (and there were many!) was oppression, in all its forms and the need to educate ourselves about, and support oppressed people, particularly women. We discussed lesbianism, and how choices for women must include all [emphasis hers] choices. We talked of how important it is for all feminists to create a 'safe' place for lesbians, because there are so few safe places, especially in small communities (Duggan n.d.).

While most of the attendees found the event to provide a safe and energizing space which recharged them for their work, a few women had left preemptively, she said. One of those – the Pictou County Women's Centre employee – subsequently made her complaint. The others had initially ignored the complaint, said Duggan, because they didn't think anyone would take it seriously.

The problem, however, has escalated. This particular woman, with the as-

sistance of local right-wing support, has participated in an active campaign to discredit her local centre, centres in the Atlantic and, ultimately, centres across Canada (mostly through the organization known as 'Real Women') (Ibid.).

There had been "a telephone and mail campaign" directed against the federal government, Duggan explained, "complaining about the funding of 'radical lesbian feminist centres.'" They were seeking the de-funding of the Pictou County Rape Crisis Centre, and were also complaining about federal funding for the regional conferences. "Feminists in the Atlantic region need your support!" Duggan wrote, encouraging SJSWC activists to write letters to the federal government voicing support for the Pictou centre.

It's unclear exactly what Duggan's role in all of this was, but given her own outspoken political lesbianism it is not unlikely that she was among those advocating a strong role for lesbians in women's centres at the conference. Duggan kept the issue on the SJSWC agenda, apprising them of the ongoing campaign against lesbians organized by REAL Women, and held meetings at her house to discuss how to respond to anti-lesbianism, REAL Women, and other homophobic and anti-feminist groups. Eventually the controversy abated, although it fueled an ongoing suspicion and stigma surrounding the presence of "radical lesbianism" at women's centres (as we have already seen, this fear had already pervaded throughout the 1970s). Meanwhile, Duggan and her comrades continued to grow the Rape Crisis Centre in St. John's.

On April 27, 1989, tragedy struck: Diane Duggan died by suicide. She'd been wrestling with a variety of personal issues at the time, but there was little doubt in anyone's mind that the pressures of playing such a visible leadership role in the community had played a role in the tragedy.

"It was totally shocking to people here," reflected Roberta Buchanan, who published excerpts from Duggan's journals in the SJSWC's newsletter at the time, by way of tribute but also in an effort to draw attention to the mental health challenges incurred by activists. Excerpts of her journals were also shared with *The Sunday Express* newspaper (Lee 1989). Its two-part coverage of Duggan's death focused on depression and mental health, but its framing of the issues caused some controversy among members of the feminist and lesbian communities.

As Gray recalled:

She was incredibly involved in the Women's Centre and incredibly involved in gay rights. It was a real shake-up in the community [when she died] because people were blaming themselves for not doing something about it. But... she didn't tell anybody how she was feeling... So it was very unsettling. She was a powerful force. While she was in St. John's she did a lot. She worked a lot at the Women's Centre and she mentored a lot of people and helped them to come to terms with their sexuality (Gray 2023).

"It was like somebody had dropped a bomb in the [lesbian] community," recalled Dopler. "It was brutal. That shook a whole community."

Lesbian organizing continues

Around the time CHAN began to dissolve in the late 1970s, a lesbian organization briefly formed in its wake. It was called Gay Organization of Women in Newfoundland (GOWN). Several lesbians from the period remember it, although they were not involved. They do recall that it was intended to be a politically active group. All the lesbians they recall being involved with it have since passed away.

According to Beth Lacey, two of the GOWN organizers included Denise Martin and Sheilagh Moore, both of whom have since died. When Lacey moved to St. John's in 1977, she heard the group was active, but never had a chance to attend a meeting during its brief lifespan.

"The only thing I really know is that Denise wanted us to start our own path, as it were," she explained. "Up to that point, everything had been mixed, so that was the first attempt to break away from the boys. Not completely breaking away from the boys, but taking our own path. The issues were a lot the same, but some were different."

The organization was evidently short-lived, and I was unable to find any material content that it produced, although it did runs ads in *The Body Politic* in 1979. GOWN would appear to represent the first exclusively lesbian organization in the province.

Following what some lesbians had referred to as the "purges" at the NSWC in the 1970s (during the conflicts between NSWC and Woman's Place), throughout the 1980s lesbians began returning to the Women's Centre (indeed they had never *really* left).

Marion Atkinson recalled that time:

The gay women started coming to the Women's Centre early on. They got support there that the gay male didn't have, because the women had a support system with other women. We didn't give a shit! You know what I mean? Fuck – come on, we're all in! And they brought issues to the Women's Centre's attention, issues that they started working on: employment, and housing.

The gay males tended to keep it much more covert and quiet. They had one little spot downtown [a bar] where we'd gather, but they didn't have a gathering place for lobbying and stuff like that. In my opinion, it was only after the gay men saw the women progressing that they got the hang of it. But they didn't have the support system that the gay women had [through the Women's Centre]. The gay women had other women to talk things over, and educate. The men didn't have that. Because all the macho men were still calling them a bunch of queers, or fags. Shit like that. So they were more quiet about it, and it took them a lot longer to organize. I think some of the gay women who were friends of the gay men kind of educated them and put these ideas in their head.

But they never had a central place to go to for organizing like the women did (Atkinson 2021).

Beth Lacey was one of the first of this newer cohort of activists in the late '70s and early '80s, and would go on to play a key role in both the feminist and queer movements.

I grew up in Grand Falls, where there was nothing and no one except me. Or so I thought. I was born in 1955, and of course in those days, there was nothing. I'm a big old dyke, so for me, I was born with dyke written across my forehead. I'm sure in the womb I was doing graffiti, like 'I Love Women' or something. So I was pretty confused in Grand Falls, you know... I liked doing boy things, like playing baseball, playing hockey, and kissing girls. But I knew I wasn't supposed to kiss girls. Even at that age (Lacey 2022).

Lacey recalls overhearing adults talk about hermaphrodites one day, and wondered whether that's what she was. She also overheard adults use the word 'homosexual.' She didn't know what it was, but had a feeling she ought to find out. So, at the age of 12 or 13, she went to the library and looked up the word 'homosexual' in the Encyclopedia Britannica.

It talked about homosexuality, but it only talked about males. So I thought — that's me! I was the female version. But [the encyclopedia] didn't talk about girls, so I didn't know if there were any more of me around or not! I wondered. But there was nobody to ask. I knew better than to ask my parents. They were good churchgoing people, you know. That's not something they would have been able to handle back in the 1960s.

It was when I went to university that I learned there were other lesbians. I was 17. Now I'd heard that there were others besides me, but I'd never met one. So I wasn't really clear on who they were or where they might be. But when I went to university, I lived in residence, and there were a couple of incidents we'll say... I was really shy, so if somebody hadn't jumped me[32] I'd probably still be in the closet (Ibid.).

Lacey spent a few semesters at MUN and then quit to do a lab course at community college. Then at the age of 19 she moved to Corner Brook. It was there she came out, and had her first serious relationship.

I came out in 1975, in Corner Brook. I was there for a couple of years working in the hospital and came out there. But there was nothing in Corner Brook at the time. There were a few people around who we knew were gay or lesbian but we didn't interact with anybody basically, mostly because my girlfriend was completely in the closet (Ibid.).

When the two split up in 1977, Lacey moved back to St. John's. She re-enrolled at Memorial University, and began dating Lynn Murphy.

"We became very out," she recalled. By this time there was an increasingly vibrant queer presence on campus, and Lacey soon met other gay and lesbian students. They would all meet daily for lunch at a self-designated table in the

---

[32] Later on in Corner Brook.

Thomson Student Centre cafeteria.

We would unite at one table, it was a huge table, and there'd be ten, twelve
of us. Everybody knew that that was our table. Nobody ever gave us hassle.
It was very obvious who we were: me in my workboots and my flannel shirt.
Back in the day things were so butch-femme. When I first came out it was all
very butch-femme. Now, I was never very into that. But... I certainly looked
more butch than Lynn. One day we were sitting at the table and I realized that
I forgot my cigarettes. So I gave Lynn the tray of food to bring back to the table,
and I ran back to get cigarettes. When I got back to the table, one of the girls –
Judy Stacey – said to me: 'What are you doing, Mary?' To Judy everyone was
Mary, whether you were male or female. She said: 'What are you doing, Mary?
Jeezus you're the butch one, you should be carrying that tray!' (Ibid.).

There was a psychology course at the time called Sexual Behaviour, and it
was one of a handful of courses where professors would sometimes lecture on
homosexuality. Lacey was a psychology major, and the professor reached out
to her and asked her to come and speak to the class.

Everybody knew I was a dyke, so when they wanted somebody to speak at
the Human Sexuality course, of course myself and Lynn went and did our best.
It was 1978 or 1979 when that happened… I was pretty butch and chubby, cer-
tainly no man's dream of a woman, and Lynn was very femme, large-breasted,
blue eyes, very pretty. And there were [people] at the back of the room who
said: 'Well I understand why she is [lesbian], but the other one could get any
man!' That was the mentality in that course (Ibid.).

Lacey's reputation as a lesbian who was not afraid to speak out publicly
was starting to spread. In 1980, the NSWC organized a Provincial Women's
Conference in St. John's, and organizers reached out to Lacey and Murphy to
ask them to do a workshop at the conference. Organizers gave the workshop
the circumspect title 'Choices', but it was intended to be about lesbianism.
When this became apparent to attendees, several of them left the room. Lacey
recalls about a dozen people attending the workshop in the end. Her overarch-
ing memory of the Conference however was about meeting Rita MacNeil. The
multi-Juno and -ECMA award-winning singer/songwriter, a member of the
Canadian Country Music Hall of Fame, had just released her second full-length
album and her career was just beginning to take off. She was the keynote guest
at that year's Provincial Women's Conference.

After giving her workshop at the Conference, Lacey's involvement with
the Women's Centre deepened and she became an active volunteer. In 1982
she was hired as Coordinator of the Women's Centre. She recalled one of the
interview questions during the hiring process for the job:

One of the questions was: 'You know a lot of things happen here, there are
a lot of accusations, how would you feel if somebody accused you of being a
lesbian?' I was sitting there thinking [laughter], and I wish I'd answered differ-
ently, but what I said was: 'Well I've certainly been called worse things than

lesbian.

But I ended up coming out to everybody at the Women's Centre, and that became a pretty safe place for women while I was there. I certainly felt safe there as a lesbian (Ibid.).

Sharon Gray – who had been involved with the early Woman's Place collective as well as NSWC – was still actively involved in the movement and recalls the gradual emergence of out lesbians at the Centre around this time. She spent a great deal of time at the Centre on Military Road, which she also recalls as being poorly insulated and extremely cold.

It was a very, very active place. That was the first place I ever met lesbians. In fact it was not in my consciousness at that age. I'd gone to university for a couple of years, and I was certainly sexually active and stuff, but it had just never occurred to me that there were women and men who didn't see things the same way. And it came as a tremendous shock to me. I don't think I was brought up particularly strictly but I was brought up in a fairly religious family, and it was never talked about. There was absolutely no conception that marriage and children was not a woman's place. That was the expectation, that a woman would get married and have children and be a support to her husband. I didn't really buy into that. I certainly didn't want to have children at that age of my life. But it was certainly refreshing to see other women who felt the same way, even women who had children.

Beth Lacey and I became best friends. She was funny as anything, and she knew that I had no conception that she was a lesbian. And she teased me about it. One time I said to Beth: 'I'm not sure if I've ever met a lesbian.' And she looked me up and she looked me down, and she said: 'Yes Sharon, you have.' And I was just like - aha (Gray 2023).

Lacey thinks she was the first publicly out lesbian at the Centre, and spent the next four years working to grow the Centre, expanding both its membership base as well as the presence of out lesbians within the organization. The 1984 'Women's Festival' – a broad-ranging "Celebration of Women" organized by the NSWC and held at the LSPU Hall from March 8-10 of that year, featured a session on "Lesbianism" on Saturday morning, facilitated by Lacey along with Sandy Pottle. "Feminism as the theory; lesbianism as the practice: A discussion of the politics of lesbianism within a feminist context and the double oppression of lesbians," explained the Festival program.

But the growing presence of lesbians was not without controversy, even within the organization.

Lynn Murphy recalls this period in the early 80s:

There was at one point a bit of backlash. There were some women that felt that we were taking over the Women's Centre, that lesbians were taking over. And then there was another group that felt we weren't being active enough! So it was a period of time with quite a bit of strife about lesbians being a big part of the group.

I feel like what happened there was after we became such a big part of it and were making demands, then some people felt like: 'Oh, that's too much.' And you get that backlash. Of course, we were the ones doing all the work! It was all lesbians who were doing the abortion rights stuff. Peg [Norman] was head of the Morgentaler Clinic and Beth [Lacey] was head of [CARAL]. We were the ones that drove women to the clinics. It was the lesbians (Murphy 2022).

Eventually, Murphy said, things resolved (for a time). The Centre was busy and there was more than enough work for everyone. As Lacey explains:

Basically the Women's Centre at that point was the last stop for any woman in the city that had any need that couldn't be satisfied, whether it was housing, reproductive rights, trying to advocate for social services, violence against women, whatever. We also ran the Rape Crisis Centre out of the Women's Centre. So there was a lot going on. And of course we spent half our time applying for money. We did a lot of research too. There was a women's health education project on the go, there was a pensions project on the go, there was a lot happening at the Status of Women. We were establishing a footing (Lacey 2022).

The Centre's Military Road location also became an unexpected social hub on Friday nights when the organization started putting off 'TGIF Fridays'. The informal gatherings were held at the Centre on Friday evenings, and often stretched into the wee hours. Peg Norman remembers them vividly.

Everybody would show up! We would take turns tending bar. What we would do is we would start off with a dozen beer from the Fountainspray, which is now the Needs store. Somebody would go over and buy a dozen beer, and we'd sell them for two bucks apiece, and when we were down to the last four, you'd take the cash and you'd go over and buy another dozen. You would do that, and the cut-off for buying beer was ten o'clock. So if it was a really fun night, and it was getting close to ten, you'd do an assessment. How many are still here? How many more beers do you think we're going to need? And bottles of wine. We used to get the great big bottles of screw-top Partager (Norman 2022).

Lacey said the events became a magnet for feminists, lesbians and even non-politically-active women throughout the city.

Slowly but surely lesbians from within the movement starting coming, and then lesbians who just knew women, who knew lesbians in the movement, you know how it happens. And all of the sudden everyone was getting together at the Women's Centre on Friday nights! TGIF Fridays became a big thing. We had all kinds of people, having a ball on Friday evenings (Lacey 2022).

Lesbians were also active within GAIN. Tree Walsh's tenure as president in 1983 saw the group hold its most expansive Pride Week yet – a full week of events. In 1985, GAIN submitted a proposal to the Office of the Secretary of State for a Lesbian Health Project. The proposal was rejected, reported GAIN's newsletter, owing "to the priorities, funding and current fiscal restraint of the Women's Programs."

NL's lesbians also had a significant impact on the national women's movement. During her tenure as Women's Centre coordinator, Lacey and one of her co-workers at the Women's Centre, Annette Clarke, attended a meeting of the National Action Committee on the Status of Women, Canada's flagship feminist organization at the time.

When I got there, they were talking about all these caucuses, and I thought, fuck – there's nothing about lesbianism here! So I asked for a lesbian caucus, not thinking it was a big deal. Well! The lesbians that came out of the woodwork then! And were they ever happy. My god, they were thrilled.

So we got together as a caucus, and the first hour was just excitement — oh my god, oh my god, oh my god. And then we were like, well as a caucus what do we want to accomplish? And what we wanted to accomplish, was to get us covered by the human rights code, by the Charter of Rights and Freedoms (Lacey 2022).

During the following day's lobby session, Members of Parliament appeared before NAC to answer a limited number of questions. The issue of which questions would get asked was always deeply political, with differing factions of the organization lobbying for their questions or concerns to be the ones raised before the MPs and ministers. The lesbian caucus developed a question without much expectation that it would make it to the floor, since they were a new caucus. To their surprise, it was one of the ones that did get asked.

In 1986, Lacey was offered a job with the Women's Policy Office, a branch of the provincial government. "After four years at the Women's Centre I was desperate to get out of there," she said. "I was about to have a nervous breakdown, you know what it's like working with NGOs. And I was the sole advocate for abortion for all the time I was at the Women's Centre."

When she left, Sandy Pottle, another lesbian. was hired to replace her. "When they hired her," recalls Lacey, "one of the older members of the Status of Women said: 'Well you know, we just had a lesbian, isn't it time to have a heterosexual again?' Oh wow — two lesbians in a row! But we did it. She was hired."

***

The year 1990 marked a catalytic moment of change for the feminist movement, in this province and across the country. As we have seen, the federal government played a significant role in the growth of feminist institutions like the Status of Women Centres by providing operational funding through the Office of the Secretary of State. Throughout the 1980s, funding continued to flow from the federal government to women's centres, but as neoliberal ideology began to take hold among the mainstream political parties, purse strings began to tighten. Funding criteria for a range of government programs began to narrow, and more strings were attached to funding in terms of what that funding could be used for. Fiscal pressures intensified when a Progressive Conservative government ousted the Liberals at the federal level in 1984. Feminists began hearing rumours that the Secretary of State funding on which they had been relying since the early 1970s might be under threat. Feminist organizations worked earnestly to strengthen their relationship with the federal government, producing copious reports on all the work that was being accomplished with these funds, meeting with federal officials to strengthen relationships and emphasize in person just how important that money was to the women of Canada.

Nevertheless, in February 1990, their worst fears were realized: the office of Secretary of State under the Progressive Conservative federal government announced the elimination of all Women's Program funding. This also led to the termination of several employees at provincial women's centres whose salaries had been funded with Secretary of State funding.

The country's feminist activists threw themselves into action. All across Canada they rallied, protested, organized petitions, mailed letters and postcards, spoke to media and politicians alike. Yet the federal government held firm in its decision. All seemed for nought.

The feminists of Newfoundland and Labrador weren't willing to let their hard-won funding go without a fight. As feminists across the country strategized how to fight the cuts, local planning meetings started at the SJSWC in February 1990. Sixty women showed up at the very first meeting, reported Peter Gullage for *The Sunday Express* in a feature titled "Winning ways: Anatomy of a political victory; or how Newfoundland women stared down the feds." Gullage put the funding cuts in context:

[T]he $1.6 million cut from the budgets of women's centres across the country was a paltry sum in the grand scheme of federal spending. After all, the National Gallery in Ottawa threw $1.7 million at the controversial abstract painting Voice of Fire *and they got to keep it... Furthermore, the $51,000 annual budget for the [St. John's] centre was already well below the level needed* (Gullage 1990).

With the federal government refusing to budge, it was time for direct action. On Monday, March 25 at 11:30am, a group of women launched an occupation of the Secretary of State's office in St. John's. "About 100 women, children and men took over the premises just before noon Monday," wrote one activist to supporters in Nova Scotia. "We have support from all local political parties (well, the Libs haven't actually shown up), numerous women's, social action and labour groups. What we lack is national press." She urged activists in other provinces to use "feminist networks" to get wider national coverage of the St. John's occupation.

By Wednesday the feds were feeling the heat. Secretary of State Gerry Weiner refused to meet with the women, but did delegate two of his staff to meet with them, and even flew representatives in from all the other women's centres in the province for the meeting. The feds made an offer to restore 75 percent of the operational funding but only as project funding.

Local activist Bonnie James, in a letter to a counterpart in Nova Scotia, wrote:

It is clear they want tighter control. All 7 [centres] have rejected this and also decided to refuse to even submit applications for projects at this time... Morale is high. More people come every day – hundreds this afternoon. About twenty stay at night. Eviction expected by the end of the week. The sun is not the only thing rising in the east! Love to all from the trenches (James 1990).

As the St. John's occupation continued, hundreds of supporters rallied outside the downtown offices, and visited the occupation force. Solidarity messages and telegrams poured in from across the country. Solidarity rallies and sit-ins took place, from Halifax to Vancouver. A key issue of contention was not just how much money might be available to women's organizations, but what it would be used for. The federal government wanted to get out of the business of providing operational funding to centres. They offered to provide significant amounts of funding, but only for specific projects. Feminists rejected this: projects and programs were no good without "the stability of a continuously run Women's Centre." As feminists continued to reject government offers, police were deployed to the sit-ins, rallies and occupations.

"The women were told to leave or be arrested... by a large contingent of Royal Newfoundland Constabulary officers on the fifth day of their around the clock occupation of the Atlantic Place offices in St. John's," reported *The Evening Telegram* (Dicks 1990). The Sunday Express reported that "ten paddy wagons and two cruisers were on hand to transport the women to the lock-up if it proved necessary" (Sunday Express 1990). After five days, with the threat of police action looming, the feminists in St. John's ended their occupation and left the Secretary of State office.

Support for the Women's Centres was strong. Support coalitions formed at local high schools and wrote letters of support. St. John's City Council even threw its support behind the protestors. The province's labour movement helped to coordinate support rallies as well. Even *The Evening Telegram* published a fiery editorial in support of the women: "[T]he decision to cut out a paltry expenditure of less than $2 million, that must have been among the best for the social value obtained of any item in the government's spending program, and was vital to the continuation of a host of women's programs, was quite wrong. Worse, it was stupid" (Telegram 1990A).

The editorial was also critical of the suggested compromise – cost-shared funding with provincial governments – as "guaranteed to breed inequity" (Ibid.).

St. John's East MP Ross Reid played an interesting role in the crisis. While stopping short of breaking ranks with his government, he spoke out ardently in support of the Women's Centres and the need for them to remain open.

According to *The Evening Telegram* coverage, he "has been working with a variety of groups to secure funding ensuring the centres remain open... Mr. Reid said the centres provide essential services to women, families and communities across Newfoundland and Labrador" (Evening Telegram 1990A).

"If core funding is not provided, then other avenues must be found and we must move forward and work together toward that end," he told the Telegram (Ibid.)

On Sunday, April 1, 1990, a "Weiner Roast" was held at Bannerman Park to protest the cuts. About 200 attended (Evening Telegram 1990B). The following morning, April 2, sixty women returned to the Secretary of State offices in St. John's demanding to meet with Weiner. They delivered a letter. And then they announced they would wait for a response – effectively resuming their occupation.

Police were called, and two and a half hours after the women arrived the RNC moved in on the protestors. Twenty of the women who refused to leave were arrested, along with two male supporters. Reporters described the scene:

At least two dozen uniformed police officers poured out of elevators on the eighth floor of Atlantic Place and marched into the office to carry out the arrests. Protestors did not resist. Two dozen supporters in the hallway sang and waved placards as the others were led outside and escorted into a police van (Canadian Press 1990A).

The day following the arrests, protestors returned. They were now locked out of the Secretary of State offices, but resumed their picket outside. The activists also set up "a display desk showing our wide support at the provincial govt building." They tried unsuccessfully to secure a meeting with federal Minister of Justice John Crosbie (a Newfoundlander), but did meet briefly with federal Fisheries Minister Bernard Valcourt who was in town. He lamented at being unable to do anything and left protestors with the perplexing advice to "Keep it up!"

"The issue was not the $1.6 million cut from Women's centres across Canada, but a move by the Federal Government to silence groups that have opposed unjust government policies," wrote the St. John's Status of Women Council in a summary of the events.

Feminists across the country took up their banners and protest placards once more, this time in support of the courageous Newfoundland feminists who had been arrested. Finally, the federal government relented, after a fashion. It announced a one-year restoration of full funding to the country's women's centres. This funding was extended again in 1991, while centres scrambled to find other sources of funding more reliable than the federal government. In Newfoundland and Labrador, operational funding was gradually transferred from the federal to the provincial government, and today it is the province which provides core funding to the SJSWC. Without the brave fight of NL's feminists, a great deal more would likely have been lost, both in this province and around the country.

"It was mostly lesbians leading the occupation," one participant told me, requesting anonymity. Following that victory, tensions between lesbians and straight women at the Centre rose again in the early 1990s.

As funding sources shifted and became more precarious, some feminists became concerned that the Centre's association with lesbians could become a liability. Sharp Dopler, who wrote a graduate thesis on the "Lesbophobia" that occurred in the Centre during this period, described the subsequent events as a "great cataclysm in the women's community which was caused by their 'There's no lesbians here! [attitude].'"

"'There's no lesbians here, don't say there's lesbians here because they won't fund us!'" is how Dopler described the concern some women had. "But the fucking lesbians were doing all the work!"

Examination of documents from the period reveal two tensions were emerging, and probably fueling each other. On the one hand was the issue of sexuality. Lesbians were becoming more visible and out. They were demanding space, presence, visibility and respect. As Pottle explained:

[Some older feminists] found it quite upsetting that people whose sexual orientation was other than straight were involved. They had troubles with recognizing sexuality as being anything that had anything to do with the women's movement. They felt that your body and anything that you do with your body, with your sexuality, that it was going to detract from [the movement] and people would scorn you for being associated with it (Pottle 2022).

On the other hand, the Centre's own growth was putting its consensus-based, collective organizing and decision-making model under strain. The tensions this produced were perhaps inflamed by funding shifts. In the wake of federal funding cuts, and with a growing focus on grants and project-based initiatives, the accounting mechanisms expected by funders likely produced pressures on an anti-hierarchical organizing collective. They increasingly had to meet external deadlines, and follow the strings regarding project timelines and outcomes set by external bodies. The Centre was also hiring a growing number of employees on a variety of short- and long-term grants, and the Steering Committee (note the non-hierarchical language – it was not then referred to as an executive or management team, or as a Board of Directors) was effectively the employer. When problems arose surrounding employees – for instance concern with employees' work, or complaints made by employees about their working conditions – there were conflicting ideas about how to deal with them. Should the Centre employ managerial human resources techniques, such as formal disciplinary procedures? Or traditional forms of anti-hierarchical feminist decision-making and consensus-building? Were some members of the Centre managers and others employees? Or were they all members of a non-hierarchical movement?

Members of the Centre were split along all of these issues. Often they intersected. As Pottle recalled:

There's always been the division within the women's movement of the women who want to occupy the positions of power and those who want to collectivize the positions of power. There were the more conservative feminists who didn't really have a problem with there being hierarchies and such. They just wanted to occupy the positions of power! (Pottle 2022).

The Centre was comprised mostly of volunteers, but did occasionally hire short-term employees. Often the grant programs used to pay employees came with various strings attached, rendering the pool of eligible applicants fairly small. The volunteers tended to be outspoken, committed feminists; but not all the hired employees shared their commitment and attitude. "[Some women] who were hired used to always complain that there were no men working at the Women's Centre!" said Pottle. "They had no consciousness about being a feminist at all."

As Gerry Rogers explained:

Sometimes we would bring in someone, hire someone with these sorts of job programs. And it would sometimes be people who really weren't suitable. Sometimes you'd throw somebody in the mix who's not a feminist, but it's a chance to give someone a job and help them make more money in what should be a supportive environment. And then they discover that they're surrounded by lesbians (Rogers 2022).

The lesbians were involved with everything, doing everything. Doing the work of the Centre. All the heterosexual people were busy going home to their husbands. We were there doing the bulk of the legwork. Putting flyers in enve-lopes, lobbying, calling, whatever. Working at the Rape Crisis Centre. Staffing the St. John's Status of Women Centre.

And at some point it came to somebody's notice just how many lesbians there were around. And there were a lot of us who were pretty butch-looking, right? The lipstick lesbians weren't as big of a thing back then. They were more rare. So one of the members of the [Women's Centre] Board said we needed to tone it down. 'What the fuck are you talking about?' [we asked]. – 'Well, you know if the mainstream thinks that this is just a place for lesbians they won't take it seriously.' – 'Are you fucking kidding me? Lesbians are doing all the work!' – 'Well, we can just downplay that part… We can't be all things to all women. We have to realize that we have limitations.' – 'Oh yeah, your big fucking homophobic limitations!' Like, fuck off.

The other side – clearly I'm on the lesbian side – the other side were talk-ing about how there was a conspiracy and that the lesbians were going to take over the St. John's Status of Women Centre, and delegitimize all the work that it had been doing – and recruit! (Dopler 2021).

With tensions rising, members of the SJSOWC struggled to maintain unity. At a steering committee meeting on June 26, 1990 it was proposed that "there is a need for a Lesbian Support group to operate from the Women's Centre.

A group could meet perhaps once a month which would provide a safe place for women to exchange information and give support...there is a great need for such a group" (SJSWC Steering Committee Minutes, June 26 1990) In the summer of 1991, the Centre struck a 'Sexual Orientation Committee.' Jennifer Mercer and Beth Lacey were two of the Committee's members, and were later interviewed by Martha Muzychka for a Canadian Research Institute for the Advancement of Women (CRIAW) newsletter.

The two women told Muzychka the "time was right for such a committee to be established, that something had to be done to address homophobia. The committee was born out of pain, and we (the committee) were overwhelmed by the responsibility to tackle homophobia in the women's community...We used a lot of humour to deflect the pain we felt"" (CRIAW 1992).

According to Muyzchka, members grappled with both external homophobia as well as their own internalized homophobia. They held a screening of the National Film Board (NFB) film Sandra's Garden. This film tackled one of the prevailing social tropes of the time, which was that homosexuality was the consequence of incest. They also organized a series of screenings of the film Pink Triangles: one session was for lesbians only, one session for straight people, and one session was for everyone.

"Our goal was to educate our community, because the lesbians felt betrayed by the women's community," Mercer told Muzychka. Lacey added: "We remember that straights and lesbians don't come to the discussion as equals. It's nothing for a straight woman to identify her sexual orientation, but it's dangerous for a lesbian to do so" (Ibid.).

Mercer emphasized to Muzychka that straight women needed to address their homophobia:

A woman coming into a feminist organization is challenged. That's what we do – we challenge all the assumptions about women and society. We do it in everything, from issues around money, childcare, or reproductive freedom. You can't imagine us having a discussion about reproductive freedom, and if someone came in, we wouldn't stop the discussion because she might be put off. But we do it about lesbians, and we don't call it homophobia. We call it making it safe for her (Ibid.).

Things eventually came to a head in June 1991. With tensions rising between straight and lesbian members, one of the Centre's employees was dismissed.[33] She subsequently filed a complaint with the Human Rights Commission, alleging sexual harassment and discrimination on the basis of political opinion. The Commission undertook a preliminary investigation which lasted over a year, and determined in March 1993 that there were grounds for a tribunal hearing to proceed. In the wake of this decision, the Centre reached a cash settlement with the complainant, and the investigation was closed.

While all of this played out, much of the Centre's work effectively ceased,

---

[33] A straight employee, according to the women I interviewed.

and the Centre closed its doors to the public for almost 18 months.

"It was a really, really horrible miscommunication," said Rogers. "It didn't have to be that way... Then the next thing you know people are inflaming it, making it worse, and so all the lesbians left the Women's Centre."

"I think some of them saw it as an opportunity to get rid of this [lesbian] element," said Pottle.

When all of this went down with the St. John's Status of Women's Council, we said to them: this is homophobia! But they said: 'We're feminists, we can't be homophobic.' The fuck you say! So it was a blow-up, right, and a lot of lesbians stopped dealing with the St. John's Status of Women Centre. We started our own organization – NAN (Newfoundland Amazon Network; Dopler 2021).

"It was ugly for a few years," recalled Norman.

In the lead-up to, during, and after the human rights complaint, the SJSWC struggled to address the concerns of lesbians. It produced the first provincial document specifically addressing the needs of lesbians. "Time for Action: A Brief Discussing the Needs of Lesbian Feminists" was published by the SJSWC with a note on the cover indicating that the "Author must remain anonymous to protect her employment." According to the brief, it was produced by the SJSWC in an effort "to be responsive to its lesbian members... The needs of the lesbian community have not been addressed specifically by the feminist movement in this province" (SJSWC n.d.).

Twenty lesbians were interviewed for the report, ranging in age from their mid-twenties to mid-fifties.

The report notes that any effort to gauge the size of the lesbian community "is made nearly impossible by the invisibility of the community." It used the commonly cited 'one in ten' estimate to suggest a population of around 8000 in St. John's. "Members of the community estimate that between four and five hundred women are 'out'," it stated (Ibid.).

The report was produced after the heyday of GALT, and identified an absence of any gay or lesbian activist group in the city at the time. "Lack of funding and difficulty in finding enough volunteers to openly work for the organizations, have been the main reasons for the demise of these groups. Volunteers are afraid of being discriminated against should their sexuality become known" (Ibid.).

While noting there was at least one gay and lesbian bar in the city's downtown, it also observed that "homophobia forces lesbians to socialize, for the most part, in their own homes" (Ibid.).

The report addressed the recent convulsions within the Centre.

Human rights complaints made against several employees were believed by many in the lesbian feminist community to be rooted in homophobia. These lesbian feminists did not feel supported by their heterosexual sisters... women felt attacked as lesbians and, in response, left their political activities within the feminist movement... There was a sense among some of the women of searching for a new base from which to operate (Ibid.).

The report also said that those interviewed felt lesbians within the community failed to respect each others' diversity – including class distinctions – leading to communication problems and a sense of isolation. "We do not accept, and work through, differences among ourselves," it stated (Ibid.).

The report flagged the urgency of amending the Human Rights Code to protect gays and lesbians. Until that was done, it warned, lesbians would continue to languish professionally and economically. "[L]egal matters facing lesbians, such as physical abuse or property rights, are often left unattended because the women involved do not wish to face a hostile and public legal system." Property rights in particular were highlighted – it was difficult, for instance, for lesbians to apply for a mortgage together. The importance of bringing the school system under the Human Rights Code was also flagged. The specific health care needs of lesbians, including mental health and counselling, were also acknowledged.

Yet the report recognized the paradox that it was difficult to fight for improvements in the legal system when doing so opened activists up to discrimination. "[Lesbians] need to lobby to get human rights protection, yet they need that protection in order to lobby safely." As so few lesbians had jobs in which they felt safe being out, "much of the political work on behalf of lesbians is being carried out by a very small number of women... There was frustration expressed with the lack of active lobbying by lesbians for their own rights, coupled with understanding of why so many women are afraid." To address this, the report recommended formation of a lesbian organization which could employ a coordinator who could safely be out and direct activism and lobbying. It also suggested forming a media watch committee (Ibid.).

Education was an important theme in the report. Several of the women interviewed:

... felt there is a great need for more community education around the issues of homophobia. The women wanted to see workshops offered, preferably by lesbian feminists, to groups such as police, social workers, health care workers, lawyers and teachers. There was some concern that the community is not ready for such education, and that there may indeed be a backlash. Several women felt it is important that we be included in the charter of rights before such education can proceed safely. There was also a strong feeling among the women interviewed that there is a need for formal education structures to recognize, and discuss, homosexuality as a positive lifestyle option... the women were concerned for young lesbians who are attempting to understand their sexuality. They felt that these women will experience needless pain because of their lack of knowledge (Ibid.).

The Report suggested promoting this kind of education at the high school level, and suggested the MUN Women's Studies department could perhaps play a role in this. It suggested pamphlets and gay and lesbian committees for high schools, workshops for students, and greater action against "homophobia in the school yards" on the part of schools (Ibid.).

While there was a gay and lesbian bar, the majority of women interviewed "stated very strongly that they feel a need for a social outlet other than a bar. Women felt that it is important to have social activities which do not centre around alcohol" (Ibid.).

How should lesbians organize around these issues? Solidarity was important, said the report.

There was a strong feeling that lesbian feminists have worked with great energy on issues that are not often of immediate concern to them, such as day care and abortion rights, and that the heterosexual feminist community must now reciprocate by working for the inclusion of sexual orientation as a prohibited ground in the charter... it is important that heterosexual feminists work under the direction of lesbian feminists in fighting for lesbian rights. Over half the women mentioned feeling betrayed by their heterosexual sisters. They felt they are not welcomed within the feminist movement. One woman believed feminists must realize that lesbians are 'a catalyst for change, and whenever there is change, there will be conflict.' ... feminists should realize that it is difficult for lesbians to speak on behalf of themselves, and that they need the support of a larger group (Ibid.).

At the same time, warned the report, lesbians need to acknowledge and respect their own diversity – in particular this meant more support for Indigenous lesbians within the broader lesbian community.

Above all, the feminist movement needed to work on community building. According to one respondent, "card games are more useful now than demonstrations," insofar as they could help bridge gaps between and among feminists. Other respondents were more militant: "Reclaim the Women's Centre" was one of the recommendations. "Community building is a first priority. Other action can grow from this," stated the report. "Lesbians need to put their own issues first" (Ibid.).

In some ways, the report was probably a last-ditch effort to re-establish a working relationship between the various factions that emerged following the human rights complaint and it may have come too late. On November 1, 1991, the Women's Centre closed its doors in the wake of the human rights complaint and investigation.

The decision to close the Centre while the investigation played out upset some of the members. A group calling themselves the "Women's Centre Support Group" tried to organize momentum among members to re-open the Centre, at least on a part-time basis, and offered to set up a volunteer staffing schedule. They emphasized the need to get events and programming rolling again "so that it will be available once again as a centre for feminist activity, discussion, and meeting between women: TGIFs, films, discussions, CR groups, lesbian awareness, a letter writing club on issues of concern to women... These could be organized by volunteers" (SJSWC Archives).

The ad hoc group also urged the Steering Committee to try to settle the human rights complaint out of court. What the Steering Committee opted to do instead was to hire Catalyst Consultants, a feminist consulting firm based in Ottawa, to undertake an organizational review of the Centre structure. A June 1992 general meeting saw members express loud concerns about an out-of-province consulting firm being hired to spearhead the review, as opposed to local members. A follow-up general meeting was organized in July to discuss "how can we have more of a local voice and ownership in the organizational review." The review, meanwhile, got underway. Catalyst conducted phone interviews with members and distributed questionnaires, and put together focus groups as well as a day-long retreat for members in September 1992.

Meanwhile, lesbians still active in the organization struggled to assert their own vision for the Centre's future. A petition was delivered to the Steering Committee on July 10, 1992, signed by 10 lesbians, demanding the establishment of a Lesbian Resource Centre to operate within the larger St. John's Status of Women's Centre, and to be run by a Lesbian Resource Centre Steering Committee.

"Our request reflects our goal of self-determination and not separatism," stated the petition letter. It stated that lesbians involved with the Centre "have felt in the last year that they have not been welcomed by their heterosexual sisters...our needs are not the same, and only members of an oppressed group can and should direct political action in their own interests."

There is no record of a response.

On December 1, 1992, Catalyst submitted its Organizational Review. It had tried to determine, without much success, whether the Centre's activists had a shared vision of what the Centre should be – education resource? Referral centre? Activist headquarters? "There was no agreement on what the Centre should be doing at this time," the report concluded. "There was very little consensus on the models" (Catalyst 1992).

However, one thing the Catalyst report did highlight was that lesbian issues – along with counselling – were among the most immediate needs.

Recently, a new gap was identified related to lesbian services. However lesbians chose to stay inside the Centre to create their space. We would suggest that this occurred for two reasons: There was no existing safe place outside to go and the Centre did not take up this issue as with all others and ensure that lesbians would have a rightful space in the outside world.

Within the lesbian community there appears to be some disagreement as to whether the Centre should be involved in developing or supporting any lesbian services. Some feel that it should be done by lesbians only, while most felt that 'there is a definite role for the feminist community to play in working with lesbian feminists to end discrimination.' The reluctance to involve heterosexuals may be in part a legacy of the human rights case and the feeling of betrayal that many lesbians have experienced.

At the membership meetings, it was clear that women supported the idea of the Centre ensuring that lesbian needs were addressed. There was also a growing understanding that because of discrimination it was important for lesbians to have the tangible support of heterosexual women in the development of services addressing the needs. Some specifically identified in the brief, Time for Action, include: ensure that sexual orientation is included in the federal and provincial Human Rights Codes; have a lesbian space for social, educational activities; engage in community building activities; and do more public education on homophobia and lesbianism (Ibid.).

The Catalyst report also addressed that there were conflicting views of how the Centre should operate. Should it be a hierarchical workplace? A non-hierarchical collective? Something in between? The women involved were also split on this subject. However, the report did suggest the human rights case was "the breaking point in a long history of poor working conditions" which it attributed to weaknesses of the non-hierarchical collective model, particularly insofar as this model had led to an unsuccessful attempt to balance being a non-hierarchical collective with being a formal employer (Ibid.).[34]

The fallout from the human rights case had also impacted the Centre's perceived ability to support women, noted the Catalyst report. "For some lesbians, the service has become increasingly inaccessible as a consequence of the lack of safety related to the human rights case."

Finally, after twenty months of internal struggle and reorganization, the Women's Centre re-opened on Thursday, September 16, 1993, with an evening social gathering – "a free beginning with exciting possibilities."

The Centre was open again and would become a vibrant source of feminist activism in subsequent years. But it had also begun an inexorable journey away from its non-hierarchical, collectivist roots toward the more hierarchical organizational structure under which it operates today, with a clear distinction between hired staff – both managers and employees - and a board of directors. And while the Centre today is a rich source of activism and support for lesbians, trans and non-binary people, along with other marginalized identities, it would take time following the "cataclysm" of the early 1990s for lesbians to return en masse. Many of them did remain involved to varying degrees when the Centre re-opened, but they now also had a new organization under which to operate.

---

[34] Personal correspondence between women involved with the Centre at that time also reveals conflicting ideas about the best organizing model. Some women who were involved with union activism felt that employees deserved the sorts of grievance procedures and structures that unionized employees had access to. Others however felt this was a move toward patriarchal bureaucracy and managerialism, and away from core values of feminist consensus-building and egalitarianism.

Newfoundland Amazon Network (NAN)

In 1991, Gary Kinsman and Patrick Barnholden left the province when Kinsman was offered a teaching position in Nova Scotia. By 1992, GALT had folded. The demand for human rights protections around sexual orientation remained unfulfilled, and now there was no longer even an organization to fight for it.

As Gerry Rogers explains:

There was nothing. There was no place to gather outside of the bar. And there were no activities specifically for lesbians. So a bunch of us decided: well let's start a group. And that we would look at doing social events, dances, but also activism. And our activism was about getting sexual orientation included in our human rights act (Rogers 2022).

The group they formed had perhaps the best name of any activist organization in the province's history: Newfoundland Amazon Network, or NAN.[35]

The Newfoundland Amazon Network was a successor of sorts to GOWN, as a lesbian-only organization. NAN was also determined to keep activism front and centre. It would come to play a central role in the fight for the human rights amendment so long sought by the province's activists.

Many of the early NAN members were teachers, and had experienced first-hand the fear and intimidation of an explicitly homophobic religious school system. Many of the early NAN meetings took place at the Hamilton Avenue home of Sue Rose and Ann Shortall, both teachers.

Ann and Sue really put themselves on the line, because they weren't protected at that time. They were not protected and they were teachers. And some people were afraid, they were afraid that there would be violence, that they would be targeted in their homes. So we were constantly struggling to figure out how to make it open and accessible but also safe (Norman 2022).

I remember all of us sitting on the floor because there wasn't enough room for all of us. We were sitting on the floor, and we were bouncing around ideas about what we needed to do. Some of the dykes weren't so much interested in political action, but most of us had been politically active in the women's movement. So we knew about activism, we knew about strategy, we knew about all that kind of stuff. Those of us who had that kind of experience led the formation [of NAN] (Rogers 2022).

Rogers had been involved as an activist in Montreal, with groups like AIDS Act Up Montreal. She brought those mainland activist experiences to her organizing work with NAN.

There was a strong consensus about the need for a telephone support line — this was the era before cell phones, and very few people had even heard of the internet. The support line — 722-DYKE – was set up on October 14, 1994,

---

[35] The word 'nan' is an informal British term for 'grandmother,' which is in common usage in NL and elsewhere.

and operated at least through 1995 (NAN's News 1994).

NAN published a newsletter as well. The November 1994 issue is full of optimism, and discusses NAN's goal of opening a Lesbian Resource Centre:

... we are hoping to rent a small modest space centrally located that would be available to all lesbians. We'd have an information board, some resource material... the space would be available for anyone who would like to use it to hold groups or meetings, e.g. a study group, a Lesbian AA group, a coming out discussion group, a group for Lesbian mothers group, a group for young dykes, for Lesbians who want to do political action, sports groups or events for just plain fun (Ibid.).

The June 1995 issue featured a letter from a "gay male" thanking NAN for a friendly reception when he accompanied a lesbian friend to one of NAN's women's dances:

I half expected to meet with overt hostility (because I knew it was a lesbian function), but what I encountered was a friendly community of lesbian women coming together in solidarity. After attending your dance and reading your impressive newsletter, I can only wish that the gay men in this city could come together in the same manner! (Nan's News 1995).

NAN's response emphasized that they welcomed men at their functions as well.[36]

Social organizing was important. NAN organized darts tournaments at the East End Club. NAN also organized women's dances, both at the Grad House on Military Road, as well as The Loft, a large venue located on the upper level of Haymarket Square on Duckworth Street. Rita Murrin was one of the DJs who frequently DJ'ed the events.

One of the challenges was navigating the balance between lesbians who were out, proud and activist; and others who were still closeted to varying degrees or didn't want to be publicly identified as lesbian.

"There were some dykes who didn't want anybody taking pictures, didn't want it announced for anybody to know that we were having these dances," said Rogers. "There was that delicate balance. Some of us were so fucking out."

NAN's activism wasn't just focused on queer rights — members were active on multiple issues. "The dykes at the time were really running the Women's Centre, and the abortion clinic," said Rogers. "There were dykes involved in AIDS activism."

Mikiki, then a young gay activist (who would later come out as trans nonbinary), summed up the vital importance of lesbian and women's activism to the broader community.

It was really important, seeing the activism going on through NGALE and the Status of Women Council, and seeing all these amazing older dykes in po-

---

[36] Some NAN activists I spoke with disagreed with this, and recall actively refusing entry to the dances to gay men who showed up.

sitions of power within community organizing and seeing how they identified and how they organized. There was intra-organizational activism and building solidarity movements and coalitions, a lot of that was done by women. It was mostly women who were doing HIV/AIDS work, and work around intimate partner violence, and violence against women.

A lot of the activism for the human rights legislation was done by women. I was involved too, and they gave me so much space. They literally taught me how to be a better feminist ally, and how to shut the fuck up and listen. But they were also so patient with me when I thought I knew everything. I was a 16-year-old faggot activist who thought they knew everything. And they were so patient and created so much space and were so gentle in reminding me that I didn't know everything, and that it actually was important to let other people take the floor – people who had history or had experience or who were directly impacted by these struggles. They had such gentle generosity. My god, what beautiful, beautiful activism these women did. Queer women have always done the heavy lifting (Mikiki 2023).

These women would also play a key role in the final battle for human rights protections around sexual orientation. We shall turn our attention back to that struggle in Chapter 6.

Chapter Four: Organizing at Memorial University

Organizing on campus

Memorial University, like many campuses throughout the world, played an important role in community queer activism over the decades, but it didn't always take place in public. When Roberta Buchanan arrived to take up a position in the English Department in 1964, there was "a total silence on the topic of homosexuality. People were afraid they would lose their job if they came out. It was a very different world," she recalled. Just like in the K-12 school system, employment contracts included 'morality' clauses which could be used to fire queer employees, although no one I interviewed had any recollection of this happening. For many years the mere threat was often sufficient to stifle public activism.

Nevertheless, the university provided a space where boundaries could be nudged. The January 22, 1965, edition of *The Muse* campus newspaper reported on a lecture given earlier that week by Lutheran pastor L.G. Thelin, who argued there was "nothing wrong with marriage between two men or two women." While he did say he considered homosexuality an "abnormal personality structure," he urged greater tolerance (The Muse 1965). While there was still no overt queer organizing at that time in NL, Canada's first formal queer organization, Association for Social Knowledge (ASK), had formed the previous year in Vancouver, and momentum was building toward the first moves to decriminalize homosexuality in 1967.

"Pastor Thelin told a student audience he approves of marriage between two homosexuals if it develops greater humanness," reported *The Muse*.

Amen.

The Muse

The Muse student newspaper was a nexus for early gay and lesbian organizing and expression. In fact, the first clear sign of queer activism on campus was a letter published in the February 1, 1974, edition of the paper, several months before the events which led to the formation of CHAN. Signed "John Novak" (the quotation marks likely indicate an alias), a fourth-year education student, the letter both announced the coming of a homophile organization on campus and exhorted students to get involved to make this possible. It's unclear whether it was written to announce an organized effort, or merely to test the waters for interest (since nothing further was heard on campus for a few years, likely the latter). Still, the idiosyncratic letter, which seems full of coded references that are inscrutable today, is revealing nonetheless. "Stop cruising those Education building and main library washrooms!" it proclaims. "Don't go to Toronto, Montreal, or Vancouver to come out. Come out at home – St. John's" (The Muse 1974).

The letter made reference to a profusion of gay professors on campus who, it said, poorly hid their sexual orientation. It also acknowledged there were some bars in the city "where gay life can be found," but lamented that those bars were not gay bars proper; they're all "predominantly straight-orientated." Time to start a homophile association at MUN, the letter proclaimed repeatedly (Ibid.). "Don't let me be a voice in the wilderness!" the author begged. "WAKE UP you gays! Come out! It's GREAT! It's legal! It's moral! Straight friends are accepting us!" (Ibid.).

The Muse writers of that period were often in the habit of penning provocative letters under aliases as a way of stirring up interest in the paper, but the letter appears sincere enough. It provoked a response two weeks later from a self-identified straight man professing to love wearing women's underwear, and inquiring whether he would be welcome in a homophile association. It's also unclear whether this letter was sincere or an in-house invention.

In the November 28, 1980, issue future *The Muse* editor, Jon Waterhouse, penned a broad-ranging essay about gay identity and homophobia on campus and in society. The piece, a first-person narrative, talks about the ignorance and biases which exist in society, and presents data and statistics from recent research. It provides some of the stereotypically 'gay' traits – "some are limp-wristed, and some affect camp accents" – while emphasizing the differences among gay people and urging the public to avoid stereotypes. "St. John's is a centre for gay people in Newfoundland," Waterhouse writes, while asserting there are no "transvestites" in Newfoundland although drag queens occasionally appear at "the Hallowe'en ball."[37] He points out many "housewives" are in fact gay and while some gay and lesbian people are promiscuous, some have settled into "longstanding 'homosexual' marriages" (Waterhouse 1980). In closing, he calls for tolerance and respect.

In the last decade, gays have become far more visible… For many, the gay still remains the dirty old man in the park. But someday gays will be openly accepted. Gays do not have to be cured; what must change is people's attitude towards this normal and harmless form of human behaviour that is an integral part of the lives of a minority in society (Ibid.).

Three years later, *The Muse* editor, Robert Stoodley, published an update on queer life on campus. His article "Gays at MUN: A Cramped Closet" ran in

---

[37] One assumes he is using "transvestite' to refer to "transgender"; in that period the terms were often confused and conflated.

the October 28, 1983, issue of the paper, and bemoaned the "near invisibility of a sizeable minority on campus" (Stoodley 1983).

"Although actual violence on campus is fairly rare, the gay individual can be continually harassed," he wrote. "Some clubs and societies are notoriously anti-gay; life in residence may be impossible for the open student" (Ibid.).

The article urges gay students to come out, quoting gay students and staff attesting to how much more rewarding life can be when they stop hiding. He does, however, note that in the absence of any organized queer society on campus (there were already several at other mainland Canadian universities) it was hard for gay and lesbian students to meet each other. Most had to go downtown to bars or dances in order to find other queer people, he observed.

He also noted a growing division in the queer community: "Being obviously gay may draw disdain from gays who try to appear straight and feel that "screaming queens" and "diesel dykes" tarnish the good image they've tried to build up. For some, however, it has its advantages" (Ibid.).

The article, which also featured an annotated guide to LGBTQ-themed books in the Queen Elizabeth II, generally referred to as the QEII, Library on campus, concludes on a note of defiance from a student named Stephen. "The world is going to have to learn to put up with me. I've gone through enough shit for being gay, but I'm a human being as much as anybody out there, with as many rights. Watch out world" (Ibid.).

The important role of the Lesbian and Gay Supplements published by *The Muse* is explored in this chapter.

Libraries and bathrooms

While some students were becoming politically active around queer issues, others took advantage of the university environment to explore their sexuality – quite literally. Without the internet or social media apps to facilitate hookups, a fascinating array of sexual practices developed. Certain bathrooms on campus – particularly in the Education Building and the QEII Library – came to be known as gay hookup spots.

"The men's washrooms at the Education Building and in the library had glory holes," recalls John Bragg, who was a student at Memorial from 1969 through 1973. "The basement washroom in the library was incredibly active and had a glory hole."

Walt Chaisson remembers well the sexual activity that flourished on campus during those years. After doing his first two years of studies at Grenfell College in Corner Brook he moved to St. John's in his third year to continue an education degree. He was still in the closet, but found plenty of opportunities for sex with men.

I went to [St. John's] in my third year, when I was 18, and oh god, all the doors came off. I found all kinds of spots on campus to have sex with other guys – in the library, the arts building, the phys ed building, you name it. You could get sex anywhere. It was really liberating for me.

I had my first sexual encounter with another man in the Education Build-ing, in the bathroom on the second floor – the small little one. And it changed my world. It was like wow. Wow. This is so much better than I thought it could be. I would find all kinds of excuses to go to the library or go 'study' or whatever, because I was living with three other people and I didn't want them to know that I was gay (Chaisson 2021).

In 1991 (as well as subsequent years), Memorial University Vice-President Administration and Finance Wayne Thistle – who was also the university's chief legal counsel – gave a presentation to the Canadian Association of Uni-versity Business Officers on some of the chief liability issues facing universities in the 1990s. The published version of this presentation flags a dozen key areas of concern, including: "Is the university at risk if homosexuals use its campus washrooms as a meeting place?" In it, Thistle explains that "at a university in Atlantic Canada" (presumably Memorial) the matter was one of persistent concern. "[I]n spite of increased security activity, the problem has not been eradicated," he wrote. He said security managers had proposed installing hid-den cameras in washrooms on campus – "or locating security personnel in false ceilings" but concluded these approaches were "somewhat drastic measures which most people find offensive and unacceptable." He suggested a more rea-sonable approach was to monitor washroom use and approach people who appear to occupy washrooms "for longer than normally necessary." He said university monitoring had revealed many of those using washrooms for sex on campus were not students, but broader community members. His particu-lar, and very homophobic, concern was that in the event university researchers were conducting experiments on children, those children being experimented upon might have to use the washroom and encounter homosexuals. He notes ultimately that efforts to control washroom use – for instance threatening users with arrest if they took longer than expected in the washroom – were probably fruitless: "more often than not, they simply locate to another venue only to repeat the conduct" (Thistle 1992).

Chaisson also remembered campus as a site for sexual activity for the broader community, as well as Memorial's efforts to crack down on campus sex.

It wasn't just university students. It was also some of the cleaning staff. And it was also people from outside. People from outside the St. John's area would come in to campus, because it wasn't locked. You could just walk in off the street, it didn't matter. Some of the people didn't even go to university. I remember one guy had on these work boots, these really worn work boots, and he just loved giving you a handjob underneath the stall and you coming on his workboots. He would have been about forty, he was in his forties at that time probably.

It was very underground. You would look for any stall that had the wall and where the partition didn't go all the way. Then [Memorial] brought in all these little metal blocking things, to block the open space. Before that there would always be a little space that you could look through and if you saw someone looking back, then you knew that it was game on. Go! (Chaisson 2021).

The library wasn't just about sex, however. In a 1994 interview with Macleans magazine, former NDP MP Svend Robinson – one of Canada's first out gay parliamentarians – famously recalled his undergrad university years: "at the University of British Columbia, he would sit at a carrel by the window in the library. The books stacked on his desk all bore the same call number: HQ 76" (Fulton 1994). The call number refers to the section containing books on homosexuality, a valuable resource in cities and towns where other queer books and magazines were still difficult to find. As that section grew at Memorial's QEII Library, queers from across the province were gradually drawn to it as well.

RM Kennedy was one of them. As a teenager, still in high school, he used to skip school and hitchhike into St. John's in order to spend time reading queer books at the university library. Kennedy's Catholic high school only had a small library, but some of the nuns took pity on the voracious young reader and gave him special permission to access the convent library, which had more books. The books were all theological in nature – on Saint Augustine, or Saint John of the Cross – but they were still books, and Kennedy devoured them. When the priest found out, however, he ordered an end to Kennedy's visits.

The priest said I could no longer have access to the library, and the reason was that only the clergy can interpret the word of God. So I got banned – from reading Catholic texts! – at the age of fifteen. So that's when I was like: 'I'm going to go and find books.' And I started skipping school to go and find books.

I didn't take anything out. I didn't have a [university] library card, so I could only sit there and look at the books, and read them. But... books were for sure an entrance for me into the world. When you're a queer in a small town, your world is so small (Kennedy 2022).

When Ramona Roberts attended Memorial in the late 1990s, the library still provided an important space for queers. She too gravitated toward the HQ shelves in the QEII library. People would carry on entire conversations in the margins of books in that section, she recalls. Sometimes people would write homophobic remarks in the margins, and other people would fire back, carrying on full debates and arguments.

Roberts had been assigned a carrel in the library, which was always full of stacks of queer-themed books. Once after stepping away briefly, she returned to her carrel and found a note on the stack of books propositioning her for a meeting in the women's bathroom. She didn't go.

In a weird remote kind of way [the library] was like a meeting place. Just

seeing the [queer] books come and go and knowing that other people besides me
were checking them out and reading them, and sometimes writing stuff back.
It was maybe the precursor to an online community – people would just write
whatever comments they wanted [in the books] (Roberts 2021).

One unlikely space which also turned into a queer haven, at least for a
time, was the campus chaplaincy. Sharp Dopler recalls attending Memorial in
the 1980s. Having been raised Catholic, they got involved in the faith community on campus, and found it a surprisingly open space, supervised by priests
whose views were rooted in liberation theology.

I was very Catholic. I was going to Mass every day, I was involved in the
chaplaincy, and I was involved in a youth group… We were into all kinds of crazy
shit there. We were doing liturgical dance, and sacred clowning, all kinds of crazy
shit. Then the Jesuits got upset because people were leaving Pius X and coming
to St. John's College [the chapel at Memorial] because Mass was more fun at St.
John's College (Dopler 2021).

Dopler initially entertained thoughts about pursuing a career in the church.
"Then this priest says to me: 'You need to understand your sexuality before
you can make a choice to change how you express your sexuality.' He said
'God made [homosexuality] too, and it's okay.' That changed everything. It
changed everything for me."

Chaisson also got a glimpse of the chaplaincy's inclusiveness during that
time, but in his case, it served to drive him away. "That's where I saw this one
person wearing a rainbow flag on his coat," he recalled. "And then I immediately thought: 'I gotta stay away from that organization. There's a gay guy
there so I can't go near there, because he may have seen me somewhere.'"

MUN GALA

When Greg Bourgeois moved from the small west coast community of Kip-
pens to St. John's to attend Memorial University in 1979, it was a big adjustment. "It was scary, but I was young, I was naïve, so I was more excited than I
was scared I guess," he reflects. The young teenager had had a more positive
and inclusive upbringing than many other queer NLers of his generation.

There's never been a closet for me. I was very fortunate. My family are
of Mi'kmaq and French descent. The Mi'kmaq side of the family – my moth-
er's side – were very accepting. When I was a child of five or six years old,
I remember being very vocal about how I loved Tarzan – the old television
show used to come on Saturday mornings. I always wanted to be Jane. My
mother's family were very accommodating. My father and my father's fam-
ily just sort of ignored it, he didn't know how to deal with it really. But
I remember my mother calling me Two Spirit. She told me that Two Spirit
meant that I had a male and a female soul, and she said I was very lucky

because I would be able to see life from both points of view. That's how she put it. Actually, I don't think she used the term Two Spirit – that term came later – but she told me I had 'two souls'. She said: 'You will have insights into things.' My mom was a very spiritual lady... and she taught me things about my heritage as a child growing up. I lost my mom at the age of twelve – she passed away from cancer – so I lost her at a very young age, but she was an amazing woman, and her sisters were all much the same, they were very loving women. So I was surrounded by a lot of female influence as a child. My community was basically my cousins, and they were great to me. It was always just sort of accepted that I was different. There were never any real issues of bullying or anything. When my mom passed away I had to take over the cooking and the cleaning and running the house. I didn't really have my own life as such until 1979 when I came in to St. John's and started university. So that was a real culture shock for me (Bourgeois 2022).

Like many NLers from outside of St. John's, he moved directly into one of the campus residences, Barnes House, when he arrived. Students roomed two to a room in those days, and residences were segregated by sex. It was not uncommon for women to stay over in the men's residences, Bourgeois recalls. Often during the first few weeks of the semester, female relatives — cousins, sisters — would stay with male residents while they looked for accommodations in town (there were fewer female residence spaces than male). Bourgeois' roommate didn't arrive in town until partway through the semester, so for the first several weeks he had a room to himself. This led to some misunderstandings. "People assumed I was a female, and that's why I was in a single room. Even with a name like Greg. I guess because of my voice and mannerisms and the fact that my hair was longer — I didn't have a moustache or a beard at that point — apparently there was a lot of controversy about whether I was male or female."

Still, he recalls, people were cordial and friendly. That changed when his roommate arrived, and his housemates learned that not only was Bourgeois a man, but he was a gay man. His roommate was from California and had no problems with it, but some of the Newfoundlanders in the house did. Unbeknownst to Bourgeois, they called a secret house meeting one night while he was at the library studying. They told the others they wanted him out of the house because he was gay.

Roy Rowsell was house president at that point, and basically Roy stood up and said: 'Well what has he done? He's been great with everyone, he has good house spirit, he was good during frosh week. He's always there to help anybody who needs any help. You've all gone to him for things.' He said: 'No, I really don't see what's wrong' (Ibid.).

The residents took a vote, and the proposal to evict Bourgeois from the house was voted down. The instigators still caused him trouble, Bourgeois said, but never to his face after that.

Not every gay resident's experience turned out as positively.

In October 1986, *The Muse* ran a gripping letter from Memorial English professor Roberta Buchanan (former member of CHAN). In it, she recounted the horrific experience of a student named 'John' living in Bowater Residence at the MUN St. John's campus. According to her account, in June during the summer semester mid-term break, when his roommate was away for the break and he was all alone:

... a group of six or seven men entered his room and beat him up. He passed out, and when he regained consciousness everything was wet, and there was 3 or 4 inches of water on the floor. [The student] was in a state of shock: he remembers wandering in a wooded area, and being taken to the Health Sciences Complex by a couple who saw him from their car. He was covered in blood; he had tried to commit suicide by slashing his arms. Why had this totally unprovoked attack been made upon him? Apparently, because he was gay (Buchanan 1986).

Homophobic slogans had also been painted on the walls of his room, Buchanan continued. She said the student spent several weeks in psychiatric care dealing with shock and depression stemming from the attack. When he recovered sufficiently to return to residence – escorted by security – to retrieve his belongings, other students told him he wasn't welcome back (Ibid.).

Buchanan's letter was full of rage toward a student body and a university that would permit such things to happen on campus. The following week *The Muse* ran a letter from another resident denying the incident she described; the author admitted John's room was flooded but denied that he was beaten up (the flooding of rooms was "common," the author said, adding cryptically that in this case the flooding was "provoked" Lundrigan 1986). Whatever the truth of the matter, Buchanan's letter invoked rage with a purpose: her letter also announced the formation of a new organization on campus, dedicated to confronting homophobia, and she urged "those who abhor homophobia, and who believe human rights and individual dignity override questions of sexual orientation, gender, colour or creed" to get involved by writing letters of support, making donations, or joining themselves. It was a striking way of announcing the arrival of Memorial University's first organized queer activists: the MUN Gay and Lesbian Alliance (GALA; (Buchanan 1986).

MUN GALA formed in the fall of 1986 with the aim of supporting gay and lesbian students, faculty and staff at the university. To celebrate the group's formation, newly opened local lesbian bar, Earhart's, provided its space free of charge for an inaugural Hallowe'en party on November 1, and donated a 40-ouncer to the group's fundraising raffle.

The group was founded by Ron Knowling, then a fourth-year undergrad studying economic history who had also served as News Editor with *The Muse*. "MUN GALA was supposed to be more of a social group than a political group," recalled Knowling 35 years later. They held some barbecues at members' homes, and Buchanan recalls giving a journal workshop to the group.

Inevitably the group wound up involved in activism. Its very existence became a matter of controversy on campus when it sought official recognition. Student clubs and societies like MUN GALA had to be approved, or 'ratified', by the MUN Students' Union (MUNSU) prior to receiving funding and permission to operate officially on campus. When MUN GALA first applied for official society status in the fall semester of 1986, their application was unanimously approved by the Students' Union. The following winter semester, in 1987, however, the group faced resistance of a sort in the form of a competing organization called 'NorMUN'.

According to coverage in *The Muse* from the period, "NorMUN's professed aim was to provide a discussion group to promote 'traditional sex roles,' counsel, and act as a group resource centre for emotional problems" (Hallett 1987). *The Muse* reporter Bob Hallett, who would go on to become a well-known musician and co-found the band Great Big Sea, covered the controversy and said NorMUN also referred to itself as "the heterosexual society." Student Union president, John Reid, accused NorMUN of seeking ratification solely to "discredit" MUN GALA, however NorMUN's application provoked a debate among the union's elected Board as to whether it was appropriate to start ratifying groups based on their "sexual preference" (Ibid.).

During the debate, MUNSU Councillor Barry Reilly argued that NorMUN represented heterosexuals and as such had the right to be ratified if they were going to start ratifying groups like GALA for homosexuals. MUNSU VP-Academic Ron Byrne fired back that heterosexuals were already "well represented" at Memorial and in the broader society. The ensuing debate also provided a platform for homophobic attacks on MUN GALA. In the end MUN GALA's application was approved (NorMUN's was rejected, although lead organizer Bill Grant promised to keep trying), however the controversy deterred Knowling and other group members from applying for ratification ever again. They continued to meet informally and hold events, but ceased to seek or hold official group status on campus (Hallett 1987).

"I thought it would be good to have an organization on campus that could provide a social focus for gay and lesbian students and create a source of pride in the community," he told Muse reporter Padraic Brake. "Unfortunately I think all the controversy stirred up by the ratification of the group destroyed any chance of this happening. I still think that there is a need for it on campus" (Ibid.).

For the following decade, most organized activism would occur through community-based groups, in which MUN students continued to play an important role. However, as Memorial's student population grew, so too did the need for a campus-based queer organization.

It wasn't just students, but staff as well who were pushing for equality at the university. Greg Bourgeois had attended Memorial as a student and in the mid-1980s he got a full-time job, working at the university library. Not long thereafter he met his first serious boyfriend, and they moved in together. This led Bourgeois to wonder whether he might be able to get health insurance coverage for his partner, the way straight couples were able to.

Nobody could really answer my question, so I got in touch with the Director of Human Resources. I figured there was no harm in asking. I was with the union [CUPE] but I never went through the union, I just went directly to Human Resources. I think that was in 1986 or 1987. I went over and I sat down with the Director in his office. He offered me a cup of coffee, and being young and naive I suppose I just went ahead and asked him. The Director said: 'There's no precedent for health care benefits for a same-sex spouse. But your points are very valid – anyone who's been co-habitating for six months are considered a common-law spouse in the heterosexual relationship, so I don't see why not. Let me check with the insurance companies for you.' So he checked with the insurance company and a day or two later he got back to me and he said: 'Well Mr. Bourgeois, why don't you come over now and fill out the paperwork for your boyfriend.' So from that point onwards that was available to same-sex couples at the university. MUN were very forward-thinking in that respect (Bourgeois 2022).

Progress wasn't as easily accomplished on every front, or at every university. As a contrast which aptly demonstrates the fickle mood of the times, the University of British Columbia came under international opprobrium when it refused to allow the use of its campus for the 'Gay Olympics.'

The 'Gay Games' as they are known today, were started by the Federation of Gay Games which was founded by gay former Olympians in San Francisco in 1982. The first two games, which are held every two years, had been held in San Francisco, and in 1986 organizers requested use of UBC facilities for a forthcoming gay Olympiad in 1990. "(It's) an issue of the community identifying (homosexuality) with the University of British Columbia," UBC President David Strangway told Canadian University Press (CUP) in defense of the decision. "One doesn't want to have an informal identity with an issue of such controversy... I don't think the university is the place to make political statements. Why would one not participate in the normal men's athletics and the normal women's athletics?" (May 1988). Members of the UBC Board of Governors also suggested if the games were held there, it could serve as a deterrent to future students and enrolment might drop.

That year's Gay Games – the first to be held outside the United States – garnered the most controversy thus far. Religious groups organized protests and spent a great deal of money on advertising campaigns attacking the games, and the BC provincial government refused to provide any funding. The games went ahead at BC Place Stadium, and they were the first Gay Games at which world records were set.

Out On Campus

In the early 1990s, the city experienced a brief dearth of organized activism. GALT had dissolved, and NGALE had not yet arisen in its wake. MUN GALA no longer existed. NAN was in the process of coming together. What queer activism went on was mostly centred around the ACNL, but the focus of that organization was the AIDS struggle. With no organized queer presence in the capital city, the St. John's Status of Women Centre, then located on Military Road, found itself the recipient of calls and letters from queer people – mostly lesbians – looking for support in the city. The Centre itself had only recently reopened following the controversy and human rights complaint pertaining to issues of sexuality. When it received inquiries about queer events or organizing, for a time the newly reopened Centre began forwarding calls and requests to a MUN student and activist named Liam Hustins (Hustins transitioned in the early 2000s, and assumed the name Liam at that time; his story is told in greater detail in Chapter 9). Recognizing the need for a more organized support network, Hustins, along with fellow MUN undergrad Mireille Sampson, established a MUN society called Out on Campus, which was formally recognized by the MUN Students' Union in early February 1995 (Harnett 1995).[38]

Student activity was at that time centred in the Thomson Student Centre, or TSC. In the early 2000s, the building was renovated and rebranded as the Bruneau Centre, and student activity moved to a newly constructed University Centre on the other side of the Prince Philip Parkway. The new building was formally named the Joseph R. Smallwood University Centre, but a combination of active resistance from some students, coupled with disinterest from others, resulted in its being referred to through most of its existence simply as the University Centre.

On the second floor of the old TSC, in a narrow corridor behind the gym (which frequently doubled as a concert arena) were a group of offices known as 'Society Row'. This was where officially ratified student groups had their offices (only a lucky dozen or so were awarded offices, out of the dozens of student societies which existed). Many societies doubled up in the cramped, closet-like rooms. Some of the last remaining closed-circuit connections to campus radio station CHMR were located in those offices. Closed-circuit connections had been installed throughout campus in the 1960s, and the station used to broadcast in lounges and cafeterias. Over the years many of those connections had broken down. In some cases, electricians doing repairs or upgrades were confused by the connections, and simply disconnected them. But along Society Row in the early 1990s you could still press a button and tune in to the radio

---

[38] By the time of its formal recognition other community groups such as NGALE and NAN had also come into existence, but community queries were still often forwarded to the campus group.

station directly in a few of those rooms.

When Out on Campus was initially ratified, there was a long waiting list of groups looking for offices, so Hustins and Sampson approached Lynn Peddle, coordinator of the Women's Resource Centre (WRC) on campus, to ask if the group could use the WRC space. She readily agreed. At the time, the Women's Resource Centre was headed up by a coordinator who was hired by the Students' Union. In the late 1990s, the group would restructure itself as a grassroots, membership-driven collective; in more recent years it has rebranded itself as Intersections: A Resource Centre for Marginalized Genders.

The WRC offered Out on Campus space in its office to meet as well as to build and store a small resource library. Ratification of student societies by MUNSU came with a small operating grant, and Sampson was eager to use the money to acquire queer books and reading material. A new alternative bookstore named Bennington Gate had recently opened in Churchill Square, a few minutes' walk from campus, and this bookshop had dedicated sections for feminist and queer literature.

"It was the first time I remembered ever seeing queer books in St. John's anywhere," recalled Sampson. "We used basically all of our budget on books and put this book collection together."

The group advertised itself by postering on campus, and attracted a small but dedicated membership.

"I remember very tiny, itty bitty meetings," said Sampson, looking back on events a quarter century later.

Out on Campus sounds very active and you think of it as being an activist group, but what most of the meetings came down to was just a tiny handful of people basically doing mental health support.

Most of the time, what I found was someone would come to me and they'd say they were a little bit out, and they were struggling with the stuff that was going wrong. One guy came out to his family, and his sister said: 'If you want to be gay that's fine but don't come near my kids.' Another guy had been married, and he was worried that if his wife knew, she would use it to prevent him from having access to his children. There were all these legal implications and family implications of coming out – it was still a really big deal.

Back then, ultimately it wasn't really activism that people on campus needed so much, it was someone to talk to. So that was most of what happened, these intimate conversations (Sampson 2021).

With a permanent home and funding, the organization grew rapidly. With growth came homophobic backlash. On Pink Triangle Day, February 14, 1996, Out on Campus launched a poster awareness campaign in recognition of the day and the ongoing struggle against homophobia. The next day many of the posters had been destroyed or defaced, with homophobic messages written over them. "Just because you have defective genes, keep it to yourself!" one said.

"You can't just kill a person anymore and get away with it," spokesperson Mireille Sampson told media in the wake of the violent messaging, reminding them that Pink Triangle Day was named after the triangle homosexuals were required to wear in Nazi concentration camps. "But people are still being gay-bashed and this direct way of oppressing needs to be addressed… Thousands of people died in gas chambers, and for enlightened students to write something like that shows that they aren't any better than those Nazis" (Murphy 1996).

The community-based NGALE had already formed by the time Out on Campus submitted its papers to the Students' Union to formally ratify. Relations between on-campus and off-campus activists would go through ups and downs as time went on, but during those early years, the relationship was a close one. NGALE promoted Out on Campus in its newsletter, and Sampson, Hustins, and other campus activists regularly attended NGALE meetings.

During NGALE's early years, however, it was the student activists who took a prominent role in public speaking and lobbying on behalf of the city's growing queer movement.

"Most of the [NGALE members] were older, maybe in their thirties or forties," recalled Sampson, who was barely 20 when she co-founded Out on Campus. "Most of them didn't want to be that public. They weren't out to their families, they weren't out to their workplaces. Whereas we [students] were the ones that didn't really care. So we ended up being the ones that were in the newspaper or on the television news or whatever."

Activism aside, peer mutual support remained a key raison d'etre for the student group. "The point that sticks in my head from back then was really the need for mental health support," said Sampson. "What people really needed was mental health support. I would think that it's still very necessary and important."

LGBT-MUN

As we have seen, Memorial University has always been a nexus through which new ideas, people and insights enter the province, and the arrival of students and staff from other provinces brought fresh activist experiences and expectations to the city, including vibrant new ideas for queer activism.

Ramona Roberts was originally from Nova Scotia, and had just completed an undergraduate degree at McGill University in Montreal. There she had minored in Women's Studies, and wanted to continue in that discipline. She felt the urge to return to the Maritimes, and since Memorial University had a well-recognized Masters program in Women's Studies, she applied and was one of the five students accepted to the program for the fall semester 1996.

While living in Montreal, Roberts had come out as lesbian. "I had had a gradual coming out process at McGill, and came to MUN looking for the queer student group, to help me continue my own journey and to make some friends," she recalled twenty-five years later. She remembers getting off the bus in front of the university, on Elizabeth Avenue. From that vantage, only the diminutive Arts & Administration Building[39] is visible, and she recalls a sense of horror when she initially thought that was the entirety of campus. It was only as she climbed the hill to the Arts Building, that the remainder of the sprawling campus revealed itself.

What proved more elusive was the queer community she sought. When she asked around whether there was a queer group, people were quick to mention Out on Campus, and many of them remembered Sampson and Hustins. But both those organizers had moved on from MUN by that point, and Out on Campus had slid into inactivity in their absence. Roberts realized to her dismay there was no active campus group. "So, like you do when you're 22, I thought: 'Well I'll just have to make one!'" she recalled. The prospect was a daunting one.

It's so easy to feel like you're the first, especially if you're young, or if you're doing something that's new for you. Or if you happen to come in at a moment where there's a gap that you're filling. It's easy to feel like there's nothing and no one else. Which can make you feel really special but also really lonely (Roberts 2021).

Roberts scheduled a meeting with an executive director at the Students' Union, to find out what was involved in creating a campus society. As she explained what sort of group she wanted to form, the executive director suddenly became furtive and urged her to come in and close the door. She recalls that, "He talked to me quite nicely, but the idea that it called for a closed-door discussion in his mind kind of gave me a sense of what things would be like."

Roberts filled in the paperwork and revived the group, this time calling it Lesbian, Gay, Bisexual and Transgender Students at MUN, or LGBT-MUN.[40] There was no office space available and a lengthy waiting list for one, so like her predecessors she approached the Women's Resource Centre, which again offered to let the group use its space for storage and private meetings. It irked Roberts that some offices appeared disused – one was even used just as a stor-

---

[39] Often just referred to as the Arts Building.

[40] For reasons that are unclear to the early organizers, the group's name was actually ratified as "LBGT-MUN" or "Lesbians, Bisexuals, Gay and Trans students At MUN" as opposed to the more common "LGBT" acronym. It is unclear why that was the case, but the atypical acronym stuck and that is how the group became known on campus. Efforts were periodically made to correct the order of the acronym and bring it in line with the more universally common LGBT, however the early LBGT phrasing inexorably returned. This confusion was only finally truly resolved when the group rebranded itself as MUN SAGA (Sexual And Gender Advocacy) in the 2010s. Because both names were used interchangeably on campus, for the purpose of continuity in this section I simply refer to the group as LGBT-MUN, even though for much of its existence the name "LBGT-MUN" was more commonly used.

age unit for the MUN Ball Hockey Team – while LGBT-MUN had a credible need for a private and safe space. Her lobbying paid off when the Students' Union relocated Student Security (a sort of student auxiliary branch of Campus Enforcement and Patrol) out of Society Row, freeing up an office which was assigned to LGBT-MUN.

Roberts personally recruited some of the group's early members. One of the courses she TA'd as a graduate student teaching assistant had an openly gay undergrad in it, named Mike Hickey (they subsequently changed their name to Mikiki and appear elsewhere in this book). She approached them, and the two went to work recruiting others. They didn't have much money, so they figured stickers would be the most cost-effective way to advertise the group. They could cram six stickers onto a piece of paper and photocopy it onto sticker sheets, so they made stickers reading 'LGBT-MUN' down the side. Most of the sticker was blank, and one of their first events was a sticker-making party where they coloured them with markers, writing different individualized messages in the empty space. Because they had neither an office nor a phone at the time, Roberts decided they could put her name and home phone number on all the stickers. The internet was still not widely used at this point, but the group obtained an email address and added that to the stickers as well.

"Then we had a very sneaky evening sticker party running around slapping them up on stuff," Roberts recalled. They put them up all over campus – on doors, walls, lockers. They focused especially on bathrooms, sticking them up inside the stalls, which they figured would provide a private and safe space for any student who wanted to copy down the phone number.

It was a little bit scary. We'd heard rumours of [queer] people having been beaten up on campus. I remember being afraid of getting pinned down in the residences. [Residence] didn't have the reputation of being a very safe space at the time. But they had those tunnels, so we'd go through the underground tunnel and then up the stairwell into each residence. We'd start at the top, slap a sticker on each stairwell door and then run like hell down to the bottom, and get as far away from there as we could before anybody came by (Ibid.).

At one point they did get stopped by a campus security officer. He said he'd seen the stickers popping up all over campus, and asked whether they were the ones responsible for them. Roberts admitted they were. The officer nodded, paused, and then awkwardly asked if they would kindly stick them on glass instead of walls, because that way they wouldn't damage the paint.

The sticker campaign produced the desired effect, Roberts said. "It worked! The stickers got stuck up, and people started calling."

When people called to express interest in getting involved, one of the challenges the group faced was vetting members before letting them in. Most of the group's members were not out, and there was a great concern that homophobes might try to infiltrate the group in order to out its members. Roberts fielded many of the calls herself, and had to navigate a tough line between being supportive, but also cautious. She recalls one occasion when a prospective member called, and as part of the vetting process she asked him questions about whether he was out to anyone. She later found out that he misinterpreted this as her suggesting that he should come out, and as a result he did wind up coming out to a family member after the telephone discussion.

It went fine for him, but I felt a responsibility there, that I should not have [said that]. But it was a difficult balance because each new person that came in was going to see all of the other people and have a way to find us again. It was a delicate question of trust. But it worked out – we didn't ever have anybody come that didn't genuinely want to be there (Ibid.).

Confidentiality was critical at the time, said Roberts. "It may actually have been a matter of safety, even life and death in some cases."

She recalls one incident when she was speaking with a trans member of the group in the TSC cafeteria. The trans student wasn't out to anyone outside of LGBT-MUN, including their family. Roberts, meanwhile, was widely recognized on campus, both for her public activism as well as her colourful, visibly striking hair styles. While they were chatting, another student from the trans member's small, rural home community approached them with a curious look, and asked the two how they knew each other.

My heart just froze. There was a bit of shuffling and mumbling about running into each other at the TSC, and the moment passed. But I remember thinking: 'Wow, this really can happen and we really do need to watch our step.' Because I had the impression from speaking with that person, that the consequences would have been very serious [if they'd been outed]. Just calling somebody by the wrong name or the wrong pronoun at the wrong time felt like a pretty big deal.

I'm happy to hear how different it is now, but there was no question in my mind that [confidentiality] was critically important. People deserve to have their own process, emotionally and socially, about coming out and transitioning – they're just sorting out their identity for themselves and expressing it. But in addition, it's not always safe to let the world know who you are. Or at least it wasn't then (Ibid.).

Because 'Ramona Roberts' was such a memorable name, and also because it was written as the contact on all the group's publicity material, members used to joke that they were 'Friends of Ramona', riffing on the famous queer epithet 'Friends of Dorothy.'

For Roberts, visibility brought concerns as well as laughs, and her experiences reflect the still-powerful stigmas of the period. She found that people off campus often read her as a man. She didn't mind, but this created problems when they read her as an effeminate man. As a consequence, she would often deliberately "butch up" her appearance, in order to be more masculine rather than risk being read as an effeminate or gay man.

"I was very alive to the possible risk of gender perception by others in different times and different spaces," she recalled. "It ranged a lot. I wasn't always afraid, but there were definitely moments."

One occasion she vividly recalls occurred when her girlfriend came to visit from Montreal. They were at a Tim Hortons off-campus. Both of them had a fairly androgynous look at the time, and while they were sitting there, two other men came in and sat down as well. The two men kept looking at them oddly, and when her girlfriend got up to use the washroom, one of the men got up and followed her. The washroom was down a narrow corridor invisible to the main seating area, and they were the only customers in the café.

I remember just feeling so paralyzed. I thought, 'If he's gone in after her, then if I go in there the other one will come after me and no one will know what happens after that.' So I couldn't go [after my girlfriend]. It was horrible to be thinking about what was happening. How long do I wait? If I go to the counter and ask for help, will anybody help me? I didn't have a cell phone, I couldn't have texted people to come or called the police on my own if I felt I needed to. So I just waited, I horribly waited.

Then the guy came back by himself, and he talked to the other guy, and I could see that he said the word 'Women's' (Ibid.).

The two men left, but they remained seated in their car outside the Tim Hortons for a long time. Eventually they drove away, but a few moments later they came back. Roberts realized they were just driving around the block, returning every few minutes to wait at the Tim Hortons. Roberts and her girlfriend – fearing the men were waiting outside to follow them – waited until the men drove around the block, and then they ran as fast as they could across the parking lot as well as an adjoining one. They made it to a nearby grocery, and from there they used a payphone to call a taxi. Once in the taxi, they made sure they weren't still being followed before finally heading home.

How right were we to be afraid? We'll never know. But I was scared for a long time after that. It was clear to me they were looking for us. And just that sense of powerlessness, wanting with all of my being to go in the bathroom after my girlfriend and just knowing that the other guy was going to come after me if I did. Then we would for sure have been on our own – we would have lost the possibility of getting any help. Stuff like that happened to other people too, but that's the one that sticks with me after all that time. That was really personal (Ibid.).

As LGBT-MUN grew, Roberts reached out to the community-based group NGALE, which was also in a major growth phase at that point. She began attending NGALE meetings, and the two groups reestablished a strong relationship. Some NGALE members who were not affiliated with the university began attending LGBT-MUN meetings as well, for the additional support and community. Trans community members in particular began coming to campus, since LGBT-MUN had a stronger trans contingent than NGALE.

Organizing both on and off campus intensified in the wake of Justice Barry's ruling in the Nolan case [see Chapter 6] and the subsequent campaign for a provincial human rights code amendment. NGALE and NAN reached out to LGBT-MUN to involve them in the lobbying process. Roberts recalls getting a phone call from Gerry Rogers in 1997, and was asked to attend a very hastily organized meeting between NGALE, NAN and provincial Minister of Labour, Kevin Aylward. She attended and spoke to the importance of the human rights amendment for students and young people. Avoiding discrimination in housing and employment was a serious concern for students, she emphasized. The Canadian Federation of Students had passed a resolution calling for a human rights amendment as well, she told them.

In 1997, the MUN Students' Union received a public presentation from LGBT-MUN, and approved a resolution to replace the student society with a fully-fledged LGBT-MUN Resource Centre. At the time the Women's Resource Centre was the only other resource centre on campus, but MUNSU formalized the 'resource centre' category as one supporting marginalized groups of students and which would provide Centres with a much larger designated space on campus and a significantly higher semesterly funding grant. LGBT-MUN was the second student group to be awarded Resource Centre status, joining the WRC in that role.

The larger presence of LGBT-MUN meant it was also a target for homophobic and transphobic attacks. In October 1997, the Thomson Student Centre was defaced with swastikas and anti-gay slogans, with LGBT-MUN bearing the brunt of the attack. Spokespersons told media that such vandalism was sadly common, and the group's posters around campus were often defaced in a similar manner (Temple & Taylor 1997).

The awareness raising clearly worked, and the little group was growing fast. In addition to their general membership meetings, they launched a women's sub-group, as well as a trans group. Given the lack of visible supports in the community, the trans group in particular drew a number of members from off-campus, and LGBT-MUN made a decision that they would not turn any non-student community members away. The sole exception to this was when they started receiving calls from under-aged youth in the K-12 school system, who had heard about the campus activism and were also looking for support. Organizers made the difficult decision not to admit under-aged youth to the meetings.[41] Fortunately, the support gap for young people was soon filled when the St. John's Status of Women Centre launched a youth group specifically for queer and questioning youth.

The presence of older (non-student) community members in the group came to be seen as a strength by Roberts and others:

I think it was probably a gift to students, particularly in the trans group, that some adults who were beyond their student years attended as well, be-

---

41 Other members had a different recollection of this, and recalled the group admitting and providing active support to underage community members.

cause it provided an opportunity for the students to see an image of a future for themselves, in a world that was barely starting to enter the internet and still didn't provide a lot of images like that (Roberts 2021).

The group wrote letters-to-the-editor in local newspapers whenever it seemed appropriate, and they also organized social activities. Roberts remembers the group's annual Christmas party being particularly important for members. Of the group's membership, most were not out to their family members, and when they returned to their home communities to celebrate the holidays with their families, they would be returning to the closet. Other group members had come out, and relationships had ruptured with their families as a result. The LGBT-MUN parties provided an opportunity for members to celebrate the holiday with their chosen friends and family, without having to hide their identities from those around them. Those spaces and events were deeply meaningful and special, recalls Roberts.

While the leadership at the Women's Resource Centre on campus had long been a source of support for queer organizers, not all WRC volunteers were equally supportive. Roberts, who volunteered for the WRC as well, recalls discussions with some women volunteers who were ambivalent or uncomfortable about the presence of lesbians and other queer people. One woman told her she felt disgusted at the idea of women having sex. That said, leading WRC organizers worked hard to try to maintain a positive and inclusive environment at the Centre, and Roberts felt they mostly succeeded.

One of the initiatives LGBT-MUN took on was production of the 'LGBT Guide to MUN'. The slim little pink-covered volume was designed to be carried around easily and privately, and contained everything from coming out stories to advice about campus to community supports for queer students.

We wanted to create something that people could carry around with them. We wanted it to be small on purpose. We wanted to make it something that people could possess secretly and read when no one else was around, and find out that they weren't alone and maybe find some resources to get them on their way, or maybe just something to help them hang on inside themselves for a little bit until the next step came along (Ibid.).

They received some financial support from both the undergrad and graduate students' unions, and left stacks of the guide outside their office for people to pick up. They left copies with the QEII Library, and the Women's Resource Centre. And, inspired by the success of their sticker campaign, they did a few guerrilla drops of copies in other strategic locations around campus. The Guide generated a lot of interest. In addition to coverage by campus media, local television news agency NTV invited Roberts to the studio to talk about the guide.

Roberts graduated and left the province in 1999, going on to pursue a successful career as a lawyer. LGBT-MUN is still thriving today, although in an effort to be more inclusive it changed its name to Sexual And Gender Advocacy (MUN-SAGA) in the 2010s. Early members, like Mikiki, will never forget how meaningful and important the group's role was for queer students and the broader community alike.

"There was such a real sense of community," they said. "I met so many other amazing, queer baby angels who were so helpful for the development and formation of my own sexual identity. And that's where I developed some of my first platonic queer same-gender friendships. It was amazing."

"A Handful of Precious Rebels": The 1991 Muse Lesbian and Gay Supplement

The morning of Friday, February 15, 1991 dawned cold, dark and dreary. As one would expect for mid-February a heavy layer of snow covered the ground. Rain was in store: 57 millimetres of it would wash away the majority of that snow by day's end.

Valentine's Day had come and gone, but Thursday evening was really just the opening act. Most students looked forward to the weekend, when Valentine's concerts and parties would spill out across campus and all over town. At the popular Bridget's Pub downtown, the Blind Pigs had played the night before and Chris Hennessey was on the lineup for tonight. Other students would head straight from class to the Strand Lounge in the Avalon Mall where they might splurge on two-for-one steaks, or enjoy the tunes of the Travelling Blueberries (a Traveling Wilburys cover band) who were playing that weekend.

A renewed organizing effort was underway among members of the queer community, who had recently put together the city's latest activist outfit: Gays and Lesbians Together (GALT). The group had had a meeting at 7:30pm the previous night in space offered up by the St. John's Status of Women's Centre, then located on Military Road. Little did they anticipate the turmoil that was about to be unleashed the next day, which would set the stage for a rampant display of homophobia and spark intense divisions among the city's queers.

Back on campus, the halls and public spaces buzzed with the excited activity typical of a Friday. This was still an era when campus was a deeply, intractably social place. These days students come and go to campus for largely functional reasons: class, library research, meeting professors and printing off assignments. Today's campus has mostly ceased to exist as a social space. Even the student centre often lies empty and sterile, but in the 1990s these spaces were lively and rambunctious. At that time, students came to campus and spent the day there, simply because it was the place for students to be. The thought of leaving campus when your classes were over would strike most students as bizarre, and possibly anti-social. Unless you had a job, what else would you do with your day besides hang out with your school friends, or perhaps make some new ones? The tunnels – largely empty these days – were packed shoulder-to-shoulder with students sitting on the floor, leaning against their respective lockers, avoiding class, chatting, flirting, playing music. Ghettoblasters blaring heavy metal and bad rock competed with homegrown guitars, harmonicas, and bodhrans.

Today the Bruneau Centre is a sterile, silent building with a hospital-like atmosphere. Renovated for corporate interests, it's rare to see students' faces unless they're dashing to or from class in one of the two large lecture halls in the building. But in 1991 – then called the Thomson Student Centre – it was the beating heart of campus. On the third floor was the large, sprawling campus and community radio station CHMR-FM. Outside its doors, a large seating area was packed with tables full of students smoking, playing cards, sharing boisterous stories with one another. Invariably you could find someone willing to sell you drugs at one of the tables; look hard enough and you'd find a generous soul willing to give them away for free.

The stairwell was also a hangout; bedecked with bizarre and abstract (locally-produced) modernist art, students perched on ledges, smoking and getting intimate with each other. University-produced signage even beseeched students to avoid blocking access to stairways with public displays of affection.

The third floor overlooked a large gym, used for concerts, rallies, and sporting events (the campus ball hockey league stank the building up Wednesday evenings, but could they ever draw a crowd!). Behind the gym was a narrow row of offices known as 'Society Row', where many of the student clubs and societies had their homes (including, a couple of years later, Out on Campus, the first iteration of LGBT-MUN). On the first floor were the MUN Students' Union offices, along with the Breezeway Bar and its two large spillover rooms: the Gold Room and the Ping Pong Room (which was exactly what its name suggested). Line-ups for the bar would begin around 11am. The bar opened at noon, but the moment its doors opened the waiting patrons would pour in, lunches in hand, to grab up tables and chairs. Some came to procure seats for friends who would join them after class. Within minutes of opening the bar would be thick with the haze of cigarette smoke, the air equally dense with the hubbub of conversation and laughter. Student employees clad in prestigious polo shirts emblazoned *Breezeway Staff* circulated with trays full of plastic beer glasses. Hulking male student bouncers flexed muscles beneath tight polo shirts at the door, presiding over the inevitable line waiting to gain entrance. It would be almost another decade before a female student filed the discrimination complaint which eventually struck down the management policy of hiring only men for security.

Back then, more than a few students would waltz in at noon and not leave until kicked out over twelve hours later when the bar closed.

The first floor also housed the university's large cafeteria, not yet privatized. Unionized employees dished out a range of dorm-style fare, but here eating was a secondary function. Professors often used this space (as well as the Breezeway) to meet with students, and socializing went on at all hours. Certain corners were almost permanent pop-up stalls for pot sales; students would brazenly offer their goods from large garbage bags full of drugs half-heartedly hidden under the tables.

On this particular day, a large GMC tracker dominated a corner of the seating area: MUNSU was selling tickets on it as a fundraiser for its Childcare Facility. The university had for years refused to provide any childcare support for students or staff, and so the Students' Union had established its own daycare centre for the university community in 1975. Demand far exceeded the capacity of the dark, moldy trailers which housed the daycare, and so MUNSU was aiming to fundraise $1 million to build a new, state-of-the-art facility.

In 1991, campus buzzed with raging debates over the (first) Gulf War which followed Iraq's invasion of Kuwait. The air campaign associated with Operation Desert Storm had begun about three weeks earlier, but American-led forces wouldn't launch the ground war for another week. Posters advertised anti-war movies and protest planning meetings, while in the food court a solitary student set up a table where he sold yellow ribbons to raise funds for the troops.

For most students, Friday was a day to kick back and party.

For volunteer staff at *The Muse* campus newspaper, the morning started like any other Friday. Volunteers straggled in in various stages of hangover throughout the late morning. Being part of an organization like *The Muse* lent you the prestige of being able to leave your bags and coat in the office, as opposed to having to use one of the lockers in the tunnel system. Volunteers would stroll in, drop off their bags and coats, chat a bit with whoever was there, then head on up to the third floor for a smoke and a game of cards.

Friday was the day the weekly paper published. Production nights were Wednesdays: a long, drawn-out affair that often stretched into the early hours of Thursday morning. On Thursday, editors and production staff rested and recovered from the all-night ordeal, while local printers Robinson-Blackmore printed off 10,000 copies of the paper. The copies showed up on campus at some point on Friday morning: bales of them, which had to be loaded onto large steel trolleys and then manually delivered around campus by volunteers throughout the morning. The arduous distribution was usually a job assigned to new recruits: the more elite and experienced writers, meanwhile, would smoke and talk and head off with their fresh copies of the paper to the Breezeway for a beer.

On this particular morning, two young writers – Craig Welsh and Andrew Smith – made a nervous beeline for the cafeteria. They were eager to observe students' reactions as they opened the paper. Because today was the day *The Muse* published its annual Lesbian and Gay Supplement.

The paper had been doing so on and off for nearly a decade, not without controversy. The supplement was first published in 1984, when Editor Robert Stoodley – an out gay man – persuaded staff to run it in recognition of the

International Year of Lesbian and Gay Actions, organized by the International Lesbian and Gay Association (ILGA, which at the time called itself IGA since no women had been present at the 1978 founding meeting; 'Lesbian' wouldn't be added to the name until 1986). The European-based ILGA organized a range of actions that year, including a march of 1000 people on the United Nations protesting for lesbian and gay rights. Stoodley learned about all this from an article in *Pink Ink*, a Toronto-based gay newspaper. He figured it was an opportune moment to expand the public face of queer activism in Newfoundland and Labrador.

His lead editorial in that first 1984 Supplement was subtly critical of previous queer organizing efforts in the city. The following are excerpts from the Supplement:

There is a gay organization in St. John's called GAIN – the Gay Association in Newfoundland. Do you know where their office is (if they have one), what they do in public, or how big their membership is? Highly unlikely. They play it safe, keep out of the public eye, and don't get noticed by anyone (Stoodley 1984A).

There is no gay group on campus, no way for gay students and faculty to get together. Taken together, this means that the gay community in St. John's is fragmented, with no means of contact except bars and the occasional dance. They have no source of news, no avenue of social contact in which to support one another.

There is no other minority in town so isolated. There are religious groups, women's support groups, organizations for various racial minorities. Gay people, estimated at 10% of the population, have no such recourse; in order to associate freely with other lesbians and gays, they must either resort to the bars or take great risks to form a circle of friends. This large minority (which numbers in the tens of thousands in Newfoundland) has no sense of solidarity.

That can end. The ground has been broken, in the form of the now-defunct CHAN (Community Homophile Association of Newfoundland) and GAIN. It's not enough, though. Gay people have to become public. They have to use the media to their advantage. They have to become visible, to refuse to be silent any longer.

And that's why the Muse is printing its first-ever Gay/Lesbian Supplement.

We, the gay men and women of Newfoundland, have been silent too long. It doesn't have to be that way. We can use 1984, our Year of Action, to make ourselves heard and understood. And maybe, in the process, we can unite and destroy our isolation (Ibid.).

We have nothing to lose but our closets! (Ibid.).

The supplement featured a mix of local articles and pieces taken from the Canadian University Press newswire. Fellow *The Muse* writer Jean Greig contributed a piece on political lesbianism. Stoodley also penned a lengthy two-page feature titled "Come Out, Come Out Wherever You Are" discussing the importance of coming out and offering some advice and scenarios for doing so. The spread, which featured several 'coming out'-themed comics penned by himself and other *The Muse* staff, also discussed their experience of homophobia at the Breezeway Bar (Stoodley 1984A).

The supplement apparently provoked quite a reaction; in an editorial looking back on it five years later then-Editor Barend Kiefte said "the general student body was outraged and the reaction was adverse. As far as the students were concerned, the paper had lost some credibility." He suggested that part of the problem was that the original Supplement had included too much opinion and not enough factual news (Kiefte 1989). Yet it was generalized homophobia that clearly drove the outrage. A letter-to-the-editor from an Artie Canon published a week after that first Supplement complained "of the continuing publicity granted to the gay population of this institution... the vast majority of the student body doesn't want to be polluted by this" (Canon 1984).

The impenetrable density of homophobic thought was even better reflected by Barry C. Parsons' response to the supplement. In a letter-to-the-editor titled "Why I won't join da Muse" he wrote: "Does the editor of the Muse think that everybody who is anti-homosexual is homophobic? Certainly they are not. They simply do not agree with the practice, propagation or proliferation of homosexuality" (Parsons 1984).

The next Lesbian and Gay Supplement, which appeared in 1989, generated even more controversy, including disagreement among the paper's own staff. It was preceded by a fevered debate among *The Muse* volunteers about whether they ought to publish one or not. Some argued it would damage the paper's image and reputation. Others argued it wasn't right for them to produce one since there were no publicly out gays or lesbians on staff. When a majority voted in favour of producing the Supplement, Co-News Editor Bernard Tobin resigned in protest (Kiefte 1989).

Yet the seven-page Supplement ran, on February 17, 1989. The lead editorial was written by "RMK & PB" (likely *The Muse* staffers RM Kennedy and Padraic Brake):

This supplement is meant to show the joy and love within the gay and lesbian community, and not just the oppression, which more often than not would get far more coverage by the mainstream media than any positive representation. Certainly one of these joys is the struggle to make it easier for other people to express this love. Hopefully, this supplement will have a part to play in that process, because it counters the shroud of myth that hangs over gay and lesbianism, and therefore counters homophobia. The lesbian and gay movement isn't about the search for tolerance from heterosexuals. It's about the demand for equality and public acceptance! (The Muse 1989).

Articles in that year's Supplement included a discussion of lesbianism as an alternative to patriarchy from Kennedy; Robin Whitaker shared a reflection on her own evolving perceptions of sexual identity; and Beth Ryan penned a feature centrespread exploring the ways in which gays and lesbians struggled to overcome discriminatory legal barriers to form families and raise children. There were articles reprinted from other papers, as well as a guide to gay and lesbian culture (music, films, books). Padraic Brake contributed two articles: a history of the campus activist group MUN Gay And Lesbian Association (GALA), and a personal reflection about heterocentrism on campus, particularly at the Breezeway Bar.

The latter article in particular (Brake 1989) stoked some of the outraged letters-to-the-editor that flooded the paper in response, many of which *The Muse* printed the following week. Stephen Mandville raged in an almost full-page homophobic rant that "This article in last week's Muse is the result of irresponsibility and tasteless attempts to somehow justify an abnormal and destructive behaviour." He warned that the Muse was seeking to normalize homosexuality, and charged that "Homosexuality in society cannot and should not be accepted as an alternative lifestyle" (Mandville 1989). Some students demanded *The Muse* publish a 'heterosexual supplement,' while others inevitably levelled the false yet then-common[42] claim that homosexuality was linked to pedophilia. Ray Van Horne submitted a lone letter of support for the Supplement (The Muse 1989). Two weeks later, an incensed student named Chris St. Croix – not yet a member of *The Muse* – wrote an eloquent refutation to Mandville's homophobic rant. St. Croix would play a lead role in the drama which was to come two years later (St. Croix 1989).

In 1990, *The Muse* published another (the second 'annual', and the third in its history) Lesbian and Gay Supplement. "Discrimination on the basis of sexuality is an issue that needs to be taken up by people of all sexual orientations," wrote Co-Editor Robin Whitaker in that issue's editorial. "Homosexuals have to refuse to remain hidden if their sexuality is to be seen as an acceptable option, but this will not happen without the support of straights who refuse to remain silent when they see others discriminated against because of their sexuality."

In that issue, Chris St. Croix – now a staff volunteer at *The Muse* – wrote a piece in which he discussed homophobia on campus, offering examples of graffiti he'd seen around MUN: "Gay Rights? No!" and "Right to die!" He observed that a campus in Nova Scotia had just elected a student union president who said he "would fight discrimination on all issues except homosexuality" (St. Croix 1990).

Whitaker also contributed an article covering a panel held on campus by the MUN Gay and Lesbian Studies Group (a sort of informal offshoot of the earlier MUN GALA). The forum was an opportunity for students and others

---

[42] While this false and hate-mongering claim appeared to have largely been laid to rest for a time, in recent years it has been resurrected by bigots and hate-mongers.

to discuss the ongoing Hughes Inquiry into child sexual abuse by Christian Brothers at the Mount Cashel Orphanage (see Chapter 5). Speakers from campus, as well as the Rape Crisis Centre, warned that the Hughes Inquiry was being used by some to justify homophobia, by incorrectly fuelling the public perception of links between homosexuality and pedophilia. Speakers argued that local media, in their efforts to play up the sensationalism of sex crimes, were ignoring the problems of institutional and patriarchal power within the Catholic Church. Others suggested the Catholic Church was deliberately trying to fuel an anti-homosexual backlash in order to divert attention from the way its own internal structures had systematically facilitated and covered up the abuse (Whitaker 1990). The article segued nicely into a two-page centrespread feature by Padraic Brake on the Catholic Church's organized efforts to perpetuate homophobia and undermine the struggle for gay and lesbian rights (Brake 1990).

Inevitably, there were complaint letters in response, which *The Muse* duly published. "Gay and lesbian communities may have a right to express their views, but not at the expense of students," wrote Rod Parsons. "Why should we fund homosexual and lesbian propaganda to help spread their perversion throughout our university?" (Parsons 1990).

One student wrote in complaining about seeing words like "AIDS", "Gay", "Lesbian", "Homosexual" and "Sex" in the headlines of a newspaper. A self-professed feminist wrote in to complain that public mention of women's masturbation denigrated women. There were letters in support: one person said: "I have a gay friend who was physically beaten because he has a healthy relationship with another man. This happened on our campus this semester" (Muise 1990). The majority of letters were critical, scathing and homophobic.

The Muse at that time was a proud collective which adhered passionately both to its journalistic raison d'etre, as well as grassroots democratic principles. Every Wednesday, volunteers gathered for an intense, hours-long meeting where literally everything was decided, from story assignments to political stances. Each year the collective would develop a 'boycott list' of companies from which they refused advertising (it was often dozens of names long). Anyone could propose the name of a company to add to the list, and each proposed boycott would be presented and then debated in excruciating detail (approved boycotts were announced in the paper). All decisions were determined by majority vote. Most writers were volunteers, with the exception of a small editorial cadre – elected each year, with a recall option if people didn't like the job they were doing – who received small honoraria, a pittance in contrast with the long hours they put in. Many of them went on to become professional journalists, but just as many graduated and never touched journalism again.

The debate at the February 13, 1991, volunteer meeting was especially passionate. Each year the paper produced several 'supplements' – focused sections of the paper dedicated to a specific theme. These supplements were also voted on. In March, around International Women's Day, the paper published a Women's Supplement. Twice a year, the paper published an Arts & Expressions supplement full of poetry, prose and graphic art. Some years there were Environmental Supplements, or Peace and Justice supplements.

The timing of the annual Lesbian and Gay Supplement was meant to coincide with Pink Triangle Day, itself scheduled to challenge "the standard, heterosexual-oriented Valentine's Day," as the supplement's introduction explained (The Muse 1991D).

What sparked concern at the meeting that week was not the plan to publish a 1991 Lesbian and Gay Supplement, but one particular item: "A Gay Man's Guide to Erotic Safer Sex." Written by two local GALT activists – Patrick Barnholden and Padraic Brake – it drew attention to the ongoing AIDS crisis and distinguished higher-risk from lower-risk sexual activities. It also provided suggestions for low-risk sexual activities, including anal intercourse with a condom and mutual masturbation. It described various sexual scenarios, as a way of demonstrating safe sex responses. Finally, it featured a visual graphic reproduced from a pamphlet originally produced by the AIDS Committee of Toronto, depicting (in shaded silhouette) two men having oral sex and discussing how to reduce the risk of HIV transmission (Barnholden & Brake 1991). The content would be considered tame and verge on boring by today's standards, but thirty years ago it was unprecedented for any provincial publication to use graphic language or visuals of that nature.

"It wasn't just some random made-up thing to cause scandal, it was a legitimate health document," Welsh explained, looking back on events thirty years later. "From today's perspective, you'd go 'Oh how cute', but from a 1991 conservative Newfoundland perspective it might as well have been hardcore porn."

The article's genesis is a powerful story in itself, fuelled by the death of a well-known queer activist. Michael Smith was described by Toronto's *NOW Magazine* as a "well-known radical faerie, anarchist, pagan, punk musician, ecologist, native solidarity activist and gay rights tactician... best known for his blending of serious political organizing and playful guerrilla theatre" (Harrison & Kirzner 1991). The British-born Smith had moved to Canada in 1982. His life and career are memorialized by the AIDS Activist History Project,[43] and a variety of powerful tributes from some of those whose lives were touched by his friendship and activism can be read on that website.

Smith died from AIDS-related causes on February 5, 1991. Patrick Barnholden, an activist with GALT in St. John's, had previously lived in Ontario and worked closely with Smith. Barnholden, his partner Gary Kinsman, and Michael Smith had all been members of AIDS Action Now! in Toronto. Barnholden wanted to attend Smith's funeral, but couldn't find a way to get to Toronto on short notice. Peter Wood, then Executive Director of the AIDS Committee of

---

43 https://aidsactivisthistory.ca/

NL, heard about Barnholden's dilemma. Wood had a plane ticket to Toronto, and offered it to Barnholden (at that time, airport security was more lax and it was quite easy to fly using someone else's plane ticket). Barnholden gratefully accepted, and flew to Toronto for Smith's funeral.

"[The funeral] was very inspiring in so many ways," recalled Barnholden. "He was an activist in so many ways, and it was a difficult time for us to lose Michael."

Barnholden returned to Newfoundland after the funeral fired up from the experience "and moved to do something." In a fit of synchronicity, the day he returned Brake contacted him asking whether he'd like to write something for the forthcoming *The Muse* supplement. Barnholden felt self-conscious about the fact he was from Ontario, "I wanted to make sure it wasn't just somebody from away [writing]." Brake agreed to co-author the piece, and the two met in an empty classroom at Memorial University on a Sunday night – a blizzard raging outside – to hammer the article out. What resulted from their work that night was "The Gay Man's Guide to Erotic Safer Sex."

"I wrote that article in the context of having come back from Michael's funeral, and I was very angry about some of the things that had happened to Michael," explained Barnholden. "And I know Michael would have loved the article."

Should *The Muse* publish it? That's what volunteers gathered to debate that Wednesday afternoon in February 1991. They gathered in the larger central office, crammed together on beat-up sofas, perched on barstools, sitting cross-legged on the floor. The concern, recalled Welsh, wasn't so much whether the content was appropriate or not – everyone involved with the paper at the time was enlightened enough to recognize how reasonable it was. But the paper re-lied on the Students' Union for most of its funding, and had a relationship with MUNSU that was tense at the best of times.

Most student councils didn't really need much of an excuse to close down a student newspaper. I think most of the staff were generally open enough that they weren't concerned or thought the material or content was wrong or bad or anything like that. I think the concern was, is this the hill you want to die on? Because it might be. Because they might close us. So are you really sure this is a story that needs to be told? Convince us that this has such importance, that it needs to run even if it could cost us everything. That's where the debate went (Welsh 2021).

Welsh can't recall whether he spoke or not – he had only joined the paper a few months prior – but he recalls that he came out of the meeting fully in support.

Knowing me, I probably went 'Fuck it, let's go.' Because I liked a good fight. And because I thought if some kid read that and went 'Oh, okay this is what I need to do to have safe sex' and we saved his life, I couldn't give a shit what everybody else thought. One kid. As long as one kid read that newspaper,

I didn't care (Ibid.).

Craig Welsh – who would go on to a professional career in journalism, serving as Assistant Editor of both *The Packet* and *The Express* newspapers in the province – had joined *The Muse* in his third year at MUN. There, at the age of twenty, he not only discovered his future career, but he also discovered gay people.

I'm sure I had met gay people in my life, but I had never met anybody that was gay and out. The Muse was my first introduction to that, where there were gay people and they were out and they didn't give a shit. So you either dealt with it, or you moved on. It was very much a growing-up experience for me. It was like – well, they're awesome, so why wouldn't I want to hang out here? (Ibid.).

"I was so oblivious to [homophobia], it genuinely astonishes me to look back on it," he reflected. Welsh grew up in the Virginia Park area of St. John's, and attended Booth Memorial High School. He didn't venture into the city's downtown until he was a university student.

Gay issues, and concerns, and people – it just wasn't something that came on the radar. I didn't even think about it. I remember seeing this little ad for GAIN [Gay Association In Newfoundland], they used to advertise in the classified section of The Telegram. It really confused me, because I didn't understand what it was. I had a very isolated view of things, until I joined the Muse (Ibid.).

He says he later learned the paper was often referred to on campus as the "fag-rag" because of its coverage of gay and lesbian issues, but at the time he joined he was unaware of its reputation.

That Wednesday, *The Muse* Production Lead, Chris St. Croix, presented his plans for the 1991 Lesbian and Gay Supplement. He doubled as coordinator for that year's supplement, although he chose to use a pseudonym in his lead editorial. He wrote:

I'm not removing [my name] to protect my parents from finding out, they know. Right now I'm protecting my parents' friends. I made a promise to my parents that I would wait until I moved away before I publicly signed anything as a gay man. My name isn't here because of a promise I made... So what I am about to write is hypocritical, and there are times when I have difficulty accepting that my anonymity is just (The Muse 1991D).

There was nothing hypocritical in the arguments St. Croix demonstrated that Wednesday, as he argued for the paper to run the 'Gay Man's Guide to Erotic Safer Sex' which they all knew would likely be controversial. Welsh says he was swept away by the young editor's passion.

Chris St. Croix was phenomenally fucking charming. I can't emphasize enough just how charming Chris St. Croix was. He's at that time probably 22 years old, a good-looking blond guy, gay, out, proud, persuasive, charming. He's standing up there, he's put this together, he's made his arguments, he's done his research. I challenge anyone to be able to stand up and say no to him. That was my recollection, that here's this very charming man standing up there making a very persuasive argument (Welsh 2021).

St. Croix was then in his fourth year at Memorial. He had started university intending to study pharmacy, but instead was drawn toward writing. He didn't get involved with *The Muse* until late in his second year, when he delivered the letter-to-the-editor he wrote in response to the homophobic reaction to the paper's 1989 Supplement. Three decades later, he reflects on that letter:

Writing that letter for the Muse is what got me in the door. I was reaching multiple breaking points with family, with being in the closet, with friends. I went to the Muse and realized these were people I wanted to hang out with. My friends were nice people but not in any way politically active. They had expectations of how life was supposed to go, and I no longer felt like that was working for me. [The Muse staff] were my people, I bonded really well with them. I was taking Russian as a minor, and went to Russia in 1989 with a bunch of students and got a boyfriend out of that trip. I ended up half coming out, and then stepping back into the closet. So all of that combined to make me primed (St. Croix 2023).

When St. Croix joined the Muse in 1989, he was quickly appointed to the position of Production Assistant. By the end of that year, he'd been promoted to Co-Production Lead, and was elected Production Lead for the 1990-91 year. During the Christmas break of 1990-91, he attended his first meeting of Canadian University Press, the national umbrella group for student newspapers (at the time the organization only permitted democratically-run papers to be members). CUP, like many of its member papers, was a staunchly left-wing organization (it drifted right in subsequent years, and many of the member papers eventually shed democratic and collective organizational models in lieu of more corporate hierarchies, wherein editors and staff were hired rather than elected). The national convention that Christmas was held in Abbotsford, British Columbia, and it was St. Croix's first real exposure to radical politics at the national student level.

That conference was the first time I got to really hang out with a bunch of queer people. It was full-on hanging out with the queer crowd all the time. The host paper was The Ubyssey [student newspaper at the University of British Columbia] and it was the leftmost of the leftmost at the time... National CUP was crazy, everyone was tearing down walls and doing shit (Ibid.).

There was an ongoing struggle within *The Ubyssey* at the time, St. Croix recalled, stemming from bisexuals feeling like they weren't being adequately represented within the queer context. This triggered a larger debate at the CUP Convention about how the organization engaged with queer issues.

"That led to the idea that we needed to have a more structured approach to how we talk about gay issues inside CUP," St. Croix explained. "This led to the question: 'Why don't we have a coordinator? We have coordinators for other things – environmental issues, Black issues – so why don't we have a coordinator?'"

Almost before he knew it, St. Croix was appointed CUP's first Lesbian, Gay and Bisexual Issues Coordinator.

St. Croix returned from the conference in January, and began work on the 1991 Lesbian and Gay Supplement. All of these experiences shaped his response when he was approached by Barnholden and Brake with their idea for the article.

We had talked about the article, and that pamphlet that was featured from the AIDS Committee of Toronto was something that I picked up at a conference in Toronto. I had the idea in my head that we needed to be more blatant about how we talk about these things. Guys of my age grew up in that shadow of AIDS. [Barnholden's] generation were a bit older. For them, a lot of people in their peer group were the people who got AIDS and were dying. It was so personal to them. My peer group was a bit later. We came of age knowing that AIDS was a thing, and by that time we were all afraid to death of sex. We'd had safer sex drilled into our heads for so long.

[My decision to run the article] was affected strongly by me deciding that once I was out I was out... I made myself a bit of a figurehead in part because over the course of the years I was at the Muse I must have talked to at least a half dozen people who were in the closet. They came up to me: 'Can I talk to you about this? And about how to deal with it?' I mean, who [else would] those people talk to? So I felt: I've already committed, I'm here. I will be as loud as I need to be so that other people can be less loud (Ibid.).

One of St. Croix's contributions to that year's supplement was a history of queer activism and a consideration of different approaches to activism. When I spoke with him, St. Croix joked that "Newfoundland gets everything five or ten years later than big centres like Toronto or Montreal," and he felt the radical, in-your-face activism of groups like GALT was an example of that. "That language hadn't really made it to Newfoundland yet, but had already started elsewhere. This question of how do we do gay protesting and make a mark?"

Not all queer activists agreed with the more radical style of activism that GALT sometimes engaged in. St. Croix observed that some of the older NL activists were critical of this newer, louder form of protest.

[They] were more into the proper polite way of being a gay activist. Volunteering with the AIDS Committee, soliciting for donations, getting businesses to do things, getting government to pass laws or speak about things in the right way. It was a contrast of an approach. [They] were coming from [an attitude of] 'We need to do everything we can within the structure of the system to get the support that gay people and people with HIV need.' Whereas my attitude was: I hadn't been playing the game that long, I hadn't worked in that polite version of it, I saw that anger was getting coverage, anger was getting more action, or at least engagement. That appealed to me. So then [Barnholden] and

[Brake] came to me and were like 'How do you feel about this? You're doing the gay and lesbian supplement, this is what our article is, how do you feel about it?' I guarantee you there was some 'Holy fucking god, are we really going to do this? Is this a thing that I'm going to advocate for?' But by then I was primed to go for it, and to say 'Look, this is what we need to do' (Ibid.).

At the February 13 *The Muse* staff meeting, St. Croix made his case and staff voted to run with the article. Friday morning, Welsh and Smith decided they wanted to catch people's reaction to the supplement when it hit the stands. So they left *The Muse* office and went downstairs to the cafeteria, and occupied a table where they could unobtrusively observe people reading the paper.

You could always tell when they hit the page. We were watching their reaction, and the reaction was generally like: 'Oh! Hee hee hee, look at this, oh my goodness!' Maybe it was because most of the people we were watching were girls, women – we didn't see a lot of men reading the paper as I recall – so they just giggled and found it sort of funny and mildly scandalous. So we went back upstairs and reported: 'Yeah, we might be okay, people aren't freaking out in the TSC. I think we're okay.'

Then by 11 o'clock all hell broke loose (Ibid.).

Welsh can't recall how it initially broke, but says it suddenly seemed they were under attack from all quarters.

A woman came into the newspaper office with a handful of newspapers and threw them at us, and called us perverts and sickos. We got reports that the Engineering Faculty took every copy of the newspaper they could find and threw it in the garbage. It started boiling. We started getting the phone calls. The students' union contacted us and asked us what the hell was going on because their phones won't stop ringing off the hook, with people demanding that the students' union shut us down (Ibid.).

The Muse was normally distributed off campus as well, including at a bookstore in the Village Mall. The shop had a shelf where local newspapers and magazines were displayed and sold, and where *The Muse* was available free for the taking. The bookstore didn't stop distributing the paper, but staff were ordered to put each individual copy in sealed plastic bags.

The scandal escalated as local media learned of the issue. Welsh says he still resents the way other news media responded:

The group that pissed me off were the local media, because they didn't have our back. They were completely content to basically gin up the reaction to it. The Telegram on Saturday put us front page, top story. I remember CBC doing a story about it, and they didn't talk to us, but they made sure they talked to everybody else who was scandalized on campus (Ibid.).

MUN President Art May, a former Deputy Minister of Fisheries in the federal government, waded into the issue when he was contacted by *The Telegram* for an interview. Instead of defending the paper or trying to de-escalate the situation, May called the supplement "pornographic writing" and warned that the paper would "single-handedly be responsible for raising tuition fees by a few percentage points" because alumni would cancel their donations to the university (Dicks 1991). The Royal Newfoundland Constabulary (RNC) announced that it would launch an investigation into the paper.

The beleaguered volunteer staff were overwhelmed as the scale of the controversy became apparent, but they remained proud and defiant. After a weekend of provincial and national news coverage, most of it critical, GALT, together with the St. John's Status of Women Council, and other supporters of the paper, held a press conference-cum-rally on Monday, February 18, at the LSPU Hall in the city's downtown.

There, supporters fired back at both the way the issue was covered as well as the homophobia and ignorance which fuelled the public outrage. One of the paper's vocal supporters was Gary Kinsman, then a professor at Memorial and today one of Canada's leading sociologists and experts on queer studies. He was also an organizer with GALT at the time. Reflecting on the events thirty years later, he remembers making the decision to speak out in support of the article — a decision which at the time could have had serious consequences for him. Some of his own colleagues were outspoken in their criticism of *The Muse*.

There were people even in the sociology department at Memorial - these liberal straight people – who said to me: 'I've done so much to support you [queer] people, and this is what you do?' These sort of comments really made me angry. There was a significant feeling of isolation. And I made a conscious decision that this [article] was really politically important and it had to be defended (Kinsman 2021).

Kinsman remembers drawing on the example of Rosa Luxembourg – the famous Polish-German theorist and revolutionary whose outspoken defence of rank-and-file rebellions during the German revolution of 1918-19 led to her assassination — for inspiration in deciding to take his stand.

Luxemburg was clear that even if she did not think a revolt was going to succeed it was her responsibility to stand on the side of the revolt. That is a bit of what I felt when the storm over the Muse supplement and article on safe sex blew up. I had to stand on the side of the authors and the Muse. The socially organized attempted 'moral panic' was curtailed and limited by the response of those defending the article and the solidarity actions on the mainland.

I felt like this was a fundamental dividing line and this article had to be defended. These so-called progressive straight people who told me 'What have you people done to our wonderful support for you?' – that really empowered me to go further with it (Ibid.).

Both Kinsman and Barnholden were frequent callers to VOCM open line shows, and were well-recognized media representatives for GALT. They knew they'd be easy targets, and it wouldn't be hard for anyone to find out where they lived. "I think we feared a bit about our own personal safety then," Kinsman said. "I mean nothing actually happened, but these things cross your mind."

Kinsman set aside his fears and fired back at the moral panic in his comments at the press conference that Monday.

"It's really unfortunate the media pounced on this and defined it immediately as being about offending people – rather than as a health education issue," he said at the press conference. "This is a brilliant illustration of how the homophobia in society is preventing us from doing the effective safe sex and AIDS education we have to do" (Harrington 1991).

Kinsman contextualized the controversial article by explaining how groups around the world were adopting the sort of educational approach reflected in the Supplement. "To work, the message must be explicit, gay, and sex-positive, actually show people how to have safe sex and use language appropriate to the community it is aimed at," he said. "This is the type of work that succeeds. This is what works" (Ibid.).

Kinsman pointed to the scandal as an example of the ways in which religious and media groups were working to suppress safe sex campaigns. "The reality is, you have to decide whether you're going to allow HIV to spread because of your 'moral' perspective, or whether you're going to seriously grapple with explicit education," he said (Ibid.).

Other speakers tore into President May for his comments describing the paper as pornographic.

"Mr. May seems to have lost sight of the fact that pornography is sexual imagery which presents a human subject as a sexual object for the use of the viewer," said Theresa [Tree] Walsh on behalf of the St. John's Status of Women Council, which ardently supported *The Muse*. "This article, and the accompanying photograph, depicts a sexuality which is mutually pleasurable and entered into freely, not one linked to violence, humiliation or ridicule" (Ibid.).

MUN Biology and Women's Studies professor, Joan Scott, was even more blunt, speaking in support of the paper. "Art May is only exciting homophobia on the campus when he should be squelching it. At cinemas, we are exposed to an avalanche of movies that are graphic, explicit and full of coercive sex and violence against women. The supplement is completely free of coercive sex" (Ibid.).

Meanwhile, *The Muse* staff fiercely criticized the response of the local journalistic community.

"Muse editor Dawn Mitchell said that despite the news conference, none of the "zillions" of journalists pestering Muse staff members seem to care about AIDS education – the point of the article in the first place. Their interests: shock value, the police investigation, the [students' union], and May's comments," reported Halifax-based Canadian University Press reporter Jeff Harrington. "It's totally amazing – they've blown it all out of proportion. On TV, we were put ahead of the Gulf War and a possible outbreak of meningitis," [Mitchell] said" (Ibid.).

Now-defunct local newspaper *The Sunday Express* published an editorial on February 16 criticizing The Muse and warning the gay and lesbian community to "take care not to lose sight of their longer-term social goals." MUN student and GALT activist Padraic Brake – one of the authors of the controversial article – fired back at the *Express* during the press conference. "What long-term goal are they referring to – that we should book funeral parlours?" he demanded (Ibid.).

While the local media was silent or complicit in the attacks on The Muse, support poured in from other campus papers across the country. Student newspapers at the University of British Columbia in Vancouver, Simon Fraser University in Victoria, McGill and Concordia University in Montreal, the University of Toronto, Dalhousie University in Halifax, Wilfred Laurier University in Waterloo, the University of Winnipeg and elsewhere all republished the controversial article as a sign of support for *The Muse* and its decision to run it. St. Croix feels that the queer networking which took place at the CUP convention six weeks earlier helped to reinforce the strong sense of solidarity with which other campus papers responded to the controversy. Some of those other papers faced backlash as well. According to one account, the printers contracted by *The Cord* newspaper at King's College refused to print the issue containing the article, and cancelled its print run. Halifax police launched an investigation into the *Dalhousie Gazette* for publishing the article, but dropped the investigation after two weeks. Student editors at *The Uniter* newspaper at the University of Winnipeg were asked to resign, and *The Cord* newspaper at Wilfred Laurier University was shut down by its students' union (Case 1991).

On Monday February 18, while *The Muse* supporters prepared for their press conference, the editors met with Students' Union President Wade Brake. He threatened to cut the paper's funding, and to impose an editorial board on the paper to control content and ensure it never published anything similar again (neither threat ever came to fruition). Later in the afternoon he met with President May. The meeting was also attended by Memorial's Dean of Student Affairs, Vice-President Administration and Finance, and the Acting Director of University Relations. The two presidents shared their mutual criticism of the supplement, but Brake also expressed "dissatisfaction" with May's incendiary comments, which he thought went too far. May refused to recant, and told *The Telegram* afterward that he stood by his previous comments, including the threats about tuition fees. "The actions of a few individuals on the staff of the Muse can have far-reaching impacts on the university as whole," he warned. He also said the university would cease to publish ads in *The Muse* (Cleary 1991).

President May seized on the issue with a vehemence that surprised many. He personally responded to most of the complaint letters that poured into his office. When members of the public wrote in support of the paper, he sent replies arguing with them on their position.

The correspondence with his office on the issue is voluminous.[44] Some members of the public wrote in to agree with his position but warned him that by making a public controversy he might wind up generating sympathy for gays and lesbians. The Royal Canadian Legion wrote a letter criticizing the supplement. "The protests to our office have come from widows and Veterans, who feel that inclusion of this article in the newspaper is degrading to the name of Memorial University, which was named to commemorate those Newfound-landers who gave their lives during World War I and World War II for the cause of freedom," said the letter from the Legion, which was cc'ed to Premier Clyde Wells [ATIPP].

Self-proclaimed Christians wrote in to complain the supplement was blasphemous. Some threatened to withdraw their children from university. The nonsensical "I'm-not-homophobic-but…" argument recurred frequently. "One might conclude from my comments that I'm homophobic," wrote one critic of the Supplement. "Quite the contrary. I have no problem with a person's sexual orientation and would defend their human rights in all fields of endeavour. However, I object to the imposition of their orientation and sexual depravity on my moral sensibilities and those of my children and grandchildren [ATIPP]."

When one Memorial graduate wrote in to criticize May on his comments, and to defend *The Muse* article as an important safe sex initiative (the author also threatened to stop donating to Memorial if it didn't respect freedom of the press), the President's Office sent a stock response letter to which May appended a personal handwritten note. "It is not clear from your letter whether you have read the material," May responded to *The Muse* supporter. "For a reaction from the wider community please refer to the attached letter from the Royal Canadian Legion." He included a copy of the Legion's letter [ATIPP].

A petition was submitted containing nearly a thousand signatures collected over four days, and complaining about *The Muse*'s representation of "small minorities."

One critic of the paper wrote to May: "I have still not seen the paper, but if the descriptions I have heard from colleagues are correct I would agree with you that it was grossly offensive, and I would strongly support your saying so [ATIPP]."

Another warned him: "If the president of a university cannot… manage the values of the institution, then emasculation will result." To this, May graced the author with another personal handwritten note: "In your penultimate sentence, you have captured exactly what I was about, i.e., attempting to manage 'the values of the institution.' I will continue to attempt to do so, and look forward to your continued support [ATIPP]."

One faculty member wrote in to criticize May: "Although I found parts of the Muse supplement were at a bathroom wall level and parts disturbing, your

---

[44] I was able to acquire the entirety of this correspondence as the result of an ATIPP request.

reported reaction was far more so... now an increase in fees may be blamed on those in our society who are homosexual, which is not what this campus or society needs." May responded with a full-page personal response criticizing The Muse content [ATIPP].

Another faculty member warned May that "While I'm inclined to withhold my [donation to MUN], it is not for the publication [of the Gay and Lesbian] supplement, but because of what I perceive as your failure to defend the free expression of ideas within the university." May responded to this with another full-page, personalized letter [ATIPP].

One student wrote in to criticize May:

Everything you are quoted as having said in the interview with the Evening Telegram was either a false conjecture or an unwarranted intrusion on students' affairs. There are many students who have lost a great deal of respect for you... [name redacted] is ignorant of the struggle of Gays and Lesbians to be fully accepted by our society. From your comments I can tell that you have a long way to go too. Maybe the page was worth the risk [ATIPP].

The letter was delivered to May with a hand-written note from his assistant. It read: "Dr. May, you indicated you saw no need to see this letter from [name redacted]. However, it is now posted on at least one bulletin board, etc [ATIPP]."

President May was eventually persuaded to tame his attack on *The Muse*. In response to one of the letters that came to his office criticizing *The Muse*, he claimed to have seen evidence that previous *The Muse* coverage of gay issues had led to the withdrawal of financial support to the university. However, he also admitted "I should not have raised the issue of fees... The fee increases will be necessary irrespective of what The Muse does or doesn't do."

Speaking at a Rotary Club luncheon that Wednesday, May finally apologized for his comments in a tersely worded statement. That, he said, would be the last he would speak to the issue (The Evening Telegram 1991C).

The police investigation never materialized either. On Tuesday February 19, RNC Public Information Officer Lieut. Robert Shannahan confirmed for the *Telegram* that an investigation was under way. "The investigation will be conducted to determine if there are reasonable and probable grounds to lay charges under the criminal code dealing with the corrupting of morals," the RNC spokesperson said. Members of *The Muse* braced themselves for the investigation, but much to their relief they heard nothing more about it from the RNC.

Missing in the ensuing controversy over the "Gay Man's Guide to Safer Sex" and its silhouette graphic was any discussion of the other important material that comprised the supplement. It opened with a boldly laid out manifesto from the Concordia Women's Collective in Montreal: "WE ARE PART OF THE LESBIAN AND GAY LIBERATION MOVEMENT" proclaimed the title in large block letters set against a shaded dark background. St. Croix led off with a poignant personal editorial. He also wrote a powerful and well-researched feature article on "The Politics of Protest: Activism – assimilation vs. confrontation" on the very subject that would characterize the ensuing public debate. He took readers through a history of confrontational activism by groups such as ACT UP and Queer Nation, contextualizing their politics and practice of direct action. This led into a discussion of local activism, and the approach of GALT which drew inspiration from the direct action tactics of its mainland colleagues.

"The need for protest is everywhere, even here in Newfoundland," wrote St. Croix. "Human rights violations are occurring every day and gay bashing is on the rise." He pointed to the provincial government's continued refusal to add sexual orientation protections to the province's human rights code.

The power of activism is strong, and no one can deny that the strides made by the gay communities in the past five or ten years have been enormous. But they haven't solved anything. Still, gay men and lesbians are ignored and discriminated against, or beaten and murdered. These groups are voicing their rage at a society which is still blatantly heterosexual and homophobic, and they're willing to do more (St. Croix 1991).

There were heartfelt narratives from contributors about the difficulties they faced due to homophobia and discrimination. One short, poignant contribution by Paul Dayson titled "One day I will have to come home" opens:

Every time I return to my parents' home for dinner or to spend time over the holidays as I approach the house, walking up the front steps, I always reach inside my jacket and take off the pink triangle pin I wear everywhere else... While I have come out to almost every person in my life that I have regular contact with I have not been able to talk to my family about my sexuality. It is something I fear... Yet the rift, symbolized by the removing of the pink triangle pin, is eroding the relationship I have with my family. Our relationship is being destroyed. I cannot deny a part of myself... (Dayson 1991).

The supplement included a full-page survey from GALT, asking gay and lesbian respondents to send in responses to the questions pertaining to their experiences and discrimination they faced. In a separate piece, Patrick Barnholden wrote a history of GALT, explaining their purpose and goals and setting that against the recent history of queer activism in Canada. Fellow GALT activist (and former *The Muse* editor) Padraic Brake contributed an extensive interview with Kinsman about "Teaching from a gay perspective at Memorial."

The supplement also offered contributions from lesbians. "Kyla", in a piece titled "To be lesbian and to hear the heterosexual roar," writes:

I am the keeper of secrets. Sitting in a class, people around me talking about the weekend, what they were up to, what their boyfriend or husband said – I am silent... And yet when I speak up, try to talk openly about my life just like all the heterosexuals do, people say that I should keep what goes on in my bedroom (or wherever) in the bedroom. Ha! Why should I when hetero-

sexuals basque in the privilege of being able to be open about their lives and their sexuality? And yet here I am, writing under an assumed name, protecting my job. I'm angry. I want straight people to look at their lives for a change. I want to stop keeping my secret by challenging the heterosexual roar (The Muse 1991E).

"Brauna" penned a personal exploration of the question "Are categories of identity even necessary?"

What took me longest to realize was that being gay was special, that being gay, in fact, had a valuable social role to play – gay people can reveal to the heterosexual culture who they are, what the 'limits' of their actions can be and maybe, hopefully, through this, that there are other possibilities for their actions and their gender and sexual identities, and maybe even that these categories of identities are not even necessary (The Muse 1991A).

A bisexual contributor shared the struggle she often faced in defending the fluidity of her sexuality in the face of criticism from other lesbians, while a straight student urged other straight students to recognize the importance of allyship and supporting their gay and lesbian friends. There was also a variety of poetry, comics, and a few reprinted articles from other student newspapers.

True to form, the paper even published its critics. Bernard Noftall provided a short rant complaining about the lack of a "heterosexual supplement": "I'm growing rather tired of activist (gay, etc.) ramming their opinion down my throat... I'm straight and happy to be so." *The Muse* editors wittily titled his contribution "Deep Throat" (Noftall 1991).

Over the next several days following the supplement's publication, letters poured into the newspaper office. *The Muse* normally published a page or two of brief letters-to-the-editor in each issue. In light of the controversy, the jaunty paper decided to print every one of the letters it received in an 11-page "Letters Supplement," abandoning word limits in order to allow the mostly outraged letter-writers to express themselves freely (*The Muse* staff did, however, permit themselves the indulgence of affixing pithy title-headings to several of the letters).

"You might be wondering what on earth we are doing with a letters supplement," wrote the Letters Editor, in a "Lettertorial" preceding the section. "It took a bunch of us about two days to type them in and it's taken me EIGHT HOURS to lay them out and we are damned if we're going to do it again" (The Muse 1991C).

The letters demonstrate the range of responses which the Lesbian and Gay Supplement provoked. *The Muse* was accused of being a GALT newsletter. Numerous self-identified straight contributors wrote in to claim that they supported gay and lesbian rights but felt the supplement's "shock value" set back the struggle for equality. The student Engineering Society cc'ed a copy of a letter they sent to the university president demanding *The Muse* be de-funded and replaced with a new student newspaper.

It is important to note that the Engineering Society is not trying to repress the rights of either gays or lesbians. It is, however, trying to protect the rights of the students in our faculty who are tired of these issues dominating every paper the Muse prints... The present editor of the Muse, Ms. Dawn Mitchell stated that at her estimate, ten percent of the university's population is homosexual. Why then does the Muse staff insist on dedicating thirty nine percent of the last issue and hence thirty nine percent of the students funding to this subject? (Ryan 1991).

R.J. French, a MUN medical student, wrote in to denounce the paper's method of providing safe sex information. "I can only hope for several things," they wrote. "First, that students grappling with their sexuality will not accept the degenerate presentation in the Muse as their only alternative. Second, that your measly publication will cease to exist" (French 1991).

Another anonymous student raged circuitously: "I hold nothing against Gays and Lesbians, but I do not agree with their sexual morals... The gay population is approx. 10%, yet you as editors feel it is ok to impose their sick, perverted means of lust on 90% of the population who think it's sick" (The Muse 1991B).

Several self-avowedly straight students wrote in to warn gays and lesbians that while they supported their rights, their interests were being undermined by content such as that featured in the Supplement and they should avoid sensationalism in future. Maureen Woodrow, chair of the MUN Ottawa Alumni Association wrote in to criticize potential damage to Memorial's reputation. Ann Marie Vaughan, student representative on the MUN Board of Regents (hand-picked by the university back then, not selected by students as is current practice), also wrote in to denounce the article and the damage it would do to Memorial's reputation. "While gay and lesbian issues are important I wonder what attention is given to women's issues, the disabled, international students, student aid, and underfunding. I am certain that these issues are not being given the same attention, and are without a doubt extremely important," wrote Vaughan. In response, *The Muse* editor Dawn Mitchell wrote in that issue's editorial "When I see statements like that, I get angry. The Muse has consistently covered these very subjects and more. Only those who pick up the paper solely... on the odd occasion when we cause a fuss, would not be aware of our attempts to wake up this campus" (Mitchell 1991).

Even Dean of Student Affairs Wayne Ludlow wrote a letter to the president of the Students' Union, enclosing a petition against the paper he'd received signed by 400 students. He cited complaints he said he'd received: "The people who contacted me considered the relevant articles to be trashy, demeaning, pornographic and totally unnecessary." He urged the Students' Union to exercise greater editorial control over what was published in the paper.

There were letters of support as well. "We were not offended by any part of the G/L Supplement," wrote Catherine and Gary Rodgers in a letter they titled

"Muse not a paper by fascists for fascists". "However we were appalled at the incredibly narrow minds of some fellow students who signed and circulated a petition in reaction to it" (Rodgers & Rodgers 1991).

Karen Hill, Ontario Bureau Chief with Canadian University Press, wrote in support and excoriated the paper's critics. "The message your critics are sending is quite clear: good manners are more important than lives, so do not speak the truth about HIV and AIDS. These are the people that will let others die in order to avoid offending sensibilities, or risk fund-raising projects" (Hill 1991).

"The controversial graphic on page 13 was less offensive than the average sexist beer ad, and it offered a much more valuable message," wrote Sandra Cowan, calling the supplement "refreshing" and "enlightening." "It is unfortunate that the Muse seems to be the only Newfoundland publication willing to deal with the issue openly, without making a moral issue out of AIDS and homosexuality" (Cowan 1991).

Another anonymous student voiced support while also criticizing the local media response:

On Friday afternoon a NTV crew interviewed students in the TSC. At first I thought it was about tuition increases but I soon found out it was about a picture published in the Gay and Lesbian Supplement. It seems that the media is trying to portray university students as immature people who are more concerned with beer chugging contests than their education and future. What's the difference between the controversial picture and many magazine ads?... Many of these depict heterosexual or group sex. Are these ads accepted by the public because they show what is considered "normal" sexual behaviour by society's standards? (The Muse 1991F).

William Kearney wrote in on the media coverage as well, asking:

Who in this city has not heard of the Gay and Lesbian Supplement? St. John's has virtually erupted over the publication of this material; and it must be noted that most of those partaking in discussion did not see the actual Muse in question but saw the front page of Saturday's Evening Telegram. The content of the twelve pages of writing cannot be accurately represented in a few choice bits as published by the Telegram (Kearney 1991).

Kearney also took aim at President May: "[M]aybe students should focus on cowardly university presidents who foresee tuition increases and attempt to cover up the reality of government cutbacks by shifting the blame to a handful of precious rebels" (Ibid.).

GALT wrote a letter of support, and so did ACT UP Montreal the following week. Perhaps the most unabashedly direct response came from Dan Hart: "Girl, this article is for and about gay men. That's a given. And that without apology. If you're heterosexual, get your own. If you're queer and all this attention is unwelcome, get a life. In other words, shit or get off the toilet" (Hart 1991)

What was notable about the controversy was that some members of the queer community also took an outspoken position against the paper, replicating in local form the broader divide between those willing to adopt confrontational tactics and those opposing such approaches. Some felt that the "Gay Man's Guide to Safer Sex" depicted an overly sexualized homosexuality.

A student who signed off as "Gay, but not today" wrote:

I am proud of the attempt to express freely the issues of my minority and try to eliminate some of the prejudices we face every day... The manner in which the project was undertaken however, left me literally disgusted. Homosexuals were presented as sex addicts with no concern for privacy or dignity. Their only concern is their next sexual encounter. I fail to see the need for excerpts of "soft" porn in the supplement... I don't expect to read it in an article supposedly aimed at the acknowledgement of the homosexual population as the boy or girl next door or the person you met in the Breezeway last week (The Muse 1991G).

Newfoundland nationalism even reared its head, as some members of the local queer community denounced the "agit-prop" tactics of groups like ACT UP and Queer Nation and likened it to a form of cultural imperialism from the mainland. Ron Knowling, a long-time gay activist in St. John's and the founder of MUN GALA in the 1980s, wrote a lengthy complaint published two weeks after the Supplement.

My first objection to this supplement is that it does not represent gay men in a fair manner. For years we have struggled to free ourselves from stereotypes which define us in an exclusively sexual manner. Activists in this city, myself included, have worked hard for YEARS to try and overcome stereotypes which referred to gay men as child molesters and perverts. The article ignores this danger... The problem arises when people who have absorbed these experiences [the deaths of loved ones to AIDS] arrive in Newfoundland filled with the righteous wrath of the AIDS crusader. AIDS is a problem. But this is not Toronto. This is Newfoundland, and the problems of AIDS must be solved in this context. To impose mainland solutions here is imperialism and exactly the same as that exercised by the United States, Great Britain or Canada. The truth is that the cultural tools exist in this province to create an AIDS campaign that reflects our experiences and nationality as Newfoundlanders... In the meantime, the damage has been done, the stereotypes have reinforced and the neutral have been polarised. Who will be left to pick up the pieces? A year from now the people who thought up this selfish prank will be back on the mainland. The local Newfoundlanders already working with the Gay community will have to. How will one of us convince a company to donate to the Newfoundland AIDS Association when this is fresh in the public mind? (Knowling, 1991).

The director of the NL AIDS Association also criticized the issue when interviewed by CBC Radio. This created problems for defenders of the paper:

when Kinsman contacted the AIDS Committee of Toronto to ask for them to support *The Muse* and its article, he was told they could not.

[They] took this stand-offish approach, like 'Personally we're really supportive of what you've done, but in terms of AIDS Committee of Toronto we can't do much because the local group, the NL AIDS Committee, has taken this hostile approach.' It's bizarre to me that [ACNL] adopted that position, but for whatever reason [they] did and stuck to it. So it did unfortunately produce some division (Kinsman 2021).

Back on campus, it took some time for the furor to diminish; the uproar would be talked about in association with *The Muse* for years. The Students' Union threatened and discussed de-funding *The Muse*, or establishing a student union-picked editorial board to control its content. Editor Dawn Mitchell skillfully mediated with MUNSU over the ensuing weeks and managed to avoid any consequences to the paper. The experience, however, was eye-opening to the student volunteers who lived through it.

There was so much going on, there was so much chaos. We used to have to have people watch the door, to make sure that people wouldn't break into the office to try to trash the place. We had people try to break into the office. I had someone call who said: 'Your grandparents must be disgusted with you.' Well, my grandmother used to write for The Compass out in Carbonear, and my grandmother was thrilled. She said it was great. 'You keep writing, Craig, you keep doing your thing. I'm really proud of you.' That's what my nan said to me.

So it was, at least from my perspective, a highly educational experience. You know it's one thing to read about people being homophobic and not treating gay people with the respect and love that they deserve. It's another thing when people want to come and fuck you up because they saw a picture in a newspaper in a safe sex article. It was illuminating for me, it was a very transformative moment (Welsh 2021).

Looking back on the controversy from the vantage of three decades later, Welsh confessed to mixed feelings over the initial decision to run the controversial article.

I've wavered sometimes over the past thirty years. Was [running the article] the right decision? And part of it was the reaction from the gay community, as I recall some of them not being happy. Was this a case of me being an outsider thinking that 'I know what you guys need', as opposed to listening to people about their actual day to day life experience, what impact it might have on them? My initial reaction was that if this saves one person, cool let's do it. That was my opinion for years, but then I got older and wondered, did we mess people up? Like maybe we didn't save some kid out there from HIV, but maybe we made some people's lives really difficult for weeks or months because we ran this supplement and caused all this controversy.

But I think I've come back to the other side of it. I was a 20-year-old kid, trying to figure out what to do and what's best and everything else. And to try and help people who were being targeted and not being loved and respected. And we did something. I think if you try and do something for a good cause and maybe it doesn't work out the way you hope it does, at least you tried to do something good. As opposed to just hating people because of who they choose to love (Ibid.).

The fallout was personal for many of those involved. Welsh's girlfriend of three years broke up with him three weeks later, which he attributes in part to the fact the crisis at the newspaper came to dominate his life during the period. He also lost a few close friendships. "A couple of friends were like, 'Why did you run that? That's disgusting.' And I was like: 'Okay, well we're done.' It was a clarifying moment. I got to see who you were by how you reacted to that. That moment was a real Rubicon for me. If I knew you and you hated that paper, I cut all ties."

The controversy didn't deter the "handful of precious rebels" at the Muse from continuing their courageous, path-breaking journalism. Nor did it curb their appetite for a Lesbian and Gay Supplement: they would go on to publish a few more supplements before abandoning the entire concept of special topic supplements a few years later. And initial disputes aside, the supplement also came to hold a special and treasured place in local queer lore. Solomon's – the city's primary gay bar at the time – got a hold of a copy, blew up each individual page and framed them. The eleven framed pages of the supplement, decorated with stars and glitter, lined the long corridor you walked through as you entered the bar. They remained there, a reminder to everyone of the courage and defiance of those "precious rebels" at *The Muse*, until the bar closed in 1996.

Chapter Five: Homophobia

Homophobia takes many forms. It's often the product of ignorance, but it can also be deliberately malicious. In Newfoundland and Labrador it has taken both of these forms.

It assumes another, less tangible form in NL history as well. There's a type of homophobia that is rooted in a sort of epistemic murk, dwelling in the tension between NL's two competing claims: that on the one hand NL is a conservative Christian society deeply resistant to change; and on the other that it is an exceptionally tolerant society in which ills such as racism or homophobia don't really exist, thanks to a shared heritage rooted in poverty and struggle that has forged us to be the friendliest people in the world. Both of these claims are myths, but myths that one often encounters. Some of the NLers I interviewed were eager to distinguish NL from the mainland and to point out that things "weren't as bad" here as there. Yet for others, NL exists only as the traumatic memory of the violently bigoted place they fled as soon as they could, never to return. The experience of many of my informants also put paid to the myth of Newfoundland being a conservative Christian society: the 1970s were just as full of drugs, sex and orgies here as they were anywhere else.

But these myths serve a useful function for the institutions of power in this place, especially when so many people buy into them. A superb example can be seen in the experience of teachers in the school system prior to the abolition of denominational education in the late 1990s. I could find no evidence of teachers actually being fired due to homophobia.[45] Yet because their contracts contained vague language with allusions to conduct and morality – because of the *perception* that NL is a conservative Christian society in which queerness would not be accepted – the majority of queer teachers silenced themselves into the closet. Let's not forget the trenchant observation of mainland queer journalist Ken Popert, writing in *The Body Politic* in the 1970s specifically about the hesitation of NL queers to be loud and proud: "[I]n St. John's, as elsewhere, the question has to be constantly posed: how much closetry is necessary, and how much is irrational? The future of every gay community can be read in its answer to this question" (Popert 1976).

This is not to ignore or downplay the very real fear, violence and repres-

---

[45] One informant did make an anecdotal claim that he knew a teacher who was fired, and another alleged that transfers to undesirable locations in the province served as a way of pressuring suspected queer teachers to quit.

sion that many queers faced, with or without being fired from jobs. Yet while it served a function of violence, this murky homophobia also operated through confusion and fear, rendering the direct application of official repression often unnecessary.[46] It was no less real in its damaging effects and consequences. And yet the fact that it operated through fear and perception – and not necessarily overt rules or public violence – enabled public institutions to deny its existence. So churches could deny their responsibility in cultivating and encouraging homophobic violence; public institutions could deny their bigoted employment practices; NL could present itself to incoming tourists as the friendliest place in the world while the same boats those eager tourists arrived on were – on their return journeys – full of queers and trans people fleeing the island and the painful bigotry they'd grown up with. In order to make sense of NL history it's crucial to understand these competing perceptions and experiences of what this place was – and is – like. How could the 'friendliest people in the world' also visit such pain and suffering on each other, and drive so many of their fellow NLers away?

Experiences varied widely of course. This chapter explores a few examples of the types of institutional discrimination that existed in this province prior to the year 2000.

Homophobia in the media

In 1978, the Canada Lesbian and Gay Rights Coalition organized protests against the CBC, which had a policy refusing to air public service announcements or ads from gay and lesbian groups. The Coalition comprised 52 groups across the country, who presented at CRTC[47] Licence Renewal hearings for the CBC demanding the national broadcaster change its policy.

"In reviewing this matter, the [CBC] has concluded that homosexuality is still considered a controversial subject. Consequently, it is the [CBC's] decision that any broadcast matter dealing with homosexuality will be dealt with in programming only, and under criteria for programming. It is not acceptable for public service announcements," wrote CBC executives, defending the policy.

The CBC's homophobic policy was introduced in 1977, as a response to a 1976 complaint from the Gay Alliance for Equality over a Halifax-based CBC station that refused to air their public service announcements. CBC had no formal policy barring gay PSAs at the time. Instead of eliminating its discriminatory practices, CBC responded to the complaint by making it formal policy to refuse such announcements. "They're getting paranoid. We're not going to

---

[46] It also operated through physical street violence, as we will see in this chapter.

[47] The Canadian Radio-Television and Telecommunication Commission is an administrative tribunal that implements laws and regulations set by the federal government, and who regulates and supervises broadcasting and telecommunications in Canada.

change our policy for gays," Montreal Public Relations Director for CBC Herbert Steinhouse told Canadian University Press in October 1978.

Discrimination was rife at the CBC not only in its journalistic and broadcasting practices, but also its workplace practices. Karl Wells is a household name in Newfoundland and Labrador. He worked with CBC from 1974 until 2007. Since the 1980s he was the weatherperson for CBC's flagship evening news program in NL, *Here and Now*, and his smiling, upbeat demeanour has been a constant for generations of NLers spanning decades.

Unbeknownst to most of those viewers Wells was engaged in an ongoing struggle against homophobia at his workplace.

"It really took its toll on me," reflects Wells, now retired. "I would come home and be very upset and I would cry. It was really hard."

"He was very stoic about everything," interjects his partner of more than forty years, Larry Kelly. "He wouldn't let on that there was anything happening. He took a lot of it home."

Wells originally had aspirations to be a professional actor. But NL's education system only went up to grade 11 at the time. When he graduated at age sixteen, he was a year too young to apply to the professional acting schools he wished to attend on the mainland. While he waited to be old enough to apply, he enrolled at Memorial University. There he got involved in radio (at campus/community radio station CHMR) and acting, and was offered a summer job at CBC in 1974. He became ensconced in life at Memorial and decided to complete his degree there after all. In summer 1975, CBC hired him back, and then in 1976 they offered him a full-time job, working at CBC Radio.

There were at least three producers in radio who were definitely gay, and one who I think was gay but wasn't out. But you'd hear other employees talking about them behind their backs, in not a nice way, and I realized right away that this was not a place where I could be announcing that I lived with a man. So I just kept quiet about it. If I'd been terribly open about it I don't think I would have gotten permanent work. I had to work there at least two years before I got a permanent job. I don't think there was any way in hell I would have been made permanent if I was talking about being down at Friends [gay bar] or whatever. There's no way (Wells 2021).

When Wells became permanent, and forged professional relationships and friendships with his co-workers, he did become more open about being gay.

I wasn't in the closet, I wouldn't say I was in the closet, but at work I never talked about my personal life. And they didn't want to know about it, because they knew that I was gay. It didn't take long for people to find out I was gay. I mean you're on television, your face is very well known, and you're going to gay bars, you're going out with a guy all the time to restaurants, shopping with a guy – hello, it's a small town (Ibid.).

He became probably the province's most widely recognized gay personality (rivalled by Tommy Sexton), and while many of the reactions to this were positive, there were bigoted and homophobic reactions as well.

I would get letters from people telling me I had to repent. People would send me tracts from the Bible, from the Old Testament, that was very common. It just all went in the garbage. People knew me – they recognized my face – and they would say 'Oh look – he's a queer.' That was said to us, we were walking up George Street one day, a beautiful sunny day and these guys were hanging out on the deck of the Rob Roy which was a bar, and one of these guys says: 'Oh look! There's that queer who works for the CBC!'

During the 1990s I would do the weather outdoors, I'd go everywhere. Sometimes I would be outdoors, like at Quidi Vidi Lake, and I'd be there with the microphone ready to go on the air, and a car would drive by and they'd roll down the windows and they'd scream out: 'Karl Wells is a faggot!' That happened several times when I was doing the weather (Ibid.).

Even some members of the gay community ostracized him, especially during the early years when they were afraid that being seen in association with someone who was so out might lead to suspicions that they too were gay.

Once there was a table of guys at a gay bar, and I stood by the table, and several of the people at the table got really uptight. They got really uncomfortable. I remember saying to one of them: 'Hi I'm Karl, what's your name?' And he responded: 'What do you want to know that for?' It was like he was talking to the Soviet secret police, or a CIA agent or something. But it was my face – I was on television, and they figured that by talking to me, somebody who was so well known, and so out in the open about who he was – they didn't want to be associated with me for fear that they would be labelled gay. Because all these people had jobs, and they were all in the closet. They went to gay bars but they weren't really out (Ibid.).

It was at his own workplace that Wells faced some of the worst discrimination. "There were some people at work that were very, very nasty and homophobic. It was horrible."

He recalled an incident with one of his co-workers on Here and Now in the early 1980s.

I was in the studio by myself, just making notes, getting ready for the weather that evening. And this guy came up to me – I hadn't even noticed him because he just walked up and the studio was very quiet, there was nobody else in there, it was dark and there were only a couple of houselights – and he walked up to me. I looked up when I realized he was there. He was almost in my face, and he said: 'You know that disease that those guys are getting in New York, with all those spots all over their body, those growths and those purple spots, and they're all dying? You're gonna get that. And you're gonna die.' Every bit of life just drained out of me. I'll never forget it. I'll remember his eyes until the day that I die, because there was nothing but pure malevolence in them. I was speechless. And then he just turned and quietly walked away. And I had to go on the air with him that night. There was no reason for it. It was completely unprovoked. It was just pure hatred (Ibid.).

Wells has reflected a lot on the homophobia he experienced at the CBC, and why a workplace that's widely presumed to be progressive would have been a magnet for such bigotry.

I think part of it was the fact that the CBC had a reputation – not only in Newfoundland and Labrador but also across Canada – for being a company that employed a lot of homosexuals. I mean, I don't think it employed any more homosexuals than other companies – the vast majority of the people who worked for CBC to this day are heterosexual – but I think because it had that reputation, it made the heterosexual employees very self-conscious and uptight. They didn't like there being any homosexuals working there, and felt that if it weren't for people like me, the company wouldn't have that reputation. I think that's how they saw it (Ibid.).

After anti-discrimination provisions were added to CBC workplace policies, Wells finally decided to take action about the homophobia he was experiencing. There was a senior producer at CBC who was particularly homophobic. Wells recalls the man ranting publicly in the newsroom when a gay bishop was ordained in the US.

He was ranting about this, talking about how disgusting it was. He was just a desk away from me. And he knew I was gay. He used to do things like that. I thought: this is homophobia. Why is he saying that a few feet away from me? Obviously it's intended for my ears – there weren't many other people in the newsroom (Ibid.).

Similar experiences continued. Another producer, just before transferring out of NL, pulled Wells aside and told him to be wary of the afore-mentioned man, that he had it out for Wells. Another producer also pulled him aside one day, and told him the man had been saying things about him behind his back. This producer told Wells he needed to be more aggressive in pushing back against the homophobic producer, who outranked Wells. "That's easy to say," said Wells, "but when you're dealing with somebody who's a powerful producer, who literally had the power to have me taken off the show, I'm not about to poke the bear and make him more angry or make him hate me more than he already does."

The final straw came in the early 2000s when Wells was in Corner Brook with a small production team, spending a week hosting the weather from different locales in that city. While there, a reporter with the *Humber Log* newspaper asked him for an interview. One of the questions she asked was: "How does it feel to be a role model for every young LGBT person in the province?" Wells thought a moment and replied: "Great! If anybody finds me to be a good role model because of what I've done in the past or because of who I am and what I do, that makes me feel wonderful."

Later that evening, Wells was hanging out with his team and a CBC communications staffer asked him how the interview went. Wells recounted his interview, including the question about being an LGBT role model. "[The CBC communications person] said – 'What?!' She appeared alarmed. She said, 'I have to phone St. John's! I have to tell the bosses in St. John's what happened!' So she did, and they freaked out. They threatened to withdraw CBC advertising from that paper."

When Wells and the team returned to St. John's, he was summoned into the office of a senior producer.

This guy got me into the office. He said: 'How are you doing?' I said: 'I'm fine.' Then he said: 'Uh-huh. You know, I know what it's like to be thought of as not like everybody else. It's like an alcoholic. You might be off the booze, but people always look at you as if to say: He's a drunk, he's doing okay now, but you never know when he might come off the wagon.'

I said: 'Well, I'm not an alcoholic.' He said: 'You know what I mean! Now tell me about this interview.' I said: 'I guess you're referring to the question I was asked.' He said: 'Yeah! How did she ask it? What did she say?' So I told him. And he said: 'You didn't have to answer the friggin' question!'

I was shaking. I was thinking: I'm in some sort of weird twilight zone here. Everything that happened over that simple question was so bizarre to me. I think they viewed it as me being outed. Which was ridiculous, because everybody in the province knew I was gay. It was bizarre to me. Why the hell do you think the woman asked me that question? It was crazy. They blamed me. It was like I had betrayed the CBC. After that the harassment from that producer got worse and worse (Ibid.).

Eventually, says Wells, "I snapped. I went to Human Resources and made a complaint."

Wells, with the support of his union, said he was facing harassment because he was gay. The HR department told him they would conduct an investigation, as they had to determine whether anyone else had witnessed or heard the harassment he cited. He gave them the names of some other CBC staffers he knew were aware of the harassment. This included one St. John's-based staffer, and some other CBC personnel who had since transferred to studios elsewhere in the country.

After several weeks, he was summoned back to the HR office. "They said: 'Karl, we believe you. But we can't prove it. There's nobody who will tell us anything that proves what you're saying is true.'"

The local CBC staffer they interviewed had told them he didn't remember anything about the incidents Wells reported. Wells asked whether they had interviewed the other people he'd suggested, who were no longer at the St. John's studio. "They said: 'No, we didn't speak with them because they're now on the mainland and we want to keep this in the family. We want to keep this in St. John's. We don't want to go outside.'

That more than anything is what drove me to take early retirement from the CBC. I left in 2007. I'd been there 31 years. I think I would have stayed, my career would have gone on longer, if I didn't feel just so frigging let down by the CBC, and the fact that I had to continue working in this environment. It was toxic. Totally toxic. I worked in a toxic environment for many of my 31 years with the CBC (Ibid.).

Since retiring from CBC, Wells has continued his media work, and remains one of the province's most prominent media personalities. He's worked as a food and restaurant critic for *The Telegram* newspaper, and hosts his own television program on Rogers Cable. He's also returned to acting, and starred in several solo and group performances. His face continues to be one of the most recognized and well-loved media presences in the province.

Yet he still has nightmares about the experiences he had at CBC, and the homophobia he experienced there. He had one such nightmare just a couple of nights before our interview, he confesses. "It had a bad effect on me... having to deal with this stuff was horrible, horrible."

Homophobia in the military

Homophobia was institutionalized in the Canadian Forces under Administrative Order 19-20, which barred homosexuals from serving in the military. Several soldiers serving in this province fell victim to the regulation in 1977, when Master Corporal Gloria Cameron – an eight-year veteran of the Canadian Forces – and eight other women were discharged under Order 19-20 for being lesbian.

Gerald Hannon interviewed Cameron for *The Body Politic*. An extensive feature on her case appeared in the September 1977 issue of the paper. She told him what had happened.

I guess it really started back in December [1976]. Though I'd known a lot of gay kids since I arrived at the base – there were at least a dozen gay women that I knew quite well; maybe half that number of gay men. Anyway two of the women decided to marry, that was last December. And they did. There was a little ceremony in one of the cabins we had access to off base (Hannon 1977).

Her discharge stemmed from the unofficial wedding ceremony held in December 1976 to celebrate the relationship of these two women. Although it was held in a private cabin at Argentia,[48] word somehow got out. So the base commander brought in a special investigative unit from Maritime Command Headquarters in Nova Scotia to look into the matter.

The two men set up office in the VIP floor of the barracks and began calling in women for interrogation. Cameron was summoned on March 2.

I was really nervous and afraid. I wanted to stay in the Forces, but I guess I'd known from the beginning what their position was on gay people. I'd just

---

[48] A WWII-era US naval base on the southwest coast of the island that continued to operate until 1994, at which Canadian Forces personnel were also stationed.

always lived with the fear of being found out... I suppose I always felt eventually I would get caught. It's not a very good way to live (Ibid.).

Cameron said that during this initial meeting her interrogators were polite and asked her whether she was a homosexual. She "denied everything" and the men appeared to accept it and let her go. Two days later she was called back in for a follow-up session, which proved dramatically different from the first interrogation. She arrived at 11:30am and was asked if she would allow them to use a lie detector test during this interrogation. She refused. The interrogation began.

So they began to question me but it wasn't just about the services, or who I knew, but they asked me about my family and my background and probed away about my grandparents and all kinds of personal things... It went on 'til eight o'clock that night and I just broke down. I cried. Mostly because I knew I was going to be kicked out. But I admitted it. I told them I was gay. But I didn't implicate anyone else (Ibid.).

After nine hours of interrogation, she was given a statement of confession to sign and released.

When the interrogation team left the base, wrote Hannon in his powerfully emotive article, "they left behind them a shattered and terrified gay community." The formerly tight-knit gay men and women were now afraid to be seen near each other, uncertain who had been found out and what inferences might be drawn from their association with each other.

On March 29 eight women were dismissed as a result of the investigation. In a touching and poignant turn of events, another woman was dismissed when she deliberately outed herself in solidarity with her comrades. Although she hadn't been implicated and had avoided suspicion, this ninth woman turned herself in, saying she was "tired of living like a rat in a hole."

Cameron, a 27-year old Master Corporal with a stellar record full of citations and commendations, who had aspired since the age of 14 to join the Canadian Forces, returned to her parents' home in Kitchener, Ontario, and decided to fight. Her parents accepted and supported her. She filed an appeal, and spoke out to media about the injustice, making herself a potential target in the process.

Her appeals were unsuccessful at the time. In 1992 – following years of activism by courageous people like Cameron – CFAO 19-20 was finally repealed. In 2017, the Canadian federal government issued an apology to those whose lives and careers were destroyed by this form of institutionalized homophobia, and a class-action suit on behalf of those affected in the Canadian Forces and RCMP led to a $145 million settlement in 2018. It doesn't change the traumatizing injustice they faced, but it is to be hoped that Gloria Cameron and the other eight soldiers whose dismissal stemmed from celebrating the love of two women, received their share of the compensation.

I attempted to get in contact with the women who were dismissed in March

1977, but was unsuccessful in tracking any of them down. I spoke with NL queer activists from the time, who recall the dismissal making the local news and being widely discussed within the queer community. Activists at the time also tried – unsuccessfully – to make contact with the women. Nevertheless, knowledge of what had happened at Argentia helped bolster the resolve of local activists to continue their fight for queer rights, more publicly than ever. We do not know how many of the women were NLers, but I was told by some of my interviewees that although they had lost contact with her, at least one of the women remained in this province for several years after, and was part of the local lesbian community.

Discrimination of this sort wasn't limited to the 1970s. There were several such cases in this province, even after the laws were purportedly changed.

Sharp Dopler came from a military family – their father was an Indigenous American soldier stationed at Argentia. There he met Dopler's mother, a Newfoundlander.

Dopler joined the Canadian Forces in 1982 and was purged fifteen years later. This was in fact after the orders barring homosexuality in the Forces had been repealed, and reveals the lingering stigma and impact of those policies.

"They would hunt us down," explained Dopler. "They would use us to harm one another. Many of us experienced sexual assault and other things, ongoing harassment, interference with our careers.

"I had never hidden being gay. I experienced a lot of being cautioned about being gay – to be quiet, to be careful. I experienced a lot of bullying from my colleagues, mostly from other queers who were afraid of getting caught. I experienced a couple of sexual assaults – 'I can fix this for you, I'll be real gentle'" (Dopler 2022).

In the last two years of their career Dopler was hired as chief security officer for a sea cadet training establishment. One of their male subordinates responded with belligerence and hostility to Dopler's supervision, and complained about Dopler to the Commanding Officer (CO).

The CO gave him a choice: he could straighten the fuck up or he could get the fuck out. So he left. He then filed a charge of abuse of authority against both myself and my commanding officer. Then he had his girlfriend, who had been a long-time friend of mine, make allegations of sexual assault against me.

I spent two years fighting to clear my name. The military police did not find evidence of sexual assault. But by then I was already damaged goods. I had been passed over for a promotion, I'd been hired back in a subordinate position, I'd been pretty much fucking humiliated. I couldn't stay there anymore. So I left, and that almost killed me, because that was the most positive part of my identity at that point (Ibid.).

When the federal government issued a public apology for the purge, Dopler was one of those who received a cash settlement.

It was absolutely surreal to sit in the House of Commons and hear those apologies. It was surreal. I don't have words to explain it. And then I got my personal apology letter which I have on the wall, and I got my Canada Pride citation which I wear with pride, and now I'm on the board of Rainbow Vets Canada so we have our own queer veterans' association which has standing.

I've heard other survivors talk about these concentrated hunts that they experienced. And the odd thing was that there was so much shame around being purged. Like the first time I was around other people who were purged was the night of the apology. The lawyers held a reception for purge survivors who wanted to be in town, and there's not a lot of words I can use to explain being with people who shared that experience. Everyone was the same - not being able to understand why. All we wanted to do was wear our uniform and serve our country (Doppler 2022).

Homophobia on the mainland

NLers have also experienced homophobia outside of the province, and been present in many of the catalytic moments of queer history around the world. Joey Shulman was born in St. John's and grew up there in the 1950s. He was living in Toronto when the Bathhouse Raids took place in 1981, and was present in one of the bathhouses that was raided. He was arrested. It was for him one of the moments which reminded him how quickly societal tolerance can shift. It was a lesson he'd initially gleaned from reading about Oscar Wilde, who one moment was celebrated by British society, and the next shunned and imprisoned. Shulman's own experience in the Bathhouse Raids underscored a similar theme.

We need to learn from our past. No matter how comfortable we get as gay people, there are always people like Hitler, people like McCarthy in the 1950s US, people like the RCMP fruit machine, the Bathhouse Raids. The Bathhouse Raids happened at a time when we felt so fucking liberated! We were out – in downtown Toronto we were living in entire apartment buildings downtown. We were fabulous, we were exploding, we were just like Mary Tyler Moore throwing our hats in the air – and then suddenly the police just clamped down!

It was horrid. Horrid. I had committed no crime as far as I was concerned. I was in a gentlemen's membership club where everyone was of age, and we were just doing what members do. We weren't doing it in a window that was open from the street. No one unknowingly was going to walk into a bathhouse and go: 'Oh my god there's homosexuals here!' So I was quite indignant.

I waited out the year on bail waiting for my trial date, and then I took a limo with great righteous indignity to the courthouse in Scarborough. I was looking forward to giving an award-winning legal performance and speech, but the cop didn't even show up. And the charge was dropped. I was furious!

Furious. Almost all of the charges were dropped, and it cost the City of Toronto close to a million dollars, and it changed a number of peoples' lives (Shulman 2022).

After the arrests many of the men were concerned their names would be published in the newspaper, since that was common practice at the time. It had happened in previous raids and had even led to suicides. Shulman, a publicist, phoned up his contacts at the papers to find out whether that was likely to happen. He was informed that normally the names would be published, but because this time the police had arrested so many men – more than 300 – it would take too much space to print all their names and therefore none of the names would be published. Shulman was out anyway and didn't feel he had anything to lose, but this came as a relief to many of the other men who'd been arrested.

"It's important for younger people to know that this was a real attempt to stop us from finding and having and sharing love," Shulman said. "And that shouldn't be allowed. People came out of that defiant. It was our Stonewall moment. We took to the streets, and won all of those rights that ensued."

Homophobia in the medical and psychiatric systems

Another form of homophobia was that institutionalized in the medical and psychiatric system. Until 1973, homosexuality was labelled a mental illness by the American Psychiatric Association (APA). The APA publishes the Diagnostic and Statistical Manual (DSM) which classifies mental disorders, and establishes the diagnostic and treatment standards followed by psychiatrists around the world.

Even after homosexuality was delisted as a mental disorder (the decision was made in 1973 and it was publicly delisted the following year), it continued to lurk in the DSM under the moniker of "sexual orientation disturbance" and various other labels until it was finally eliminated entirely in 2013. Furthermore, it was not uncommon for diagnoses of "depression" or "nervous breakdown" to be related to sexual orientation (experiencing the social trauma of homophobia doubtless fuelled depression, anxiety and 'nervous breakdowns' in some cases of queer people seeking mental health support). For instance, if someone growing up as the only queer in a small outport community found themselves depressed by the isolation and homophobia they experienced, and then wound up being admitted to a psychiatric facility and undergoing electroshock therapy for their depression, it's hard to ignore the visceral connection between their sexuality and the 'therapy' they were provided.

All of this meant that even after 1974 some gays and lesbians found themselves institutionalized – both voluntarily and involuntarily – for being queer.

The first time Wendy Williams encountered a lesbian, it was as a student in the Nursing program at Memorial University. "Her admitting diagnosis at the then mental hospital was 'lesbian'," she recalled.

Ellen Balka recalls meeting several women during her youth in the United States and Canada who had been institutionalized for their sexual orientation. When she moved to Newfoundland, she met a woman here who sought treatment for depression linked to her sexual orientation.

The woman very consciously chose not to come out and elected to go into the mental hospital and have shock treatment to deal with her depression rather than come out. That was in the early 1990s. Homophobia was still enough of an issue that somebody who was incredibly capable and bright and knew lesbians… she chose to get shock treatment, rather than deal with being a lesbian (Balka 2021).

Anne Escott, one of the founders of CHAN, also had a run-in with the psychiatric regime as a teenager in the 1960s. She had been seeing a psychiatrist in St. John's following the death of her father. She was on a light regime of antipsychotics to help with the severe depression she'd experienced following his death the year before. She was in Grade 10 at this time, and one day during a session with the psychiatrist she confessed her attraction to other women. She was completely unprepared for his reaction.

I just mentioned that to him and immediately by Monday I was in a psychiatric ward at St. Clare's and I was moved from 100 mg a day to 400 mg a day of largactil which I eventually took myself off of in first-year university. But I was [in the psychiatric ward] about ten days. Because I mentioned being gay (Escott 2022).

The lingering association between homosexuality and mental illness had other consequences as well. While mental illness has always been stigmatized, this blurred history made many in the queer community even more hesitant to seek help for mental health concerns.

There was such a stigma around mental health issues in the LGBT community because of the whole idea that your sexuality was considered a mental illness. So as someone with a mental illness, when I was younger, there was a lot of stigma around that. And it was a difficult time because people with mental illness were not accepted.

I had a friend whose parents were very religious – they were Pentecostal. And when he was 19 or 20 they brought him to a psychiatrist. They said: 'Look, our son is gay. What can we do about this – what can you do about this to change it?' The psychiatrist told his parents that it was their problem and they had to accept that he was gay and there was nothing wrong with him. But that traumatized him. He became for a while a very severe alcoholic (Baggs 2022).

Gemma Hickey, who today is a nationally-recognized activist, had a similarly traumatic experience as a teenager in the 1990s.

I had a really hard time in high school dealing with my sexuality. I was assigned female at birth and at the time I became a teenager I never knew trans people existed. It wasn't really talked about. Now I was always a tomboy when I was a kid and I had crushes on girls and that became more apparent to me when I hit adolescence. I had boyfriends, but I always found myself daydreaming about girls. And when I daydreamed it would be me as a boy, being with these girls. But there was no language for that, there were no terms or anything that I felt I could identify with outside of lesbian. I was Roman Catholic and my family were very devout, so I thought: 'If I'm gay then that's wrong.' So I talked to my doctor and he referred me to this therapist who was sharing an office with him.

I didn't realize I was getting into conversion therapy as such. I went to my doctor after my first sexual experience with a girl, when I was fifteen years old. I liked it 'too much' and it really messed me up. I felt like I was sick, I felt like I had a disease. And I kept it all in. When I had that first sexual experience, it really freaked me out. And I'd internalized so much homophobia that I myself became very freaked out about people who were gay around me. So I had to talk to someone. And I talked to my family doctor. I told him, and he said: 'Well there's a doctor I can refer you to who's renting space from me here, if you'd like to see her.' I thought – sure, it can't hurt. But it hurt. Big-time.

I went to see her, and she wasn't advertising as a conversion therapist, but she was very Catholic. She was very involved with the Catholic community. It took me a little while to tell her about why I went to my doctor and what I was doing there with her, and I was so nervous. I was really scared to death about talking about it. It was really hard – I was moving around on my chair and trying to get the words out. Finally I told her. And then she started doing this type of therapy with me. There was no electro-shock or anything like that, although she did prescribe me anti-depressants. She basically said that my attraction to girls was rooted in the desire to be like them. Which is ridiculous – I never wanted to be like a girl. But she said this was all based on Carl Jung, and that I desired qualities in the same sex, that I wanted to be like. Basically it was like reprogramming my brain. She gave me a lot of material to read, told me to pray – it was all rooted very much in Catholicism and in changing the programming in my brain. That went on for a while and nothing changed, I didn't feel differently. So I attempted suicide.

Luckily I survived. I attempted suicide in my senior year of high school. I went to a party, drank a lot of alcohol, took whatever pills I could find in the medicine cabinet. Had my friends not made a call and I been rushed to the hospital, I would not be here today. When I was in hospital, in the psychiatric ward at the Health Sciences Centre to recover, the psychiatrist sent me home after a couple of weeks. I told him what I felt was wrong with me, and he said: 'There's nothing wrong with you! Go on home out of it. There's nothing wrong with homosexuality, I can't believe you're in here.' And it was just so freeing. It really was. Also when I was in hospital I had a crush on this nurse who was lesbian. I've stayed in touch with her, and she's been a big support to me. When I made it through my senior year I was able to meet her and her partner and brought my grad album to show them that I made it. It was just so nice. I hadn't known anyone who was lesbian before that. In hospital she took a special interest in me and it was really nice to have that. That, coupled with the psychiatrist in the same ward who told me there was nothing wrong with me, it all gave me that confidence to be able to be out.

So when I got out of hospital I came out as lesbian. I realized I had a lot of internalized homophobia, but the majority of people – my family, friends, teachers – were all fine. And when I came to university, it was a whole new world. So then I vowed to do whatever I could to try to bring awareness to this harmful so-called therapy (Hickey 2022).

Sharing information about one's sexuality was a dangerous gamble. It could lead to traumatic outcomes of the sorts experienced by Hickey and Escott. But some doctors could be supportive. Robin Stagg, a folklore student at Memorial, recounted the experience of one of the gay men he interviewed from the Bonavista region of the province. This man grew up in the 1950s and spent a summer in St. John's receiving medical treatment unrelated to his sexuality (this would have been about 1972). There he told one of his doctors that he was gay. "His doctor then gave him information about homosexuality, and introduced him to social workers who then provided him with the names of bars and a few restaurants that were frequented by gays" (Stagg 1994).

Balka encountered institutionalized discrimination of another sort in the medical system when she had surgery in May 1993 at the Health Sciences Centre in St. John's. When she was asked to provide the name of her next-of-kin, the hospital refused to let her enter the name of her partner, Wendy Williams. After the surgery, they also refused to let Williams into the recovery room. The experience, recalls Balka, was "traumatic."

Six months later Balka had to return for more surgery, so this time she met with hospital officials in advance to find a way for her partner to be allowed into the recovery room.

They had twenty different options of relationships that I could select. But because Wendy was a woman's name, and I was a woman, they wouldn't let me use 'spouse.' And we went through all the twenty things. One was 'guardian,' but she couldn't be my guardian because that was a legal term. And on and on and on. One of them was 'ward,' as in I could be a criminal and she could be legally responsible for me (Balka 2021).

In the end, she thinks they selected 'ward,' in order to ensure the hospital would let Williams into the recovery room.

Homophobia on the streets and in politics

Wendy Williams faced a dilemma of a different sort when she became the first provincial politician to be publicly out. Elected to represent Ward 1 in the

St. John's municipal election held on November 13, 1990, she began a relationship with Ellen Balka (then head of the MUN Women's Studies program) during her tenure in office. When the November 9, 1993 municipal election rolled around, she knew she wanted to run again but was unsure whether to do so as an out lesbian.

She discussed what to do with her partner, as well as close friends. Although there were a few out politicians in Canada at the time, she wasn't aware of them. The only out politician she'd heard of was Diane Sands, a Democratic member of the Montana state legislature in the United States. Williams flew to Montana and met with Sands, to get a sense of how she had handled things. She found that Sands had a massive support network in place. Sands also didn't have any children: one of Williams' concerns was what impact it could have on her two children if she ran as an out politician. She sought the advice of other politicians she knew, and received mixed messages: some encouraged her to be out, others advised her not to.

In the end, Williams did come out publicly, although without making a formal public announcement. She did so by going dancing with her partner at a public concert. Balka remembered the night fondly: it was at a venue called The Loft, located on the top floor of 223 Duckworth Street (known as Haymarket Square), and the local reggae band Pressure Drop was playing.

So I never came out and said I was a lesbian, I just showed up. And then when I went to events I took Ellen as my partner. I represented St. John's City Council at a municipalities meeting, and Ellen came as my partner to the dinner and dance. I was on the board of the Cancer Agency, I took Ellen as a partner to events that I went with. I never lost a friend over it, I didn't lose anybody in my family. I mean some of them weren't so sure, but Ellen was invited to all the family functions and I took her to events and represented City Council and nobody on my council ever challenged that (W. Williams 2021).

Williams did, however, lose her seat in the subsequent municipal election to Sean Hanrahan, a local businessman.

Homophobic attacks were still a common reality in the 1990s. Two gay men going by the pseudonyms Paul and Clyde reported to *The Telegram*'s Tracy Barron in 1994 that "Once when we left a bar three men chased us down the street and confronted us. There was one guy who wanted to kill us, the other guy was fifty-fifty and the other guy stood back a bit," said the 31-year-old Clyde. While Paul, 30, tried to reason with the trio, Clyde was able to get away and hail down a cab. He drove back to rescue Paul, who leapt into the cab. The two escaped almost physically unscathed – Paul had taken a punch before the taxi pulled up – but incidents like this contributed to a constant psychological wear on the city's queers (Barron 1994).

"It was awful," Clyde told Barron, adding that he'd had several friends hospitalized with injuries sustained during homophobic attacks. "It is a horrible feeling when people want to kill you just because you're gay. Now I'm careful. When I leave a place, I'm always with people" (Ibid.).

In a 1985 court case involving the death of a gay man in St. John's (the court ruled the death manslaughter), the defense attorney cited other homophobic attacks during the sentencing hearing when he argued for a lenient sentence. One of them involved a man who:

... was eighteen years of age, he was six foot four, he had three or four convictions for narcotics. He engaged in assault against a fellow five foot two or three, outside a club on Water Street which is known for the frequenting of homosexuals. His reason for attacking the individual was that the fellow was a homosexual, and that was his only reason. He punched the fellow, after the fellow was knocked down he kicked him repeatedly. He broke his jaw and bruised him seriously. I don't recall the judge involved, but he sentenced him to five days in jail for it.[49]

Violence like this was also chronicled in *Outlook*, the bi-monthly newsletter produced by NGALE. Paul Barton[50] related several attacks in the March/April, 1996 issue, in an article titled "The Dark Side of Being Gay."

For as long as I can remember, the east end of Water Street and Duckworth Street, as well as the area surrounding the Newfoundland Telephone Building, has attracted gay men. Before the Journey's End was built, the area was much more isolated and private than it is now, and this may have been the reason gays like myself were attracted to the area. Whatever the reason, gay men flock to the area especially in the evenings and weekends, usually looking for other men to engage in anonymous sex with (Barton 1996).

Lately, he warned, the area had attracted a new breed of visitor: the skateboarder. "Until recently, gay cruising and the skateboarders have co-existed. As of late there appears to be a faction of the skateboarder types that have taken a liking to harassing gays" (Ibid.).

Early one Sunday morning, he reported, two gay men were walking home along east Duckworth Street when they were assaulted by a half dozen young men in front of the Sir Humphrey Gilbert Building. They escaped and used the pay phone located at the top of Hill O'Chips to call the police. A police car responded to their call, but the officers refused to let the men file a report. "Police said that the men had been drinking and they didn't believe their story, even though the two men showed visible signs of being beaten" (Ibid.).

On another Saturday night, a 21-year-old man walking alone on Duckworth Street was attacked by a group of four young men in baggy clothing, who shoved him around yelling slurs like "queer" and "fag." When the man escaped and used a payphone to call police, he was told no units were available

---

[49] I am presently in the process of researching this and several related cases for future publication.

[50] This may have been a pseudonym. Several of the contributors to Outlook – and to other queer publications – used pseudonyms, and no one I interviewed from this period who worked with NGALE had any recollection of anyone by this name

to help him (Ibid.).

The same night, another man was attacked while sitting in his car on Water Street just down from the War Memorial. A group of four young men – possibly the same ones – carrying skateboards attacked the car, yelling homophobic obscenities at the driver, who quickly drove away.

Much of the gay-bashing that goes on remains unreported. Many gays have a fear of police, possibly because of tales of police harassment, or they are not completely out and open to report this type of crime to the police and often when it is reported there is no action taken, or the gay man is subjected to more harassment by the police themselves" (Ibid.).

Another type of attack that was reported involved gay men cruising the area being lured in by homophobes and then attacked. Barton reported the case of a "good-looking man" who was seen standing outside the Journey's End hotel parking garage – "it was very apparent that he was trying to get someone to stop and pick him up." Several cars did stop, and as soon as they did, they were rushed by additional men hiding in the garage, who threw rocks and bottles at the cars. In another case, two gay men walking by the area were ambushed by a gang of young men, dragged behind the building and badly beaten (Ibid.).

"Even lone young men feel the need to harass gays," wrote Barton. "They can often be seen standing around the Newfoundland Telephone Building, smiling, trying to attract attention. When you stop, you are either verbally or physically assaulted" (Ibid.).

Cruising was dangerous enough already. Barton said it was common for gay men to pick up strangers, have sex, and then find their pockets had been emptied during the encounter. Sometimes they would be beaten and robbed; other times pickpocketed. It happened to Barton himself on one occasion. When he reported it to the police, at first they accused him of soliciting the services of a prostitute. He persisted and eventually, he says, they became more helpful. They in fact caught the thief and charged him. He was sentenced to six months in prison, but Barton never got his money back.

"There are dangers out there, and we've got to work together to help one another," wrote Barton. "If we see one of our own in trouble, we've got to lend a hand. It could be just driving up and offering a ride out of harm's way or stopping at a phone booth and calling the police" (Ibid.).

Derrick Bishop remembers the close call experienced by a friend of his.

A friend of mine got picked up one night, he was cruising downtown and he got picked up by an individual who drove to an area of St. John's that was kind of secluded, up around Pippy Park. And then the individual in the car said to him: 'Well you got in the wrong car tonight!' And he started threatening him, but my friend jumped out of the car and basically ran all the way home, which was quite a distance. He ran through the woods so the individual couldn't follow him with the car or hit him with the car. He managed to escape, thankfully. He was very lucky to get out of that one alive, I think (Bishop 2021).

A folklore research paper on "Gay Lore" from 1979 preserved in the Folklore and Language Archives at Memorial University features interviews with some local gay men. One of them recounted the dangers they faced in the city's downtown:

[A] friend of mine who was leaving the 'Seabreeze' [which] was a gay bar a couple of years back before the 'Deck' and 'Friends.' One evening when he was leaving the bar he was attacked by a few guys and he lost a face full of teeth, et cetera. So he was beaten up kind of badly. And the problem there, he felt, he didn't report it. He felt that there was little that could be done about it. That the authorities would not look into it whether that's because he's gay or because that type of thing just goes on (Reardon 1979).

Ron Knowling is a solid, six-foot-two, 180-pound man who says his size meant he usually felt secure walking around the city's downtown in the 1980s. Even he recalls being attacked on occasion:

There was one incident when I was at Madames [gay bar] and some guys came into the bar and started picking up beer bottles and throwing them at people. One of the walls of the bar was rock, and so these guys were throwing beer bottles around and they were exploding. I remember one guy grabbing me and hitting me, and I went across one of those tabletop video games that they used to have in bars. Fortunately it wasn't a great punch, so I just ended up with a bit of blood from some glass that cut my ear. It looked more dramatic than it was. There were always stories going around about people being attacked. It's important to understand that this stuff was going on (Knowling 2021).

Greg Bourgeois recalls drivers of vehicles yelling slurs at him sometimes when he walked downtown, and was attacked once on his way into Friends bar in the early 1980s.

I was on Duckworth Street and this guy who was probably twice my size grabbed me. He walked past me and grabbed my arm, swung me around and called me faggot and went to punch me. But it didn't work. I kind of ducked, and when he swung me around I used my body weight against him, I sort of went into him and threw him off balance and then I hit him and he went down and I just turned and ran. I was very fortunate there. That happened in the alleyway going down to go into Friends. But just a few steps down and I was amongst a bunch of people and I was safe (Bourgeois 2022).

"We weren't safe on George Street. We knew that," recalled Lori Seay, of the late '80s and early '90s.

There was a bad bashing at the Sundance and another at the bottom of the stairs on George Street. It was not safe, certainly not for anybody who got read as queer. I was safe — I'm femme — but I remember walking home with my girlfriend and a crowd of kids followed us screaming at us because they clocked that we were both women (Seay 2022).

There was a phrase they used to use — '100-yard queer' — referring to whether someone could be clocked as gay from a distance.

"There was so much street-level harassment on George Street, we just avoided George Street like the plague," said Seay. "The packs of roaming drunk teenage boys were terrifying for everyone, really. Especially women. But for queer people, ten times ten times more."

Andy Wells was mayor of St. John's from 1997-2008. Although a controversial figure, he was a staunch ally of the queer community. He once famously tried to fire one of the Commissionaires who provided security at St. John's City Hall, when the man refused to raise a pride flag during Pride Week. In the end the Commissionaire was transferred away from City Hall. In the 1990s, before human rights were even extended to gays and lesbians, Wells and his wife would often show up at Solomons and spend the night dancing. Seay recalls feeling reassured by his presence.

"It felt like, Andy had our backs," said Seay.

Sheilagh O'Leary is the city's Deputy Mayor today, but as someone who grew up ensconced in the queer community, she remembers how common homophobic attacks were.

It was just an accepted thing. Everybody knew – if you were out by yourself, and if somebody was gay – especially young gay men – and if you were out on the road by yourself, you were a prime target. If you looked in any way, shape or form like you might identify differently, then you were a walking target (O'Leary 2022).

Michael Riehl recalls one weekend when someone pulled the fire alarm at Solomons, a gay bar which operated in the early 1990s. Patrons had to exit quickly, and the fire alarm attracted a large crowd of curious passers-by. There was widespread panic among patrons, he explained, that they might be outed while pouring out of the bar into the street – they might be seen by family or friends to whom they were not out. Others feared violence from gay-bashers outside the bar. Rumours also spread that someone had pulled the fire alarm deliberately for that purpose – to force patrons to come out and show themselves.

While the cause of the fire alarm was never determined – was it homophobic gay-bashers, or some drunk patron accidentally hitting the alarm on their way out? - Riehl remembers how a collective sense of outrage over the possibility it was homophobes galvanized several community members into action. The following week, he and several others showed up to act as impromptu security. Their plan was to form an ad hoc security squad to protect patrons in the event of a fire alarm being pulled. Their intention was to shield patrons from public scrutiny and protect them from any gay-bashers who might be waiting.

A bunch of us in the community – I was one of them – went to Solomons the next week in case the fire alarm was pulled to say: 'You looking at something? You want to come?' We were mad! It was like the drag queens getting mad at Stonewall. I was going to be there to support, I was going to stand there, and I was gonna say: This is my ground. This is our ground (Riehl 2021).

"At that time it was really common to be gay-bashed and for the police not to respond quickly," explained Roger Baggs. He'll never forget the homophobic attack he witnessed one night from his apartment on Duckworth Street. It overlooked Solomon's Lane, the narrow alley containing The Ship Inn and farther below, Solomons.

One night a bunch of people were coming up from Solomons, and then these other guys were walking up from Duckworth Street. The two groups met on the corner, and there was a lot of debris lying around on the street at the time – pieces of wood and things like that. One of the guys took a piece of two-by-four and cracked it over this other guy's head. He went right down flat on the ground. Somebody screamed, and then those guys basically started hitting everybody with the two-by-fours. I had a landline at the time and I picked up the phone and called 9-1-1 and told them what was going on and to get down there right away. So the paddy wagon showed up and everybody who was there was put in the paddy wagon! The police didn't ask them any questions, just gathered everybody up and threw them in the paddy wagon. It should have been obvious who was injured and who wasn't, I mean that guy is lucky to be alive. It was scary! You had to watch yourself… I knew somebody else who was involved in a bashing. They were common. When you came out of Solomons, you had to get out of there fast! It was not a safe place. Like you'd think you were living in a safe place here in Newfoundland, but it's not (Baggs 2022).

Far from confronting these forms of homophobic violence, the police often perpetrated a homophobia of their own.

Particularly back in the early days St. John's wasn't as friendly, and Newfoundland wasn't as friendly toward gay people as people now like to kind of create in their minds. "Some people nowadays think: 'Oh, St. John's was so open and so welcoming and all of that stuff.' No it wasn't. Some police officers could be brutal. In the early days they would harass people all the time. They would just drive around downtown and if they thought you were gay or if they thought you were cruising or something like that, they'd get out sometimes and shine a light. Even in the early 1990s* (Kelly 2021).

In June 1995, gay-bashing became a crime at the federal level with Bill C-41. That didn't necessarily change things on the ground in Newfoundland and Labrador. By the mid-1990s, there were frequent efforts by gay and lesbian activists to forge relationships with the RNC and RCMP and encourage police officers to take homophobic harassment and violence seriously. Such efforts faced a two-pronged challenge: on the one hand, activists had to persuade police officers to take complaints from the province's gays and lesbians seriously. On the other hand, they had to persuade victims of homophobic violence to file complaints with the police. Years of police ignoring homophobia meant the province's queer community did not trust the police or consider it a realistic and safe option to file formal complaints. In the early 1990s the NL AIDS Committee wrote the RNC with a formal request that the force establish a permanent liaison officer for the LGBT community. They did not receive a reply.

Following Brian Nolan's human rights complaint (explored in Chapter 6), the Royal Newfoundland Constabulary did finally reach out to NGALE for some training and support. Derrick Bishop was on the group's executive at the time.

I got asked by the Chief of Police to speak to the police. The police chief and those in the administration wanted to educate the rank and file about lesbian and gay issues. So I was asked to speak to a large group of police officers. I did, and it was not an entirely pleasant experience. There were two officers – out of a large number – who were making comments while I was presenting. While I was talking. And they were not quiet comments, they weren't whispering, but they were basically talking back and forth while I was presenting, and they were very rude. And I think the comments they were making had to do with the Brian Nolan case. They were very nasty. But afterwards some police officers came up to me and apologized for the behaviour of these two people. They said they were ashamed that these two officers would do that. So there were some changes that were occurring in people's attitudes at the time (Bishop 2021).

And when NGALE held its fourth Annual General Meeting in April 1998 the Royal Newfoundland Constabulary was invited to address the meeting on the second day, following the keynote. Deputy Chief Ches Oliver was supposed to attend, but his place was taken by Sgt. Robert Shannahan from Police-Community Relations.

Mikiki may have been the first high school graduate in the province to attend high school grad with a same-sex partner. That was at Gonzaga, a former Catholic high school in St. John's run by the Jesuits (denominational education had been abolished the year prior to Mikiki's graduation, but its dismantling was a gradual process). It was an experience which encapsulated both the gains which queer activism was achieving, as well as the pervasive threats which still existed.

I carried a piece of steel reinforcement bar in my backpack for most of high school because I was told that there were people who were specifically looking to hurt me. There were specific guys that I had been told if they ever found me they would kick the shit out of me. When I went to my senior high school prom with a guy, we put a bunch of baseball bats in the back of the van, because we were anticipating that we were going to get bashed over there. So there was still a very real threat of violence.

I love that [my same-sex prom date] got no media pick-up, that it wasn't a controversy. My parents were brought in by the principal, Father Leonard Attila. He was this super handsome, gigantic Italian bear. He brought my parents in, and he explained to my parents why I was allowed to bring a same-gender partner to the prom. He said the only reason he brought them in was to talk about concerns for the safety of my two younger siblings who were going to be continu-

ing at that school for the next two or three years. So here was this Jesuit priest, who was the principal of the school, explaining to my parents: 'Of COURSE they'll take their same-gender partner to the prom! It's the '90s!

But the principal of Brother Rice high school, in September of the following year, said in his opening address in reference to the prom that they wouldn't tolerate any 'shenanigans' like what happened at Gonzaga the year before. He specifically said that there would be no tolerance for same sex prom dates (Mikiki 2023).

The Impact of Mount Cashel

"I can't say it strongly enough — the Mount Cashel orphanage was a dark cloud over any gay movement, any gay or AIDS stuff," said Bernardus Stromer-Chaos, who chaired the board of the AIDS Committee of NL in the early 1990s.

It was huge. The church in Newfoundland had been a very dominant, trusting force. People in the outports would bring their children to church, their kids who were being sexually abused. There was such enormous trust in the church. The priests, they were the men you would wipe the chair for and give the best chair in the house. That actually happened in the 1980s! People were practically clicking their heels in obedience.

So after Mount Cashel the social political landscape changed a lot. And [the Liberal government] responded to that. Because people were pissed off, they were disappointed, they were angry, they were sad, they didn't know how to talk about it (Stromer-Chaos 2022).

Mount Cashel was an orphanage in St. John's which operated between 1898 and 1989. It was run by the Congregation of Christian Brothers, a Catholic order. In its later decades, the majority of its residents were not only orphans but included 'wards of the state' – boys who had either been removed from their families or in many cases given up by low-income families who could not afford to look after them.

"Mount Cashel had a very disciplinarian regime and the boys endured physical punishment and violence, and it was in this context that sexual assaults and harassment from the Brothers took place," wrote Kinsman (Kinsman 1993).

Numerous unsuccessful efforts were made by the boys and others to alert authorities and the public to the ongoing abuse. In the early 1970s, social workers and doctors reported the abuse to authorities, to no avail. In 1975, the Royal Newfoundland Constabulary opened an investigation but it was killed later that year on the orders of the Chief of Police, despite numerous accounts of abuse that were collected from residents and even confessions from some of the Christian Brothers. The following year, one of the investigating officers was ordered to doctor his initial investigation report. In 1976, two *The Evening Telegram* journalists investigated the sexual abuse and prepared to break the news, but the publisher killed their story before it could go to print. During this period, the NL Justice Department was also complicit in the cover-up and doctoring of investigative reports (Higgins 2012).

Other efforts to expose the abuse ensued, also largely unsuccessful, until the news broke on an open-line phone-in radio show in 1989. In response, the NL Justice Department, then headed up by Progressive Conservative minister Lynn Verge, re-opened the quashed 1975 investigation. This led to a public inquiry and in 1989 the orphanage was closed and later demolished (a large grocery store now stands on the site). Several Christian Brothers were charged and tens of millions of dollars were paid out to more than 100 former residents who were abused; related lawsuits continue to work their way through the courts today (Ibid.). The Catholic Church's initial response to the investigation in the 1970s was to transfer the Brothers under investigation to other jurisdictions, with the outcome that they continued their abuse elsewhere (Kinsman 1993). The revelations of abuse at Mount Cashel opened the door to subsequent investigations elsewhere, revealing an ongoing pattern of physical and sexual abuse perpetrated by church officials throughout the world.

It's important to emphasize that what happened at Mount Cashel had nothing to do with homosexuality. These were crimes of power perpetrated and covered up by influential male-run institutions: the Catholic Church; the Royal Newfoundland Constabulary; the NL Department of Justice. It merits mention here because of the manner in which the investigation and subsequent revelations impacted the queer community. To put it bluntly, these institutions of power sought to pin the blame on "homosexuals" rather than on their own failure to uphold public trust, integrity, and due process.

The Hughes Commission relied on reports produced by police and social service agencies which were written from, and embodied, anti-gay stand-points. For instance, the title of the police detective's initial 1975 report was 'Homosexual Acts and Child Abuse at Mount Cashel Orphanage.' This reflected the active criminalization of homosexual activities that has long plagued police practice. Documents from social service agencies also designated homosexuality as a problem... This description of the problem as a 'homosexual' one was thus already in the texts and evidence the Commission depended on, and it remained unchallenged. The Commission simply built upon this prior definition of homosexual activity as a criminal or social problem. This is how heterosexism – the ideology and practice that defines heterosexuality as 'normal' and 'natural' and lesbians and gays as 'abnormal' and 'sick' – entered into work of the Commission; this theme of homosexuality being a problem was reflected in the way the media framed stories... Through this reliance on texts that already pre-package homosexuality as a problem, the Commission and the media came to take up this same anti-gay standpoint (Kinsman 1993).

Rather than focussing on the frightening abuse of social power by those entrusted with authority over young people, the media has tended to focus on the homosexual, or deviant, character of the men involved. Although we know very little about these men's sexual identities, few defined themselves as 'homosexuals'. Contrast the 'homosexualization' of these men with the way men who commit sexual assaults against girls are covered in the media: their 'heterosexuality' is never focussed upon as a problem, even though heterosexual men account for the vast majority of those who sexually assault and harass young people (Ibid.).

The outcome of this, warned Kinsman, was an observable increase in gay-bashing. In addition, "the provincial government continues to use the suggestion that we are a danger to young people in denying basic human rights protection to lesbians and gays" (Ibid.).

Karl Wells worked at CBC during this period, and reflects on the scandal:

During the Mount Cashel tragedy some people somehow or other conflated being a pedophile with being gay. During the Hughes hearings quite often victims would refer to the perpetrators as being gay. They weren't gay – they were child molesters. They were pedophiles. And there are heterosexual pedophiles and there are homosexual pedophiles. But somehow or other they conflated being gay with being a child molester and you had people looking at you differently again. All through that Mount Cashel tragedy which went on and on and on and on (Wells 2021).

Activists and allies at the time pushed back hard against this framing of the abuse at Mount Cashel. Ron Knowling was one of the founding members of GALA-MUN and subsequently involved with its successor, a group calling itself the Gay and Lesbian Studies Group. On February 13, 1990, the group held a public forum at Memorial University called "The Hughes Commission and the Lesbian and Gay Community." It was an opportunity for the city's queers to voice their concerns about how the police and church were trying to frame their abuse of authority. The panel included Peg Norman, then working with the St. John's Status of Women Centre and Rape Crisis Centre, along with Kinsman, who was then teaching sociology at Memorial.

"The blame must not be shifted onto already oppressed groups," Norman said, according to coverage of the event in *The Muse* (Whitaker 1990). At the panel, Kinsman noted that this conflation was appearing with growing frequency in student research papers as well.

"'Where's the power issue?' [Knowling] asked, saying he thought the problem at Mount Cashel occurred because priests and Christian Brothers had a lot of power in an institution that was not open to public scrutiny," reported *The Muse*. "Panelists suggested the coverage of problems of child abuse in the R.C. Church may have encouraged an anti-homosexual backlash in society," continued the coverage (Ibid.).

"[English professor] Roberta Buchanan, who chaired the forum, suggested the Hughes Commission is being used to draw attention away from something she says many people don't want to face: the problem of abuse within families in our society" (Ibid.).

"I was very concerned about Mount Cashel," Knowling recalls over three decades later.

It was all framed within the idea that these were homosexual acts. But a rape is a rape is a rape. It's not a homosexual rape, or a heterosexual rape. It's not a homosexual molestation or a heterosexual molestation. But it was all being framed within the context of [homosexuality]. And the media were incredibly ignorant of how they were fueling a homophobic panic. It was a real discussion which was ongoing at the time. There was some really vile sloppy reporting going on and it didn't help the situation (Knowling 2021).

WaterLily, a feminist publication in operation at that time, also took repeated aim at the Hughes Inquiry in news coverage and commentary. Feminist activists hoped to use the Hughes Inquiry to draw attention to the ways in which police, justice department and church also downplayed or ignored issues of violence against women, seeking to emphasize the ways in which the Mount Cashel abuse and coverup reflected a systemic problem rooted in patriarchy.

Child sexual abuse offenders are predominantly heterosexual males. Victims of child sexual abuse are predominantly female. Why then, do homosexuals get blamed for all of this and much more besides? The portrayal of homosexuality as the problem at Mount Cashel by the media and [Hughes] commission council has taken away from the real issue of abuse of power... The church must take an active role in helping dispel the myths surrounding who is responsible for the abuse. They helped create the atmosphere and conditions that are often attractive to potential sex offenders – status and authority, social acceptance, and secrecy and access to children. The church must also take responsibility for its part in doing nothing to prevent it from happening in the first place (Keats 1989).

National feminist organization Women's Legal Education and Action Fund (LEAF) also tried to draw the attention of the Hughes Commission onto the broader issue of abuse of power within patriarchy, underscoring that what facilitated the abuse at Mount Cashel had nothing to do with homosexuality but everything to do with the impunity of powerful men and male-dominated institutions.

LEAF's submission will... demonstrate that where allegations of physical and sexual abuse against women were reported to persons in authority with a legal or moral obligation to respond, in some cases there has been no response, or an inappropriate response, by the system. Women and young girls are most frequently the victims of sexual and violent crimes against the person, these crimes being largely perpetrated by men... It will be LEAF's submission that the criminal justice system in Newfoundland, as well as in other regions of Canada, has not responded to the needs of women of all ages with respect

to physical and sexual assault and that the administration of justice has af-
fected female victims of violence by further stigmatizing and alienating them
(Greene 1989).

Stromer-Chaos, a long-serving activist with the AIDS Committee who also
served on its board, observed that the Mount Cashel tragedy and the way the
church tried to conflate it with homosexuality also created tremendous problems for AIDS activists. He feels it was a key reason the provincial government
– especially the Liberals – were hesitant to support or fund initiatives around
AIDS.

The Mount Cashel orphanage was a big issue. I cannot state it more strong-
ly – Mount Cashel was a dark cloud over the gay movement, over any gay or
AIDS stuff. We [ACNL] weren't getting any money, or at least very little money,
from the provincial government. We had a hard time getting legitimacy. People
wouldn't come forward. People were afraid. I'm certain Mount Cashel was a
factor. It changed the socio-political landscape a lot (Stromer-Chaos 2022).

"Mount Cashel in some ways and in some peoples' minds conflated the
issue of gay and lesbian with child abuse," said St. John's lawyer Lynn Moore.
"Which it was not about at all. It was about power and control."

Today Moore is a well-known local lawyer who has been involved in class-
action suits on behalf of some of the victims. She began her career as a lawyer
watching the Mount Cashel trials. She started law school in 1989, the year it all
became public. During her second summer of law school, she attended court
and took notes on the Mount Cashel cases as part of her studies. "It was very,
very horrible in terms of what the survivors were relaying and how the defence lawyers were cross-examining. It was very, very upsetting and I would
go home from work and cry at night and then get up in the morning and go
back and do it again with my brave face."

Ultimately, the experience wound up shaping Moore's career.

I think it had a huge impact on me. The trials were so horrible, and the law-
yer that I watched was so masterful and so compassionate to the survivors,
that I thought: 'I want to do that, I want to be able to talk to people about
what to expect.' I wanted those cases, which a lot of people didn't want, and
now that's pretty well what I do full time, except from the civil side (Moore
2022).

The readiness of local media to conflate a variety of abuses of power with
homosexuality was apparent in other cases as well, observed Moore. She cited
cases in which convictions of indecent assault by men against other men were
reported by local newspapers as "homosexual activity" rather than abuse or
assault. In other cases, she noted, such acts were described in the newspapers
with the bizarre label of "immoral practices".

The framing of what happened as "homosexuality" rather than a systemic
problem with the Catholic Church underscores the Church's powerful influence in NL as well as elsewhere, says Moore.

I was raised as a Catholic and the level of indoctrination was substantial. We went to Mass once a week, we started every day with prayers, we had to go to confession – this was part of my school curriculum! And of course religion was taught. But until I think grade 12 it was always Catholicism that was the subject of religion. And I remember as a six-year-old being told the crucifixion story. I was in grade one. There were generations of children that were told the only good women were virgins.

I remember in high school having debates with our teachers about birth control. At the time the church was selling the Billings method, which involved people having to keep track of their cycles and their temperature and at a certain point in the month – when you were most likely to conceive – that was when you had to abstain. And prior to this rhythm had been the method – so you just watch your cycle and you avoid [sex]. So the classrooms were filled with little babies, because it didn't work, you know? I remember saying to one teacher: 'So what you're saying is that God made us to have these sexual desires and urges, and at the time that they're most insistent, you're saying that we shouldn't act on them.' And she said: 'Are you a bunch of animals?'

The church, to my way of thinking, to the present day, has never really gotten its head around the fact that it is a patriarchal institution that oppresses not only women but trans people and gay people and lesbian people. There's a lot of oppressive behaviour... they continue to not understand the depth of the problem that their institution is facing (Ibid.).

The Village Mall

What has come to be known as the 'Village Mall affair' is a complex incident involving homophobia, moral panic, journalistic ethics and public sex. It should be stated at the outset that public sex in the province was rife in the 1990s; as someone who was a teenager during this period, I remember it well. Teenagers had sex at drive-in movies and in and around schools. When I attended Memorial University as an undergraduate, public sex and public intimacy was an accepted reality, sometimes joked about and sometimes subjected to scrutiny and critique by policymakers. Every semester, university officials would beseech students to stop blocking public spaces with intimate acts, and I recall numerous occasions of couples covered in blankets in public or semi-public spaces (bars, food courts, empty classrooms) in the University Centre having sex. Students' union officials were warned to be careful entering society rooms as they were frequently used for sexual encounters. Local scenic spots like Signal Hill were widely known as go-to spots for romantic and sexual trysts.

Such behaviour was widely tolerated, because it was heterosexual in nature. A different standard was applied to same-sex public sex, however. As community members attested to earlier in this chapter, police would prowl known sex sites looking for homosexuals engaging in sex. University officers produced entire reports on the threat posed by homosexuals – not heterosexuals – engaging in public sex at university. There was a clear double standard: heterosexual public sex was something to be laughed at, joked about, a matter of bemused resignation that was largely tolerated, especially among the young, as a matter of natural youthful and human behaviour. Same-sex public sex, however, was a threat to be feared and punished.

The other important reality to bear in mind is that space for same-sex displays of affection or intimacy was all but non-existent in NL at the time. There was the occasional gay bar or gay dance that would be organized, but they paled in frequency and accessibility compared to all the opportunities and spaces available to straight partners. There was also little opportunity for queer people to meet each other. In an era before the internet or dating apps, the only way to find other queer people was to go to places where you had heard they might be found; queer hangouts passed on through oral lore and rumour. There one had to take the initiative to proposition others one found there, and hope that you might find a potential partner. Taboo, stigma, hypocritical double-standards and fear all combined to limit and restrict the ways in which queer people could find each other or express intimacy, desire, care and love for each other.

The Village Mall is a large shopping complex in the west end of St. John's. Part of a once-booming shopping mall trend (in 1980 over a third of retail sales in the city were cornered by the Village and its more centre-city rival, the Avalon Mall), it's now a pale reflection of its former self. Shuttered retail spaces abound; some shops remain but these days it seems to be the lunchtime teenage clientele from the high school across the street which keeps it alive.

Once upon a time, however, the Village Mall was booming, full of the latest, trendiest fashion outlets, retail chains, busy eateries, a games arcade, and a legendary fountain.

And in 1993 it became the centre of a maelstrom of controversy.

According to court records reviewed by researcher Michael Jackman, on February 8, 1993, RNC officers met to discuss allegations of young men being solicited for sex in and around the Village Mall. The RNC, in consultation with police in other jurisdictions, apparently considered constructing a viewing platform behind the male washrooms, but the architectural layout rendered this difficult.

"This option and the idea of having an undercover officer were dismissed because of the potential to raise suspicions amongst workers in the mall who were themselves suspected of cruising the washrooms for sex," wrote Jackman in a summary of the case published in *The Independent* twenty-five years later. On February 21, a secret video camera was installed in the bathroom, and a month later a second one was added. These cameras were designed to capture images of people using the washroom and entering stalls. The cameras remained until April 13 (Jackman 2018).

Initially 10 men were charged in early May, but dozens more saw their names appear in The Evening Telegram and on the evening news in the weeks that followed. By mid-May, newspapers and television reports were saying that there were 60 men caught on tape, but that little more than half could be identified and would face charges. In nearly all cases, the laying of charges and subsequent convictions were reported in **The Evening Telegram.** *Amongst those charged was one of the RNC's own officers who quickly resigned his post and left the force. Other men saw their employment terminated, while their family members took leave from positions to avoid humiliation and to deal with the emotional and practical effects of the scandal. Such impacts were ultimately more severe than the fines imposed by the courts which ranged from $300 to $1,500* (Ibid.).

Ultimately, 36 men were charged with committing indecent acts, according to police records; 34 of them were named in the press. Charges against one man were withdrawn and one man successfully appealed his conviction as the camera failed to provide a clear enough view to substantiate the charges.

Jackman was 10 years old when the story initially broke. He watched television news coverage of the events as a child. I spoke to him about his subsequent research into the case, as well as his own experience of those events as a child.

"I didn't understand exactly what was wrong, but I knew they were doing something bad in the washrooms and it had to do with sex," he recalled 25 years later. "It was much later that I came to see it as part of a wider phenomenon of regulating sex in public."

Jackman grew up to pursue graduate studies at Memorial and then York University in Toronto. Today he teaches and conducts scholarship at the University of Vienna in Austria. Before that, he returned to St. John's to do postdoctoral work in the city, including the most in-depth research yet on what happened at the Village Mall.

By pure coincidence, his post-doc research coincided with the eruption of a 2018 public debate around the Village Mall investigation. That year, St. John's Pride Co-Chair Noah Davis-Power demanded an apology from the RNC and the provincial Department of Justice for their role in the 1993 sting operation. When an apology was not forthcoming, St. John's Pride threatened to bar sitting MHAs and uniformed police officers from participating in the Pride Parade. The controversy divided members of the public as well as the queer community itself. A caller to local radio station VOCM identified himself as the person who, as a minor, had been propositioned for sex at the Village Mall, and whose parents made the complaint to police which precipitated the investigation. Meanwhile, scrutiny also fell on the role of media and journalists from the period, who found themselves called to account for their own role in publicizing the names and addresses of the men who were charged (Jackman 2016).

"It was really journalists – if you want to blame anyone it was *The Evening Telegram*, it was the CBC," Jackman told me. He acknowledged that reporters from the period said they were just doing their job, and that it was routine practice to publicize the names of those charged with crimes.

I didn't quite buy that. Because they put it on the front page of the Telegram several times, and they scrolled the names and ages and home addresses of people on [CBC's] Here and Now one after the other. And I think that really contributed to the hysteria surrounding it. Not just that it disclosed personal information but that it gave the public something to talk about and something to be scandalized about, something to feel was a threat to public safety and a threat to morality and all these things. I think journalists at the time... spun it into this major news story and very selectively drew parallels to Mount Cashel and created a moral panic.

Where did the police err? I think if you put up a sign that said 'Please do not have sex in the washrooms, you are under surveillance' the men might have moved elsewhere. It's the same as putting signs in a store saying 'Do not steal – you are under surveillance.' I mean of course you probably shouldn't go in and steal stuff from a store, but the response shouldn't be 'We're going to let people steal stuff and keep track of it and then we're going to do a huge crackdown and allow the journalists to put names and addresses and everything in their papers.' That's heavy-handed and it treats the problem as something that is best dealt with through severe punishment rather than prevention (Jackman 2022).

Allusions to Mount Cashel were overt and public, Jackman pointed out. CBC did streeters interviewing members of the public about the events, and multiple persons drew connections to Mount Cashel, which still lingered heavily in the public consciousness.

"[These men] didn't go to prison for what they did, these were pretty light charges – comparable to parking fines or driving into a fire hydrant or something," he said. "So there was a huge discrepancy between what the charges were, and the penalties they faced, and the social impact that the gossip mill had on people's lives."

Another noteworthy dimension of the Village Mall case is the fact that activists during that time largely ignored it. It was only 25 years later that St. John's Pride sought to make an issue out of it. Where were the queer activists 25 years earlier?

"There was no community response, or at least no trace of it," said Jackman. There were probably a variety of reasons for this, he said, but he did speculate on one potential cause. "My impression is that a lot of these men were in heterosexual relationships, they were married men. I don't know if gay and lesbian activists would have taken on that sort of issue unless it was very clear that these were gay men and they were being attacked in some way."

He contrasted the Village Mall cases with that of Brian Nolan's complaint against the RNC (discussed in Chapter 6).

That was a police officer harassing a person, so it's very clear then that you're dealing with issues of identity which in some cases were more manageable and I think more appealing to gays and lesbians at the time – to say 'I'm being attacked,' these are 'my people.' I don't know if you would have the same pushback with a bunch of men who may or may not be gay-identified. Even today. In the Toronto Bathhouse raids you had a community response and an organization that took it on, because those were gay institutions in a sense, they weren't parks or washrooms. So the location is perhaps important in how people thought about that as a community issue, as a gay and lesbian issue (Ibid.).

Tom Mills, a former Director of Public Prosecutions for the province, agrees that it poses important questions.

How many of those men were gay? I don't know. There are men who simply have sex with men on occasion. They swear up and down that they are not bisexual and that they are not gay. And who am I to challenge that person's self-identification?

It's always been a struggle for me, because as a member of the queer community, what duty or allegiance do I owe, and to who?... I have a lot of problems with the Village Mall cases for all sorts of reasons. But I would draw a distinction between the Village Mall and the Toronto bathhouse raids because those were police coming in en masse unannounced to arrest everyone on the premises... That didn't happen at the Village Mall. People were videotaped. Now, should they have been videotaped? What are the privacy issues? Was it about prevention, or was it about detection? These are very important questions (Mills 2021).

Mikiki, who was a child when the Village Mall affair happened, heard about it in the news but had a very different relationship with it, one shaped by their own experience of growing up in a homophobic environment in which sexuality was an unspoken and taboo subject both at home and at school.

When the Village Mall scandal was happening, I would in the middle of the night go and take yesterday's newspaper out of the trash and I would find the articles about the Village Mall and I would cut them out and I would put them in a suitcase and I would bury it under a tree, under the bows of a fir tree across the street. Because they listed all of the names of everyone they arrested. I would go through it. I realize now that this behaviour was totally abusive, but at the time, as a 12-year-old fag who was trying to figure out my identity, I would go through the phone book – because they also listed their address in the newspaper, in the Telegram – I would go through the phone book, I would find their phone number, and I would call them. Just so that I could hear their voice. Because I needed to know that there was someone else out there like me. Now I had proof, that there was someone else out there like me. But I realize now that this would probably have just been seen as harassment by those folks, that's brutal when I think about it in retrospect. I was a squeaky-voiced little 12-year-old, I don't remember if I even tried having a conversation about being queer.

I was learning about my own sexuality, and now I had empirical evidence – here was empirical evidence that other people understood what I was feeling. I wanted help figuring out what that meant. I didn't understand the implications of the criminal prosecution, I didn't see it as a threat to myself. I just saw it as – there are other gay people, and therefore I need to find other gay people (Mikiki 2023).

Homophobia in politics

Homophobia reared its head in the sphere of politics, as well. There are other examples of this in the chapters of this book focusing on the struggle for human rights legislation, but a very public case from the 1988 federal election offers a potent example.

Ross Reid is a former Canadian politician who served as Progressive Conservative Member of Parliament for the federal district of St. John's East from 1988-1993; he was federal Minister of Fisheries and Oceans during part of this period. Born in St. John's in 1952, he did his university studies in Ontario before returning to St. John's in 1975 to work for John Crosbie, then a provincial MHA for the Progressive Conservative party. Reid continued to work as an assistant to Crosbie when the iconic politician moved to federal politics, serving as chief of staff when Crosbie was federal Justice Minister and Fisheries Minister, and later also serving as an advisor to Prime Minister Brian Mulroney.

In 1988, Reid decided to enter electoral politics himself. He put his hat in the ring to run as Progressive Conservative candidate in the district of St. John's East in the 1988 federal election. The candidacy was contested, and Reid defeated a former provincial cabinet minister to become the PC candidate. A wave of homophobic gossip nearly derailed his campaign.

Rumours began swirling during the candidacy nomination. The real trouble began, Reid recalls, when Prime Minister Brian Mulroney arrived for a whirlwind campaign stop in St. John's. Following a rally at the Newfoundland Hotel, Reid found himself cornered by four journalists.

"Their questions were along the lines of: 'the story is that your campaign is not very active, it's not very busy, and the reason is because you won't deny that you're gay and people won't work with you because of that,'" he recalled.

Someone had obviously contacted the media and planted the story. And what the media were really asking him was: *are you gay?* Put on the spot, Reid refused to deny that he was gay.

"My friends knew I was gay, my family knew it, everyone knew I was gay," he explained. To this day he doesn't know who fed the story to media; whether it was political enemies within his own party or opponents from other parties. "I don't know if they knew I was gay, or they guessed, or maybe they just figured 'Let's throw it on the wall and see if it sticks.' I've never been able to answer that, I've never particularly tried to answer it. But it was pretty grim."

What he is particularly critical of is the way that some of the media jumped on the issue.

CBC's performance in all of that was pretty shameful, terrible. And other media quite quickly rallied around it. I was 'news maker of the week!' So there was a fair bit of national attention. And on a personal level it was pretty rough, because it became a real football... it really affected me. It really sort of jarred me a bit.

CBC called and wanted to do an interview. I talked to them, and said 'Okay I'll do the interview.' [The producer] said: 'We'll give you a chance to say exactly what you've said to me.' Well that's not what happened. So needless to say that fomented it. It came down to where people were saying: 'Oh I'm not going to work for him until he denies it.' Provincial members were not happy.

Right after the CBC piece came out, the annual meeting of the provincial [Progressive Conservative] party was in Corner Brook that weekend. So I'm sitting on the plane, going to Deer Lake, and you know the old expression 'your ears are burning'? Well my ears were burning off the sides of my head! It's all anybody was talking about. I could hear it. And if I couldn't hear it, I could feel it. I could sense it. So I went out, I did a day of that and then I had to come back (Reid 2021).

Reid returned to attend the Conception Bay South Firemen's Ball on a Saturday night. As soon as he got back to St. John's, he received a message from John Crosbie, his political mentor and friend. Crosbie told him to come over and see him the following evening, on Sunday night.

I can remember how we sat down in his living room and he said: 'Well what's going on here? They all want you to deny you're gay.' And I said: 'I'm not going to deny I'm gay. I can't deny I'm gay and I'm not going to!' I was going to refuse to answer the question, because that would just feed it. And [Crosbie] never hesitated once [in his support]. I never got anything less than one hundred percent support from him (Ibid.).

Crosbie and NL Premier Brian Peckford – Ross was running for the federal PCs, but the provincial government under Peckford was also Progressive Conservative – brainstormed what to do. There was a large-scale meeting planned for that Thursday night for PC supporters and campaign workers. They decided they needed to use the opportunity to quash the homophobia once and for all.

So Crosbie and Peckford got on the phone. The campaign was encouraging people to go to this meeting, and Crosbie and Peckford got on the phone and their message was: 'Get your ass in there and support [Reid]!' Between the two of them, the provincial cabinet was on orders to be there, as much of the provincial caucus as could be there was expected to be there, and it was wonderful for me personally. It was great for the campaign frankly, but it meant a lot personally, because I wasn't just all alone out there... Peckford was very supportive during that period. [Prime Minister] Mulroney was also very, very sympathetic, all through the thing (Ibid.).

As organizers prepared for the Thursday meeting, the story lingered in the media and there were a range of reactions from journalists. Early on during the controversy John Nolan, a former politician and broadcaster with CJON, was given a story to read on-air about it. After he did so, he phoned up Reid to apologize, and to say that he refused to read the story on-air again.

Another woman came in and she sat down and she burst into tears, because her husband had just told her that he was gay. I spent 45 minutes with her, and we didn't talk about me at all. I told her: 'We all know people who have come out of marriages for all kinds of different reasons. It's got nothing to do with you. So don't feel ashamed. I know it's inevitable and it's easy to feel that way, but don't feel ashamed, it's not your fault. This is something that he's dealing with and perhaps should have dealt with a long time before' (Ibid.).

Reid also received calls of support, some of which surprised him. There were calls and notes of support from older PC politicians – "small-c conservatives" – from around the country. Svend Robinson, an NDP MP from British Columbia and an out gay man, called him up to let him know that he had the support of the federal NDP through the ordeal. Even Jack Harris, the incumbent NDP MP against whom Reid was running in the election, phoned him up. Reid was touched by the strong and sincere show of support from his political opponent, and it presaged a friendship between the two men which has lasted to the present day.

It was still unclear how the Progressive Conservative membership, and the general public, would react. Shortly before the big rally planned for Thursday night, Reid got a phone call from Kevin Parsons. Parsons was a provincial PC MHA and former mayor of the town of Flatrock. He was widely known, and active both in Conservative politics as well as the Catholic Church. He was the man who had introduced Pope John Paul II during the papal visit to Flatrock in 1984, a keystone moment for the province's Catholics.

Some [Conservatives] were leery. This was 1988, rural Newfoundland, a lot of it Catholic. But then the night [the meeting] was happening, I got a call from Kevin Parsons, the guy that introduced the pope in Flatrock in 1984. He phoned me up at 6 o'clock that night, just as everybody was sort of preparing to trundle off to the headquarters on Torbay Road. And he said: 'I want to introduce you tonight.' I said: 'Kevin that's very kind of you.' And he said to me: 'Who am I to judge you? Who am I to say what's good or bad? I don't know what my children do, it's none of my business, it's their business! They're adults. This is the same thing. And I would like to introduce you tonight.' I replied: 'Kevin, absolutely.'

When we got there, the place was jammed. There were 400 people there, and I was told there were more than 100 people outside that they couldn't let in. The place was blocked. There were TV cameras everywhere. It was the days of smoking, so the air was full of cigarette smoke. Kevin [Parsons] did the intro-

duction. Then Peckford got up, and he was all fired up. And then Crosbie got up,
and he was just outrageously funny (Ibid.).

Crosbie deployed his trademark humour to tackle the homophobia head
on, mimicking and satirizing the journalists who had launched the controversy,
and who had thought it appropriate to ask veiled questions about someone's
sexuality.

'Imagine' – *Crosbie said* – *'Someone asking me if I was a* **heterosexual!***' He*
said that in front of 400 people. He was a progressive guy. And then after that,
it wasn't an issue. Going door to door, out and around, in public debates that
were on the go, it was never mentioned (Ibid.).

Reid went on to win the seat, which he held until 1993. He was in the federal government in 1992, when the government – about to lose a court case in
the matter – repealed regulations barring homosexuality in the Canadian Forces, finally ending what is now referred to as the LGBT Purge. The Progressive
Conservative federal government's decision to abandon the case upset some
right-leaning Conservative members, he recalls.

When they stood up and announced that all prosecutions and investiga-
tions involving gay men and women in the military would be ceased, and that
it would not be a problem for somebody joining the military, that caused a
bit of a stir from some of my colleagues. So I brought together a little group
of people that I knew who were like-minded – *in those days the Progressive*
Conservative party actually was progressive in large hunks – *and [the opposi-*
tion] went away. And the world didn't end, funnily enough. It carried on, right?
(Ibid.).

He's quick to emphasize that he can't take full credit for quelling opposition within the party. "It was a pretty broad party. Back then it actually was
progressive. But there was certainly a rump on the right. So whenever it looked
like there was a group on the right that was coming together, I would convene
a group on the left."

Ross went on to play varied roles in federal and provincial politics for many
years. For the past decade he has worked as an international consultant on human rights and democratic development, working in Iraq, Afghanistan, Bosnia
and Herzegovina, Kosovo, Ukraine, and elsewhere. Looking back on the events
of 35 years ago, he emphasizes the important role played by his colleagues and
even people he didn't know at all, who stood up – even across political lines
– to offer unwavering support when homophobia reared its ugly head. In the
end, he feels it brought the campaign, and the party, even closer together.

If anything it invigorated people. And now people knew I was gay, people
who had had no idea I was gay. At the end of it, it was obviously affirming. I
mean you're pretty raw, you're pretty whacked, in those days the campaigns
were seven weeks long, or even longer. So you've been doing this, and you're
sort of hollowed out by the end of it. But having gone through all of that and
seeing the support, and seeing the response – *primarily here but also right*
across the country – *it was good. It meant a lot* (Ibid.).

Chapter Six: Fighting and Winning Human Rights

As we have seen, as late as 1995 it was not illegal to discriminate against someone on the basis of their sexual orientation in Newfoundland and Labrador. Every province has its own human rights legislation, which lays out the grounds on which it is illegal to discriminate against someone – for instance, on the basis of their gender, disability, and so forth. These human rights acts enumerate the specific "prohibited grounds of discrimination" which vary from province to province, although many are similar.

Quebec was the first province, and in fact the first jurisdiction in the world larger than a city, to introduce a prohibition against discrimination on the basis of sexual orientation. This effectively made it illegal to discriminate against someone because they were gay or lesbian; discrimination on the basis of gender identity – or transphobia – is a more recently prohibited form of discrimination, dating only to the past decade in most provinces and 2013 in NL. Quebec brought in its legislation on sexual orientation protection in 1977, twenty years before Newfoundland and Labrador would follow suit. NL was the third last province to prohibit discrimination on the basis of sexual orientation, and it was a long, hard struggle.

The province's Human Rights Association (NL HRA) was founded in 1968, its original mandate to educate the public about human rights. 1968 was the International Year of Human Rights, designated such by the United Nations on the twentieth anniversary of the UN Charter of Rights. The NL Liberal government struck the NL HRA to raise awareness about the anniversary and the importance of human rights. The nomenclature is confusing: originally, this association, which later became known as the NL Human Rights *Association*, was initially called the NL Human Rights *Commission*. A year later, in 1969, NL passed its first Human Rights Code. That year, leadership of the Commission (as it was then called) passed to Dr. Biswarup Bhattarachya, a psychiatrist working at the Waterford Hospital. He was an ardent campaigner for human rights,[51] and began remolding this commission into an activist, advocacy group, and its name was changed to NL Human Rights *Association* (Clement 2012).

Meanwhile, the NL government moved slowly in giving its legislation – the Human Rights Act – teeth. In 1971, a Human Rights Commissioner was hired, but the office really only served to vet complaints and make recommendations to the Minister of Labour. It wasn't until 1974 that a standing commit-

---

[51] But not sexual orientation protections.

tee was established — called the NL Human Rights *Committee* (soon renamed to *Commission*) — and a full-time investigator would not be hired until 1982. The distinction between these similarly titled bodies is important. The group which for most of its existence was known as the NL Human Rights *Association* (although its original name had briefly been NL Human Rights Commission) was a community organization, often led by fervent activists but without any actual powers in law. The NL Human Rights *Commission*, on the other hand, as established in 1974, was an independent agency of government, which eventually acquired the powers to investigate and issue legally binding rulings in certain complaints cases.

Dominique Clement observes that NL's 'human rights state' — by which he refers to the regime of policies and processes providing for the enforcement of human rights — paled by comparison with other provinces, especially in its early years. NL was one of the last provinces to adopt human rights legislation and he attributes this to "the perceived lack of ethnic or racial discrimination" – a view which was rife among policymakers – as well as the fact that many of the organizations fighting for human rights in other provinces had no presence in this one (Clement 2012). Once NL did enact legislation, its efficacy was undermined by a lack of effective enforcement mechanisms as well as a lack of resources and staff.

"Newfoundland stood out in the 1970s for starving its human rights program" writes Clement (Ibid.). The community-based Human Rights *Association*, by contrast, has a vibrant history, driven by an array of committed volunteer community activists until its dissolution in 2013. Following its creation in 1968, it didn't take long for the Association to become a magnet for complaints of all sorts. As Clement observes, "at times the [Association] even appeared to be doing the Commission's work" (Ibid.).

Dr. Bhattacharya was the first president of the Association, a human rights advocate who would criticize subsequent boards for not being sufficiently outspoken. Nevertheless, sexual orientation remained off the agenda during the Association's early years. According to lesbian activists from the period, some of the Association's leadership in its early years considered lesbianism "sensationalism" and were concerned that feminists not associate themselves with it. When the Association made a submission to the provincial government in October 1972 urging amendments to the provincial Human Rights Code, they pushed for protections around sex, marital status, political opinion, and pregnancy. Sexual orientation was not yet on their radar.

The Association took confrontational stances early on, criticizing the RNC for photographing participants at protest rallies; the chief of police responded brusquely that there was no law preventing them from doing so, and they would continue. The Association even held a public seminar at City Hall on June 11, 1973 on the topic of "Police Methods." There, in addition to discussing the photographing of protestors, the Native People's Association also presented a brief criticizing the police for their lack of Indigenous language facility and flagging that as a human rights concern. NLHRA Directors stated that "the Chief of Police, in a letter addressed to the Human Rights Association dated May 7th, 1973, has stated that the law enforcement agencies have the right to use whatever methods they may for the purpose of protecting the innocent (NLHRA 1973)."

The Association's scope was wide: they lobbied on behalf of Indigenous women who at the time would lose their status if they married non-Indigenous men (1973); they called for removal of the word "savages" in the provincial coat of arms (1974); and they adopted resolutions on behalf of the Indigenous Ache people of Paraguay (1973), for instance (NLHRA).

They investigated dozens of cases a year, and without any guidebook or procedure many of the investigations were ad hoc. Without any legal authority, there was little the Association could actually do besides refer complainants to other bodies or bring the weight of moral authority to bear on behalf of those seeking their help. They essentially vetted many of the complaints that would subsequently go to the province's Human Rights Commission. In some cases, a letter or phone call from the Association would be enough to bring about the desired outcome. "We can only act by making things public," a Board member reflected in the minutes of a 1973 meeting (Ibid.).

The range of complaints they received was astonishing, and in some cases amusing. A resident of Lawn submitted a complaint that the neighbouring town of St. Lawrence had better television reception than his community, while a resident of Carmanville complained that he had been requesting use of the town's bulldozer for three years to no effect. A St. John's resident complained that he'd been sold a rusty car and demanded restitution from the car dealer. A junior car salesman, meanwhile, sought protection when his employer told him he must get a haircut or be fired (Ibid.).

Most of the complaints were more serious in nature. In the mid-70s, the Association dealt with the issue of "persons of another nationality not being permitted to enter local bars," according to a 1976 report. Indeed, the scope of racism the Association encountered was such that one of their earliest public seminars in 1974 was on "Racism in Newfoundland" (Ibid.). While policymakers insisted NL did not need more robust human rights mechanisms because racism was not a problem here, the complaints rolling in to the Association indicate otherwise.

Of particular concern to the Association and queer people alike was the problem of the province's denominational education system. This holdover from the Confederation negotiations set the stage for numerous human rights violations, although none of them were considered violations of the law at the time. As Clement observes, "The Newfoundland [human rights] legislation was also noteworthy because it exempted all educational institutions… only in Newfoundland did religious groups hold a monopoly over public education" (Clement 2012).

The province's schools were run by faith-based school boards, and religious-based discrimination against both students and staff were fully sanctioned under this system. For instance, students who were of the same faith as the school their parents applied to on their behalf would be given priority in applications. This became a problem for parents seeking to put their children in the very few French Immersion programs offered in the province, or schools that were more geographically convenient for parents.

For staff, problems stemmed from the abhorred 'morality clause', also referred to as the 'lifestyles clause.' This clause in teachers' contracts stipulated that "A contract of employment made between a School Board and a teacher may only be terminated without notice by the School Board, where there is gross misconduct, insubordination or neglect of duty on the part of the teacher, or any similar just cause..." (Kelleherr 1982).

"Just cause" was not defined, but came to be used as a catch-all for firing teachers whose behaviours or identities ran counter to their employer's interpretation of morality, which was often based on their employer's interpretation of faith-based morality. The Roman Catholic school board, in particular, used the clause to fire teachers who divorced, changed their faith, or married outside of the denomination. Although no documented cases have been found of teachers in this province being fired for being gay or lesbian, it was a constant and ever-present fear on the part of queer teachers that if they were outed, they might lose their jobs under this clause (Ibid.).

The Association grappled with this clause from their earliest days. It was a repeated subject of discussion at the group's annual general meetings. In 1976, media approached the Association seeking their take on the clause, since it was the subject of intense debate between the school boards and the Newfoundland Teachers' Association (NTA). Because the NTA hadn't approached the Association for support, the Association demurred from taking an official position on the debate, but did respond to the issue by organizing a public seminar: "To what extent does the employer have the right to interfere with the personal lifestyle of his employees?" Several of the representatives of the denominational education system who were invited to speak at the event declined to attend (Ibid.).

While there is no record of the NTA formally approaching the Association on the issue, individual teachers did. In 1975, a teacher with the Roman Catholic School Board was fired for marrying a non-Catholic. He appealed the decision, and an arbitration board upheld his dismissal by a 2-1 vote. Another Catholic teacher in Grand Falls was fired for the same reason. That same year, a teacher was denied a position with the Roman Catholic School Board because she wasn't Catholic (she was Hindu, but there was no Hindu school board in the province). In 1977, and again in 1979, the Pentecostal school board fired teachers under the religion clause. And these are only the ones who brought their cases forward to the Association (Ibid.).

When the Canadian Human Rights Commission produced a pamphlet which stated that religion was a prohibited ground of discrimination in Canada, the Association responded with a letter tartly asking them to correct the pamphlet. "In fact there are very qualified people who are refused employment almost every day of the week by school boards in this province because of their religion... the rest of the country [ought to be] aware that religious discrimination is still very much alive and well in Newfoundland," stated the letter (Kelleher 1982).

In the 1980s, a further problem arose: amid pressure for change, churches sought to retrench their control over the system by insisting that candidates for school board elections must be of the same designated faith as the school board to which they sought election. For the Roman Catholic and Pentecostal school boards, this meant candidates had to be of those respective faiths. For the Avalon Consolidated School Board — an amalgamated school board which was typically more liberal in its operations — it still meant that candidates had to be a member of one of the official partner denominations: United, Anglican, Salvation Army, Presbyterian or Moravian. As HRA literature from the period indicated, this excluded a wide range of faiths – Jews, Muslims, Hindus, Buddhists, Confucionists, atheists/agnostics, Lutherans, Baptists, Orthodox, Mormons, Mennonites, and others – from being eligible to run for any of the province's school boards. Several members of the excluded faiths submitted nomination papers and were rejected as ineligible; they then submitted complaints to the Association. In response, the Association adopted a vocal public stance against the system, and in 1985 undertook a campaign of media ads urging voters to vote for a specific pool of school board candidates who had all committed to changing the exclusionist policy if elected (NLHRA 1985). The Association's campaign was endorsed and supported by the Association for New Canadians, the Multicultural Women's Association, and the Newfoundland Sikh Association, all of whom provided financial assistance.

No evidence has surfaced that queer teachers were actually fired for their sexuality, however the possibility — the fear — was enough to keep most of them in the closet. Because there was no human rights legislation prohibiting discrimination on the basis of sexual orientation, there was nothing to prevent them from being fired over their sexuality, and no legal recourse for them if they were. Lynn Murphy, who was an outspoken lesbian activist in her early twenties, attested to the fearful environment this created for teachers. She experienced it firsthand when she got a job with the Roman Catholic School Board in 1983. "When I got my job at the school board, I had to go back in the closet," she said. "Or I would have been fired instantly. No discussion, no rights, nothing. That was a hard period of time... My work put me back in the closet."

Retired teacher Colin Wilson said that when school boards moved against gay employees, they did so with a subtlety intended to disguise their true motives.

During the 1980s and 1990s I had friends that were gay teachers, and they were sent to schools that [the school board] knew they'd want to leave. They never really fired you – they moved you to a school that was either hard to get to or had transportation problems, or where you had to move to [in a more remote part of the province]. They moved you to schools that they knew you didn't want, hoping to frustrate you enough that you'd quit. Most of my gay friends that were teachers, they all quit and they all went to Ontario. And there they got the best kind of jobs with the best kind of pay... I was lucky, I never had any problems (Wilson 2022).

The Association's first documented brush with sexual orientation rights appears to have been in 1986, when Brian Nolan, an Air Canada employee, contacted them complaining that he had been denied a flight pass for his same-sex common-law partner of five years. Flight passes were a perk of airline employees at the time, who could use them for flights for family members. Nolan's complaint was ground-breaking, as not only were sexual orientation rights not in the provincial human rights code at the time, but same-sex benefits (or marriage) weren't even on the agenda of most queer activists. The Association responded to Nolan's complaint by informing him that flight passes were an informal benefit that weren't guaranteed by Air Canada's collective agreements, and therefore it was unlikely he would have grounds for a formal complaint. The case was dropped – but Nolan would go on to play a key role in the fight for human rights protections a few years later, as we shall see (Ibid.).

Fighting for change

As the 1980s progressed, the voices calling for change became louder. In November 1980, the Canadian Human Rights Commission submitted its report to the Special Joint Committee on the Constitution of Canada, which was considering what to put into the country's forthcoming Charter of Rights and Freedoms. The report called for the inclusion of protections for gays and lesbians in the Charter: "A list of enumerated grounds which does not include marital status/situation de famille, physical or mental handicap, political belief and sexual orientation does not offer adequate protection," it stated bluntly (Canadian Human Rights Commission 1980).

NL activists participated in the fight for human rights at the national level. On August 26, 1985, Wallace Upward, on behalf of GAIN, spoke at a public hearing at the Holiday Inn in St. John's for the House of Commons Special Committee on Equality (Sub-Committee on Equality Rights), chaired by Liberal MP Sheila Finestone. The federal government was reviewing the new Charter's equality rights and held hearings across the country. Upward argued for the Charter to include sexual orientation as a prohibited ground. In his presentation he bluntly enumerated the intense – and still legal – discriminations queers were subject to in this province. Gay teachers risked being fired if they were outed. Gay parents were faced with difficult and costly custody battles to maintain access to their children if they were outed. He cited cases of LGBT people being evicted, or refused housing, in St. John's when their sexual orientation was discovered. He said that gay organizations like GAIN were frequently refused rental space for their meetings and socials. In 1984, he said, GAIN had been refused advertising in all local and provincial newspapers except for *The Evening Telegram*. He said there was "particularly harsh discrimination" in hiring in the Canadian Forces and the RCMP (Bulgin 1985).

Finestone responded by describing GAIN's presentation as "a well thought-out, concise and helpful submission." She added that gays and lesbians in St. John's "should be encouraged by the number and organizational ability of lesbian and gay groups across the country" (Ibid.).

Iona Bulgin, who covered the hearing in an article for *The Body Politic*, said that while Finestone (a Liberal MP) appeared sympathetic to GAIN, her Progressive Conservative committee colleague MP Roger Clinch was hostile in his comments to the group, and chose to argue with GAIN representatives. "If all the desired categories were to be listed, would not Section 15 itself eventually become a form of discrimination?" he argued disdainfully. Upward responded diplomatically that "to ensure future protection against discrimination, the Section must be left open to further discussion and future generations" (Ibid.).

The sub-committee received fifty submissions at the St. John's hearing, but GAIN's was the only one that focused primarily on sexual orientation. Two of the other groups present at the session – the Provincial Advisory Council on the Status of Women, and the St. John's Status of Women Council – also expressed their support for GAIN's position, and for the insertion of sexual orientation protections in the Charter. The SJSOWC presentation stated that:

Homosexuals are particularly vulnerable when choosing litigation as a means to establish precedents. Section 15(1) [of the Charter] does not include sexual orientation as an enumerated ground for discrimination. It is popular to think that the absence of this ground is different than giving permission to discriminate on this issue. As Equality Issues in Federal Law states, though, the Canadian Forces has policies excluding homosexuals from enrolment and will discharge them if discovered. The lack of enumerated grounds then offers little or no protection and it is difficult for homosexuals to litigate because they aren't equal before the law. Homosexuals will leave themselves open to discrimination if they pursue this course of action. We think that sexual orientation as a basis for discrimination is unacceptable" (SJSOWC 1985).

In their conclusion, SJSOWC reiterated:

The Charter itself will need reform since it does not prohibit discrimination on the grounds of sexual orientation and marital status. These two issues must be included immediately. Sexual orientation is of particular importance as without protection homosexuals have no recourse; if they choose litigation and it fails, they are at great risk (Ibid.).

The Provincial Advisory Council on the Status of Women (PACSW) brief, titled "Women and Equal Rights," was delivered by PACSW president Ann Bell and administrator Dorothy Robbins. At that time, only Quebec prohibited discrimination on the basis of sexual orientation, but PACSW called on those protections to be extended federally. "[PACSW] believes that it is not reasonable to refuse a person employment, accommodation, or any other individual right, on the basis of sexual orientation. Your Committee should make such a recommendation to Parliament" (PACSW 1985). In the end, it did.

Marion Atkinson had been deeply involved with the Newfoundland (later St. John's) Status of Women Council both as a volunteer and employee. She also worked for the Human Rights Association from 1984-1989. It was during her tenure there that the Association increasingly focused its attention on homophobia. The Canadian Federation of Civil Liberties and Human Rights Association – a national body with which the NLHRA was affiliated – had already in February 1982 adopted a policy on sexual orientation. This policy advocated for provincial associations to lobby to include sexual orientation as a prohibited ground of discrimination in their provincial human rights legislation. At an HRA meeting on April 16, 1985 the NLHRA adopted the national policy.

Referring to sexual orientation complaints, Atkinson recalled:

While I was there we took on the whole load of it. Employment, housing, hiring practices, because the [gay] male was at a real disadvantage. Moreso than the women. See the women could cover it up easier. And they did. They had to. Even the language around gay life was very derogatory... it was mainly housing issues, and work issues. Discrimination at work. Those were the two main things. Back then if somebody made a derogatory statement to you, people didn't dwell on it. They just let it go, to keep the peace. The environment was totally different. Today you'd get told off if you tried that with anybody, which is as it should be. But back then it was all kept very quiet and low-key. But you saw a turnaround with the younger gay people. They didn't give a damn. The older ones were still very fearful of coming out, and they would try to hide it (Atkinson 2021).

Once the Association began taking on cases involving homophobia, the trickle quickly turned into a flood. While Atkinson said the Association faced a maelstrom of complaints from queer folks in the mid to late 1980s spanning all areas of public life, discrimination in housing really stood out to her as a problem.

We were finding that a lot of gay people couldn't find an apartment. Oh yes, that was happening. Or if it was found out that they were gay, the landlord would give them their notice. They'd come to us because the Human Rights Commission couldn't do anything about it, because there was nothing in the Human Rights Act. What we did, we tried to negotiate with the landlord or whoever it was. But because we didn't have any legal power to back us up, that didn't go too good. So we realized that we had to go the legislative route (Ibid.).

Another early concern of the NLHRA was the matter of local media publishing the names of men charged with sexual offenses involving other men. Jack Harris was a lawyer who'd had informal contact with CHAN in its early years, and would later go on to become a federal MP for the New Democratic Party as well as leader of the provincial NDP, during which time he would be an outspoken advocate for queer rights. He served briefly on the NLHRA Board in 1984-85 and raised the matter of media publishing the names of sex offenders. Sex offenders' names were not published when the offenses involved crimes committed against women, he noted – only when the offenses were homosexual in nature. This was a discriminatory double standard, he observed. It was also a practice which had come under fire by queer rights advocates across the country, and which raised significant controversy during the subsequent Village Mall cases in 1991, which were examined in Chapter 5. At Harris' behest, for a period the NLHRA undertook monitoring of local media to document media practices surrounding coverage of cases involving men charged with sexual offenses against other men. After a few months of monitoring, the NLHRA determined that it was difficult to discern any regular pattern or policy behind media decisions to publish sex offenders' names; it appeared to be done on a random, ad hoc basis with no rhyme or reason. They determined to continue monitoring the situation, but the issue appears to have dropped off the radar once Harris left the NLHRA (NLHRA 1984).

The broader concern surrounding sexual orientation protections remained, however. Atkinson and some of the Association's board members conducted a review of human rights codes from across the country, drawing anti-homophobia language from the best of them. They also realized where they could combine efforts. For instance, single women – particularly single mothers – were also facing discrimination in housing; landlords didn't think they would have the money to pay their rent, and refused to rent to them. The Association was already working on a lobbying campaign against housing discrimination toward single mothers, so they realized they could expand it to also include housing discrimination against gay people.

In 1985 the Association met with the provincial Minister of Justice to provide an analysis of the provincial Human Rights Act, at which time they argued for the inclusion of sexual orientation as a prohibited ground of discrimination. The Minister struck a Human Rights Legislative Review Committee to do a broad overhaul of the Act, on which the Association was given a seat. Atkinson said they "fought hard" for the inclusion of sexual orientation as a prohibited ground, but they "did meet some opposition on this committee." Apparently, government argued that sexual orientation protections were *implied* in the Charter of Rights and Freedoms and therefore didn't need to be explicitly stated in provincial legislation. The Association countered that this was inadequate and needed to be clearly articulated in both federal and provincial legislation. During these lobbying initiatives, Atkinson stated, the Association maintained contact "with local gay groups to ensure our goals are not at cross-purposes."

GAIN set its sights on reform at both the federal and provincial level. In 1985, GAIN wrote to provincial Progressive Conservative Minister of Justice Gerry Ottenheimer to request that sexual orientation be added as a prohibited ground of discrimination in the NL Human Rights Act. There is no record of whether a reply was received. On January 29, 1986, GAIN's "political section" met to discuss an ambitious initiative to contact every member of the NL House of Assembly to gauge their position on amending the NL Human Rights Act. They also worked on a brief and letter to send to NL's newly appointed Progressive Conservative Justice Minister Lynn Verge (GAIN 1986).

Verge was a trailblazer in provincial politics. Before entering politics, Verge, a lawyer with degrees from both Memorial University and Dalhousie Law School, served as president of the Corner Brook Status of Women Council and was also on the executive of the National Action Committee on the Status of Women. Elected to the House of Assembly in 1979 at the age of 28, she become one of the province's first ever female cabinet ministers when she was named Minister of Education following her win.[52] In 1985, Verge became Minister of Justice and Attorney General, a post she held until the PC's were defeated by the Liberals in 1989. Verge made it a costly win for the Liberals: she personally squared off against Liberal leader Clyde Wells in the district of Humber East, and although his party won the election, he himself was defeated by Verge in the district race (Liberal MHA Eddie Joyce would subsequently resign in the district of Bay of Islands, allowing Wells to run there in a by-election and win a seat). Verge continued her political career, becoming PC Party leader in 1995 and the first female party leader in the province's history. In the following year's provincial election, newly minted NL Liberal leader Brian Tobin won a Liberal majority government. Verge lost her own seat, leaving politics thereafter (Payne 1991).

Cathy Murphy remembers Verge well; the two were involved in feminist activism in the early days of the province's women's centres.

She was very sharp, very smart. I remember having a conversation with some of the men who worked for her in the Department of Education.[53] One of those guys talked to me about his first meeting with Lynn Verge. He said it was a real wake-up call to him and the other men that was in the meeting with him, because they were used to dealing with ministers who really didn't know much about education, and probably cared even less. But he said the first meeting he had with her, he learned that first day to take her very seriously. Because she asked the kind of questions that new ministers ask, and they answered just

---

[52] Hazel Newhook was named Minister of Consumer Affairs and the Environment in the same cabinet.

[53] Verge was Minister of Education before being appointed Minister of Justice.

the way they answer those ministers – partly dismissively, you know. But he said he knew she was different that very day, because when she got an answer that wasn't in enough depth for her, she asked a second time. And he said she then ended up asking a third time. By the time she asked a third time her face was red, he said – but in the end it was his face that was red, because he knew to never ever go into a meeting with her again without having his answers prepared and his research done. There wasn't going to be any snow-jobs with her! (Murphy 2022).

Marion Atkinson disagreed with Verge's party affiliation – although both were deeply involved in the women's movement, Verge's politics were too conservative for her – but they were next door neighbours and she developed a deep respect for her. She said she's never forgotten the day after the final election Verge lost. The former provincial party leader packed up her office into the back of a pick-up truck all by herself in the middle of a snowstorm, and drove it home. Atkinson came out, shocked that no one from the party had offered to help her. The two women unpacked Verge's pickup, and then Atkinson invited her over for a pot of soup. "Lynn was fine," she said with a smile. "She was conservative as hell, except when it came to women. But she kept an open mind."

When she was Justice Minister in the 1980s, Verge emerged as an unexpected ally to the province's queer activists. She responded positively to GAIN's request for a meeting, and in March, during her first year as Justice Minister, she received a brief outlining the group's request for a human rights code amendment. "The recommendation has been firmly noted," her office acknowledged, but made no commitments about whether it would be acted upon. The provincial Human Rights Association – the civil society body – issued a statement in January 1986 recommending the provincial government amend the NL Human Rights Act to include sexual orientation. Atkinson – then director of the association – commended GAIN "with a wholehearted endorsement of their efforts." The province's Human Rights Commission – the agency of government – also issued a formal recommendation that the province include sexual orientation within the Human Rights Act. Momentum was building (Evening Telegram 1987A).

GAIN's 1987 report to the Minister outlined the types of discrimination gays and lesbians faced in the province "on a regular basis":

Hotels, for example, suddenly find they have no vacancy when a gay couple seeks accommodation. Public houses and bars exclude patrons they suspect of being gay. Office buildings and community centres refuse to rent to gay organisations and business meetings. Hospitals may refuse visitation privileges in Intensive Care/Coronary Care Units to the lover of a gay patient. Printers have refused to publish gay newsletters, newspapers refuse to carry advertisements for gay organizations and radio stations refuse to broadcast public service announcements of gay meetings (GAIN 1987).

The report also unpacked at considerable length the false association between homosexuality and pedophilia, emphasizing that it was far more common for sexual predators to be heterosexual than homosexual.

Another frequently heard accusation is that gay people 'recruit' adolescents to homosexuality. Although researchers do not agree on the causes of either heterosexuality or homosexuality, there is general agreement about what does not cause it. One cannot recruit either a gay person to heterosexuality or a heterosexual person to homosexuality (Ibid.).

The 20-page brief despatches a variety of other myths and stigmas, reflecting some of the common falsehoods and misunderstandings still prevalent in the period.

GAIN's presentation had a greater impact on Minister Verge than they realized. Beth Lacey, a former coordinator of the St. John's Status of Women Council, was, in 1987, working in the Women's Policy Office (an agency of the provincial government) and was known to many of her colleagues as an out lesbian. One day not long after GAIN's presentation, she got a call at her office. It was Minister Verge.

"Beth, what are you doing?" asked the minister.

"Working!" replied Lacey.

"Come on over, I want to talk to you about something," the minister responded.

Lacey was confused.

"It was quite unusual for a minister to call you to their office," she reflected, 35 years later. "You know, I'm a lowly employee and she's calling me over to talk to me?"

When Lacey got to the minister's office, Verge looked at her and bluntly asked, "Beth, what can we do? How do we get this through? What do we need to do to get gay rights recognized?" She was referring to GAIN's proposal to add sexual orientation protections to the Human Rights Code. Verge, it turned out, was determined to try to make it happen. "She was keen, very keen on it," recalled Lacey. "She did a lot of stuff behind the scenes. But it didn't happen on her watch."

Verge would continue the fight even after she was no longer justice minister. When asked by media some years later why she hadn't brought forward legislation while she was minister, she said she had tried but failed to muster the necessary support among her cabinet colleagues.

Lacey had a personal encounter with one of those colleagues. In 1986 the Provincial Advisory Council on the Status of Women, headed then by Anne Bell, met with the Minister Responsible for the Status of Women. As an employee of the Women's Policy Office, Lacey attended the meeting. One of the PACSW members raised the issue of adding sexual orientation to the provincial human rights code.

And [the Minister] — here I am sitting at the table, everybody knows I'm a lesbian — [the Minister] says 'Well, I think that's a disease. And I don't think that should even be considered.' I sat there, for I don't know how long. I left as soon as I could. I didn't go back to work that day. Then I went back in on Monday, and I met with my two bosses — the Assistant Deputy Minister and the Director of the Women's Policy Office. And I said, 'I am never going to be put in a position like that again. My principles will always outweigh anything else. I need you to know that, because if it happens again I will not respond that way. You can let me go now if you want, but that's the last time I'm dealing with it that way.' But they were 100 percent behind me. So that was a really good thing. But, I had been out for so long! I was gobsmacked. I didn't have a word in my mouth (Lacey 2022).[54]

It was during this period that the New Democratic Party became the province's first political party to come out in support of a human rights amendment around sexual orientation. At its June 7-8, 1986, provincial convention in St. John's, the party adopted a resolution to support the struggle of gays and lesbians for equal rights, including the adoption of changes to the province's human rights code. The party recognized that:

...lesbians and gay men in the province have no protection in the provincial or federal human rights codes, or federal Charter of Rights, and have and will continue to suffer discrimination in housing, employment and other aspects of their daily lives... the New Democratic Party make a commitment to lesbians and gay men in their struggle for equal rights by adopting party policy to support them in their effort towards equality (Paddock 1986).

"We considered it very important that there be protection against sexual discrimination for gay men and women," St. John's East district association delegate Rosemary House told national queer magazine *The Body Politic*. "We wanted the NDP to show its support for the gay community and our concern for human rights" (Ibid.). At the time, the NDP only held one seat in the provincial legislature; Peter Fenwick was MHA for the district of Menihek, although Gene Long would also be elected to represent St. John's East in a byelection later that year.

Interestingly, the provincial Liberals appear to have also briefly endorsed adding sexual orientation protections to the Human Rights Code, but only for a brief period before their election win. When the National Action Committee on the Status of Women wrote the provincial parties asking for their position on sexual orientation protections, MHA Kevin Aylward responded on behalf of the NL Liberals: "Our position, with reference to inclusion of "sexual orientation" in the Human Rights Code, is that we support the inclusion of "sexual orientation"...Every person deserves the respect they need to become a wanted and contributing member of our society." But this support was not to last; after their election win the Liberals backed away from this commitment. Aylward's letter is dated June 17, 1987, the same month Clyde Wells became leader of the party.

---

[54] The views of people in the 1980s and 1990s may not reflect their views today.

Public opinion was also shifting in a positive way. According to a September 1985 national Gallup poll, over 70 percent of Canadians believed discrimination on the grounds of sexual orientation should be illegal. The poll also revealed 71 percent support for this in the Atlantic region.

Verge was still working behind the scenes to try to muster cabinet support among her PC colleagues to bring forward a human rights amendment. In 1989, the provincial Progressive Conservatives were defeated and replaced by a Liberal provincial government. Activists soon found the Liberals even more resistant to bringing in human rights protections for gays and lesbians than their Progressive Conservative predecessors. The St. John's Status of Women Council and other feminist groups organized a Provincial Women's Lobby session, and met with newly elected Premier Clyde Wells and members of his cabinet on June 19, 1989, two months after their election win.

The Provincial Women's Lobby was a remarkable undertaking that deserves mention in its own right. The first such lobby took place in 1984, after those attending a provincial meeting of Status of Women Councils in Labrador City highlighted the need for regular meetings with MHAs and passed a resolution to undertake a provincial lobby. They were held in 1984, 1987, 1989, and 1991. By the early 1990s, the Provincial Women's Lobby had grown into an astonishing advocacy machine. In 1988-89, the budget for the event was $20,000, which included teleconference expenses, transportation, space, and accommodations rentals. During the 1980s, participants included not just the SJSWC, but groups such as Women For Change, Single Parents Association, Single Mothers Against Poverty, Women and Words (a literary organization), Native Friendship Centre, Women's Institutes, and more. "Any women's group that agrees with equality for women is eligible to join," stated a call-out for participants in 1991 (SJSOWC 1991).

In 1987, committee chair Wendy Williams reported on the organizing committee's approach that year. Planning began in August of the previous year, for a lobby session in March. First, invitations were mailed out to a wide range of women-serving organizations throughout the province asking if they would like to be involved. These invitations also solicited advice on what key issues should be raised. For those groups that responded and expressed interest in participating, teleconference sessions were held every four weeks, normally Sunday evenings. Technology was not so advanced in those days, and people did not have equipment in their homes for teleconferencing and most telephones were not capable of such things. So regional offices would have to be found, often in hospitals or schools where the technology existed, and women would have to go to those offices for the teleconference meetings. This was particularly challenging for women in rural areas, who would often have to travel considerable distances. "We met through snowstorms, freezing rain and fog on the teleconference hookup," wrote Williams. In addition to province-wide meetings, sometimes more focused regional meetings were held as well, to work through issues of importance to local regions. Women participating throughout the province educated themselves thoroughly on all the issues to be raised, and shared information about where their local MHA and other local politicians stood on the issues. In the pre-Internet era, this type of information was hard to come by, and only accessible from those on the ground in different parts of the province. There was no email in those days: information exchange had to take place through postal mail or telephone.

The lobby session Williams supervised in March 1987 was an elaborate event in and of itself, running from Saturday, March 21 to Monday, March 23. Women poured into the city from all over the province to participate. Headquarters for the lobbyists was the Littledale Conference Centre in the west end of St. John's. The event was an opportunity for the women participants to connect with each other in person as well, and they took full advantage of the conference centre facilities. On the evening of March 21, there was a swimming session to open things off, followed by a banquet ("a nice banquet with very stimulating discussion" wrote facilitator Dorothy Inglis in the planning proposal). The next day things kicked into action in earnest ("we will work very hard from early to late" wrote Inglis). There was a three-hour workshop that began at 9:00am where issues and strategies were reviewed. After a 40-minute lunch, another three-hour workshop. After a one-hour break for dinner, the evening was devoted to practice lobby sessions, where participants did a live-action rehearsal.

The next day was the lobby session itself. At 9:00am, a convoy of taxis arrived at the Conference Centre to transport the women to the House of Assembly. There, they spent an hour meeting first with the NDP. Then at 11:00am they met with the Progressive Conservative government. Then at 12:00pm noon they met with the Liberal opposition. At 1:00pm the lobbyists held a press conference for media.

It was at the 1987 Provincial Women's Lobby that women's groups began to pose questions about sexual orientation rights. Their question began with a preamble:

We would like to support the Human Rights Association and Human Rights Commission in urging the provincial government to move forward quickly to include sexual orientation as grounds for non-discrimination in the Newfoundland Human Rights Code. For too long homosexuals have been victims of obvious discrimination. Inclusion of non-discrimination on the grounds of sexual orientation in the Human Rights Code would be an important first step towards eradicating homophobic reactions in our society and a necessary step if we are to show respect for all persons (Ibid.).

And then the questions. For the governing party: "Mr. Premier – I would like to ask what would your government do to increase quicker changes in the Newfoundland Human Rights Code?"

And for the opposition parties: "We would like to ask if your party supports this and will your party apply pressure to the government to ensure that sexual orientation is prohibited as a grounds for discrimination in the human rights code."

The lobby report includes the politicians' responses. Premier Brian Peckford, on behalf of the Progressive Conservative government, deferred the question to Justice Minister Lynn Verge – "because she is doing a revamping of the Human Rights Code right now and has brought certain suggestions to Cabinet over the last month or so (Ibid.)."

Minister Verge replied diplomatically:

With the benefit of recommendations from the Human Rights Association and the Human Rights Commission, as well as a small committee comprising of representatives from those two groups and the Provincial Advisory Council on the Status of Women and the public... I have proposed to cabinet a complete revamping of the Human Rights Code – major changes in the structure so that it clearly complies with the Charter of Rights and Freedoms so that investigation, prosecution and adjudication are separated and to get to your point looking at lengthening the code and expanding the protection so the issue you raised that specifically setting out sexual orientation as a prohibitive ground of discrimination is being looked at and I appreciate your recommendation (Ibid.).

When the question was posed to the Liberal opposition, the response came from Leader of the Opposition MHA Leo Barry:

[O]n this issue I don't think there has been a position taken by caucus – my own personal opinion is that I believe it should be included as a ground on which discrimination should be prohibited, but I can't commit caucus until we have had that submitted to caucus and discussed and a caucus position taken. We will do that as quickly as possible and respond back to you (Ibid.).

The response is illuminating in hindsight: Barry would go on to play a pivotal role in the drama to come, as we shall see.

The women lobbyists included their rebuttal to Barry:

We would ask that it be would be done as quickly as possible because if we are looking at the issue as a human rights issue and not as a gay rights issue then it becomes very important that we don't let society practice discrimination by obliterating two little words 'sexual orientation' from our own code. So it would be very important for anybody considering the Liberal Party in the near future to know where they stand on that issue and there is no reason in our province, after seeing Manitoba and Ontario include sexual orientation inter code – there is no reason why our province have to be last on this issue and we would be very interested in knowing where the Liberal Party stands as soon as possible (Ibid.).

As for the NDP? Party leader Peter Fenwick gave the clearest, most unequivocal answer of all:

The answer is yes. We have very clear policy on that – that discrimina-

*tion on the basis of sexual orientation should not be used in order to deny
people the same rights that everybody else in society has. I've gotten into some
pretty curious arguments with some right wing groups out of British Columbia
who finally ended up accusing me of being a homosexual as a result of that
argument, but I don't think that's a major problem from my perspective. The
fact of the matter is, you are quite right, that kind of discrimination has to be
eliminated. I've heard arguments that people say 'well, you don't want your
children being taught by homosexuals' – I say, 'I don't want my children being
attacked by homosexuals and I don't want them attacked by a heterosexual
either'. And that's really the important part of it. That a homosexual and a
heterosexual should have exactly the same rights, but should be bound by the
same laws as well* (Ibid.).

NDP MHA Gene Long jumped in with a comment as well:

*Just to add, in bringing it forward and putting pressure on getting it into
the code – that is something that we're prepared to do immediately, whenever
people are wanting to come forward to that – I had a person talk to me about
that last week so we are willing to help speed up that process of forcing the
government to respond on that question* (Ibid.).

Two years later, at the 1989 Provincial Women's Lobby session, held at the
Rabbittown Community Centre, the women asked whether the newly elected
Liberal government would add a sexual orientation amendment to the provin-
cial human rights code. Peg Norman, then working with the Mokami Status of
Women Council and Libra House in Happy Valley-Goose Bay, posed the ques-
tion, contextualizing it against the Mount Cashel inquiry:

*We applaud the efforts of both Church and Government in looking into the
issues of child sexual abuse in this Province. However, there is a very real danger indicated by recent news reports that increased homophobic reactions will
divert attention from the real issue of the abuse of power by adult males in positions of authority and trust. While it is true that two-thirds of child sexual
abusers are heterosexual males, we are concerned that public misconceptions
will label this a homosexual crime unless Government takes a leading role in
establishing the truth. To prevent this clouding of the real issue, we feel that
the Government can help to eliminate this problem by taking positive action.
I would like to direct my question to the Premier. Will your Government move
quickly to introduce an amendment to include sexual orientation into the Human Rights Code during this House sitting?* (Ibid.).

Newly elected Liberal Premier Clyde Wells responded:

*The simple answer to that I would have to say is no. We will not introduce
it during this House sitting. Whether we will introduce it in the future and when
in the future it will be introduced we will have to determine after taking a look
at the overall issues and everything that is concerned and everything that will
flow out of it. The extent to which there will be public hearings or an opportunity for public discussion we have not yet decided. We have not yet looked at*

the issue as at this stage and have not looked at it specifically. I do not know exactly when we will get around to it, probably by fall some time we will get around to looking at the issues. One of the things the Government intends to do is get back to presenting draft legislation for everything that it proposes to the public for an opportunity for public discussion on all of these issues before we give them any law. Telling the group we met just before this that in the past the legislature had the practice of introducing a piece of legislation one day that may involve a massive public change, a major public change, with no opportunity for public debate and only to have the change implemented in two or three days and go through the legislature very quickly with no opportunity for public debate. In all areas where it is a significant public move that affects the public and where there is a variety of opinions on the issue, we intend to ensure that there is an adequate level of public input before moving to introduce legislation or start to implement legislation. So that is one area where we will provide for ample opportunity for public debate (Ibid.).

Joyce Hancock offered a rebuttal, taking the Liberals to task over their failure to develop any stance on the issue as a party:

I am also a part of the National Women's Lobby Group and one of the things that we have been doing over the past two or three years is looking at changes and the need to look at the Canadian Human Rights Code and that we said in our background paper that the Human Rights Code of Manitoba, Ontario and Quebec have protection. I noticed in your opening statement that you spoke of wanting to hear the opinions of people regardless of sex, colour, race and creed so that the dignity of all Newfoundlanders are protected. I think we need to move very quickly on this and I recognize that talking about something like this in caucus is, of course, timely but one thing I am concerned with at the last lobby, the Liberal Party at that time had not a policy in terms, they had the new leader at that time, Mr. [Leo] Barry, said that they did not have a policy and that they would get back to people and let them know what the policy was overall as soon as possible. I am a little upset that that has not happened because there has been some moves taken to educate. I know papers were given to Members who are here now, members of the Party who became elected this time, and you have had that kind of information and are able to educate internally so that there can be some policy developed because regardless of sexual orientation, the fallout from what is happening now, whether it is Church or Government-instituted, looking at sexual abuse. [If] we do not recognize and the Government does not take a lead, the homophobic fallout from that is going to be very dangerous and because ten to fifteen percent (10-15%) of Newfoundlanders and Labradorians do not have this protection, I think that the Government has to take a lead and that public reactions will stem from that. We all know that (Ibid.).

Premier Wells responded:

I appreciate your concerns. I have to say to you that the Government that

I lead intends to do what is right for all the people in the Province and to make sure that we come to the right conclusion but we also admit up front that within us we do not have the right answer, the absolute right answer to everything and we want input from society as a whole and there will be an opportunity for public input and for legislative action that will flow out to respond to the issue (Ibid.).

What did the opposition parties have to say? Norman posed a variation of the question to them: "Will your Party support an amendment to the Human Rights Code to include sexual orientation and see that it is raised during the sitting of the House?"

MHA Tom Rideout responded for the Progressive Conservatives:

I cannot, in all honesty, tell you today that our Party would or would not support an amendment to the Human Rights Code on sexual orientation. I can tell you that there in the past when we were Government, there has been on this issue and perhaps one or two others that might come up today that there certainly has not been any consensus among the Members or supporters of the Party. What we have done and what I will encourage the Party to do during the tenure as leader, at least, is to re-visit and re-look the number of issues including this one that we never taken a position on before and see if the Party is prepared to take positions but at this point in time I would be less than honest if I said to you that the Party has a position for or against. It does not. Our Party on this particular issue has been split among individuals by and large, I suspect, the same way that society has been split up (Ibid.).

Hancock responded to Rideout, refusing to let the PCs off the hook.

I am wondering if, you know, the last time we lobbied your Party was in power and we heard the same kind of thing. We heard that it was going to be looked at and I think the words 'as soon as possible' were used in terms of getting back to us. I think what you heard in the question was that it is no longer just a concern that the dignity of all the Newfoundlanders be considered here. I think what we are going to see is the extreme fallout from the enquiries whether they are Church initiated enquiries or Government initiated enquiries and I think the big losers in this are the people who work and are part of our communities and whether there is a split in the way, I think it is time that we look at it so we know where what is happening in the Party and where to lobby to get the change because nobody has asked, those of us who work on the issue, nobody has asked us to educate the Party. Nobody has asked for any of that and I am wondering could we expect some action soon in terms of discussion and maybe to use those of us who work on the issue to educate those people who are within your Party who may be able to [inaudible] (Ibid.).

Rideout replied, revealing the internal disagreements which had hampered Verge's efforts to bring forward the amendment:

Well, during the last review of the Human Rights Code, the Provincial Human Rights Code, it was looked into in great depth and the Government, which was us at the time, agreed to move in some areas but agreed not to move in others simply because there was not a consensus in Government but I would hope that over the next year or so this Party will go through, not hope, but will, in fact, go through a major new policy development initiatives, policy development in the social areas and in the resource areas and hopefully as a result of that renewal and revitalization new policy positions will be developed by the Party. What will come on an issue like this, Joyce, I really do not know. As I said earlier, supporters of the Party are split just as inconsistently as is society at large on this particular question. Some are openminded on it, some have closed minds on it and I do not know if it is possible to have closed minds opened up and listen or not but I would be less than honest if I did not tell you that this is a very divisive question within the Party and I suspect that it is in most groups in Newfoundland and Labrador (Ibid.).

PC MHA Lynn Verge, the former Justice Minister who had tried unsuccessfully to get her cabinet colleagues to support sexual orientation rights, jumped in as well:

I would just like to add that in dealing with homophobic fallout from the publicity of the child sexual assault cases, there might be another way that Government could help educate people and that is by having the kind of Premier's Task Force or high-profiled major Government study on the problems of male violence against women and children that we called for when we were in the Government and Tom Rideout was Premier. We called for that kind of study coupled with immediate action on another front. I will get into that later. But one of the reasons for wanting to have a major study was to educate the Government as well as the public about why these violent crimes are being perpetrated against children and women and that kind of process might get it across to people that have to do with abusive power and that the majority of offenders are heterosexual males (Ibid.).

As they took the reins of government, the Liberal position on sexual orientation rights appeared to harden, and it seemed opponents to same-sex rights had gotten the upper hand in caucus. In 1990, the Liberal government brought forward amendments to the NL Human Rights Code that would render its protections more expansive, applying not only to place-specific services but to service access more broadly. The amendments would also provide limited exceptions for exclusions, in the case for instance of organizations that wanted to be gender-specific or for the designation of gender-specific washrooms; the provincial Human Rights Commission, Human Rights Association, and Provincial Advisory Council on the Status of Women all opposed gender-segregated exclusions. The Liberals' amendments did not, at this point, seek to expand the prohibited grounds of discrimination to include sexual orientation. This omission sparked a short but fierce debate in the House of Assembly.

Lynn Verge – then Leader of the PC Opposition – used the opportunity to criticize government over its lack of protections for gays and lesbians. At the bill's second reading on November 29, 1990, she said:

The Code prohibits only certain types of discrimination. There is no mention made of the most insidious types of discrimination, namely, discrimination against groups which are relatively powerless and weak in our society, groups that are misunderstood and frequently abused. One such group is gays and lesbians (Verge 1990A).

When debate on the bill continued the following day, November 30, she continued her demand for the inclusion of gay and lesbian rights. Liberal Justice Minister Paul Dicks, she said:

...has defended this glaring omission on the grounds that extending human rights protections to gays and lesbians is not popular. Now, the people who are most vulnerable in our society, the individuals most likely to be persecuted are not popular by definition. Jews were not popular in Nazi Germany. And I would say to the Minister and the Government that it is people who are not popular, who are not powerful, who are not well understood and appreciated, who need the protection of the Human Rights Code the most. Most of the individuals in this House are powerful, command respect, and will probably never need a legal guarantee of human rights because of their privileged positions in society. But there are many other individuals, including gays and lesbians – and I am not suggesting that there aren't homosexuals in this House of Assembly – people throughout the province who are discriminated against on a daily basis and they have no protection under our Human Rights legislation (Verge 1990B).

In response, Dicks first criticized Verge for not having brought in those protections, if she felt so strongly about it, when she had an opportunity to do so two years earlier as Justice Minister. He also questioned the very notion of sexual orientation, claimed that such discrimination did not exist in Newfoundland and Labrador, and leveled the time-worn and bogus association of homosexuals with pedophiles.

What is a sexual orientation? Would it include a sexual orientation toward children? Would it include a sexual orientation toward animals?... There is perhaps a body of medical opinion that would suggest that pedophilia is a different disorder than homosexuality, but are we prepared to say that we are going to prevent Big Brothers, Big Sisters, and organizations which have this type of concern, from screening people on a sexual preference basis, particularly when it is undefined as to whether sexual orientation – as a term, I would also include pedophilia and other types of disorders like that (Dicks 1990).

"I have been in this office now for a year and a half and... I have not received any individuals or any person who has written to me and complained that they have been the victim of discrimination because they are homosexual" (Ibid.). He did go on to then mention two such cases he heard of in the media – one a case of two women kicked out of a downtown club because they were lesbian; the other of two men kicked out of a club because they were dancing together – but said he did not know the facts, it had not been reported to him, and laws should only be brought in to deal with problems that were real.[55]

There the legislative debate would effectively rest for the next five years.

Lesbians take action

The campaign for a human rights amendment wasn't the only issue around which activists were mobilizing. Women's organizations were starting to place a stronger emphasis on addressing lesbians' concerns. While lesbians had always played key roles in virtually all women's organizations in the province, few of these organizations had officially acknowledged lesbian-specific issues in setting their agendas and lobbying for change. This began to change in the early 1990s. The St. John's Status of Women Council had published its research document "Time for Action: A Brief Discussing the Needs of Lesbian Feminists." The provincial Human Rights Association also prepared a policy paper on the needs of feminists. In response to these initiatives, the PACSW, as an arms'-length agency of the provincial government, published its own position paper "Out of the Closet and Into the Light: Improving the Status of Lesbians in Newfoundland and Labrador" in December 1992. In it, PACSW acknowledged that in March of that year it had:

...decided to set sexual orientation and the status of lesbians in New-foundland and Labrador as a priority for research and lobbying... in response to requests from members of the lesbian community in St. John's that women's organizations use their position of safety and privilege to advocate on behalf of lesbians, and to help lobby for the inclusion of sexual orientation as a prohibited ground for discrimination in the provincial Human Rights Code (PACSW 1992).

The PACSW brief, written by researcher Martha Muzychka, acknowledged that it built on previous briefs and research compiled by GALT, GAIN, SJSOWC, and NL HRA. PACSW initially tried to organize focus groups as part of their research, but abandoned this strategy because the lesbians they reached out to were concerned about confidentiality and didn't feel safe meeting in focus groups. Instead, they conducted one-on-one interviews. The data they collected was telling. One woman said she'd hidden her sexual orientation because she feared it would jeopardize her immigration status. Others addressed the problem of custody battles for children. Because many lesbians lost custody of their children in court battles after coming out, apparently it was not uncommon for ex-husbands to threaten court action unless the women agreed to surrender any claim to child support. In other words, they had to trade child support for joint custody. The women interviewed also criticized the social pressure they

---

[55] Paul Dicks was interviewed about this issue in 2023, and his reflections are discussed later in this chapter.

felt to withhold their sexual orientation from their children until they were teenagers. They said this led to even greater resentment from the child because they felt betrayed that their parent had withheld the truth for so long. "One woman summed up the situation as 'lose them or lie to them'" (Ibid.).

The women pointed out that simply adding sexual orientation protections to the Human Rights Code wouldn't resolve all the problems they faced unless there was a more comprehensive legislative review. For instance, even if discrimination was illegal, how would child custody, wills and inheritance, and other family law provisions be handled without legal mechanisms acknowledging same-sex partner benefits and marriage? It was noted that in some jurisdictions, the separation of lesbian couples had led to court cases where their partnership was treated as a business relationship, with consequences that were very different from what the outcome would have been if they were considered marital relationships.

The Newfoundland Amazon Network (NAN) was also in operation at this time, with connections and a presence in all of these other advocacy groups, helping to ensure the concerns and experience of lesbians – and all queers – were on the radar wherever possible. NAN would ultimately come to play a vital role in the final denouement of this struggle. But let us not get ahead of ourselves.

The fight continues

Returning to the early '90s, the fight for a human rights amendment continued, despite the Liberals' intransigence. On March 17, 1991 GAIN's successor organization, Gays and Lesbians Together (GALT), brought Svend Robinson – an out gay NDP Member of Parliament from British Columbia – to give a presentation at St. John's City Hall on the need for NL to pass a human rights amendment. The media attending the event were asked not to take photos of the audience. Also speaking at the event, GALT spokesperson Brenda Ponic cited Justice Minister Paul Dicks' arguments – which he apparently made on CBC Radio as well – that he did not believe discrimination against gays and lesbians was a problem in Newfoundland since no one had ever presented such complaints to him. His comments were easily refuted, she said, by the survey of the province's gays and lesbians conducted by GALT in February that revealed 87 percent of respondents had experienced some form of homophobic discrimination. The survey also showed 22 percent of those cases involved workplace discrimination and harassment. At the forum several audience members also shared experiences of discrimination and harassment they had experienced, reported Jennifer Silk in *The Muse*.

GALT kept up political pressure for a human rights amendment amid mixed messaging from the new Liberal government. GALT spokesperson Patrick Barnholden was interviewed by *The Evening Telegram* on May 16, 1991, and said GALT had been informed by Justice Minister Paul Dicks that a "gay rights clause" was being seriously considered. However, Barnholden also pointed out that Premier Clyde Wells had flatly rejected the idea when he met with the women's lobby a month earlier (Jackson 1991).

GALT's Brenda Ponic received first-hand experience of the homophobia that was still rampant among Liberal politicians. She attended a meeting that year representing the St. John's Status of Women Centre. She was supposed to give a presentation about the proposed human rights amendment to a large group of politicians and activists.

I remember being outside, and waiting to go in. And then there was some MHA – I don't even know his name – and he knew I was going in to speak, and he came up to me and he said: 'Brenda, we cannot have gays in the human rights, because they violate children!' And I was just like: 'What the hell are you talking about?' I got so mad at him in the hallway outside. He was an asshole, we had an assholish back and forth. And then when I went in to do my thing, I was on fire, because I was so pissed off at him. I just remember his snarling disgust and patronizing attitude. And I was so shocked, because it was like – you can say that kind of stuff? Really? It was just so overt! (Ponic 2022).

NAN activist Ann Shortall also attended a lobby session with the Liberal cabinet that year, and remembers it well. A teacher at the School for the Deaf, she explained to the premier the fear under which gay and lesbian teachers operated, without human rights protections. "I remember sitting there and saying 'Well I can't be fired because I work at the School for the Deaf, so I'm under the provincial government.' And Clyde Wells looked at me and he said: 'Oh yes you can!'"

Then the group asked Premier Wells whether he would consider adding sexual orientation to the provincial Human Rights Act. "Clyde Wells said outright, 'Not while I'm premier,' recalled Shortall. "And true to his word, it didn't happen while he was premier."

On June 26, 1991, GALT held a press conference denouncing the provincial government's refusal to add sexual orientation to the provincial human rights code. They accused Premier Wells of being the one responsible for blocking efforts to amend the legislation. The press conference featured not only members of GALT, Gary Kinsman, Padraic Brake, and Brenda Ponic, but also Progressive Conservative MHA Lynn Verge, who joined the activists and spoke to the PC Party's support for an amendment. It was here that media asked her why the PCs – who were the governing party from 1972-1989 – hadn't amended the Code while they were in office. As stated above, she responded that she had previously tried, but failed, to muster enough support from her colleagues in government to amend the Code at that time.

In 1991, GALT activists Gary Kinsman and Sharpe Doppler met with Minister Dicks to discuss their brief and the need for sexual orientation protections. The meeting did not go well. Following the meeting, Kinsman talked to CBC reporters:

We were quite disappointed with what came out of the meeting. It's quite clear that Paul Dicks believes there's not a majority in cabinet [in support of] sexual orientation protections at this time, that they discussed it not so long ago in the past and I don't think he's seriously interested in reopening it. What he's interested in doing is producing as many small administrative technical arguments on why he feels sexual orientation protections might not be nec-essary... Instead they come up with and he comes up with relatively spuri-ous arguments, for instance that we should wait for the federal government to introduce sexual orientation protection into the charter, or that it might not really be necessary or that there's some problem with the wording, all of these types of arguments get raised (Kinsman 1991).

If government was serious about giving the idea fair consideration, they would establish a committee to study the proposal, but they were not even will-ing to do that, Kinsman said.

[Dicks] was very clear to say that he personally couldn't tell us anything about his own personal views because of cabinet solidarity... But having said that, the actual arguments that he's producing... are very dangerous ones, because they feed into all of the bigoted attitudes that some minority of the population has about lesbians and gays. So they actually are arguments that could be used by people who want to discriminate against us in the future... They weren't just saying no to a piece of human rights legislation. They were actually in many ways saying yes to discrimination against lesbians and gay men. They weren't saying that in so many words but that's the implication. That the type of discrimination and violence that goes on will continue and the government is basically giving a green light to it. And we think that is deplor-able and we'll be back here many times I'm sure to try and change their minds (Kinsman 1991).

"What are they afraid of?" asked Doppler. "Why are they afraid to even look into sexual orientation legislation? What's the fear?"

Looking back on these events thirty years later, Kinsman summed up his assessment of the roadblocks GALT activists and allies encountered from the provincial government.

The key barriers were that [the Liberal government] largely subscribed to pretty reactionary views, pretty awful views, on lesbians and gay men and trans people and gender diverse people. They were holding on to a very moral conservative type of position and they did not want to move on human rights protection. Human rights protection is really quite limited and it doesn't actu-ally accomplish that much. But it was happening in other provinces, there was lots of organizing going on across the so-called Canadian state around this, but the Newfoundland government was really pretty adamant that they didn't want to make this type of change. And they perpetuated some of the worst arguments around childcare workers and teachers supposedly being a threat to younger people (Kinsman 2023).

The struggle wasn't only taking place in the halls of legislatures, but in the public sphere as well. Radio talk shows were a frequent space in which public issues were debated. Dopler, an activist at the St. John's Status of Women Centre, was frequently recruited to handle media because of their quick wit and sharp tongue. Peg Norman, another SJSOWC activist and one of the founders of NAN, remembers one incident well, when Doppler went on the radio to talk about the need for sexual orientation protections.

It was on the CBC Crosstalk show one day. I was at the Morgentaler Clinic, working, and it's lunchtime so I have the radio on. So I'm listening to Dopler, who's talking about queer rights, and then somebody phoned in and started quoting scripture. They were quoting scriptures, prohibitions against men lying with men. Chapter and verse – they were really into it. And Doppler just, without raising their voice, was just like: 'Well, chapter and verse such-and-such says this about not eating the flesh of swine. But it's pretty likely you had bacon and eggs this morning for breakfast, isn't it sir?' I just burst out laughing. Doppler was fearless, and funny, just really really funny (Norman 2022).

In 1992, even though sexual orientation was not yet part of the province's Human Rights Act, the NL Human Rights Commission agreed to begin accepting complaints on the basis of sexual orientation (previously such complaints would have simply been rejected out of hand). Without an amendment securing sexual orientation protections in legislation, however, there was little point in submitting a complaint. As accounts of violent homophobic attacks in the 1990s reveal, discrimination was still rampant. Turning to the state for support was not considered a viable strategy for most queers given the lack of laws or policies to protect them.

After GALT folded around 1992 (following the departure of several key members who left the province), there was not only no legislation, there was also no organization advocating for it. The gap — while a serious concern for activists — wouldn't last long. First NAN would form, as lesbians mobilized to keep the activist agenda alive. A couple of years later, Newfoundland Gays And Lesbians for Equality (NGALE) would form, with the specific intent of fighting for a human rights amendment. What would catalyze both groups into action was a horrifying event that occurred the night of July 7, 1993.

In some other provinces, amending provincial human rights codes to include sexual orientation as a prohibited ground of discrimination came as the result of debates and lobbying at the level of provincial legislatures. But in NL, the breakthrough moment came not in the form of legislation – Clyde Wells' Liberal government was still refusing to move forward on the issue – but as the result of a human rights complaint filed by a courageous, determined 39-year-old airline employee: Brian Nolan.

The Brian Nolan Case[56]

The morning of July 7, 1993, began early for Brian Nolan. Over the next 36 hours a series of events would be put into motion that would change life forever for gay and lesbian people in the province, and Brian would be at the heart of it.

In the dark early morning hours, he focused on wiping the sleep from his eyes and getting ready for work. It was a Wednesday, and Brian was working a shift and a half. He was an airline employee, and worked at the Air Canada ticketing counter at the St. John's International Airport. He normally worked from 9am-5pm, but had offered to cover part of a co-worker's shift, and so he had to be at work at the airport at 5am. He made it, and the next twelve hours passed uneventfully.

As 5pm rolled around, Brian was picked up from work by his partner, Shawn Hyde. That night they were going to celebrate the birthday of a close mutual friend, Lynn Andrews. Brian and Shawn made a quick stop to grab some sub sandwiches for supper, and then stopped at the liquor store to get a flask of gin for the party.

Lynn Andrews lived on Prescott Street in downtown St. John's. Brian and Shawn had been roommates with her at Prescott Street before moving into a house of their own in Paradise, a small community just outside of town. They still had their keys to the house on Prescott Street, where they often stayed if they needed to overnight in St. John's.

They got to Prescott Street around 5:30pm. Brian immediately took a long soak in the bath, to unwind and freshen up after his long day at work. After his bath, the gin was opened and the birthday celebrations commenced. Around 7pm, Lynn's roommate Geoff Parsons got home and joined them. By 8:30pm the gin was almost gone between the four of them, and so Brian popped across the street to get a dozen beer. It was decided to add some Chinese food to the mix, and so they made a telephone order, which arrived around 9pm. Beer, gin, and Chinese take-out: all the makings of a fine birthday party for a group of young friends in the early '90s.

By 11:30pm the food was gone. Brian, ever the conscientious houseguest, cleaned up the scene of the party. He and Shawn didn't always get to spend the night in St. John's any more, and they wanted to make the most of it. So, after the kitchen and living room were tidied up Brian and Shawn headed downtown to see some live music at the Ship Inn.

At the Ship, Brian and Shawn ran into another mutual friend of theirs, Ron

---

[56] The narrative of events depicted in this section has been reconstructed through a summary and synthesis of court records, media coverage and interviews pertaining to the case. Unless otherwise stated, information in this section is from RNC Public Complaints Commission 1994.

Knowling. The three of them stayed at the Ship for around an hour, and then decided to pop down the lane to see what was happening at Solomon's. Solomon's was the city's gay dance club at the time, and it was located at the bottom of Solomon's Lane where it intersects with Water Street. Today the space is an upscale housewares shop called Home on Water. But back then, it was a large dance club – larger than the present-day shop, since it encompassed much of the building's first floor.

It was a Wednesday night, so Solomon's wasn't particularly busy. It was filled to less than half of its usual capacity that evening. Brian, Shawn and Ron took seats at the bar, where they chatted together over a beer. Other friends occasionally popped by to say hello. There was a brief incident where two customers became belligerent toward the bartender, who called the police. The unruly customers were gone by the time the police showed up. Four officers – three men and one woman – strolled into the bar. The bartender explained what had happened, and that the unruly customers were gone. The officers looked around the bar for a few moments, and then departed.

It was around 1:45am when Brian decided to call it a night. He'd been up since before 5am, and had to work another shift the next day, although not until 2pm. Shawn and Ron decided to stick around for a few more beer, but Brian preferred to get home and get some sleep before his shift the next day.

Brian left the bar. Prescott Street should only have been a five-minute walk – just up Solomon's Lane, past the Ship, across Duckworth Street and then he'd be home. But between him and his destination were the four RNC police officers who had been in the club earlier. They had lingered outside after they left the bar, and when Brian exited, he saw them lounging against the iron railing of the steps leading up the lane. The following account of what happened next is based on his testimony during the legal proceedings which followed.

As he approached the steps, he wondered why the officers were standing around. He paused to see if there might have been an accident. Then he realized the officers were all staring at him intently. This made him nervous. He'd never had encounters with the police before, but knew they did not always have a positive reputation in the queer community.

The fact that one of them was a woman made him feel a little safer, he recalled. As he reached the steps, it was the woman officer – Constable Krista Day – who approached him.

"What's the matter, faggot?" she said, according to his later testimony. "Have you got no place to go, faggot? We've got just the place for you!"

Then Constable Day grabbed Nolan by the lapel of his jacket and began dragging him toward the nearby police car, which was parked across from the entrance to Solomon's Lane. She kicked him as well, he later testified, propelling him forward. One of the other officers – Constable Hickey - also grabbed him, and the two shoved him into the back of the police car. The two other officers stood back, watching.

Brian was terrified, and did not say a word. Nor did the officers ask him anything – they didn't ask his name, address, or where he was going. They didn't ask him whether he was sober or request that he do a sobriety test. It seemed he was being arrested, but they gave him no reason for the arrest. The tone in Constable Day's voice, he testified, "displayed an obvious prejudice and he felt any protest on his part would have brought physical retribution."

The officers drove Brian to the lockup. Constable Day continued her verbal abuse during the ride, he said, pouring out homophobic invective against the young man in the back seat. Brian sat in terrified silence.

They arrived and he was taken into the lock-up. In a state of shock, he followed the instructions he was given, handing over his shoes, money, belt and other belongings. Then he was taken to a cell. He said that once he was locked inside, he actually felt a little safer now that there were bars between himself and the RNC officers who had abused him.

Sitting there in silence, the sense of shock he felt gradually shifted into a sense of outrage. He'd been picked up at random off the street after exiting a gay club, beaten and abused, and then arrested for no reason by these officers. He got up, banged on the cell doors and called for someone to get a supervisor. He could hear officers talking just beyond the cell, but they ignored him. After shouting for a short time, he gave up, and lay down on the hard mattress provided. Three other people were in the cell, all sleeping. His own exhaustion eventually got the better of him, and he dozed off for a few short hours.

The next morning, he was awakened by prison security guards, who had come to release him. He was brought to the main counter to be given back his belongings. He was asked to sign a register indicating he was being released. At this point, Brian spoke up. He said he was not signing anything until he was given the names of the officers who had brought him in, especially the female officer. He explained that she had verbally harassed him. The prison guard told him he wasn't getting any names, and to sign the form and get out. Brian repeated his request that he be given the name of the officer who had arrested him. At this point, he later testified, another warden came up alongside him.

He grabbed my right wrist and twisted my arm painfully upward behind my back. He then came around to my left side, still holding my arm behind my back, and kneed me in the stomach. This was followed by a punch, a bit lower, from the spot where he had hit me with his knee. He then grabbed me by the neck, pulled me backwards while holding me by the twisted arm, and yanked me towards the cell. He then forced me around and shoved me through the cell door, face down, onto a mattress on the floor (Stacey 1994).

"He said: 'Maybe another day in the cell will help you sign [the release form], faggot" (Ibid.).

While this went on, he recalled, one of the prison guards did something else unusual.

[One of] the prison guards involved lifted a book up to her face when the

boys started beating on me, and basically I thought: 'Oh she's been through this before, she's covering her face so she can tell the truth in court that she saw nothing.' That's exactly what happened. She took a book up, when the first guy grabbed me [...] she took a book that she just happened to have right there, and she opened it up, and she put it over her face. It was a deliberate act of: 'Go for it boys, I'm not going to rat on you because I'm seeing nothing' (Ibid.).

A short time later, the guards returned. They took him back out of his cell, and again Brian demanded the name of the officer who had arrested him. This time the guards finally provided it – Constable Krista Day.

Brian finally emerged into the morning light and walked the ten minutes from the lock-up to Prescott Street. Shawn, who had assumed that Brian had run into friends on the way home and stayed somewhere else for the night, woke up at 7am to see Brian standing in the bedroom doorway. Brian looked "like a ghost," he recalled in the RNC Public Complaints Commission report (1994). "He was white and looked to be in shock... He had difficulty getting words out, he was so upset and cried several times in the process."

***

Brian Nolan is originally from Sweet Bay, but grew up in Gander. Immediately after graduating high school, he moved to St. John's. He got a job working as a flight agent for Air Canada. Flight agents were unionized with the Canadian Auto Workers union (CAW).[57] Brian threw himself into union activism as a young man. The labour movement was one of the spaces in which some queer rights activism was going on (although not all unions were as progressive as others). This union training was pivotal in preparing him for the struggle ahead.

"My union background, my union training, and my union activism was really instrumental in leading me to go ahead with it and to fight it," he reflected, looking back on events nearly thirty years later.

One of Brian's friends and supporters at the time was Mary Shortall. She was a co-worker who went on to become President of the NL Federation of Labour. At the time she did work as an education peer facilitator with the CAW. She vividly remembers Brian's state of mind after his encounter with the police.

He was very, very traumatized by it. Exceptionally traumatized. At the time there were a lot of people in the system who didn't believe him. When Brian would tell the story to officials, people didn't always believe that it happened. It became a big struggle for him. I think that part empowered him to tell his story at whatever cost. His commitment was really strong (Shortall 2022).

In the days following his arrest and beating, Brian mulled over what course of action to take. As much as he felt a burning desire to fight the homophobia he'd experienced, it still wasn't an easy decision to make. "I was very deter-

---

[57] In NL the CAW was affiliated with the Fisheries Food and Allied Workers union, the FFAW — today it's part of Unifor.

mined that I was going to take action, and follow it through," he reflected, nearly three decades after the events of that night. "But I was very scared."

He reached out to the community-based Human Rights Association (as opposed to the Human Rights Commission, which was the government agency). Ivan Morgan said he still remembers the day Brian walked into their office, and the horror he felt on hearing his account. The Association had met with other victims of homophobic violence before – Morgan recalls meetings with men who had swollen faces and stitches from beatings they'd received. In the end, no one had ever been comfortable facing the public scrutiny that a human rights complaint would bring.

"Then Brian Nolan walks into my office, he sits down and he says: 'I'm good to go,'" Morgan said. He called the other staff and an emergency Board meeting was held, at which point they determined to provide Nolan whatever support he needed. His union was supportive as well.

There were other considerations — Brian and Shawn weren't out to everyone, and filing a complaint would shine a public spotlight on their relationship. Brian was more publicly out, but still felt the need to give his mother, then in her seventies, a heads up about what was coming. "My mom was one hundred percent supportive," he recalled. "'Nail the bastards to the wall!' she said."

Shawn was not out to his family, so the two of them visited Shawn's parents. They told them about the looming case, and about Brian's having been attacked because he was gay. "It was funny," recalled Brian. Shawn's mother, seemingly oblivious to the fact they were trying to tell her that her son Shawn was also gay, shrugged at the news. "Sure everyone knows Brian's gay!" she responded.

One of the things that Brian struggled with was the fact he had friends who were police officers.

One of the fears I had in those weeks was that I know people who are RNC officers, I know people who are police officers, and they're good people. Part of me felt guilty about attacking the police force itself. Even though part of me knew it was right. But – what about the good ones? And then I came to the conclusion that, you know, if they're that good, why are they allowing their buddies to do this? Why are they defending them? So I processed all that through my head and came around to the decision [to fight] (Nolan 2022).

On July 19, 1993, Brian filed a complaint with the RNC, against the four officers he encountered that night: Constables Krista Clarke (Day), Larry Hickey, Glenn Barry and Lester Parsons.

His complaint made three allegations against Constable Day: that she had arrested and detained him without sufficient cause; that she used unnecessary force; and that she was discourteous to a member of the public by calling him "faggot," "queer" and other derogatory terms (Stacey 1994B).

He also made two allegations against each of the other three officers: that they aided and abetted Constable Day in her violation of the RNC Act by failing to act to prevent a wrongful arrest; and that they also aided and abetted her by failing to stop her from using unnecessary force (Ibid.).

The complaint first went to the Chief of Police, E.J. Coady, who assigned RNC Lieutenant Duffett to investigate the matter. Duffett informed the four officers of the nature of the complaint and asked them to provide a response. Before the end of the following day, all four officers had submitted responses. Duffett subsequently submitted a report to Chief Coady.

At the same time, the RNC initiated an investigation into Brian's allegations of assault from the HMP prison guards. Staff Sergeant L. Peyton was assigned to that investigation. Based on this investigation, assault charges were laid against one of the guards, Owen Devereaux. The Justice Department decided Devereaux would be allowed to stay on the job during the trial. He was "a very good corrections officer," stated an official with the department (Dimmock 1994B).

Brian testified against Devereaux, recounting the assault and the derogatory language used. Robert Pinsent, then a trainee guard at Her Majesty's Penitentiary (HMP), testified in support of his colleague and flatly denied Brian's account. "Nothing like that (assault) happened that day," said Pinsent. "No kicks, punches or anything. He was being held" (Whiffen 1994).

Pinsent said Brian refused to sign the release form and began pounding his fist on the counter. "He was ranting and raving," said Pinsent. "He was cursing and swearing and would not sign." Devereaux was ultimately found not guilty of assault, but he did face internal disciplinary action (RNC Public Complaints Commission 1994).

"Unlike the RNC they did not have an independent body to investigate," said Nolan. "It was they said-they said. They had four of them backing each other up and my story had no other witness. So that case was pretty much thrown out, because they said it didn't happen."

Brian focused his energies on the RNC complaint. During this time, Brian refused to let his complaints be handled confidentially. He worried that if the matter remained shrouded in secrecy, that's where things would stay, and he wanted to shine a light on what he considered to be systemic homophobia in the RNC and at the HMP. He spoke candidly to media when they approached him. Media reciprocated his openness by providing steady, ongoing coverage of the proceedings against the police.

Looking back on it, Brian feels the majority of media coverage was respectful, but there were times when well-meaning reporters still disappointed him. "The worst part of it was that the press would say things like 'Well-known homosexual Brian Nolan.' They didn't say 'Well-known heterosexual Sergeant so-and-so.' So the press was still a bit naïve in those days. There was frustrating stuff like that," he said.

Another complicated development was that some members of the queer community didn't seem pleased with the public stand that Brian was taking.

There seemed to be a fear from some quarters that challenging the RNC in this way risked rupturing whatever tenuous relationship there was between the police and the queer community. It might deter queer people from reporting attacks to the police, they suggested. Gerard Yetman from the AIDS Committee of NL appeared to express such a concern in an interview on August 9, 1993. "So far in the last four months we've had six attacks on gays and three attempts on lesbians and only one of those cases was reported," he told Telegram reporter Mark Vaughan-Williams. "The Brian Nolan case has put us at a standstill in our work" (Vaughan-Jackson 1993E).

"There was a bit of, 'Why are you bringing this up again?'" reflected Brian, looking back on events. "I think there was a bit of: 'This might cause more backlash.' And a legitimate worry it was. Some people said: 'Well, you know, you're throwing it in their face and they're going to be more difficult to deal with now.'"

Perhaps some were also concerned that it might stoke further aggression from police officers, who still commonly raided gay clubs like Solomon's on the pretext of checking for under-age customers. Others, however, applauded the courageous stand Brian was making, and followed the proceedings with baited breath. In addition to his colleagues in the labour movement, the local lesbian community were very supportive, he feels. He remembers regular visits from the likes of Tree Walsh, Susan Rose and Ann Shortall, among others who dropped in regularly offering to help with writing, media prep, and other work.

I think they had experienced so much themselves that they were more than eager to help. And lots of strangers came out of the blue, lots of straight people, lots of people who you would not have expected to be supportive of the movement. They came forward and said 'You know it's great you're doing this, it's about time it got done' (Nolan 2022).

Three months after filing his complaint, Brian received a formal response: the Chief had dismissed the complaint as unfounded (Dimmock 1993C). Nevertheless, the RNC was feeling the heat. In early 1993, prior to Brian's assault, the AIDS Committee had tried to address the problem of 'gay-bashing' and people's reluctance to report it. AIDS Committee Executive Director Gerard Yetman wrote the RNC asking that they assign a permanent liaison officer to handle complaints from the queer community. The RNC ignored this request. Following Brian's complaint they suddenly announced they would put in place two liaison officers to handle complaints specifically "from the homosexual community."

His complaint had been dismissed by Chief Coady, but Brian was not prepared to give up. On October 20, he filed an appeal with the Police Complaints Commission against the Chief's dismissal of his complaint.

The RNC Police Complaints Commission was itself a very new entity. It began operations May 1, 1993, less than three months before Brian filed his complaint. The Commission had been formed in the wake of the Mount Cashel child sexual abuse inquiry. RNC mishandling of complaints regarding child sexual abuse and police participation in the ensuing cover-up had spurred a realization that the police force needed greater public oversight (Evening Telegram 1991A; Loney 1992). In response, Justice Minister Ed Roberts announced the formation of a quasi-independent RNC Police Complaints Commission (Loney 1993B). He appointed former Memorial University president Dr. Leslie Harris to serve as the first Commissioner (Loney 1993A). So when Brian appealed the Chief's dismissal of his complaint, the matter wound up in Dr. Harris' lap. It was the first complaint the Commission had received in its brief existence.

The Commission itself was not without controversy. It had already been criticized for a perceived lack of independence from police culture (Hebbard 1992). At least three of the Commission's investigators were former police officers, including one from the RNC. Justice Minister Roberts was also slammed for having appointed an all-male panel of adjudicators. All six were male lawyers (Smith 1993).

Roberts defended the appointments, responding weakly that "government did not deliberately exclude women." In response to growing calls to appoint some women to the Commission, he said that to do so would require government to amend the legislation to expand the size of the Commission (Ibid.).

Roberts' defense of the appointments also pointed a glaring light at structural inequities in the provincial justice system. Eligibility requirements to serve on the Commission stipulated a minimum 10 years of experience practicing law in the province. The pool of women lawyers who met that criterion was extremely small, Roberts claimed (Ibid.).

The Telegram reporter Jennifer Smith revealed the stark numbers in her investigation of the matter: of 400 people called to the bar in the province between 1956 and 1985, only 35 were women. And of the shortlist of potential adjudicators reviewed for the RNC Complaints Commission appointments, only 2 of the 25 candidates were women. "We try to be sensitive. We are not perfect. I am not perfect. That's why we are reviewing this," Roberts told Smith (Ibid.).

The issue became a political hot topic. In December 1993, provincial NDP leader Jack Harris moved an amendment to boost the number of adjudicators for the RNC Complaints Commission from 6 to 12. The amendment passed.

This didn't satisfy the opposition however. Progressive Conservative MHA Lynn Verge called the situation an "insult to women," and said the amendments fell "far short of what's required to achieve gender equity or geographic balance." She argued they ought to open up the eligibility requirements to include non-lawyers with relevant experience, in order to include both more women and greater representation from around the province (Vaughan-Jackson 1993C).

Roberts fired back at Verge's critique: "We don't believe in quotas. Ms. Verge seems to like quotas. We don't believe in quotas, we believe in merit"

(Ibid.). Following the expansion of the Commission, four of the new appointees were women (Evening Telegram 1994).

The Commission's early operations revealed both a need for the body – in the first year of operations, 81 complaints were filed against RNC officers – but also raised questions about its effectiveness. Of the 81 complaints, only one resulted in disciplinary action (Express 1995; Jackson 1995). Before Brian's complaint could go to an adjudicator, the Commissioner first had to make an effort to resolve it informally. Commissioner Harris tried to pursue a settlement between the two sides, but it quickly became apparent a settlement would not be possible to achieve.

"I am satisfied that there is an extreme conflict of testimony [between the police and the complainant]," Harris reported. "There is no meeting of minds" (Dimmock 1994B). So, as per the legislation, Harris referred the matter to an adjudicator. On January 20, 1994, J. David Eaton was selected as adjudicator for the complaint. "Let him decide who is lying," said Harris bluntly.

At the same time, Brian procured the services of local lawyer Gregory Stack and filed a civil suit against the RNC (Dimmock 1993E; Vaughan-Jackson 1993B). "That decision [to bring a civil suit] was made way back when this initially happened," Brian told The Telegram reporter Mark Vaughan-Jackson. "I was a little wary as to whether an internal investigation would bring justice (Vaughan-Jackson 1993B).

"The dismissal [of the RNC complaint] didn't come as a big surprise. But I did naively hold out a tiny little hope that they might uncover what happened," he said (Ibid.).

Brian was immensely busy, fighting for justice on multiple fronts. When he initially decided to fight back, he had no idea it would turn into such a multi-pronged struggle.

When I made the complaint and wrote the letter, I was very naïve. It was only after it all started that I realized, this was like five processes happening all at once! It was very frustrating to be going through so many different processes, and many disappointments in each one, and not understanding what the differences were. It was quite complicated and I can see why somebody would not want to go through it. It wasn't so much a sequence of events as an intertwining vine, with all of it happening all at once. They were all so intertwined and also all happening at the same time so it became very frustrating, very complicated.

I was run ragged! I was tired of it and there were so many times that I said: 'Why the fuck did I do this?' If I had known how complicated it would have been, I would not have done it. Or at least, I certainly felt that way a number of times (Nolan 2022).

Yet he persevered. In his appeal to the RNC Complaints Commission, he now singled out Chief Coady in strongly worded language. "I feel very strongly that the Chief of Police is deliberately ignoring the alleged problem of homophobia and prejudice within his department in an attempt to save face," Nolan wrote (Dimmock 1993B). If this problem was not addressed, he warned, it could lead to serious injury or death for gay men or women in the future. As he told *The Express*:

The whole (investigation) seems to be leaning toward a belief on the part of the (RNC) that they're the true and good, and I'm the bad guy. I got that feeling all the way through the investigation and I do expect that the report will follow through in the same vein (Dimmock 1993B).

The RNC was making him feel like he was the one on trial, not the police officers who assaulted him, he said.

As the hearings commenced under Eaton's supervision, the RNC defendants first sought to have the appeal dismissed through a number of legal maneuvers and procedural ploys. These were all dismissed by the adjudicator. During the hearings, the adjudicator heard from both sides. Each of them were provided legal representation. Lawyer Brad Wicks represented the officers, and Norm Whalen, former President of the NL Human Rights Association, represented Brian. Whalen told the hearing that Nolan's arrest was the "most traumatic thing that ever happened to him in his life" (Stacey 1994). As Whalen told the hearing:

It's a serious matter, but more than anything else it's a matter of conscious-ness-raising and education and tolerance and setting a standard of conduct and behaviour for police officers. Nolan said he hopes his complaint will result in greater police tolerance for minority groups such as homosexuals. 'I want to address a great injustice, [Nolan] said. I'm not seeking vengeance' (Stacey 1994A).

Brian hoped that the outcome of his complaint would lead to the Department of Justice instituting human rights training for both RNC officers as well as wardens at the HMP.

Wicks – defending the officers – argued that Brian had been tired and drunk, and that perhaps he didn't like the RNC. He said all this could have contributed to his having a different memory of the night from the officers. "Brian Nolan's account cannot be given any weight," argued Wicks. "These four police officers are all sworn to uphold the law and fulfill their duties under the law and their experience and training should be given considerable weight."

Wicks argued the charges against the officers should be dropped and Brian should have to pay all the legal fees associated with the complaint process.

The hearings were eagerly followed by the province's media. Gary Dimmock, reporting for the Sunday Express, provided a bird's-eye view of the proceedings.

Seated for most of the hearing in a huddled group, the police officers whispered to one another during Friday's informal hearing, sometimes using police codes like 10-62 (meaning someone is listening). While one scribbled notes, the other police officers tried to determine whether their presence was necessary at this week's gathering – a meeting to set a date for a formal inquiry (Dimmock 1994E).

In making their defense, the officers provided further details on what transpired before the encounter with Brian. All four officers had been assigned to downtown patrol that night. Constables Day and Hickey were in one police car, while Constables Barry and Parsons were driving the larger police van that was used to transport multiple people.

Constables Barry and Parsons received the initial call about a disturbance at Solomon's. The bartender who called the RNC knew the two troublemakers and had given their names to the dispatcher (neither of them was Brian, Shawn or Ron). The dispatcher did not pass the names on to the officers. Constables Day and Hickey overheard the call and decided on their own volition to join in as a backup unit. They arrived first, and waited for Barry and Parsons. When they all got there and assembled outside the bar, Parsons informed the others that they were about to enter a gay bar – he did so, he said, so that they would not be surprised at what they saw inside. The other three responded that they already knew that Solomon's was a gay bar. As they approached the bar, they noticed someone sitting on the steps just outside. He seemed drunk, they testified, and they assumed this was one of the people responsible for the disturbance, but they ignored him and entered the bar instead. The bartender explained to Constable Barry what had happened, while the others observed activity in the bar. A couple of minutes later, they said, they left the bar (Stacey 1994E).

From that point on, their statements disagreed both with Nolan's, and also with each other's. The officers claimed that they saw a drunk man outside the bar before they went in, but they ignored him because they were concerned about what was happening inside the bar. When they left the bar, they said they saw a man at the stairs and assumed it was the same one (this was Nolan, they said). They said the man appeared drunk. Constables Day and Hickey called out to him, and when he ignored them, they ran after him. They said the man brushed Constable Day's hand off his shoulder when the officers caught up with him, and began shouting about being harassed. They put him in the car and drove him to the lockup, where they left him for processing. They denied making any derogatory comments to him (Ibid.).

The four prison guards who were present during Nolan's detention also testified. Morris Power was on duty when Nolan was brought in. It was his last shift as a correctional officer before being promoted to lieutenant. At 7am, he was relieved by Correctional Officer Barry Whitty, who would be the one to release Nolan. Correctional Officers Owen Devereaux and Robert Pinsent, then in training, were also present throughout this period (Stacey 1994C).

They all claimed that Brian had been clearly intoxicated when he was brought in. They said they did not offer him the right to make a phone call because they felt he was too drunk to use the phone. They said he complained about sexual harassment when he was being processed, and they attributed this to his purported drunkenness. When he was released the next morning, they said Nolan demanded the names of the arresting officers, including the woman who called him "faggot." Whitty said he told Brian that Constable Hickey was the arresting officer and he did not know the name of the woman. Devereaux did know the name of the woman, but refused to provide it. They said at this point Nolan became upset and hostile, and so they restrained him and put him back in the cell for a short time (Stacey 1994C).

As the hearings proceeded, inconsistencies emerged in the officers' testimonies. Constable Day initially testified that she arrested Brian. But Constable Parsons said it was Constable Hickey who arrested him. Parsons also said he was the one who put Brian in the police car, while Day said it was Hickey who had put Brian in the car. Hickey also said the officers first saw Nolan when they left Solomon's Bar. But Day said they saw him before they entered the bar.

Additionally, Constable Day told investigators that Nolan sat in silence when he was being driven to the lockup. Constable Hickey, who was in the same car, told investigators that he babbled drunkenly. Constable Day also told investigators that Nolan asked for the officers' names at the lockup, and not only did she and Hickey give him their names, but she said Hickey also offered Nolan a business card. Hickey, however, told investigators that he ignored everything Nolan said and had no further engagement with him after he put him in the car.

Brian's friend Lynn Andrews – whose house Brian was staying at that fateful night – testified about his fraught condition after he was released from the lock-up. "He was upset, distressed, crying and traumatized. I've never seen him like that before," she said.

Correctional Officer Owen Devereaux also testified. "This is the first instance in my 10 years at the lockup that I've heard someone say the reason he was arrested was because he's gay," he said (Stacey 1994C).

Brian's lawyer, Norm Whalen, zeroed in on Devereaux's initial refusal to give Brian the name of Constable Day. His questioning revealed that Devereaux was not unaware of her name, as he told Brian that night, but that he deliberately withheld it (Ibid.).

"Why didn't you simply tell him it was Krista Clarke Day?" Whalen asked during cross-examination (Ibid.).

"If I had given him her name it would have been like I was agreeing that she said that," Devereaux responded (Ibid.).

The appeal dragged on for two long years. Dr. Theodore B. Hoekman, an Associate Professor at the MUN School of Medicine, was called on to address claims regarding Brian's purported drunkenness. None of the officers had bothered to test Brian's drunkenness when they arrested him, so Hoekman made estimations based on the memories of those who were around Brian that night. They estimated he had had two 12-ounce drinks of gin and seven regular strength beer between 6pm and 2am. He had also consumed a considerable quantity of food during this period. All of this was not enough to make him extremely intoxicated, Hoekman felt.

Finally, on August 30, 1996, Eaton issued his decision in the case.

He dismissed Brian's allegation that the officers had used excessive force. Any arrest, he explained, would necessarily involve the use of force – simply touching someone is defined as use of force. From what Nolan described, the actions of the officers, Eaton said, did not sound like excessive force was used in arresting him. The more salient question, Eaton observed, was whether Brian should have been arrested at all.

To this end, he analyzed the Detention of Intoxicated Persons (DIP) Act at some length. This legislation permits officers to detain intoxicated persons who are causing a public nuisance or who they believe may be a danger to themselves or others. Eaton emphasized that this does not give officers broad sanction to arrest drunk people. There must be a safety concern involved. There must also be reasonable grounds for the officers to reach this decision.

Eaton said that based on the evidence and analysis provided, it was clear Brian had quite a bit to drink that night, but it did not sound like he could be classified as extremely intoxicated. This was based in part on Dr. Hoekman's analysis, but also on the testimony of Brian's friends. They unanimously reported that whenever Brian became heavily intoxicated, without fail he would begin to sing. That night, they all noted, he had not yet reached the stage at which he began to sing, and therefore he was likely not too intoxicated. Neither Shawn nor Ron said he seemed too intoxicated to make his own way home; they had no concerns about his state of mind when he left the bar. While the prison guards had said Brian was intoxicated, they also reported that he was not "falling down drunk." Eaton noted it was curious they had volunteered the information that they didn't offer Brian the use of a phone because he was too drunk to use it. Normally, Eaton observed, anyone brought in to the 'drunk tank' would be too intoxicated to use a phone, so it was curious that the wardens had volunteered that fact as a way to emphasize Brian's drunkenness.

Eaton observed problems with Constable Day's testimony. She said she told Brian he was not allowed to be drunk in public and that's why she was arresting him. That's not what the Act says, Eaton pointed out – it's not illegal to be drunk in public unless there's a public nuisance or safety hazard involved. He said that based on Day's testimony, he did not think she actually understood the Act and her responsibilities under it. Furthermore, if – as she testified – she had seen a man from 50 feet away upon her arrival at the bar and thought he ought to be detained under the Act, why had she not immediately taken action? An arrest should only have been made if there was a safety concern involved, and if there was a safety concern involved, she should have taken immediate action, not gone into the bar and waited until after to act.

Constable Hickey had made the same claims. He said he was concerned

Brian might have wandered into traffic and hurt himself. But why was Hickey only concerned about this possibility after leaving the bar, and not when they first arrived, asked Eaton? Hickey also said he thought Brian was one of the men the bartender reported as causing a public nuisance. Yet the officers were given descriptions of the troublemakers by the bartender, and Brian did not match either man's description. By the officers' own admission, they did not ask him for his name, where he was going, or whether he was with friends. There was no apparent effort made to determine whether he was a danger to either himself or others. There was, Eaton emphasized, no reasonable basis for them to think Brian was either a public nuisance or a safety concern.

Eaton also noted there was a clear discrepancy between the two sides on the sequence of events. The officers said Brian was intoxicated and outside the bar when they first arrived, and Brian said he was arrested immediately after exiting the bar. Eaton determined that Brian's account was the more believable, in part because of the various contradictions in the officers' testimony, and in part thanks to the testimony of a Paul McCormick, who had also been at Solomons that night. McCormick, who had not been drinking that night, left the bar moments before Brian did. McCormick confirmed Brian's testimony that the officers had been lounging on the guardrails by the steps. He also testified that he saw Brian leave after he did; he then turned the other direction and got into a car. All of this corroborated Brian's account of the moments leading up to the encounter.

On the allegation of being detained without reasonable cause, Eaton ruled in Brian's favour. He concluded that Constables Day and Hickey detained Brian "without having good and sufficient cause to do so. They made assumptions rather than inquiries, and either did not fully understand the requirements or the purpose of the D.I.P. Act, or were not concerned about them" (Vaughan-Jackson 1994).

On Brian's complaint about the derogatory language used against him by Constable Day, Eaton also offered a restrained ruling in Brian's favour. As stated in Eaton's decision:

Cst. Day, in giving her evidence, demonstrated a lack of appreciation for or sensitivity to appropriate terminology used to describe homosexuals. She stated that she did not see any difference between the words 'gay,' 'homosexual' or 'queer' – just letters. They all mean the same thing to her. Considering all of this evidence, I am satisfied on a balance of probabilities that Cst. Day called Mr. Nolan 'faggot' sometime during her dealings with him. I am not prepared to conclude that the verbal abuse was as vicious as Mr. Nolan suggests (Ibid.).

In conclusion, Eaton's ruling was a mixed bag. It did find some of Brian's allegations to be proven: the allegation against Constable Day for using derogatory remarks and the allegation against Constables Day and Hickey for having arrested Brian without good and sufficient cause. It is important to note that in his complaint, Brian had charged as well that he felt his arrest was a form of sexual harassment and that he had been singled out because he was gay. Eaton said he couldn't rule out the possibility that this was a factor, but there was insufficient evidence to satisfy him that the arrest was motivated by Brian's sexuality. Rather, Eaton ruled that the arrest was improper because it failed to meet the criteria for an arrest under the DIP Act.

While I cannot rule out the possibility that [homosexuality] was a factor, I quite firmly believe that the arrest was a result of unfounded assumptions, a failure to conduct proper inquiry, a failure to pay any attention to clear evidence (ie. that it was not Mr. Nolan who caused the disturbance) and a failure to understand the D.I.P. Act (RNC Public Complaints Commission 1994).

Eaton was deeply concerned, he said, about what seemed to be a lack of training given to officers about the DIP Act and how to enforce it. He said the prison guards' testimonies indicated there were several 'regulars' who frequently spent their nights in the lock-up – if they were being arrested for drunkenness, why were none of them being brought to a rehab centre, he asked? It seemed the officers were simply locking up drunk people, rather than making any effort to determine whether they were actually safety concerns or public nuisances. He urged a review of the situation to take place, and proper training developed for officers.

Eaton ordered that Constables Day and Hickey each receive a five-day suspension without pay for the improper detention. For the use of derogatory language, he gave Constable Day an additional two-day suspension without pay.

"Deprivation of liberty is a serious matter," he wrote in his ruling. "Members of the public have a legitimate expectation that they will not be detained without good and sufficient reason. For this expectation to be satisfied, police officers must know, understand and respect the limits of their authority to detain people" (Ibid.).

The officers, he said, had failed to live up to this standard.

Brian's victory made headlines across the province. "This is a major, major victory," he told Telegram reporter Mark Vaughan-Jackson. "I didn't expect to win anything. I went into it thinking it would be a victory just to bring it to public attention and make them think twice about doing it again (Vaughan-Jackson 1994).

"It's a victory for the entire gay community and for any minority community," he said (Ibid.).

Looking back on events three decades later, Nolan has a more ambivalent attitude about the outcome of his complaint to the Police Complaints Commission.

When I found out they were suspended it was wonderful. At least there was a recognition. But I didn't think it went far enough... I wanted to press forward with a civil suit, and [the Police Complaints Commission lawyers] discouraged me. They talked me out of it.

I felt like they were saying, 'Okay well we'll rap their fingers, we'll keep them happy, we'll keep the gay movement happy by rapping them on the knuckles, but we don't want to go any further than that.' So I felt that the [Police Complaints] Commission itself wasn't really strong enough... I felt like they were a bit of the old boys' club themselves.

That was the sort of vibe I got. This might be unfair to them, but it's certainly what I felt – that I had them working for me now, and what's happening is good from my perspective, but it's not good enough, but I better shut up or I'll get nothing. By nothing, I mean results. So I kind of accepted their 'Back off... you should leave it alone.' I wish I hadn't. But I was exhausted, so I kind of succumbed to their suggestion. I did it reluctantly, but I did it (Nolan 2022).

There the matter might have rested: a few days' suspension for two of the officers for the ordeal Brian went through. But that wasn't the end of it, because in addition to his complaint to the RNC Public Complaints Commission, he had also filed a separate complaint to the Newfoundland and Labrador Human Rights Commission.

Brian's chances with a human rights complaint did not look good at first. According to documents obtained by the now-defunct *The Sunday Express* newspaper, the Human Rights Commission sought a legal opinion as to whether Brian's complaint might hold up. The initial legal opinion said it would not. The Human Rights Code prohibits discrimination in the provision of a service to individuals, and the legal opinion suggested that neither police nor penitentiary guards provide a service to individuals. If they do offer a service – protection – then the complaint would have to be against the officers who watched Brian's assault and refused to offer that protection, which in this case would have been against their own fellow officers. It would be difficult to prove, stated the opinion, that penitentiary guards are supposed to provide a service of protection to the general public (Dimmock 1994A).

The internal report revealed the Commission was torn about how to handle Brian's complaint. The complaint was "not a matter for investigation under Human Rights legislation," it stated baldly. Yet Commission Executive Director Gladys Vivian was reluctant to simply dismiss it. She indicated that she believed portions of the legislation "should be read as if they included the words 'sexual orientation' as a prohibited ground of discrimination." She also equivocated: "Even so, however, I do not think Mr. Nolan's complaint properly falls under either of the three sections" (Ibid.). When the report was leaked, revealing these internal debates, she refused to speak to media about it.

By December 21, documents obtained by *The Express* revealed the Commission had finally swung around to a consensus that they would accept the case. "Newfoundland's Human Rights Commission has done an about face by agreeing to accept a gay man's complaint against the RNC and the city lockup," reported Gary Dimmock in *The Express* (Ibid.).

And so, in spite of the negative legal opinion, five months after receiving his complaint the Human Rights Commission decided to proceed and accept the complaint. It would be an uphill battle, since it was questionable whether a complaint on the basis of sexual orientation would hold up at all. Discrimination on the basis of sexual orientation was not prohibited at the time in the NL Human Rights Code – successive provincial governments had steadfastly resisted including it, despite growing pressure from community groups. Nonetheless, in light of growing public awareness of the issue and the fact that other provinces had succeeded in 'reading in' sexual orientation as an implied right (even if not literally stated in the Act), the Commission had been accepting complaints on the basis of sexual orientation since the fall of 1992. Brian's would be one of the first.

I spoke with the current Executive Director of the NL Human Rights Commission to trace what would have been the trajectory of Brian's complaint once the Commission decided to accept it. Carey Majid, originally from Ontario, obtained her law degree from the University of New Brunswick. After working for a time in Ottawa, she moved to St. John's in 2001. After spending some time in private practice in the city, she was hired as Executive Director for the Commission in 2009.

Majid explained that once the Commission decided to accept Nolan's complaint, it would have informed the provincial Department of Justice that it was accepting the complaint for investigation, and that in doing so it was 'reading in' sexual orientation.

What does it mean to 'read in' sexual orientation (or any right)? Pieces of legislation like the Charter of Rights and Freedoms, or the NL Human Rights Act, list out, or enumerate, various prohibited grounds of discrimination. These include things like gender, race, religion, disability. It is illegal to discriminate, for instance in the provision of a public service, on those grounds. The NL Human Rights Act at that time did not list 'sexual orientation' as one of the prohibited grounds. That doesn't mean that the intention to not discriminate on that basis wasn't there," explained Majid, "perhaps it's just that the particular terms or concepts didn't exist when the legislation was written.

In Canada, a principle of constitutional or statutory interpretation is called the 'living tree doctrine.' Human Rights legislation is supposed to be interpreted in a broad and purposive approach. The law is continually evolving as society evolves.

'Reading in' is an approach that the courts – and only the courts – can take to read in, or read down, or do all these different things, to move the law forward. The courts are not meant to legislate, but they are meant to interpret the legislation. So what they're saying here is that the provinces have human rights legislation, that the goal of protecting human rights is extremely important, and they set out these certain groups of people… they've picked these things, and now the courts are saying that something can be added to a piece of legislation to make sure it conforms to the constitution or charter (Majid 2022).

They're saying the legislature meant to protect the human rights of all people of personal characteristics that are immutable. The original intent of the legislature was to protect everybody for things they can't change. So we're going to read in sexual orientation... to say that's what the legislature actually intended when they set up these human rights legislation. [It's] meant to protect these people too (Ibid.).

Majid offers the example of gender identity and gender expression. Although the NL Human Rights Act was not amended to include gender identity and gender expression as prohibited grounds of discrimination until 2013, the Commission had already been accepting complaints based on those grounds for several years before the legislation changed, interpreting the NL Human Rights Act – its own enabling legislation – to include gender identity and gender expression in the definition of sex.

Once the Commission signaled their intention to 'read in' sexual orientation into the NL Human Rights Code – by accepting Brian's case back in 1993 – the provincial government had the opportunity to appeal this decision; in other words, to say that the Commission shouldn't accept the complaint because sexual orientation was not explicitly written into the legislation. Then the two parties would go to court, and a judge would have to decide whether the Commission was right in 'reading in' sexual orientation in its interpretation of the NL Human Rights Act.

That's exactly what happened. The provincial government appealed the Human Rights Commission's intent to accept Brian's complaint, and the matter went to the NL Supreme Court to decide whether, indeed, sexual orientation protections would be 'read in' to human rights legislation in this province. That decision fell to Justice Leo Barry.

Barry was an interesting character who, like then-Premier Clyde Wells, had experience in both party politics and the court room. Originally from Red Island, NL, he graduated from Dalhousie Law School in 1967, receiving a Masters from Yale Law School the following year. He promptly dove into provincial politics, first as a Progressive Conservative. Elected as MHA for Placentia West in 1972, he was subsequently appointed Minister of Mines and Energy under Premier Frank Moores. He was defeated in the 1975 election but re-elected as MHA in 1979 (after an unsuccessful party leadership bid) and was reappointed Energy Minister under PC Premier Brian Peckford. In 1981, he resigned from Cabinet over policy disagreements with Peckford, and in 1984 he crossed the floor to join the Liberal Party. That same year he was selected as the province's Liberal party leader. His tenure – during which the Liberals increased their seat count but failed to win government – lasted until 1987. A caucus revolt while he was on a trip out of province led to his eventual resignation, and Clyde Wells was selected to replace him at a leadership convention that summer. Wells would go on to win a Liberal majority government in 1989. Barry, meanwhile, returned to the courtroom.

It was Barry who wound up presiding over Brian Nolan's complaint against the RNC. The matter went before Judge Barry to determine whether the NL Human Rights Commission had the right to 'read in' sexual orientation to the NL Human Rights Act.

After two years of legal back and forth, Nolan's complaint against the RNC finally concluded on August 23, 1995 when Justice Leo Barry ruled in Nolan's favour (Newfoundland v. Newfoundland 1995). Not only did Barry find merit in Nolan's complaint, he caused a political earthquake by intensifying pressure on the provincial government to amend the province's human rights code.

This triggered a local iteration of the long-standing tug-of-war between courts and governments over the legislative power invested in each. It is generally accepted that courts interpret the law, however Barry's ruling in the Nolan case dramatically increased pressure on the provincial government to update NL's human rights legislation. According to Majid, if society had advanced to the point where courts were reading in a right not explicitly stated in the legislation, the proper thing for a government to do is to update its legislation to reflect current practice. This would require a Liberal provincial cabinet that was still clearly divided on the subject of sexual orientation protections to swallow their personal divisions and unite behind the kind of human rights amendment that community groups had been calling for since the 1970s.

In his landmark ruling issued on August 23, 1995, Justice Barry laid down the law – quite literally – for the province. Not only was sexual orientation an analogous right to those already in legislation, he stated, but its specific omission could be seen as establishing the grounds for discrimination against a class of persons, which in itself was antithetical to the purposes of human rights legislation (Ibid.).

Looking at homosexuals as a group... they have suffered discrimination arising from stereotyping, historical disadvantage and vulnerability to political and social prejudice As human beings they are entitled to have their human dignity preserved. They are entitled to protection from this discrimination, which could properly be described, in the words of McIntyre, J.... as among 'the most common and probably the most socially destructive and historically practiced bases of discrimination'. One must conclude, therefore, that the Code has a glaring omission because of its failure to include 'sexual orientation' in its prohibited grounds of discrimination. One must further conclude that this glaring omission is itself discriminatory, in that it 'reinforce[s] negative stereotyping and prejudice thereby perpetuating and implicitly condoning its occurrence'... Accordingly, I cannot see how the exclusion of 'sexual orientation' is relevant to promotion of the functional values of the Code. I find, to the contrary, that exclusion conflicts with those values and undermines the worthy objectives of the Legislature by implicitly condoning attacks upon the human dignity of homosexuals. As such, the exclusion must be viewed as discriminatory and in violation of s. 15(1) (Ibid.).

Barry anticipated government's reaction to his ruling, and argued it was within his jurisdiction to make this determination.

I do not take this to be a usurpation of the legislative function. The New-foundland Legislature adopted the Charter in 1982. It must, therefore, be taken to have approved the role given the courts by the Charter to ensure that provincial legislation conforms with the Charter and does not discriminate on grounds expressly prohibited by s. 15(1) of the Charter or analogous grounds (Ibid.).

The accomplishment was what Brian had sought from the beginning — a recognition of the impact of systemic homophobia, and a concrete commitment to sexual orientation protections in the province. He personally got nothing out of it, no money or material compensation, and this decision marked the end of his long battle for justice. Having established that sexual orientation protections were to be read into the human rights code henceforth – in other words, that Brian's complaint could be received – his complaint itself was then promptly thrown out because it did not meet the much more narrow criteria of having involved a failure to provide a service. In other words, Brian had succeeded in getting the courts to acknowledge the *principle* that discrimination on the basis of sexual orientation was a human rights violation; but his own complaint failed to meet the narrow criteria of an eligible complaint. The two-year fight had succeeded in finally getting sexual orientation protections read into the provincial human rights code – something community groups had been fighting to achieve for more than two decades.

"I was ecstatic," Brian reflects today, thinking back on the events. "That was fabulous. That was – wow. That was the icing on the cake, even though the cake fell flat in the oven. That was really good, that really put my mind at ease. For all that I had wished I hadn't done it, I was now finally really glad that I did."

It was a victory, not just for Brian but for gays and lesbians throughout the entire province. It did come at a price for Brian; the fight was far from easy, and his experience of assault left him traumatized. Even today he's reluctant to talk about it. He shares the fact that years after the event, while showing around some visiting friends from away, he came face to face with one of the former prison guards, working as a volunteer guide at a tourist site.

"I ran outside, and I threw up," he recalls. "The residual effect – it's traumatic."

Nevertheless, his achievement was a victory. Activists did soon learn the fight was far from over. Fired up by Brian's struggle, his colleagues in the labour movement invited him to speak at an NL Federation of Labour (NLFL) provincial convention in the late 1990s. Brian's friend, Ron Knowling, was working for the NLFL at the time and was asked to draft an LGBTQ policy resolution for the Federation, to be presented to delegates from unions across the province to vote on at the convention.

Mary Shortall was at the Convention when Brian spoke:

I remember Brian going up to tell his story at the Convention, and it wasn't easy... it was a brand-new issue really, any type of gender or sexual harassment. Unions were starting to develop policies but it was all really new. I remember being in workshops with labour leaders who did not want to be there, and who were not really on board with some of the issues and the realities of how the workplace had to change. During those early to mid 1990s there was a lot of resistance and a lot of push-back against what the rest of us knew had to happen in workplaces. There was a lot of pushback. So education was key (Shortall 2022).

The matter was further complicated by the fact that the prison guards against whom Brian had filed complaints were unionized as members of the Newfoundland and Labrador Association of Public and Private Employees (NAPE) – and their union local was at the Convention. NAPE is the largest union in the province, and some NAPE members felt an obligation to support the prison guards.

So when Brian spoke at the Federation convention it was met with resistance. There were members who felt that they were being blamed because they worked in the system, and there were some members who didn't support gay rights to begin with... There was all kinds of discussion happening in those days, so it wasn't extraordinary that there was some pushback, but it was horrible to see it unfold there because people were very emotional about it. That had the tendency to polarize the debate on the floor. So when Brian told his story, it caused some discussion and it was really emotional (Ibid.).

Despite knowing he would face pushback from some of the delegates, Brian got up to share his story with the hundreds of attendees present. Shortall says she'll never forget that moment.

Brian was really, really scared. So myself and [another CAW member] flanked him. We went up beside him and encouraged him and helped him tell his story. We stayed beside him while this all happened. And there were people who came up who continued to argue against what he was saying, but you could really see a transformation in the discussion. You had to have these really uncomfortable discussions, in order to create the kinds of discussion and debate that people had been denied while they were growing up. So the debate that happened there was really important in terms of how the NL [labour movement] progressed. But it was very, very difficult, and if Brian hadn't done it, I don't think it would have happened the same way. But at the same time you can see the toll that it takes on someone, when they have the courage to stand up and do that in front of a somewhat hostile crowd. These people are supposed to be your friends and your comrades but then there's a hostility there that you weren't expecting. That's got to be soul-sucking, when you put everything into it.

There were some people who were really angry and some people got up on the mic and spoke really angrily. But then others got up to the mic and took them on. Some people left the room – some members got angry and walked out. I don't know for sure that they were all prison guards but that was one angry group. There was still a lot of homophobia, and I can't imagine the courage you needed to get up and speak. It was pretty dramatic (Ibid.).

"It almost created a kind of rift in the labour movement," recalled Knowling, who was also there. "A lot of members turned their backs and walked out. But in the end cooler heads prevailed."

As Shortall explained:

The discussion did turn around. And I think that out of that there came a lot of support and a lot of commitment to enact things like affirmative action, and to bargain same-sex rights in collective agreements. That was the beginning of that conversation, and I think it was a real shift for the labour movement. I think it really empowered those of us who were doing that work as new activists. It wasn't only because of how I felt about Brian's courage – I was so proud of it – but it also made you understand exactly why you need to stand up and have your friends with you, and keep fighting for these things and keeping having those uncomfortable conversations because that's what makes a difference. Today, when we see ultra-right ideology start to creep back into the labour movement, now more than ever we need to be vigilant against that and we need to keep having these conversations and keep engaging our members. Because if you're not engaging, then that's where that sort of things creeps in (Shortall 2022).

The experience has also given Nolan a new awareness of how difficult it is to fight for change, even when the tools for justice supposedly exist.

One thing I got out of this is how the bureaucracy is so complicated. It might be legitimately so, I don't know. But it's so complicated and so overwhelming and so threatening. I can see why it's so difficult for people to go through with complaints against police or whatever bureaucracy is causing the problems. It's really difficult to fight, it's really difficult to go through it. As they say, in every rape case the difficulty of fighting the system is in itself an injustice.

Sometimes people ask me, 'Should I go through with a complaint?' And I say: 'Here's my story. I'm not saying yes or no, but you better be ready for a hell of a lot of work and trouble and torment and sadness and frustration if you do go. And if you're ready for that, then I would love for you to go through with it. But if you can't handle that, and if it'll hurt you as much as you're already hurt, then maybe it's best to leave it alone.' It's a terrible thing to say. But it reflects my experience, and it feels fair to share it (Nolan 2022).

Thanks to Brian Nolan's courageous fight, and the ruling issued by Justice Leo Barry, the courts had had their say: sexual orientation rights must be read into the NL Human Rights Code. But it remained for the province to actually amend the Code to permanently entrench those rights through legislation. That would require a final concerted effort from all of the province's queer activist groups, working together as never before.

NGALE, NAN and the Human Rights Struggle

When Brian Nolan began his fight, there was a vacuum in queer organizing in the province. GALT had ceased to exist. NAN had emerged from the internal struggles at the St. John's Status of Women Centre, but still had a relatively low profile and was concentrating on organizing the city's lesbian community. The ACNL was primarily focused on the AIDS struggle, but in the absence of any other organized queer group its activists wound up doing double duty in the fight against homophobia.

"Apart from the gay clubs, there wasn't really much else on the go," explained ACNL Executive Director Gerard Yetman.

It seemed that the AIDS Committee was looked upon as the gay organization. That's where a lot of gay men would come to volunteer, to socialize, and I think the AIDS Committee also became a home to the lesbian community. We had a lot of gay men and lesbians. They were the ones that were losing their friends. And they were also not afraid (Yetman 2022).

The attack on Brian Nolan – and the public fight for justice that he began – quickly dominated discussion at the ACNL. One of the ACNL's new employees was a young man named Brian Hodder. Hodder was a former schoolteacher from Marystown. After finishing high school, he moved to St. John's to attend Memorial, graduating with a teaching degree in 1987. He immediately returned to Marystown, and started teaching at his former high school. That was when, in his early twenties, he met his partner and realized he was gay. As the province was still in the grips of the denominational education system, he felt a growing dissonance in his role as a teacher in an environment where he couldn't come out as gay.

I remember [another teacher] in the school on a regular basis would get up in the middle of the staff room and pontificate about the Bible and gays. I'd just be sitting there cringing and feeling like I can't say anything. Funnily enough, after I left, at least two other teachers that I had taught with came out to me. Neither one of us knew [that the other was gay]. I pretty much came out when I left, but I think people had it figured out anyway. It's just funny that there were a group of us there that never spoke to one another. So when I moved [to St. John's] and did come out, [I said] you know what? I'm not shutting up any more. I'm not going back to that position of feeling silenced any more (Hodder 2022).

No sooner had Hodder and his partner moved to St. John's, than they met Jack Clark, a well-known member of the community widely remembered for his talented piano-playing at local venues. They were sitting at Classic Cafe,

Hodder recalled, in its old location on Duckworth Street. "[Jack] walked by, he looked – he cruised us I guess – and he came over and introduced himself. That was one of the first friends we made. And one of the first things he told us was that he had AIDS."

It was Hodder's first real exposure to AIDS. Clark befriended Hodder and his partner, and introduced them to his social circle. Most of them were volunteering with the ACNL, and as Hodder didn't then have a job, he threw himself into the volunteer work there as well. Pretty soon that led to a job with the organization, and he worked there for four and a half years.

It was early on during Hodder's time at the ACNL when Nolan's case hit the media. Volunteers and workers at the ACNL felt they needed to do something to speak up and address the issue of violence in the community. So they organized a community forum on a Wednesday night to talk about the attack, about the problem of homophobic violence in the community, and what they could do about it.

At the public forum, speakers pointed out that there needed to be an organization to tackle the problem. So the ACNL set up another meeting for a week's time, in its offices, to launch a new group.

That's when NGALE [Newfoundland Gays And Lesbians for Equality] started. It came out of an event in which people were frustrated that there was no place to speak up, no support for people who had gone through these incidents. It was not the first gay-bashing incident that we had been aware of, but there was no venue where people could turn for support, for advocacy, for connection, for community-building.

There was a conversation around safety, around the police, and the fact these were police officers who had done this. If you weren't safe with police officers, then where were you going to find safety? That's what really started it. The impact of [Nolan's case] was such that it caused people to say – enough! It was the impetus that got things started with NGALE. It was almost our Stonewall in a way (Ibid.).

About twenty people showed up at that first meeting. There were not a lot of women, Hodder recalls — this was because NAN was already in operation and most of the activist lesbians were involved with that group. Some women did show up, and one of them was elected president of NGALE. A week later she stepped down, and Hodder was nominated to fill the role.

The prospect of kickstarting a new organization was a daunting one, but ACNL Executive Director Gerard Yetman, Hodder's boss, told him not to feel overwhelmed, and that he was welcome to do NGALE work as part of his work duties at the ACNL.

One of the group's first acts was to set up a toll-free long distance phone support line.

There was nothing outside St. John's. Corner Brook had some activists, but there wasn't much. That was why the phone line was so important for me when

I became active, because it was a venue that people could reach out. We didn't have the internet, so phone was the only way that it could happen... It was really important that people outside of St. John's had a place where they could call for support. Because I grew up in rural Newfoundland, I knew what it was like to feel like you're probably the only [queer] person in the community. But you're not – you just don't know it (Ibid.).

They set up regular training sessions for phone line volunteers, and operated the phone line one night a week. As Hodder recalls, "Some of the conversations I remember having with people were just about having someone at the end of a phone line that they knew they could talk about what they were going through with. I think we saved lives."

Hodder reached out to NAN, and the two organizations forged a loose but supportive working relationship. Among other collaborations, which included political lobbying, they would jointly organize Pride Week for the next few years.

Looking back on those events, Hodder said he was especially grateful for the leadership role NAN played during NGALE's early years. As the slightly older sister to NGALE, and with plenty of experienced activists in its ranks, he feels NAN was the stronger political advocacy force at the time. Their organizers helped open doors for the younger, less experienced NGALE activists.

We worked hand-in-hand with NAN. They had insider people, women that worked in government departments who were able to do the groundwork in setting up meetings. I remember us meeting Clyde Wells, who was premier at the time. We met with Wells at Confederation Building about the need to include [sexual orientation protections] and the impact that it would have. He gave a politician's answer, which was that yes this makes sense, it'll be something that we'll work on. To give the man credit, he sat, he was respectful, he listened. I think the writing was on the wall, because [sexual orientation protections] had happened in other provinces.

But I give a lot of the credit on those meetings to Beth Lacey and the other women at NAN. They were really good at organizing. They had a lot of the ins on how you set up meetings, and how you meet (Ibid.).

The presence of two groups did create some uncertainties for NGALE's efforts to be inclusive to women without undermining NAN. While some lesbians did get involved with NGALE, NAN itself made it clear they intended to remain a separate organization. "We really made an effort to include women," said Hodder.

NAN would work with us but they were very clear that they wanted their own space. Some of that may have come from previous iterations where I don't think women always felt safe in male environments.

NAN was the stronger organization at the time. They provided a very strong community for women – they had their own dances, they had their own organizations. They would work with us – it wasn't like we weren't welcome

– but they didn't want to be part of one single group. We did have a number of women [in NGALE] throughout the years, but it took a while for that number to become a little more equitable (Ibid.).

The advocacy and support scene was growing. A local branch of Parents and Friends of Lesbians and Gays (PFLAG) also formed that summer and held its first meetings.

As president, Hodder quickly became a fixture in the province's media. In addition to doing interviews on behalf of NGALE, he began writing monthly columns on queer issues in *The Evening Telegram*. That came about thanks to Lynn Barter, an *Evening Telegram* editor who was also serving on the ACNL Board of Directors. Hodder was chatting with her one day and mentioned there was no voice for the queer community in the paper. She told him to write a sample column and she'd bring it to her bosses. A week later it was in print, and he's continued as a columnist with the paper to the present day.

That was something that was always, and still is, very important to me – that we're part of a broader community. If we're to ever make any changes, the people in the broader community need to hear our voices on a regular basis.

I always said: I am a voice. I'm not the only one. Feel free to disagree. Some people thought I was pushing things too far, some people thought I didn't push things far enough. That's just the nature of what happens when you do advocacy (Ibid.).

One of the early issues NGALE had to grapple with was the presence of ever-younger queer-identifying youth who were interested in being involved. Historically, homophobes and bigots had tarred queer people with an entirely false and manufactured association with pedophilia, so there had long been a sensitivity around the presence of youth in queer activism. But the youth of the 1990s weren't willing to let themselves be excluded, despite the concerns of some older queer activists.

Mikiki was one of the youth activists who helped pave the way. They came out as gay in 1995, in high school. From 1992 to 1996, they attended Gonzaga High School, which was a Catholic Jesuit institution until the dismantling of the denominational education system, which happened during their time there.

"I'm really thankful that happened," they recall, referring to the abolition of denominational education.

It was a combination of that, plus Ellen coming out on television, plus RuPaul – all of it helped, and suddenly it became cool to have a gay best friend in the early to mid 1990s.

So there was that, plus I started hanging out with a bunch of riot grrrls, and started getting involved in activism through Youth for Social Justice. I started hanging around downtown at the Oxfam office near the War Memorial, and met a bunch of very articulate and active hard-left folks from all over St. John's (Mikiki 2023).

Mikiki wasn't yet out, but got involved in doing sexual and reproductive health education work through Youth for Social Justice (YSJ). The group, which was run by youth and affiliated with Oxfam, did sex education workshops in high schools, including some outside of town. Then Mikiki attended a Youth for Social Justice camp – they jokingly referred to it as 'baby anarchist training camp' - which had a focused gender and sexuality day.

We had done a sexuality workshop in the morning, and then during the lunchbreak two of my friends cornered me in the bunkroom. They said: 'You had a lot of interesting things to say during the workshop, we're just wondering if you're gay.' And I was like: 'Yup.' Essentially I just needed someone to ask that question. And then, once I had been asked – once I had been given that permission – then I very quickly started speaking out loud (Ibid.).

Youth for Social Justice had forged a working relationship with NGALE, and proposed that Mikiki should serve as a youth rep for NGALE. It would be the first formal youth position within any of the province's queer activist groups, and it sparked considerable debate.

I was the youngest member by ten years. I remember they had to have executive meetings to decide whether they would allow me to participate. They were concerned that they were going to be branded as pedophiles. This was a couple of years after the Village Mall scandal, and [other homophobic scandals]. So there was a lot of conversation publicly around the role of queer adults in what [homophobes] called 'grooming' and 'recruiting.' So there was a lot of fear because I was the only kid.

But that was exactly the problem. I was a kid, and there was no space and no conversation around [sexuality]. The idea of having [gay] mentors who could have provided guidance was completely off the table because of their fear of being labelled a sexual predator (Ibid.).

Mikiki observed that because known and established older queer activists were hesitant to engage with, educate or even be around youth out of fear of being labelled a pedophile, this actually increased the likelihood that queer youth seeking to understand or explore their sexuality would wind up in risky situations.

But it generated all these complex and I think actually rich and robust questions about the place and representation – or lack of representation – around youth, and queer youth sexuality. I was the only one who was out among my age group in the city, at least for the first year or two. But then [some others] came out, and then it hit a critical mass of youth who were out. And then in the mid 1990s we saw a lot of queer youth taking up activist positions. So there was this very aggressive, explicit claiming of our right to hold sexual space as young people. It was very important to me to be publicly queer and that meant also being publicly sexual (Ibid.).

In its second year of operation, NGALE launched its own newsletter. They also organized dances and social events. They held car washes and other fundraisers to raise money to operate a phone support line (which launched in April

1995). They held film screenings at the Avalon Mall cinemas, bringing in queer themed films like *Priscilla Queen of the Desert* and *Jeffrey*.

In December 1995, NAN and NGALE held a joint Christmas party at the LSPU Hall, featuring a potluck and dance. "It was more about community-building," explained Hodder.

It was about support. There were a lot of people that came that didn't really find a place in the community. A lot of them weren't really into the downtown bar scene, so they were just looking for a place to connect with people, to explore. I think that's what NGALE provided, on top of the advocacy (Hodder 2022).

The advocacy, however, was also key.

NGALE also forged links at the national level, establishing a close working relationship with Equality for Gays and Lesbians Everywhere (EGALE), which had become the leading national queer rights group. When EGALE was initially setting itself up, NGALE donated $100 to help the national group secure an office. While EGALE fought for a federal human rights amendment around sexual orientation, NGALE focused on the provincial legislative fight, and both groups reinforced each other's efforts. In November 1995, a little over two months after Justice Barry issued his ruling in Nolan's human rights complaint, NGALE reps took part in a three-day national strategy session in Ottawa focused on the human rights struggle (Barron 1995). Earlier that year EGALE reps also visited St. John's to provide training and conduct strategy sessions with provincial activists. Activist momentum was building again (Evening Telegram 1995).

In early 1996, Hodder wrote the leaders of the three provincial political parties asking them whether they would endorse amending the human rights code, and also whether they would support the extension of health care and benefits to same-sex partners. Lynn Verge, on behalf of the Progressive Conservatives, wrote back a strong endorsement of amending the Human Rights Code but said benefits should be left to collective bargaining with workplace unions. Jack Harris, on behalf of the NDP, wrote back his endorsement. From the provincial Liberals, now under Brian Tobin's leadership, there was no response (NGALE 1996).

In 1996, NGALE also filed a complaint with the CRTC when a local cable channel refused to accept gay-themed advertisements. By that point, a phone support line was also in operation in Corner Brook, operated by a group calling itself the Bisexual, Gay and Lesbian Association for Support (BGLAS).

After mulling over Justice Barry's decision for several months, on April 26, 1996, the provincial government announced that it would appeal his ruling. NL was by this time one of only three provinces which had not yet explicitly added sexual orientation to their human rights codes. Alberta and Prince Edward Island were the other two, along with the Territory of Nunavut.

The announcement only added fuel to the activists' fire. Two months later, on June 23, over a hundred people attended the annual St. John's Pride Week March for Freedom, and speakers included Jack Harris, leader of the provincial NDP, Joyce Hancock, head of the Provincial Advisory Council on the Status of Women, and Dale LeDrew, on behalf of the United Church, along with local activists like NGALE's Michael Riehl and MUN's Out on Campus rep Mireille Sampson. They called on government to respect the Barry decision and adopt anti-discrimination legislation. That same month, NDP leader Jack Harris formally asked the provincial government to introduce a human rights code amendment around sexual orientation. In response, Liberal Labour Minister Kevin Aylward replied that government might consider doing so in the fall.

NGALE was plugged into other ongoing struggles as well. Events were held throughout that summer's St. John's Pride Week to raise funds for another legal battle, being conducted by the Vancouver-based queer bookstore Little Sisters. The venerable BC institution, which had been around since 1983, was routinely targeted by Canada Customs and often had shipments of queer-themed material coming from the United States and elsewhere labeled "obscene" and seized at the border. In addition to the clear homophobia driving such seizures, it also became apparent that customs officials were targeting independent queer booksellers, since the same materials were left untouched when shipped to major commercial bookstore chains. Little Sisters took the federal government to court in 1990 in a landmark case that stretched over ten years. The final ruling by the Supreme Court of Canada, issued on December 15, 2000, ruled that while the Government of Canada retained the right to designate and seize material it considered "obscene," it had wrongly targeted and discriminated against Little Sisters. The ruling also placed a new onus on government to prove the material was obscene (Zeidler 2019).

Back in Newfoundland, even though the Liberal government was busy fighting the Barry decision, its own agencies were getting on board with combatting homophobia. On December 17, 1996, the Provincial Women's Conference – organized by the Women's Policy Office, an agency of the provincial government – invited NAN to organize a two-hour caucus during the Conference. This included a session on how to lobby government to respect the Barry decision and get anti-discrimination legislation passed.

Although momentum remained strong in the wake of the Barry decision, a movement relying on volunteers was at constant risk of burnout. On April 29, 1997, a report in the *Humber Log* warned that the Les-Bi-Gay support line operating on the west coast of the island might have to close in April, as it was down to a single volunteer. "Since its inception three years ago, it's estimated the line received between 3000 - 4000 calls from all over the west coast, and saved numerous lives," the article explained. And on June 22, 1997, about 50 people marched down Cochrane Street to Water Street in the City's annual March for Freedom as part of St. John's Gay and Lesbian Pride Week – a far smaller crowd than had attended the same event the preceding year, in the wake of the Barry ruling and government's decision to appeal it.

Meanwhile, the fight to get the provincial government to respect Barry's decision and pass official anti-discrimination legislation continued. Provincial Liberal labour minister Kevin Aylward had issued a government response immediately following the ruling pledging to respect it and to introduce the required human rights amendment. Yet a truculent attitude prevailed among members of the Liberal government, some of whom remained defiantly homophobic. Others were opposed to what they considered the usurpation of legislative authority by the courts. The following year, the NL Liberal government filed an appeal against the Supreme Court decision just before their deadline for doing so expired (Cleary 1996). Furthermore, the NL government took its fight national, applying for intervenor status in a human rights case in Alberta involving a teacher who was fired because he was gay. The NL government got involved specifically to argue against 'reading in' sexual orientation rights in that case (Hilliard 1997).

NGALE was loudly critical of these acts. The NL government shouldn't be wasting public funds fighting against human rights either in this province or any other, argued the group's spokespersons. While NGALE acknowledged that having the legislature pass equality laws was preferable to having the courts 'read in' anti-discrimination, the mixed messages from the province were bewildering. In the same year, the Liberal government both committed to bringing in legislation, and also filed appeal against its obligation to do so (Ibid.).

"We're wondering if one head of government knows what the other head is doing," commented NGALE's Brian Hodder in *The Evening Telegram* on June 17, 1997 (Ibid.).

Local media held government's feet to the fire. "Labor Minister Kevin Aylward may not keep his pledge," wrote Ryan Cleary in *The Evening Telegram*, observing that government kept promising the legislation but failing to deliver. Aylward had promised to bring forward legislation in early 1996. "But the leaves have changed color, dropped dead and still no act," Cleary wrote (Cleary 1996A).

On April 4-7, 1997, NAN put off "The First Provincial Lesbian & Bisexual Women's Conference", to be held at a secret location that would only be shared with registrants. "The purpose of the meeting," according to registration materials, "was to strategize how to achieve protections under the provincial human rights code." They brought in Yvette Perreault, co-author of the book *Stepping Out of Line: A Workbook on Lesbianism and Feminism*, and Deb Parent, an activist with the Toronto Rape Crisis Centre, to facilitate the conference. NAN's activism received national prominence a few years later when the right-wing national news publication *The National Post* published an "expose" on hundreds of thousands of dollars in federal funds that had been provided to "lobby groups for lesbians." The January 4, 2000, article attacked such use of public funds, which had included a $4000 grant to NAN for "a two-day session for the purpose of identifying the human rights issues affecting lesbians, developing strategies to address those issues, and taking responsibility as individuals and as a committee to implement the strategies."

The federal Liberal government finally acted on its promise to pass a human rights amendment at the federal level, holding its second vote on the legislation on May 1, 1996. Less than half the Newfoundland and Labrador MPs supported the bill. Liberal MP George Baker voted against his own government. Liberal MPs Jean Payne, Bonnie Hickey and Gerry Byrne voted in favour of the human rights legislation. Fellow Liberal MPs Fred Mifflin, Larry O'Brien and Roger Simmons didn't show up to vote. All told, only three Liberal MPs from this province voted in support of the human rights amendment: Payne, Hickey and Byrne.

Wells' administration never did pass the human rights amendment called for by Barry and so many others. That role would fall to his successor, Liberal premier Brian Tobin. At first, he too dragged his feet. For each of its first four sittings in the House of Assembly, the Tobin government promised it would amend the human rights legislation but failed to do so.

NDP leader Jack Harris was vociferous in his demands for the amendment. "I think that government is stalling the legislation deliberately," he told *The Evening Telegram* on May 8, 1997. "Either we have a homophobic government or we have somebody influencing government who is homophobic or doesn't want them to pass this legislation. The amendment has been made in the past so it's not a question of drafting problems, it's simply a question of political will" (Hilliard 1997).

In response, Liberal cabinet minister Kevin Aylward said he was working hard to drum up adequate support within the cabinet and caucus to pass the legislation. When government re-convened for the fall sitting of the House of Assembly that year, there was still no sign of the legislation. "The frustration level is extremely high," SJSWC spokesperson Dawn Onishenko told media. By this point the Progressive Conservatives were also outspoken in their demands for a queer rights amendment, and were brow-beating the Liberals over their failure to act. "We are usually always last to come on stream in various areas," Opposition Leader Loyola Sullivan told media. "We seem reluctant to be leaders and always want to be followers" (Macafee 1997).

In the end, it was NAN that came to play a key role in getting the legislation passed. NAN, like NGALE, had been writing politicians urging them to support the legislation. Finally, Gerry Rogers wrote to Premier Brian Tobin himself. As she recalls, "I said: 'We are this group of lesbians, and our human rights act has to change.' I wrote the letter and asked him to meet with us, I said that we wanted a meeting between him and a number of lesbians."

Tobin agreed to set it up. He didn't attend the meeting himself, but he strongly urged his entire cabinet to go. Most of them did, along with several other MHAs. Rogers facilitated the meeting, and adopted an unorthodox approach.

I thought the best way to deal with this is to tell stories — people's life stories. There were at least a good dozen of us [lesbians]. What I asked people to do, I had two different colours of paper, cut in strips. And I asked all the ministers and the MHAs to write down any questions that they had about gays and lesbians. And then on a different coloured paper, all the horrible things that they heard. And then we put them into bowls. And I started off by saying that there's so much mythology out there about us – myths like 'gays and lesbians shouldn't have children.' But we do. 'Gays and lesbians should not be teaching our children.' But we do. Each time I hit one of those things, I would ask someone to speak, who was a teacher. Or who had kids. Or who was a nurse. Or who was a mother. I asked them to personalize everything. And then in between each story, we'd pull out the worst thing you ever heard about gays and lesbians, and we would talk about that. And then we'd pull out another question that you had about gays and lesbians. So it was safe for anybody to say anything and ask anything — and we would address it. We would speak to it.

I think that's what got it for us, telling our stories and speaking our truths. I said [to the MHAs] 'It's evident you don't want us teaching your children. But we are. And we're doing a fine job.' And then someone told the story of trying to take care of their mother in a long-term care home. That was very moving, because it personalized us. It de-monsterized us. And the MHAs had to listen. They had to be polite. It was our meeting. And they had to be polite because [Premier] Tobin told them they had to be (Rogers 2022).

Not everyone agreed with Rogers' approach. She recalled that some women at the meeting, representing other agencies and advocacy groups, felt the approach was childish and too much like playing games. She said some of them were very angry with her. "[They] were really angry and upset and didn't think this would work," she recalls. But she holds by the way she facilitated the session.

Because I came from making documentaries, I knew how important the stories were. And busting those myths. That's what we did. Instead of just writing dry briefs about it. We said: 'Here's someone taking care of her mother inside long-term care. Here's a teacher. Here's a parent' (Ibid.).

Another important aspect of Tobin's leadership, say some of the NAN activists, was the prominent role played by women in his cabinet. Sandra Kelly, Joan Marie Aylward and Julie Bettney were all relatively young cabinet ministers. While Tobin is still often associated with his role in the offshore fishery 'Turbot Wars', he also instituted some of the most progressive and fundamental shifts in the province's social fabric. He took on the denominational school system, holding a provincial referendum to change Newfoundland and Labrador's Terms of Union with Canada. The referendum passed, and the denominational school system was dismantled, replaced by an ostensibly secular one. His government also brought in the first permanent provincial funding for the Morgentaler Clinic which provided abortions, ignoring the outcries of angry anti-choice activists including the still-powerful churches. His government also took action on adding sexual orientation rights to the provincial human rights act. NAN's Peg Norman attributes the role of strong young women support-ers like Kelly, Aylward, Bettney, and even Tobin's wife Jodean, as playing an important role in moving these initiatives forward.

Paul Dicks is no longer involved in politics; he's returned to the legal realm. I spoke with him about those years. He declined to comment on behind-the-scenes debates, invoking the principle of cabinet secrecy.

The thing to realize with cabinet ministers is that you have to defend the government's position...I'm conservative fiscally but I'm very liberal in personal rights, so if I said things [opposing same-sex rights] I was probably reflecting [government's position]. You're conveying the message that govern-ment wanted to put out there at that time, and government's decisions.

While I was in cabinet I probably disagreed with government on 50 percent of the decisions I was forced to defend (Dicks 2023).

While Dicks wouldn't discuss the specifics of cabinet debates, he did of-fer broad reflections on the period and its politics. He pointed in particular to the influence of organized religion on the provincial government in the early 1990s.

At the time there were a lot of factors playing, and there was a strong reli-gious element," he said. "The churches still had a lot of credibility and [sexual orientation protections] were generally resisted. A number of people in cabinet and government were from more evangelical denominations. The mainstream Protestant denominations had generally been more receptive to it.

The reason we were able to do it in the late 1990s was the churches lost credibility after the Hughes Inquiry [into clerical abuse at Mount Cashel]. With the clerical abuses becoming such a matter of prominence with the gen-eral public, it opened the way for people to have a more liberal view of what social rights should be, and personal rights, the personal liberties that people should have...and to limit the extent to which society should intrude on peo-ples' personal decisions.

Here you had clerics who were saying: 'Oh gays - isn't this terrible?' Mean-while they were the ones abusing children. So then people said – 'What?' It led people to question the things they were told.

"By the mid-1990s when Tobin came back I think people were saying: Let's move on, we don't have the right to intrude on peoples' personal lives (Ibid.).

Dicks pointed out that Tobin returned to the province from several years as a federal politician in Ottawa, where same-sex rights were by then well-estab-lished. He also observed that with the closure of the NL cod fishery in 1992 due to overfishing, many NLers had to leave the province for work as well. There was a process of depopulation in rural NL during this period, with former fishers and their families relocating elsewhere in the country, some of them to parts of the country with a more liberal social milieu around queer rights. The increased contact between NL and other parts of Canada due to labour migration may have helped to liberalize attitudes in rural NL.

Dicks points to the period from 1989-1996 as one of profound social change in the province. Some of this was due to Mount Cashel, but to other shifts as well. Growing media coverage of queer rights struggles elsewhere in Canada and the US played a part, he feels, along with political changes within the province.

The other thing we did was denominational reform. We did away with denominational schools. That sent a message to the public. The first time around it was strongly opposed but we had two referendums and by the second time it was done people had asked themselves the question of why we were discriminating against people based on their religion by sending them to different schools. And that led to other questions, like what right do we have to intrude on peoples' personal right to their sex lives?

So you kind of inculcated – not a revolutionary, that word is too strong – but you inculcated a necessary and for some people a radical shift in their thinking to be more accepting of these things. If you don't discriminate on the basis of religious affiliation for education, why are we discriminating on the basis of sexual orientation? These things follow each other (Ibid.).

Eliminating denominational education was key to this process, Dicks feels. He pointed out that generations of NLers had surrounded themselves by people of the same religious denomination – in schools, in communities – and this merely reinforced prevailing traditions and attitudes. Once NLers began having to engage with others who held differing views – even differences as minor as Catholics and Protestants – it began opening minds, he says.

It wasn't only the school system, it was in the health care system too. The Salvation Army had their own hospitals, St. Clare's was the Roman Catholic one, the General Hospital was the Protestant one. It crossed every major sector, certainly the influential sectors. All these things changed. We brought all the hospitals together too at the time.

It was a process of liberalisation. In some ways it was like the Quiet Revolution in Quebec in the 1960s. Now it wasn't as anti-clerical as it was in Quebec but it was a period of social liberalisation in Newfoundland in many ways. The change in the school system was radical. The school system had been around since the 1850s and a lot of people were very resistant to that. But that was part of the social change, the courts as well. It's hard to put a finger on one thing but it was a time when people became more progressive in their thinking generally. Even Sunday shopping – that was another thing that was resisted! The stores were closed on Sundays, but we decided we'd allow Sunday opening. Well I tell you, a lot of people from the evangelical denominations were very opposed to that! So you allow store sales on Sunday, how radical is that? And now you had Catholics and Protestants, Jewish and other people going to the same school. How radical is that? It was a process. And also around that time abortion was still a matter of concern, but that was part of it as well. All of this was a way of saying to people: You don't have a right to intrude into other peoples' personal choices. There are areas of personal behaviour that society should not be intruding into. And on the other side of the equation is the idea that you don't have a right to discriminate in terms of public funding of things.

I think it was a reflection of a general social awareness, a change in attitudes so that people would be more tolerant. And the other thing is that once you say the churches had no right in the state, that gives the state the right to make laws that are fair to everybody across the whole spectrum of political funding and personal rights.

We couldn't do it in the early part of the 1990s, but we could in the later '90s and that was a good thing. It was all part of a process, flowering in the later 1990s.

The social progression of things sometimes takes a lot longer than it should. Most people are conservative. They don't want things to change, because they'd rather have the current situation and certainty, than change it and not know what the consequences might be. Even if the consequences might be better, they still don't want that (Ibid.).

***

I also spoke with former Premier Clyde Wells in 2023 about the 1990s struggle for queer rights in the province.

"I remember there being issues, but I don't remember the details," he said. He remembers a discussion about same-sex adoption happening in Cabinet, but he doesn't remember the details – and even if he did, he would respect the principle of Cabinet confidence and not divulge details, he said.

"That was 25 or 30 years ago...I don't remember too much in the way of detail of it," he stated.

But what he does remember – a tone of exasperation still emerges in his voice as he speaks of it – is the influence of the churches. When I refer to the "power" of the churches he's quick to correct me: "I wouldn't say power, I would say practices and attitudes of the churches, because they assumed the right to influence and dominate and affect people, and affect the lives of people...they didn't have much in the way of powers in terms of statute, but everybody responded positively to the requests or direction of the churches and that was the problem."

Wells shared his analysis of the historical position of the churches. He attributes their influence to a socio-political attitude that emerged in Newfoundland as an effort to prevent the sectarian violence that plagued the European countries from which NL's white European immigrants came. As Catholics and Protestants battled each other – often literally – in countries like England and Ireland, in NL the principle of religious accommodation took root in colonial institutions. Elites became fixated on balancing the influence and presence of the three principal Christian denominations: Catholic, Anglican, and what Wells says former Premier Joey Smallwood referred to as 'non-conformists' (Presbyterians, Methodists, United, Salvation Army, and others). Cabinet positions in government were doled out according to the principle of maintaining a strict balance between these three groups. So were senior bureaucratic posts. Each of the three groups had its own education system, its own hospitals, its own Supreme Court judges, its own statutory holidays. The result of this attempt to prevent sectarian violence, was a structure of Christian sectarian accommodation that gave the Christian churches deep roots in NL's civil infrastructure.

"Newfoundland had been used for a couple of centuries to this kind of division and acceptance and allocation to avoid physical violence," explained Wells. "The whole culture in Newfoundland was aware of that and accepting of it as a means of accommodating religious difference. I thought it was inappropriate and I thought it was wrong."

Wells grew up acutely aware of the impact of this system on education. As a child he attended a one-room Anglican school in Stephenville Crossing. "Across the pond there was a ten or twelve room Roman Catholic school, with skilled and educated teachers...well-educated, well-trained, but we couldn't go there because we were not of the Roman Catholic faith," he recalled.

When Wells got to Grade 7, a makeshift partition was erected in the one-room school to make half of it a high school. The school got a new principal, who had only completed a Grade 11 education and had another six weeks of summer school to prepare him to be principal.

"A government that maintains that kind of a system is not doing right. It's just unfair to people...It was grossly unfair and an inappropriate thing to do, and I couldn't see any purpose being served by it. So I was determined that we would eliminate that system. And we did."

It took time. When Wells began his political career, serving in Premier Joey Smallwood's government, he witnessed first-hand how obsessively Smallwood fixated on maintaining that strict balance.

"I thought it was offensive because I thought in itself it was discriminatory – it wasn't appointment on the basis of merit, it was on the basis of religious affiliation. But there was a kind of pardonable – I wouldn't say acceptable, but a kind of pardonable – motivation to avoid disruption and physical violence."

When Wells became premier, he was determined the system needed to change.

"I remember the head of one particular faith coming to see me and expressing the view that there was not an adequate number of representatives from his faith in cabinet – my recollection is that there were none! And I just told him:

'Look, this is not a religious administration. This is a public administration and it has to be structured and run on the basis of what's in the best public interest. And the best public interest is not promoting equality of representation on the basis of denomination."

The effort to accommodate a balance among Christian denominations in the education system was also costing the province a fortune, Wells recalled.

"One of the first decisions we had to make [as a government] involved a school that had become affected by dampness and it had to be eliminated and a new school built. That was going to cost $3.5 million or so to build a new school. But in order to do it, we had to put up another $8 million for the other denominations to make sure they got the same proportionate amount of money – even though they didn't need it! I mean, that's not a very sensible way to run a government."

Wells' tenure laid the groundwork for eliminating the denominational education system, a process that came to fruition during the term of his successor, Brian Tobin.

Queer activists I spoke with still express a bitter resentment at the resistance of the provincial Liberal government to legislating queer rights during those years. Many of them felt it was rooted in homophobia – and insofar as ignorance can be a form of homophobia, it probably was. But in speaking with former politicians like Clyde Wells and Paul Dicks, I did not detect any hostility toward queer activism; on the contrary, they spoke very positively of the improvements that activists won.

I suspect – and this is a purely subjective speculation – they were so consumed by their own political priorities they simply failed to recognize how important the queer liberation struggle was, and how deeply impacted so many people were. This is underscored by the fact they barely seemed to remember the activism that went on during those years. There is, perhaps, a lesson here for contemporary activists. Overcoming homophobia was only part of the struggle; getting politicians to prioritize and understand the urgency of a change is perhaps an equally difficult part of the struggle. With the Wells government preoccupied with dismantling some of the institutional roots of church influence on NL politics and society (in the education sector for instance), they didn't seem to consider equality for queer NLers a priority (opposition from homophobic members of government was clearly also a factor). The irony is that both struggles shared deep roots – an effort to undermine the historical influence of the Christian churches – yet provincial politicians either failed or chose not to recognise the interrelationship of those struggles.

There was also perhaps a fear – some might call it a cynical one – that too much change too fast could jeopardize other political priorities. Wells echoed Dicks' beliefs as to the gradual pace of change.

"The only thing I can say to you is that the approach to change and adjustment in the [human rights] laws, I expect, would have been treated the same way as we did on a normal basis of reasonable transition and not just suddenly saying 'We don't give a damn what thirty or fifty percent of the population think, we're going to do this anyway.' Governments don't usually operate that way and those that do usually end up with a lot of other difficulties that flow from it...changes of that magnitude [as the denominational education system] can only acceptably take place or should only acceptably take place in a reasonable space of time. That doesn't mean you can drag it out forever. But if you try to make the change so extensive immediately it sometimes creates a backlash."

An incident sticks out in Wells' memory, and he shares it toward the end of our interview. Every year high school students had to write a sort of public exam at the end of the year, and the only government testing centre in Stephenville Crossing was at the Catholic school. So the Anglican students had to write their exams in the Catholic school.

"That school was full of empty desks – because the other grades would have been out [for the summer] – but incredible as it seems, we used to bring our own desks and chairs over from the Anglican school to the classroom where exams were written," he recalls with a wry laugh. "Then in the fall the older boys had to go back and retrieve the desks and chairs. I remember one time when I was in grade ten or eleven I went over with one of the older students, and he knocked on the door and this very gracious nun came to the door. And he said to her: "Sister, we have come to get the Church of England chairs.""

Wells laughs in recalling the incident, but for him it underscores the sort of attitude which fueled division both along the lines of faith as well as sexuality.

"It just amplifies how silly and unacceptable that kind of division of people is. That applies also to LGBTQ rights as well. On what earthly basis should these people be treated any differently? Nevertheless, we do. And it takes time to change. And fortunately, this has been a time of great change."

***

Finally, on December 9, 1997 – the day before International Human Rights Day – Bill 21, an Act to Amend the Human Rights Code, passed its third and final reading in the provincial House of Assembly.

A press conference was put together by several of the groups who had contributed to this hard-won victory: NGALE, NAN, ACNL, the St. John's Status of Women Centre, the Human Rights Commission, the Human Rights Association, and Amnesty International. Delegates from all three political parties attended the event. There, NGALE representatives celebrated their victory but also pointed out the fight wasn't yet over – the matter of same-sex benefits remained an ongoing struggle.

NGALE also organized an impromptu party to celebrate the event. Shortall, to whom Premier Wells had flatly rejected the notion of an amendment six years earlier, was at home that night with her partner Sue Rose, watching

Premier Tobin sign the bill into law on the television news. "We were watching that on television and we were so happy," she recalls.

NGALE continued its work in the ensuing years. It incorporated as a charitable organization in late 1997. One of the important services it provided in the mid to late 1990s was its phone support line. Before NGALE had raised its own operating funds for a phone line, the group piggy-backed its phone line off of the ACNL. The ACNL had received funding to operate a 1-800 toll-free information number, and the organization agreed to let NGALE use its phone line a couple of nights a week.

"There was a core group of us who did the phone line," recalled Michael Riehl.

It was three hours a night. Some nights you'd get a flood of phone calls, some nights you'd get none. You would get people outside of St. John's who were very lonely. This was before the Internet. It was very hard to meet people. There were people you'd get on the phone line, and they'd say: 'Oh I want to meet up!' But you couldn't do that. We were there to help provide information (Riehl 2022).

There were malicious rumours circulating that the support line was a phone sex line, and so the NGALE volunteers adopted strict protocols to combat homophobic gossip. They were forbidden from arranging in-person meetings with callers, or providing personal contact information. They made sure they worked in teams, so there would always be witnesses present. Training sessions in mental health support and suicide prevention were organized for volunteers.

"The thing I remember is all these people calling up and saying things like: 'My family says I'm going to hell' or 'It's against the Bible, I need to get therapy' or 'It's evil to be gay' or 'they say I'm a pedophile,'" recalled Riehl. "There were all these different stories that were coming from callers."

Derrick Bishop also helped out on the line.

Sometimes people would call and you might be on the one phone call the whole evening. Because they just wanted to talk to somebody. They were lonely. Some of those people would also then write letters. I remember a letter came in from one person explaining their plight – they were from the Northern Peninsula and dealing with [being gay] in a very small community, so it was a real challenge for them (Bishop 2021).

Although then just 17 years old, Mikiki also helped out on the phone line.

Oh my lord, we would definitely get calls. There were multiple calls a night for each of us. But also there was a lot of just hanging around and shooting the shit. We would get calls from folks who had found the number in Wayves magazine and were planning trips to Newfoundland, folks coming in as tourists... We would also get calls from folks in Central, especially Central Newfoundland, like Gander and Grand Falls, who had come to town for an appointment or a flight and heard about us from somewhere. But there was a lot of people who just wanted to call and say: 'I am one too.' They just needed to hear someone else's voice (Mikiki 2023).

At the start of the school year in September 1998, NGALE launched a Homophobia Awareness Project, coordinated by the group's Education Committee Chair Faye Freeman and in association with the Provincial Strategy Against Violence, which was headed at that time by long-time NAN/SJSOWC activist Beth Lacey. Information packages were sent out to schools and students were encouraged to participate in a poster-making contest and submit anti-homophobia posters (Muscheid 1998). The outcome of that project stirred some controversy as well when no entries were received from the St. John's-based Avalon East School Board, leading organizers to speculate that school board officials may have suppressed the campaign. In the end, all the prizes went to Labrador students (Hedderson & Labonte 1999; Leblanc 1998).

"Some schools were very supportive and they put it out in their schools, but in others the letter never got past the principal's desk," recalled Bishop. "But a lot of the kids got involved. I think it was very successful, the fact that you got any of the schools and kids involved was a success, I think."

NGALE was invited to a number of schools as well as university classes to give presentations. Churches also reached out to the organization. The Salvation Army had a notoriously homophobic reputation, but nevertheless some of the provincial officers invited NGALE to present to their training officers.

It was very well received. There were people crying when I told them my story, or about some of the issues that were happening in the gay community. They were crying, visibly crying and upset by the hurt that people experienced, and the suffering that people had had. Many of them came up to me after and said: 'I know our church doesn't accept this officially, but I'm so appreciative of what you taught me today, and my attitude has changed' (Bishop 2021).

Other experiences were not as positive. Bishop remembers being invited to a United Church to give a presentation to members of the congregation.

The first time I went there were two or three people who were very hostile. Extremely hostile. I was very surprised actually by how hostile they were. And the anger! I thought one man was going to have a stroke. But we went back a second time, and I remember a woman who was very hostile. She got up and went to the bathroom, and on her way back she went out of her way to give me a shove and almost knocked me out of my seat. I know it was deliberate. There was such hostility in the room that night, that one person who had grown up in that church said to me when it was over: 'Derrick will you walk me to my car when we leave here? I don't feel safe.' He was afraid for his physical safety, and I had to walk him to his car, that's how intimidating some of these people were (Ibid.).

With the passage of the human rights amendment, NGALE's relationship with provincial institutions began warming up as well. The provincial government started reaching out to NGALE, seeking the group's advice and feedback on preliminary versions of legislation dealing with same-sex benefits and adoption. The Royal Newfoundland Constabulary attended and spoke at NGALE General Meetings about the work they were doing to support the queer community and tackle homophobia. In 1999, St. John's City Council approved NGALE's proposal to fly the Pride flag at City Hall during Pride Week. That year NGALE also launched the Annual Gay Pride Awards, which for the next few years celebrated people or organizations who contributed in notable ways to the queer community and queer struggle in the province. In early 1998, NGALE set its sights on a new goal: a permanent headquarters and centre for the queer community. It established a building fund, adopting a resolution that set aside 30 percent of all new revenue to go into the fund.

Unfortunately, the building never came about. After the passage of the human rights amendment, attendance at NGALE functions began to slowly wane. Several of its most seasoned activists either moved on to other work, left the province, or became involved with the national advocacy group EGALE. NAN also quietly faded away, as its members took on other roles or left the province. Queer advocacy had, by the early 2000s, shifted to the fight for same-sex marriage and benefits, which was being led predominantly by EGALE Canada along with a host of local and national allies. NGALE stalwarts continued to meet for a few more years, but momentum had shifted to newer community organizations, many of which had – following passage of the human rights amendment – now developed their own queer-themed initiatives. By the early 2000s, NGALE ceased to exist.

Still, its members are proud, even astonished, when they look back at what they accomplished during those years.

We were lucky to be there at that time. Things were more happy than sad. And we did things. We had a group, a very core motivated group, but unfortunately we didn't cultivate it amongst the younger crowd who in theory could have or should have stepped into our shoes as we aged and drifted away (Riehl 2022).

The campaigns and the activism came to dominate the lives of many of those volunteers during the final years of the twentieth century. Many of them were involved in multiple groups: NGALE, NAN, PFLAG, ACNL, and more. The campaigns came one after another: the human rights campaign, the same-sex marriage campaign, AIDS activism, trans rights activism. "Sometimes I just can't believe that we did all these things, but we did, didn't we," reflected Riehl. "We found the time. We found the time to do it, and we did it. It was important. It was important work.

"When you're involved, you're involved," he said. "You don't just do one thing, you're involved in a lot of different things. Because the community needs you."

Chapter Seven: AIDS Changes Everything

Betty Ralph remembers the day in fall 1981 when one of her gay friends dropped in to Neville's Framing. She co-owned the framing shop along with her friend Billy Neville. The acquaintance who popped in showed her a copy of *The Body Politic* which had a headline article on something called the "gay cancer." He asked her to read it and see what she thought of it.

When I read that article, I thought well, it's a virus or something. But as for saying it's just for gay men, I just couldn't believe that. I thought, nothing comes for just one section of people, that's a myth right there. But you know how religion affects people. Still I couldn't comprehend how people could jump on the bandwagon and actually think that. It was beyond me. But that was how it was presented in the early years.

Let's be honest, anyone that was living in the gay community knew life was hard enough. You didn't need anything else to make life harder. So you knew right away this was going to be a headache (Ralph 2022).

That article in *The Body Politic*, written by two Toronto-based physicians, was in fact a detailed criticism of how media were ignoring facts and data and instead using what we now call AIDS to stoke a homophobic public panic (Lewis & Coates 1981). Things would get much worse before they got better. Already the *Globe and Mail* had emulated its American counterparts, running articles fueling public panic about what it called "the gay plague" (Globe and Mail 1982).

As the public panic around AIDS grew, Newfoundland and Labrador's gay and lesbian activists found themselves working overtime to dispel myths and fake news. They also expended tremendous energy to support those infected by the virus. During the 1980s and early '90s, the provincial government effectively buried its head in the sand and ignored the crisis as long as possible, which is to say, until its indisputable spread through the heterosexual population accelerated. The province's powerful religious establishment did a tremendous deal of damage by blocking efforts to provide safe sex education or combat homophobia. After a solid decade of disastrous negligence – mitigated only by the efforts of an army of volunteers from the queer community and allies – common sense finally prevailed and the crisis gradually came under control. Hundreds of lives would be lost in the process in this province.

As news of AIDS spread in the 1980s, the province's media did little to quell the growing public panic. A representative sample of what passed for public dialogue at the time can be seen in a letter published by *The Evening Telegram* on December 7, 1985. A contributor going by the name "Shaggy Hair" complained that gays were not taking the disease seriously, and expressed concern that he – a straight man – could contract the disease via a razor cut at the barbershop (this was a common urban legend at the time). Interviewed by *The Evening Telegram*, the province's Director of Medical Services, Dr. David Severs, responded that he considered such an infection route to be possible, although he downplayed the likelihood (Evening Telegram 1985).

News about AIDS, photocopied and retyped articles, packed GAIN's newsletters in the 1980s as the epidemic spread. With so much uncertainty and panicked misinformation circulating about AIDS, GAIN activists felt they needed to do something. So did local public health officials. In 1985, officials with the Red Cross contacted GAIN requesting a meeting. Tree Walsh, who was president of GAIN, attended along with three other members of the group. The meeting had been scheduled for late in the evening.

The four of us went in, we went down the hallway to the boardroom, and they had the table set up horseshoe style. They sat on that side and we sat way over there on the other side with a big gap in the middle. Not just one table, but on opposite sides of the room. Which amused us greatly.

We sat down, and they said... 'We're asking gay men not to have sex.' We looked at each other, and the b'ys just burst out laughing. And I said: 'Well how do you propose to do that?' 'Well, we were wondering if you could intervene,' they said. I said: 'Do you think we know all the queers? We don't know all the gays in Newfoundland! We may be in touch with some, but we don't know everybody! And everybody doesn't know us! We're just a small little St. John's get-up here. We just call ourselves the Gay Association In Newfoundland because that's what you do when you're a townie, you say you run Newfoundland.

Anyway, they couldn't answer a thing. We asked them: 'Are you going to ask men if they're gay?' 'No,' they said, 'It's unconstitutional.' So I said: 'Okay, so that means you're going to ask all men [not to have sex]?' 'Oh no,' they said, 'Just gay men. It's just sodomy that we're worried about.' Well the [GAIN] b'ys just crushed him then: 'You think straight men don't engage in sodomy with gay men?' they asked. Well they just went apoplectic then, they didn't know what to say to that! Then I asked: 'Does this apply to lesbians?' And they all looked at each other – they never had one answer. Not one. They didn't know if it applied to lesbians. Then they told us: 'Nobody knows this meeting is happening. None of the staff know.' They kept it a big secret. So we said: 'Well that's nice, but we're doing a press release as soon as we leave here tonight!' And we did. The b'ys were right pissy and pissed off with them then, we were all getting so pissed off with them, because they didn't know a thing! 'Ask the gay men not to have sex?' Well, I was just finished with them then

(Walsh 2021).

In the end, GAIN offered to make a public request to the province's gay men to refrain from donating organs or blood (Evening Telegram 1985). Initially, many of GAIN's representatives as well as medical officials believed, incorrectly, that lesbians were not affected by AIDS and could safely donate blood and organs. These notions of course are now recognized to be medically inaccurate – women can also contract and transmit HIV, and the unscientific bias against blood or organ donations from men who have sex with men has lingered to the present day.

On April 3, 1987, the provincial government took action, after a fashion, by passing an amendment to the Communicable Disease Act which required doctors to report cases of HIV/AIDS to government. This would have significant consequences, insofar as the disease's addition to the list of communicable diseases, as opposed to infectious diseases, coupled with a lack of human rights protections would be used as justification for firing employees who became HIV positive (Whelan 1987A). Doctors were also now required to provide a range of demographic data on patients but did not have to submit their names. Provincial Health Minister Dr. Hugh Twomey defended government's respect for patient confidentiality with the grim yet accurate observation: "We are more dangerous to people who have AIDS than they are to us" (Evening Telegram 1987C).

In a manner eerily prescient of the more recent Covid-19 pandemic, newspapers carried regular updates on numbers of infections and deaths. On April 26, 1987, *The Sunday Express* reported that in the previous 15 months three NLers had died and 50 others tested positive for AIDS, and said the reported numbers were fueling a panic. On April 17, 1988, it reported that 8 cases of HIV had been reported at Memorial University, according to health officials there (Strowbridge 1988). Memorial's Director of Medical Services spoke out in a Telegram article on May 28, 1988, accusing the NL government of being slow to help AIDS patients (Hillier 1988D).

The provincial government began to slowly recognize the scale of the crisis, thanks to the relentless pressure of community-based activist groups. In October 1987, the government launched an education campaign directed at its own staff, inserting an AIDS awareness pamphlet – "New Facts of Life" produced by the Canadian Public Health Association – into the pay envelopes of public employees (Evening Telegram 1987).

Throughout this, it was community organizers who were doing the real work around AIDS education and support.

NL AIDS Association comes together

Gerard Yetman was a student in Toronto when he first started seeing AIDS education posters popping up in the city's gay bars, and noticed the growing availability and promotion of condoms. When he completed his university studies and returned home to Newfoundland in 1985, the issue still wasn't really on the radar in his home province. "I really wasn't introduced to the AIDS concept [at that time], or realized the impact that so many of the people around me were HIV positive and I didn't know it," he reflects, almost forty years later.

Yetman credits an older generation of gay Newfoundland men, who had been living in Toronto and witnessed the grassroots mobilization in response to the virus' spread there, as being the ones who raised the alarm in this province. They began organizing informally, gathering together to discuss what to do about the lack of AIDS-related awareness and response in this province. After returning from Toronto, Yetman got a job as a social worker on Bell Island but lived in St. John's. One day his friend Diane McLendon encouraged him to come to a meeting several of them were having in town, about AIDS. "Oh, I don't want to get involved in that," he remembers telling her. She was persistent, offered him a joint, and persuaded him to go. That meeting changed his life, and set the course of his work and activism for the next four decades.

"I got really hooked," he recalls. "A lot of it was that these were my friends, they needed help, and there was no way they were going to get help unless we formed something and did something."

The group they formed was called the Newfoundland and Labrador AIDS Association. At first the group met informally in each other's homes, concentrating on the need to support people living with HIV – driving them to hospital, cooking meals and doing laundry. As their volunteer base grew and they began contemplating large-scale fundraisers, they decided they ought to incorporate and establish some degree of formality. The group of ad hoc community members had little experience in forming and running structured organizations. This would prove a strength in some respects, enabling them to think outside the box and succeed in ambitious endeavours. But it also posed challenges. Their very incorporation faced them with just such a challenge, but also reveals the creative ways they learned to respond.

During a meeting one night at Yetman's house, they started filling out the paperwork to incorporate their organization. That's when they discovered it would cost them $100 to incorporate. That was a significant amount of money, and they brainstormed how to go about raising the funds. They settled upon an unorthodox idea: they would enter a boat race.

The Quidi Vidi Non-Motorized Boat Race was coming up, and the prize money was $100. It was the perfect solution. They just needed to win. Also, they needed a boat.

The intrepid volunteers approached Kingsbridge Service Station in the city's downtown, which donated a batch of inner tubes to the effort. The group took them to the Royal Newfoundland Constabulary parking lot, and put the inner tubes together to form a giant life preserver, which they spray-painted yellow and orange so that it resembled the real thing. Betty Ralph still wears a jean jacket stained yellow from when one of the volunteers accidentally brushed the preserver against her back.

They now had a 'boat,' but they needed to propel it across the lake without the use of a motor. Two of their volunteers had experience scuba diving, so they suggested they could push the giant life-preserver across the lake. They created costumes for the scuba divers, so that they resembled sharks.

And we had guys in the life preserver. The guys in the life preserver were people living with HIV. And we brought the life preserver across Quidi Vidi Lake, with these two divers with the shark fins. The idea was that the sharks were the HIV, and the [gay men] were in the ACNL life preserver. And we won! We won and we got the $100 and that's how we paid for our incorporation (Yetman 2022).

The group was now incorporated – thanks to the prize money from the boat race – but they needed an executive and board of directors. On January 26, 1988, Wally Upward, president of GAIN, and Yetman organized a meeting at the Health Sciences Centre to elect a formal board. Newfoundland and Labrador and Prince Edward Island were the only two provinces at that time without an official community-based AIDS group, Upward explained to attendees, including media.[58] They intended to set up an information hotline and formally affiliate with the Canadian AIDS Society at the national level (Evening Telegram 1988).

The group needed to elect an executive and board. Yetman, who by now had assumed a leading role in the fledgling organization, felt that it would be a wiser public relations move to not have gay men in a public leadership role, given the lingering stigma surrounding homosexuality. So, two women volunteers were elected into the leadership roles. Betty Ralph became President and Diane McLendon became Vice-President.

It was very strategic. We knew that we needed to take action. But we also realized that, as gay men, there wasn't much acceptance. There certainly was a lot of stigma... so we knew at the time that if gay men led this, we weren't going to get traction. We weren't going to get the support that we needed. We knew that the message we were trying to get out there was never going to happen. That's why we strategically had these two women – married women. We realized that if we were going to get the sympathy of the public, women are going to get that. In particular, married women who were raising families would listen. So that was the reason (Ibid.).

For Ralph, another benefit to having women lead the organization was to convey the message that AIDS was everyone's concern. "We didn't want to la-

---

[58] In fact, the Canadian AIDS Society reports the NL AIDS Association being an affiliate since 1986, so this is possibly a mistake made by one of the presenters or by the journalist who reported on the meeting. (Canadian AIDS Society 2023)

bel it as a gay man's disease. So rather than have the faces of people who would be prejudiced against, myself and [McLendon] put our names in for the top jobs," she recalled. "That way the faces showed it's everyone's disease."

The organization had no money, but it had a growing team of volunteers who proved willing to devote tireless reserves of energy into the fight. None of them were paid at first; not even the executives and organizers. The tasks varied widely, from fundraising to checking on patients, doing laundry for them, and cooking. They set up a buddy system, connecting patients with each other as well as with volunteers from the association. It was critical, they realized, to prevent people from becoming isolated once they were diagnosed. Those who were HIV-positive often either lost their jobs, or had to leave them as their health deteriorated. As the roster of patients grew, the Association made sure they kept track of everyone, and had volunteers to support their needs, even if that just meant having someone to talk to.

"We did whatever we could," recalled Bernard Stromer-Chaos, one of the volunteers who later served on the ACNL Board.

We cooked dinners, we brought dinners, in the morning we went to a funeral, in the afternoon we had to bring food to somebody. Pick people up at the airport. We had no money, and we got no recognition. Whatever. It was really tough. We just did it. We went from one situation to another situation to another situation. Constantly. There was a lot of what I call haphazard reactionary intervention (Stromer-Chaos 2022).

Lori Seay was one of the volunteers. She, like many, volunteered because the disease hit home in a very literal way.

We were losing friends. People were getting so sick. And people were really poor. We were all really poor. So people would get sick and not have the nutrition and secure housing and everything they needed to stay stable. None of the drugs or health support we have now. But it was a pretty mutual, caring crowd. When people would get sick, we'd take turns sleeping on the floor with them. Doing grocery runs. Organizing big Thanksgiving dinners. Taking care of each other (Seay 2022).

Volunteer burnout was a constant concern, but Ralph and other organizers were astonished at how willing their volunteers were to devote hours to the task on a daily basis, even while working full-time jobs. Ralph thinks it probably helped that none of them were getting paid for their work — it underscored that this was a humanitarian venture that put people at the centre, driven by and for the community. While media and government fixated on numbers — numbers of people infected, numbers of deaths — the volunteers actively resisted this reduction of the disease to statistics. This meant constantly pushing back against media narratives, and emphasizing that patients were people, not numbers.

To me they weren't numbers. They were faces. They were people. That makes a difference to you, because when you believe in something, it's much easier to fight... We had so many [volunteers], and they came from all walks of life, both the gay community and the lesbian community. Everyone, once they saw, would come on board to help (Ralph 2022).

AIDS was still little understood in the 1980s, and the activists were desperate for credible information. All they had to go on was conflicting information published in magazines and newspapers. Ralph read in one article that San Francisco was one of the first places where AIDS had been identified. So, she hunted down the phone number for the People With AIDS (PWA) Coalition in San Francisco.

I phoned them up, because the way I looked at it, it hit their area first, and they had more information than we did. And this is one thing I found: they didn't mind talking to you. I explained where we were to, and how we were on this little island, and I said: 'Believe me b'ys – I can do with whatever information ye can give me!' They were really good. They were right on board. They sent me everything. So we learnt from them many things which helped (Ibid.).

While education was important, and GAIN was already active on that front, the AIDS Association decided to focus its mandate on patient support. "Our mandate was to support people, because some people were on their own, so having someone to talk to was important," said Ralph. "And having someone that wasn't going to judge them. There was to be no judgement."

Many of the patients were young, and also poor. Fundraising to provide medical support and drugs for the patients became an immediate priority of the AIDS Association. Ralph began hitting up local restaurants, asking them whether they'd be willing to hold fundraising dinners for the group.

At first everyone kept saying no one was going to want to come on board, because there was fear. There was fear of how it was spread. Some people thought that if someone came in your house and drank out of a cup [they would get infected]. You had all those fearful things on the go, and you had to be able to speak with confidence, explain that it wasn't going to be spread that way (Ibid.).

One of the first dinners was held at the Curry House, a local Indian restaurant. "I didn't mind being the one that knocks at the door," recalled Ralph. "So I went to the gentleman that ran it, and he was very receptive. He had some concerns and asked questions - I told him I'd prefer any concerns or questions, you ask them to me face, don't go getting nervous!"

The event was so successful, they had to have two sittings. Ralph sold tickets in advance for either vegetarian or non-vegetarian meals, and the Association and the restaurant split the funds. The Curry House owner was so pleased with the event he invited them to schedule more.

Shortly after that event, another local restaurant, the Continental Cafe, heard about it and phoned Ralph up. "They were kind of upset I didn't go to them first," Ralph laughed. So she organized another dinner, and again demand was so strong they had two sittings. Dinner fundraisers became a popular mainstay of the group's efforts.

They leapt at any opportunity to raise money. Artists donated works to the group, on which they sold tickets. Friends was a popular local gay bar at the time, and Ralph suggested to the group that they approach Friends to hold an event as well. There was some concern from members that a gay bar would be afraid to hold an event that would associate them with AIDS.

"Everyone kept saying: 'You're not going to get their support.' But I said: 'Oh go on, I'll walk up to them, I'll ask anyone!' So I went to them, and I said to them: 'This is your community!' But no, they were on-side, they had no problem with it at all." The Association organized a drag show there, and Friends let them keep all the profits from the door.

Everyone we actually approached to do stuff had a very positive and respectful attitude. But I think it's also because we approached them with respect. Sometimes you can get too wrapped up and be too radical. There's a time for that! But there's a time to be cordial too. Everyone was amazed that the responses were so good. But I think it's because everyone realized that sooner or later there wasn't going to be too many of us on the island that didn't know someone [with HIV]. That brings home a whole new reality. There [were] many things after being written in books or TV – The Band Played On, Philadelphia – so really, you're after seeing what your reality is going to be too. Once you seen all of that, you realized that you have to work together. But I guess it was our determination, too (Ibid.).

Committees and Associations

While AIDS activists hit the ground running in NL, sorting out the institutional structures under which they would organize took time. The AIDS Association of NL was the first group to organize, comprised of grassroots activists. It was formed in 1986 by Ralph, Yetman, and others, and incorporated in 1988. In 1989, the provincial government finally decided it needed to take action, and formed a new body: the AIDS Committee of NL. Government wanted the AIDS Committee to focus its role on education. After some initial fumbling, internal problems and rapid staff turnover, government recruited someone with experience to take over the Committee: a Nova Scotian activist named Peter Wood. Under his leadership, the Committee would become a formidable force.

Wood was an activist well known throughout Canada. He had a background in theatre, where he had worked in set and costume design prior to his own HIV diagnosis in June of 1986. At the time he was diagnosed, there were 13 official cases in Nova Scotia. Less than five years later, the province would have the fourth highest rate per capita in Canada.

The 6-foot tall, rake-thin Wood hailed from the very first generation of HIV activists, and had been a founding member of the Nova Scotia People Living

With AIDS group. Those he met in Newfoundland knew him as a wildly intelligent, no-holds-barred fighter; but when he was first diagnosed with HIV it sent him into a spiral of depression. He was living in Halifax at the time, and had been a regular at the parish led by Robert Petite (introduced in Chapter 1). Wood was diagnosed around the time Petite took over the parish, and in his depression he had stopped attending church. The former rector of the parish met with Petite when he took over, and told him that he was worried about Wood.

"He had learned that Peter had been diagnosed with AIDS and was incredibly worried about him," recalled Petite.

He was worried about him not only because he had HIV but also he had become extraordinarily depressed. He kind of holed himself up in his apartment with all the windows barred and drapes over the windows, basically in the darkness.

The former rector came to me and said: 'I'm worried, I wonder if you might visit Peter.' Peter was living near the Halifax Commons at the time, and so I went and knocked and he wouldn't answer the door. But I kept coming back. I think I came back three times before I finally got him to open the door.

He was depressed and holed up in his apartment. It was a very dark time in his life and he didn't really have a community around him. He was away from close family, and I think the help that I provided was simply being there for him. Taking him for who he was. I liked his energy – we were both extroverts, we were both Newfoundlanders, he developed a trust in me that I certainly appreciated, and we worked very well together. That first meeting began really quite a lengthy and wonderful friendship together. It led to Peter taking an incredibly active role in spearheading the community's response to the AIDS epidemic at the time (Petite 2022).

After Petite helped him through the bouts of depression and thoughts of suicide with which he struggled after his diagnosis, Wood became determined to fight, and banded together with other Nova Scotians to form the NS People Living With AIDS group. In its early years, the organization operated out of living rooms and without any formal funding, much like the AIDS Association of NL was doing in its early years. Wood was a member of the National Action Committee on AIDS, and served on the Board of Directors of the Canadian AIDS Society (a national umbrella group formed in 1986). Wood was also the founding chair of the Canadian Persons Living With HIV Network (KFF Health News 2001). Among his other claims to fame was having burned an effigy of federal health minister Jake Epp at an AIDS Action Now! protest in Toronto in 1988 (Gullage 1991).

Petite described Wood as "our Larry Kramer."

He was bold and aggressive and angry and assertive and used nasty language that really got people's attention. He was a real force to be reckoned with. He and I got on like a house on fire, I don't think we ever had a quarrel about anything. We formed a very close friendship and did a lot of good work together. I can't impress upon you enough the importance of Peter Wood in this whole thing. And what a wonderful man he was. He was angry, but he had good reason to be angry about so many things. But he was a wonderful soul (Petite 2022).

Trudy Parsons, who volunteered with the ACNL, recalled him as a serious, deeply intelligent man. Every conversation she had with him was one where she learned something new, she said. He had a very strong personality, she recalled. "But he was often right."

Wood once complained to friends that Parsons was too flippant and perky around the office – he even called her a bubblehead. When she heard about it and called him out on it, he apologized. He explained that all his previous work around HIV had been done with gay men, and he wasn't used to working with women. As the months passed, they became quite close.

"He had a great deal of heartache, loneliness and survivor's guilt," Parsons recalled. By the time they met, most of his friends had died of AIDS; he was in fact the last surviving member of the founding cohort of PWA Nova Scotia.

"Peter was a seasoned activist," recalled Yetman.

He was a gay activist for many years in Halifax, and he was a very eloquent speaker. He'd had a lot of experience, and was one of the founders of the AIDS Coalition of Nova Scotia. So when Peter came here he had already had all that experience of forming an organization and running an organization (Yetman 2022).

Wood had experience making governments listen. Working out of a small, cramped office in Churchill Square, he slowly began opening doors for AIDS activists, particularly in the area of education and awareness.

But education wasn't enough, said Ralph, looking back at events over three decades later.

Education is fine, however what about the people who are living with it? You had to have supports for them. You had to have a grassroots organization that wasn't afraid… You couldn't just educate people. You couldn't forget the people who were living with it. That can quite easily happen, and I didn't want that, because that wasn't what [activism] was supposed to be. It was supposed to be about humanity (Ralph 2022).

In addition to what it fundraised, the AIDS Association received federal funding from Health and Welfare Canada. But it received no provincial funding. The province directed its own funding – what little there was — to the AIDS Committee.

The existence of two AIDS-related organizations with differing, poorly articulated mandates, one around education, one around patient support, generated friction at times. Activists with the AIDS Association, who were working around the clock to fundraise and provide support for those living with HIV, were frustrated that government seemed to be ignoring the situation of those patients. Ralph complained to The Sunday Express in 1991 that government ignored the Association and its requests.

"They see us as someone who is just out to be a thorn in their side," she said. She said that provincial health officials blamed the Association for creating a panic by saying the number of people with HIV was higher than official government counts (Gullage 1991).

Gary Kinsman, also speaking on behalf of the AIDS Association, complained to media that government was refusing to listen to their requests for anonymous testing, or to provide funding for more effective drug treatments. He acknowledged that education and awareness were improving thanks both to their work and that of the AIDS Committee, but expressed frustration at the duplication of efforts, saying that both groups needed to start working more closely together. At the same time, Kinsman criticized media for depicting the two groups as "warring factions that would never unite," and refused to answer questions about differences between the two groups (Ibid.).

Nevertheless, *The Sunday Express'* Peter Gullage summed up his impressions: "One [group] operates at the street level and is financed by donations, while the other is… funded and works the political boardrooms" (Ibid.).

While the AIDS Association and AIDS Committee struggled to reach an accommodation with each other, some of the province's medical establishment comprised a third column of sorts that was critical of both groups. Dr. Christian Sauve, who worked at the General Hospital in St. John's, chastised the AIDS Committee when interviewed by The Sunday Express in 1991. Sauve boasted of having been one of the first Canadian doctors to work with AIDS patients, in Florida in the early 1980s. He argued the situation in NL was under control and accused both groups of fueling unnecessary panics (Ibid.).

Mr. Wood… came here after we were following patients already for years and we had established our clinic and everything was running well, and he decided to make a lot of problems. If Mr. Wood thinks he's helping the situation by doing that, I think he's damn wrong… I would expect somebody like that to be more respectful of people who have training in that, and would ask questions instead of making declarations (Ibid.).

Dr. Sauve's comments struck at the heart of a dissonance between the medical establishment and people living with HIV. Establishment doctors in essence argued that people living with HIV should shut up and listen to medical 'experts.' AIDS activists, on the other hand, argued that their first-hand lived experience – coupled with the homophobia that was still widely pervasive in the medical establishment — gave them a level of expertise that should not be ignored.

"At this point, I know as much or more about AIDS than many, many doctors and especially general practitioners," Wood fired back in response to Sauve's comments. Wood wasn't afraid to criticize the government that had recruited him, either. He said he'd been repeatedly brushed off by the provincial health minister, and this type of behaviour reminded him of what he'd witnessed in

Nova Scotia shortly before infection rates soared in that province (Ibid.).

"We've [activists] never been wrong, and the naysayers in government have been wrong every time. And what are the consequences of being wrong?" he warned (Ibid.).

This was something on which both the AIDS Committee and the AIDS Association agreed. Kinsman and other Association activists met with provincial health officials in 1990. They tried to convince government of the scale of the looming crisis, and Kinsman drew on his own previous experience as a Toronto-based activist to urge the NL government to take action before it was too late.

"Basically the response we got was 'That's not the way it's done here. What we do is respond to problems when they emerge.' That was said in a fairly strong way to us," he told *The Sunday Express* (Ibid.). As an example of government inaction, Kinsman told reporters that a critical blood monitoring machine used to take cell counts for HIV-infected patients had broken down the previous fall, and the province had taken no action to fill the gap. Months later, they were still debating whether it would be more cost-effective to try to fix the broken machine, or buy a new one, he said. Meanwhile, patients were left in the lurch (Ibid.).

Wood agreed with Kinsman's assessment: "If [government] knew anything about cost, they'd be putting money into prevention," he warned (Ibid.).

Wood also recognized the duplication of efforts going on across the two groups, and that they might be more effective working together. Despite the fact they now worked for separate organizations, both Wood and Kinsman had previous experience working together as activists. Wood reached out to the Association, and raised the idea of merging the two groups.

Ralph remembers the meeting held by both groups, together with government officials, to discuss this proposal. The Association was open to the idea of merging, she said, since it brought the prospect of additional funds and open doors. Although it had government funding, lately the Commission had started putting off fundraisers, and community members had pointed out there wasn't enough money and resources for two AIDS organizations to be competing for it. The Commission suggested merging the two boards, dissolving the Association, and uniting their efforts.

Ralph recognized the importance of establishing an organization capable of long-term planning and growth, because AIDS "wasn't going to be going away any time soon." The Association's community activists did have one over-arching demand, on which they drew a line in the sand: government had to provide funds to go toward people living with AIDS. The provincial government agreed to designate a portion of funding for direct support of people living with AIDS, and so the two groups merged to form the AIDS Committee of Newfoundland and Labrador.

Wood was the Executive Director of the now merged AIDS Committee of

NL (ACNL). With their new budget, the ACNL was able to hire Wally Upward into the role of Education Coordinator — a role he'd already been carrying out in a volunteer capacity with the Association and also in his capacity as a lead organizer with GAIN. In addition, the ACNL created a position for HIV Counselor, to provide support for those living with AIDS. Yetman quit his job as a social worker to enter the HIV Counselor position. When Wood eventually left the Committee to move back to Nova Scotia, the Executive Director role fell to Yetman, who continued double service as HIV Counselor.

Wood died on October 4, 2001, from lymphoma as a result of AIDS. He was 54.

Thanks to the 1991 merger, there was now a single united organization to lead the fight for action on AIDS. The Committee brought its funding and connections with government to the new organization, while the Association brought its fearless determination and tireless volunteer community activists.

As per the merger agreement, a Family Support Program was established through the AIDS Committee which collected funds that were disbursed to people living with AIDS. In 1991, the Program gave $6358 in assistance to 31 people (Baird 1992). The newly revamped Committee became more community-focused, as well. There was an active Women and AIDS component of the group which met, as well as a quilting group. The Committee brought in speakers, produced a newsletter, and did workshops for pastoral workers who might wind up treating AIDS patients.

Still, support from the province remained inadequate, and the organization struggled to alert government to the scale of the crisis. In 1992, Wood and Yetman held a joint meeting with several provincial cabinet ministers, Social Services, Health, Education, and Justice, to discuss the AIDS crisis. "Anything is a start at this point, because [now] there is nothing," commented Yetman after the meeting (Ibid.).

After Yetman became Executive Director of the AIDS Committee, he brought Bernardus Stromer-Chaos on as Chair of the Board, and the two would forge a productive working relationship over the next several years. Stromer-Chaos (whose story is told in greater detail in Chapter 11) worked for the Department of Justice, and was a Dutchman with a reputation for treading on tradition. As a 'Come-From-Away' (CFA, as those not born in NL were sometimes derogatorily referred to at the time) he felt a certain freedom in ignoring unwritten rules and norms. "I had no allegiance to names, locations, outport cities, hierarchies," he recalled. "To me it was all a blank screen. So I would just do things. I got so much flak from my co-workers, because I embarrassed them, but I became known for it. I broke all the golden rules."

He offered an example of this rule-breaking: as a probation officer he used to have to write pre-sentencing reports. His colleagues would always complain about the Crown Prosecutor's office, because that office would often send their reports back demanding changes. "They would always bitch and complain about the Crown," he said. When it happened to Stromer-Chaos he wasn't as patient, and instead of just venting with his immediate co-workers, he went straight to the Head Crown Prosecutor himself. "I went over to him and I said: 'What is it that you want actually?' I think I was a little too Dutch for him. Because he replied: 'Do you know what? You're the first person ever to come to the Crown and ask us this question.'"

Stromer-Chaos would apply this same directness to his work with the AIDS Committee.

The ACNL had scores of volunteers at this time, but they tended to come from particular demographics. There were lots of young people, students, and out gay and lesbian activists. When it came to working professionals, many remained in the closet. They would donate generously to the organization, but did not want to be associated with it publicly.

"A lot of quote unquote professional people were not out [as gay]," explained Stromer-Chaos.

They were afraid that they may lose their job, and they may lose their house, whatever the fuck. So the professional class — whatever that means — and the so-called educated class — whatever that means — weren't out, and would not go to the AIDS Committee. Or would not want to have any dealings with it.

A lot of professionals would leave the province to get tested outside the province, because they didn't want to come out. So we were dealing with the economically disadvantaged people. Like sex workers.

It was a very difficult, sensitive period. Because in those days if you had AIDS you had to come out of the closet for being gay. And in some cases you had to come out of the closet for having been sexually abused. How do you protect these clients, and how do you push forward the organization's mandate? So it was very difficult. We didn't really get any legitimacy until about 1990 when the straights started getting HIV (Stromer-Chaos 2022).

Supporting the dying

Counseling and palliative care became a central focus of the newly merged Committee in its early years. "From 1990 until about 1996 we were a palliative care organization," said Yetman. "At that time AIDS patients couldn't go into the palliative care units. There was a lot of fear. I'd say more fear than stigma."

Ralph remembers the fear. Her own mother approached her one day, and said that several of the elderly ladies in her church were afraid of taking Communion, because they were worried that they would get AIDS from sharing the blood of Christ. An astonished Ralph told her mother that they might do well to be worried about catching something from sharing the same glass, but that it wouldn't be AIDS.

AIDS patients weren't allowed into palliative care, so the Committee put together a team of volunteers to go into patients' homes and help take care of them. Many of the volunteers were nurses, including several palliative care nurses who put in extra hours after their work day looking after people living with AIDS. Several student nurses volunteered their time as well. Other volunteers were relatives of patients who had died of AIDS; having learned firsthand about the disease and having cared for their loved ones, they extended this care to other patients in their communities. ACNL provided the sole palliative care support for AIDS patients until St. Clare's Hospital agreed to open up its palliative care unit to AIDS patients in 1995. Even then, there remained several patients who were reticent to enter the hospital's palliative care unit due to its historical hostility toward queer people and those living with AIDS so the ACNL and its army of volunteers continued to look after them in their own homes.

ACNL volunteers also played an important role as patient advocates. Patients often didn't have the strength to advocate for themselves. Both Yetman and Ralph emphasized the importance of having support people present when patients received diagnoses.

"When you hear that you're HIV positive, you go into total denial," explained Yetman. "A lot of people go into total denial, a lot of people don't really understand, and don't hear anything after that."

As Ralph explained:

When they're about to tell you something you don't want to hear, it's more devastating when you're alone, than when you got someone there who you know is going to be there for you through the whole ride. If they wanted to fight, you had to try to help them fight. Sending someone into a medical system that's already sick, they don't have energy enough to fight for themselves. Some days they just have enough energy to get out of bed. Not to stand up and fight. And we were willing to fight, believe me (Ralph 2022).

While HIV is treatable now, at the time very few patients lived more than a couple of years after their diagnosis. Often patients would wait until they were already quite sick before they got tested. In some cases, this was due to fear and denial. But it was also because they were worried about being outed, and facing both homophobia along with the stigma of AIDS. Many were afraid of losing their jobs if it became known they were HIV positive. This fear was particularly acute for queer and trans sex workers, whose entire livelihood would be jeopardized if they were known to be HIV positive. Newfoundland and Labrador being a small place pervasive with gossip, those who could afford to often flew to the mainland to be tested.

Few of the early activists had any training in palliative care or counselling, but they taught themselves and learned by trial and error. "You had to keep them thinking kind of positive," said Ralph.

What I discovered is that sometimes what you said to people made a big difference. You had to basically realize what each individual was like, and try to use positive reinforcement that would work for them. What worked for one don't work for another.

You also had to be aware of the fact that no matter how much you didn't want people to die, a lot of these people were going to die. And then you had to realize you had to try to talk about death. Now how many people wants to talk about death? But it's to make it go easier... if you start saying things that puts death in a certain light to people, the fear isn't there the same. But because our society refuses to talk about so much, then you see the fear, when it's happening. So you had to do conversations, but you had to do them lightly. And I could do it in all different lights. It didn't matter whether you wanted it from the Christian side or whether you wanted it from the crystal side. Everyone's got something they believe in (Ralph 2022).

Ralph would seek out counsellors or spiritual guides she thought might be able to help different patients, and request their assistance.

But there was one thing. When I asked anyone to talk to someone, I was really blunt. I would say to them, 'I don't want anyone showing up to someone who was gay and going on with this hellfire and damnation.' You had to be normal! I would say that to them. I told them: 'I'm wondering if you could [talk to a patient], however I have to be blunt. I do not want you going in and telling them that they're condemned. No one is condemning anyone. These individuals is already after putting up with enough shit from people. So if you're willing to do it for me, you follow these guidelines.' Well, they knew that the feedback would come back to me, and I would go after them (Ibid.).

When Bernardus Stromer-Chaos became involved with the NL AIDS Committee, he had no training in palliative care but people turned to him because he did have a background in counselling. "Suddenly overnight I became the palliative expert in how gay men were supposed to die," he recalls wryly. He recalled one incident in particular that moved him very deeply, involving a client who came to his house for a therapy session.

He came to my house, he was exhausted, he was tired and exhausted, his T-count was the shits. Normally I do an hour [of therapy], but of course I was going to let him talk as long as he wanted. And I wasn't a therapist – I was just a person sitting there. Anyway, he had this imagination. And he believed that he was going to go into this village, and he was waiting for the horse. Then he was going to get on the horse. And when he got on the horse, he was going to ride out of the village and that's when he was going to die. That's what he told me. What am I supposed to say? So, I supported him. But his doctor called me and told me that he was histrionic. And I just fucking lost it with her. I was very mouthy, because she was so clinical, she was very medical and clinical about this issue. I just lost it with her... because to me it didn't matter [if the patient believed that].

Two or three weeks later I got a call from this outport mother [of the patient he had seen]. She said: 'My son is asking for you. Can you come to the hospital now?' So I went to the hospital. The parents were there, and they knew their son was going to die. I went to his bed, and he said: 'The horse is in the village. But I can't get on it!' So I said to him: 'Well, why don't we get a chair? Then you can step on the chair, and then you can try to sit on the horse.' 'Oh yeah, yeah, that's a good idea,' he said. So that's what we did – I got a chair. Then I left the room, and his parents went back in. And ten minutes later he died (Stromer-Chaos 2022).

In many cases, the activists had to look after funeral arrangements as well. Many patients were ostracized by both family and community, either for being gay, or being HIV-positive, or both, and had no one to take care of their final arrangements. In other cases, churches would refuse to bury AIDS patients, claiming the bodies would contaminate the soil and infect others.

"A lot of people died," said Stromer-Chaos.

And there was a lot of unpleasant response to that. In some cases, parents would refuse to pick them up. Funeral homes would not bury them. So what did we do? We paid out of our pockets. I remember one case, there was this guy in Vancouver who had AIDS. And he just wanted to die in Newfoundland. Long story short, we managed to scrape the money together to fly him home. And within 24 or 36 hours he died. But not at his family's home (Ibid.).

The family would not accept him, even at the end.

Stromer-Chaos recalled another story he was told by a patient whose partner had also died of AIDS. "He was living with his lover, he told me. He had been living with his lover for years and years and years. And the day his lover died, the in-laws told him to get out of the house."

Even today Ralph turns fiery when she recalls the homophobia that many AIDS patients had to deal with.

I always looked at the gay community as a community to applaud. I even said that to someone – 'Rather than condemn people and point your finger and look down on people, don't you think that you should stand up and applaud them? Because after all when it hit San Francisco... they stood up to say that there is something going on! Rather than look at them and condemn them, don't you think you owe them?' Because no one else was standing up! Everyone else was keeping it covered up. They stood up, they brought awareness to it, and now they're being condemned? Because that's how it felt, especially with some people. It was a sad time (Ralph 2022).

Ralph remembers the first AIDS funeral she attended as though it were yesterday. Her friend Bob Day, a Newfoundlander, had died in Toronto, where he'd been living. His partner brought his ashes back to St. John's.

He requested that he was going to be cremated, and then we were going to spread his ashes. He wanted us to show up at sunrise on Signal Hill. I can remember us all gathering on the top of Signal Hill, and walking down those steps. [Bob] used to go up there, and there was a place where he used to sit and just think on life, and that's where he found his peace. So that's where we were going to spread his ashes from. It was a really nice still morning, and as we all walked down over the steps, all I could think on was that it was like a death march. All you could hear was us marching in unison. Even though it was probably two dozen of us, it sounded like just one footstep echoing. To me that was really something. Everyone was so still as they walked in silence. That's exactly how it was. And he was the first (Ibid.).

Ralph was to see many more funerals in her life, but that first one stuck with her.

Most of them were only young, in their twenties, which was sad because you were only just becoming an adult. The oldest that I knew was 45 years old. The majority of them were in their twenties, thirties. It was heart-wrenching. To watch so many people, and I kept thinking, they're only starting their lives. You don't know how much was in their life to give. They were just starting off. And to lose so much youth at such young ages, was just mind boggling. You didn't expect it to be like that (Ibid.).

"I saw fourteen of my friends disappear from HIV," said Roger Baggs.

They died. Fourteen guys who were on the scene with me – all dead. And those were guys I knew. There were so many guys who died. I knew one guy, his parents were very prominent in the community, and he died all by himself in a hospital in Halifax. And a lot of other Newfoundlanders died by themselves in Casey House in Toronto. I worked with the AIDS Committee, and I was doing palliative care work when I was nineteen years old! It was eye-opening. It changed me. When one person passed away it hit me harder than I thought, and I had a little breakdown and ended up in the hospital… because I was grieving. I could see how people thought it was too much for me, but it hardened me up in a way psychologically, it toughened me up. I saw HIV and AIDS first-hand and I had guys who I had dated pass away. It was difficult, such a difficult time (Baggs 2022).

Seay agrees. "There's a whole missing generation of people. If you look at a picture of us all at the bar in 1991, today the men are gone. Almost all of them are dead."

Petite, now living in Chicago, has a similar recollection. Many of his Nova Scotian and Newfoundlander friends and parishioners died during his years as a priest in Halifax.

I have a photograph that was presented to me when I left Halifax. It's a collage of people's heads, that was blown up really big. There may have been 25-30 people in that picture, both men and women. Within two years of my arrival in Chicago, every male in that photograph was gone. Everybody had died (Petite 2022).

"Everybody's dead," said Barry Nichols, recalling the friends he met in the St. John's gay community when he came out in 1979. "Everybody I knew is dead. It's like, where did everybody go? So many people died in the AIDS pandemic. Honestly I lost tons and tons of people. I don't know how I escaped it myself. I cry about it sometimes, it's so sad."

Educating the public

While the activists threw themselves into the fight, the ongoing stigma against homosexuality in the province made their work tremendously difficult.

In a 1987 interview with *The Evening Telegram*'s Maudie Whelan, Wally Upward, then president of GAIN as well as chairman of the AIDS Association, talked about the phone information line the group operated. He said they received calls from all over the island as well as coastal Labrador, and that half the calls they received were from married men who were bisexual. Because they were closeted, they kept their gay relationships secret from their wives. Even though they slept with different men throughout the year, "they deny it's part of their sexuality." This was a common response to homophobia at the time, but the arrival of AIDS put everyone involved in such relationships at risk.

"Homophobia," said Upward, "is a problem to be dealt with" (Whelan 1987D).

In the same interview, Upward said that he and his brother had gone around St. John's distributing 200 copies of the informational booklet "AIDS: What Every Canadian Should Know" to doctors' offices. Two of the doctors, he said, refused to allow the books in their waiting rooms (Ibid.).

"Government officials, medical experts and AIDS activists say many NLers are ill informed about the AIDS epidemic. Around the province, many still believe AIDS is a medical crisis linked to the San Francisco gay community," Upward told *The Sunday Express* reporter Linda Strowbridge in May 1987. "People are a little apathetic about it because they say there are only five AIDS cases in Newfoundland and it's still considered to be a gay disease... so they don't worry about it" (Strowbridge 1987).

The refusal of educators and policymakers to accept the reality of youth sexuality posed another risk that activists had to tackle. In an interview with *The Express*' Anna Dwyer in 1992, Upward explained that he concentrated his education initiatives on younger grades because informal surveys of students which he conducted suggested that younger students, 12 or 13 years old, were having more sex than older students, 16-17 years of age. He speculated younger students were experimenting more, while older students were settling into longer, more stable relationships.

I go into the schools because I talk very frankly and very openly and because most of the teachers, even if they have the ability and the knowledge, they don't feel comfortable talking about it and passing out condoms. We have this island mentality that we don't have homosexuals here, we don't have prostitutes here and that we don't have drug users in Newfoundland. Well we have all the things big cities have, it's just that most people don't see it (Dwyer 1992).

Because neither government nor school boards had any consistent approach to AIDS education in the early years, activists like Upward had to approach schools individually and often negotiate their way in with the principals on a case-by-case basis. Often, they would receive idiosyncratic instructions from principals about what they could or could not say to students. One principal, Upward recalled, wasn't too troubled by condoms but was frantic that he not tell students to get an abortion if they were infected and got pregnant. "I think what they're afraid of is that people will push homosexuality when they get into the classroom," he told Dwyer.

In another interview with *The Evening Telegram*, Upward wrestled with the differing attitudes among policymakers surrounding AIDS activism and gay activism, expressing his frustration that it was more acceptable to talk about the "AIDS cause" than it was to talk about "the gay cause," or discrimination experienced by gays and lesbians. At other times, activists struggled to distinguish AIDS activism from queer activism, he said. "The AIDS Committee is not a gay organization," he emphasized. Nonetheless, in the public eye at least, both were inextricably linked.

It was really difficult. The schools were church-based, so it was pretty hard to deliver education when you weren't allowed to talk about human anatomy. You weren't allowed to bring condoms into the school, and in a lot of schools you weren't allowed to talk about condoms. So it was pretty difficult. Usually the principal would be standing in the classroom while you're giving your little lecture. That happened lots of times (Yetman 2021).

As the virus continued to spread, things gradually began opening up, Yetman recalls.

We had a lot of young teachers – a lot of gay teachers in the schools who couldn't come out or they'd lose their jobs. But at least they'd get us in. It was a dynamic at the time that homosexuality just was not accepted, and while these institutions [churches] would never do anything to hurt you – as they saw it – they didn't do anything to help us either (Yetman 2022).

Yetman and Stromer-Chaos continued to use the ACNL Board of Directors in a very strategic manner. Yetman personally recruited Board members, inviting community members to join and telling them why their presence would be helpful. He recruited both a nun and a priest to the Board. He recruited doctors.

Bringing a priest onto the board gave us legitimacy in the eyes of the public. [I built] up the board with people with credibility and links that could open up other doors. For an organization that was confronted with so much stigma and discrimination, this was one way – I figured it was the quickest way – to knock down barriers (Ibid.).

Yetman was similarly strategic when it came to education and outreach efforts.

I took the approach of building communities from the inside out. When I was trying to get into towns, what I would always do was I would go and meet whoever was the religious leader. And I'd go meet the mayor. The movers and shakers of the community would be the ones I would go and meet with. I'd talk to them about HIV, about how important it is to get education to the kids. Being from St. Mary's – a small town – myself, I was always able to speak to the fact that I grew up in a small town. I was a very closeted gay boy. And we have them everywhere. They could be your own children. That was my approach to getting into towns (Ibid.).

Even as news about AIDS spread, activists in the province continued to face resistance from many of the Christian churches. The journalists covering the crisis were among the more educated people on the topic, and they played an important role not just by reporting, but also by calling for action. In a May 3, 1987, op-ed for *The Sunday Express*, journalist Linda Strowbridge warned that "essential public education about AIDS is being blocked by religious disputes, and public sensitivities... Government has so far chosen to remain silent about AIDS... Concerns about public sensitivities and morality debates must be set aside, so that Newfoundland can tackle a medical reality. Like it or not, hiding from the facts never changes them" (Strowbridge 1987).

Many of the province's religious leaders were brazen and unapologetic in their fight against safe sex, in particular condoms. In a joint pastoral letter released in March 1987, church elders from across the province "condemned AIDS commercials, articles and speeches, promoting the use of condoms as a campaign to 'encourage promiscuity, condone an immoral lifestyle and contribute to the further spread of AIDS'," reported *The Sunday Express'* Linda Strowbridge on November 15, 1987. Yet there was dissension among church ranks, she reported. Catholic curriculum planners with the Roman Catholic school board broke ranks and recommended Catholic junior high school students be taught about AIDS prevention through the use of condoms (Ibid.).

James McGettigan, Family Studies Coordinator for the Roman Catholic School Board, was one of those recommending the move, Strowbridge reported. "It would be morally wrong not to give children the information about sexual safety," he told her. "We would be guilty of negligence if we don't mention condoms" (Ibid.).

In fall 1987, the provincial Department of Education added a unit on AIDS to the Grade 9 course 'Adolescence: Relationships and Sexuality' taught in the province's public schools (Whelan 1987C).

Meanwhile, the province's newly appointed Director of Disease Control, Dr. Faith Stratton, took the firmest line yet on AIDS, adamant that it was time for public education in schools no matter what the churches thought of it.

"The people who (would be) upset are the people who are not informed, the people who do not understand what is happening," the young doctor told *The Evening Telegram.* "They do not understand the disease and are not open to listening or understanding."

Appointed Chief Medical Officer of Health in 1986, Dr. Stratton brought a fact-based approach to the job of tackling AIDS, resisting both the outrage of organized religion as well as intrusive demands from the province's media that might violate the privacy of patients.

"Our decisions (about releasing information on AIDS victims) are based on logic, not on emotion," she told *The Sunday Express* as she refused to divulge information on those who had died. This came shortly after a 60-year-old man died at the General Hospital in St. John's and was discovered after his death to have been suffering from AIDS (Yaffe 1987A).

She said that earlier that year she'd received a deluge of calls and letters from people in the Port de Grave region, including politicians and business owners, after an AIDS patient from that area died. She said they were panicked and looking for information, and while she refused to divulge personal information pertaining to the victim, she reassured all those who called that AIDS was not transmitted through casual contact (Ibid.).

"The increasing incidence of AIDS in Newfoundland is creating a mood of fear, panic and hysteria, particularly in those communities where AIDS victims have died," she told Barbara Yaffe with *The Sunday Express* (Ibid.).

It was in 1987 as well that Department of Public Health laboratories began offering HIV test analysis locally for the first time, through the Miller Centre in St. John's. Prior to that point, the only laboratory testing within the province was available through the Red Cross in St. John's. Public Health had offered tests, but they had to be sent out of province (often to Halifax) for analysis. Demand for tests in NL was doubling every year and ran into the hundreds by early 1987; the addition of local testing capacity marked a ramping up of efforts by Public Health. Yet to obtain a test still required a referral from a physician (Whelan 1987B).

Pressure from within the medical community began to build for something to be done. Dr. Ian Bowmer, a professor at Memorial University's School of Medicine and Director of Student Health Services for the university, excoriated the provincial government when he spoke out at a medical conference in May 1988: "Newfoundland has been slow in developing support systems to help those suffering with AIDS or exposed to the AIDS virus," he said, declaring that GAIN was the group doing the most in the province to raise awareness (Hillier 1988).

Fighting to improve care for AIDS patients

The story of Rick Bennett and Greg Brace, two Newfoundland residents who died of AIDS, was told in multiple newspapers of the time: first by Tracy Barron

(1995b) in *The Evening Telegram,* and then by Dave Cochrane (1996) in *The Muse.*

Bennett and Brace were a couple who both contracted HIV while living on the mainland. They lived with the disease for 12 years, in Toronto and Vancouver. When Brace's condition began to deteriorate, Bennett told *The Evening Telegram,* "he wanted to return home to Newfoundland to die with his family by his side" (Barron 1995).

But they both struggled with the decision. As Bennett explained:

When you come back to Newfoundland, as opposed to other provinces in Canada, you can be sure that your life expectancy is going to decrease by at least a year because of the lack of services and programs and everything else. They don't take as good care of their HIV patients as the rest of the country (Ibid.).

He said that because of the lack of widespread awareness of the disease, as well as the prevailing stigma, AIDS patients often had to educate themselves. He said elsewhere in the country, doctors welcomed the initiative shown by AIDS patients in self-education, and acknowledged their own shortcomings when it came to knowledge and training. They worked with patients, he said, to develop treatment plans. Not so in Newfoundland, said Bennett. Here, many doctors resisted self-educated patients. They insisted on imposing their own ideas and wouldn't listen to the patients, who often knew more about their condition than the doctors.

Bennett and Brace, like other AIDS patients from this province, faced an impossible dilemma. They wanted to be in their home and around family in their final years and months, but had to consider that it would almost certainly speed up their demise to return to Newfoundland and Labrador. They decided to return nonetheless. Interviewed following their arrival in the province, Bennett said that after returning and experiencing the abysmal state of the medical system in this province and its treatment of AIDS patients firsthand, he and Brace were second-guessing their decision and thinking about returning to the mainland. "But time is short," he said (Ibid.).

As it turned out, Bennett died in March 1996 of kidney failure brought on by AIDS. He died before Brace, who spoke to Dave Cochrane at *The Muse* about his partner's death later that year (Cochrane 1996).

Bennett and Brace, like dozens of other ex-pat Newfoundlanders, moved home when their condition worsened. Others chose to stay away, either because they feared the stigma and poor treatment for which the province was known, or because they had no supportive and welcoming family to return to. In a 1992 interview with *The Express,* Upward reported that at Casey House, a hospice for AIDS patients in Toronto, the second largest demographic of people who had died there were Newfoundlanders (Dwyer 1992).

The AIDS crisis affected society in other ways too. As patients and their advocates struggled with treatment options – there was both a dearth of effective treatments, and yet a profusion of ever-changing experimental options – many of them came to acknowledge the beneficial effects of marijuana in treating the myriad symptoms and bringing some degree of comfort to patients. Yet marijuana was still criminalized at that point. AIDS organizations, including the NL AIDS Association, took on a lead role in lobbying for more accessible policies surrounding medical marijuana.

The Department of Health wasn't the only government body with a role to play in AIDS treatment. The Department of Social Services was responsible for welfare and other social support payments. The blanket policies the department used were not equipped for supporting patients with HIV/AIDS, advocates warned. There was an implicit assumption built into the province's social services system that people requiring welfare were elderly and had either large families and children to help them, or savings from a lifetime of employment. The system was simply not designed for supporting a growing demographic of young, single, terminally ill people. Many of the necessary medications for HIV/AIDS patients were not covered by Medicare. Patients were incurring bills of $2800 a month or more for medications simply to stay alive (Flynn 1997).

"Are we going to do as we have done with just about everything else in Newfoundland – wait until it's too late as we have done with our fishery?" asked Yetman bitterly in a June, 1992 interview with *The Evening Telegram*'s Moira Baird (Baird 1992).

Department of Social Services policies put AIDS patients in a difficult situation, and not just because of the lack of funding for medicines. Social assistance recipients were provided access to a drug card that paid for some of their vital medication – but only if they were unemployed. The consequence of this is that many patients were forced to give up their jobs in order to receive the drug card that enabled them to access life-saving medications.

"For a lot of people, there comes a point where they have to make a decision – if they want their drugs they're going to have to quit their job and go on social assistance because they can't afford the drugs," explained Yetman to *The Evening Telegram*.

Our system is encouraging people to get out of the workforce. And in my personal opinion, that encourages death in people because they lose control of their lives, they become dependent on a system.

Once you lose control, you're losing self-esteem, self-respect and you're also dealing with a terminal illness for which you know – at this point – there's no cure. So, these people end up suffering severe trauma, severe psychological strain and stress which in turn deteriorates the immune system (Ibid.).

AIDS capital of Newfoundland

On July 12, 1991, the province's first HIV-positive baby was born, garnering front-page headlines ("It was only a matter of time," said Dr. Stratton to

The Evening Telegram). In October 1991, the province broached another grim milestone with the first known woman to die of AIDS in the province. Stratton pointed out that other women may have died of the disease but their families may have covered up, or not known, that they had AIDS (Ryan 1991). Urban myths continued to perpetuate that the disease affected only men. And gossip and innuendo of all sorts continued to obfuscate educational efforts. In the case of the woman who died in October 1991, Betty Ralph of the NL AIDS Association told *The Evening Telegram* that rumours of her death began circulating three years earlier, when she'd first been diagnosed. It created "quite a bit of chaos" for the woman to have to contend with widely circulated rumours of her death while she struggled with the disease. Rumours also circulated that she had contracted the disease because she was hemophiliac or a drug user – neither of which was true, said Ralph. She said the woman had in fact contracted HIV through heterosexual sex in her teens (Ibid.).

"When a straight woman dies, maybe it will hit home to them," Ralph told *The Evening Telegram* bitterly. "But somehow, I doubt it. I don't know what it will take to show people. I guess a lot more people have to become statistics before people will believe it. I hate to say it but that's what it takes to make people realize how serious this is" (Ibid.).

As activists continued to apply pressure and government mulled over how seriously to take the AIDS crisis, a sudden surge of cases in Conception Bay North transformed the political and social landscape (Bailey 1995). In 1988, the region reported its first two HIV cases. By 1997, the region garnered national headlines as health officials identified 42 local cases, 31 of them women, and warned there could be as many as 150 cases in the region (Sullivan 1995, Sweet 1997). As cases skyrocketed, government was torn in its public response. At a workshop panel held in early 1993 in Upper Island Cove, a public health nurse denied there was any AIDS epidemic in Conception Bay North (Flynn 1993). On the ground, health officials launched a massive education and testing campaign beginning in 1990. In 1994-95, a concerted public health campaign managed to double the numbers of people being tested in the area. In April 1995, the Canadian Red Cross issued a blanket ban on blood donations from the region, after it was identified as a high-risk area (Sweet 1997).

"In the AIDS capital of Newfoundland, everyone knows sex can be deadly, but few people seem to be taking precautions before becoming intimate," wrote Deana Stokes Sullivan in *The Evening Telegram* on March 26, 1995.

The simple truth that the disease was spreading through heterosexual sex continued to defy popular belief, in the community but also in more educated circles. The theory was proposed that a special, unique strain of HIV was circulating in CBN, and public health officials launched a study to investigate the notion (Barron 1995B).

"The spread with which, and the ease with which this transmission appeared to have occurred raised questions based on the fact that certain strains of HIV may be more efficiently transmitted through heterosexual intercourse," Dr. Sam Ratnum, director of the Newfoundland Public Health Laboratory, told *The Evening Telegram* on December 1, 1995. The study concluded that this was not the case (Ibid.).

"What we have here is a type B strain – the same strain that is prevalent elsewhere in the country. So there is nothing unusual about our situation," concluded Dr. Ratnum (Ibid.).

The situation took a further twist in 1992, when the justice system began wading into the epidemic. Raymond Mercer of Upper Island Cove, in CBN, was charged and convicted of criminal negligence causing bodily harm for knowingly infecting two Conception Bay North women with the HIV virus. One of the women was 15 when she was infected. The other woman was a 22-year-old who subsequently moved to Toronto. She was diagnosed early after she noticed symptoms and got tested in Toronto, which enabled her to receive treatment earlier than most (R. v. Mercer 1993).

Mercer was initially only sentenced to 2.5 years, but upon appeal the sentence was increased to 11 years. The previous judge had erred by not considering the importance of deterrence in sentencing Mercer, ruled the NL Supreme Court of Appeal judge (Ibid.).

"This man knowingly and deliberately caused grievous bodily harm to two young women which will lead to their untimely deaths. His crimes are even more exacerbating when considered in the light of his callous and ruthless deception of his victims," stated the judge (Ibid.). In October 1999, Mercer was denied parole.

In a similar case, Harold Williams of Shea Heights in St. John's was charged with a criminal offence for infecting a woman with HIV. He was found guilty on April 26, 2000 by Judge Malcolm Rowe (Belec 2000).

The sudden involvement of the NL justice system had a profound national impact. Some local activists speculate that it was all the panic and media attention around the CBN outbreak that generated a feeling of pressure among law enforcement officials that they needed to do something. Others speculate that it was in part due to the justice system's complicity in covering up sexual abuse at Mount Cashel that officials felt pressure to now be seen to be proactive about something. The move to criminalize HIV transmission suddenly posed a new threat to patients across the country, especially those who might not have known they were positive. HIV-positive sex workers in particular faced an untenable situation: doing sex work was the only way they could afford the HIV medications they needed to survive. Disclosing their status would cut off their income and ability to access life-saving medications. Not disclosing would now put them at further risk of criminal charges.

The surge in CBN came with profound social cost both for AIDS patients as well as residents of the area. Many people viciously (and wrongly) blamed the local surge on ex-pat Newfoundlanders – especially gay men – who contracted the disease outside the province and then came home to die. In St. John's, university students from CBN lied about their region of origin, and job applicants were often asked if they were from the area. A woman from CBN reported being hired by a St. John's bar but warned by her employers not to tell anyone where she was from. Members of a rock band from Bay Roberts (a town in CBN) were booked to play a show in downtown St. John's and upon arrival discovered they were being advertised as being from Corner Brook. The bar was afraid no one would show up if patrons knew the band was from CBN (Flynn 1994).

Even children were not exempt from this treatment. The mother of a Bay Roberts high school student complained to *The Evening Telegram* on November 4, 1994, that her daughter had been viciously ostracized at a high school volleyball tournament in Bonavista when other students learned she was from CBN (Ibid.).

Eventually, by 1997, all the education and outreach efforts appeared to be paying off as infection rates started to drop. "Conception Bay North may finally be able to shed its reputation as the AIDS capital of Newfoundland," wrote Barb Sweet in *The Evening Telegram* on October 21, 1997.

Activists and health officials continued to struggle on the front lines. The CBN outbreak underscored how Newfoundland and Labrador's infection spread assumed demographic qualities unique in Canada. By 1992, the province had the second lowest incidence of AIDS in the country, at 35.1 cases per million people. But it also had the highest rate of teenage HIV infection in the country, and the second highest rate of female infection in the country. In an interview with *The Express* that year, Upward raged against the myths he felt were fuelling this spread (Gullage 1991).

"It's no good sticking our heads into the sand and saying 'We're Newfoundlanders, this is not going to be our problem,'" he said. "You don't have to be gay and you don't have to be a mainlander. We have our own homegrown problems right here in this province and it's going to get worse" (Ibid.).

Organizing for awareness

It wasn't just government inaction that frustrated the activists, but the clear evidence of homophobia that still permeated government. Ralph recalled one meeting with public health officials which the provincial minister of health also attended, and at which he said something that set her off with particular vehemence. They were discussing a particularly sad case involving a schoolteacher from a small community who had died. Shortly before his death, the community learned he had AIDS.

"The people were so uninformed. His poor parents, who were senior citizens, were treated cruelly. They put a quarantine [sign] on their door. Now why would you do that? There was so much fear – fear was dominating," Ralph recalled.

The schoolteacher had bought a new car not long before his death, but his parents were unable to sell it; no one would buy a car belonging to someone who had died of AIDS.

The activists described this incident to the health minister at their meeting. He responded by denying that there were many of "those people" on the island. Ralph turned and tore into him.

I asked him: 'What do you mean by 'those people'? What do you mean, we don't have many of 'those people' on the island? You really don't know! And you're the minister of health!' That to me was the wrong attitude. I didn't appreciate that. And I knows the b'ys that were sat there with me definitely didn't appreciate it (Ralph 2022).

The stigma they encountered in government meetings was part of a wider problem, though. "What surprised me the most was that it was educated people," said Ralph. "If it was someone that lived in a small isolated community, well I could understand that at times, because you didn't have the information. But if you're educated, there's no reason for you to be so ignorant."

Susan Rose, some of whose colleagues knew or suspected her to be a lesbian when she worked as a schoolteacher in the 1990s, recalls one colleague who refused to sit next to her in staff meetings because he was afraid of catching AIDS.

As a teenager, RM Kennedy was coming to terms with his own sexuality while growing up in Conception Bay North, the epicentre of the crisis. "I definitely remember that the first time I really heard the word homosexual, like where it became a concrete concept, was definitely during the AIDS crisis," he recalled.

Bay Roberts was about ten kilometres away, that's where we went to get groceries and things like that. There was a man who tested positive, and he ran the bread store – he had this little bread store. He got run out of town. The bread shop got shut down, he tested positive... I remember everybody talked about it. 'You can't go to the bread shop because he's got AIDS, because he's a homosexual' [they said] (Kennedy 2022).

When word got out that her business partner, Billy Neville, was HIV positive, Ralph noticed a drop in some of their regular customers.

I did have customers that left. Someone said to me: 'Do you realize that so-and-so and so-and-so and so-and-so are not coming to your shop any more? And I thought, well yes. And they said to me: 'That's because they know about Bill.' And I said to them: 'Oh well! C'est la vie' (Ralph 2022).

But people surprised her as well.

I really noticed, that some people you'd think would be more open-minded – nope. And the people you thought would run in the opposite direction? Turned out to be people that would stand alongside you. That's when I really

discovered that what you see is not always what you get. Just because some-
one is conservative and presents themselves very conservatively, doesn't mean
they're ignorant. And people who seem very open-minded, sometimes are not
as open-minded as you think they are! (Ibid.).

As activists countered misinformation and pushed for change, and as infection rates rose, the churches began to feel the pressure and started reining in
their active opposition to public education and health measures. Yet they still
refrained from actively supporting those initiatives. That, for Yetman, wasn't
good enough.

"Our churches are not supporting publicly – publicly is very important,"
he told *The Evening Telegram* in June 1992. "It's very nice that they say 'We are
supportive. We don't reject anybody.' That is fine. But how does the person sitting home in isolation know that?"

Many activists were open in their scathing condemnation of government.
In a May 1994 interview with *The Evening Telegram*, Bonnie Belec reported that
the AIDS Committee was in good shape "no thanks to the province." In 1993,
the group fundraised roughly $20,000, she reported, which was disbursed to
40 people living with AIDS in the province. The federal government was also
kicking in some support, including $170,000 to support the group's operations.
The province, she said witheringly, gave nothing (Belec 1994).

Testing blood

In the early years of the crisis, on February 6, 1986, GAIN helped to coordinate a meeting at the Health Sciences Centre, billed as "a discussion concerning
the problems surrounding having the blood test done to see if you have been
exposed to the AIDS virus." Blood tests would be offered immediately following the meeting to anyone wishing to have them.

The problem GAIN activists wanted to tackle was the lack of anonymous
testing. The lack of anonymous tests had two consequences: on the one hand,
people refused to get tested. At the same time, those who could afford it left the
province to be tested (Jackson 1992, The Packet 1999). Karl Wells recalls that as
an out gay man who loved to travel, some of his colleagues assumed he was
HIV positive because of his frequent trips outside the province. They assumed
he was receiving treatment elsewhere.

According to Ralph:

Anonymity was key. Anonymity was what everyone wanted. We were
trying to get more people tested, because I knew we had a lot more people
walking around with HIV than what we realized. And a lot of people were
asymptomatic. But it was a real issue, that people didn't even want to go in
to be tested. That was because people would see them, in the Health Sciences
Complex (Ralph 2022).

Eventually, she said, advocates persuaded some of the public health officials to adopt a numbering system; patients would be referred to by numbers,
and results would be released by numbers. Only the doctor would have a confidential file linking name and number. This helped increase testing numbers,
she said. So did increased awareness.

Those who refused to get tested were sometimes blamed by others for contributing to the spread of the disease. Ralph, looking back on events, says she
never judged people for refusing to get tested. She also didn't blame those who
were HIV-positive from hiding that fact from those close to them.

*You had to watch it, because – jobs. That was the biggest fear and why a
lot of people never came out earlier. No matter what anyone says, I'm sorry but
you have to pay your bills. You have to live. Don't go condemning someone,
because you're not going to be paying their bills for them!*

*Some people would get upset, and say: 'I don't know why so-and-so [won't
get tested].' B'ys, live in the real world. There are negative people out there.
And if you got a job, you can't just come out. You might want to, but you got
to be realistic too. So if somebody didn't want to say something [about their
HIV status], to me that made no difference* (Ibid.).

Former volunteers with the ACNL I interviewed confessed to having to
make difficult ethical decisions in their daily work and lives. Because of their
ACNL volunteer work they often knew about patients' HIV status while those
patients kept their HIV-positive status hidden from others. Sometimes volunteers would see patients at the local clubs, hooking up with or going home
with people (including the volunteers' own friends). Should they warn their
friends, or even strangers, that the person they were going home with was HIV
positive? It might save someone's life. It would also mean violating their commitment to confidentiality. Volunteers had to navigate these difficult ethical
decisions on their own. Some of those I spoke with did indeed sometimes warn
people, divulging a patient's status in the process. Others placed confidentiality first, and looked the other way. Many of them stopped going out to the
clubs entirely, so as to avoid being put into situations that might require them
to make these difficult choices.

The stigma and pressure were immense. Trudy Parsons, who joined the
AIDS Committee, gave public talks where she candidly shared her thoughts
of suicide after being diagnosed with HIV. "I had it all planned out. I thought
of using a gun, but then again I was afraid of guns. I thought if I was to shoot
myself there would be a lot of blood around. How would people clean it up? I
didn't want anyone to be HIV positive because of me."

Fighting AIDS on campus

With its own medical clinic administering to thousands of students from across the province and beyond, Memorial University also came under pressure to play a more proactive role in education and protection. University officials struck an advisory committee on AIDS in 1988 but the committee soon came under fire from queer activists on campus (Whitaker 1988). The MUN Gay And Lesbian Association (GALA) publicly criticized the fact no out gay activists were appointed to the committee.

"Even though AIDS is not a 'gay disease' the homosexual community has been dealing with it since 1981, which is seven years more than the university has," MUN GALA president Ron Knowling told *The Muse* in January 1988. "So it should have a valuable contribution to make" (Whitaker 1988).

Dr. Russell Harper, chair of the committee and Director of Student Health, defended the committee, arguing that it already had nine members and any more would make it ineffective. He said he had discussed the committee's composition at length with Memorial's president and vice-president.

"There was no way to represent every group in the university, the homosexual sector was not the only one omitted," he said. Harper also suggested that since the "homosexual sector" had been dealing with the disease for so long and educated themselves so well, they were perhaps less in need of support from the committee. Knowling fired back that gay organizations were the ones already doing all the work around AIDS, but they were doing it without any institutional support or resources. Now the university was setting up its own brand-new committee with resources and money without involving the groups that were already doing the same work (Ibid.).

"Many people's reactions to the AIDS issue is due to homophobia," Knowling pointed out. "The whole issue is tied up with sex and sexuality, and this makes it hard to judge people's reactions. In the interest of fairness and equality it would seem proper to have a member of the homosexual community of MUN on the committee" (Ibid.).

In September 1989, the MUN Students' Union (MUNSU) made provincial headlines by announcing plans to distribute free condoms, in addition to educational pamphlets, to each of the roughly 2500 first-year students, an initiative made possible in part through federal funding. MUNSU President Robin Russell chose her words carefully, conscious of the fierce animosity of the province's religious leadership to such initiatives. She told *The Evening Telegram*: "We are not promoting promiscuity... We only want to educate and create awareness among students. Students are not taking it as seriously as they should" (Will 1989).

That year, MUNSU took the lead in installing condom machines in the Breezeway Bar on campus, which the students' union owned and operated. In the first five months, Breezeway Manager Gary Clarke told *The Evening Telegram*, they sold 587 condoms at a cost of 75 cents each, with the women's washroom selling twice as many as the men's. The students' union also entered into negotiations with the university administration in an attempt to persuade them to install condom machines in other washrooms on campus (Ibid.).

The give-aways to first years included a bookmark demonstrating the proper way to put on a condom. This generated complaints from religious groups both on and off campus. An elected representative on the union's board was interviewed by *The Evening Telegram*, and his comments reflected the pressure some union representatives felt. He said it was a good idea to put condom machines in the bathroom for those who want to use them, "but they shouldn't give them out for free if some people are going to be offended" (Ibid.).

Meanwhile, as awareness slowly grew, an array of grassroots communities began organizing to fill the gap which lingered from government underfunding of support programs for people with AIDS. "Walks for AIDS" became a frequent undertaking in a growing number of communities across the province, raising funds for individuals and families dealing with HIV/AIDS as well as organizations like the NL AIDS Committee. The AIDS Candlelight Memorial and Mobilization was launched, and Memorial University launched an official AIDS/STDs Awareness Week.

There were creative education efforts, too. In August 1992, the provincial Oxfam branch brought the South African-based puppet troupe Puppets Against AIDS to the province for a month-long tour. The tour inspired a local group of young people to form their own puppet troupe for the same purpose. JIGSIMBIZA, comprised of Becky Moyes, Denise Hann, Andreae Prozesky, Geoff Shinkle, Leslie Thompson, Temma Frecker, and Tristram Clarke, modeled their work off the South African troupe, but fused with local culture. They took their show on the road across Canada in the summer of 1996 (Vaughan-Jackson 1996).

On April 14, 1989, the Canadian Rights and Liberties Federation and the NL Human Rights Association jointly put off an AIDS conference at the Hotel Newfoundland in St. John's titled "Striking a Balance: Responses to AIDS." On November 30, 1989, the Institute for Social and Economic Research (ISER) located at Memorial University held a conference titled "AIDS, the Social Sciences, and the Local Community." All these initiatives contributed to pushing back the stigma and ignorance that still surrounded the subject.

But widespread stigma lingered. In 1990, a poll of 548 medical students conducted by University of Toronto professor Kathryn Taylor found that half of them believed it should be acceptable to refuse to treat HIV patients. 70 percent of them had negative attitudes toward lesbians and gays, and one in six responded that they would not want their child to be in the same room as someone who was HIV positive. The homophobia revealed by the survey was roundly denounced by Toronto-based AIDS activists.

Discrimination at work

Today, discrimination against people with HIV is against the law in Canada. That was not the case during the AIDS panic of the 1980s and 1990s. In May 1988, the Canadian Human Rights Commission adopted and published its 'Policy on AIDS', which argued against discrimination but also stated that it would recognize being HIV-free as a Bona Fide Job Requirement in certain circumstances, permitting employers to fire or refuse to hire people with HIV into those positions (CHRC 1988).

The prevarication of provincial institutions when it came to protecting the human rights of people with AIDS was demonstrated by Memorial University, whose Board of Regents adopted an AIDS/HIV Policy on November 10, 1988. While it offered guarantees that students would not be discriminated against in university admissions decisions on the basis of HIV status, it left decisions about on-campus housing applications up to the discretion of the Director of Housing along with the Director of Student Health Services, to be determined "on a case-by-case basis." Students who were HIV positive were "requested" to inform Student Health Services.

There were further caveats: "As with any behaviour which clearly threatens the safety and welfare of others, a student with HIV infection/AIDS who knowingly engages in behaviour which is likely to transmit the virus to others, or in any way deliberately endangers the safety of others, will be subject to disciplinary review" (Board of Regents 1988).

Protections for university employees were somewhat stronger, guaranteeing non-discrimination in hiring and stating that "An employee shall not refuse to work with, teach, provide care for or service to a person with HIV infection/ AIDS by reason of that fact alone" (Ibid.). Confidentiality was promised on a "need-to-know" basis. Memorial president Dr. Leslie Harris meanwhile established a MUN Presidential Committee on AIDS to provide advice.

On August 15, 1992, the NL Employers Council spoke out in an article in *The Evening Telegram*, calling on local businesses not to discriminate against employees with HIV/AIDS. "We would encourage all business people to give fair and responsible consideration without discrimination against anybody," said Jim Pitcher, president of the Council. "As an organization we must provide access for disabled people and also persons with AIDS." He urged businesses to contact the ACNL for advice and for help in developing workplace policies.

It wasn't an idle concern. In 1988, Trudy Parsons, a 23-year-old employee with Comcare Canada Limited, was fired after she tested positive for HIV. Parsons was not one to take discrimination without fighting back.

Parsons, from Bay Roberts, was well acquainted with AIDS before her own diagnosis. A close high school friend of hers had been diagnosed with HIV. So when Parsons moved to St. John's, eager to find a volunteering commitment, she contacted the AIDS Committee in addition to other local volunteer agencies. The AIDS Committee was the only one that contacted her back, and so she started volunteering with them.

She instantly fell in love with the group. "You could smoke in their office and drink all the coffee that you wanted to," she recalled, thirty years later. "And it was really social so it was a lot of fun. It was really social. It was like a big old party happening all the time."

The Committee was brimming with volunteers, and Parsons says many of them have remained close friends to the present day. The group's strength, she feels, was the effort organizers made to make everyone feel welcome, and to ensure the environment was as social and upbeat as possible.

It was very welcoming. Like you'd go in thinking this is going to be really sad and really serious, and every preconceived notion that I had about that experience was not at all what happened.

We used to have parties at the AIDS Committee, when the building was closed, and we used to do that a lot. Big parties. Nowadays when you have a party at a non-profit you usually can't even have alcohol.

Back in the day you had to print off your own pamphlets and fold them and there'd be this big table of people sitting around having wonderful conversation and smoking cigarettes and joking around and folding pamphlets. I used to be a volunteer coordinator in another organization after, and we started getting those resource materials done outside the office, and it really took away from the liveliness of an organization. Like, that's an important piece to keep (Parsons 2022).

When she first started volunteering for the ACNL, Parsons was working at a local bar, making good money, she recalls. She wanted to go into nursing, and so she decided to leave that job for a lower-paying job with Comcare Canada Limited, in the hopes it would better position her to enter nursing. Comcare was a homecare company, which among other things, had a provincial contract to provide services for people with HIV/AIDS. When Parsons began working with them, she was at first the only employee of theirs who was willing to work with AIDS patients. All the other employees refused.

In the early fall of 1991, not too long after she started working with Comcare, Parsons was contacted by public health officials and informed she'd been identified through contact tracing as someone who had had sex with a person who'd been diagnosed with HIV. Several months earlier, Parsons recalled, she had worked up the courage to ask a local doctor, who was testing her for other STIs, to test her for HIV as well. He refused, and laughed her out of his office, telling her there was no way she could have HIV.

When Parsons did the test following the contact tracing, the tests all had to be sent to the mainland. Normally this process took two weeks, but because of the large number of tests being done at that time, it took six weeks for her results to be returned.

Parsons spent those six weeks coming to terms with the possibility she might be HIV positive. The public health nurse who contacted her shared her personal home phone number with Parsons. Parsons spent hours on the phone with the nurse in the evenings, asking every question that came to her mind.

When the results came back, she learned she was HIV-positive.

"My benefit has always been that I've been very naïve in my life, and I still am," Parsons reflected. Having come to terms with the likelihood that she was positive during those six weeks of waiting for her test results, she now spoke openly at work about her HIV diagnosis. She never imagined it could lead to her losing her job. She had the impression her local colleagues were okay with it. But when word of her HIV positive status got to the company's national headquarters, the response was swift and unforgiving.

At the end of a 12-hour overnight shift, Parsons was told to come into the office before going home. She asked if she could shower and change first, but was told no, she had to return to the office immediately. When she walked in that night, she recalls, she thought she was going to be given a raise; her performance had always been highly praised by her supervisors. Instead they asked her point-blank: "Are you HIV positive?" She told them yes. They said in that case she couldn't work any more shifts for them.

Parsons, floored, fired back that if she was available for work and they weren't going to call her in for shifts, they still had to pay her. She can't recall where she got that idea, but said the company didn't dispute it: they told her to leave but she would continue receiving a paycheque.

Parsons immediately contacted the AIDS Committee and told Peter Wood what had happened. Wood told her to keep him informed, and if they tried to fire her, to let him know the instant it happened.

She was suspended from work, but still receiving a paycheque. The situation forced her to tell her family. She was still coming to terms with the situation herself, but given the fact she was now suspended with pay, she felt she needed to tell her family before they found out from anyone else.

A few weeks passed, and then three days before Christmas she received a letter from Comcare officially terminating her employment. As soon as she read the letter, Parsons made a bee-line for the AIDS Committee office. She walked in, and found Wood sitting there working. She told him what had happened. He sat there a moment staring at her. Then without saying a word, he calmly rose and walked around the office, ripping down every poster that bore the Comcare logo on it. He slowly and deliberately gathered every one of the company's posters and pamphlets, and he threw every single one in the garbage.

"That one act made me feel really calm," recalled Parsons, still moved to this day. "It said okay – I have people that are on my side and know that this is very terribly wrong."

Having disposed of the company's materials, he sat back down. "What do you want to do about it?" he asked her.

I said, I don't even know, but I can't let this go! My thing was, if I let this go, then it's going to set a precedent for me allowing other people to treat me badly over something that I really can't control. And it's ultimately none of their business. I knew I had to nip that in the bud right away. I couldn't let that go. I didn't

want to do any of this shit, I really didn't. But I knew that if I let it go, I couldn't
live with myself. It was about my dignity and my sense of self-worth.

So we talked about it, and he went over some ideas about what might
happen, and we decided that in the new year we would file the human rights
complaint (Ibid.).

The complaint process was a difficult one, she recalled. During the course
of her complaint, she learned of at least two other complaints that had been
filed over HIV-related job discrimination in the city – a pianist who used to
play at local bars, and a woman who'd been fired from a fast-food restaurant.

Parsons approached the Human Rights Association, the community-based
group which played more of an activist role than the government-affiliated
Human Rights Commission, and they recommended that she obtain a lawyer.
"But no lawyers would take it," she said. "They wouldn't touch it."

Unable to find a lawyer on her own, she met directly with the Human
Rights Commission herself in January 1992 and filed a complaint against Comcare. She later expanded the complaint to include the provincial Department
of Social Services. She wanted financial compensation from Comcare, but from
the government she wanted a change to legislation to prevent companies from
discriminating against employees on the basis of their HIV status. The Commission at first suggested she settle for $1500 and drop the request for legisla-
tive change. Her complaint was difficult for them, she said, because although
it was in part against the company that fired her, she also wanted the provincial
government held responsible over its failure to enact legislation to prevent job-
related discrimination.

"I felt like [the Commission] was frustrated with me and didn't want to be
bothered," she said. "I was told that if it went to tribunal, that I would lose."

Unable to find a lawyer to support her with the process, and fighting the
case on her own, she was often bewildered by the legal language used by the
government, Comcare, and Human Rights Commission alike. "I didn't understand the language. And nobody else that I knew did either. Like I didn't understand what the heck they were saying. Even the Human Rights Commission, even the way that they communicated was, I just didn't understand."

Wood tried to help, especially in handling the media around her complaint.
In a joint interview with *The Evening Telegram*, Wood expressed the ACNL's
outrage at her dismissal. "AIDS is not just a mainland disease or a gay disease,"
he told *The Evening Telegram* reporter Craig Jackson. Parsons, meanwhile, accused the company of targeting her because she was willing to be open about
her HIV status (Jackson 1993).

"I really don't think I was fired due to HIV. I think I was fired because I was
willing to admit I was HIV-positive," she told Jackson. "I've been angry and
bitter and I probably will be until the day I die" (Ibid.).

The Evening Telegram reached out to Comcare for comment. Lewis Nick-
erson, the company's national Vice-President Administration, claimed the

company had no choice, and were required by law to fire Parsons because the province's Day Care and Homemaker Services Act stipulated that a health care company cannot employ someone who has a communicable disease. HIV was classified as such a disease under the Act (Ibid.).

Government approached her "many times" seeking to settle outside the human rights tribunal process, Parsons said. On March 25, 1993, the Department of Social Services offered to compensate her for lost wages and benefits, as well as provide compensation for humiliation, in order to avoid a formal human rights complaint hearing. "Only I never went in looking for a financial settlement [from government]. I went in wanting the legislation to be changed. I wanted the company to give me a financial settlement."

In the end Parsons agreed to settle privately. She received a financial settlement of $12,000 from Comcare – one of the highest discrimination-related settlements in Newfoundland at the time, she was told – and she said the provincial government also signed a document committing to enact changes to legislation to de-list AIDS from the Communicable Disease Act (which allowed HIV-free status to be considered a bona fide job requirement) and move it to the Infectious Disease Act instead.

For Parsons, the victory was bittersweet. "I'm disgusted to live in a province that discriminates against the normal taxpayer I want to be," she told *The Evening Telegram*. She complained that the province had seemed like it was dragging out efforts to amend the Act. Comcare itself got off pretty easy, which annoyed Parsons, leaving the provincial government to shoulder the bulk of the financial compensation. The company was only required to make a $2500 contribution to the NL AIDS Committee (Ibid.).

Parsons was later featured in the NFB film *Thinking Positive*, produced in 1993, the same year famed Codco actor and comedian Tommy Sexton died.

Outreach and education work continues

After being laid off by Comcare, Parsons threw herself into HIV education and prevention work with the ACNL, traveling the province and speaking openly about her experience living with HIV. "Back then just to say publicly that you were HIV positive was an act of activism," she reflected. "All you had to do was show up, and say: I am."

So Parsons showed up – from one end of the island to the other. For years, this meant she was constantly on the road.

We would go where people were. The smaller communities were so much easier to work with. The larger the community, the harder they were to work with. We would go wherever we were asked to go, and oftentimes the smaller communities would be like 'nobody ever comes here!' so they'd just be grateful that you cared enough to show up! They didn't take you for granted.

Not that it wasn't difficult. Every time I would do an evening session with the adults, some drunk guy would jump up and say: 'You're a whore! I wouldn't have sex with you!' and then storm out. That worked in my favour though, because I was young, and I was very tiny, and I looked frail, and people don't like it when you yell at somebody who looks like they're a teenager. So all of a sudden the energy in the room would change to be all [supportive] (Parsons 2022).

Parsons worked with a couple of other women to develop a proposal for a Women and AIDS Project, which received funding from Health Canada. They were able to coordinate a few retreats for groups of 25-50 women, including HIV positive women.

Parsons often went into communities on her own, and also experienced the phenomenon of teachers and principals trying to control what she said during sessions with students.

I would be alone, and oftentimes the principal and the guidance counsellor were men. They would get me into a room and sit me in a chair and they wouldn't sit down, they'd stand over me and tell me what I could and couldn't say. I don't know what they thought I was going to tell people. They would tell me all the things I couldn't talk about – 'Don't talk about anal sex!' Like, I'm not going give a guide, you guys! Good grief! (Ibid.).

Parsons said the ACNL began getting the schools to sign an agreement stipulating that although the schools could set guidelines around what material could be presented, presenters would be allowed to honestly answer any questions asked by students.

So as soon as I got on stage I'd be like: 'Guess what? I was told not to talk about this, this and this. But if you ask, then I have to answer!' Then the men would be like – 'We're not going to invite you back any more!' To which I replied: 'I know! And I don't care – I'll probably be dead next year, so I don't care if you're not going to invite me back!' (Ibid.).

Parsons, and the other AIDS educators, also quickly discovered that students were starved for information on a wide range of subjects, which were being censored by the denominational education system. This included a lot of content not even related to AIDS. When the ACNL activists showed up at schools, students would find ways to approach them with a broad range of questions.

The things that young people, the youth, would spring on me was like – 'I think I'm gay' or 'I think I have an eating disorder' or 'I'm being molested at home.' They'd whisper it in your ear. You'd be walking by them and they'd lean in and they'd go: 'I think I'm gay' and you'd go: 'Okay!' I'd just tell them: 'It's not always going to be this way. Things change and you're not always going to stay here. It'll be okay.' I mean, what do you say? It was wild. It's so different now than what it was then. Sometimes we don't take a pause to acknowledge the huge shift that's happened. More shifting of course needs to happen, but we've come a long way!

So I started bringing resources about those things. They could get the HIV stuff from the public health department, from their school, we could mail them all that stuff. But what I brought with me was the other stuff (Ibid.).

The more education work Parsons did, the more she came to realize the young people in schools were often her closest allies; they were often more open-minded and accepting than the adults she encountered. One of her most frightening experiences occurred in the community of Traytown. She had to spend a few days in the area, so she tried to rent a motel room. Everyone knew she was coming to do AIDS education, and the person running the motel refused to put her up in the main building, instead giving her a self-contained cabin on the edge of the property. It didn't have a phone, and hadn't even been cleared of snow – she had to trudge through snowdrifts to get to it.

As she sat alone in the cabin that night, she heard noises outside. Local men from the community were driving around her cabin on skidoos, throwing rocks at her cabin.

It was terrifying! I didn't have a phone in the room, so I asked the [receptionist], and she asked: 'What do you need a phone for?' I explained what was happening. I called Gerard [Yetman] at the AIDS Committee, and I told him, and he goes: 'Well do you want to come home?' And I said: 'No, I want to finish what I came here to do.' But I was afraid. I was so afraid. I mean I was like a hundred pounds soaking wet. So he said: 'Do you want me to come?' And I said no — I didn't want to be rescued either (Ibid.).

The next day, when she spoke at a local high school, she told the students about what she had experienced the night before. That evening she returned to the cabin, wondering if the harassment would continue. What happened instead was that several of the teenagers she'd spoken to earlier in the day showed up unexpectedly at her door. Worried about her, and disgusted at the behaviour of the adults in the community, they showed up so she wouldn't be alone that evening. "So the teenagers would show up in the evenings," Parsons recalled, "some of the boys and some of the girls, and they'd sit and stay, until it was time for me to go to bed. And [the harassment] stopped. They were great. The kids were so good. I have a deep abiding respect for young people."

Dealing with death

While dealing with the strangers in small communities was challenging, debates and disagreements also arose among volunteers themselves. Those involved in the movement, patients and allies alike, often argued over their preferred choice of terminology. One of the arguments was between the term People With AIDS (PWA) or People Living with AIDS (PLA). Others argued against both terms.

"There were people who were like, 'I'm not living, I'm dying!' explained

Parsons. "And they were dying. They didn't want to use the L any more, they wanted to use the D."

As patients struggled to come to terms with their very real mortality, their community realized the importance of celebrating every possible moment while people were alive.

The idea was — let's have some fun, at any opportunity that we can. We would take people out of the hospital, out of palliative care, and bring them to a party. And sometimes they would die a few days later. They were very, very ill. Peter [Wood] used to tell us that when he was in Nova Scotia, they would bring sex workers in to the palliative care unit. And I was told — see I was trained by gay men, and I was told — if somebody needs that, you have to arrange it. I said: 'Okay, I don't know anything about that, but I'll figure it out.' So they would do all kinds of stuff! They were good guys (Parsons 2022).

The psychological burden of working so closely with death took its toll on the volunteers. "We would spend time in palliative care with people we'd never met before, because their own families wouldn't come. Or their families wouldn't accept that they were ill and then they'd want to argue about it. I mean, the person was very clearly dying," said Parsons.

I feel like we didn't [cope]. There was a lot of burnout. There were times when the environment was very toxic too. It was good and it was bad. People were dying pretty quickly. It was a lot of death. You'd go to three funerals in the run of a week. So you couldn't stop to think about them. Once somebody was dead, you moved on to the next person. And that was it. There wasn't time – how do you grieve that many people? By the time I was 24 I stopped counting, and I think the number of funerals I'd attended by that point was 74. I was 24 years old. You had to stop counting (Ibid.).

In 1992, CBC-NL produced a half-hour documentary called *The Death of Ray Condon*. Condon, originally from Calvert on the island, had been a schoolteacher in Labrador West when he received a positive HIV test result in 1991 at the age of 46. He dedicated the remainder of his life to public education, traveling both the island and Labrador and speaking at schools and other venues. He spoke openly about his life as a gay man and about his experience with AIDS. He also allowed a CBC-NL camera crew to follow him until his death in 1992. The documentary produced after his death was a clear and sympathetic portrait of a gay man and his final year struggling with AIDS.

Yet the stigma faced by those diagnosed with HIV was immense. Parsons recalled one community around the bay that she visited with Yetman and Upward, to put off a workshop on a weekend. As they set up their materials and locals started filtering in, Parsons detected a strange atmosphere in the room.

They were acting weird. I didn't know what was going on. They wouldn't make eye contact with me. Usually people will nod at you, or speak, or stare at you because they're mad. But they looked like they were holding a lot of guilt and shame and I couldn't figure out why. They weren't even sitting with each other — they were all sitting with their backs to each other, or turned away. I was like, what the fuck is going on?

Then a fisherman guy comes in and he's in his gear and he stomps on in, and I thought: 'Oh great, he's gonna give me a hard time.' Because he came in all [aggressive]. So we changed the order of speaking, and I got up right away, and I said: 'There's something going on here. What is it? You guys look like you're in a lot of pain.' Then this woman turns around to the guy in the fisherman clothing, and says: 'Are we gonna tell her?' And he goes: 'Yep.'

Then he says: 'We're ashamed.' And I was like: 'Okay, well we're here to talk about difficult things.' That was my mantra — 'We can talk about difficult things.' So they talked about a gentleman that had come home [with AIDS], and they had crucified him. They just crucified him. The whole town. I can't remember the stuff that they did, but it was shocking. Absolutely shocking. They just did everything that they could to make the rest of his life as uncomfortable as possible. Like throwing rocks at his house in the middle of the night, and all kinds of really weird, fucked up things. And they were embarrassed about that. They were very brave in telling it though. I couldn't believe that they were sitting there, and telling it. They were so brave! And they were committed to never behaving that way again. Like there were big grown men crying to break their hearts over their shitty behaviour. It was something else. And it was more than just HIV, it was about homophobia, and it was about a man being what they considered sissy. It was all of that too.

Of course, they couldn't make amends with him — he had died. So I was kind of the substitute — let's tell this girl, this HIV-positive girl, our terrible things, and see if we can get some absolution or some fucking shit, I don't know. I know that I didn't respond with shock. I was like: 'Wow, well that's heavy.' I wanted them to change. I told them: 'You're being very brave. You're being very brave.'

I mean, what I was thinking in my head might have been very different from what was coming out of my mouth. But you can't shut a community down by judging them. Because more people are going to come home. Because another effeminate gay man is going to come home. Whether he's HIV-positive, who knows. But if they're willing to talk about it, then we've got to have space for that. I really did believe that they were being very brave though. They were showing the ugliest pieces of themselves. Most of us don't do that. And they were very, very committed to doing better and being better (Ibid.).

Doing AIDS-related education and activism took its toll on Parsons, psychologically but in other ways too. By her willingness to speak out publicly as an HIV-positive woman, Parsons became a target for bigots. She frequently received hate mail and death threats. The people sending hate mail found the addresses of her relatives and friends, and sent them hate mail as well. They made harassing and threatening phone calls to her mother. As she was crossing the street downtown one day, a driver suddenly accelerated and tried to run her over. She doesn't know if that was because of her activism, but because she was easily recognizable and had been on television, she suspects that it was.

The AIDS Committee were concerned for her safety in the face of all this harassment, and arranged for police protection on multiple occasions when she received death threats. This might stop the harassment for short periods, but as soon as the police were redeployed, the harassment would begin again.

My mother was afraid. She was so afraid. So I stopped telling her the things that were scary that happened, because there was nothing she could do about it and I wasn't going to stop anyway. There was no point in telling her. And I stopped talking about [the harassment] publicly, because you don't want that to show up in media, because she's going to hear about it.

I was going by the seat of my pants. In the beginning I was told that I was going to [die] within four to seven years, and that the last three or four years would be very bad. So I was running on [a feeling] that I have to do as much good stuff as I possibly can to make up for one mistake. For being human (Ibid.).

Billy Neville and Betty Ralph: A story of friendship and AIDS

Betty Ralph was already deeply involved in AIDS activism long before her business partner, Billy Neville, tested positive for HIV. Neville was an artist and businessman whom Gerard Yetman remembers as being one of the pillars of the gay community he looked up to as a young man; one of many gay elders lost to the disease. Neville had gone to Concordia University in Montreal and obtained a fine arts degree there. He was an award-winning photographer, and also involved in the Newfoundland Independent Filmmakers' Cooperative (NIFCO).

"He was always arts-inclined," recalled Ralph. "He had this natural artistic flair, that's the only way to describe it. It was natural. He was born with it. He was born talented."

Neville also had a practical streak. He realized he needed a source of income in order to pursue his artistic interests, and so he went into the framing business, opening Neville's Framing with himself and Ralph as co-owners. They had met as students at Memorial University, and become fast friends. In 1981, he asked her to go into business with him, and she agreed. On March 15, 1981, the two friends opened Neville's Framing.

In addition to being a talented artist, Neville was also an out gay man. "He wasn't closeted by no stretch of the imagination," said Ralph. "He was out. He was what I would call a very proud gay man."

Ralph recalled their shop's first location, which was on the corner of Prescott and Gower Street, farther down the road than the business's present spot. At the time, she said, there were gangs of "young street urchins" hanging out and roaming in the area, and they used to lurk outside the business and yell out homophobic insults at the shop, and at customers going inside.

"Sometimes they'd be saying stuff, and Billy would go out and he would go right over and say to them: 'Say that to my face!' Well of course they wouldn't now, would they?"

Gerry Rogers and Peg Norman, who lived near the shop, remember Neville's pet dog, a wiry terrier named Duckie Dog. "It was the funniest looking little dog," recalled Rogers. It had the run of the downtown, and would randomly show up at people's houses, expecting to be let in and stay the night. People couldn't say no to it, Rogers said. "He was just Duckie Dog! This funny, funny little dog."

Sandy Pottle was good friends with Neville as well.

Everybody knew Bill. He was a real good friend and he hung out with us quite a bit and was always present. He was full of fun. He was one of the most fun people you could ever meet. He was always looking for a good time and he was very creative with his picture framing business, and a very artistic man. He was a lovely person. He always seemed to be happy (Pottle 2022).

On a bright sunny day in January 1989, Ralph was working in the shop. She had a workbench by the window, and was enjoying putting together frames under the warm rays of morning sunshine. Neville had been out that morning, and when he entered the shop, he came right over to Ralph.

"I got to talk to you," he said. Ralph intuited instantly what it was about. She suggested they leave the shop and go back to his place to talk. When they got there, he told her: he'd tested positive.

"Well that's life, I guess we'll deal with it the best way we can," replied Ralph.

"It's a good thing, my dear, that when I got this news today it was bright and sunny," Neville replied. "Because if it wasn't, I don't know if I would have come back."

Ralph, together with another male friend of Neville's, went together with him to his first specialist appointment, to provide support through the experience. Ralph remembers being interrogated by the doctor when they first arrived; he wanted to make sure she understood what AIDS was. The doctor was surprised that a friend and business partner would want to sit in through the appointment; it was more common, she was told, for patients to be abandoned by friends and family members after testing positive.

At first, Neville's intention was to take what medications were available and try to continue running the business with Ralph. The problem, Ralph explained, was that the most widely available medications, the only ones available in Newfoundland and Labrador, were not very effective. It was the more experimental medications not yet approved for widespread use which were showing more promise. These were inaccessible to people in a province like NL. The only people who could access the drug trials were those in larger centres like Toronto.

In 1990, a friend from Ottawa came to visit Neville in St. John's. He spoke frankly to Ralph during his visit. "He said to me: 'Whatever chance Billy's got of having a decent quality of life, he has to get to the mainland. For the drug trials."

The two managed to convince Neville to relocate to Toronto. His friend from Ottawa had driven down, and offered to drive Neville back with him and put him up. Ralph packed him a suitcase. Neville agreed to the plan.

Neville also had a sister living in Toronto, who offered to put him up for a while too. Once he was in Toronto, he got approved for access to the drug trials, and was able to find a small bed-sitting room on Jarvis Street in downtown Toronto, in the gay village.

Ralph continued to look out for her friend, even from St. John's. She phoned him daily to check on his status. She also coordinated a network of acquaintances in Toronto; in the event she couldn't get ahold of him, she would call up one of those friends and ask them to check on Neville in person. There had a been a case, she said, of a young Newfoundlander living with AIDS in Toronto who didn't have many connections and had died alone in his apartment, without anyone checking on him. His body was found several days later when other tenants reported the smell coming from his apartment.

"He passed away, he was by himself, no one checked on him regularly. I remember when [Billy] phoned and told me that. I'll always remember Billy saying to me: 'Betty, don't let that happen to me.'"

Living with HIV was like being on a roller-coaster, explained Ralph. "It was a ride. It wasn't like a smooth road. It was a lot of ups and a lot of downs. It reminded me of a roller coaster, with someone's health. One day they'd be all right, and then all of a sudden they didn't have enough energy to get out of bed."

Whenever Neville's health deteriorated, Ralph would get on a plane and fly up to Toronto to look after him until he got better. She nursed him back to health a few times that way.

In the summer of 1993, things were looking up. Neville had found a nicer, larger one-bedroom apartment he was preparing to move into. Ralph's younger brother offered to head up to Toronto and paint it for him. Then Neville's health took a turn for the worse. Having looked after him during other recent bouts of ill-health, Ralph had a feeling this might be his last chance of returning home. This was the dilemma faced by many Newfoundlanders and Labradorians as their health deteriorated: deciding if and when to make what might be their final journey home.

In the summer of 1993 I knew he had to come home, because I knew he was to the point where time wasn't on his side. And I knew when time wasn't on your side, the day that you feel good when you got up, is the day you had to go to the airport to get on that plane. You couldn't say: 'Oh, I feel all right now.' No, this was your one chance to get home. You either had to pay for someone to fly down with them, or send them to the airport by themselves and if they looked really sick, nine chances out of ten they were not going to be let on the plane. So you got a very narrow window of opportunity to bring someone back home. Otherwise, they'll die where they're to.

And he did phone [to come home]. I told him that's fine, just phone and book the ticket and everything will be looked after for you. Just give me the info. There will be no if's and's or but's about it, just do it. So he did. And when he came home I could see that he was a lot sicker looking even than the last time I seen him. So I knew he wasn't going back. I knew this was the last trip (Ralph 2022).

A friend had agreed to fly back to St. John's with Neville to look after him during the journey, and Ralph picked them up at the airport. She drove them back to her house, where Neville would be staying. He still hadn't made up his own mind about whether he wanted to stay, or return to Toronto. "I thought: 'he ain't going back.' But what I said was: 'We'll see!' That was always my answer. Because I didn't want to come out and be adamant, because you don't want to take away someone's rights either."

Neville met with his doctors in St. John's, and they also pulled Ralph aside to tell her that he shouldn't attempt to fly back to Toronto.

I told them: 'Well it's his choice. I don't think he should, but I do not have the right to say to him that you can't go back. I don't think anyone has that right to say to people.' Eventually Billy realized. He said to me: 'I realize it's not a good idea for me to go back.' I said to him: 'Well it's your choice!' He said: 'I don't think I'll be going back. I think I'm going to stay and see what the rest of this year will be like for me. And then I'll decide (Ibid.).

Ralph's brother had just finished painting the new apartment in Toronto, and as he showed it to the building owner, he told the incredulous landlord that Neville would not be returning, and that he hoped someone else would enjoy the freshly painted apartment.

Ralph moved Neville into the top floor apartment of her house. He was on the third floor, and her apartment was on the first. "At that time he was using a walking cane," she recalls, "and I'd always put the cane by his bed and say to him: 'Now you knows any time in the night that you needs anything, tap that old cane and you'll see how quick I can fly up over the stairs!'"

She installed a second roll-out hideaway bed in Neville's apartment, as there were an array of friends who wanted to spend time with him during his final months. Many of them spent the night chatting and recalling old times until the late hours, and then they'd roll out the second bed and spend the night in the apartment with him.

That way everyone had a chance to say their own goodbyes in their own time, in privacy too. Now, he couldn't stand for people crying. So I had to be stern with people. I said to them: 'When you go up to see him, please don't cry. When you're in the same room with him, talking to him, you be full of life!' I told them: *'If you got to cry, leave the room. If you don't, I'll bury you! I'll have no other recourse but to bury you.' That was too draining on him, he didn't want people to be down, he didn't want people to bust out crying in front of him. So I was like the shield between them. It was me that told them: 'Don't do that! I'll have to bury you, because we can't have that. He's got to have a good space.' I knew it was the end of his journey, so I had to make sure that everything was in order* (Ibid.).

In late 1993, Billy Neville died.

Neville and Ralph had discussed funerary preparations before his death. His family was Catholic, so for the sake of his mother he wanted a Catholic funeral, although he also requested cremation. He also wanted there to be a party, and Ralph followed through on her commitment to make sure his final wishes were followed to the letter.

Ralph had been to many AIDS-related funerals already, and had crossed paths with homophobic priests and dour undertakers alike.

Back in those days, even if you did have a church funeral, some of them were all hellfire and brimstone. They would – on the pulpit! – make people feel that the person in the casket was there because of their own fault, or that they were not Jesus' child, based on the fact that they were gay and lived a gay life. So I didn't go to many of the services that took place in church, but I went to the funeral homes.

I remember walking into one funeral home, and it was really quiet and of course me goes in and says: 'My god we're all some morbid in here to-night!' And no one laughed. It was really awkward! I was thinking: 'Oh my Jesus!' Then some of the b'ys shows up, and I says to them: 'Do they have another place where we can go and gather? Because this is not what this person wanted. This is what all these other people wants!' And someone says: 'My god I'm some glad you showed up!' So I went and asked the un-dertaker, and he told us: 'Oh yes, there's a room downstairs you can go and you can socialize in if you like, as a group' (Ibid.).

The dichotomy, she said, was between family members who sought to ig-nore the fact their deceased relative was gay or had died of AIDS, and the per-son's friends and chosen family, who wanted to celebrate them for who they truly were.

So that's what we started doing. We would gather downstairs in most of the funeral homes where people had passed, and we would have our own memories of that person. It would be like a celebration. That made people feel much better. Someone would bring a book with photos in it, and you would flip through it, and you would remember the times and talk and laugh. That's the way it should be – it was their last celebration (Ibid.).

Ralph took an especially hands-on role in organizing her friend Billy Nev-ille's funeral. It had to take place at the Basilica in St. John's, as that was the family parish. But she didn't approve of the priest there, so she found another, more inclusive and open-minded priest she thought would do a better job. She met with that priest, explained that she wanted him to preside over Billy's funeral, and asked him to deal with his superiors to make it happen. The priest agreed, and obtained permission to preside over the funeral.

A problem arose, however, over Billy's cremation. Although it's common practice today, in 1993 it was frowned upon to have ashes, in lieu of a body in a casket, at a funeral service. Again, Ralph prevailed on the priest to find a way to make it happen, and he obtained permission.

More than anything, Billy's friends wanted to make certain the funeral truly was a celebration of his life in all of its aspects.

It was the funeral that he wanted, and he was going to get it. But it was also something for the gay community. Up to that time, at most of the religious funerals... [priests] were preaching hellfire and brimstone and damnation and basically being negative. What did this do to the people sat in that church, so many of those people also living with HIV and AIDS themselves? When they got up there with that holier-than-thou condemnation, they were hurting a lot of people. So I saw [Billy's funeral] as payback. He was having it the way he wanted, and it was going to be in a church, and it was going to be presided over by a bona fide clergy, and we were going to have it our way! I don't think the poor priest realized it, but he was fine. I said to him – look, if there's a problem, it's not your problem, it's mine. You come to me and I'll go straighten them out.'

I thought it was time for [gay] people to sit in the pew and actually feel good, even though the event they're at might be sad, but they shouldn't walk out feeling like a piece of garbage. And that's what was happening. So I told [the priest]: 'I know we're breaking some of the rules, but rules were made to be broken – especially some of them' (Ibid.).

For the service, Ralph brought in a table that Billy had hand-made himself, and put his ashes on it. Glen Rockwood, a good friend of Neville's, gave the eulogy.

Everything you weren't supposed to talk about in a church, we talked about. Because to me, this wasn't just a funeral for Bill. It was also a time for the gay community to heal and realize they're worth something... [we talked about how] he was a proud gay man. [Rockwood] gave the eulogy from his heart, and it was magnificent. And everyone who was in that church that night, when you looked around, you could see the pride in them. Because it was the first time a service actually acknowledged them. I was scared that the poor priest would get ragged on because it was done this way, but the gay community had to be made to feel good. I was tired of negativity. And then we went back to the house and we had a party. That's exactly what we done. We celebrated his life (Ibid.).

Chapter Eight: Encountering Queer and Trans Archives (A Prequel to Chapter Nine)

In the Centre for Newfoundland Studies (CNS) at Memorial University of NL, there is a file folder labelled "Homosexuals."

The creased, battered legal-size file folder is found among the CNS Vertical Files. It contains clippings, 251 in total, spanning the gamut of queer history in Newfoundland and Labrador.

The file itself is an artifact, a relic handled reverently by those who know of its existence. The strata of items it contains is constantly shifting, jumbled and re-ordered every time someone leafs through it. It speaks to the tumultuous changes of the past four decades, chronicling the fight for human rights, same-sex marriage, the AIDS crisis, and more. The file contents themselves speak to prolific changes in archival mediums during that period as well. There are newspaper clippings, the oldest among them carefully printed, cut and pasted onto protective cardboard backs. The time-consuming care this required was eventually abandoned and clippings thrown in haphazardly, folded and bent, with dates and provenance (usually) scrawled hastily somewhere on the item. When the Internet appeared, news articles were printed from websites. There are pamphlets, minutes of meetings and conference agendas, photocopied excerpts of books.

This age-worn file folder has sat in the archives since 1986. Within the title "Homosexuals" are subsumed bits of data spanning the gamut of queer identity: gays, lesbians, transgender folks. The folder originally had a different name: "G.A.I.N." (Gay Association in Newfoundland) was erased and replaced by the more all-embracing label of the [mid-1980s] moment: "Homosexuals."

There are other file folders in the CNS for the would-be queer historian: files on "AIDS" (three thick folders, sub-divided by time period); folders on the "Royal Newfoundland Constabulary" (here will be found most of the files pertaining to Brian Nolan's human rights case explored in Chapter 6). There are individual biography files – some of them containing nothing but an elusive, single photograph. But "Homosexuals" is the point of departure for most researchers who seek to orient themselves in the province's queer history.[59]

---

[59] As this manuscript is going to print, a new initiative calling itself the "NL Queer Research Initiative," has undertaken the project of scanning some of the queer archival holdings in the QEII Library and elsewhere and making them publicly available on the Internet. While this will be welcomed by some researchers, it has also raised complex and controversial issues of consent, safety, copyright, right of response, and individual and community ownership over archival materials.

At least half a dozen different librarians have contributed to its contents over the years; probably more. It is one of more than 9000 vertical files; one of more than 40,000 files in the entire CNS. So much history lies hidden between the stained, folded edges of this single queer relic, standing defiantly against the march of digital progress.

I was not the first to immerse myself in the treasures dispensed by this fickle file folder. I won't be the last. It's curious to think of who else may have leafed through its holdings over the years, and what their relationship might have been with its contents.

One of those people is Daze Jefferies. Jefferies is a multi-disciplinary scholar, artist, poet, musician, and much more. Much of her work focuses on trans and sex worker histories in the province. In 2019, she co-curated the archival-artistic queer history exhibit *A Hole So Big It Became the Sky* with Spanish-Canadian artist Coco Guzmán at Eastern Edge Gallery in St. John's. Her graduate thesis "Fishy fragments: trans women's worlds in Ktaqamkuk/Newfoundland" engages with the province's trans history; as does her 2018 contribution to the collection *Autoethnography and Feminist Theory at the Water's Edge: Unsettled Islands*. Her poetry and music offer inspiration and solace to many, myself included. Whenever I speak with Jefferies, I find my mind shifting imperceptibly into a higher intellectual gear; we've trod many of the same thorny paths and I am grateful to have had her as a colleague. We met some years ago, and have stayed in touch, sharing our respective work on the province's queer history.

Throughout the process of writing this book, I grappled with unexpected challenges. There were multi-layered ethical choices to be made, often involving confidential material and knowledges that I could not share with others. There was the circuitous research path: riddled with dead-ends, with hints, with false leads. There was the problem of historical events remembered differently by different people; sometimes even documented differently by different media. Above all, there was the psychological burden of grappling with a century-long history of loss, violence, repression.

Nowhere did I grapple with these issues as deeply as researching the following chapter on trans history in the province. It's a history that is inspiring in many ways, but it contains disproportionate layers of pain.

In 2022, I sat down with Jefferies and we discussed the fraught process of researching trans and queer history in this province. It's important, I feel, for readers to understand not only how these knowledges are researched and constructed, but to know as well the affective burdens and ethical dilemmas faced by the researcher. And so on a warm spring night Jefferies and I sat down in her quaint Georgetown apartment. She took a platter of peanut-butter chocolate chip cookies out of the oven, I turned on my digital recorder, and we shared.

RHEA: Tell me first of all how you entered into your work on queer and trans history in this province.

DAZE: I engage with this work as a trans bay girl. My archival journey exists in fragments, and my approach to archives is fragmented. At seventeen, when I moved to St. John's for my undergraduate studies and I began to find queer community on campus, I started wondering about intergenerational connections – specifically, what seemed to be a lack of trans elders in community gatherings and spaces. I was looking for guidance with my own transition, and I didn't really know older trans women who were visible or participating in or organizing queer social life.

What I understood as a lack of trans women's presence in community organizing in St. John's speaks to a larger contested terrain about intergenerational mis/connections in queer and trans life. I remember having a conversation with you in 2015 about gaps in the historical record, and I had been thinking about belonging and the im/possibility of trying to place myself in a past about which I desired to know more. I was studying folklore and oral history and I was really interested in doing historical research and ethnographic fieldwork, but as an artist I was approaching things from a creative and emotional framework. I was using poetry and sound to ask questions about haunting and absence and ghosts and history. My community was primarily other young trans people, those my age, in Newfoundland and Labrador. I was struggling to make sense of transness in a rural geography, and I hoped that turning to history could help me situate my life in a specific place-based context.

But it wasn't that simple. It seemed like there was a real dearth of material engaging with trans lives in Newfoundland and Labrador, and so I wanted to begin sitting with and attempting to tend to some of those gaps in my undergraduate studies. I thought that I could try to piece things together in some way. That ethic or approach has changed significantly over the years.

In graduate school, I was mentored by Sonja Boon, and I was interested in thinking with creative histories. We really interrogated feminist, anti-colonial, and queer approaches to engaging with fragmented records of marginalized communities or exploited communities or communities that have been overlooked or subjugated or erased within the historical record. I was thinking about the geographical context that shapes trans history in Newfoundland and Labrador in particular. I thought a lot about outmigration, the HIV/AIDS crisis, rural silence, and ends of life caused by political, medico-legal, and economic failures. I didn't have extensive archival training or experience, so my engagements were a learning process, but they taught and offered me so much.

As I started spending time in the Centre for Newfoundland Studies, I worked with the "Homosexuals" folder several times, because it was just so packed, until I stumbled upon that one fragment of an article from *The Telegram* – "Transsexuals treated unfairly" – about Dawn [Hartman] and Jennifer [Crandell – both of whom appear in subsequent chapters]. I must have missed or overlooked it three times before it actually held my focus. That was in 2018, and I was able to reach out to Dawn and Jennifer to connect and follow up about the work. At that time, I was also dealing with intense grieving, from the unexpected death of my partner and colleague Yuvi, and I was approaching history as a way to heal in some ways. I think that doing archival work about trans and sex worker history, as a grieving trans sex worker, has profoundly shaped my worldview and sense of reality. The weight of responsibility and care that the work would require was impossible for me to fulfil. So working with archival fragments became important, because fragments invited my relationality and creative response.

But there was no way to prepare for the amount of pain that shaped the historical narrative. The medico-legal neglect, the loss, the violence. These stories are so easily captured by media, and they articulate trans history as one of immense struggle. In the process of living with the death of my partner, I was grieving for Newfoundland and Labrador trans women and sex workers. By that point, my small graduate stipend had run dry, and survival sex provided my only steady income. I was pulled between worlds, I felt completely outside of my body, and part of the process of dealing with grief was spending hours at the Centre for Newfoundland Studies, spending hours digging through microfilm in the basement of the QEII, spending hours scouring advanced Google searches with specific terms – "transgendered Newfoundland", "transsexual Newfoundland", "transsexual" with both one and two s's – scouring the Internet Archive's Wayback Machine, learning, listening, longing.

At the same time, I was also living through a revolution of trans activism in St. John's. The formation of the Trans Needs Coalition, the addition of gender identity and expression to the provincial Human Rights Code, organizing trans marches, the presence of activists and artists like Jude Benoit and Violet Drake, Two-Spirit-led organizing, trans support groups, PFLAG support meetings, clothing swaps, house parties, all kinds of gatherings – these formations were so integral to keeping people alive and to offering that sense of family and community. They were living history.

There has been so much collective energy calling for justice. But what I've struggled with most in this ongoing process have been the ethical layers of resurfacing painful histories. Specifically, the narratives of trans women and sex workers who have lost their lives to violence or who have chosen to leave the world because of structural and social barriers. I keep trying to figure out how to honour and live better with the ghosts while not necessarily telling their stories, because they aren't mine to share. I would love to hear about your relationship with encountering these difficult narratives and how we might move forward.

RHEA: It's been an evolving process for me. I think when I went into it, I didn't realize how fraught it would be. When I encountered stories like the one in Dr. Hoenig's research in the 1970s [discussed in Chapter 9] I felt this flaming indignation, a sense of anger. I felt this protective wrath for the trans people I encountered in the historical record and the way that they had been treated. And I felt this desire to honour their memory. I didn't want them to simply linger there in these historical records which didn't do them justice at all. And which probably did them a lot of harm. That was my initial surge of feeling. But of course the more I got into this work, I went through so many different shifts of feelings.

Hearing you talk about grief, I realize now it was also grief that propelled my own research in some ways. After coming out as trans, I struggled with some of the things I felt I had lost, perhaps as a result – not as a result of being trans, but as a result of the transphobia of the world we live in, and relationships that had been ruptured in part due to my own experience of gender dysphoria. I think I too turned to the archives to try to contextualize myself. It's sometimes easier to feel things for or about other people, than to deal with your own feelings. Burying myself in archival work helped. It also helped me to feel part of something bigger, at a time when I was finding it difficult to find queer and trans community here in the city. The Covid pandemic was in full swing, so I was also grieving all the losses the pandemic experience brought with it, the sense of rupture. The archives became a sanctuary, a fraught refuge of sorts.

I remember reading your Master's thesis and I was struck by the intensity of feeling and emotion in it. It was so powerfully written. I could sense that you were feeling a lot of things and you expressed those emotions so incredibly, I was bowled over by the feelings that came off the page. And it was only as I got further into my own research that I started feeling that as well. I remember hearing Alexandria Tucker's account of what she went through in the US [discussed in Chapter 9], and that shattered me. Reading the obituary sites for Alexandria and others, I was in tears, I would sometimes spiral into a depression that would linger for days. Those intense feelings stayed with me. Trying to reconcile the tragedies of twenty or thirty years ago with the ongoing violence against trans people that we are seeing on the news today, it produced an almost insurmountable wall of grief, a sense of being surrounded by violence. I started feeling an existential exhaustion – that's how I described it at one point. Eventually it was just the momentum of the project that kept me going, the feeling that I had to figure out a way to get this all out, to get these stories out. It was a real roller coaster of emotions. I was going to ask you how you dealt with that, but I know there is no single way, it's an ongoing process. Sometimes it still leaves me feeling really messed up.

DAZE: Creative practice has been the only way that I have been able to process and move forward. I still struggle with the ethics of the work, because as a young researcher I had no idea that I would encounter so many world-shattering narratives. I keep believing in the resistance, strength, and self-determination of trans women and sex workers that escape archival capture. And I keep trying to let go of the hurt of the past while holding on to those who came before. In that way, counter-archival ethics live in me and give me hope.

The works of trans scholar Viviane Namaste and Black cultural historian

Saidiya Hartman have really shaped my engagements with history. Hartman's book *Wayward Lives, Beautiful Experiments* is a counter-archival journey through young Black women's search for freedom in the early 20th century against the brutality of racism and misogynoir and what she calls the afterlife of slavery. She opens up a past that is legible for those who exist in the margins of archival materials. She gives so much through the process of withholding.

Encountering different kinds of loss and violence in the historical record has helped me to imagine and speculate and dream beyond the limitations of archival collections. I was really lucky to study with scholars like Sonja Boon who were able to hold me up in the process and who recognized how hurt I was by the material, and that I couldn't turn back. My mentors and professors and colleagues held me together and shared a lot of knowledge with me and encouraged an autoethnographic approach: reading the history through my own position in the world, and not shying away from the emotions, not shying away from the impact that the research had on my everyday life. Maybe it would have been different if I wasn't grieving and if I wasn't doing survival sex the whole time. It would probably be very different. Seeing losses of life over and over and over, I felt like I was breaking down. And creative practice held me up.

I still wrestle with various questions: Is it my place to do this work? What can I attempt to say? What should be withheld? I feel like I'm living with ghosts. To make sense of many voices from the research process, I've made illustrations, imagining faces and figurations to bring the body back into the narrative, even if what has been available to me is only a name or a sentence. This has been a particularly grounding method for relation with the many sex workers who've been criminalized or have gone missing or whose descriptions appear in the magistrate's court section of early to mid-twentieth century issues of *The Telegram*. There has been no justice for sex workers in Newfoundland and Labrador, who can teach us all so much about survival and community.

The idea of the counter-archive is important to me, because I think there's freedom in it, and I think that there's radical potential in a community-based approach to refusing the limitations of a dominant culture that decides what is documented or overlooked. It allows a community to remember and to dream and to challenge history on their own terms. And it also holds possibility for the future. I think about the audience of the work as well. Is this work for 2SLG-BTQIA+ community, or is it for the general public's gaze and consumption? My work is for queer and trans community. So what role does the counter-archive play in that context?

RHEA: I want to come back to that point, but on the topic of archives first let me say that one of the challenges I encountered was dealing with memory. This was a broad challenge throughout the work, because I would interview people, and they would tell me these vivid stories. But then I would go back and I would compare their stories to media coverage and other archival records, and would realize their stories didn't neatly match up, they clashed with archival records. So then I would struggle with how to reconcile peoples' memories with what the archival documents seemed to say. I would sometimes go back to people, but I would feel awful going back to them and saying: 'Are you sure you remembered this correctly, because it seemed that this is the way it actually happened.' So there was that dissonance that arose a number of times. Sometimes people would say: 'No, this is what I remember, regardless of what the archives say.' Other times they'd say 'Oh yes you're right,' and it would help them piece together something that had sat in their memory in a different way for so long. Which posed additional questions for me – why did they remember it that way? Why was this particular sliver of memory lodged so intensely in their heads, while other seemingly – to me - more important events were forgotten? What is to be learned, not just from what we remember, but from the way we remember it? So all of that was something I wrestled with. Because on one hand I didn't want to doubt or challenge people's memories and their experience of events – they were so generous in sharing very personal, often traumatic memories with me - but on the other hand how do I reconcile that with the data? So there is that challenge to keep in mind when dealing with archives, and when producing a history that others will read. I think to throw away someone's memory of events just because it doesn't mesh with published facts can be a form of violence, especially in queer and trans community. Trans lives have been deeply harmed by so-called experts having the audacity to tell us what we feel or why we feel it, and trying to impose their often incorrect version of objective reality over our very real subjective experience of the world. Those are forms of violence. I think all memories belong in the archive, even if it is difficult to understand exactly where and how and what their role is. But I think what you're referring to by the counter-archive is a different project. Tell me about it.

DAZE: In my life, a counter-archival approach represents what might have been. The speculative method is a form of resisting the brutality and quiet of the historical record. It registers the unknowable, the secretive, the silent, and the stealthy. It acknowledges how many trans women and sex workers have desired to forgo institutional capture. And I want to respect them by not filling gaps, but imagining a past by using fragments as a guide. Counter-archival practice recognizes that there is no singular history. Queer scholars like Cory Thorne have explored how much queer knowledge in Newfoundland and Labrador is shaped by intergenerational exchange and rumour and gossip, about how stories are transferred and take on new forms. And maybe it's okay that they distort claims to truth and change in complicated ways, because it registers how histories are lived and embodied. Even if they challenge the media record – who's to say that the media record was accurate? For me, a counter-archival approach takes all of this into account and believes in the agency of historical actors and community voices to change the past, and in so doing to change the future as well.

I also think a lot about what it means to assemble lived knowledge and to make historical narratives accessible to community. Most of the people I hold close to my heart have never been to the Centre for Newfoundland Studies. I've been the mediator and the sharer because of my educational privileges, because of the time commitments involved, because of the affective pull. I've shared a lot with others about gay and lesbian history, but I've withheld so much about trans and sex worker history because the stories are unfathomable. My thesis research and writing were overwhelmed by pain. And so with/holding is another key term in my process. The holding of the work is an act of care. Being with, and holding, but also withholding. Being selective about what can be shared and with whom. What can be resurfaced, and for whom. I think that with/holding is important in many ways, especially with sacred community knowledge that might really harm people if it emerges in the wrong context. It's about sitting with the conflicting narratives and dealing with the fact that multiple truths can be possible at the same time. The silences make space for other encounters and narratives.

RHEA: I'd like to come back to that idea of with/holding in a bit. But something I was thinking when you were talking about the historical record, about archives, is that I think a lot of people don't fully have a grasp of how archives and the historical record is produced. Even in our own community, I would sometimes explain how I was doing a queer history of Newfoundland and the response would be: 'Oh that's going to be a really short book, not much of a queer history here!' I remember that happening and it was a terrible start to the interview because I wanted to yell: 'No! It's such a rich history!' But that's the perception even some people have in the queer community, that our community has no history.

The other thing I encountered oftentimes was I'd be asking people about things that happened in the past, and they'd say: 'Oh yes this and this happened, I don't remember the details but you can go find it in the archives.' So there's this perception that somewhere out there is an archive that contains everything – all knowledge, everything that ever happened. And that's not the case! Like you said, it's fragments, and there's so much that isn't there. There's even stuff that used to be there – for example the online archives of CBC and other news agencies – stuff that was around five years ago is gone, it's wiped. Many local newspapers were never properly archived in the first place; some have vanished entirely. *The Telegram* and its precursors exist on microfilm but have never been properly indexed. And even the Internet Wayback Machine is getting eroded increasingly due to privacy or copyright claims. Many government records and other institutional archives have been lost or destroyed. So there's this perception that everything is archived somewhere, and that's not the case. People just don't realize that we are the ones producing this history, we are the ones actively building these archives, and producing them in ways that reflect our interests and priorities and interpretations. It's just quite sobering to think on that. If you don't tell me something, and if I don't document it, then for all intents and purposes it vanishes.

DAZE: Absolutely. And in a province where archival and historical endeavours seem to be increasingly undervalued and underfunded. I have to believe that someone will remember, someone will journal, someone will record, someone will accumulate, someone will share. And so much of the past can't be resurfaced or recalled. The fragments survive with their own power. The voices begin to come through. I've been interested in oral history for a long time, and I've helped organized two different queer and trans oral history projects with support from many, including Dale Jarvis at Heritage NL, the curatorial collective RetroFlex (Kai Bryan, Jason Wells and Jason Penney), and the team at Eastern Edge Gallery. What I love about oral history is that it registers the voice and memory in specific embodiments of the past. Everyone remembers differently, everyone describes and emplaces the past in unique ways. But some gaps can never be filled. And maybe they shouldn't be filled.

What is the potential of silence? What is the potential of the ephemeral? These are some of the bigger questions that I'm left with as I think about ghosts and as I think about consent and the historical record. Who consents? How does a life that is lost consent to entanglement or relationship with the researcher or writer? In my thesis, I opened the introduction with a paragraph to Alexandria. I was letting the weight of grief out of my body, and at the same time I didn't have her consent. Even though I find myself trying to communicate with her ghost and others all the time. I want to keep learning in this work, what it means to engage with lives who are connected to a community of people, in the living present. Lives that shape a living history. While also understanding my own need to release and let go of historical knowledge that hurts me. It's been a learning process. There have been shortcomings and many moments of pause. There have also been lessons for deeper engagement. I feel responsibilities in this work.

One thing I'm hoping for is more collaboration, because I felt so lonely as a grad student. Violet Drake and I lived together for a few years, and we co-grieved and co-processed a lot of things. And when you and I reconnected in early 2022, we had a shared resonance about the difficulties and challenges, about our own agency and our own desire for the work, while also struggling with how to honour and show respect for those who have produced these histories, and for those who have so intimately touched our lives in this present moment. The sacrifices that have been made for us to survive, to write stories, to be held in this world.

RHEA: You've spoken about ghosts, but I also frequently find myself wondering, what are our responsibilities to the living? I wrestled with this the more I got into my own research. On the one hand, when I initially got into it, I felt a real anger at a lot of the families of these trans people I was researching. In a sense, I didn't care about the families who had hurt and rejected their trans relatives. When I call up the family and friends of now-deceased trans people and ask them to share those people's stories, they sometimes respond with these platitudes about respecting family privacy. This made me so angry – I had to swallow that anger, but I felt it in such a deep way. I struggled with peoples' sense of obligation to 'respect the family' versus my desire to protect the memory of these trans folks *from* their family. Asking for family privacy seemed to me to be a form of ongoing violence against the trans people who had been silenced against their will. Refusal to talk about now deceased trans people seemed like a continuation of these families' or friends' refusals to acknowledge them – and again, an ongoing act of violence against them. The urge to silence, to privacy, to protect the family or community, was a form of violence that killed queer and trans people. So while I had to pretend to be sensitive to these families or friends, and I had to be respectful, I sometimes felt very angry, I felt like the effort to acquire and tell the story of a trans person's life was a way to rescue them from the clutches of the violence around them, including the violence of the family. I know so many people who experienced terrible hurt from their families. Mind you, plenty of friends and family were wonderful, and supportive, and eager to share these stories. But some were not. And so I struggled with that.

But I also struggled with the realization that I was causing some people harm by asking about these stories. I realized that when I approached people out of the blue, asking about events of thirty, forty, fifty years ago, I was triggering all these painful memories in people. There were people who burst into tears, or broke down emotionally, during our first conversation, almost before I could even ask them any questions! There were some folks who agreed to an interview but then they would reschedule and reschedule and reschedule and weeks or months later they would explain that psychologically they just hadn't been ready for the interview, that they needed to prepare themselves, and that's why it took so long. I realized that I was placing a big burden on the people I was asking questions to. I was dredging up these painful memories. I felt it was necessary, because I felt that the people and the events I was asking about hadn't been done justice in the past, and that their experiences could inform and guide the present in important ways. But I also realized this was really hurting people in the present, people who had healed and moved on. So I wrestled with those feelings. I felt a responsibility to the ghosts, but what responsibility did I have to the people who were still living?

DAZE: I still struggle with these questions. That's why I love oral history projects, because people have their own agency, and if they want to show up they will. And if they want to share, they will. Oral history projects are kind of similar to a peer circle or support group, but the levels of confidentiality are different, and people still have the agency to ask for their story back. Whereas working with documents charts its own course. Working with community charts its own course. Working with the body charts its own course as well. But I think sometimes there are points when you just have to say no, I can't go any further. And that's okay. I can't go any further for now, and that's okay. And this is an incomplete work. It's a work that will be built on. It's a work that has been in progress by many people before us, for decades. It's a work that we're picking up pieces of and pushing them a little bit further. Compiling and assembling and encountering a little bit deeper. It's living history, it's living on its own terms. History will be known on its own terms, and it has its own power, and that requires believing in ghosts, it requires believing in those fragments. Maybe that piece of Jennifer and Dawn's article in the *Homosexuals* folder didn't want to meet me those first few times. Maybe that document has power. Maybe it wanted to stick to another page. Maybe I wasn't ready to find it until 2018. Or maybe the microfilm, maybe that film reader wanted to turn itself off. Who knows?

RHEA: Speaking of ghosts! What you were saying earlier about with/holding really resonated. We've previously discussed some cases involving trans folk from earlier decades, and the challenge of figuring out how to write about them in ways that are comprehensible, and not hurtful, for those in the present. I remember one case in particular that we discussed. I initially felt quite confident that there was a way to tell that story. But then the more I thought about it, and tossed around ideas of how to do that, the less confident I felt. And I still do think there is a way for that story to be told, but I was also still deeply concerned. Because I was cognizant of how the history I'm producing intersects with the present. And I kept thinking about how regardless of how I might try to present some of these cases, I worried about how they could be misunderstood, misused or appropriated. Trans folks had to struggle with a great deal of ignorance, violence and abuse in those earlier years – and there was no perfect way to respond to that violence. Sometimes they had to do things to survive, or make choices that today could easily be taken out of context. Given all the violent bigots out there – TERFs and the like – I don't want to offer cursory snapshots of complex cases that could be deliberately misinterpreted or misused to put queer or trans people in a negative light. And yet on the other hand, I do feel this historian's urge, this journalist's urge, to tell the whole story and simply put all the facts out there and trust in people to interpret them, or in my own ability to mediate the complex facts for readers. Navigating that has been difficult. There are various examples of people doing things that were illegal or that could be construed as unethical in some ways, but having very good reasons to do so, especially in the past, in a historical context. So telling those stories in the present becomes very challenging. I began to grasp what you were talking about earlier in regards to with/holding. It makes me nervous sometimes when people think it's sufficient for archivists to simply digitize everything and put it online. If people are just going to grab things and put them online for the world to see, how is that being mediated? But then that also makes me think, well maybe we should be the ones telling these stories before someone else gets to them. We can provide context and hope that will help with the way the story is told. I don't know. It's so complicated.

DAZE: It really is complicated. And the thing is, it wasn't so hard to encounter a lot of these historical knowledges. It just took time. I share your concerns about contemporary archival projects. But I think the weight of trans history, the weight of transphobia, the weight of gender-based violence, the weight of fear, turns upon those moments in the historical record. Troubling trans narratives that were widely circulated in Newfoundland and Labrador media in the 1980s and 1990s have been experienced and likely passed on by many. They might be forgotten by a number of folks who engaged with the text, but there's something that remains in the cultural psyche. So what does that mean for the historical context? Regarding your effort to find ways of navigating these ethical choices, where are you at with that process?

RHEA: My writing style tends to be: get it all out there and then figure out how to refine it. So I first write these things up in great detail, but then I struggle with what to remove – what to leave out. What to with/hold. As I said, I also always struggle with this journalist's instinct that the truth matters. And I know 'truth' is a slippery, relative concept; there's no such thing, et cetera, but for me it's important that everything be out there – the raw facts and data, as much as we are able to present them. But I also recognize that sometimes that is not necessarily the best thing. So I wrestle with this a lot, because I do feel the urge as a journalist to make sure everything is told in as great and as complete detail as possible.

DAZE: Right. But you have an ethical commitment and I think that's at the heart of the work. It's non-exploitative and you're grappling with the challenges. I think that's maybe where the difference lies. That's the potential of the work, because you care about it and you care about how it's going to be engaged with.

RHEA: Sometimes I come across material that I'm surprised even made it into the archive – personal or private material that somehow slipped through. On one level I'm thrilled by the additional level of detail it allows; by the fact that it gives me a more complete understanding of what happened in the past. But of course I can't always use it, due to copyright or legal reasons. But then you're left with the burden of knowing. You know these things that you are not allowed to use. Sometimes it's for ethical reasons, sometimes it's for copyright reasons, sometimes it's for other legal reasons and sometimes it's just because you feel uncomfortable putting it out there for all the reasons we've discussed. I've had to do all of those things with this book. But I feel like I'm going to feel some sense of guilt putting a book out there and knowing that I withheld things, even if I could not use things for legal reasons.

DAZE: I struggle with that with/holding process as well. Withholding is a key term that becomes important when discussing power dynamics and op-

pression and hierarchies. And I've had to think about what it means to with/
hold historical knowledge that I feel I shouldn't know, but that I've been able to
encounter through my own time commitment and positionality. When I'm left
with a narrative that I feel can't be resurfaced on simple terms. Releasing such
knowledges through written or spoken or body language can be difficult. Visu-
ality is different. If I am unprepared to process a pain of the past, if something
has really hurt me and I need to let it out, an abstract visual means will often
bring me peace. The ethical layers that shape that process of withholding are
what's most important to me. The narratives we hold on to are going to come
out at some point with people that we trust; with people who understand the
intensity of that knowing. So it's about *who* is able to know. It's about access.
Who has access to these inner worlds?

Some of these decisions are also in the hands of the archivists. At the institutional level, so many things are gatekept and withheld. It takes various
forms of networking and trust to gain access to material. So, from the institutional domain to the community level – where lots of folks don't trust institutions with their knowledges for all the valid reasons that we know – these
are ongoing troubles of history-making and cultural documentation. That's the
messiness of the historical project. I think it helps to emphasize in the narrative
how it is constructed from many different fragments, and from many different
community voices that are sometimes at odds with each other, but together as
an assemblage they create this really fascinating story about queer and trans
histories. It's about how we remember together. It's about how we remember
with the historical record and without it. It's about how we remember with and
without each other. And the fallibility of memory is something that's important
to acknowledge.

RHEA: What do you believe is important about the fallibility of memory?

DAZE: Memory is something that lives and loops. It is revisited and revised. Thinking about this requires us to wrestle with people's anxieties and
desires. It requires us to recognize how narratives are carried and change over
time. For me, plurality is important. Registering the multiple and the im/pos-
sible. The might-have-been and the yet-to-come. Memories produce cultural,
social, historical, and political knowledge of any given moment. Shifting and
complicated and fishy memories are encounters with lives in movement.

Encounter is a word that we're both using. It's a word that's really special
to me. I really don't like the word *uncover*. I don't like the word *recover* either,
because it puts too much emphasis on the individual agency of the researcher
or writer. What we've been doing, these are *encounters* with a presence that has
been lived. And that word – *encounter* – registers the power dynamics at play.
The time commitment of engagement. It registers what is trusted and what
is mistrusted. It registers how a document, a person, a community has will.
That's why encounters are important.

RHEA: Yes. And there are multiple encounters over time. There are things

I am encountering for the first time, and which no one I know of has encountered before – but that is not to say they have not ever been encountered before. Or that others are not encountering them simultaneously, in different ways, from different angles. Or that they will not be encountered in the future, in entirely new ways. And each encounter has a valence, a quality, a uniqueness of its own. It's not just the first encounter – or the first published encounter – that matters. Although there is always a risk that initial encounters will set a template or framework for future encounters; something which I think it's important to resist. Every encounter ought to be on its own terms, although it can be informed by previous encounters.

And these encounters of which we speak – they are not merely encounters with documents, or with historical moments and experiences. They are also – as you have been pointing out – encounters with ghosts. I want to also comment on that, because I've encountered – I've felt - those ghosts so viscerally as well, so often. The more you learn about a person from history, from the archive; and the more you spend time encountering that person – the things they produced or the things produced about them – the more real they become to me, regardless of when they lived and whether I ever even met them. They take shape as a person, and grow as a presence in my memory, in my consciousness. When we talk about the ghosts of trans people, I still feel that anger and that pain and that weight in reading about people's histories, but there's also something reassuring about encountering these ghosts as well. Some people talk about the concept of 'affinity ancestors' – those who came before you and shape you, and whose ghosts sometimes walk with you, even if they are not blood ancestors. I feel like I have encountered some of those during this process, and these encounters have changed me. Ultimately, I feel they have strengthened me. I think about Alexandria all the time now. And that's a presence that I did not have before in my life. But now there's this powerful, courageous, very human, very amazing Newfoundland trans woman who is so often in my thoughts. Almost like a guardian angel, in a way. There's something to that presence. I didn't have that before. And I mean there are aspects to her story that are very, deeply tragic, but I feel I've gained somehow by encountering it. I've learned from her, and with her. It's like I feel, in a way, that I'm travelling with her.

DAZE: That's so beautiful! Being *with* the knowledge, being *with* someone, being *with* a ghost. And *holding* on to what has touched you so profoundly while also working within the limits of what can be known and shared. I feel deeply altered and forever moved by the past several years of my life, by the time I've spent being with trans women and sex workers of the historical past. I've learned a lot of things that have really hurt me, but they've also offered me hope. Alexandria's forthcoming autobiography, written with and by her partner Kris Elder, will have a life of its own and it will register the power and the breadth and the beauty of her life in her own words. That keeps her memory in movement.

I think about this short poem that Dawn Hartmann wrote in one of her pieces for *The Telegram*. It's this moment of hope for the future, and a glimpse into a world lived otherwise. I think about how the past and present and future are entangled and what our responsibilities are. Because the work that we're doing also challenges linear time. I think about how these different historical and temporal contexts match up sometimes to create really beautiful moments. The creation of this book is one of those moments for you. The creation of artwork is one of those moments for me. And the creation of community-based collaborative projects can be more. As fraught and complex as our work sometimes is, these are all beautiful moments that flow from each encounter.

Chapter Nine: Trans Lives, Trans Activism

There is documentation of trans people with connections to this province stretching back decades. I met, or encountered through other people I interviewed, trans NLers who left the province in order to transition as far back as the 1980s. Some of them declined to interview or participate in this research, a decision I understand perfectly well given the difficult memories that period probably evokes for them, and their desire to leave that part of their lives behind.

This chapter explores some dimensions of trans-specific history in this province. Owing to the lack of widespread media coverage or medical documentation pertaining to trans people in this province during that era (with some exceptions, as we will see), much of this chapter tells this story by chronicling the lives of several trans people who had connections to this province. These stories have been put together through media archives, court records, and interviews with the individuals themselves or their families and friends. The snapshots of their lives provided in this chapter offer an insight into the lived experiences of trans folks during this period. These sections also honour and celebrate the remarkable lives they lived.

One of the earliest documented references to trans people in Newfoundland and Labrador is a curious article published in a psychiatry journal in 1974.

Dr. Julius "John" Hoenig was a psychiatrist born into a Jewish family in Czechoslovakia in 1916. He attended medical school in Prague but fled to the United Kingdom when Nazi Germany invaded his homeland. He completed medical studies in Glasgow and joined the British army for the remaining years of the war. Following the war he returned to psychiatry, eventually settling into a 12-year career at Manchester University. It was there he participated in early research on transgender patients. From at least the early 1960s the University of Manchester Psychiatry Department worked with dozens of trans patients, and Dr. Hoenig was one of the people involved in this research (Fernando & Srinivasan 2009).

In 1967, the Memorial University of Newfoundland Medical School was established, and Dr. Hoenig was recruited the following year as head of psychiatry. He relocated to St. John's, but continued working with his former colleagues on analyses of their research on trans patients in Manchester, publishing a number of articles and studies from this work (Ibid.).

It appears his interest in transgender patients was aroused in Newfoundland and Labrador as well. In 1974, an article appeared in the now defunct journal *Psychiatria Clinica* titled "Sexual and Other Abnormalities in the Family of a Transsexual." The article was co-authored by Hoenig and Elaine Duggan. Duggan was a social scientist by training, and in 1970 was one of the first two students to graduate from Memorial with a degree in Social Work. Much of her early work focused on resettlement of rural communities.

The article by Hoenig and Duggan is a curious beast. Its subject is a 17-year-old patient, assigned male at birth, who has been admitted to hospital: "the patient had been feeling depressed because he could not accept his male gender role. He believed that although he possessed a male body, mentally he was female." The article discusses this patient, but the real star of the article is the patient's mother: "an intelligent and thoughtful person, who was struck by the high incidence in the family of what she thought were inherited disorders. Led by her curiosity she had made inquiries and in doing so had sharpened her powers of observation making her an excellent medical witness" (Hoenig & Duggan 1974).

The authors put an impressive scientific sheen on describing what basically amounts to family gossip.

Most of the content of the article is based on what the mother told them. She provided what in essence was a sexual history of 117 members of her extended family. One must bear in mind homosexuality and 'transgenderism' were incorrectly classified as 'disorders' during that era, and so the authors hypothesize on some of the possible factors driving the various 'disorders' which the mother chronicles. Her story chronicles incest and sexual abuse among family members, in addition to gender non-conformity, homosexuality and transgenderism.

The article would be laughable by today's scientific standards, and how much of the mother's tale is believable is impossible to tell. It does, however, speak to the widespread extent of some degree of sexual and gender non-conformity (and awareness of these topics) in even the most rural corners of the province during the early twentieth century.

It also raises questions around whether Dr. Hoenig was conducting research locally around gender identity in this province. Following his retirement from Memorial in 1980, he moved to Toronto. There he worked with the Clarke Institute and the Centre for Addictions and Mental Health, which was the go-to spot for treating Canadian transgender patients for many years (as recently as 2019 patients from this province had to travel to CAMH to be approved for publicly funded gender affirming surgery). Dr. Hoenig played a role in developing protocols around treatment of trans patients at the Clarke Institute, so he clearly retained an active interest in the subject over the years (Fernando & Srinivasan 2009). One of his doctoral students at Memorial, Uma Srinivasan, completed a PhD in Medicine in 1981 studying "the prevalence of effeminacy" among a group of young boys aged 6-12 who were receiving treatment (for unrelated issues) at the Janeway Children's Hospital in St. John's. The study was based on a combination of interviews (with the boys and their families) and direct observation (analyzing what the children drew, what toys they played with, and so forth). The study, shockingly primitive by today's standards, would probably not even be permitted under modern ethical research norms. Nonetheless, it speaks to the sustained interest of Dr. Hoenig and his colleagues in gender identity research in the province (Sreenivasan 1981).

Dr. Hoenig retired from the Clarke Institute in 1992 following a stroke, and died in 2009. Despite making inquiries, I was unable to find any trail of personal or research documents left following his death.

While the medical archives do not provide much additional information about the period (future research may reveal more information), media archives also contribute to the story of Newfoundland and Labrador's trans history. One of the first stories they tell is that of Jeanie Sheppard.

Jeanie Sheppard (Nov. 14, 1957 – Dec. 16, 1980)

Once upon a time, there used to be a community in Sandy Point. Sandy Point is located on the west coast of the island. It's now an island itself, after a storm in 1951 destroyed the land bridge connecting it to the rest of the island. Efforts were made to prevent "The Gap" from eroding further, but were eventually abandoned. Over the ensuing years, the already shrinking community there was largely resettled in nearby St. George's; the last two permanent residents left in 1973 (Downer 1997).

Jeanie Sheppard[60] was born in Sandy Point in 1957. Her family eventually grew to include fifteen siblings. They were often paired up; she was assigned responsibility for looking after her younger sister Sharron. Her parents would send them out of the house in the morning and tell them to find a way to occupy themselves in the outdoors. Once out in the wilderness, they would trade clothing. Her sister was eager to wear the pants and be a tomboy, while Jeanie loved swirling around the beach in her sister's skirt. The island was sparsely populated, enabling them to keep their secret safe.

"We came from an island, and you might as well call it a deserted island," recalled Sharron. "We had lamps, there was no electricity, we had wells and outhouses and stuff like that."

[When Jeanie] put the dress on it didn't mean nothing to me, I was five. I just used to laugh. But nobody else would know. And she used to always watch mom getting dressed to go out and watch her putting on makeup and stuff like that. Me, I was the tomboy so I was out chasing the b'ys and climbing trees. We were like opposites (Sheppard 2022).

---

60 Jeanie is also referred to at times in media reports as Jeanie Shelley Boushard (a stage name) or Jeanie Sheppard Boushard Fox (her married name).

They also became very close. "If you understood me and Jeanie's relationship, it would be like twins," explained Sharron. "That's how close we were."

In the 1960s, the provincial government began efforts to relocate the community, offering residents money to sell their land and move to nearby St. George's on the mainland, where it would be easier to provide centralized services. Jeanie's family opted to move to St. George's, but only for a short time. It was both too big and too small – it lacked the small-town cohesion of their former community, yet wasn't big enough to offer adequate educational and employment opportunities for all the newly arrived residents. After about six months there, Jeanie's parents decided to take their government money and relocate the family to Toronto. There, Jeanie's father got a job as a construction worker outside of town, and her mother looked after short-term boarders. Their house became a sort of waystation for newly arrived Newfoundlanders, who would board for a few weeks or months while getting their bearings in the big city.

Their house was in downtown Toronto, not far from the city's 'gay village' centred around Yonge Street. It didn't take long for a teenaged Jeanie, still pre-transition, to discover the gay clubs on Yonge Street. Sharron and Jeanie retained a close relationship, and sometimes when Jeanie was left alone to babysit Sharron, Jeanie would sneak off with her to gay clubs like Club David's, an iconic gay and drag bar that operated in the mid-1970s.

"She used to babysit me, and she used to sneak me out and into David's on downtown Yonge Street, so I used to go to the gay bars too!" laughed her sister, remembering.

Jeanie charted her own ad hoc path through transition, during a period when not even the term was widely used. When she was in high school, she stopped using her masculine birth name and instead adopted the more androgynous Billie. She began wearing her hair long and paying more attention to her appearance, although she still presented as a man. Eventually she came out to her family as a woman.

"If that's the way you feel, then do it. Why be unhappy when you know you could be happy," her brother Albert Sheppard responded at the time, according to a later interview with the *Monmouth County Daily Register*. "She came up to me when she was about 16 or so and told me she wanted to be a woman. I said if that was what she wanted and if that would make her happy, then it was fine with me" (Graves 1980).

Sharron doesn't actually remember a particular coming out moment for Jeanie. She said Jeanie may have had one-on-one conversations with some of her family, but says her own memory is that Jeanie's transition was simply a fluid and open act, and one that the family matter-of-factly accepted.

It wasn't like she had to tell anybody. It wasn't like she had to stay in a closet. She was just like my sister from day one anyway. It wasn't just in a name, it was the way she acted, the way she was, what she used to do. She was doing it all her life, you know? She told mom first, but there was no 'Holy Jesus' moment or anything like that. And neither with dad. It was just like: 'That's who you are.' We all accepted her the way she was. I just figured that's the way it was supposed to be – family is family, friends are friends, and I love you as you are, I didn't give a shit what you got in the bottom or on the top or wherever. It's just who she was (Sheppard 2022).

Jeanie began performing at nightclubs, first in Toronto and then Montreal. David's was one of the spots where she performed. Sharron attended some of her shows. What she remembers in particular was Jeanie's talent at making her own clothes.

"Jeanie used to make her own costumes," explained Sharron.

She stayed in the basement, and she had her sewing stuff and her costumes there. She could take one costume and fit it on to another and it would be like – wow. She was quite the seamstress. She used to make her own things, like her pants – she used to make huge bell bottoms but she would cut the sides out, or put different cloth inside, really pretty colours and stuff. She made tops, put different buttons on shirts, she loved doing stuff like that. I know that if she was alive today she would have been somebody very important in the fashion world – she loved that stuff.

The girls used to come on [stage] and they were so gorgeous! My god, they were beautiful. And the costumes these girls made were fabulous. And they could sing – they would sing their songs, and Jeanie often used to sing for me too (Ibid.).

One of Jeanie's favourite songs, Sharron recalls, was Blondie's 'Heart of Glass,' which she integrated into a show she used to put off at the Manatee club, another famous queer nightclub in downtown Toronto. She had another performance that was centred around her pop culture namesake.

I remember this one outfit she had, it was an 'I Dream of Jeannie' costume. With her hair all up and a veil and everything, just like in 'I Dream of Jeannie.' And those see-through pants – she made everything just like it. I said: 'Oh my god are you really going to wear that?' And she says: 'Yeah! I made it, so I'm gonna wear it!' All her costumes were so beautiful and they were all home-made. She was so talented in that way.

She was so beautiful. And then when she had her boobs done, I used to look at them and feel them and poke at them. I used to go: 'Oh my god I want those!' And she would say: 'Well you're already a girl so when you develop that's what you're going to get.'

Just growing up with her was such a beautiful memory. It was very beautiful. We shared a lot. She was both the big sister and the mom that I needed. I was the youngest of sixteen, and when we moved to Ontario it was hard for my parents to get grounded so it was left up to other people to take care of me, and Jeanie was that person. She just used to amaze me. She was such a good spirit. Laughing, joking, carrying on and just being so funny (Ibid.).

By that point Jeanie fully presented as a woman, but she still enjoyed having fun with gender play.

Sometimes she used to sit down, and I used to have my girlfriends over, and she used to come in and I'd say: 'Hey sis how's it going?' And then she'd talk like a man, and my girlfriends would look at her and go: 'Holy shit you sounded just like a guy!' She used to do that and it was to die for. She was the devil too, she was so funny. Also with mom and dad's friends – they'd be at the bar and she would come in and do the same thing [speaking like a man]. And they'd be craning their necks around looking to see 'Who the hell was that?' She had a real flair for life, I tell you. It was awesome (Ibid.).

Jeanie eventually began spending more time in Montreal. She fell in love with a local man and they moved in together, living in the north of the city. There she became a well-known drag performer at venues like PJ's and Cafe Cleopatre. PJ's had more of an Anglophone clientele, and Jeanie became particularly well-known for her Wonder Woman routine there, along with a "space show."

Steven Cairney was a DJ at the club, and he and Jeanie became close friends.

She had that Linda Carter [Wonder Woman] look. She had the same kind of look – dark hair, and she was just stunning. Such a beauty. And so passable. We both were, but her moreso than I. And she had been trans for quite a few years before I met her. Even her voice was very soft and feminine... her facial features were very strong, she had a strong jaw-line and high cheekbones and beautiful eyes and long dark curly wavy hair. Nice full lips. She was a real beauty.

The trans community was very small, and we had a lot of friends in common, and then we became best friends. She was just such a nice person. She had such a big heart, and was so funny and fun to be with. It was impossible not to like her. She was just such a warm person, and so friendly and helpful (Cairney 2022).

They had a mutual friend, he recalls, who was self-conscious about her looks. "Jeanie always made her feel so good. That's what Jeanie tended to do to people."

Cairney still treasures a birthday card she gave him once. He was transitioning at the time, and used the name Cindy. She spelt out the name on the card, expanding on each and every letter. "She wrote 'C is for Caring, and I is for...'," he recalled. "And she wrote me so many other things, cards about 'Having a friend like you...' and what it meant. She was so, so nice to me. My heart was broken when she died."

She often talked about her Newfoundland origins, Cairney recalls. It was something that was very important to her. "She was a proud Newfie. She still had a Newfie accent, and she was very close to her family who accepted her as a woman. She was a Newfie and a proud Newfie."

Most of the trans community Jeanie and Cairney were part of in Montreal worked as drag performers or sex workers, he explained. "Most of the drag shows were actually done by trans people, not drag queens," he said. "They were mostly trans people doing the shows. We were a pretty tight-knit community. But it was very underground."

It was in Montreal that Jeanie met Robert Fox, a trucker from the United States. Following what family members described as a "whirlwind courtship" Jeanie and Fox returned to his hometown of Howell, New Jersey, and were married. At the time New Jersey required genital inspections of women by a medical professional before marriage (a policy common in many American jurisdictions in the early twentieth century as part of a campaign against venereal disease). Because there was no formal legal infrastructure around name and gender transitions at the time, and because Jeanie had not yet completed her vaginoplasty surgeries, this could have posed a barrier to the couple's marriage plans. But Jeanie apparently feigned shy and managed to sweet-talk the doctor into signing his approval without actually carrying out the inspection (Brenoff & Berry 1983).

The marriage soon ran into problems. Accounts provided by family members to media described Fox as overprotective and jealous. He'd been married previously, and had two children, an 18-year-old daughter and a 13-year-old son, from a previous marriage that ended in divorce. The children had gone to live with their mother following the divorce, but after Fox and Jeanie's wedding, the daughter moved back in with them and apparently forged a close relationship with Jeanie.

That was Cairney's recollection as well. He stayed in regular contact with Jeanie when she moved to the US. "From what Jeanie told me [the children] really, really cared for her," he said.

According to court testimony reported in the *Asbury Park Press*, Fox said Jeanie had been the one who insisted on coming out to the children.

'I was totally against it,' Fox said. 'She told me that she had only been wrong once about telling someone – telling someone who couldn't accept it. She insisted my daughter was ready and should be told.'

Fox recalled that his wife went into the kitchen where his daughter was and he heard a scream. When he ran into the kitchen, he found the two hugging each other (Ibid.).

Jeanie subsequently told her stepson as well.

Family members described Fox as "moody," "strange," and said "he followed [Jeanie] everywhere, except when she went to the bathroom." A few months after the wedding, Jeanie told family members on the phone that she wasn't happy and felt the marriage wasn't working out (Graven 1980).

Jeanie had already undergone two transition-related surgeries in Toronto, and was scheduled for a final surgery there in early 1981. "It was the most important thing in her life," Sharron told reporters after her death (Graven 1980).

She planned to spend Christmas with her family before going in for the operation.

The jealous and controlling Fox decided he didn't want her returning to Toronto. They argued and fought, and Jeanie told her family she'd had to "break down and cry" to persuade him to let her go (Ibid.).

She was scheduled to leave for Toronto on Monday, December 16, 1980. That afternoon at around 5:00pm, as she packed her suitcase, Fox again argued with her. He found what was later described in court as a packet of "diary-like letters" (Brenoff & Berry 1983) from someone who was apparently a former lover and close friend. Fox drew a handgun and shot and killed her.

Fox's daughter had stayed at a friend's house overnight, oblivious to the murder that took place after she left the home. The next morning, she telephoned home, and after speaking with her father she gathered what had happened and she phoned the police. A nearly 12-hour siege of the Fox residence ensued. Late that night, Fox's brother persuaded him to surrender to police. When they entered the house, they found Jeanie's body. It was flown back to Toronto for burial (Sheehan & Graven 1980).

Sharron remembers the day of Jeanie's murder in vivid detail. Over four decades later, she still speaks through tears.

"It was a nightmare. Jeanie was coming home for Christmas, and I couldn't wait. I just couldn't wait. She was supposed to be home, and she'd told us what time she would be over at mom's. And then she never showed up, she never made it. And never made it. And never made it (Shepperd 2022).

Sharron and a mutual friend phoned all of their family members and friends, wondering whether perhaps Jeanie had gone to someone else's house from the airport. When no one reported hearing from her, they tried calling Jeanie's house in New Jersey; Fox sometimes answered but either hung up or told them that she had already left. Sharron called the airport and learned that the flight had arrived hours earlier. She eventually called the Toronto police to report that her sister was supposed to have come home hours earlier but was missing. She doesn't remember whether she called the New Jersey police too, but does recall that it was a couple of hours later that the police phoned her parents' house. They explained something was going on at the Fox residence and that shots had been reported.

So I was scared. I got scared then. Then when he surrendered and they found her body, that's when they said there was a person there and it has to be your sister. That was a nightmare. It was like everybody was running around and talking but none of it seemed real, none of it was real to me. I needed to see it. I needed proof. When they called and said they needed somebody to go and identify her body, I wanted to be the one to go. But my brother said I couldn't, because of how she was shot. Once he went and done that, and I got the confirmation I needed, it was like my entire heart and soul just dropped (Ibid.).

Monmouth County prosecutors tried their best to obtain justice against

Jeanie's killer. A first murder trial against Fox ended in a mistrial in July 1981. A second trial in February 1982 also ended in mistrial. In July 1982, a third trial finally saw Fox convicted of manslaughter and sentenced to five years' probation (Brenoff & Berry 1983).

Predictably, defense attorneys portrayed Jeanie in as negative a light as possible during those trials. Fox claimed temporary insanity caused by the discovery of correspondence between her and her former lover. During the third trial, some of Jeanie's friends from Montreal also testified. Cairney was among them. He testified that Jeanie's murder "figured prominently" in his subsequent decision to detransition (Ashbury Park Press 1982). Monmouth County prosecutors said they were "outraged" by the leniency of the manslaughter sentence, and appealed it. It was upheld in June 1983 (Brenoff & Berry 1983).

Jeanie's friend Steve Cairney attended her funeral in Toronto, and there he met her family for the first time. He was struck by their love and acceptance of Jeanie. "It was amazing. Even today it would be amazing, because the trans community unfortunately do not get the support that they should. But in the 1970s? In Newfoundland? For a family to be that supportive was almost unheard of."

Cairney's own mother had been heartbroken when he came out as a trans woman, he said. It was about two years after Jeanie's death that he made the decision to detransition, and reassumed his birth name of Steven. Her murder had played a part in that decision, as he testified. So did the death of a close friend.

Jeanie's death definitely played a factor but it wasn't the only thing. There also was a friend of mine who died by suicide at my apartment. He jumped off my balcony. He wanted to transition but felt that he was too masculine. He was kind of envious that I was able to [pass] and he wasn't. Then one day I was with him [at my apartment], and all of the sudden he went in my bedroom and I couldn't find him and I looked and he had jumped off the balcony... so there were a few things that played into me deciding to [detransition]. I just thought it was probably the best for an easier life, not to continue (Cairney 2022).

More than forty years later, Jeanie's memory is still vividly alive for those who knew and loved her.

"She's someone I still think of all the time, and it's been forty odd years," reflected Cairney. "But I still think of her frequently... Once you got to know her, you couldn't not like her. She was remarkable."

She was a beautiful soul. She was my heart. She was the most beautiful heart that you'd ever meet. She loved everybody, she helped everybody, and if she got mad, the way she'd get mad is she'd just look at you and say 'Whatever' and then leave. She wasn't a confrontational kind of person. She was always happy-go-lucky, she'd just shrug and say: 'There's more to life than that shit.' We had such good times. Such really good times.

When she left this world I didn't have anybody. I needed somebody to guide me when I got to the boyfriend stage, but I didn't have anybody and it was hard for me. I always wished I could talk to her again, just for a minute or something. But she had a good life. What she had was good. I just wish she could have been here for the rest of it (Shepperd 2022).

Liam Hustins (August 21, 1973 - July 30, 2004)

Liam Hustins was an activist, writer, performer, and artist originally from St. John's. He came out as lesbian in the early 1990s, and co-founded Out On Campus, the first queer group on the Memorial University campus run exclusively by students and, for a period, one of the province's pre-eminent LGBTQ rights groups. Later in the 1990s, he left the province, and wound up in Toronto. There his work and activism took a different direction, and in the early 2000s he came out as trans and transitioned. Liam died young but is still widely remembered both in this province and Toronto, where a memorial is inscribed with his name at the iconic Buddies in Bad Times theatre.

Hustins' activism began not long after enrolling as an undergrad at Memorial University in 1991. He moved into a large shared house in the city's downtown. One of his roommates there was Ted Martin, another undergrad.

It was a tall, skinny, three-storey building and there was a whole bunch of people living in there. It was very much a party house. We spent a lot of time hanging out. There was a lot of that first-year university trying to figure out where your gender and sexuality sat. We spent a lot of time curled up in our rooms on the bed having heart-to-heart conversations... about gender and sexuality (Martin 2022).

Both Hustins and Martin got involved with the extended circle of students involved with *The Muse* student newspaper. Campus life was a full-time affair in those days, with the hours between classes packed with socializing and creative work.

Liam and I would hang out in the old food court at MUN, along with a few other people. There was a table just as you came into the food court on the left-hand side, and it was one of the only tables that had bench seating. Those of us who were there very early would claim that table first thing in the morning and there would be people at that table throughout the rest of the day. This was back when you could still smoke in the food court. We played a lot of cards (Ibid.).

Hustins was also an ace ping-pong player, he recalls. "His family had a ping-pong table in their basement and he would whoop my ass anytime we played. I remember playing ping-pong and smoking drugs at his house when his parents were out of town."

"Liam was very bubbly, very excitable. He had the best grin. There was something very fae about him at times."

Both Hustins and Martin discovered the gay club scene together – Solomons was the venue of choice in the early 1990s. Hustins came out as lesbian, and together with Mireille Sampson co-founded the campus-based organization Out On Campus in 1994 (its establishment was officially ratified by MUNSU in 1995). The community-based NGALE had been formed in 1993, but Out On Campus maintained a louder, more visible presence, and organizers at the St. John's Status of Women Centre often referred queries from gays and lesbians directly to the campus group. Out On Campus played a key role in Pride Week celebrations in 1995 and Hustins served as one of the primary media spokespersons.

Gemma Hickey was one of the young students Hustins recruited to the organization. Hickey, who recalls feeling isolated and alone when they started university at Memorial, met Hustins early on through a mutual friend.

Liam just seemed really cool. He used to sit at the table and would roll cigarettes old-school, like take the tobacco out from the pocket, roll it, smoke it, no filter. That was Liam. We were opposites – I was a little preppy kid just out of high school – but for some reason Liam wanted to hang out with me and we hit it off. Everyone was in love with Liam – men, women, everyone.

Liam was larger than life. Just this huge personality, this huge presence. I wanted to be like Liam. So confident, so self-assured, just very handsome. At the time Liam identified as a butch lesbian and had this curly thick dark hair, always wore a black leather jacket, jeans ripped at the knees, and just looked so cool. Black boots, had a strut, a lot of bravado, but it just seemed so natural.

Liam and I hit it off right away. Liam said: 'We need to get something on the go on campus for people like us'... So we came up with the idea to form this group called Out On Campus. That was Liam. It couldn't just be a group with a name that was different – it had to be OUT. We're all OUT. Coming out. You had to be OUT! That was just Liam in a nutshell.

I was fresh out of the gate in terms of activism – back then I knew nothing. I hadn't come out to all of my extended family and friends. So I was still a bit nervous about being [out] in public... So Liam said to me: 'You know, you can be involved, but you don't have to be out, you don't have to put your name on any of the documents. You can still be a part of this and be a founding member and contribute in lots of other ways.' So I said okay. Then there was this society fair on campus, and Liam wanted me to stay at the booth for a bit to talk to people and that sort of thing. Of course, I was really nervous about it. There were a lot of people [at MUNL] that I hadn't come out to in high school, that didn't know I identified at that time as a lesbian. And I remember the sign that Liam drew up for the group – it had the triangle on it and it said Out On Campus in pink and black. People came by and just looked at the sign, looked back at me, looked at the sign, looked back at me, and I was like: 'Yup.' There was nowhere for me hide really. So I think that experience really gave me the

push I needed to get more involved. It was as if Liam gave me that permission,
gave me that push. Liam pushed and brought me to where I needed to be at that
time. I don't think anyone else had that kind of influence on me in that way.
So the roots of my activism – a lot of it is rooted in trauma I've experienced,
and trying to turn it around, but it's also because of Liam's presence in my life.
Liam was a real inspiration (Hickey 2022).

Mireille Sampson, with whom Hustins co-founded Out on Campus, retains similar impressions.

Liam was just a remarkably brave and generous person. Nothing seemed to
stop him. He was just going to live. [Despite] all of the crap that he had happen
to him in his life, he just kept going. And not just going, but really living loud
and out there and full. And he would always help anybody. There was no bit-
terness and there was a kindness and he always had this thing about looking
out for other people. There was consideration for other people. He always put
other people first. He was that kind of person (Sampson 2021).

Liam never graduated from Memorial, but in the mid-1990s acquired a
small motorcycle and set off to see the country. He spent time in Vancouver,
and enrolled for a period at Fairview Community College in Alberta, where he
studied small engine repair, a topic inspired by his love of the motorcycle. He
rode his Yamaha 500 back and forth between Vancouver and St. John's three or
four times, friends recall. Then, in 1997, Liam made his way to Toronto, the city
that would become his new home.

Patricia Bandak met Liam early on during his time in Toronto. The two
dated casually for a time but went on to become deeply close friends.

Liam was always generous, kind, open-hearted, very friendly, super smart.
Just a very nice person, and always very open and welcoming to everyone. He
would get a lot of people together to do fun things all the time. He'd always
include everyone he knew, and invite them everywhere (Bandak 2022).

She recalls an expedition he organized to Gay Day at Canada's Wonder-
land, during which he pulled together a couple of dozen people to take a bus
to the event. Another time he helped Bandak organize an expedition of 21 lesbians to go white-water rafting in Ottawa.

"That was such a fun trip," she recalls. "Liam played music all the way
there. He played the same song the whole way there because he loved it so
much. He was just very fun."

Aimee Finlay was a young undergraduate student doing visual studies at
the University of Toronto. She was at Buddies in Bad Times Theatre one night
when she met Liam. Liam was there with Bandak, and Bandak noticed the two
younger people staring at each other throughout the show. Bandak approached
Finlay and told her that Liam liked her. Liam and Finlay exchanged numbers
and shortly thereafter went out on a date. They fell in love almost instantly.

For our first date alone we went to the Horseshoe Tavern. From that first
date we were just kind of tied at the hip. I was living up on Bloor Street in

Little Korea, but spending all my time at Liam's apartment in Parkdale. So very quickly I ended up moving in with him. We were very, very much in love (Finlay 2022).

One of the things that attracted her to Liam was his generous, inclusive nature.

Liam was an includer in everything. He was a skateboarder, but I am not a natural skateboarder. So if I had been dating anybody else, they would have been like: 'I'm going skateboarding with my pals.' But not Liam. Instead Liam said: 'You're getting a longboard! I'm taking you shopping right now and you're going to learn to skateboard!' And so I did. Was I good? No — I was terrible. But it didn't matter. Liam had a little gang, and we'd all go out, and we'd skateboard through the city, and we'd be terrible. But Liam would say: 'It's okay!'

And Liam was good. Like, he wasn't incredible, and he didn't learn to skateboard as a child, but his attitude was: 'We're doing this and we will not be excluded from it!' That was typical Liam. He was very playful and loved animation, collectible toys, all of that stuff. He loved the movie Toy Story.

Liam was just so generous. He always looked out for the underdog before it was cool to do so. He had Indigenous peoples' rights at the forefront of his mind all the time, and sex workers' rights, and rights of women. I think he really felt kinship with the underdog in any situation and was always looking out to bring up people around him who might have less privilege or harder lives or harder sets of circumstances before them.

I was a bi femme and in the queer community sometimes femme women are thought of as not queer enough. Liam was never like that. He and I were very, passionately in love. It was young love, we had amazing chemistry, we adored each other, we fell hard for each other. He could be generous and giving - almost to a fault, about which he would always say: 'It's the Newfoundlander in me!' He would give the shirt off his back to anybody that needed it, without question (Ibid.).

Bandak remembers how quickly the couple bonded after she introduced them.

They were a great couple from the moment they met. They were a great couple, just beautiful. Aimee's gorgeous, she's a stunning redhead, and Liam was very handsome. Liam adored Aimee, and Aimee adored Liam. You could see the love between them. They were a beautiful couple (Bandak 2022).

Nigel Wynne met Liam in the summer of 1998, before either of them transitioned. They met during Toronto Pride Week; "MegaPride" was that year's ostentatious theme. Wynne had just moved to Toronto the previous year and come out as lesbian. He'd recently had a difficult break-up, and didn't have any friends in the city. Early on a Sunday morning in late June, Wynne was walking aimlessly down the road, feeling sad about his situation, when he encountered two individuals sitting on the side of the road. It was Liam and a friend.

These two little punks sitting on the side of the road just asked me who

I was. They were really nice to me. They said: 'We've got a skateboard street gang if you want to join.' I said: 'I don't know how to skateboard.' They were like: 'That's fine, you can still join.' So they invited me to go out skating with them the following week in the evening. This was before cellphones, so they told me where to meet them, and I just had to arrive and hope they would be there. And they were (Wynne 2022).

Wynne borrowed a skateboard, and did his best to follow the others' lead: he very much wanted to make friends with this gang of skater punks he'd encountered.

I was riding on one of their skateboards, and at one point I wound up in front, in the lead. We were approaching the streetcar tracks at Spadina and College. I saw the criss-crossing streetcar tracks, and figured I needed to go over them really fast. So I started speeding up, and then made it across the tracks — ticka-ticka-ticka-ticka. When I got across, and turned around, they were all just stopped in front of the tracks with their mouths open, shocked. They said: 'Nobody skates over streetcar tracks! You're supposed to stop and walk over the streetcar tracks!' So after doing that, I was in.

Liam told me: 'You have to think of a skateboard name. If you can't think of one by the next time we see you, then we'll give you one.' I didn't want to come up with a name, but I had a t-shirt that said 'Manc' – I was from Manchester. I was wearing it the next time I saw them, and they were like: 'What does Manc mean?' I said: 'It's just a person from Manchester.' So they chose that as my skateboard name. That's how I got the name 'Manc,' and a lot of people in Toronto call me that now. You could say that Liam and the others gave me my name. It was nice (Ibid.).

Wynne rapidly became close friends with Liam's gang, and especially with Liam.

They were always very inviting to new people. I would sometimes get jealous of that; I'd want to be special. I'd say to Liam: 'Do they have to come and hang out with us?' But Liam would always tell me: 'Yes, everyone is welcome to hang out with us. Always. It's an open invite. The door is always open, and whatever we have we share.' That was very much Liam's approach to life.

He was very, very open. Very warm, very accepting, very forgiving (Ibid.).

Hustins was rapidly making a name for himself in the creative community. He began attending Clit Lit, a queer spoken word event. It was there he met Elizabeth Ruth, a published author and writing instructor who organized the events and became somewhat of a mentor to him. She remembers his avid involvement in the monthly events.

I met Liam sometime near the end of the 1990s on Church Street, in the heart of Toronto's gay neighbourhood. I hosted a queer reading series there, at a club called The Red Spot. I don't remember our introduction or on which night Liam first took to the microphone to share his stories. What I do recall is that every month, when community gathered, he was always at a table, front and centre, grinning ear-to-ear, cheering on other readers. To me, he seemed like a hard shell with a soft centre, a no-bullshit, high-octane personality that was perpetually about to bubble over. At the end of one event, he approached me, tempted to get up on that stage. He was a storyteller, not a writer, he said. He came from Newfoundland. Would he fit in? Words were words, I told him, certain the audience would be as appreciative of his contribution as he was of everyone else's. A month later, he did just that, and the crowd loved him. Of course they did. He was open, down to earth, authentic. With his big personality and Newfoundland expressions, he went on to become a crowd favourite and one of the few among us with a serious passion for science fiction and speculative fiction.

Back then, my partner Shannon and I rented the first floor of an old brick house on Dovercourt Road. Liam came for supper one night with his partner, Aimee. The four of us sat around a small table in a bright yellow kitchen, laughing. I remember thinking Liam liked to laugh, and to drink, perhaps too much. It seemed to me he was searching for something he hadn't yet found. We all were. He wanted to talk writing and gender and sex, and about his big love for his first home, Newfoundland. He made sure we understood that Newfoundland was still its own nation, with its own history and culture. He was fiercely proud of that. Now, re-reading Liam's short story, "Cold Steel Utensil", published in Bent On Writing: Contemporary Queer Tales, I see the subtext, so much of who he was becoming. I wish he'd had the chance to get there and enjoy the view (Ruth 2022).

Hustins had already self-published an illustrated chapbook, but his contribution to the *Bent on Writing* anthology in 2002 was his first published work of fiction in Toronto. He volunteered with the Merril Collection of Science Fiction, Speculation and Fantasy, which is one of the world's largest collections of speculative fiction (part of the Toronto Public Library). He served on its Board, and became editor for *Sol Rising*, the Collection's newsletter. This gave him access to meet and interview other authors, emerging and big-name alike. He organized a workshop for beginning horror writers through the Merril as well.

Liam really wanted to be a writer. He was determined. When he landed in Toronto he applied for a job at Xtra Magazine. He poured all his heart and soul into his application to 'Extra Magazine' and wrote to them about how much he would love to be a part of the 'Extra team.' He eventually got a one-page reply from someone at the mag. The letter basically said: 'It's called Xtra.' Liam was pretty devastated by his mistake but was able to laugh about it a few years later (Finlay 2022).

Liam did eventually go on to write for *Xtra*, as well as *Rue Morgue* horror magazine. His artistic interests were varied. He worked for a time at a printshop, and became good friends with the owners, who Wynne says became like family to him. Often, he would stay after the shop closed, working there on his own artistic projects late into the night. At the time, his partner Aimee worked at an independent fashion retail outlet located on the same block. After work she would sometimes work on her visual design projects for school in the print-shop with Liam's aid. Liam also loved designing and producing vinyl decals; he designed and printed the decorations for his gang's skateboards at that shop. Jamie Fraser Books, a well known used and rare book dealership, was located in the same building, and Liam also worked for a time in the bookshop (as did Aimee). It was there that he greatly expanded his own collection of science fiction and horror books, which eventually grew to encompass over 5000 volumes. Fraser was president of the Merril Collection board at the time, and it was through him that Liam got involved with the library.

"Writing was definitely his first love, but he also liked painting," recalled Wynne. Art intersected well with his skater punk ethos. Wylie remembers Hustins growing incensed at The Gap clothing store when it began appropriating punk fashion elements.

"We felt it was appropriating queer fetish wear," explained Wynne. "These days people wear studded collars all the time, but at the time we felt they were marketing things that came out of the queer community." Hustins spray painted the Gap shop window one night in downtown Toronto; Wynne described it as an elaborate and politicized statement against the Gap's appropriation of queer culture and regrets that he never took a photo. The two fled the scene as soon as they were done, and spent the night carousing nearby, never realizing until they got home that their spray-paint-splattered clothing and bags would have easily identified them as the culprits.

"He always talked about wanting to get a van, rob a Shoppers Drug Mart and take all the Tampax and give them out to people for free," remembered Wynne.

"He was artistic, very artistic," recalled Bandak. In addition to her job as a courier, Bandak was a freelance photographer. She documented Toronto's gay and lesbian scene in her earlier years, and then later transitioned to focusing on nude photography. One of the shows she organized was a collaborative art event featuring work by herself, Finlay, and Liam. "Liam made computer parts into a collage," she recalled.

Carey Gray is owner of Aslan Leather, a leather store in Toronto. Finlay worked with him for a time early in her relationship with Liam. Gray, Hustins and Wynne formed a strip group called the Throbbing Rods, and put off some shows around the city, including a large performance at Toronto's Opera House. They also took the show on the road, including some performances in the US.

"It was great, it was fucking awesome," recalled Gray. "I made these packing pouches, I made stripper pants for all of us, and we did it to AC/DC's 'I'm Gonna Rock You All Night Long' and stuff. It was really hot. Manc [Wynne] did all the choreography. He was fantastic."

Wynne remembers those shows well, and laughs when recalling them.

I'm not a big dancer or anything, and I don't like being the centre of attention. But we knew what song we were going to use, and I said 'Well how about we just take turns dancing individually to the song, and we'll pick our best moves, each other's favourite moves, and we'll do that.' So I said: 'Who wants to go first?' And the two of them were like: 'I'll go first! I'll go first!' So I knew I would never have to dance alone. I just watched them and wrote down all the moves I'd be able to do, and then after they'd both danced around, I said 'Okay I think we have enough here.' So I kind of choreographed it. That was a really cool experience. We all did it together, that was a really good, awesome experience. Carey had made us jeans with velcro all the way down the sides, so we could rip them off and throw them over our heads. Then at the end it revealed the packing, kind of like underwear. It was cool (Wynne 2022).

Everyone who knew Hustins remembers how important his Newfoundland identity was to him.

Let me tell you one thing – Liam was very proud of being from Newfoundland. He would mention it all the time, and told me that I should go there, that he would love to take me there. Liam was so proud of where he was from. He was very proud of Newfoundland. Super proud. Loved it. He was proud of his heritage from there and being from there (Bandak 2022).

He was really proud to have come from Newfoundland. He gave me a Newfoundland flag and made me an honorary Newf, even though I had never been screeched in. He was really proud to come from Newfoundland. When I picture Newfoundland, it's through Liam's eyes. He would talk about the ocean, this amazing ocean with massive rocks and waves smashing up against them all the time (Wynne 2022).

Wynne got a first-hand dose of Newfoundland culture when Liam's parents came to visit him in Toronto. They brought moose meat, cod tongues, and cod cheeks, and hosted a home-cooked feast for Liam and his friends. "His mom taught me to pronounce Newfoundland," recalls Wynne. "It was the first time I'd had cod tongues and cheeks."

Finlay also remembers how central his cultural identity was to Liam.

Liam was a passionate Newfoundlander. He let everybody know that he was a Newfoundlander, and he was so proud of it. It was hard for him that it was expensive and not easy [to travel home]. My maternal grandmother is from Codroy Valley and so he would always tease me that I was a baywop and he was a townie. He loved that, and it was one of the first things that we connected on. He loved Newfoundland. But I think it was bittersweet. I think he would have loved to have had a life in Newfoundland, but he knew that it was not likely that he would ever settle back there. He had such a full and vibrant life in Toronto (Finlay 2022).

When Liam's younger sister Nancy-Louise moved to Ottawa for school, he was grateful for the chance to spend more time with her, recalls Finlay. The two developed a close relationship, and Liam and Aimee often took trips to Ottawa to visit his sister, who was studying to be a lawyer.

"He was so proud of her," recalls Finlay. "He was very proud of her. He adored her. That was a very important relationship for him. They really developed a beautiful friendship."

In January 2002, Wynne's father, who lived in the UK, died.

"Liam was the first person I told," he recalled. Liam left work immediately and went to find Wynne. "I stayed in his apartment, kind of catatonic, until my plane left three days later," said Wynne. "Liam just played backgammon with me non-stop."

Wynne returned to England for a few days for his father's funeral. The day before the funeral service, Liam phoned him from Toronto.

Liam called to say that the funeral was going to go okay and that he was thinking of me. But then he told me that he had decided to transition. He was going to be called Liam now. He said it was partly my dad's dying that had shown him that life was for living, and he had to live his best life (Wynne 2022).

At the time, Wynne didn't take the news well. He was going through a difficult emotional period due to his father's death, and wished Liam hadn't chosen that occasion to share such personal news with him. Over time, he said, Liam's decision to transition positioned him to help other trans people in Toronto – including Wynne himself.

He was one of the first of our circle to transition. A lot of trans guys who are my friends now, it was Liam who opened a lot of the doors for them. He told them who to talk to, told them how to access services, and so on. This meant that by the time I transitioned ten years later... my path was very easy, because those he had mentored and helped could then in turn mentor me back. A lot of people went to Liam for help and advice, and just to talk. Just for someone to talk to. He definitely provided that (Wynne 2022).

Liam wasn't the first person I knew that was trans, but I think he was the second person. He opened the doors for a lot of people to become comfortable with being trans. He was very supportive for anyone who had those decisions to make, and he was very helpful to anyone who was going through that stuff. He would be like a brother to them. And he was really happy after he transitioned, he was super happy (Bandak 2022).

Unbeknownst to many of his friends however, Liam was also struggling. Finlay was among the few who witnessed it.

He was so happy on the outside, and I think what's really hard for some of his social acquaintances is that a lot of people saw Liam so happy – here he was transitioning, and had a job, had a partner, had a fairly good relationship with his family – but behind closed doors Liam could be very sad. I think his suicide was shocking because people didn't see it coming. He wasn't depressed day to day... he was very successful for his age and he was very loved. But behind closed doors... we partied hard, we'd be out drinking, and on the town, and dancing, and being crazy, and then we'd be on our way home and he would be on the sidewalk in absolute tears. He really enjoyed pub life and drinking life and bar culture, but he would often come home very sad. The people in our social circle did not see that (Finlay 2022).

The regular drinking became one of the things Finlay and Liam argued about. He'd experienced sexual abuse as well as abusive relationships in the past. "These two things were very hard for Liam, very internalized," Finlay recalled. It was only toward the end of his life that he started therapy.

Gray, who transitioned several years after Liam, feels that the lack of public supports for trans people at the time exacerbated some of the pressures and anxiety Liam experienced.

He had anxiety, and when you go on T [testosterone] it's like you go through puberty all over again… He transitioned, but he was so scared to go to the bathroom in the men's rooms. He was scared to go into the stall and take a piss. Aimee would [tell him to] bring frozen grapes so that it sounded like he was taking a shit. Today there's guys that can have access to bottom surgery, but you didn't have that twenty years ago. It wasn't available.

Today I'm on all these [trans] groups on Facebook and other places, and the guys are all: 'What's happening to me?' They always ask questions, and there's lots of people commenting and helping them. But we didn't have that back then. Liam didn't have that. It was early in the days of the internet, and he didn't have what we have today.

When he died, I had been planning to transition, but then I decided 'I'm not fucking doing it.' I had turned forty and was ready – I was going by 'he', and people called me Mr. Gray which was great – but I just didn't do it. So I wound up waiting until I was 49. Because of his death, and the death of [another trans man who died by suicide]. It's a hard thing to talk about (Gray 2022).

The lack of supports and community for trans men at the time probably contributed to Liam's increasing alcohol use, Gray feels.

We didn't have a lot of money, I don't even remember us eating much for dinner – all of our money went to beer and booze. We were very in love, we had a lot of fun, we had a wonderful group of friends, we partied and danced and felt alive. But we didn't always take the best care of ourselves. Part of that was our youth, and part of that was from the abuse.

I think that Liam's suicide came from a place of his sexual abuse and [re-lationship] abuse that he suffered. Certainly not from his sexuality or gender identity. I think that alcoholism made things seem really dire for him, it would make things seem insurmountable. When he was sober and happy he could deal with things and look at all the successes in his life and the happiness and the friends, but… when he'd been at the pub since 6pm knocking back pints and got home at midnight, that's when he would be very sad and go to a dark place.

We had a lot of fun, but I think the self-care that would have helped him have greater mental stability wasn't there. We were just very young and our whole friend group – we were all partying and at the bars. We all felt on top of the world. As queer people, I think the places that we socialize are often bars and bar culture, because you don't have that aspect of your life in other places where people meet and socialize. That was hard for Liam. I don't know, maybe everybody's youths are like that.

After he died, for the next six or seven years he was at the forefront of my mind every day before I reached a point where I could emotionally move beyond it. But I think Liam was actually very happy – he loved the world and he had so much joy around life and friends and family. He was a very passionate person (Finlay 2022).

Chosen family is important in queer community, and Liam and Aimee built that into their lives as well. When an apartment below Liam and Aimee's place became vacant, they arranged for Bandak to move in. Wynne was also a constant presence in their lives.

"We used to call Nigel [Wynne] our adopted child," Finlay recounts with a laugh. "For a few years he stayed on our couch probably four nights a week, no joke. He almost lived in our one-bedroom apartment. We were all so very close. I think Liam would love the fact that we are all still friends."

"We had a big community," explained Bandak.

We'd have parties on my deck all the time, my group of friends and his group of friends. And he was happy most of the time. The only time I didn't see him happy was when he was drinking and drank too much. He was very happy most of the time but the drinking was a problem and would take him in a different place mentally. But that was just a small part of who he was. Through all of that he was fantastic, a great person, fun, kind, smart, always fun to be around. And well-loved (Bandak 2022).

The love within their close-knit circle of friends was mutual. Liam and Aimee organized a fortieth birthday party for Bandak, which she remembers vividly and fondly. The young couple organized it at a large event space on Queen Street West and packed all three floors of the hybrid venue. Over 150 people attended, including many of Bandak's friends from Montreal whom Liam and Aimee invited.

"It was the sweetest thing ever," Bandak reflects, still deeply moved. In addition to organizing the party, Liam gave her a very special gift.

Liam knew that I loved Madonna, and so for my birthday he gave me the Madonna book, Sex. I hadn't bought it because it was so expensive. I wished I had. But Liam collected books – first editions and stuff, he collected first editions for the value of them. So he had collected the Madonna book, but he knew that I'd always wanted it, and so he gave it to me. Brand new. Because he knew how much I loved Madonna. That was probably one of the nicest gifts anyone ever gave me. That party was amazing and that gift was amazing. That's how sweet Liam was. I still have the book. I'm going to hold on to it until the day that I die (Bandak 2022).

Gemma Hickey, who later transitioned as well, also reconnected with Liam before his death.

Liam had come out as trans and was just as gorgeous and just as larger than life — just so real, so brave. He started hormone therapy and transition with the same kind of vigour and fearlessness as when he said 'We gotta start something on campus.' Same kind of approach – 'This is what we're gonna do!' (Hickey 2022).

"I had a lot of gender dysphoria over the years," said Hickey. Hickey described struggling with dysphoria and gender identity, a struggle exacerbated by the experience of childhood sexual abuse. "My mind went to Liam, and how brave Liam was, for making those changes at a time when the rest of us, myself included, weren't there yet. I felt that because Liam went there, I could go there. So I started hormone therapy."

Hickey's activism is well known throughout Canada; following leadership roles in NGALE, PFLAG and EGALE they created the Pathways Foundation for survivors of clergy abuse, led legal and human rights challenges around same-sex unions, gender-neutral passports, and more. "I credit Liam for pushing me in this direction – Liam had a profound impact on me and the advocacy work that I do."

Mireille Sampson, with whom Liam co-founded Out on Campus in St. John's, was similarly impacted by their relationship.

Liam was just a remarkably brave and generous person. Nothing seemed to stop him. He was just going to live his life. All of the crap that had happened to him in his life, he just kept going. And not just going, but really living loud and out there and full. And he would always help anybody. There was no bitterness and there was a kindness and consideration – he always had this thing about looking out for other people. He put other people first. He was that kind of a person (Sampson 2021).

On July 30, 2004, Liam passed away in Toronto.

A service was held in St. John's, and another one in Toronto on what would have been his 31st birthday. Over 150 people attended. Wynne performed a rendition of "Danny Boy," Liam's favourite song. "It was a long, loud and raucous affair, and one that Liam would have really enjoyed," wrote *Sol Rising* editor Sabrina Fried in a tribute published in the newsletter. His ashes were scattered in the Atlantic Ocean.

"He was definitely well-loved and well-remembered among lots of people across the community," said Wynne. "Even today people who have only been here in Toronto a few years, they'll hear his name and they're like: 'Who's this Liam guy?' He was very well-known and very loved."

Alexandria Tucker (July 23, 1974 - April 14, 2005)

Alexandria Tucker was born on July 23, 1974. She had two siblings: an older brother named Marty and a younger sister named Kelly. Marty was two years older than Alexandria, and Kelly two years younger.

"Our dad was a raging alcoholic and was very abusive to my mother," explained Kelly. "So mom fled my father when I was five. She had to pick up and start anew. We had nothing."

After the separation they stayed with friends of their mother's for a while, and eventually settled into a new house in Kilbride, on Chatman Crescent by the Lion's Club. In 1987, as a young teenager, Alexandria began studying martial arts at Jerry Lee's NL Shotokan. She studied aikido, jiu-jitsu, and shotokan karate. She excelled at the martial arts.

"Jerry Lee was one of Alex's mentors and really took Alex under his wing," recalled Kelly.

That whole family were so supportive and lovely and were a really big part of Alex's life. It really gave Alex something to channel her energy and frustrations into. She really dove into it.

Alex was almost an anomaly in our family. She was so different from the rest of us. My mom's a smoker, I'm a smoker, my brother is a smoker, but Alex would never touch it. My mom always used to roll her own cigarettes, and would keep a hundred cigarettes rolled. I remember waking up one morning, and Alex had stayed up all night long writing 'cancer stick' in little tiny letters over every single cigarette. All down the shaft of the cigarette: 'cancer stick cancer stick cancer stick.' A hundred cigarettes — it must have taken her all night to do that! It was quite funny.

Alex never drank either. She was so focused, so great in school. She had her own car at sixteen! She was so different from the rest of us (Tucker 2022).

Colin Williams was one of Alex's high school teachers at Beaconsfield High School in St. John's. He has similar memories of Alex's singular focus. Williams was a dog breeder on the side, and bred Lhasa Apsos. He hired Alex to come over on the weekends and help with cleaning up the grounds and kennels.

She helped me clean up around the kennel and the garden, and would stay and have a Pepsi after. She didn't smoke, she didn't drink, she didn't do any drugs. She was an excellent student, very outgoing, very athletic. She was in excellent shape, was very active in martial arts and excellent at it... Later she worked for my brother at one of our Irving [gas] stations, on Water Street. She was unbelievably dependable, she showed up, she was honest, she didn't take time off... just a real all-round nice person.

She was determined, focused, very careful over her appearance. She always had her hair cut and always dressed meticulously (C. Williams 2022).

It wasn't until her final year of high school in 1993, at the age of seventeen, that Alexandria came out as trans to her sister, Kelly.

"I remember it very well. Alex had a girlfriend – they'd been together forever, for years and years, throughout high school. One Hallowe'en they all went downtown to this Hallowe'en party, and Alex dressed up as a woman. She showed me her Hallowe'en costume, and I was like: 'Damn – you look hot!' She had blonde hair, she just looked so good! Of course, it wasn't just a Hallowe'en costume – it was an opportunity to dress like herself without anybody questioning it.

Anyway, she went out and had a great time. Then two weeks later I was home by myself, and I was sitting in the living room. Mom was at work, our brother Marty had moved away and was living in Toronto, so it was just Alex and I. And Alex came upstairs dressed in her Hallowe'en costume. I said: 'What are you doing? Hallowe'en was like so two weeks ago! What are you doing?' And she replied: 'This is me.' I said: 'I don't get it.' Alex was probably the first transgender person I ever saw or ever met. This was Newfoundland… this was my first introduction to anything that was really different. I remember just looking, and saying – 'Go on! Don't be so silly!' And Alex sat down and she cried and she said: 'No, this is me. This is who I am.' And then she sat down with me and explained it all to me. I embraced her, and I said: 'Just be whoever you are, all right?'

But it was hard, because Mom didn't know, nobody knew. I was the only one with this information. I had to keep this secret for Alex. That was really difficult. I could see how she was struggling. She was living in the basement, and she kind of shut herself off from the family – she would come upstairs and blurt out something nasty and go back downstairs. But it all made sense to me after that. Anyway, a week later Alex and her girlfriend broke up. And Alex just laid in my arms and wept. I think it was really one of the first times in our lives where we felt really close to one another. Because she'd been so closed off from us (Tucker 2022).

It would be years before Alex came out to the rest of her family. Kelly found it difficult to see Alex struggling with dysphoria and know what was going on, but have to keep it secret from other family members.

I will never forget how sour Alex was on graduation day. It was high school graduation and she was in a tux. She'd already come out to me, and was in this tux and was so angry. My poor mom had no idea what was going on. I was like: 'Oh my god, I feel for you…' It was a very exciting and special day for my mom, but I remember that day with my little old nan and Alex just being so mad (Ibid.).

After high school, Alex struggled to find ways to make a tolerable life in Newfoundland. She began studies at Memorial University, and began looking for community.

"She tried to dive into the gay community," recalled Kelly. "It was very underground, in bars, but Alex had some good times and connected with some great people. But it just wasn't open. It was all secret, in this shroud of darkness. And that was very lonely, to be living this double life."

According to her later partner Kris Elder, Alex did try reaching out to a local psychiatrist to inquire about hormones and medical transition. Kris doesn't know who it was that Alex contacted, but the psychiatrist apparently told her that her best hope would be to leave the province. So, at the age of nineteen Alexandria moved to Victoria, BC, to transition.

Alex kept a personal journal, which is being annotated and edited for publication as part of a forthcoming book by her partner Kris. This is an excerpt from that journal, provided by permission:

Spending many a summer isolated and contemplating my future, weighing out my desires over reality, I delved deep into what it meant to be a human being. I knew there were Boys on one side of the spectrum and then Girls of course on the other, but I could not explain where I fit into this monochrome illustration, having felt female all my young life only to find out that for sure I was anatomically an XY male. I was both devastated and extremely confused all at one time. It was however within this confused state that I made some of the best decisions of my young life. Decisions that I now look back upon and thank myself profusely for having made so young.

Regardless of how well things were going, nevertheless that one nagging question that lingered in my mind from the moment I first put a name to my discomfort, always came bubbling back to the surface. Were my family and friends, and Newfoundland for that matter, ready to accept me, the only transsexual in the world, into their lives?

Although I regard the months I spent alone with much deference for my ability to clear my head, I was never able to answer that one question. All I could think of was just how disgusted I was in that being only 15 years old I was left to fend for myself. No doctor wanted to help me with this problem I lay on their table. Their only solution was to suggest I move to a larger city where they would know what to do for me. "Then again you could always visit the Waterford hospital," one woman said with evident abhorrence in her voice. The Waterford Hospital was a place well known for housing some of Newfoundland's most mentally ill, and I did not see how she came to the conclusion that I was in need of such treatment.

I guess in retrospect, Newfoundland was not ready for me and although I said before that I did not leave in fear, as I look back, I know now that I did. I not only walked away with my back stiffly turned on a town that to this day I long for, I ran. I ran with all my might. I had to get out, off the rock and find what remnants of the person I knew I was. That is, should she still exist.

I ran with immense fear. This fear was the innate fear that society instills into us all from birth, coupled with my own inability to articulate accurately with educative authority to my family what I was feeling. It was this fear of the unknown that won out in the end and took from me the family that I did not wish to lose. I boarded a plane and headed West.

Kelly followed her there soon after. Kelly, Alex, and Alex's girlfriend at the time rented a house together in Victoria. Alex's then-girlfriend, an American, also had two young children from a previous marriage, and one of the kids lived with them as well.

Whereas Kelly was younger and still enjoyed partying - she has memories of coming home late at night and fighting with Alex over their make-up; "regular sister stuff" - Alex was becoming more of a homebody, she recalls. Alex was intent on establishing a home and helping to raise her partner's kids. By 1998, she was two years into a college degree in psychology and sociology at Camosun College. She became involved with the Victoria chapter of the Transsexual Women's Support Group. She was taking hormones, and had plans for surgery. "I considered myself female, I presented as female, everyone in my community respected that fact and treated me accordingly," she told the hosts of GenderTalk, a US-based radio program focusing on transgender issues founded in 1997 by Nancy Nangeroni and which ran until 2006.

A custody battle was brewing over her partner's two children. According to Tucker, the woman's ex-husband hadn't originally sought custody but his parents, the children's grandparents, wanted the kids. There had been hearings with a judge in Montana, who made his sympathies clear.

"We had gone to court on several issues, and the judge in the case, his last comments were that he would have a hard time giving these kids over to two Canadians," recounted Tucker to GenderTalk.

During the June 1998 reading break, Tucker went to Montana. She had visited previously, and had met her partner's family, including the father of her partner's children. Worried that her relationship with the children's mother was complicating the custody dispute, she decided to meet with her partner's ex-husband to offer to step back from the relationship if that would help resolve the custody dispute. Tucker went to his workplace - he worked part-time as a labourer - to meet with him. She described to GenderTalk what happened next.

The first thing I said when I saw him was, I want to talk to you about the kids... There were people in his work and we were outside the front door, over to the right-hand side of the building... when I turned back to him he said: 'You're never going to see my kids again.' It was midway through that sentence that I felt the knife coming at me and it went into my brow and tore up to my skull (Ibid.).

As a trained martial artist, Tucker instinctively responded, and tried to grab the weapon. The two wrestled over the knife. The ex-husband cut his hand on the knife in trying to grab it; the two were by now covered in blood. Tucker broke off the handle of the knife, then managed to escape the ex-husband's hold and ran. As she scrambled across the road, dodging between moving vehicles, toward her parked car, she looked back and saw the ex-husband standing, watching her.

"I ran to my vehicle, and I'm in a panic, I don't know what to do, I've just been attacked, and I panicked. I'd never been involved in such an incident. So I headed toward the police department."

It was a small town and the police station was only a short drive away, seven minutes according to current maps, but during those minutes Tucker's assailant returned to his workplace, his blood dripping all over the pavement as he walked back to work. His colleagues called the police, saying that he had been attacked and identifying Tucker as the attacker.

As Tucker approached the police station, three police cars squealed up and surrounded her. Officers leapt out of the car and surrounded her with guns pointed in her direction.

I was dragged out of my vehicle by gunpoint, I was pressed into the ground with a boot to my neck, with a gun pressed up against the back of my head. I had no weapon, they were in the process of checking me and still there were three officers with weapons pointed at me... I was afraid I was going to be shot (Ibid.).

Tucker was shoved into the back of a police car.

I'm told that I'm not under arrest, yet I had just been put in there at gunpoint and there's handcuffs burning holes into the backs of my arms. I was hogtied essentially and thrown into the back of the car, bleeding from my forehead and unable to move... I was brought to the county jail, where they discovered I had [hormones] in my car. They demanded to know what the drugs were for, and I had to [explain] the process. They believed they were looking for a male – that's what the ex-husband stated – and they had me. So because of that I was stripped, and for protesting against being stripped after not being charged with anything, I was beaten... I was in shock (Ibid.).

She told them that she was the one who had been attacked, and that she wanted to file charges. "They just said: 'You're going to prison.' They persisted with the threats and with telling me where I was going. They had already made up their mind what was happening to me."

Tucker demanded to see an attorney. She and her partner in fact had a local attorney they'd been using in the custody case. After being held for two hours Tucker was finally permitted a phone call. She reached her partner's mother, who sent the attorney over. The police refused to let the attorney see her. They told the attorney Tucker was "too emotionally disturbed" to see anyone. Tucker said the police interrogated her and audiotaped the interrogation without her knowledge and without her lawyer present. Her lawyer later tried, unsuccessfully, to have the secret recording removed from evidence.

Alex's injuries included a sprained ankle and a 1.5-inch stab wound above her right eye that was sewn shut with twelve stitches. After she was stripped and beaten at the police station, police photographed her naked body, as photographic evidence of her state of transition. This horrific experience constituted a source of significant trauma for Alex in later years.

Her bail was set at $150,000, and she spent seven months in a men's county jail awaiting trial. She described the horrifying seven-month ordeal to the GenderTalk hosts. Not only was she sexually assaulted by prisoners and guards alike, she says:

I was housed in an area with two sex offenders at one point, and a man who had beaten a woman and left her in a ditch for dead… I often received clothing that had semen and snot all over them. There were days I went without food and water. There was one three-week period that I spent living in the library – three days of that period I was not permitted to go to the washroom, and I had to go in a wastepaper basket, both urinate and defecate. I was left in there for three days (Ibid.).

After seven months of torture and her hearing repeatedly postponed, she was finally called in to a meeting with prison officials and a man who claimed to be an immigration officer. They said they were offering her a plea agreement: if she agreed to sign a paper saying she was guilty, she would immediately be taken to the US border and released. She would be free to go on condition of never returning to the United States.

"I would have admitted to anything at that time, to get out," she said.

They brought in this immigration officer, [he said] I have the immigration papers here. He signed them in front of me, he gave me his sales-pitch. He must have been a really good salesperson. He told me that [if I sign] right away they'll be at court waiting for me and they'll deport me immediately. I would have said anything, to go home to my family (Ibid.).

It was all a ruse. Once she had signed the guilty confession, they instead brought her in front of a judge — the same judge who had said he didn't want to release the children to two Canadians – and, armed with the coerced confession, he sentenced her to ten years in the Montana State Prison for Men, with seven years suspended, for the assault charge. She was sentenced for an additional two years at the state prison for use of a weapon. The sentences were to run consecutively. The judge also stated in the sentencing hearing that "under this arrangement… you will be out of prison in a short time and spend the rest of your time in Canada. Six months sounds like at the most and then you will be deported."

This did not happen; Alex was incarcerated for more than two years and was not released until August 14, 2000. The causes for this extended period of incarceration are presently under investigation by her partner Kris.

It was while in prison that Alexandria came out to the rest of her family.

Alex sent a letter to my mother from jail when she was in the penitentiary in Montana. That's how my mom found out – Alex wrote it in a letter and sent it. And mom responded well. She said: 'I love you. I just love you and I want you to be happy and safe, and I don't understand it but I respect you and love you and I'll do my best to get it.' And the same with [our brother] Marty. Marty was very much like: 'Hey, I love you, you're my family and you mean the world to me.' They looked out for each other. Myself and Marty and my aunt drove down to Montana to try to figure all this out… so Alex told Marty face to face. And then my mom got the letter in the mail (Tucker 2022).

In describing the horrific sequence of events to GenderTalk, Tucker maintained an equanimity toward the ex-husband, in spite of what he did to her.

Coming from small-town Newfoundland, here in Canada, we're taught that you don't hurt someone that you love. I saw [the ex-husband] as the father of the children I was raising. He was a family member to me. This was the last thing I ever expected… However my heart breaks for the man, because he felt like nothing. His parents made him feel less than dirt. That's the saddest part of this situation – I wasn't the only victim here. In the long scope of things so also was the ex-husband, because of his parents' abuse and the religious intolerance (GenderTalk 2022).

Eventually Tucker managed to get a medical claim to a federal magistrate over the conditions she was being kept in. The prison had already lost cases of that nature, so Tucker surmised that they didn't want to risk further investigation. Instead, they finally agreed to send her back to Canada. An article in *The Times Colonist* described how "U.S. Penitentiary staff took her in prison garb to the Canadian border at Milk River, Alta., and told her to start walking" (Paterson 2003).

Kelly remembers the day Alex arrived back in Canada.

It was awful, it was really awful. Alex called me from a pay phone, and I was at work. She said: 'I'm at the US border' – they just dropped her off with nothing. No money, nothing – just dropped her off in the middle of nowhere. So she had to make her own way back. I can't remember if I sent money, or if mom sent money, but anyway she was able to get back and she showed up at my work. I remember going to hug her and hold her, and she just cringed. She tightened up into a ball and pulled away from me, and cringed at the touch of another person. It was so fucking sad. She was a fraction of the person who had left. Alex always had a bright, beautiful smile and could light up a room. They sent back someone totally different (Tucker 2022).

Back in Canada, Tucker worked hard to put her life back together. The post-traumatic stress she experienced from her ordeal in prison took its toll.

She was very different in our house, at least at the beginning when she just got out of jail. She would hoard her broccoli – like she wouldn't leave it in the fridge – and if the toothpaste was squeezed the wrong way she would throw it in the garbage. She would just stay in her room a lot.

But then Kris came along (Ibid.).

Kris Elder had been introduced to Alex by mutual friends. The two formed a fast connection, and were soon in a romantic relationship.

"Kris really lit up Alex's world," recalled Kelly. "She changed it and helped her accept who she was as a person because Kris was so accepting. Kris had a beautiful community around her that was diverse, they lived their truth. Kris really helped Alex accept herself and heal. She was a big, big part of Alex's healing."

The post-traumatic stress Alex experienced had caused friction and distance between the two sisters, and their relationship became strained for a period. Then late one night the new couple showed up on Kelly's doorstep.

The two of them had been having a couple of drinks and they showed up giggling at my door. It was eleven o'clock at night and that was my first time meeting Kris. They came in, and we just shared some lovely time together. Kris was so wonderful. She's a very lovely person, who loved Alex fiercely (Ibid.).

Alexandria moved in with Kris and the two worked closely together in activism, volunteering and other pursuits. Alexandria became an outspoken advocate for the queer community. She drew on her martial arts background and received a start-up business loan to launch Pride Warriors Canada (Shikiken Bushi Ryu Karate-do), a "GLBTIA-focused community self defense program." It operated out of a local community centre and also held sessions at a public park. She got involved again with the Victoria branch of the Transsexual Women's Support Group, although her criminal record did create tensions with some members, as well as the Victoria Pride Society. She was elected to the Board of the Victoria Pride Society, but toward the end of her tenure became an outspoken critic over the Society's lack of support for queer people of colour and Indigenous queers. In 2002 she was one of the invited speakers for Victoria's Take Back the Night March.

In 2002, Alexandria was fired from her job shortly before she was scheduled for gender confirmation surgery in Montreal. According to Elder, she felt the firing was discriminatory, but was unable to prove it. When she was denied Employment Insurance support, she filed an appeal on the basis of her looming surgery – the lengthy recovery period would render her unable to work for a time – and won the appeal. She worked with the Transgender Alliance Society to produce a transgender resource and support guide for the Victoria area. When she was subsequently hired as an administrative staff person at the University of Victoria, she dove into volunteer work with her CUPE union local, as well. She continued her undergraduate studies at University of Victoria.

Keenan Pinder met Alex in 2001, at a series of consultations put off by the B.C. Justice Institute to build a strategy to improve life for trans people. The two forged a close friendship which continued after they both returned home to Victoria.

In Victoria there's a really tight-knit trans community and Alex and I would often go to the university and speak to the university classes about trans issues. It was like Trans 101, just getting them used to the idea that trans people do exist and this is how to refer to us and be respectful and all that kind of thing. We would do things like that together (Pinder 2022).

Alex also tried to kickstart a legal fund for trans people, but it never came to fruition. As Pinder recalled, "She was big on ideas and she was a force to be reckoned with. She had a great spirit, and she was really larger than life. She would light up a room when she entered it. She was beautiful all around."

Alex and Pinder formed a local group called Genderqueers, which was intended to serve both a social and activist function for its members. They protested a local coffeeshop where members had transphobic encounters, and also organized a leaflet campaign against a local gay bar which had transphobic bathroom policies. They did fundraising and helped members attend conferences and events.

"There weren't very many of us but we tried to bring awareness where we could," recalled Pinder.

Much of her activism took place outside of structured groups. According to Elder:

Alexandria was a friend to homeless people, buskers, and people asking for spare change. She would give them money, buy them coffee, spend time chatting with them, and find out more about their stories and lives. Sometimes we would go downtown and we would take someone out for a meal and have a chat together. We met some lovely folks from other provinces who were trying to survive on our streets. She was very outgoing... When I say she would give them money, I mean that she would give them the last of the money left in her wallet. We couldn't afford this but we did it anyways because we both saw the humanity in people and how close to homelessness we all could be with life being so expensive in the city.

She tried to help out when some homeless people were camped out at this heritage building called Spiral Island and then they got kicked out by the city so they went and protested at the City Hall. This was fall 2001. We did some video work down there and she interviewed some folks off camera and tried to be an ally (Elder 2022).

She also sought to take the US government to court over her treatment in Montana. Her hope was that if the case made it to the US Supreme Court, it might bring about change (ABC News 2003; Advocate 2002). It was an uphill battle. She didn't have the financial or logistical resources this required, and was turned down by over 35 law firms that she approached, including the American Civil Liberties Union (ACLU) and the Lesbian Defence Fund. "Due to the magnitude of my case, and due to the magnitude of the violations in my case, they just don't have the money to proceed with such a case," Tucker explained to GenderTalk Radio. Nevertheless, she persisted. "I'm doing this on my own without resources and without assistance, but I'm very thankful that I made it this far. I don't plan on going away until justice is served."

"It's not the first [time something like this has happened], and it won't be the last until people stand up and say 'What you're doing is wrong,' and hold the constitution to the paper that it's written on," she said. "I'm [considered] a gender terrorist because I have a mind and because I'm speaking what I feel... I'm lucky that I didn't disappear, and I'm lucky that I'm here to tell you my story."

The untreated post-traumatic stress she experienced as a result of the ordeal finally proved too much. On April 14, 2005, Alexandria Tucker died by suicide.

Before her death, Alexandria made a final trip back to Newfoundland, together with Kris. Alexandria showed her partner the city in which she had grown up; Kris recounts Alex's astonishment and delight that St. John's finally had its first sushi restaurant. They had kept their arrival date a secret, and made a surprise visit to Alex's mother, who had remarried and was then living in Hants Harbour.

"My mom didn't even know she was coming," recalled Kelly, laughing at the memory.

Alex just knocked on my mom's door in Hants Harbour – knock knock knock. My mom was sitting there with her husband, and a couple of her friends were there. Alex and Kris knocked on the door, and mom comes in and says: 'There's two ladies at the door, I don't know who they are!' She came out, and the minute she saw Alex she just embraced her and put her arms around her. Then she called up all her friends to come over and have a party (Tucker 2022).

The following is a brief excerpt from the travel diary Alex and Kris kept of their trip, shared with permission.

Our trip to Newfoundland in the summer of 2004 was Alexandria's first time back home in ten years, and her first time seeing her mother in over five years. The last time Alex and her mother laid eyes on each other was when Alex was incarcerated in Montana and her mother testified on her behalf at the sentencing hearing in district court.

Alexandria and I arrived in Hant's Harbour and stopped by the post office to inquire about directions to her mom's place. The postmistress told us to follow the road up the hill and the house would be at the top. We found it right away and drove into the yard and got out. We surprised her mom and husband by showing up a day earlier than they had expected.

Her mom held her arms out to Alex and said: "Look at you, Alex, aren't you gorgeous, my gorgeous daughter, look at you."

It was a very loving and sweet, warm welcome. Alex was so happy, it meant the world to her to see her mom again and to be so lovingly embraced and welcomed back home. We were both teary eyed, and I was so glad to meet her mom and husband after all this time. They treated us to a lovely baked Cod and boiled potatoes meal. We felt like we had finally really arrived now in Newfoundland."

Alex and Kris revisited many of the important people and places from her childhood. They visited Colin Williams and had dinner at his house. Alex reconnected with Jerry Lee, her martial arts instructor. Alex met with other childhood friends as well.

Her death – and more importantly, her life, in all its kindness, strength and courage – would have a profound impact on people across Canada, reverberating all the way back to Newfoundland and Labrador. After her death, Pinder, together with his friend Noah Adams, organized a cross-Canada cycling tour called the Trans Cycling Odyssey. The goal was to raise awareness and support of transgender mental health (Bruner 2006). Pinder and Adams cycled across the country, holding workshops and public events in large centres along the way. They told Tucker's story, and spoke about the need for supports for trans people and mental health.

It felt like for a lot of people it was the first time they had a chance to meet and get together with other trans people and talk about not just suicidality but talk about being trans with other trans people. In some cases it was a sort of unifying event. I remember being told that in Ottawa it was a real unifying point for the trans community there (Adams 2022).

When they reached Newfoundland, they visited with Tucker's family. They also held a workshop at Memorial University.

I certainly remember the workshop at Memorial University. There was this really young trans guy, he must have been seventeen or eighteen. He was very quiet, but then he spoke up and talked about his experience. Somebody told me after that that was the first time they had heard him speak (Ibid.).

They tried repeatedly to connect with CBC, but received no response to their queries, Adams said. NTV however provided extensive coverage of their tour. Adams recalls the reporter being very emotionally moved by Tucker's story. Adams and Pinder visited the famous George Street, and found themselves welcomed by patrons at some of the local bars who recognized them from the evening news. Everyone was friendly and supportive, he recalls. More than fifty people showed up for the workshop they held at Memorial University, the largest turnout of any in the country.

After Alex's death, Kelly and Kris spread part of her ashes in East Sooke Park in British Columbia. "We hiked into East Sooke Park and went down to this beautiful flat rock and we had a small ceremony for Alex there," Kelly said. The following summer, Kelly, her mother, and brother hiked into Gros Morne National Park on the west coast of Newfoundland to spread the remainder of her ashes. Kelly brought her newborn daughter along as well. "It was a beautiful, beautiful day," she recalled.

"A lot of her life choices were not hers to make," reflected Kelly. "Alex struggled to find out who she was, but after she did, it was the trauma of jail that really shifted the trajectory of her life. She didn't lose the battle because of being transgender, it was the trauma that was inflicted upon her."

Alex was a firm believer in reincarnation, she said, and believed she would return.

One of Kelly's strongest memories of her sister was of a Thanksgiving dinner at Alexandria and Kris' house. They had a Thanksgiving potluck every year with family and friends, at which Alex always had a pot of vegetarian Jiggs Dinner simmering on the side.

They invited me over one time for Thanksgiving dinner. I came over and Alex's laugh would just fill the space. I remember all their friends were there, people were playing music in the corner, their home was so lovely. Plants every-where. They were making t-shirts in the basement. They were just so creative, the two of them together. There was art and there was poetry everywhere, they made such a beautiful home. You could see how much they loved each other.

We were there, and Alex pulled out the turkey from the oven, and it was tofurkey! I was like: 'What the hell! Alex, what has happened to you? You're serving tofurkey? That just should never even be a thing!'

I remember when I said that, her laugh – it was just the two of us in the kitchen – she just burst out laughing. I'll never forget that moment. Their little kitchen with the sun shining in and Alex's golden curly hair, just so happy and peaceful, serving me this tofurkey. In a house full of laughter (Tucker 2022).

NGALE and trans activism in the late 1990s

During the early decades of queer activism in the province, a broad lack of awareness around gender identity was challenging for trans and non-binary NLers who tried to get involved in the queer community. RM Kennedy moved from Brigus to St. John's to attend Memorial University in 1988.

I tried really hard to be a lesbian. But I'm not. And I felt really uncomfort-able. When I was pre-pubescent it was very clear to me that I thought of my-self as male, masculine, whatever. Trans was not a concept that I really had a word for. And then through puberty it was really hard, and that's partly why I left. Then the cringeworthy part is that when I finally left home, and spent those years in St. John's, and tried to be a lesbian, when I think about it there's a lot of bad feelings associated with it. Certainly the women's community in St. John's in the late 1980s was not a place that felt very positive for me in a lot of ways, because there was no trans discourse. And it just didn't feel right. Even though I tried – I tried! And it was really only when I left Newfoundland that I realized – okay, I think I know what this is now.

[In Newfoundland] I had a feeling that something just didn't feel right for me. I mean the most I would have encountered would have been drag. That's as close as we would get to trans back then, and of course many drag queens are trans – many are not, but many are – and even that was really defiant.

I remember there being a lot of biphobia [in the Newfoundland lesbian community], and that was part of my lack of comfort. There was definitely a big strong strain of lesbian nationalism that didn't make it a very hospitable environment for being trans... I mean my word for it is lesbian nationalism, but it's this view where masculinity is just bad, and that if you're a trans woman you're too masculine, and if you're a trans man you shouldn't be mas-culine. There was this little undercurrent of men-are-bad. It's the most insidi-ous form of transphobia within feminism.

I even remember times in the 1990s and 2000s when I would make an effort to go back and see people I knew, and it still kind of had that. There was still a real discomfort with trans people. My feeling is that it's probably changed a lot in the past five or ten years, but even ten years ago people were uncomfortable (Kennedy 2022).

Kennedy's experience was echoed by other members of the queer community in the 1980s and 1990s with whom I spoke; people who identified as gay or lesbian during their time in Newfoundland, and often with a sense that it didn't feel quite right, but once they left the province and encountered a more inclusive and gender-variant community, would come out as trans, non-binary or gender-diverse.

By the time Newfoundland Gays And Lesbians for Equality (NGALE) was formed in 1993 (see Chapter 6 for more details), some of the province's queer activists had a better, but still very basic, understanding of gender identity and the needs of their trans members. NGALE's political lobbying was still directed toward human rights protections around sexual orientation, not gender identity. Members took action, writing letters, speaking to media, when their trans members encountered barriers like doctors refusing to provide hormone access. It would not be until 2013 that gender identity and gender expression protections were enshrined in the province's human rights code, although in the years leading up to 2013 trans people who experienced discrimination could, in certain circumstances, file complaints on the basis of sex or sexual orientation. Although NGALE did not take a direct role in articulating and fighting for the rights of trans members, it did provide a vital source of community and support for those members, many of whom were struggling to transition on their own. Their struggles and achievements would begin to forge the path toward gender-affirming health care that exists today. Three of NGALE's early trans members in particular, Dawn Hartmann, Felicia Faye, and Jenn Crandall (along with her partner Katherine Walters), would play a key role in this process, which we will examine in the remainder of this chapter.

***

Jennifer Crandall was originally from Nova Scotia, born in a small village called Advocate Harbour in Cumberland County. Following a difficult childhood in that small rural community, Jennifer left home and wound up in British Columbia, where she lived for 35 years "in male form." She had also been in the military, worked in pulp mills, and had owned her own cabinet making business. By the mid-1990s Jennifer was running a gym where she trained powerlifters, football players and other athletes.

In 1995, Jennifer met a feisty young Newfoundlander named Katherine Walters. Katherine, who was separated and heading toward divorce, had been living in BC since the early 1990s. Both of them were avid customers at Ariana's Bookstore, an alternative bookshop located in Chilliwack that held a dear place for many in the community. The bookstore was facing financial difficulties, and the owner convened a meeting of supportive customers to discuss its future.

At the meeting, Jennifer caught Katherine's eye because of her mischievous manner of goading a couple of the other customers into arguments with each other. Katherine "stared at Jennifer knowingly, with a raised eyebrow whenever this happened," Katherine recalled. "I've been busted!" thought Jennifer at the time.

After the meeting, the two were introduced to each other, and they became fast friends. Jennifer was married, so their friendship was casual at first. By 1997, Katherine had developed more serious feelings for Jennifer. On the drive home after attending an event together in Vancouver, she confessed her feelings. Jennifer admitted she shared similar feelings. She was still married, but her relationship had been deteriorating for some time. The next morning, she phoned Katherine.

"I've done it," she said. "Can you come pick me up?"

"I thought to myself, 'Done what?'," recalled Katherine. "But then I said: 'I'll come pick you up.' And we've been together ever since."

For a year, they lived together as a heterosexual couple. Just days after their first anniversary, Jennifer worked up the nerve to talk to Katherine.

I knew nothing about transgenderism and was taken aback by Jennifer's revelations, but remained calm. One thing I was sure about were my feelings for her, so I rallied my courage and the next day gave Jennifer a makeover. Off came the beard, up went the hair, out came the makeup and a more feminine outfit, and Jennifer literally appeared. Any doubts I had had about what this might mean to us were extinguished. Jennifer had never looked so happy (Walters 2022).

They scoured the internet looking for information and support, without finding much. They also found they were treated differently when out in public.

Jennifer was a far cry from her former persona as a macho, guy's guy, and people did not know how to respond, especially Jennifer's children. I quickly became protective of Jennifer. I also found myself questioning my own sexual preferences and identity, a process that would take years to unfold (Ibid.).

While they had a few good friends who supported them, they knew Chilliwack wouldn't be home for much longer.

Katherine decided she wanted to leave BC following her first and only earthquake experience there. While it was only a minor tremor, it helped make up her mind. "I can take a lot of crap in my life, but homes that move like that are not in my playbook," she quipped, recalling the event.

When Katherine's boss announced shortly after that she was retiring, the couple took it as confirmation of their growing desire to leave BC. Katherine's family were all in Newfoundland, and Jennifer, who had never been there, was curious to go. In early 1996, they mailed 84 boxes to Katherine's mother and at the end of March 1996, climbed aboard their old Ford Tempo to drive across the country.

"It was an adventure to say the least," recalled Walters. At the top of Lake Superior, they got snowed in but found shelter at a tiny, family run motel. Their car gave out at one point, but coasted into the parking lot of a repair shop.

"We knew for certain that having survived that trip, and still being friends, we were solid. We were good!" said Katherine.

Eventually the couple arrived in St. John's, to a city where the sight of openly lesbian couples was still relatively uncommon, and trans women even more so. Katherine's brother and sister were receptive to her new partner, but acceptance would take longer with the rest of the family.

As Jennifer continued her transition in St. John's, the reaction she encountered was far from positive. She recalled looking for a job after her arrival. "I was told that I was unemployable, unwanted," she explained. "I was told I should go back to Toronto with the rest of the freaks. That there was no place for the likes of me in Newfoundland."

Transition in the 1990s was a fraught process, and the public health care system's approach to gender-affirming care was primitive, rooted in ignorance and phobias. Requests for access to publicly funded surgery had to be approved by the Canadian Association for Mental Health (CAMH) in Toronto; prospective applicants had to "live as" the "opposite gender" for two years, and then travel to Toronto to be examined by psychiatrists there at their own expense. For transgender women, the process was deeply misogynistic; a board of primarily male psychiatrists applied a profoundly sexist and misogynistic lens to this work, requiring trans people to exhibit ludicrous portrayals of a very narrowly conceived gender binary. Approvals or rejections were often quite arbitrary. Some trans people spent years trying to win approval under these misguided regulations. The only alternative was to pay privately for surgery, often in other countries, which was financially out of reach for many.

Hormone access was also a hit and miss game at this time too. A range of medical professionals could, theoretically, have provided hormone prescriptions in the province. In practice, most refused out of ignorance or fear.

Jennifer's experience is an example of the sort of ordeal trans people experienced in the province. She said that she, along with a couple of other trans women, had several individual meetings with a local psychiatrist.

"Eventually he recommended that the three of us be given hormone treatments. Shortly after that, I went to his office where he read a note to me from the [people] in charge at Eastern Health, and the note read: 'We will have none of this here in Newfoundland. These people can go back to Toronto with the rest of their like.'

There were four endocrinologists in the city at the time. Not one would even walk in the room with me. So the three of us went our separate ways... Dawn went south to the US where she was able to access services there. And

Felicia [died][61] (Crandall 2022).

Jennifer eventually managed to obtain access to hormones through an unorthodox route. Desperate following the health care system's rejection of her request, she booked an appointment with a local doctor.

I went to this GP, I laid down a piece of paper with a phone number on it, and I said 'This is the phone number of a man down on Water Street who will get me whatever drugs I want. And I'll self-administer them. Or you can write me a prescription and you can keep an eye on me.' So she wrote the prescription (Ibid.).

In reality, the phone number she'd written down was her own; it was all an elaborate bluff. But it worked. "I basically blackmailed the MD."

***

Dawn Hartman was born in Illinois in 1945.

"I knew as a child, by age four, that there was something totally different about me," she reflected. "But I lived in a family where you don't talk about anything. I had a father who was an alcoholic and a bigot, a racist, a homophobe, the whole deal."

In 1965, with her classmates being drafted for the Vietnam War, she proactively enlisted as that gave her more control over her options in the US military – she hoped to avoid being sent directly to the front lines of combat. After initially training as a nuclear power technician, she wound up working as a communications technician at a naval base. After completing her tour of duty, she was hired by a university research group to work in the relatively new field of computer development. She had married during her stint in the military, and now had children, and was also wrestling with alcoholism. When her father died of a heart condition brought on by his own alcoholism, it was a clarifying moment for her.

"I realized, standing in this little room with dad on the gurney and [my brother] on one side and I on the other… I realized that's exactly how I was going to end up. That was the end, I realized. And I came to realize that I had to become myself. That I had to be real," Hartman recalled.

She was sober from that day forward. She also came out as a trans woman to her wife, who did not take the news well. So she moved out, into a large old Victorian mansion that was divided into self-contained apartments. In the apartment across the hall from hers lived a young woman named Lori. The two became fast friends, and began seeing each other. Dawn came out to her as trans early on in their relationship, and Lori was fully supportive.

Several months after they met, Lori, who worked in counselling psychol-

---

[61] In fact, Dawn [Hartman] informed me that before returning she did manage to access hormones thanks to a prescription she had from an American doctor, which she took to a local Walmart. She suspects it was the first time they'd encountered such a prescription. The problem faced by local trans women was that they could not obtain prescriptions in the first place.

ogy, was offered an internship at Memorial University of Newfoundland. She asked Dawn to accompany her, and so the two moved to St. John's in 1997.

Dawn fell in love with Newfoundland. "I found Newfoundland to be like heaven on earth," she recalls. "If you so much as looked like you were going to cross the street, traffic would stop both ways. I couldn't believe it – I was like, what the hell is this? This is like no place I've been before!"

Lori and Dawn rented an apartment on Victoria Street in the city's downtown core. Upon meeting the couple, Lori's university colleagues told Dawn about NGALE, and suggested she might like to get involved with the group.

I was in transition, and NGALE was really a wonderful support group of fabulous people. I had been socialized male, and the women [at NGALE] helped socialize me as a female. And that was so good. So my experience was one of support and friendship. And I'm still friends with so many of the people of NGALE. So my experience in Newfoundland was wonderful (Hartman 2022).

When it came time for the couple to leave, Dawn applied to jobs, hoping to be able to stay and settle in the province. She was a US citizen, and Canadians were given priority for many of the jobs she applied for, so she was unable to stay. But the Newfoundland experience stuck with her, and when she returned to the US, she tried to find somewhere in that country as similar to Newfoundland as possible. The combination of geography and social conscience led her to Vermont, where she lives to this day. She remains in contact with many of her Newfoundland friends, and returned for a lengthy visit in 2013.

During the period she lived in NL, provincial government services didn't yet have any formal infrastructure prepared to deal with transition matters like name or sex marker changes. Dawn had been given what she called a "get out of jail free letter" by her gender therapist in Chicago, to take with her to Newfoundland. "[I]t described me as someone who's not dangerous and that I was in transition and that it was totally appropriate for me and that I should be afforded all the facilities normally afforded to any woman."

When she arrived in St. John's, she needed to get a Canadian driver's license. So, she went to the Department of Motor Vehicles and showed them the letter. It was the officials' first time encountering something of this nature, but she says they shrugged and happily provided her a provincial driver's license in her requested name and female sex designation.

"I had a perm – I looked pretty good in the photo," Dawn recalls with a smile. These processes have subsequently become bureaucratized, and in some ways made more difficult and legalistic. Dawn's relatively easy acquisition of the license in 1997 heartened other members of NGALE. Dawn also did a legal name change in Newfoundland, after learning that the province did not appear to require all the complex legal and bureaucratic undertakings that she had encountered in the US. After legally changing her name here, she was then more easily able to get it recognized by American institutions when she returned to that country.

Dawn has fond memories of NGALE's social events, and of travelling around the province; she had positive and friendly encounters wherever she went. She feels NGALE's presence played a vital role in her positive experience, and in the lives of other queer members during those years.

It was crucial. Crucial. Totally required. People had to grow up and understand that not everybody is what you see in a mirror. Not everybody's going to be the same, and that we all have value. We all have incredible value. And to try and diminish someone or change someone is an act of tyranny and abuse.

I had some contact with the gay community back in Illinois before I left. One of the [trans] girls entered a blind date contest on a Chicago radio station and was murdered by the person who took her out. That was frightening. Homophobia was just awful. So I'm incredibly grateful for NGALE. It was crucial for me to have the support of people. The Newfoundlanders were nice and kind, but there wasn't anybody I could talk to about [being trans]. Of course the hairdressers were a lot of fun – I got this gorgeous curly perm, I have never looked so good in my life (Ibid.).

***

Katherine Walters and Jennifer Crandall became friends with Dawn during her time in the province. After her departure, in September 1999, Katherine got a job with Grenfell Regional Health, and so she and her partner Jennifer Crandall moved to St. Anthony.

"St. Anthony was not a friendly town," Jennifer recalled. Both she and Katherine are tall women, and she remembers the first day they took a stroll through town, hand in hand. Walking through the shopping mall, people stopped and stared.

"It turned their world upside down," Katherine said.

"I walked up to one woman, and I said: 'Did your mother teach you that it was okay to stare like that?'" recalled Jennifer. "And she just continued to look at me. I thought, 'Oh my god, what's in the water here? Where have we landed?' It wasn't a friendly place."

"The first apartment we were living in, that first Christmas, I was standing in front of the living room window, in the apartment, and something caught my eye – a sort of flash," recounted Katherine.

I looked down and there was a red dot in the center of my chest. I learned later that somebody had gotten a new laser sight for their rifle for Christmas and decided they'd give the two strange girls in the apartment building a little fright. I dropped to the floor, lowered the blinds, told Jennifer to get down and called the RCMP. They found the owner of the laser sight; he'd been having a few drinks with friends.

St. Anthony was rough. We wouldn't go anywhere alone. Somebody tried to run Jenn off the road with their car one day when she was out walking (Walters 2022).

While the town didn't give them a friendly welcome, Katherine's workplace was a different story. One of the psychologists employed there, originally from Colombia, proved far more open-minded and supportive than those they'd met in St. John's.

He was irate about what Jennifer had encountered in St. John's. He said: 'psychologists write prescriptions for hormone therapy all the time, what's the big deal?' He was a very bright light in a very dark time for us... his belief was that no one should be allowed to suffer, and allowing someone to suffer because you are ignorant is no excuse. The mental health team [in St. Anthony] turned out to be a real source of advocacy (Ibid.).

Katherine was the Quality Improvement Coordinator for Grenfell Regional Health Services and approached the Mental Health Team about inviting Jennifer in as a citizen advocate. It was clear that transgender folk in the province were in dire need of a service path, a process for transition that didn't require them to fight every step of the way, and the Mental Health Team went to work to address this.

"We actually created the service path for trans folks up there – in friggin' St. Anthony!" explained Katherine. Word began to spread about the supportive, gender affirming health care team on the Northern Peninsula. Patients and medical professionals alike began traveling from St. John's to St. Anthony to seek training and support — a reversal from the usual rural-to-urban trajectory. "People wound up driving from St. John's to St. Anthony to see us. I did education sessions for the medical staff, and if any medical students came through, we got our hands on them too."

Planned Parenthood NL, based in St. John's, heard about the work they were doing and flew Jennifer back to the capital to give a presentation at a conference they put off for staff in health-related fields. She remembers being struck by a young teenager who gave a moving speech just before her. She found herself wondering what she could offer that might be different. When it came time for her to speak, she took an unorthodox approach and decided, she said, to try closing the gap between speakers and audience. "I came down off the stage and I wandered among the tables, saying: 'It's okay – you can touch me. I'm not contagious, trust me.' I kept that up until I got captured by a table full of med students, and then there were just hugs all around."

The team they worked with in St. Anthony recognized the importance of providing training and establishing protocols to support trans people in the province. For Katherine and Jennifer, this work was personal, driven by the memory of their friend Felicia who had died by suicide after encountering several barriers in her transition. The more they continued their work, the more it confirmed to them that the province was full of trans people, many of them suffering in silence. Katherine has a vivid memory of one person in particular.

This poor individual had so many moments of mental health crisis, yet nobody had identified what was at the root of all this. Then he met us. I remember the day that he showed up at our house, it was almost midnight, he pulled in the driveway, he was clearly distraught, and he said: 'I just needed to find out that you're real.' I said, 'Come in, I'll make you a cup of tea.' I said: 'There's nothing wrong with you. The rest of the world doesn't understand what they're looking at, but let me tell you, you're fine. We've just got to get the rest of the world to catch up with you.'

That was an a-ha moment for us. We realized – there has got to be a service path. We have to educate people because this person has suffered for fucking years because they have never had someone recognize what their experience was. It was a real sort of: 'Oh my god I can't believe this is happening' moment (Ibid.).

Mikiki, who was one of the first out gay youth activists in the province (they came out in high school in 1995), reflected on the impact, both personal and systemic, that the lack of trans-inclusive education and awareness had on people growing up trans, non-binary or gender-diverse during that period.

There were trans people, but they weren't identifying yet. I identify as trans and non-binary and I had this conversation with my dad over the phone when I was 27. He said: 'Do you remember when you used to wear this sarong that you made out of a bedspread, and you wore all these skirts and makeup around the house?' I replied: 'Yes, and you threatened to kick me out of the house all the time.' My dad is actually super progressive and very hard left, but I had fights with him when I was a teenager. So then he said: 'I've been thinking about our history and your adolescence and I want to apologize.' I said: 'Thank you for your apology, but I don't accept it. I don't know who I would be and how I would be moving in the world today if I had felt safe and if I had had the space to do that exploration.'

I mean, I had at that point had a decade of sexuality and sexual history and identity and public-facing gender presentation as a sexual person programmed into my body, written into my body. So to then start unpacking all of that, I just didn't have the balls, or the ovaries, you know? I didn't have the bravery. There were definitely moments where I had tried to do some of that - I always identified as genderqueer. But to try to actually put that into practice, was a different matter (Mikiki 2023).

Felicia Faye

Felicia Faye was one of NGALE's first trans members.

"Felicia came to an NGALE meeting as a person who was just starting to transition," recalled Derrick Bishop. It was 1997.

She wanted support with transition, and people who she felt could be supportive. She attended NGALE meetings for a period of time and was involved in social events. But she had some difficulty in family acceptance, which was not that uncommon. A lot of the support she needed was around how to deal with a former marriage partner who was not acknowledging the transition, and parents and siblings. She went through some very difficult periods (Bishop 2023).

There were also children involved from a pre-transition marriage, and the lack of acceptance and support from her family took its toll. Her work environment, friends recall, was a different matter.

She worked in construction, and construction workers are often seen as rough and tumble people. But from conversations we had, it seemed she was very much accepted by her co-workers. It wasn't an issue with them. I know she was certainly out to her co-workers and from what I gathered, from what she said, it was not an issue amongst them (Ibid.).

Bishop remembers her attending the New Year's Eve galas that NGALE put off in the late 1990s.

Those events were significant for her because she could be totally out and amongst people who were totally accepting. I remember how strikingly attractive she was – both in terms of appearance and personality.

She was a lovely individual. Felicia was very warm and accepting. She was very lovable, and very loving... we both went to Prince of Wales high school; she was a year or two ahead of me. We had discussions about high school and how we had felt as teenagers struggling with issues that we had, when there was absolutely no support for anybody at that time. This would have been the very early 1970s when we were in high school, and you thought you were the only person in the world like this. And you tried everything in your power to put it out of your mind and deny it. I know I tried for seven years, and Felicia certainly tried as well and finally came to the point of saying 'No, this is not who I am, and I have to be true to myself' (Ibid.).

Two of Felicia's friends were Jennifer Crandall and Katherine Walters. They were present at the first NGALE support meeting that Felicia attended.

"That was the only time I saw trepidation," recalls Katherine. "I remember how nervous she was about being there."

"She didn't speak much," recalled Jennifer. "I can't remember her speaking at all. But she sat there and slowly melted down over the course of the evening, from the tight indrawn shoulders, to slowly relaxing, realizing that it's okay. And she looked at us a lot."

Meeting other trans people had a profound impact on her, said Jennifer. In an era prior to widespread Internet and social media use, in-person meetings were the only sort of validation many trans people encountered. But that didn't make daily discrimination any easier to deal with.

"I knew that she had a young son and that she was married," recalled Katherine. "And she told us that her family wasn't receptive in any way, shape or form. She moved out and moved into an apartment at the top of Brazil Street."

Jennifer feels things were more difficult for Felicia because, unlike the other trans women involved with NGALE, Felicia's roots were in St. John's. It was easier for new arrivals without family or social networks in the province to avoid unsupportive friends or relatives.

My family was all in the greater Vancouver area or Halifax area and they had no influence on me. If people don't want to talk to you, then they can't give you negative energy constantly. [Felicia] didn't have that distance. Those people were in her face every day, making her feel shitty. There was lots of pressure. I know that she had undergone shock treatments and aversion therapy. That was common at the time. I dodged that bullet several times as a child.

But nobody wants to talk about bad stuff that happened in the past. It's like nobody must ever know. Nobody wants to look in that mirror.

The poor girl went through hell. Eventually she hit a spot where it went too far. If she'd had some distance, some physical distance from her family so that they weren't in her face every day, then there might have been some time to decompress (Crandall 2023).

Felicia was not unlike a lot of people of her generation. Remember that the Internet was still in its infancy, and a lot of people didn't know how to navigate it. And if you confided to a doctor or a counselor, how much did they know about any of this? We had to really go looking for information, and it wasn't easy to find. Once the Internet arrived it was easier for folks to discover that they were normal, that there were other folks like them out there. But up until that point, it was very easy to convince them that there was something inherently wrong with them that needed to be fixed. And Felicia bought into that for a long time. She was motivated to accept a lot of these outrageous behavioural therapies.

There was a whole generation of people who bought into the myth that there was something wrong with them that needed to be fixed. They created personas and lived in deep cover for decades, trying to survive. A lot of the trans folks that we met early on [in Newfoundland] had lived in deep cover for decades to survive. And then there's all the trouble that causes – the challenges with relationships and a whole host of things (Walters 2022).

On Easter Weekend 1999, Felicia died.

"We all took it kind of difficult," said Bishop. "This was a suicide, and those of us that were very involved found it difficult to process."

"When Derrick [Bishop] called me to say what had happened to her, I emitted some kind of strange sound, it felt just like I had been gutted," said Katherine, her voice still shaking over two decades later. "And I remember the crush of humanity there at Carnell's [Funeral Home] on Kenmount Road."

The memorial service was held in Felicia's deadname, and the photos displayed were all taken prior to her transition. It was a jarring experience for those who had shown up to pay their respects to Felicia.

"For those of us who knew Felicia, it was like we were awash in a sea of humanity who had never met her," recounted Katherine. "It was like something out of the Twilight Zone. We all got together after, we met and had trauma counseling as a group afterwards. Derrick Bishop from NGALE organized it, because he was worried about the effect of grief on all of us."

Katherine said the tragic experience was part of what gave her and Jennifer the drive to push for change in St. Anthony. "I think that's why we got so determined – we wanted a service path because we didn't want anything like that to happen again."

But for both women, the memory of Felicia that lingers most powerfully is of the time they drove her to a coffee night hosted by NGALE. "When I think of Felicia I see a large group of people," recalls Jennifer. "We're all sitting in a coffee shop, kind of commandeering the place. And she's in the middle, smiling and happy."

She had by then moved out on her own, and was living in her small apartment on Brazil Street, recalls Katherine.

I remember picking her up there. She was getting ready for a little [NGALE] gathering at a coffee shop, and she wore a red coat that she had found and matching boots with stilettos. It was priceless. Just the look on her face – it was all so fresh and so new and she was so joyful. I couldn't take my eyes off her that night because the joy was just so pure. The joy of being in the company of people who accepted who she was, on her terms. It was awe-inspiring, really (Walters 2023).

The service path that exists today in the province would take years, and a great deal of struggle, to develop. Much of the present system of gender-affirming care in the province is less than a decade old. For trans people, reaching out to medical professionals in Newfoundland and Labrador prior to the 2010s was much like a game of Russian roulette. Many professionals were overtly hostile to trans people, leading to the sorts of encounters which drove Alexandria Tucker, and many others, out of the province to seek transition-related care elsewhere. For some trans NLers, these negative encounters contributed directly or indirectly to their deaths. A handful of open-minded psychiatrists did attempt to put trans patients in contact with sympathetic surgeons, but the systemic barriers were high. One St. John's doctor I spoke with from the period, who requested to remain anonymous, acknowledged that trans patients were sometimes referred to them by supportive health care practitioners, in the hopes they could do surgery for them locally. This doctor expressed their frustration:

There was no support for these folks in the 1990s. There was no funding so in fact I did little surgery at that time, as most patients could not afford it. The requirements for these patients to see a psychiatrist in Toronto prior to any surgery made this impossible (Anon. 2022).

The work done by Jennifer and Katherine – and inspired by the experiences of others like Felicia - would help to build the foundation upon which today's service path developed. The work they did with Planned Parenthood NL, along with the training and awareness raising done in St. Anthony and elsewhere, helped open the minds of an emerging generation of health care professionals about the needs of trans patients and the ethical imperative to support them in an affirming, accepting manner. That work planted the seeds upon which today's path to accessing gender-affirming care would be built.

Chapter Ten: Gay Bars and Social Scenes

On April 9, 1976, the #1 hit single in the United States was "Disco Lady" by legendary Stax Records recording artist Johnnie Taylor, "the philosopher of soul." In the UK, it was "Save Your Kisses For Me" by Brotherhood of Man, the four-person pop outfit that would go on to win Eurovision '76 and feature on the theme to the Brady Bunch. In Canada, the top song was Gary Wright's "Dream Weaver."

Were one of those songs playing on the night of April 9, 1976, at the Waterfront Club in downtown St. John's? That was the night of "an act of discrimination against gays... which should go down in the textbooks of Nfld. history," according to CHAN's *About Face* newsletter (About Face 1976).

Ironically, the Waterfront Club was, at the time, the go-to spot for many in the queer community. The run-down harbourfront bar at 161 Water Street had been frequented by queer folks, especially gay men, since it opened in 1970. Many of those who frequented it at the time are today hesitant to call it a 'gay bar' — queerness wasn't celebrated there, but it was tolerated, which set it apart from most other local venues.

"That was one of the original places where gay people hung out," recalled Barry Nichols. "I didn't even know it was until one of my friends took me there for a drink on Saturday afternoon. We used to go out and drink on Saturday afternoons because, well, you were cruising all the time."

"It was kind of a sleazy bar," recalled Brian Caines, who used to go there until he left Newfoundland in 1974.

It was pretty rudimentary. It had regular old geezers from the east end of St. John's who used to drink there. But they were pretty friendly with gay people being around. I don't remember a lot of hostility around it. I remember dancing there and those old geezers would just sit there drinking their beer (Caines 2022).

Not so that Friday night in April 1976. The bar was packed as usual. At about a quarter to eleven – fuelled perhaps by some combination of love, defiance and drink – two men got up to dance with each other. Shortly thereafter, they were approached by management and told to get off the dance floor. Another gay man who was on the dance floor was also told to finish his beer and leave. Any straight couples that were dancing were ignored; only the same-sex couples and a known gay patron were singled out and told to leave the dance floor.

Word spread quickly in the packed club. Angered by the treatment of these men, half an hour later a group of about 20 gay patrons got up en masse and moved to the dance floor, where they began dancing with each other in defiance of management. Less than two minutes later the managers were back, yelling and ordering them all off the floor. What ensued was a rowdy mass exodus: joined by other queer patrons, they not only left the dance floor but grabbed their coats and marched out of the club in protest. The makeshift mob proceeded down the street to a nearby club, the Sea Breeze.

The Sea Breeze had previously been known as the Fogo-A-GoGo Disco-theque, and was located just down the road at 189 Water Street, on the corner of Baird's Cove. "Swing with the beautiful people/ Dance on the steel floor / To fantastic dancing lights" ran a 1972 ad in *The Muse*. It also had a reputation for being tolerant of queer patrons. Patrons of both bars disagree as to which was the "original gay bar" though perhaps neither truly deserves the title, given their ambivalent and semi-closeted approach to the role. By 1976 this bar, now known as the Sea Breeze, was down on its luck, and when the angry queer mob from the Waterfront showed up, it eagerly welcomed the large influx of new customers. Would they be allowed to dance with each other, the newcomers in-quired of Sea Breeze management. Most certainly, they were assured. The Sea Breeze was in precarious financial straits, and its management was disinclined to say no to such a large group of prospective customers.

Just a few years previous, it would have been unheard of to imagine same-sex couples dancing with each other in a downtown bar. But there was a new sense of defiance in the air; the homophobia of Waterfront management sparked outrage and a determination to fight. CHAN moved quickly, turning the spontaneous walkout into an organized boycott. Organizers wrote up a pe-tition which was signed by dozens of patrons and submitted to the Waterfront managers. According to Wish Leonard, the manager refused to accept the peti-tion when he delivered it.

"[E]ven if it does not change the policy of the Waterfront, it has brought gays closer together and a fuller sense of gay unity and community has result-ed," observed the newsletter article covering this sequence of events (Ibid.).

CHAN organizers also reached out to the Sea Breeze to ensure manage-ment's goodwill was genuine. They "made it clear that St. John's gays expected the same casual rights that straights take for granted: the right to touch, to show affection, to dance together," wrote Ken Popert in a summary of these events for national queer magazine *The Body Politic* (Popert 1976). If The Sea Breeze was willing to respect those rights, then CHAN promised them an as-sured and steady clientele from the city's queer community.

The Sea Breeze agreed. The Waterfront swiftly came to regret its actions, replaced its management and indicated to the boycott organizers that the bar would welcome back gay patrons and show greater tolerance. Many of those patrons refused to return, however, and The Sea Breeze became the city's new unofficial gay club. By 1977, it was even running ads in CHAN's *About Face* newsletter, promoting itself as the "Gayest Spot In Town." Looking back on events with the vantage of hindsight, one might debate whether it was a tri-umph of activism or the first glimmerings of rainbow capitalism.

The transition was not entirely smooth. Word got out that The Sea Breeze was welcoming gay patrons, and it became the target of homophobic attacks. "A number of greasers" began showing up at the bar, looking to pick fights with gay clients. The Sea Breeze responded by hiring additional bouncers with specific instructions to watch out for homophobic activity and keep homophobes out of the bar. The additional security measures worked, for a time. Eventually, in order to keep out homophobic patrons looking for a fight, The Sea Breeze converted itself from a bar into a private members' club. From August 31, 1976, private membership cards were issued to regular patrons. New members, gay or straight, could be signed up if existing patrons could vouch for them. Members could also bring guests into the club with them. This model would be adopted periodically by other gay clubs that appeared in the following years, including Friends and The Upper Deck (Ibid.). The new manager at the Waterfront was also now encouraging the former clientele to return.

"In no time at all, it seemed, Water Street had a number of gay or gay-friendly bars," remarked Leonard, looking back on the sequence of events.

However, the commitment of Sea Breeze's owners to provide a gay-positive environment appeared to waver. In early 1977, *The Body Politic* published a news update reporting on strife between clients and management.

The Sea Breeze is virtually the only night spot frequented by gays in the city and its manager... has been giving patrons a hard time lately. But despite his statement 'there shall be no waltzing between males in this club at any time,' the waltzing goes on without interference and the club continues to be the most popular gay night spot in town (Leonard 1977A).

Neither The Waterfront nor The Sea Breeze officially self-identified as 'gay bars,' although they both benefited immensely from a (usually) tolerant attitude and a loyal queer clientele. This attitude frustrated CHAN organizers like Leonard.

Since the inception of the Waterfront as a club on Water Street, it has always been frequented by gays. Within recent years, gays have made up some 70% of the club's clientele... 15% of the remaining portion of the clientele are people who move in the gay circle and hang out with the gays. This means that approximately 85% of the club's business could be attributed either directly or indirectly to gays. Why then does the management refuse to admit that it's a gay bar? And more importantly, why should gays continue to frequent a bar and almost wholly support it, while the management hauls in their money and hopes that they will remain hidden in 'a closet in the corner'? (About Face 1976).

Karl Wells also feels it's important to remember that the gay bars of St. John's were not gay bars strictly defined.

There was no such thing in St. John's or in Newfoundland as a bar that was exclusively gay. I don't care what anybody says, it just didn't exist. All of these bars were open to anybody that wanted to go in. It might be that on some nights most of the people there were gay. Some nights it was fifty-fifty, or thirty percent gay. But there was no such thing as an exclusively gay bar. I've [heard it said that] Friends was St. John's' first exclusive gay bar. That's absolutely wrong. They would not have made any money, none of these bars would have made a penny if they were exclusively gay... there's no bar in St. John's that can survive exclusively on a gay clientele or even an LGBTQ2S+ clientele (Wells 2021).

Gay bar or no, momentum was growing for more inclusive spaces in the city's downtown, and a more overt embrace of queer positivity would be adopted by The Upper Deck, which opened at 208 Water Street in October 1977. The opening night featured a drag show.

"The owners of The Upper Deck say they will run the place as a gay bar as long as they get enough gay patronage," wrote Wish Leonard in *The Body Politic*. "Two other clubs in the city frequented by gays, the Sea Breeze and the Waterfront, do not wish to be categorized as gay establishments" (Leonard 1977B).

Betty Ralph remembered the Upper Deck well. It was the first gay club she attended as a student at Memorial University. She was brought there by friends one night, and when they got to the door the others all pulled out membership cards. Ralph didn't have one. The bouncer explained it was operating as a members' club, and customers needed to produce a membership card to enter. Because she was with other members who vouched for her, she was told she could sign up for a membership card on the spot. She eagerly signed up.

Not everyone did. Ralph recalled that some of her gay friends wouldn't go to the bar because they were afraid of signing up for a membership. They were worried that if their name was on the membership list, it might get leaked, or police might raid the club and seize the membership list. The private membership club approach worked in some respects by allowing management to control who was in the club (and keep homophobes out), but it also had the effect of deterring some customers who were afraid of having their names on the membership rolls.

"Friends used to have membership cards too," remembered Sheilagh O'Leary. "Remember it was a very dangerous time. So it was a way to keep it kind of safe in the bar. So there were little membership cards, but they also had a little slat in the door, so that they could look out the door and see who was in the lineup."

Shortly after getting her membership, Ralph was in a sociology class at Memorial University, waiting for the professor to show up. One of the other students in the class called out to her, and said in a loud voice (so as to be heard by everyone) that they'd heard she'd been seen at the Upper Deck on the weekend – a gay club! It might have been delivered in a joking tone but it was a barbed homophobic comment.

"Yeah, it was like high school," Ralph laughed, remembering the moment. "And I knew there was people in my class who were definitely gay, and they weren't out, and they were probably wondering: 'Oh my god, what now?'"

Ralph decided to nip that bit of incipient homophobia in the bud, and pulled out her membership card. She slapped it down proudly on her desk. "Yeah, I got a membership card to a gay club – what's the problem?" she responded defiantly.

At this point the professor entered the room, and asked what they were all talking about. Ralph explained. Curious, the professor asked if he could see the membership card as well. She handed it over, and then the membership card made the round of the classroom, with students studying it closely.

"I couldn't understand the big deal!" Ralph said. "But they all thought it was strange that I didn't mind."

Why Queer Bars Matter

As should be apparent by now, safe and inclusive spaces for queer people in the province, including the capital of St. John's, were rare. For many, the gay bars came to provide a pivotal space for meeting friends and partners, and building community.

"The [gay] bars were everything. We had nowhere else to go," reflected Lori Seay, who lived in downtown St. John's in the late 1980s and 1990s.

"We hung out together, we partied together, we took care of one another," recalled Sharp Dopler, who also frequented the city's downtown gay bars in the 1980s and early '90s.

I remember my first breakup, and the boys taking care of me. I was heartbroken, and the boys were like: 'That's all right my darling, she was a bit tenuous, we'll find you something better.'

We had no filters. We had no boundaries. We were really handsy with one another. I would walk into the bar and one of the boys would honk my tits. And I'd grab him by the basket. We were just like puppies in a pile, we were that comfortable with one another. For me, having been on the outside most of my life, having been bullied most of my life, finding that kind of community was life-changing (Dopler 2021).

"Us non-heterosexuals, we didn't have anything good," explained Rita Mae, who was one of the city's first lesbian DJs.

We didn't have nice places to go into. We had to hide in the back corner all the time.

My gay family became my family. When you didn't get love and respect from your [blood] family, let me tell you something – you got it when you walked through the doors of that bar. You got it. That was the only place that we were safe, where we felt safe, where we could be ourselves, where we could do our own thing – it was amazing. It was just amazing. Oh I loved it. I just loved it there (Mae 2022).

For those visiting or moving to Newfoundland from outside the province, finding this sort of queer community could be a challenge. In the summer of

1982, two members of the Lesbian Mothers Defence Funds began a cross-country cycling trip in order to raise funds for the group, which provided support for lesbians facing custody battles. They concluded their cross-country journey by rolling into St. John's on August 1, 1982. A celebration ensued – but first they had to find their queer community. They described the experience for *The Body Politic*.

'By the time we hit Newfoundland they really 'screeched us in,' Cheryl laughed, referring to a process that involved a long party and lots of Newfoundland's home brew. But first they had to find the right Newfoundlanders (they had arrived with a crucial phone number mis-copied). 'We got up our nerve to ask the waitress at the first place we stopped. She wasn't gay herself, but she knew gay people and told us how to find the clubs.' The first place they tried was empty. The second, Club Max, had just opened the night before and that was where they found the women from Gay Association In Newfoundland who gave them the fine Atlantic welcome (The Body Politic 1982).

Tom Mills began going to the city's gay bars in the mid 1970s, and draws a distinction between the smaller, more intimate gay pubs and the larger dance clubs which later became popular among queer and straight patrons alike.

The distinction that I would make is that those smaller bars – like the Fogo-a-Gogo and the Alley Pub – they were smaller and they were gayer. There weren't going to be a lot of straight people at those bars. You knew going in what this bar was about. It wasn't fancy, they tended to be smaller, there wasn't necessarily a sexual element to it but it was a queer space, in almost the old traditional sense. It seems that the other bars that came later, which were bigger dance bars, you would have a larger overall number of gay people, but you would also have a larger number of straight people. And it was more about the party. Yes it was maybe majority gay, and known as a gay bar, but there would be straight people there. I can remember going to those places with straight friends. It was more of a party bar that had a lot of straight people. They were on Water Street so they had presence – I'm thinking of places like Madames, Private Eyes, or even earlier.

There seemed to be a shift between the mid-1970s and the late 1970s. I remember a difference in the atmosphere in the bars. You would more frequently see women in those bars. It seemed that there were more of the downtown regulars, people who were downtown partying late at night and just sort of dropped in. And they had coat checks, or some form of doorman. They had a little bit more control. Places like Club Max – they were popular bars, everybody was going to them, and I think they would probably be identified as gay bars but they had more of a disco-y, larger crowd.

The age range is one thing that stands out to me when we talk about these bars. These smaller bars would have men who would be in their 60s, or maybe a bit older. And then younger men. And there would be an intermingling back and forth. I knew a lot of those older men to talk to them, and I never felt like they were hitting on me. But it allowed an intergenerational exchange. You'd encounter [CBC producers and lawyers] there. You wouldn't see those kinds of guys if you went to somewhere like Solomons or Club Max, which was a younger, more party-type crowd... The younger crowd was the more mixed crowd. You had more lesbians. You'd have people who were possibly straight but maybe they were bisexual or maybe they were allies or maybe they were just there for a good time (Mills 2021).

The downtown gay scene has been a template for my life

Sheilagh O'Leary is a well-known character in the province: artist, activist, and at the time of this writing she serves as Deputy Mayor of St. John's. But her earliest community involvement was in the city's queer club scene.

"I was very involved in the local downtown gay scene in the 80's and it has been a template for my life," she reflects.

In the 1970s and '80s I would sneak down in high school, trying to go down to Friends to dance, because it was the scene. I used to sneak in underaged. I didn't care about drinking or anything else, it was all about the dance. Me and a buddy of mine used to put on our headbands and our dangly earrings and run downtown to see if we could get into the bar. We'd go dance, buy one drink and then dance dance dance and then make our way home again.

It was very eye-opening for somebody who came from a very middle-class Catholic family. I was obviously searching for community. It was a time of real awakening, of sexual freedom for people in the gay scene, but it was also inclusive of people who weren't necessarily gay. It embraced what I guess would now just be called queerness. Anything that was alternative lifestyle, anybody who had different attitudes. And it was fun! It was a time where people really needed to let loose. Especially where being gay was so taboo. It was so taboo! Gay-bashing happened regularly, with people getting hauled into back alleys because of the way they looked or acted – there was zero tolerance for [difference]. I mean, we know that queer culture – and gays and lesbians – are age-old, they've been part of society since time eternal. But everything was so restrictive at that point in time. And as a result of that restriction, I think it helped create the nugget of an explosive community that fostered a scene that was just all about discovery and freedom.

A lot of young gay men and women coming from around the bay found themselves in that scene. It was the exodus – 'taking the gay from the bay.' Small rural communities weren't able to deal with it at the time, or at least many weren't. Whether it was Catholic or Pentecostal, they were not accepting of anybody who was queer, so the [downtown bar scene] kind of embraced all of that (O'Leary 2022).

Marion Atkinson said she and her women friends often headed directly for the gay bars when they went downtown in the 1970s and '80s. Even though several of them were straight, they much preferred the environment provided by the gay bar scene. The straight bars, she said, were always sexualized and women in particular were routinely sexually harassed. Not so at the gay bars.

It was wonderful, because they were good fun and I never had to worry about anyone putting the make on me. You were having fun for the sake of having fun. And they were marvellous places. Oh my god the fun you'd have there. They were just happy places where people could relax and just enjoy themselves (Atkinson 2021).

Not everyone felt as positive about the intense growth of the city's gay bars when they exploded in the late 1970s. Some of the CHAN activists introduced in Chapter 2 felt the rise of downtown gay bars contributed to the disintegration of their own community-building efforts. When Gerard Yetman moved back to Newfoundland from Toronto in 1985, he lamented the fact that bars seemed to dominate the city's gay social scene.

When I went to [Ontario] I realized wow, there's gay sports. There's gay literary clubs. There were gay youth groups, there was even a gay art group. But we didn't have anything like that in St. John's. I think because everything was centred around clubs, it was all centred around drinking. And I think that in many ways it was somewhat detrimental to our community because I think a lot of us developed alcohol problems during that time (Yetman 2022).

Mills had a similar observation.

I think that many of us experienced various forms of trauma as younger people that could range anywhere from being overly represented in sexual assault victim cases, to harassment, to rejection by family to our own internal turmoil – our own lack of identity and our own lack of role models. Many of us are vulnerable even today, and in our younger years even more so. I think that unfortunately, our meeting space being one that was fuelled by alcohol and being provided by people who were making money off alcohol – and we were vulnerable to begin with – it led to excessive drinking culture sometimes, which would have very detrimental impacts on us in our lives and in our later years. I say that because I think that we have to be careful not to glorify the bars. We have to recognize that even though this was a wonderful thing and here we all were – one big happy rainbow family – while there's elements of truth to that, there are also elements of people becoming severely addicted to both alcohol and drugs, there's people being incredibly depressed, there were suicidal people, and so the bar life contributed to that. When it came to AIDS and STDs, some people let down their guards because of alcohol and drug consumption, and that allowed us to be even more victimized, and put us in even more vulnerable situations. So the bars are both good – in that they offer this milieu – but with that milieu came other dangers, which we were particularly vulnerable to. It also divided us to some extent – you'd have the gay people who didn't want to drink who wouldn't go there (Mills 2021).

For those who did go out to the bars, the lifestyle could be taxing. O'Leary worked in the bars, lived above and beside some of the bars, and had room-mates who also worked and danced at the bars.

You worked, you lived, and you played. I probably never saw daylight for a couple of years, because the bars used to open up at 7:00pm, but nobody would show up until 10:00pm or 11:00pm. Then you'd be bartending and dancing and doing it all, you'd be in and amongst it all, and then the bars would close, but oftentimes they'd go late and they would just lock the doors and then it was an opportunity for all of us to just dance dance dance. So I just lived there. Then by the time daylight came, you'd go home, you'd have a snack, you'd crash, and then you'd wake up again when the sun was going down. And you would start the whole routine again. There was a period of time where I'm sure I never saw the sun. But I got lots of dancing in (O'Leary 2022).

Tree Walsh vividly recalls the early gay bar scene vividly, and in particular the intensity with which it was embraced by the community in the pre-AIDS era.

The bar scene was nuts because there'd be nobody there till after midnight, and then the queers would start showing up. And then of course once the bars closed everybody showed up! And then it was gays-on-display night. And it was hedonistic! I mean there were straights doing each other in the corners, and then there were the guys and their glory holes, because it was pre-AIDS. Sex was just fucking everywhere (Walsh 2021).

Bars weren't the only queer spaces, however. For many within the queer community, house parties played an important role in maintaining community and connection. Ellen Balka recalls moving to Newfoundland on Boxing Day in 1990. Two days later, she attended a New Year's Eve party held by Peg Nor-man. Norman then lived in an apartment over the Fountainspray convenience store across from Bannerman Park on Military Road. Balka recalls it as a heady immersion into St. John's lesbian community.

I arrived in town and days later I was at a party that was a largely lesbian party. I pretty well met just about all the lesbians in town that were around in St. John's at that time and were out. I met all sorts of people at that party. And everybody knew, because I was at that party, that I was there and that I was a lesbian (Balka 2021).

Barry Nichols also recalls being taken to a house party by a friend of his in 1979, which, to his surprise, turned out to be full of older gay men.

There were a bunch of older gay men who were all queens and stuff. It was one of the most incredible evenings I had. It was like being taken to an inner sanctum of all these people who had suffered. I'd say they were probably twenty years older than me, so they had suffered so much. I never knew their names, but at the time I thought 'What a resource this is, that's disappearing' (Nichols 2021).

Ann Shortall and her then-partner, Sue Rose, often hosted dinner events and house parties. Shortall pointed out that dinner parties were important in the queer community because unlike straight couples, queer couples were still unable to show affection in restaurants or most public venues. When Shortall remembers those events, some still make her laugh.

We hosted a party when Ellen came out. That was a really big deal, so we had a coming out party at mine and Sue's house. We watched the Ellen coming out [episode] and then we had our own coming out party where we all had to sing, we had to make up a song about how we came out of the closet. It was all a big deal back then. It was a really big deal.

I think there was a lot of damage, personal damage done in terms of mental health because it was a different time and I think there was a price to pay for the secrets that we had to keep and the way that we lived. I think a lot of addiction issues happened, things like that. Like even going out to supper, it was different because in the straight world you couldn't be yourself, for the most part. And so we hosted dinners every weekend, or a bunch of us got together and we would have dinners, nice fancy dinners and things like that. I mean yes we went out to eat too, but even that felt restrictive where we couldn't be ourselves fully (Shortall 2022).

Rita Mae got her start DJ'ing events at the St. John's Status of Women Centre. A single mother with a young child, she wound up living in one of the apartments above the Women's Centre for roughly eight years.

I lived up over the Women's Centre, and I used to open up the place in the mornings, and put on the coffee. They helped me – the rent was low, so I could make it. So that's where I started out. Not in the bars of Newfoundland. We started getting the women together at the Women's Centre. We would have beer bashes at the Women's Centre. We'd probably be killed if we tried to do it now – we had no license, we had no nothing, we just did it. I had one turntable, and records, and I would bring it down into the Women's Centre, and I would play the women music. And they'd dance. So that started to become very popular. Everybody wanted to come to the Women's Centre (Mae 2022).

The popular TGIF beer bashes at the Women's Centre were mentioned in Chapter 3. When Mae eventually moved out of the Women's Centre into a house of her own, she continued putting off events in her own home. She acquired a disco ball, lights and industrial speaker systems, and the events quickly became too large to hold in her own house. She put off women's dances in local community spaces like the Grad House, the LSPU Hall, and the Masonic Temple. The events were private, yet hundreds of women would show up. When Mae organized one, the information spread quickly by word of mouth throughout the community. Mae also kept a little phone book with the phone numbers of attendees. Whenever she noticed someone new at one of her dances, she approached them for their phone number.

It's almost primitive to me that we had to do that, because there was no poster, there was no Facebook, we had nothing. We had nothing. It's almost sad when I think about it, because we were hiding. We all hid. We were all hiding.

We had to be that way. My friends were teachers and social workers and doctors. People of our sexual preference weren't looked at as a good thing. We had to hide. There's women today that still hide. Because of the discrimination. Oh my god the discrimination, we certainly were discriminated against (Ibid.).

"We never called the gay bars by their names when we were in public," said Roger Baggs.

You'd either not talk about them, or you would say things like: 'Are you going to the club the weekend?' You would never say 'I'm going to Private Eyes' or 'I'm going to Solomons'… gay people and lesbian people would always say: 'Are you going to the club?' You kind of whispered it, like it was a big secret (Baggs 2022).

For some queer folks, especially in the early years, going to a gay bar constituted too much risk. They stuck with house parties, or with secretive private dances like those organized by Mae.

"There's people who would never go downtown, but they'd come to a women's dance," said Mae. "That's how I became so popular, because many of the women wouldn't go out. They wouldn't go to a bar. It was too much. The privacy had to be kept."

But for others, especially younger people, it was the bar scene that provided community. Lori Seay, who now lives in Victoria BC, is astonished at the variety of queer spaces available to young people her daughter's age.

"There was none of that," she recalled, of her own late teenage years. "It was just us finding each other, mostly in women's studies courses or downtown at the bars."

Still, she looks back on it fondly. "It was a great exciting time. We were this little tribe of people. Everyone knew everyone and we all lived out of each other's back pockets… the queer scene was very familial."

Dallas Noftall, who grew up in the city's gay club scene a decade before Seay, had a similar recollection of its importance.

The club scene was so vital, so vibrant. The camaraderie, the little community that we had - it's how we would find each other… We were an absolutely wild tribe, and we still love each other today, many of us are still in contact today. I waited and snuck out as many school nights as I possibly could – I was out that window and down to the bar. I found where I belonged and I found my people. I didn't find it in the living rooms of older gay women like some did, but I definitely found where I belonged when I went to the bars. That's where I mostly found open-minded bisexual women and gay men. Mostly gay men. The gay men were beautiful and wonderful. I loved them, I loved them so much (Noftall 2022).

For some though, especially professionals who feared discrimination if they were outed, going to a gay bar was a fraught experience. It brought access to community and support, but also the danger of being seen and outed. Colin Williams found community at The Zone, a large dance club which opened in 1994 and operated until 2010.

"There were other gay bars but I never went to them," recalled Williams, who was employed as a high school teacher in St. John's at the time.

That's because I never went to places that you couldn't get into and out of discreetly. If it was on the open street then I didn't visit there because we didn't want to be seen going in or coming out. Whereas The Zone was more or less secluded. You could get in there without too many people seeing you (C. Williams 2022).

Police raids

Raids of gay bars by police were a common occurrence in St. John's as elsewhere. There were important distinctions however. While the raids were undoubtedly a form of homophobia – and were often carried out in extremely homophobic ways – there are important ways in which they were distinct from their American counterparts, and also from other forms of homophobic policing like the Bathhouse Raids. In those other jurisdictions and places, bars would be raided and patrons arrested en masse just for being there.

In the case of NL police raids, notes Tom Mills, who served as the province's Director of Public Prosecutions in the 1990s, raids were conducted under the auspices of the NL Liquor Control Act. Police would seek out violations of the Act, for instance underaged patrons, and while a bar might be shut down and patrons evicted, the direct target would be the bartender and bar owner. Police would shut down the venue and issue a summons to the bartender to appear in court at a future date.

That is not to take away from the subjective experience of people who may have been in the bar in terms of how they felt or what may have been said to them which may have been totally inappropriate. I don't doubt that there were homophobic remarks made. There would have been a sensitivity around checking ID's – even if [police] said they were looking at it for age, they would have been looking at your name and address. There's a dichotomy between how we may have perceived it, and how another person may have (Mills 2021).

"There were lots of police raids," recalls O'Leary.

Although we also had lots of police [dancing in the clubs]. There were gay cops there, gay judges, you name it – they were all there and they were gay. There they were. But the raids certainly happened a lot. And there were always people keeping an eye out for it. Especially because [Friends] was kept as an after-hours bar. They basically closed the door and kept it going until the wee hours of the morning. So there were raids, they used to happen (O'Leary 2022).

Greg Bourgeois was under-aged when he started going to Friends as a university student.

Everyone called it the gay bar, although after midnight a lot of the clientele were straight, because they would come to the bar to dance after the others bars closed. So there were always a number of us that were under-aged. Of course, there were policemen on the police force who were gay as well, so they would often let management know if there was going to be a raid in the bar that night. On those nights, the doorman wouldn't let anybody in who he suspected was underage. Otherwise the deal was, you could come in and dance and socialize in the bar, as an underage individual, as long as you paid your cover. You got pop or water for free, but you weren't supposed to drink. And that was only on nights when they knew there wasn't going to be a raid.

Now of course there were underage people who had false IDs, who got in on the nights that they knew there was going to be a raid, and they often ended up getting caught and then they'd shut down the bar for a couple of weeks. That never happened to me – I never had a fake ID. But for the most part the underaged people paid attention to this and respected it and did what they were supposed to do, what they asked us to do.

The funny thing is, the day I turned nineteen and was legally allowed to drink, I went down to the bar but I didn't have any ID on me. The guy who was on the door that night said: 'Greg, you can't come in tonight because we're going to have a raid.' I said: 'Tonight is actually my nineteenth birthday!' So he said: 'Oh! Well show me your ID.' The only ID I had at that time was my MUN ID, it had your year of birth on it, but I didn't have it on me. So I had to walk all the way back to my apartment, and then walk all the way back to the bar, and when I got there there had been a raid, they'd found a couple of underaged people and the police were escorting them out, and the bar was shut down for the night. So I ended up having to go to a straight bar that night for my birthday drink – my first legal drink (Bourgeois 2022).

"The cops used to raid the bars," explained Walsh.

I remember being down to the bar when it happened, I don't know how many bars the cops would raid. But you'd be in there and all of the sudden the lights would come on and people would say 'Ooh, the cops are here!' And whoever was smoking a joint in the bathroom had to get outta there as quick as they could.

I remember one night they had all the lights on and everybody is drunk and they've been partying and the cops can't get a good count – they'd all get different numbers. So the cops said: 'Okay, everybody on one side of the room!' And then [a woman] who was one of the sauciest fuckers I ever met in my life, she stood up on a table and she said: 'All the boys get on one side and all the girls get on the other side – meanwhile the cops are yelling 'Get down!' – and she continues: 'And the bisexuals can all get in the middle!' She was loaded.[62] *Anyway they counted us again, three times they counted us, and it turned out the place wasn't overcrowded after all. Well then the place just went up: 'Get out! Get out you fucking bastards, get out of here!' And the cops would get right in your face, just to intimidate you. How many times that happened.*

And now people say 'We want the cops in Pride.' In Pride! You don't know what they did. They can come in their civvies, that's fine, but don't wear that goddamn uniform here, Jesus Christ (Walsh 2021).

In Chapter 2, NGALE activist Michael Riehl described members of the community spontaneously forming what were essentially self-defense squads during a period when The Zone was being subjected to frequent fire alarms. The imperative to protect queer bars – and queer space – was one Mills reflected on as well.

The bars were the only place in which [queer] people got to interact. They played a pivotal role in allowing people to interact and bringing people from different backgrounds and different ages together to interact and get to know each other and learn stuff. It was the bar that provided the space for interface. And that's why I suspect that we as members of the queer community have a heightened sense and a heightened fear when we hear that the police have been at one of those bars. For us it's not just a place to drink. It's a safe place, if you will. I don't think we can forget that. Others might perceive it differently, but we would see it perhaps more (Mills 2021).

Gay Guides and Main Drags

In Toronto, tabloid newspaper coverage of the gay scene underwent a remarkable mid-century shift, as some of the gossipy columns discussing gays, lesbians and trans people started to be written from the perspective of those they covered. While couched in a campy, light-hearted and deliberately scandalous style, this new breed of tabloid column was subtly sympathetic to its queer subject matter. Instead of being written *about* scandalous queers, the columns began to be written *by* and *for* queers.

A case in point was the creatively titled weekly tabloid Tab. As early as 1956, it ran a column called "Toronto Fairy-Go-Round" authored by a writer called Bettina. The column stopped in 1959 but was reborn in 1963 under the title "The Gay Set," and penned by a Lady Bessborough. In 1967, the column

---

62 This story was told to me multiple times by different people who remembered it in different ways. According to one telling, the woman said: "All the boys get on one side, and all the girls get on the other, and if you don't know what you are then get in the middle!" While the story is often retold with an element of humour, patrons recall that the act of dividing men and women for the purpose of checking IDs was a deliberate act of homophobic and transphobic violence, with police officers making fun of people of all genders who didn't conform to normative gendered styles.

was taken over by Duke Gaylord, who authored pieces as late as 1985.

The May 27, 1978, The Gay Set featured a guest columnist under the name Avonda, writing from St. John's, Newfoundland. Avonda offered readers a rollicking snapshot of the gay club scene in downtown St. John's at that time.

Not all the gays in Canada are to be glimpsed in the big cities like Montreal, Toronto and Vancouver," they wrote. "[T]heir sisters in the boondocks are multiplying fast... St. John's is so actively gay that some people view the situation with alarm... (Gaylord 1978).

Beginning with North America's "primeval main drag – Water Street" Avonda showcased the key gay venues. The Sea Breeze catered "mostly to the leather types" and featured "the odd brawl but they're quickly brought under control." The Upper Deck was "a must;" a "cruisy place" featuring the occasional drag show. Stage 3 Disco also featured occasional drag shows. The Waterfront had been renamed The King's Head Pub and had "lost some of its gay quality but nonetheless is still frequented by some of the regular gays." Avonda also recommended the upstairs bar at the Hotel Newfoundland, and the Holiday Inn at 10:30pm (this was where Jack Clark, a well-known member of the community, was known to perform piano; (Ibid.).

The east end of Water Street was recommended for cruising: "it's not heavily policed." Avonda demurred on the subject of Memorial University. "Forget the University – that's a myth," they wrote (this was patently incorrect, as we have seen). Avonda criticized CHAN for being "not too organized" but promised visiting queers a warm welcome nonetheless (Ibid.).

Newfoundland's gay community is made up of friendly, dependable people. I have yet to hear of any of them engaged in a major brawl with each other. To be honest, the 'Queens' are not that bitchy... There are no rip-offs among the gay community. You will be safe. After all, this is God's country (Ibid.).

St. John's Downtown Gay Bar Scene

Some of the province's earliest organized queer activism emerged out of the bar scene, much as was the case in other locales such as New York City's famous Stonewall Inn. Some of those keystone moments include the boycott of the Waterfront Club, and the march on Trapper John's and George Street organized by GALT in 1990 (discussed in Chapter 2).

While recognizing the complexity of calling any of them a 'gay bar', the following section covers some of the key venues that played a role in queer community between the 1970s and 1990s, from the perspectives of some of those who frequented them.

The Grad House

In 1971, the newly formed Graduate Students' Union at Memorial University purchased a sprawling, 20-room house located at 112 Military Road. The $52,000 mortgage, then a considerable amount, was their response to a lack of support from Memorial's administration for the housing needs of a small but growing graduate student population. MUN frowned on grad students living in residence on campus – the party-like dorms were considered unsuitable for serious scholars – but provided no other solutions. So, the GSU took matters into their own hands.

The large old house located at 112 Military Road (beside Bannerman Park) was effectively a mansion constructed in the Second Imperial Style between 1870 and 1880. Originally known as Park House, it was home to various prime ministers of Newfoundland, including Sir Frederick Carter and John Kent. Other notable residents over the years included the Ayre merchant family, as well as the family of Liberal politician and Lieutenant-Governor Ed Roberts (when he was a child). The Conservative Club used to meet in the house as well. After the GSU purchased it in 1971, it would become a controversial asset for the union. It was in constant need of repair, and the GSU found itself perpetually short of funds to address the house's problems. For the last decade of its ownership, the GSU engaged in a near-constant debate over whether to sell the house. Finally in 1996, the GSU sold the house – which was then in need of tens of thousands of dollars' worth of repair – and leased the newly vacated Feild Hall on the Memorial campus.

For the 25 years of its existence, the Grad House, as it became known, not only served as a residence but became a critically important hub for community organizing and engagement. In addition to renting out some of the building's 20 rooms as low-cost office spaces to local community organizations, two large rooms on the first floor served as lounges and were frequently booked by community groups for meetings or social events. There was also a bar. The GSU's progressive-minded leadership had no qualms about renting or giving the space for free to queer organizations, and it's quite possible that same-sex dances, drag shows, and fundraisers for the city's queer and feminist organizations outnumbered other events during the 25-year lifespan of the space.

Fogo-a-Gogo / *Sea Breeze*

The Fogo-A-Gogo has already been mentioned. It operated from the early 1970s and later changed its name to the Sea Breeze and welcomed the influx of new customers from CHAN's 1976 boycott of the Waterfront Club. But even as the Fogo-A-Gogo it had attracted a queer clientele. It was one of the first queer bars Karl Wells recalls spending time at. "It was slightly seedy, but it was a bar where gay people could go and not get beaten up or thrown out," he said.

"Fogo-a-Gogo was known as a place where the drug crowd – pot users et cetera – hung out," recalled Wish Leonard. "I was there only once, and it was just a crowded, noisy place."

Marion Atkinson had fond memories of the spot; she used to go with a couple of young women she was friends with. "It was a little underground place, a little basement. Oh my god it was a great spot. It was a lively, civilized spot. And it was mainly gay people."

"The first bar that we went to was the Sea Breeze," remembered Joan Dewling.

I'll always remember the Sea Breeze because it wasn't a gay bar as such but we were tolerated and we were kind of on one side of the room and the straight people were on the other side of the room. And invariably people would come in and go 'That's the gay side, so we'll go over here [to the straight side].' And then often those same people would end up on the gay side within a few weeks. But that was the first bar (Dewling 2022).

"The Sea Breeze was the gay disco bar before Upper Deck and Friends," recalled Nichols.

It seemed to me like the first gay bar. Both The Welcome Inn and the King's Head [Waterfront Club] were kind of gay bars, but Sea Breeze actually seemed like an out gay bar. A straight friend of mine and his girlfriend used to go there – they liked to go to drink and they liked music and eclectic environments. So they loved going there. But one night a guy who was gay came over to them and he said: 'Why don't you heterosexuals go to your own bar and leave this space to us?' They thought this was very rude, but I guess he thought they were there to gawk at people (Nichols 2021).

The Brahma Room

The Brahma Room was a shorter-lived venture remembered by some as being contemporary to Friends; patrons suspect it was put out of business by the more popular Friends. According to one patron, interviewed by MUN folklore student Georgina Reardon in 1979:

[Y]ou must remember that when the Brahma Room was in operation, they were very tacky. They catered to strictly gay... at the Brahma Room you went, you had a bunch of butch dykes who were very cliquish. You had a bunch of gays who were there who were into the drag scene, it was cliquish. Everything was cliquish about it (Reardon 1979).

Another patron interviewed by Riordan said that "although the Brahma Room was cliquish it was at least a stronghold for gays" (Ibid.).

Upper Deck/Friends/Madames

The Upper Deck, which opened at 208 Water Street in October 1977, was more willing to embrace the label of gay bar than its predecessors. It subsequently changed its name to Friends; many patrons tended to use the two names interchangeably. In 1983, following a shift in management, it underwent a further transformation, adopting the name Madames.

Nichols recalls the place with a rueful laugh:

The entrance was on the back at the second level, and if you can picture that alley without concrete, it was a fucking mudslide. All gravel and mud. You had to go in there and you had to watch out for your life that you didn't slip in the mud on the hill because it was just like a dirty old alley. There's a side entrance to the second level on the [paved] steps now, but that wasn't there and you used to have to go right to the back of it, the big boarded up fence, and you used to go in through the mud fields to get right to the back of it. That was quite exciting too. And then it got so popular, and it became Friends.

Friends became really popular because of the mixture of people there. But it kind of moved up from being an underground type of low-life alternative bar to being an attractive 'Oh let's go out and see that place!' type of bar. Because the word got out about how cool and incredible it was. So then it became like Studio 54. Bob [Bobby Davis] the bouncer would have to stand outside and pick people and let them in. It was the craziest fucking thing in the world. So there we were lining up, like it was Studio 54. That was fabulous (Nichols 2021).

Dallas Noftall, who eventually went on to become a professional DJ herself in Toronto, will never forget her first visit to Friends. She went with a young gay friend of hers, and as she walked up the stairs and flung open the door, the new wave hit "Da Da Da" by German band Trio came on. Inside were dozens of sweaty, dancing queer bodies, she recalls.

I opened that door and bam! It was something I never ever dreamed possible. It hands down beat any of the straight bars or clubs, it was just phenomenal and alive and exciting and it was so filled with euphoria and culture and a bit of everything. I opened that door and I was gobsmacked. When people opened up the door at the top of the stairs and saw the lights and the music and the joy, it was so sexy and fun and vital and vibrant. Nobody was ashamed, and nobody was hiding. We were there, and we were alive! It was vital. It was absolutely beautiful.

Friends and Madames were cutting edge, extremely inclusive. They had it all, they were like a small version of Studio 54. People came in with their spiked hair, their piercings, they came to express themselves and they were loud and proud on that dance floor and in that bar (Noftall 2022).

Wish Leonard frequented Friends, as well as its predecessor The Upper Deck. He has vivid memories of a local man named Oliver who did drag performances there. Oliver went on to perform drag in Montreal, and later died of AIDS. One of the performances Leonard remembers involved Oliver doing an impression of American singer Anita Bryant – notorious for her virulent homophobia and campaigns against gay rights – which ended with the crushing of Bryant's LP underfoot.

John Guiney Yallop first visited the bar for a Hallowe'en event. "Even though I was out, I had never been to a bar," he recalled. "I was dressed up in costume so it felt kind of safe, because nobody knew who I was."

There were two ways to get into Friends. You could come in right at the level of the dance floor, which was upstairs, and you came in through the back off Water Street. Or you could enter from the front door on Water Street but then you had to go up the stairs – two flights of stairs, one to get your coat checked and then on up to the dance floor. The dance floor was kind of dark (Yallop 2022).

"There were lots of people who went to Friends, including lots of straight people," recalled Karl Wells.

It was a disco bar and it played Donna Summer and Gloria Gaynor, all those people, and it had multiple levels, it was a happening place. There was so much energy in that place. It was an exciting place to be, really exciting. Occasionally people would come in drag. Anything goes there, it was that kind of bar (Wells 2021).

"Friends was a disco and people went there and danced their chops off," recalled Sandy Pottle. "Mostly they went very late at night, which I wasn't always up for. But when I did go out there I managed to stay out until just about dawn. I had a really good time there. It was just such a relief to have a place where you could go and see your friends and that sort of thing."

"It was very eclectic," recalled Greg Bourgeois.

All the people who were involved in the arts, like all the actors and actresses and artists, musicians, everybody like that went to Friends. Tommy Sexton, and the whole Codco crowd, and all the musicians who weren't playing somewhere else in town on a particular night would always end up there before the bar closed. When you came in to the bar on the second level from the alleyway, there was a small bar and there was a sort of sit-down area and it had quiet music. So that part was more like a pub, or a speakeasy. People would sit there and smoke and have a drink, but there was no dance floor. If you went up a small circular staircase to the third floor, that's where the dance floor was and there was another bar up there. It wasn't a very large bar, but it was almost like a second home for us. It was right above what today is the Rose and Thistle. We were down there pretty much every Thursday, Friday, Saturday night – it was our social life (Bourgeois 2022).

Sheilagh O'Leary had her first exposure to the city's queer culture at Friends as well.

So here was this bar – it was the place to be. It was an unbelievably fun time, if you were somebody who liked to dance. And it didn't just cater to the gay community, it was for anybody who was alternative, a little bit more eccentric, anybody who was looking for something outside of the norm. So it drew in a lot of really interesting characters. Even as a straight woman, I just felt – okay, I've found my people.

I had lots of friends who were coming out at the same time, people I knew through school and people I was living with, so it was a real time of exposure. It was a real time of freedom, and fun, and joy in celebrating identity. No matter what that identity was. There was lots of drag going on, trans was happening, there was lots of lesbian culture, butch and femme was going on at that point in time. There was everything. It was such a mixed bag. But because it had all been so encapsulated, so enclosed and so taboo and so forbidden, it made it almost more explosive. And [Friends] was a bit of a safe zone, for people to go and express themselves freely. It was a point of connection between many different kinds of communities… there were also a number of little spots around but this dance club certainly was the epicentre of the culture — it welcomed everybody.

Once I was exposed to it, there was no going back. I just wanted to dance, I loved dancing. And here was this community – as soon as I found this bar, and the people within this bar, I just knew this was it – I'd found my people. It allowed me to be whoever I wanted to be. Most of the people who frequented the bar and who I became great friends with were people who had had to fight a lot of demons in order to get to that place in the first place. In order to overcome their sexuality, their identity - I thought these were such brave, courageous, powerful people who just pushed through it all. These were the people I wanted to be around. It was an unbelievable time of exposure and self-awareness (O'Leary 2022).

Several of the bar's former patrons shared memories of a friendly relationship that developed between the queer community centred on Friends, and some of the local biker gangs. O'Leary was one of them.

"Because all these things intertwined, it wasn't just a heyday of wonderful sexual freedom, but there was also a lot of drugs and things that happened. And there used to be a biker bar called The Roxy down on Water Street. They had a big burly biker clientele who you would not ever associate with the gay scene, but interestingly enough a lot of the bikers from the Roxy used to come [to Friends]. They wanted to go to a place after hours, and this was the after hours bar, so they used to come over and they'd all come and stay in the bar. So you'd have this incredible contrast of people, but everybody got along!

There was a sort of caretaking that happened, an unwritten rule or relationship [between the bikers and the queer clientele]. I don't know if the owners orchestrated it, but there was never any conflict, and the bikers kind of helped to keep things safe. It was interesting how we had this ability to cohabitate in the same space and without conflict (Ibid.).

After a few years living and working on the mainland following his graduation from Memorial University, Barry Nichols moved back to St. John's in 1979. It was where he eventually came out. He retains vivid memories of Friends.

St. John's was thriving in terms of the gay scene. I started hanging around Friends which was the gay bar at the time. It was very mixed and that's what attracted me to it. Being gay was still underground. The bar was very alternative and mixed, so there were people there who were hustlers and sex workers and drug dealers and a whole range of madness, but everybody had that edge of tolerance. That's the kind of place it was. So if you were a right-wing drug dealer you wouldn't hang out there because you wouldn't want to be associated with it. But if you had a whatever-will-be-will-be type of attitude, then that was the place. It was very exciting, it was incredibly exciting, because you had all these very alternative types of crowds, and of course when you're going to a bar you get to know people, if it's the place you always go. So it was very exciting, it was incredibly exciting! I can't believe how exhilarating it was for that time and period. Not just for sexual orientation, but just the freedom! If you were at all anti-establishment, then it was the place to be. You felt like you could hang up those masks at the door and just go in and be yourself (Nichols 2021).

"There would sometimes be guest DJ's," recalled O'Leary.

The DJ'ing was taken very seriously. The cast from Another World[63] used to come all the time. We all grew up on it; Another World was THE soap opera. They had a lot of queer staff and queer actors. And they found this club – I don't know how they made the connection. But they used to come often (O'Leary 2022).

Nichols got himself an apartment and became good friends with the rental agent who looked after the apartment for a local company. She was straight, but the two of them often spent their time downtown at Friends. Nichols himself had not yet come out as gay.

At that time there was a community of people, we lived downtown and it was a real community in the sense that we all knew each other. The other thing I loved about it is that there was only the one bar, so gay women went there as much as men. So you got to meet everybody, you became friends with a whole bunch of people and sometimes you developed really good friendships – just because you're drunk together, you're foolish, and bonding happens.

Judy Stacey was a very tall woman, very large and had a deep voice and she was scary. She was a stereotypical diesel dyke. I used to talk to her sometimes... and she used to always snarl at me because I was hanging out with this other woman who she found very attractive. And then one night she came over and gave me a lecture about how I should just come out as a faggot and leave the women to her. And then she said: 'I'm so pissed off with you I could shove a fucking beer bottle down your throat.' We become really good friends after that.

I spent a lot of time at the bar, because when you're younger you can do that – I was working every day and spending every night at the bar. Then eventually I determined that I was gay (Nichols 2021).

For some patrons, the bar became the safe space in which they shared stories of the not-so-safe-space which comprised most of the rest of the city.

There was this guy who was not a drag queen but was totally femme. He

---

[63] A popular American television soap opera which ran from 1964 – 1999.

always wore makeup and he had this huge fur coat that he loved. One night at the bar he's there and has his fur coat on the chair. And he says: 'My god, coming down tonight two of these guys jumped out of a car and threw me in a ditch!' He was so resilient though. These guys punched him and pushed him into a ditch. 'Me and me fur coat!' he said. But he was totally so rising above it, so refusing to let that affect who he was. He was such a hero to me in that way, he had this great sense of humour and loved to laugh at the challenges that life threw his way. He was very engaged, very extroverted. He moved to Montreal after. All the people from that period, most of us moved away because of employment or needing something bigger, because you can only live at the bar for so long, and there was nothing else here (Ibid.).

Another frequent patron, Nichols remembers, would also show up in the most unique outfits.

He was into his own world, he created his own outfits and loved to come out and dance and things. On a typical night he would show up wrapped totally in saran wrap with tinfoil underwear. He was incredible. This was in 1979, 1980. He'd wear fishhooks as earrings, and when he was dancing, you'd have to watch out for him because these big drop earrings with fishhooks would be flying!

Friends was a cool bar, anybody who was cool went there, no matter what your sexual orientation was. One time somebody I knew from MUN was at the bar, they were standing near to me and my current boyfriend, and we were talking and he was saying: 'I just don't understand how two men can do that together' and stuff like that, so we all just talked about that. Which was really cool – like that's a great conversation to be having in a bar in 1979 with a straight person that you know, for whom this is all foreign. It was an age of discovery, for everybody – not just gay people. It was an age of discovery for straight people to understand what homosexuality was too. And because of the nature of the bar, you were cross-fertilized that way. People who were cool and not closed off were exploring life, and then they got to see that the reality is different from the notions and beliefs they had been programmed with. That was such an important function of the bar. And you didn't have any rednecks there who were going to beat gays up because there were bouncers there as well, and [the rednecks] wouldn't have survived (Ibid.).

Club Max

Club Max, which opened at 128 Water Street, sought to capitalize on a scene that had already been well primed by Friends and Upper Deck. For many who went there, gay and straight alike, it was the most sensational club to ever appear in the province; NL's version of Studio 54. Others found it a little *too* cool and trendy, and missed the more familial, community feel of Friends. The larger venue brought a more diverse (and straight) crowd, but it retained the unmistakable, underlying vibe of a queer club.

"We went to Club Max a lot," recalled Karl Wells. "That was a great bar, really great. That was an exciting place to be. It was a lot of fun. It wasn't a gay bar, but a lot of gays went there, and a lot of gays worked there – I think everybody behind the bar was gay."

"Club Max was kind of the dance club 2.0," said O'Leary, whose roommate worked there. "Except for it was more open to the straight community, and it was less exclusive."

Less exclusive around sexuality, perhaps, but class was still an issue.

"Club Max was pretty exclusive," recalls Noftall. "They were a little snobby, and you really had to have money and know people to get in there, so sneaking in was way more difficult."

Nichols had a similar impression, and missed the community feel of Friends. "I didn't like it at all. They had gone from the organic feel to a mainland disco type of thing. It was more pretentious."

The Alley Pub

The bar located at 164 Water Street went by a variety of names in the 1980s. Originally the Night Cap Lounge, in 1982 it became known as The Alley Pub. During the mid-1980s it was known as Kibizers, and then toward the end of the 1980s it reverted to The New Alley Pub. But through all these rebrandings it was known as a "little queer pub."

"The Alley Pub became Kibizers after. It was an after-hours bar, you'd drift down there after the queer bar closed," recalled Walsh. "Because it would be open until the sun came up, because they got the black paint on the window and all that. And they had a jukebox. It wasn't bad, I used to spend a fair bit of time there."

"I tended bar at the Alley Pub and let me tell you, that was a scene," recalled Lori Seay. "It was a little queer pub.

"The Alley was definitely older working class, sex workers, more like what we think of when we think of those 'darker days,'" recalled Seay. The nearby Brother TI Murphy Centre hosted Alcoholics Anonymous (AA) meetings, and she frequently had customers who were closeted gay men pretending to their wives to be attending AA meetings there.

They'd tell me their stories and I'd pour them light beer – I wasn't pouring hard liquor for someone who's supposed to be in AA! There were also a lot of guys who did street level sex work. You can imagine how wildly physically dangerous that was at the time. Those guys would come in between jobs and it was a pretty wonderful, judgement-free zone for a lot of people I think (Seay 2022).

Tom Mills also remembered The Alley Pub.

That was the pub that we would go to late at night. It was a very popular late-night bar. You had to go to the back door because they would have the front door closed, and there was a fire exit. You'd go up the fire escape to get in, and they'd let you in, and you'd have to knock on the door, they'd see who it was, and not everybody was getting in. It was that kind of establishment. There was very little space – not a lot to it. There was that kind of atmosphere (Mills 2021).

Lesbian clubs

For a period in the '80s and '90s there was also a profusion of lesbian bars in the city's downtown. Katz (376 Water St) and Earharts (379 Duckworth St) were two of them.

"The political dykes would hang out at Earharts," recalled Rogers.

Noftall remembers going to Katz, and while she appreciated the bar for what it was, she can't help but contrast it with what she felt was the more inclusive and welcoming environment of Friends.

I remember when they opened that beautiful bar [Katz]. It was on the second floor so you had to go upstairs. Friends was very narrow, but Katz was very wide open. But when you walked up the stairs of Katz, and you walked in the door, the place was beautiful – the bar was huge, the dance floor was big, the collective area was great – but you would walk in and whether it was two or fifty or eighty people there, you had the glaring eyes of all the lesbians on you. All eyes were on the door examining everyone who walked in and giving a look of approval or disapproval, and then they continued on as if you didn't exist.

It was a very, very different experience. Eventually as it got packed and as people got their drink on, then it became friendlier and more fun, but it didn't have the impact that Friends or Madames had. Friends and Madames had a huge impact. Katz had a huge impact too, but again it was older, glaring, more judgemental lesbians. They were a hard egg to crack, that community. But it was a beautiful bar. Katz was definitely the superior space (Noftall 2022).

"There were a few lesbian clubs," recalled O'Leary.

But the lesbian bars tended to be a little less prominent. A little bit more laid back, and a little bit more obscured. And it was interesting because at the time, when you'd go into the bar, you'd see all the young gay men who would be out full-on on the dance floor. All of them would be out there. But I think a lot of the younger lesbian women at the time kind of laid back a little more. You could certainly see the divide, and I think that was probably part of the necessity of having lesbian clubs – so that there could be a special space, a safe space for lesbians (O'Leary 2022).

Another woman who requested anonymity shared a similar observation: "The gay men had the clubs, and lesbians had the women's dances," she explained.

Priscillas

Priscillas operated in the late 1980s at 379 Duckworth Street. For a brief period, the address hosted neighbouring bars for gay men and lesbians.

"I would say the first time I went down to an LGBTQ bar was when I was sixteen," recalled Roger Baggs.

It was on a dare, and there were a bunch of us hanging out together – two girls and a guy. We were 15, 16 years old. And we decided to go down to this bar on Duckworth Street known as Priscillas. It was known as a gay bar for men, and upstairs was a bar for lesbian women called Katz.

So we went to Priscillas one night but it was on a Wednesday night. One of us knew the person on the door, so we slipped in and it was the first time that I went there. With two girls and a guy. I asked the guy if he wanted to dance. That was the first time I danced with a guy in my life. And it was in public, and the lights were flashing, and it was really – wow. It was a very different experience for me.

Priscillas was very small. When you came in there were some tables, not very many, and then in the back there was a dance floor, and then on the left-hand side there were some tables and things like that, and some couches, and there was a small bar in the back as well. It was a really compact bar. I don't know how I got there, I don't know how I got home, but I remember going! (Baggs 2022).

Private Eyes

Baggs, and many other queer clubgoers, have fond memories of Private Eyes, one of the premier queer dance clubs from the late 1980s. It was located at 186 Water Street, an upstairs venue with a storied history. It was a piano bar in the early 1980s, and for a couple of years in the mid '80s became a popular venue called The Oil Patch Club, in homage to the province's offshore oil boom. After operating for a brief period under the name Checkers, it became Private Eyes in 1987, and operated until the early 1990s (another queer bar, The Outpost, would operate out of the venue in later years). The bar was located above Erin's Pub, a popular Irish Newfoundland folk club, and the entrances to each venue were next to each other, sometimes leading to awkward encounters between patrons. The entire front of Erin's Pub was comprised of a glass window, providing patrons there with a clear view of clubgoers heading toward Private Eyes, especially if there happened to be a lineup at either venue. Despite this drawback, the bar became wildly popular in the queer community.

"Private Eyes was fantastic," recalled Baggs.

I frequented Private Eyes in the late 1980s, when I was 18, 19, 20 years old.

It was right above Erin's Pub. That upstairs spot used to be called Liquid Ice, but before it was Liquid Ice it was Private Eyes. Same layout, although they had a fireplace in the back, and a pool table. And they bought these big discount airport chairs, they were in the back. And then there was a big bar on the front, on the first floor. And then a big dance floor. And a really tiny staircase. Then up the tiny staircase was a second floor, and another bar up there, and the bathrooms. It was quite the bar. Tommy Sexton was there a lot, he used to hang out in the bathroom and smoke cigarettes all night long, and everybody would be talking to him.

Private Eyes was great, although it was also scary at times. At that time, we had no human rights in the LGBTQ community. I mean, homosexuality was decriminalized but there were no human rights. So we'd get to the door to go in and there'd be a lineup at Erin's Pub, and everybody there would glare at us when we walked in that door. So you'd go in, and you'd go in so fast and then you'd also leave so fast, because you were afraid.

I learned to vogue there. I was in a vogueing competition and I was number two! My friend Paul was number one – he won. He was really good at it. He used to do this little technique, he'd start and stop these poses, and with the flashing lights it created these optical illusions that made it look like he was having pictures taken of him, and between the flashes of darkness and light he'd be in different poses. It was very captivating. And then this fellow William, from Hong Kong, he got third place.

I was just a youngster, a little club kid with my Le Chateau clothes on and my hair teased, and we'd wear makeup and we'd dress up and have a crisis every Friday night about what we were going to wear. There were a lot of straight people who went there too, guys with their girlfriends, and a lot of young women went there too. I met a lot of guys there, and I dated a lot of them casually.

The music was all eighties music. This was 1989, so it was all Kylie Minogue, Stock Aitken Waterman, Jody Watley, Soul to Soul. George Michael did his second solo album, Madonna came out with Vogue. They would sometimes play the scattered older song too, but it was quite happening, quite something. They had this big video screen that would come down and you could watch all the videos on the video screen. It was incredible for the time!

It would always be packed, and it was open on Thursday, Friday, Saturday and Sunday nights. So you could go there four nights a week if you wanted to. There was nowhere else to go really, if you wanted to meet people. There was no internet. If you wanted to meet people or socialize or feel normal or be in a safe place, there was nowhere else to go. Nowhere.

Sometimes straight people would come in and say weird things. They'd say things like: 'This can't be real!' I remember that plain as day, some of them saying 'This isn't real, this can't be real.' They would say that to us! What they meant, I think, is that here we were all having a good time and we all looked like a million dollars and the mood was so positive... and the straight people would say: 'This isn't real – this isn't what life is like!' But I think they were *just really shocked by the fact that we were enjoying ourselves. Because back then, gay people were so oppressed. When we left the bar, we had to go back to our regular jobs, and a lot of us were so poor. I was working at Subway and making $4 an hour. My friend Paul was poor and was a waiter. All the gay guys were in the service industry, and they were all poor. We would spend all our money on looking good on the weekends, buying our shirts at Le Chateau. But Private Eyes was such a great place* (Baggs 2022).

The East End Club

The East End Club at 110 Water Street opened in 1970 and operated until the early 1990s. During the 1980s it was located directly across from the TI Murphy Centre, a community centre offering adult basic education and other community services. The East End Club became particularly popular among the lesbian community; its owners are remembered by many patrons as enthusiastically supportive of the community. The venue hosted dart nights as well as women's nights. It was the venue of choice following lesbian sporting events.

"The East End Club was where all the sporty dykes went," said Peg Norman.

Lynn Murphy had a similar recollection. "The East End Club tended to be the jock type lesbians," she said. She joined a local women's baseball league, and the players often retired to the East End Club after games. At first only a few of them, like Murphy, were out; some used to bring their boyfriends with them. Within a couple years, she said, they had all come out.

The Carriageworks

The Carriageworks was a former carriage factory on George Street built by Philip Wall in 1892. In 1979 it was re-opened as a bar and restaurant and became particular popular with the lesbian community. Peg Norman remembers going to see Kate Best perform there.

Kate would be playing, just her solo guitar, singing, and you'd get some men who would be at the bar being just rowdy. And there was always some dyke who was brazen enough to go up to them and tell them to shut the fuck up (Norman 2022).

Solomons

The venue spanning 156-160 Water Street always flirted with the queer community, and during the early 1990s it hosted the city's premier queer dance club, Solomons. In the early 1980s it was a bar sometimes frequented by gay men called Side Tracked. As Solomons, it operated until 1994; mere days after it closed, Zone 216 opened down the road at 216 Water Street, and most of the DJs, staff and clubgoers made a smooth transition from one club to the other.

"It was a very different sort of gay bar dance scene back then," reflected Ted Martin.

I remember going out to the gay bars, and it was an amazing sense of freedom the first time you go. Being there with your friends, at that time, it was this weird juxtaposition of a safe and dangerous space. Because this was also the era of AIDS and HIV, it was the early 1990s, there was still gay-bashing, still a lot of adamant anti-gay sentiment.

I remember going into Solomons, I remember the first time I ever danced with a guy, grinding with a guy on the dance floor. I remember going into Solomons, sitting in the back room at Solomons and being subjected to a lot of breeder jokes. I remember this guy who called himself Bill-From-The-Hill. He was a gay guy from Shea Heights – 'up on top of the hill!' He was one tough motherfucker. There was gay-bashing and stuff happening at the time, and I remember one instance where Bill gave as good as he got. He was quite the character. I also remember a gay ex-RCMP officer, a gay ex-cop (Martin 2022).

"It was the only real gay bar," recalled Chris St. Croix.

It was what I would have expected a gay bar to be at that time. A little bit like a haven for a bunch of people who didn't have anywhere else to go, a little bit full-on crazy dance bar kind of vibe. Not particularly cruisy in that way that gay bars could be… It was a good mixed crowd in the sense that you could bring straight people with you and have a good time, but also it was still very much a gay space. Drag culture didn't have much of a hold at that point.

It was Newfoundland so everyone who was gay of all attitudes and backgrounds really only had one place to go, and that was Solomons. It was the '80s for gods sake, we were very preppy. I went deep on preppiness and Benetton shirts and the whole vibe. But at the same time, you had people coming in from Carbonear, who were very much like: 'I don't want to be here necessarily – I don't want to be in this bar – but I want to meet someone who I might have a relationship with.' So that mix made it interesting in the sense that there was a mix of cultures there. But that also made it difficult to have any sort of identity behind it. When I went to Halifax, I saw what could happen when you had bars that could be more niche in terms of what they wanted to do.

But in the days before apps and things, if you wanted to meet anyone, that was where you went (St. Croix 2023).

Zone 216

"The Zone was on the third storey of an old building," recalled Colin Williams.

We were always afraid, when we'd get in there and be dancing, that the whole floor was going to collapse and we'd all wind up down in the basement.

But when you got in there and you'd hear Donna Summers, when we heard those tunes come on – well sacred heart of Jesus b'y, there wouldn't be a soul having a drink! We'd all be out on the floor shoving our hands up in the air, dancing to Cher or Diana Ross or somebody else. There was a great sense of community, even though we weren't close to each other. If you were gay you kept to yourself, but then you'd go to the bar, and you'd bump into all these people that you knew from varying professions and it was a very safe place to go.

There were straight people came there but they came there mainly because of the music, later on at night when the straight bars closed. When the straight bars closed, they all came to the gay bars. And then it was just dancing till daylight, you know what I mean? (C. Williams 2022).

"That was before the gay bars were packed with straight people," recalled Seay. "There were some cool straight kids, townies, who might come in for a scuff with a boyfriend or something. But in that space, in the late '80s and '90s, it was a queer space. We far outnumbered the folks who were 'there for the music.'"

Anyone who frequented the gay bar scene of that era remembers Bobby Davis. His presence spanned much of the era discussed in this chapter; he worked at Friends, Solomons, Zone 216 and other venues too.

"He was a legend," recalled Seay, who occasionally covered bar at Solomons. Davis was working there as the bouncer when she was hired in the late '80s, and he took a shine to her.

We were the closest bar off the waterfront. So when the Russian boats docked off the harbour we would be the first bar they hit. You can imagine the disaster when these Russian guys walk into a bar and realize they're in a queer bar. I had a guy come in one night and he was by himself. I couldn't tell if he made a mistake or was checking things out, so I was kind of chatting with him. And he got very homophobic, and really nasty. He grabbed me – sexually assaulted me. Bobby Davis was on top of that guy with a cue ball in his hand in two minutes. The gentleman was divorced from his wallet. Bobby said to me 'You're not working – get in the car!' So I got in Bobby's car and we drove up to some sketchy apartment. He brought a bag of the weakest weed you ever smoked and he was like: 'Fuck that guy!' I said, 'Bobby Davis, you are a hero. You are a legend my friend.' That's who he was (Seay 2022).

Davis also refereed women's ball hockey, a sport which was wildly popular among the province's lesbians. "He was a big old queen, almost as round as he was tall, but you didn't fucking mess with him," recalled Sharp Dopler.

"I remember one of the times I got grabbed at the bar. I was on the door and I would do the early shift and Bobby would do the later shift." That night a customer wheedled his way in without paying cover by saying he just had to look for a friend. When Dopler found him drinking in the bar and demanded he pay cover, the man assaulted and threatened them. Without any backup, Doppler resumed their post on the door.

I waited until Bobby came in. Bobby comes in and he says: 'How's it going my love?' I said: 'Did you win at Bingo?' 'No,' he says. So I says: 'See that feller there? He hasn't paid his cover charge and he picked me up by my throat.' Bobby says: 'Oh really? All right I'll just go take a wander around now.' So off he goes. About an hour later this guy [the customer from earlier] comes up to me and he says: 'I gotta apologize.' Even though Bobby wasn't very big, Bobby had wandered over to him, and now this fellow was practically crying, begging me to accept his apology (Dopler 2021).

Dopler wasn't yet out when they first went to a gay bar in downtown St. John's. They went with a male friend, and Bobby was on the door.

Bobby was the first person to greet me that day I first went to the gay bar. I walked in and I was all nervous. 'Hello my darling!' he said. 'What brings you here?' 'I'm just going to have a beer with my buddy.' Bobby looked me up and looked me down. 'It's all right my dear,' he said, 'it'll be all right once they figures out what ya are and what you're about.' And sure enough. He was a constant (Ibid.).

In a small place like St. John's, nightlife community often spilled over into the daytime world as well. "Bobby Davis moved every fag and dyke in the city at that time," recalled Seay. "Anyone who was moving, Bobby would come and take care of us. He had worked for CN Railways for years, and if people had a sick relative on the mainland, he would get them a train pass."

Many of the other friendships and relationships fomented by the bar scene extended into daily life as well, with members of the community looking after each other. Seay recalls another friend she met through the bars.

He was a gorgeous, brassy sex worker – a really great guy. He would have orphans' Thanksgiving every year. He had a house on Angel Place, and he would take in everyone who wasn't welcome with their families. Mostly it was men who were cast out of their families. So there was a lot of chosen family. And a lot of raucous, absinthe-fuelled Thanksgivings (Seay 2022).

There were other queer spaces as the 1980s unfolded. Mary Jane's health food store opened in the 1970s, and the origin story of that space – whose original owner played a pivotal role in the feminist movement – is told in Chapter 3. Even after Mary Jane herself had left the province however, the shop continued to serve a central function in the queer community. It was the spot at which to find queer publications like *The Body Politic* and other queer books, magazines and newsletters. For many, it was also a place to find community.

Mary Jane's was a pivotal place. It was like a dykes' cabal. Mary Jane's was a revelation for me. And it was one of those places where there were also straight guys who were cool with gay people. That was a new thing, because we were quite a closed community. Making friends with straight people who were totally down with gay people was really revelatory for me (Seay 2022).

The Strand

For several years The Strand Lounge operated in the Avalon Mall, serving as a restaurant and bar that also offered live entertainment. In the late 1970s, The Strand opened a second location in Atlantic Place downtown, and then a third location in the Village Mall in the city's west end (these later two locations only lasted for a couple of years). One of the popular acts to perform there was The Great Imposters, a drag troupe formed in Ontario in 1972 which toured the country for more than three decades, headed up by notable drag stars like Rusty Ryan and Michelle du Barry.

Barry Nichols remembers the sensation they caused when they came to St. John's. He had moved into an apartment near the Village Mall with a friend from university, Everett Reid, from Chapel Arm,who was also gay. When they heard that The Great Imposters were coming, they were delirious with excitement. "We were like 'Oh my god that's incredible, we've got to get tickets to go!' This was in 1980, at The Strand in the Village Mall!"

Unbeknownst to them, the owners of The Strand rented an apartment in their building in which they put up visiting performers. So, one night when Nichols and his roommate returned home, they discovered the drag performers running around their building.

They were in our building! So we ran into them and we invited them to dinner one night. And they accepted! We were so excited of course. Everett was this beautiful man and everybody fell in love with him, so he was a great person to have as a friend because he used to make people melt and he was very approachable and stuff. My brother happened to be visiting at the time, and he had worked in restaurants in Toronto so he knew cooking, and so he made this huge Lebanese meal for them. It was incredible. They enjoyed it and they couldn't stop cracking jokes the whole time. It was so great.

Then we went to their show, and Rusty gets up – he does an opening monologue to warm up the crowd and stuff – and even though back then people were rednecks the crowd was really responsive! So Rusty gets up and talks about how fabulous the people they'd met here were, and this one group even had them over for 'lesbian food.' It was great. That was such a rich, strong, positive thing to happen in gay life here in 1980 (Nichols 2022).

Newfoundland Press Club

One occasionally queer space that wasn't fixed in location was the Newfoundland Press Club. This was, as the name suggests, a social and professional networking association run by and for the province's journalists. It's come and gone throughout the twentieth century, sometimes setting up shop in fixed locations for a time. For a period in the 1950s it was located in the Colonial Building on Military Road; later that same decade it moved to Duckworth Street. At other times it had no fixed location, and the group's executive would book spaces specifically for lectures or parties. One such occasion, described by then-VOCM reporter Nix Wadden in his memoir *Yesterday's News*, was a fashion show put off by the Press Club on November 19, 1959. The event "was billed as a fur fashion show, complete with floor show", only "the models were feminine only in attire, with Madame Edgar Squires, Mamselle Charlotte Bursey and Señorita Belle Squires emerging as the stars of the show." The event, featuring an array of prominent local journalists in drag, caused some initial controversy not due to their gender-bending but because local fur companies mistook the ads and thought the "Continental Furriers of Montreal" (a non-existent group promoted in the ads) was a mainland Canadian company coming to undermine their business. Press Club organizers met with local fur executives to smooth their ruffled feathers, and the relieved local businesses donated some of their furs for the drag show (Wadden 2008).

Cruising

The complex politics of public sex, the right to claim sexual space and presence, and queer sexuality are too complicated to explore in depth here, but suffice it to say that cruising, or seeking sexual partners, was an important component of sexuality for some in the queer community, especially gay men. Cruising was driven by a variety of factors, not least of which was the fact that there were so few public spaces in which gay men could find and meet each other. There were no such things as dating apps in the twentieth century and so for many men, cruising provided an opportunity to find sexual partners.

A variety of cruising spots in the city have been cited in the literature or were raised in interviews I conducted. Because of their accessible nature, public washrooms were a common cruising site. The public washrooms in the Village Mall were obviously one common cruising area until the RNC operation in the early 1990s (see Chapter 5), as were a variety of washrooms at Memorial University (see Chapter 4). The public washrooms at Bannerman Park were another site where cruising was common (Stagg 1994).

Barry Nichols recalled the cafeteria at Woolworth's Department Store on Water Street in the city's downtown as another common cruising area in the 1970s and '80s.

Woolworths was another cruising area. The lunch counter – Holy Jesus yes!

That's where you'd go Saturday afternoons to pick up somebody. Downtown. We'd go there and you'd find the occasional [hook-up], you'd sit there where you'd see all the regular older guys there having their chips (Nichols 2021).

The east end of Water Street in downtown St. John's was well-known for many years as a gay cruising spot, as was the War Memorial. As Michael Riehl explains:

You kept walking past the War Memorial down Water Street and [Harbour Drive], and it's a dead end. And it would be hilarious, because the car would go down there, turn around, and come back. Car goes down, turns around and comes back. It was called 'the fruit loop.' That's what we called it.

But the thing is, you had to be brave to walk down the fruit loop, because you didn't know what was going to happen. Was there somebody there actually looking to hook up? Was there somebody there waiting to bash you? If there was one person there you might start talking to them. But if you see three people, you just keep walking. You don't even look at them, you just keep on walking. Because you don't know what's going on.

There were stories of people on the fruit loop who had things thrown at them from a car. People in cars would throw a chicken box or a bottle of pop or something at them. Unfortunately, this stuff happened. You had to protect yourself. Remember this was before the Internet - people were trying to figure out how to meet people, because you're looking for human contact, right? (Riehl 2022).

"If you were cruising you'd pick somebody up, or you'd get picked up in a car quite often, because Water Street East was where all the gays went," explained Wells.

And I'll tell you there were some very prominent people who were gay – lots of judges and lawyers and executives and other people who picked people up or who got picked up. And you would drive somewhere and park, and do your thing. So there were a few places that were prominent parking areas, and quite often you'd probably be parked and all of a sudden a police car would pull up and there might be three, four cars parked, and the cops would get out and shine a light in the car or whatever. It was stressful (Wells 2021).

Sports

For some in the queer community, sports teams offered another space in which to organize. Sports teams were especially popular in the lesbian community. There were a variety of women's sports teams in the city formed around workplaces or groups of friends, and so lesbians formed their own sports teams as a way of building and maintaining community, and having fun. Sports teams offered a way to gather outside of the alcohol-fueled environment of the bar scene, although alcohol was often an important part of sporting events, and the teams often celebrated with each other after games.

Tree Walsh has vivid memories of at least two lesbian softball teams from the 1980s.

The Diesel Dykes and The Babes. We used to play up in Shamrock Field where the Sobeys [grocery store] is now. Every Sunday we'd play softball there. Totally disorganized. I'd bring my car in, I had a Honda Accord hatchback… I'd open up the Hatchback and supply the music, we had the beer in the dug-outs, we were all sot. It was bad. But we had fun.

I remember one time we had been out in Makinsons – a bunch of women had gone and rented a cabin. Oh my god what a maggoty time we had. We had had a few catches [of fish] and stuff so everything was on the picnic table and it poured! So we had to get back to town for our games and our gloves were all full and heavy because of the water, and our hands were freezing out in the field. Such a cold wind blowing on our gloves, but we didn't care (Walsh 2021).

Rita Mae, who began DJ'ing Friday nights at the Women's Centre and later put off her own private women's events, was also involved with a women's softball team and a floor hockey team – comprised primarily of lesbians – and sometimes used her events as fundraisers for the teams.

We never had no money. We'd play against all the women's teams in St. John's, and they would kill us. We'd go out there, they'd have all their uniforms on – socks and all the good things, the gloves and everything – and we didn't even have matching t-shirts. So we used to have these beer bashes so that we could try to get a t-shirt. So that we could get socks (Mae 2022).

Chapter Eleven: Pushing Boundaries in the Arts

Political activism wasn't the only front in the fight against homophobia. Even before the establishment of formal activist groups, the province's artists had been pushing boundaries and expanding NLers consciousness around a variety of subjects, sexuality among them. Every play that broached issues of sexuality or sexual and gender identity; every artist who wasn't afraid to buck norms and demonstrate alternative ways of moving in the world; all helped to create space for empathy, understanding, and change.

Tommy Sexton

Few artists encapsulate this role as clearly as Tommy Sexton. His name is iconic in Newfoundland and Labrador and beyond. A shelter operated by the ACNL bears his name. His face is still widely recognized in the province; streaming videos of his skits are shared far and wide on social media when they migrate onto the internet. But who *was* Tommy?

"Tommy Sexton was a brilliant, trail-blazing gay comedian who was nationally famous in the 1980s and early 1990s," explains Andrew Sampson, a journalist and writer who's working on the first full-length biography of the man. Born in 1957, Tommy moved to Toronto after quitting school in Grade 10 to pursue an acting career. In 1973, he co-founded the Codco comedy troupe, which initially put off theatre comedy. He joined Wonderful Grand Band[64] in 1979. He appeared in a variety of other film, stage and television performances. In 1986, Codco was picked up by CBC for television, which eventually brought it to screens across the country. The final season was produced in 1993. Later that same year, Sexton died of complications brought on by AIDS.

"What's so interesting about Tommy is that in a time when most people's public personas and their private ones were so at odds with each other, Tommy's public persona was his private persona," explained Sampson. "He was always just remarkably himself."

Tommy grew up in a large Catholic family with eight siblings; his parents were from Fogo Island and St. Mary's. Tommy mined his family, his friends, his lovers, and the broader political sphere for material that he incorporated into his work. He didn't hesitate to showcase the issues and dilemmas real people were dealing with at the time, no matter how taboo or outre they might be considered. At a time when queer characters in film, literature and television

---

[64] WGB, which was originally the backing band on the television show "The Root Cellar" featuring Greg Malone and Mary Walsh, also consisted of well-known NL musicians including Sandy Morris and Ron Hynes.

remained predominantly tragic, Tommy and his colleagues brought a queer sensibility to comedy, using humour to tackle issues that were often directly rooted in queer community and experience. He even deployed this method in response to his own looming mortality.

"When Tommy was diagnosed with HIV, he processed that death sentence – because that's what it was in those days – by again using it as grist for the mill," said Sampson. "So there are sketches on Codco that are about characters who have HIV. He used that perspective to make others laugh and to draw attention to the stigma faced by many PWA."

What initially drew Sampson, and many others, to Tommy was how proudly out he was in an era where queerness was still widely considered taboo and most people were in the closet. "How the hell did he have the fortitude and the courage to be who he was so unapologetically, in the 1970s and 1980s? At a time when the Roman Catholic Church had Newfoundlanders in a firm kind of chokehold? Yet he was there. And he was unapologetic about it."

The impact of Tommy's presence on the provincial and national stage cannot be understated, Sampson says.

It's hard to really understand just how beloved Tommy would have been then. He was a household name. When people saw Tommy on the street they would go up to him and ask for an autograph. So this well-known public figure was sort of exposing everyday people to what it looked like to be a gay person in the province (Sampson 2022).

Michael Riehl, one of the organizers with NGALE in the 1990s, feels Codco and Sexton in particular played an important role in normalizing queer culture and presence in the province. "I think stuff like [Codco] helped protect us," he said. "It helped tie us to the arts community, and showed us as colourful, fun. Maybe it helped bring more supporters in the background. It gave us allies in the back."

Sampson emphasizes however that Tommy's accomplishments were not a one-person show. He was comedic partners with Greg Malone, and much of their work was produced together. Codco itself operated as a collective, with members participating in the development of every sketch.

So if we're talking about Codco, in terms of their effect on Newfoundland queer history, I think we have to talk about how the entire troupe was extremely gender-bending. They had a queer sensibility. There's an interview where Tommy actually said that nobody in Codco lived a conventional heterosexual life. This crew was the counterculture. Half of them were vegans – in the 1970s! They had a very queer sensibility and their comedy – in regards to issues of sexuality and gender – always punched up and not down. And those sketches still hold up pretty well today (Ibid.).

In a November 1984 review for the show "Two Foolish To Talk About," produced by Greg Malone and Tommy Sexton, John Moreau wrote in *The Body Politic*: "Sexton, who half-jokingly says 'All the best performers are gay,' is happy doing Two Foolish because it gives him the freedom to do openly gay mate-rial. Both Malone and Sexton say their mission is 'To take gays to the world,' and to make them seem 'like a normal aberration in life.'" The show was tour-ing Canada to "rave reviews," wrote Moreau.

While the repressive social environment of post-Confederation Newfound-land and Labrador drove some queer NLers into activism, it also shaped the attitude of those who took to the stage. Sampson says Codco's development was also deeply shaped by the way NLers were being marginalized by the rest of Canada.

Newfoundlanders were the butt of the joke, seen as less than, stupid, free-loaders... that had a big effect on the provincial psyche. Especially when they all moved to Toronto. There's a quote I've heard – I can't recall from who – that they moved to Toronto as Canadians and returned as Newfoundlanders. Codco was a response to that. A way to celebrate their own culture while also poking fun of it.

I think what happened was [Codco members] all met each other, they were all in the right place at the right time, they were part of that first generation to come of age after Confederation, which was an extremely transformative time in Newfoundland society. It was an era of assimilation. These were people who still held on to their Newfoundland identity. They could see some of the stuff that Premier Smallwood did and the effect it was having on their prov-ince, and by the time they got together in the early 1970s they started to ask questions about it. And they grew up in the denominational school system, where the absolute moral authority of the church was unquestioned. So when you do that for eighteen years, and you get out into the world and you start to move away from that dogma, it's like it's been a dam all your life, and now it's broken open and it's flooding and they were ready to really just say and do anything (Sampson 2022).

While Tommy's life was remarkable in numerous respects, his death also came to have a special meaning. In October 1993, two months before his death, Tommy did a candid interview with CBC about being HIV positive.

He puts a face to the illness, for a lot of people who probably just saw AIDS as something to be afraid of, as something to fear. I think it does change something when somebody like Tommy, who has that kind of public platform, speaks out and tells the world what's happening to him (Ibid.).

For many in the province, including Sampson, Tommy Sexton remains a role model today.

What I also really like about Tommy is that he's somebody who, if he could have his time back and if he could choose what his life would be, I think he would choose to be gay every single time. He loved being gay. He loved what it represented. He loved having lovers. He loved men (Ibid.).

Maxim Mazumdar

The province's arts and culture field owes an outsized debt of gratitude to Maxim Mazumdar, a passionate actor, director and playwright who for the space of about a decade brought the province's theatre to a global stage – quite literally.

Mazumdar was born in Mumbai (then Bombay) India in 1952. As a young boy, and despite a speech impediment, he enrolled in the Campion Dramatic Academy. The following year, at age 13, he was already appearing on stage in leading roles with a professional Bombay theatre company.

Following the death of his father in 1969, Mazumdar, along with his mother and brother, migrated to Canada, where he enrolled at Loyola College, later absorbed into Concordia University. While there he co-founded Raven Productions, a theatrical group that performed at venues around Montreal. The group sparked international notoriety when they staged a production of Edward Albee's "Who's Afraid of Virginia Woolf?" in which the play's female protagonist (Martha) was replaced by a man (Marty) played by Mazumdar. The play was only staged once: after the first performance, Albee himself threatened to sue them over the same-sex presentation of his play, and they had to cancel the show. (The Body Politic 1974)

"Some critics have suggested that the destructive relationship portrayed in the play is actually a disguised homosexual relationship," reported *The Body Politic* in an unattributed article (The Body Politic 1974). "It is not clear whether Albee was trying to escape the imputation of homosexuality or whether he found objectionable the projection of the destructiveness of straight marriage onto gay relationships."

Following graduation, Mazumdar – together with Jordan Deitcher, a classmate of his from Loyola and lifelong friend - co-founded a new group, Phoenix Theatre. Only in his early twenties, the young Mazumdar threw himself into the theatrical world with creative abandon. One of his best-known original works was *Oscar Remembered*, a one-man play in which he takes the role of Lord Alfred Douglas, or 'Bosie' as he was known, the lover of Oscar Wilde. Wilde's persecution as a gay man came about at the hands of Bosie's furious and homophobic father, the Marquis of Queensberry, who prosecuted Wilde in the courts. Wilde wound up serving a two-year prison sentence with hard labour for his homosexuality; the experience broke both his spirit and his health, and he died three years after his release, at the age of 46.

Today, Wilde's persecution is recognized as the disgraceful act of homophobia which it was, and Wilde's reputation has been elevated by queer and straight fans alike. But in the 1970s, homosexuality was still stigmatized and Wilde's name carried an aura of scandal and disrepute. Mazumdar's play was one of the early creative works that presented Wilde in a different light, daringly reframing his role in a positive and heroic way.

"The idea of doing a one-man entertainment on Wilde was the most inviting because of the risk involved," wrote Mazumdar in an introduction to the script. "What depth lay beneath the jewelled words, the conflicting biographies, the chameleon-like letters – this haunted me" (Mazumdar 1977).

Mazumdar debuted the play in Montreal. One of the spectators at that show was William Hutt. Considered Canada's greatest classical actor, the openly gay Hutt had headlined stages from New York to London, and shared stages with the crème de la crème of classical theatre: Peter Ustinov, Alec Guinness, John Gielgud. Hutt was so taken by Mazumdar's work that he contacted Robin Phillips, director of the Stratford Shakespeare Festival, and urged him to invite Mazumdar to perform the work at the Stratford Festival's Third Stage in 1975. He did, and brought the young actor and playwright to a global audience.

"Not since the great days of the Dominion Drama Festival has the accomplishment of a young actor won such attention," wrote Herbert Whittaker, theatre critic for *The Globe and Mail*. "This study of Wilde's martyrdom is a truly remarkable accomplishment for a 22-year old Montrealer who found an audience beyond his local audience in the country's most eminent theatre" (Ibid.).

Soon the play was touring the continent. "There… is a poignancy to this story of two men who outlived both their youth and beauty," wrote Michiko Kakutani, theatre critic for *The New York Times*, of a 1981 performance at New York's Provincetown Playhouse (Kakutani 1981).

Joey Shulman was Mazumdar's publicist, and he was a Newfoundlander himself, who still proudly refers to himself as "the gay Jew of Newfoundland." Shulman's father was an American employed at a US military base in the province, who remained in the province after his tour of duty and went to work for VOCM. Joey says his father, who hosted a morning show, has been described as the man who brought morning radio to Newfoundland. The innovative broadcaster also used to do live coverage of the annual Tely 10 race in St. John's, driving ahead of the participants and broadcasting from the back of a truck. Joey's mother came from a large Jewish family which had emigrated to Newfoundland at the turn of the century from Eastern Europe; his grandmother Esther Wilansky opened the long-running Model Shop in downtown St. John's. She was also a talented and energetic fundraiser for a variety of community causes. Joey tells the story of how, when the Beth-El Synagogue in St. John's (NL's only synagogue) was being built in the 1950s, a dispute broke out between conservative-minded Jews and more progressive Jews as to whether it should be designed in the traditional manner with separate spaces for men and women, or with mixed seating. His grandmother, who was helping to spearhead fundraising for the project, was a progressive-minded woman who wanted mixed seating, but the more conservative men refused and determined that sexes would be separate. Whereupon Esther informed them that in that case they could fundraise for it on their own. The men reconsidered their position in light of this threat, and the synagogue was built with mixed seating.

Shulman grew up in St. John's during the 1950s, but his family moved to Toronto in 1958. It was there, at the age of 14, that he came out as gay. He became ensconced in the theatre world, as well as the queer community. He was one of the men arrested during Toronto's infamous Bathhouse Raids in 1981 (a story told in Chapter 5). When he met Mazumdar, he was working as an organizer and promoter in the arts. He had just left the Toronto Dance Company, and opened his own public relations firm. Mazumdar was his first client.

"Do you know the expression in the het[erosexual] world - 'chick magnet'?" he asked, reflecting on those early years of Mazumdar's career.

Saying the word 'Oscar Wilde' in the 1970s when Maxim was touring, you might as well have said 'Queers gather here'... People would show up with green carnations – which was the sort of inner circle signal that you were a follower of Oscar Wilde – and it was wonderful. It really opened the door to a whole underworld of small theatre (Shulman 2022).

Mazumdar was an astonishing, confident actor with a photographic memory, said Shulman. He particularly excelled at one-man shows.

"He was a master craftsman," he said. "He had a beautiful cultured British accent, he was a very good storyteller, amusing, ebullient – he could carry a room seemingly effortlessly."

Mazumdar's growing reputation came to the attention of organizers of the Newfoundland Drama Festival, who invited him to adjudicate the festival in 1978. His infectious enthusiasm was so well received they invited him back the following year. They also outlined for him one of their problems. Each year, the festival's top students received as prizes scholarships to pursue further theatrical training. The problem was that the only place they could receive such training was outside of the province, and the scholarships were insufficient to cover the costs of transportation, room and board at mainland institutions for students from Newfoundland and Labrador. So, year after year, the scholarships were returned unused, and the winners were unable to carry their theatrical training forward.

Mazumdar, who was coming to deeply enjoy his time in Newfoundland, came up with an idea – an ambitious one. He approached Louise Walsh, wife of Stephenville's mayor, with a proposal: he would establish a Provincial Drama School in Stephenville. That way, students could receive professional theatrical training without leaving the province. He immediately secured several grants from provincial supporters of the arts, and began reaching out to his contacts in the theatre world to secure faculty and instructors for the school. In the space of barely two months, he'd secured thousands of dollars in funding and had more than three dozen talented students enrolled. The College of the North Atlantic in Stephenville wasn't used during the summer, so he secured use of the facility for the three-week long drama school. Other local venues, ranging from bars to the regional Arts and Culture Centre, were secured for performances.

What Mazumdar created became the model for a subsequent wave of summer-time theatrical festivals that are still held throughout the province today.

It was his passionate vision and drive that revealed how successful theatre festivals could be, and showed the provincial business community that they could also be financially lucrative. In addition to the students and staff, scores of out-of-province visitors flew in each year to attend the festival, filling up local motels and boarding houses, and spending copious amounts of money in local establishments. This form of tourism is a well-worn model now, but Mazumdar was one of the pioneers who worked hard to sell the idea to a then-skeptical business community. Many of those subsequent theatre festivals were formed by Mazumdar's students.

"It brought tourists in," explained Cheryl Stagg, a close friend of Mazumdar's who worked with him on the Stephenville Festival in an administrative capacity during those years.

Our audience was maybe 15 percent from Newfoundland – the rest were from the Atlantic provinces, Ontario, and the eastern seaboard of the United States. It was a source of economic development for this region.

After that, I can't tell you exactly how many other summer theatre festivals and projects of one form or another started up in NL. They began to appear especially in small rural areas throughout the province within several short years after the Stephenville project had become fairly well established. The wonderful thing about it was that the theatre experience was brought to relatively isolated populations which would not otherwise have had theatre in their lives. The province is much richer for it (Stagg 2023).

Mazumdar's dedication to the province went beyond the Festival. He also launched a program called Theatre in the Schools, through which he would take graduates of the Provincial Drama Academy on the road across the province, and even by boat to Labrador. The troupe, who crashed in local residents' homes, would spent 20 weeks a year touring schools from one end of the province to the other, performing an eclectic hodge-podge of theatrical performances.

All the bustling arts energy on the west coast attracted other tours and performers as well; many of them queer. Sometimes all that was required to rescue repressed queer NLers from their small towns was the presence and example of these visitors. Shulman recalls once touring the island with a troupe from the Toronto Dance Theatre which included the well-known Indigenous dancer Rene Highway, who died of AIDS-related causes in 1990.

We're in Grand Falls, and I'm shopping with Rene Highway. He was really hot to look at – he had very long hair that he wore very proudly. We're going up and down the aisles and this young grocery employee, a stock guy who was stamping prices on cans in aisle five is suddenly there in aisle six too. And aisle seven. And he's smiling, and Rene's smiling back, and I was like – 'Go for it!' So we got him tickets to the show that night and he spent the night with Rene. Then suddenly he was on the bus with us to the next town! It was all very lovely. But I'm sure his heart was broken when we had to gently burst the bubble that we were getting on a plane and didn't have a ticket for him. He was crestfallen (Shulman 2022).

Shulman also remembers that one year The Great Imposters, the troupe of drag performers from Ontario, were touring the island including the west coast. Shulman had previously worked with members of the troupe in various other performative capacities on the mainland, and when he contacted them, they eagerly agreed to help put off some classes for the Drama School students. The sessions were equally impactful for the veteran drag performers, he explained. "When they came to that class, they were over the moon," he recalled. "It was like therapy for them. They talked about their repressed childhoods, and how they would have killed for an opportunity like this when they were growing up. I think that resonated a lot with the kids who were in the class."

Successful though it was, funding the summer theatre program was a challenging endeavour.

"When you start with zero dollars in September and have to come up with $300,000 or so by May, and you live in a community of 7500 people, where do you go?" reflected Bragg. With advertising, sales and administrative experience gained while operating the local weekly newspaper, she took on a key role in raising the money for Mazumdar's project. Using complimentary tickets she acquired from Air Canada, she traveled to Halifax, Toronto, Montreal, and western Canada.

I'd go see all the major, big companies that had a history of giving to the arts. I'd tell them: 'I come from rural Newfoundland, from a town of 7500 people, and I'd like for you to give me $10,000. Anyway, it worked. I think they gave it to me based on just guts alone. Often these people would say to me they'd never had an application from Newfoundland before! Sometimes I got it on that basis. I'd go to downtown Toronto, I'd go to a pay phone, I'd call a company and ask them if I could have an appointment. They'd say: 'What time would be good for you?' And I'd say: 'Well I'm in your building right now, just downstairs.' And it worked! They'd say, come on up!

Sometimes Maxim would come with me and we'd go in to see some corporate person. They were always impressed with him. He'd do all the talking, and he was so full of enthusiasm that it was infectious! (Stagg 2022).

Mazumdar's reputation, coupled with his extensive range of contacts in the theatrical sphere around the world, paid off well for the province. He recruited performers and instructors of such renown and calibre as had never graced provincial stages before, nor likely since. Among them were renowned British director Wendy Toye, Broadway choreographer Larry Fuller (of "Evita" fame), American playwright Eric Bently, as well as Sir Anton Dolin, John Gilpin.

Gilpin was a British actor and dancer who joined the Stephenville Festival in 1980. He was leading dancer with London's Festival and Royal Ballet from 1950-1972, and partnered with most of the leading ballerinas of his time. He'd been awarded the Prix Vaslav Nijinsky, the Etoile d'Or, and the Queen Elizabeth Coronation Award. He performed with the American Ballet Theatre, Chicago Ballet, La Scala Milan, the Pittsburgh Ballet Theatre, and more. At the 1980 Festival, he performed with NL actors Terri Snelgrove and Jeff Pitcher in

Invitation to the Dance, a play written by Mazumdar and based on Gilpin's own life.

In 1981, Gilpin – a close friend of the Queen Mother - was invited to the wedding breakfast for Prince Charles and Lady Diana. But he was in Newfoundland, with star billing in The Stephenville Festival's production of "Oh! Coward" on the same date, and didn't dare risk his friend Mazumdar's ire by leaving the festival for anything as mundane as a royal wedding. So, he simply handed on his hand-written invitation from Buckingham Palace to Stagg as a souvenir, and stood up the royal couple. Gilpin later married Princess Antoinette of Monaco.

Dolin was a famous British ballet dancer and choreographer who had been knighted for his work in theatre and dance. He had, in fact, been a former lover of Sir Alfred Douglas, Oscar Wilde's lover. When Mazumdar was performing Oscar Remembered in Toronto, Shulman, his publicist, learned that Dolin was in town, and arranged a meeting between the two – Mazumdar who played Douglas' lover in the play, and Dolin who had been Douglas' lover in real life – as a sort of press stunt to promote the performance. Dolin and Mazumdar hit it off and became fast friends, and Mazumdar pressed him into service for the Stephenville Festival as well.

The Stephenville Festival's alumni read like a who's who of NL performing arts: Jean House, Amy House, Peter Soucy, Jeff Pitcher, Terri Snelgrove, Lisa Moore, Don Dunphy, Berni Stapleton, Gerard MacIsaac, Pete Soucy and more. Likewise, the instructors: Michael Sinelnikoff, Thom Sokoloski, Julie Rank, Eric Bentley, Desmond Graham. Students came not just from Newfoundland but were also accepted from across Canada and the US. Spectators showed up in Stephenville from all over the world. Premier Brian Peckford flew in from St. John's and gave a short but inspired speech to the audience during the intermission of a performance of Hamlet. "The play is the thing!" he proclaimed enthusiastically.

The Provincial Drama School wasn't a stand-offish affair; Mazumdar and his colleagues ensured the institution played an integrated role in the community. In 1980, for instance, there was a parade through town featuring students and staff in costume, with brightly decorated floats depicting the shows appearing on stage that year; local residents were invited to dress up and join in. The marchers gave out candy to spectators, and local businesses offered special discounts. "Everybody in Stephenville is getting into the act, so don't be left out!" wrote Joey Shulman in "News From Big Blue", a Festival column that ran in *The Western Star* for the duration of the week-long event. Lead dancer John Gilpin, meanwhile, gave a talk to the Stephenville Rotary Club. Students broke into impromptu guerrilla performances at the local mall.

And they had fun.

"Campers and swimmers at Barachois Park got a free serenade on Sunday when the choir from Our Town broke into hymns on the beach," wrote Shulman. "Pete Soucy was covered in sand and Vicky Dawe demonstrated her two years of judo training on a poor unsuspecting soul."

Doctors and nurses at the local Sir Thomas Roddick Hospital in Stephenville, meanwhile, found themselves working overtime to attend to the needs of students in the physically demanding drama school, dealing with an array of breaks, sprains and pulled muscles.

The workload was prodigious. They worked literally around the clock, with overnight crews disassembling and reassembling stages and lighting for three different stages. This ensured visitors could maximize their trips, and see as many as seven shows in three days.

"Students at the Big Blue start every morning, except Sunday, at 9 a.m. for a crazy warmup that includes pushups, situps and lots of stretching," wrote Shulman. Then they attended acting workshops and lectures for the remainder of the day, in addition to rehearsing for their own performances. On several nights during performance week, students would be up until sunrise at allnight decorating parties, creating and decorating stage sets for the shows.

It wasn't just students who were worked hard. During the 1980 season, Mazumdar was not only responsible for supervising the entire festival, but also for teaching a voice class, playing Hamlet, and directing the premiere of his own production Invitation to the Dance. "Why all this overstretched activity? Simply put, the financial realities of setting up a new, untried festival demanded it," he wrote (Mazumdar 1981).

Invitation to the Dance represents an effort not just to honour the life of another pioneering queer artist, John Gilpin, but also to grapple with fundamental questions about the point of art and theatre. Mazumdar wrote it while grappling with a series of personal crises, and following a suicide attempt.

No work that I was producing in Canada, either as an author or actor, seemed to be of any consequence. I suddenly felt life and work were a trap set by a diabolical critic who smiled benignly on failure and nervous breakdowns.

Perhaps, during such bleak times we do our most intense work in order to survive the Black Phase. The pain of life bleeds into art. I emerged several rewrites later stronger and more determined to ignore the banal critical restrictions that growing artists in Canada are impeded by (Ibid.).

However taxing, the work was a success. Shulman judged Gilpin's performance – thirty years after his public retirement from the stage – one of his best. British stage and film actor, Edward Atienza, was invited to the dress rehearsal to give feedback, and when he broke down in tears at the end the performers knew they'd gotten it right (Ibid.).

[Invitation to the Dance] contains the belief that life is more important than death and that there is movement even in immobility. The life of an artist is riddled with the unknown. It is important, however, not to let that make us afraid (Ibid.).

During the early years, Mazumdar stayed with Stagg's family in their home during his months in Newfoundland; he eventually bought a house in Corner

Brook. The two became close friends. She vividly recalls the weeks he stayed at her house. They would do administrative work for the theatre festival after dinner, until midnight or 1:00am in the morning. Then she would go to bed. She recalls waking up on multiple occasions at 3 in the morning, and she could hear him in the dining room below her bedroom, practicing lines.

Stagg often asked him why, of all the places in the world he could have lived and thrived, he chose Stephenville, Newfoundland. At first he dodged the question, joking that he loved the Kraft Dinner she fed him (he was also, she said, addicted to a well-known NL treat called Jam-Jams, made by Purity Factories, and would consume them by the boxful in a single sitting). One night he gave her a more honest answer.

'The two years on the road [touring Oscar Remembered] did it for me. I lived out of a suitcase for two years,' he told me. He said it was the first time since he was a child that he had lived in a house with people and there were children around and he felt like he was part of a family. So that's what it was. He just felt very comfortable and very happy (Stagg 2022).

Mazumdar was a perfectionist, she emphasized. While he was fun-loving and knew how to have a good time, he also demanded the most exacting standards from those with whom he worked, students and professionals alike.

He ran a really tight ship. He aimed for perfection. He changed the lives of a lot of people in rural Newfoundland, and fully understood the value of exposing people to the arts. He would sometimes make the time to take a production or two on the road to more remote rural communities within travelling distance from Stephenville, such as Burgeo and Port aux Basques. The shows were enthusiastically received in those communities and the effort much appreciated (Stagg 2023).

Sometimes when they made fundraising presentations to prospective donors, Mazumdar would spontaneously throw in additional performance commitments or ideas.

"Why did you tell them we were going to do that? Why have I not heard of this before?" she would ask him scoldingly after the meeting. "And he would reply: 'Because it gives me more incentive to make sure it happens. Once I say it aloud I feel that I have made a commitment and will make sure that I deliver on it."

"He was a pretty amazing person," she reflects. "He was just high octane, he was so high energy. I don't know how he did it."

Mazumdar had a lung condition known as pulmonary fibrosis, which required him to periodically see medical specialists in Montreal for treatment. In April of 1988, while in Halifax to direct a production for a local theatre group in that city, he decided to see a pulmonary specialist there. Not knowing the specific nature of his condition, they did a bronchostomy on him, which can cause serious aggravation to the lungs for those with pulmonary fibrosis, and be tremendously dangerous. His lungs began spasming, and he lost consciousness.

Stagg was in Montreal representing the Stephenville Festival at an arts conference there, preparing for the tenth anniversary of the festival. She had a four-hour stopover in Halifax on her way home, and Mazumdar had asked her to meet with him there during the stopover to discuss the status of the anniversary celebration plans. When he missed their meeting, she was puzzled by this uncharacteristic lapse, but when she was unable to reach him by telephone she continued her journey home. She was met at Stephenville Airport with a message that he was in hospital in Halifax fighting for his life and that his doctors were attempting to contact her because he had told them, before falling into a coma, that she was his next of kin. She got on the next flight back to Halifax two hours later. By the time she arrived, he'd had a tracheotomy, but had also experienced brain damage. He regained consciousness briefly after Stagg's arrival, but became comatose again within hours. She remained at his bedside for nine days, along with his two close friends Richard Lambert and Edmund McLean. On April 28, 1988, at the age of 36, Maxim Mazumdar died.

Mazumdar's death has often been attributed to AIDS, and he's even appeared in AIDS memorials. Following his death, newspapers across the country, aware of his homosexuality, perhaps, drew their own conclusions and published articles attributing his tragically young death to AIDS, even though this information was incorrect. Stagg and those close to him were too busy dealing with his affairs and grappling with his death to bother correcting the newspapers. When she later met with his family, they discussed what to do about the matter of his death having been reported as being due to AIDS. Already his name was being used in AIDS fundraisers, and they considered at length the fact his death seemed to have galvanized AIDS activism and fundraising within the arts community. There was also to be considered the negative consequences of a public refutation of this cause of death. In the end, they decided to allow the incorrect accounts of his death to stand, by simply choosing to silently ignore them and not refute them.

"If it served a purpose to give more attention to the AIDS crisis that was going on at the time, I don't think he'd mind," said Stagg. "His name was being used to a good purpose."

The more we spoke, the more memories Stagg recounted of Mazumdar's playful and mischievous nature. She remembered a story related to her by his good friend Edmund McLean about a trip he and Maxim had taken to a BMW dealership in Halifax only months before his death, where Maxim planned to lease a vehicle to replace his tiny aged Honda. Maxim took a cream-coloured vehicle with chocolate leather interior out for a test drive. At one point during the test drive he stopped and asked McLean to stand on the sidewalk so that Maxim could drive by a couple of times for McLean to see how he looked in the car, and whether the colours looked good on him.

One time I went to a fundraising cabaret that he did in which he performed a selection of music from various shows, one of which was the song "Pick a Pocket or Two" from the musical "Oliver." It was in this little cabaret space and as he started the song he began pulling these long strings of scarves knotted together out of the pocket of the oversized overcoat he was wearing. I thought, 'Geez, I've got one like that.' And then the next one came out, and I thought, 'Gee I've got one like that too.' And when he got to number ten or twelve, I thought 'Son of a gun! He went into my bedroom and he stole my scarves!' And he was on stage singing this song but his eyes were glued onto me, because he saw my eyes as I was watching the scarves, and by the time I realized 'Those are my scarves!' and looked back up to his face, his eyes were glittering with glee. When I shot a look to his face his eyes were focussed on me and were absolutely dancing with laughter at the fast one he'd pulled on me!

Another time I was reorganizing the clothing in the Festival's wardrobe bank when I came upon a long gown that I believed was mine. Now, I had a closet full of long gowns, because when I first moved to Stephenville and they had dances or anything like that, people wore long gowns. So I had a closet full of long gowns. And one day I went into the costume bank and there it was hanging. As I continued with my work I came upon several others. He had gone into my closet and he took all my long gowns and he put them in the costume bank! So I picked one up and I went out to the office and I said 'What is this doing in the costume bank?' And he said: 'Oh Cheryl, you know perfectly well you were never going to wear that again!' That's what he was like. He was full of joy. He was full of energy and enthusiasm for the Festival and felt he was harmlessly helping to put my belongings to better use!

I would say to him sometimes: 'Why do you drive yourself so hard? This is way more than anyone expects of you. Why are you in such a hurry?' In a rare solemn moment he indicated to me that he felt he did not have long to achieve his plans and dreams. He said he was concerned that he did not have much time left. After his death, I found a copy of a magazine article [in which] he was quoted as having told the interviewer that he had once had a premonition that he would die at age 33. He managed to get three extra years! (Stagg 2023).

Theatre and Film

Theatre was pushing boundaries in St. John's as well. In January 1986, Cathy Jones, of Codco fame, brought her solo show A Wedding in Texas And Other Stories to the LSPU Hall. One of the "other stories" was Outport Lesbian, also featuring Lois Brown as Jones' lover.[65] According to a review of the show published in GAIN's newsletter:

Outport Lesbian is as daring and radically different as you would see in any theatre across the country. In this work Jones effectively captures the isolation and loneliness of a lesbian who dares try to express herself freely. The scene works not because of its shock value (although to see two women kissing

---

[65] A music video, featured in this performance, has lived on and migrated online, where it presently enjoys great popularity. https://www.youtube.com/watch?v=YGCNFxFc6bc

*on film is certainly an attraction) but because it makes a statement that even
the most closeted gays have a dream of expressing; that is, not being ashamed
of your feelings* (GAIN 1986).

In 1996, the play Charlie and the Angel received a glowing write-up in
NGALE's newsletter; written by Jacob Chaos and starring Jody Richardson, as
a gay man and would-be suicide, Chuck Herriott, as Charlie's boyfriend Michael, and Smith, as a deceased drag queen who is the protagonist's guardian
angel. Chaos said he wrote the play "to get on a stool, get in a dress, sing a song
and know that everyone paid."

His partner, Bernardus Stromer-Chaos, also had vivid memories of the
play's run: "He was in full drag, and we invited all the drag queens of St. John's
to come, for free – and they did. The house was sold out. We didn't make any
money but we just enjoyed doing it."

Later that year, the play Lemons was put off at the LSPU Hall and also centred around queer themes. Directed by Danielle Irvine and starring Leah Lewis, Sean Panting, Stephen Cochrane, and a host of others, the play was about
an openly gay man, played by Lewis, who was open to everyone except his
brother. It also featured "a classic fag-hag" and a "closeted man on the verge
of swinging open the door" according to an anonymous review in the NGALE
newsletter which called it "a must-see" and awarded it 9.5 out of 10 triangles
(Outlook 1996).

Meanwhile at Memorial's campus/community radio station CHMR-FM,
Gillian Strong launched a queer radio program called "Under the Rainbow" in
1996. She wasn't the first: Ron Knowling had already hosted a queer radio program called Indecent Exposures in the early 1990s, and probably others too.

That year's Pride Week '96 included a queer-themed poetry and literature
night at the Ship Inn.

Robert Chafe, along with Jillian Keilley and Petrina Bromley, wrote and
staged another queer-themed play the following year in 1997, called Under
Wraps: A Spoke Opera. Put off by Artistic Fraud of Newfoundland, it centred
around two gay protagonists, played by Chafe and Stephen Cochrane.

All the arts were getting into the act. In 1998, the Eastern Edge Gallery
hosted an exhibit of homoerotic art called Jack Was Ev'ry Inch a Sailor. In ensuing years, the Gallery would become known as a bastion for politically and
socially progressive art.

While the St. John's Status of Women Centre had put off Women's Film
Festivals periodically, in 1989, Memorial University professor Noreen Golfman
brought women's filmmaking to a more ambitious level when she founded the
St. John's International Women's Film and Video Festival.

According to Golfman, in its earliest years organizers were focused primarily on addressing the gender gap in women's representation in film-making.

**Women were simply not in the filmmaking game, not behind the camera or
in any significant way above the line, and so the main mission was showcasing**

[women] creators. We were not then thinking consciously of diversity or inclusion in the ways we do now (Golfman 2021).

For the first decade, she says, they struggled to even find and obtain films by women. They forged connections with the National Film Board, as well as other women's festivals. They tapped into a variety of women's creative and professional networks, seeking films and creators.

It was during that first decade, Golfman says, that organizers came to be aware of the burgeoning field of queer film-making.

We started receiving a few solidly queer-centric submissions, all, to my memory, highly personal short films, about coming out and/or self-acceptance. It was exciting to see these films and to recognize ourselves as a welcome site for lesbian content. That changed our whole way of thinking about what we were doing, what our larger purpose might be, and how we might be expanding our audiences.

I have a really vivid memory of introducing one of those films at the LSPU Hall to a full house of boisterous purple-t-shirt-wearing women who were practically screaming with giddy anticipation at the film they were about to see. Those films and the experience of showing them made us much more self-conscious about the festival's role in making such work public and accessible (Ibid.).

Reflecting on the festival's history, Golfman now recognizes that their small working committee was predominantly straight, cisgender, and white. She brought filmmaker Gerry Rogers, a well-known feminist/lesbian activist, onto the working committee, which was transitioning into a formal, not-for-profit board of directors.

Gerry did a lot to help shape our thinking about alternative content, lesbian and queer content. I was determined to expand the board – and eventually paid staff – to ensure we would always have lesbian representation and such has been the case ever since. Today the board — and staff — are far more representative and diverse than I would ever then have imagined was possible (Ibid.).

The same gradual shift applied to Indigenous festival content, she notes, with the caveat that that process was also impacted by an array of federal programs and funding grants.

The shift in the festival's history from a strictly gender-centred approach to programming to a more expansive one somewhat parallels what was happening in other social spheres and activities. I like to think the festival was ahead of other social and arts organizational platforms, and that we took on a broader vision with gusto and determination (Ibid.).

The importance of the arts in supporting, protecting and nurturing queer culture cannot be overstated. For many NLers growing up in repressive environments, it was the one sanctuary in which they could explore identities and grasp at being themselves. The arts environment was often more tolerant and inclusive than other environments. It also provided hope and inspiration during a more violent and repressive era. Joey Shulman spoke to the importance of the arts, drawing on his own experience and identity as "the gay Jew from Newfoundland":

The arts allows people to come out so gently. You get to play roles. You get to literally test out costumes and see how they fit... I will absolutely advocate to my grave the importance of stimulating the artistic side, the expressive side, the non-mathematical, the not-scientific, the not-industrial, that which is not geared towards 'You're going to fill this hole or this square peg or fit into this machinery.' That which is in fact going to entertain the machinery, or stimulate the machinery, or encourage or soothe or ease the pain of the machinery. That's what the arts do.

When I was a teacher in Banff in their arts administration program, there was a woman who was a survivor of the Nazi Holocaust. She was an older woman who volunteered with a small arts organization in a small community. In the class there were younger people who were complaining about the challenges of public relations and fundraising for the arts – they said that they found it really hard to compete with fundraisers for cancer and heart disease and epilepsy, all of these really pull-at-the-heartstrings and hard-times causes. It was hard to compete with them, they said, because we were just the arts. And this woman – who had been a Holocaust survivor as a child – she stood up and she said: 'In our darkest hour, when we had nothing to hope for, someone would recite some poetry. Or someone would sing. Or someone would bring an instrument they had – maybe they were part of a concentration camp orchestra. Or they would scrawl words using charcoal onto a piece of paper – they'd journal and write, and in this way they would have profound conversations about the politics of the day. And we did all this while we were starving! This was what kept us going.' I walked away from that classroom thinking: 'I don't have to apologize to anyone that I'm taking a dollar away from a cure for cancer. Our commitment to the arts is of equal value' (Shulman 2022).

An Artists' Love Story

Bernardus Stromer-Chaos was a Dutch man who moved to Canada in the 1970s. He'd been out as a gay man for most of his life. His grandfather was a German lawyer who was also gay, and had married a Dutch medical doctor. Both were queer, and it was a well-suited match. "They met in London, England at a gay club. And they married each other deliberately, not because it was illegal to be gay in Holland, but as my grandmother used to say: 'I just want a man on my arm to go to the theatre.'"

Stromer-Chaos also had a great-great-aunt who had been lesbian, and lived openly with her lover; they were part of the circle of French artists which included Claude Cahun and Marcel Moore. He had a number of other gay relatives, most of whom had lived fairly openly in the Netherlands. His childhood, consequently, was one filled with tolerance and acceptance for a broad variety of lifestyles. "We had cross-dressing parties, and I knew my parents had had same-sex experiences."

When Stromer-Chaos moved to Canada for graduate studies, he was surprised at how closeted Canadians still were. "I thought it was a bit juvenile. People would get drunk and have sex and the next day they would deny it. It took me a while to figure that out."

Stromer-Chaos enrolled at the Ontario Institute for Studies in Education (OISE) in Toronto. He eventually accumulated three undergraduate degrees, in psychology, fine arts, and special education, as well as a Masters in counselling psychology. He became deeply involved with the queer activism going on in Toronto, and became part of the gay liberation movement in that city in the 1970s. "We were organizing ourselves, we were coming off of the pink pages, we started to identify who was gay friendly. We started developing a network. So I guess in somebody's eyes, we were getting too powerful."

In October 1979, the Toronto Police Services launched a series of raids on the growing movement, targeting known activists. This was shortly before the more well-known 'Bathhouse Raids.' The raids were intended to cow queer activists into silence. "The Toronto Police raided a whole bunch of private homes, including my home," Stromer-Chaos said. "They absolutely destroyed it. And I mean destroyed it! They stole stuff and I never got the money back. So everybody went straight back in the closet and shut up."

But not Stromer-Chaos. He was among those arrested, and was brought to police headquarters and photographed there. He was advised to plead guilty, and was told that if he did so he would just get a slap on the wrist and be released on unsupervised probation. He refused.

I said no. I fought the damn case. Because I wasn't guilty of anything! Period. I didn't get too much sympathy from the gay community at all. None – because everybody was afraid. They were afraid of losing their jobs. It took me about a year and cost me $25,000 to have the case thrown out. My parents wanted me to move back to Holland because they thought it was absurd. I said no. I was already Canadian then, and I decided to stick it out (Stromer-Chaos 2022).

Stromer-Chaos, fed up by the way his fellow activists had turned their backs on him when he fought the police, moved to Halifax. There too he had friends who turned their backs on him, out of fear over his record of having been arrested. He was determined not to let that fear control his own behaviour. When he applied for jobs, including government jobs, there was always a question on the application forms asking whether he had been arrested. He always wrote down yes.

I didn't care about the consequences. I did not care. And this is the funny thing — nobody else cared either! Even in the justice department. My grand-

mother used to say: 'Do whatever it is you need to do, because they're go-
ing to talk about you anyway.' So that's what I did! And my mother used to
say: 'Look everybody straight in the eyes, and tell it like it is.' And I do. I do
(Ibid.).

While living in Halifax, Bernardus had a roommate who one day started
telling him about an incredible young actor he ought to meet, named Jacob
Chaos. After a couple of missed opportunities, Bernardus finally did meet him
at an event at Dalhousie University. It was love at first sight. "I completely,
instantly knew – that was it," he recalls.

Soon after the two met again at a friend's apartment, and Bernardus said
they began talking as though continuing a conversation they'd been having
their entire lives.

That was it. We just knew. That was it. This was during the AIDS period,
so we never actually had any sexual contact for about six months. We went out
to the theatre, we went to the movies, we went out eating, we slept sometimes
together but no sex. We proceeded with caution. And then we found a way to
have intimacy, and then we had safe sex. This was before we knew about safe
sex. There were no HIV tests, it had barely existed, but Jacob had some anxiety
about it so for years and years we had safe sex without realizing that we were
having safe sex.

Jacob was a geek before geeks existed. He was more of a geek than I was.
I used to call it the 'N-factor' – the Newfie factor. Because he was very witty.
Very witty. He could take the piss out of me. Which I loved. I loved it when he
took the piss out of me. I was more of a serious person, but I loved it when he
did that.

But he was very tenacious and serious in his theatre work. He always had
a job. He would fly to PEI, he'd fly to St. John's, he'd fly to Halifax, he'd fly
to Vancouver. To Europe. Once when we were living in Toronto he spent six
weeks in PEI, then came home for a week and then he went for seven weeks in
Vancouver. So he was gone a lot. But that gave me time to do my art. That's
how we lived (Ibid.).

Jacob had grown up on the west coast of the island. There he'd gotten involved as a young teenager with the burgeoning theatre scene being built by
Maxim Mazumdar.

It was like a medium, a place for gay men. There were straights too but it was
pretty well run by gay guys… There, on the west coast around Corner Brook, were
all these artists, these theatre people, and patrons of the arts – including gay arts
of course. We lived there for a while as well, and I would say they were even more
sophisticated than the townies [in St. John's], in terms of the arts (Ibid.).

Jacob had known he was gay from a young age, and left home at the age of
15 to move to Halifax, where he attended university. He paid for it all himself,
working and getting scholarships. He did the theatre program there, completing it when he was only nineteen. He eventually went on to get another un-

dergrad degree in German and German film studies, as well as a Masters in writing. He was prolific with languages, and learned to speak German, Dutch, Spanish, French and Sanskrit.

Many of Jacob's friends knew he was gay, but it was after meeting and falling in love with Bernardus that he came out to his family. "He was very clear," explained Bernardus. "He said: 'I'm gay, so you have a choice to make here. Either you accept me, or you will never see me again.'"

We were a match made. We were a force to contend with, the two of us. People couldn't play us off. We were nerds and geeks before geeks and nerds were chic. The instant we met we started talking to each other as if just picking up a conversation from the day before. And we carried on that conversation until the day he died. We never shut up until the day he died (Ibid.).

Jacob had gotten a scholarship to study at a theatre program in Banff, but then the couple moved back to Toronto together. "We found this most interesting alternative space to live in," explained Bernardus. "It was basically a bombed-out area where rave parties were happening. But we turned it into a palace."

After living together on the mainland, Bernardus suggested they head to Europe for a while. They had no plan, job or destination, but wanted to go and see where life took them.

"We were big risk-takers," recalls Bernardus, a fond smile in his voice. They flew to Holland, and bought a car. They had plans to drive through the Middle East, but first headed toward Austria. While in Salzburg, Jacob was drinking his coffee and reading the morning newspaper one morning and read about the looming war in Yugoslavia, which was on the verge of collapsing into civil war.

"So we looked at each other and said: 'Oh, let's go and watch the war!'" recalled Bernardus. "So we drove into Yugoslavia. And we started photographing the war."

The conflict was in its earliest days, and so the two decided to stick around and document the growing conflict through their photography work. But the conflict escalated quickly.

We were absolutely nuts – it got really bad. We had to drop the car into a ravine and then we broke into a German hotel – everybody there had evacuated – and we spent four days there alone, hiding in the hotel and trying to figure out how to get the hell out of the country. The bombs were flying all around us (Ibid.).

The two eventually managed to slip out of the conflict zone, and escaped into Italy, winding up in Rome.

"That's what our relationship was like," said Bernardus, smiling fondly. Returning to Canada, they decided to move back to Jacob's home in Newfoundland. They moved to Corner Brook, and then relocated to St. John's. For a time, they lived on Franklyn Avenue in the centre-city area. Bernardus remembers the silent, tacit acceptance that eventually came after he and Jacob moved in.

"We never announced that we were gay, but the neighbours knew," he recalled. He said they got stern looks and angry glares from neighbours when they first moved in, clearly signalling the disapproval of those around them. For some reason, things changed after the first several weeks. He remembers one day hearing a loud knock on their fence. He went out, and found an elderly lady, one of their neighbours, standing there with two loaves of bread.

And this elderly lady gave us these two breads. She didn't say a word. And then she walked away. Every two or three weeks from then on, she would give us two breads. 'For the boys,' she said. So that was their way of accepting us. We would then say: 'Thank you very much, it tastes great!' And that was it. We all moved on with our lives (Ibid.).

While working for the John Howard Society for a period, Bernardus decided he wanted to bring up the issue of same-sex benefits. There was no anti-discrimination legislation at the time to guarantee such rights, but he read over his contract, and noticed that his employment contract guaranteed no discrimination on the basis of gender. So he went to the director and told him that he would like same-sex benefits for his partner, since the contract guaranteed no discrimination based on gender. The director brought the matter to the board of directors, and three weeks later the board agreed. However, the entire organization, with close to fifty employees, Bernardus recalls, had to switch insurance providers in order to do so.

Neither of them had any difficulty finding work – Jacob was sought after in acting and other creative fields.

He produced plays and theatre – he did the play Charlie and the Angel – he made movies, he flew here, he flew there, whatever – it didn't matter that he was gone. We believed in never standing in each other's way. Ever. It brings to mind Psalm 42 – 'As you turn a deer toward streams of water, so do you turn my soul toward yourself' (Ibid.).

Bernardus' combination of education and experience was eagerly welcomed in the province, and he found a variety of jobs working in the field of justice, corrections, incarceration and rehabilitation. He worked with the John Howard Society, and was also hired by the NL Department of Justice, where he was put in charge of developing and implementing some of the first sex offender intervention programs in the corrections system. His deep involvement in AIDS activism is discussed in Chapter 7. He continued to apply his uniquely blunt Dutch straightforwardness to his work in the field of justice, thriving on the fact he didn't know or care what the social norms were in the deeply familial, hierarchical workplaces of NL bureaucracy.

He recalls one particular assignment he was given, to fly to Labrador to set up a sex offender program for Indigenous communities there. The experience left an impact on him. He'd had misgivings even before he left about the appropriateness of simply transposing a program designed in St. John's onto an Indigenous community without any culturally-appropriate discussions or input from the community.

"I thought the whole concept of it was ridiculous, but I was told to go. And when I got there, I made a big mistake."

He showed up wearing jeans and a plaid shirt, and carrying his favourite shoulder-bag. It was a lovely old vintage Newfoundland government bag from years earlier that he had found someone throwing out one day. He'd cleaned it up and carried it everywhere with him.

So I walked into this building. The women were on the left, and the men were on the right. They were all sitting on the floor. But as soon as they saw my bag, the mood instantly changed. The women started screeching. It was like they were keening. They were screaming at me (Ibid.).

The bag had triggered painful memories among many of the women, who associated the bag with cruelties perpetrated by Newfoundland government agents in earlier years. The women began screaming at him about the pain they'd endured – about families separated, and other forms of colonial violence.

I didn't say a word. I just let them scream. And when they were finished, I stood up in the middle and I also started to cry. I cried about the loss of my family in the Nazi concentration camps. I told them: 'I don't understand your pain, but I do understand what pain is.' I told them I was gay, I told them I was Jewish, I shared all of my shit. I started bawling my eyes out. I was crying, the women were crying, and then the men started crying too. Here we were, they were all crying, they were sitting in this cold damp building, and I'm supposed to implement this white man's program? It didn't make any sense! And so then I said to them: 'I'm leaving now.' And I left, I turned around and left – I went back to St. John's. I got shit from my bosses in St. John's. But I told them: 'You just shut your mouths. We are fucking white people, we have colonized these people, we killed off the Beothucks, now you're fucking telling me to impose a white-based intervention program?' I said: 'You're fucking cracked.' And I walked out of the office. Later one of them came to me and said: 'You didn't have to be so harsh.' I said: 'I don't care!'

Three weeks later I got a call from the community to come back. We sat in a circle, and we talked. And I let them completely design their own program of how to deal with sex offenders, incorporating certain elements of our existing program. And the Elders became part of the program too. And then we used that program in the prison system there (Ibid.).

Impressed by his work, Bernardus was approached by the Justice Department and offered a job to do a broader overhaul of the provincial prison system. But the work he'd done so far had taken a serious toll on him, and his relationship.

I would come home, and Jacob knew not to talk to me for at least half an hour. I would take a drink and go to my room and write some poetry. I heard fucking horrible stuff every day, and I was working in the dark, trying to figure out how to deal with this stuff. Then in the evenings I would go to the AIDS Committee. Not every evening, but many. I had to write poetry; it was the only way for me to get this stuff out. One time I was writing a piece of poetry and I completely broke down.

That's when Jacob said: 'That's enough.' I had talked to him about the program, and about taking the job. I knew it would be a hard job and I would face a lot of opposition. And he said: 'No. You're not going to do it.' So I said: 'Okay.' And we left (Ibid.).

They left Newfoundland and flew to Vancouver. Jacob's career was thriving. He was getting more work in film and appeared to be on the cusp of breaking big in the acting scene.

"Jacob was doing really well in the movies, he had lots of guest roles," explained Bernardus. Eventually he got offered a lead role in a film which promised to pay well and advance him professionally. Then he got a copy of the screenplay. As he read it, he realized the film was rife with misogynistic violence. "He learned that in the first scene he would cut open this woman's throat. And he said no. He said: 'I'm not going to do that.' As a result, he became blacklisted. He was blacklisted and no longer invited to do auditions."

Jacob's refusal to participate in a film that was laced with misogynistic violence against women cost him his North American acting career. He later wrote a beautiful and poignant poem about the experience, titled Red Sells. He continued doing theatre, but was no longer offered acting roles in film. Facing ostracism in Canada because of his principled position against violence against women in film, he and Bernardus decided it was time to relocate again. This time, they headed south – to South America.

"We went to South America without a job," chuckles Bernardus. "We went there illegally, and we worked there illegally. But within three months we were legal."

They headed first to Ecuador, where Bernardus got a job teaching at a university. But they didn't particularly like it and so they moved on to Chile, where they both got jobs at a university. Jacob resumed his theatrical career as well, setting up Teatro Chaos, the first English-language professional theatre company in the country. He also received a contract to do the recorded English vocals for language labs in all the university-level English courses, effectively becoming the voice of English-language instruction in Chile. He started doing theatre workshops as well. Once more, Jacob's career was taking off, and he appeared poised on the cusp of success.

"And then he got a cough, and everything came crashing down," said Bernardus. The cough got worse, and on New Year's Eve Bernardus took him to the hospital where he was admitted. Four days later they were given the news that Jacob was HIV positive.

That's when the whole world crashed for me. Jacob was on a high in terms of his career. Truly on a high. He was producing, producing, producing. He was producing his own plays, he was happy. My place in the relationship was to make sure everything else was in order, so he didn't have to think about it. I was very good at organizing and promoting. And I was working at the university. He could just walk on the stage, do his thing, and walk off. He was on a high. The year that he died, we had four big contracts lined up. We had such a good life. We were looking at buying a building – the first floor would have been a theatre, the second floor would have been a studio, the third floor would have been our apartment.

All of that collapsed. Completely collapsed (Ibid.).

Jacob's cough became serious, exacerbated by his HIV-positive status, and his health went downhill quickly.

In the last few weeks he couldn't even speak any more, and so we filled up six notebooks between the two of us. When I spoke to him, I could see him trying to speak, I could see him struggling, and so I started to write. I wrote to him, and he could write back. We filled up six full notebooks between the two of us (Ibid.).

With Jacob dying, Bernardus felt obliged to contact his family. Jacob had not been on close terms with them, but some of his relatives flew to Chile just before he died. Jacob and Bernardus had lived an openly gay life; all of their theatre and university colleagues knew they were a gay couple. When Jacob's blood relatives arrived, Bernardus received a quick reminder that he had no legal rights vis-a-vis his life partner.

We were openly gay, at the university, everything. No problems at all. None. But the day he died, I remember sitting there with the [university] president and the other deans, and they were all talking to the brother. I had no rights at all. I had no legal entitlement to him (Ibid.).

Bernardus needed to leave Chile, he did not feel he could continue living in the place they'd made home without his partner, but he wasn't willing to leave Jacob. Jacob had been cremated, and the family wanted the ashes. Legally, it was their right. But Bernardus managed to charm some of the staff, and persuade them to give him the ashes privately. Then he acquired a large, beautiful wooden box, which he filled with dirt. That was the box that was given to the family. Bernardus put Jacob's ashes in a second wooden box, and was able to spirit them out of the country; they remain with him to this day.

"A love like that happens only once," he said.

AFTERWORD

Queer history is always in a state of becoming. The skewed, distorted documentation and interpretation of the past which emerged during the heyday of white, ciscentric, heterosexist, male Euro-colonial historicism means queer history was buried in an assortment of disguises. Clues and whispers lie strewn about the archives; cultural signifiers half-buried, awaiting interpretation and recognition. Daze Jefferies reminds us not to use terms like "discover" or "uncover" when we talk about history; these are *encounters* waiting for us, at both a personal and collective, social level. Reminders of what has always been; encountered again and again; encountered for the first and for the nth time.

This work has been an attempt to share some of my own encounters with this past, and to facilitate further encounters between this past and readers like yourself. I am humbly aware of the fact this work could not have existed without the labour and effort of an army of queer elders, queer researchers, and queer community who helped to make it possible. I am also humbly aware of the fact this work may contain errors, gaps, and distortions that time and further research will hopefully clarify.

But I will conclude by also asserting – very proudly and loudly – the importance of this work, especially at this moment in time.

Learning and promoting queer history is, of course, necessary to ensure that queer youth and residents of all ages see themselves represented in the histories of this place. But it is also a necessary corrective to the biased and distorted histories of Newfoundland and Labrador (and elsewhere) that have predominated in the past. In the same way that we must do a better job of representing the experience of women, Indigenous peoples, and other communities in our histories, we must ensure that the important queer dimensions of our history are incorporated and reflected in our broader understanding of NL's past, present and future.

We live now in a moment where fascism is rearing its ugly head once again more publicly than it has at any point since the demise of Nazi Germany. And just as with its twentieth century Nazi adherents, fascism once again operates through a process of dividing communities, preying on irrational fears and targeting any threats to its totalitarian Christian white masculinist roots.

The cyclical, repetitive nature of historical encounters is rendered all the more obvious by the ways in which fascists uncreatively draw from their own history. Slurs used in the 1980s are recycled again today; bigoted ideas exposed and disposed of decades ago by rational experts rear their heads again. Today's far-right sometimes seems as though it emerges wholesale from a time machine: from 1930s Germany; 1970s Florida; 1980s Brixton. We must know this history in order to recognize it. Children must learn this history – the younger the better – so they may protect themselves from its simplistic, deceptive, destructive lures.

In closing, I would urge you to share this history, teach this history, ensure this history is encountered over and over again by as many as possible. I encourage you to build upon it yourselves. And if you are fortunate enough to be a member of the communities whose histories are presented here, I plead with you to remember your fellow travelers in the struggle for liberation, dignity and autonomy. There is a reason today's fascists are terrified of queer liberation, and it's because in the seeds of that liberation struggle lie the seeds of other communities' liberation. And in the struggles of those communities, lie the seeds of our own liberation. The binary grip of ciscentrism, heterocentrism, and patriarchy is an echo of other binary forms of contestation and oppression along the lines of skin colour, ethnicity, religious belief, and so many more. Colonial thinking is encoded in a binary world, and recognizable in all the different guises oppression wears. Loosening the shackles of one form of oppression reverberates along this interconnected chain, and offers space for other oppressed groups to seek their own freedom. UK-based, Black non-binary writer Travis Alabanza reminds us "that as a cisgender world grapples with a community refusing to be hidden, they must try to reinstate their power by doing what an often colonial gender project knows how to do: divide and regulate." We must not allow ourselves to be divided, and we must leave no one behind in this struggle. Rising violence is a sign of fear and desperation: not just that one community might win its liberation, but that we all might. "At least that would help me make sense of the violence," writes Alabanza. "Of course gender non-conformity and deviation from a binary would attract hurt and cause disruption if it was also a leaving behind of white supremacy. The magnitude matches the cause" (Alabanza 2023).

So let us remember the magnitude of the work we do and the significance of our very existence; let us feel the thrill commensurate with both; and let us carry on this important struggle with pride, humility and love. Stay loud, stay proud, and shine forever.

BIBLIOGRAPHY

ABC News
2003. Prisons face dilemma with transgender inmates. Jan 22, 2023. <https://abcnews. go.com/US/story?id=90919&page=1>.

About Face
1976. Newsletter. Apr 03, 1976, 2(3).

Adams, J.
2009. Alan Jarvis: wit, charm, looks – and a fatal flaw. *The Globe and Mail*.

Advocate
2002. Former prisoner undergoing sex change files suit. *Advocate*. Aug 29, 2022.

Alabanza, T.
2023. *None of the Above: Reflections on Life Beyond the Binary*. The Feminist Press.

Anderson, D.
1997. Laura Sabia, 1916-1996. *Canadian Woman Studies*, 17(1):31.

Andrieux, J.
2013. *The White Fleet: A History of the Portuguese Handliners*. St. John's: Flanker Press.

Art Gallery of Nova Scotia.
2006. *Two Artists Time Forgot*. Halifax: Art Gallery of Nova Scotia.

ArQuives
1993. Tom Warner fonds. Audio cassette of interviews. 2003-047/11T

Bailey, I.
1995. Local doctor fears 'AIDS capital' label. *The Evening Telegram*, Apr 5, 1995.

Baird, M.
1992. Newfoundland does have an AIDS problem. *The Evening Telegram*, Jun 28, 1992.

Barnholden, P. & P. Brake
1991. A gay man's guide to erotic safer sex. *The Muse*, Feb 15, 1991.

Barron, T.
1996. Priest's views border on hate literature, gays say. *The Evening Telegram*, Oct 31, 1996.
1995a. Gays, lesbians taking on feds to get equality. *The Evening Telegram*, Nov 17, 1995.
1995b. No special AIDS stain in C.B.N. *The Evening Telegram*, Dec 01, 1995.

Bartlett, D.
2007. "Harold Horwood." *The Canadian Encyclopedia*.

Barton, P.
1996. The dark side of being gay. NGALE: Outlook Newsletter. Mar/Apr.

Bebout, R.
2003. *Promiscuous Affection: A Life in the Bar, 1969-2000*. Self-published. <www.rbebout.com/ bar/into.htm>.

Belec, B.
2000. Timing key in HIV trial. *The Evening Telegram*, Apr 12, 2000.
1995. Ruling gives gays protection in code. *The Evening Telegram*. Aug 25. 1995.
1994. AIDS group in good shape no thanks to province. *The Evening Telegram*, May 02, 1994.

Berry, E.
2023. 'Her power became a catalyst for my own': the power of Sylvia Plath. *The Guardian*, Feb 11, 223.

Board of Regents
1988. Guidelines respecting HIV infection and AIDS. Memorial University, Nov 10,

1988.

Bouzane, L.

1990. Memories of the struggle for Matrimonial Property Legislation. *Waterlily*, 2(3):9.

Brake, P.

1990. Homosexuality and the church. *The Muse*, Feb 16, 1990.

Brenoff, A. & C. Berry

1983. Fox seeks to clear his name. *Ashbury Park Press*, Jun 12, 1983.

Bruner, S.

2006. Cross-Canada Odyssey. *Xtra Magazine*, Mar 29, 2006.

Buchanan, R.

1986. Prejudice and assault: Is this a university? *The Muse*, Oct 17, 1986.

Bulgin, I.

1985. Newfoundland gays urge board reading of Charter rights. *The Body Politic*, Nov 1985.

Canadian Human Rights Commission (CHRC)

1988. Acquired Immunodeficiency Syndrome (AIDS): Policy & Background Notes. May 1998.

1980. Presentation by the Canadian Human Rights Commission to the Special Joint Committee of the Constitution of Canada. Nov 1980.

Canadian Press

1990. Newfoundland police charge 20 protesting women's centre cuts. Apr 03, 1990.

Cannon, A.

1984. Aaarrgghh!! *The Muse*, Apr 03, 1984.

Case, T.

1991. Sex and the newspaper. *Editor & Publisher*, Mar 30, 1991.

Catalyst

1992. St. John's Women's Centre Organizational Review: Final Options Report. *Catalyst*, Dec 01, 1992.

CFUW

2023. Dr. Laura Villela Sabia, O.C. 1916-1996. <cfuw.org/bio-past-presidents/dr-laura-sabia-o-c-1916-1996/>.

Cleary, R.

1996a. Grits not ready with changes to rights code. *The Evening Telegram*, Apr 15, 1996.

1996b. Human Rights Code best addressed by province. *The Evening Telegram*, Apr 25, 1996.

1991. Students' union to oversee content of MUN newspaper. *The Evening Telegram*, Feb 19, 1991.

Clement, D.

2012. Equality Deferred: The Origins of the Newfoundland Human Rights State. *Acadiensis*, 41(1): 102-127.

Cochrane, D.

1996. AIDS care lacking in Atlantic Provinces. *The Muse*, Sep 13, 1996.

Cowan, S.

1991. Gay and Lesbian Supplement refreshing. *The Muse*, Feb 22, 1991.

CRIAW

1992. The St. John's Women's Centre addresses the issue of homophobia. CRIAW Newsletter, 12(3):3.

Dayson, P.

1991. One day I will have to come home. *The Muse*, Feb 15, 1991.

Dewar, E.

2020. Reflections on the Second Wave: A Feminist Journalist Remembers Herself. Personal Blog. <https://elainedewar.blogspot.com/2020/03/part-iii-reflections-on-second-wave.

html>.

Dicks, P.

1990. Human Rights. House of Assembly. Hansard 41st General Assembly Second Session 1990-1991. Newfoundland and Labrador, Nov 30, 1990.

Dicks, W.

1991. Lesbian, gay issue of MUN newspaper may cause fee hike. *The Evening Telegram*, Feb 16, 1991.

1990a. Police break up office occupation. *The Evening Telegram*, Mar 31, 1990.

1990b. Support pouring in for protestors. *The Evening Telegram*, Mar 30, 1990.

Dimmock, G.

1994a. Commission accepts Nolan's complaint. *The Express*, Feb 16, 1994.

1994b. Complaints commission to hold inquiry into allegations of misconduct by RNC officers. *The Express*, Jan 26, 1994.

1994c. No complaint lies against officer who allegedly assaulted man, analysis says. *The Express*, Feb 23, 1994.

1994d. RNC charge pen guard. *The Express*, May 19, 1994.

1994e. RNC officers deny charges. *The Express*, Mar 30, 1994.

1993a. Complainant feels he's on trial, not police. *The Express*, Oct 06, 1993.

1993b. Complainant files appeal with PCC. *The Express*, Oct 27, 1993.

1993c. Lack of evidence to back alleged allegations, RNC probe finds. *The Express*, Oct 27, 1993.

1993d. RNC's internal probe in its final stages. *The Express*, Sep 29, 1993.

1993e. Victim of alleged assault to sue RNC. *The Express*, Nov 10, 1993.

Dopler, S.

1996. Lesbophobia in feminist organizations: an examination of the effect of organizational structure and sociopolitical context on the expression of lesbophobia. Carleton University.

Downer, D.

1997. *Turbulent Tides: A Social History of Sandy Point*. ESP Press.

Dwyer, A.

1992. Battling virus by educating. *The Express*, Jul 15, 1992.

Fernando, M.L.D. & U. Sirinivasan

2009. Julius Hoenig. *BMJ*, 339:b3715-b3715. <https://doi.org/10.1136/bmj.b3715>.

Flynn, M.

1994. AIDS fear hurting CBN youth. *The Evening Telegram*, Nov 04, 1994.

1993. No HIV infection epidemic in C.B.N. area, nurse says. *The Evening Telegram*, Jan 14, 1993.

French, RJ.

1991. Muse staffers are less than talented. *The Muse*, Feb 22, 1991.

Fulton, E.K.

1994. Gay and Proud. *Maclean's*, 107:36-39.

GAIN

1987. A Presentation from the Gay Association in Newfoundland to the Minister of Justice of Newfoundland and Labrador in Favour of Including the Term 'Sexual Orientation' in the Newfoundland & Labrador Human Rights Code.

1986. Gain Newsletter, Jan 25, 1986.

Gaylord, D.

1978. A visit with the gay community of St. John's Nfld. *Tab*, 23(4):8.

GALT

1991. Here to stay: Lesbians and gays in Newfoundland and Labrador fighting for our rights.

Gendertalk

2002. Radio Program. #377, Sep 16, 2002. <http://www.gendertalk.com/radio/programs/350/gt377.shtml>.

Globe and Mail

1982. Four cases of the 'gay plague' have surfaced in Canada (Montreal, Vancouver and Ontario). *Globe and Mail*, Jul 21, 1982.

Goodhand, M.

2017. *Runaway Wives and Rogue Feminists: The Origins of the Women's Shelter Movement in Canada*. Fernwood Publishing.

Goundrey, S.

1975. A History of the Newfoundland Status of Women Council from Apr 1972-Jan 1975. Newfoundland Status of Women Council.

Graven, M.

1980. Kin of murdered transsexual says they knew of no ex-lover. *The Daily Register*, Dec 18, 1980.

Gray, S.

1972. Still a need for consciousness-raising. St. John's Status of Women Centre Newsletter.

Greene, S.

1989. Presentation to Hughes Inquiry prepared. *Waterlily*, 1990:15.

Gullage, P.

1991. Lessons unlearned. *The Sunday Express*, Mar 17, 1991.

1990. Winning ways: Anatomy of a political vistory; or how Newfoundland women stared down the feds. *The Sunday Express*, May 27, 1990.

Hallett, B.

1987. MUN GALA ratified by CSU, NORMUN nixed. *The Muse*, Jan 30, 1987.

Hannon, G.

1997. ...deemed necessary to discriminate... *The Body Politic*, Sep 1977.

Hanrahan, C.

2018. *Unchained Man: the Arctic life and times of Captain Robert Abram Bartlett*. Portugal Cove-St. Phillips: Boulder Publications.

Harnett, C.

1995. Out on Campus provides gays, lesbians with support at Memorial University. *The Evening Telegram*, Feb 13, 1995.

Harrington, H.

1991. Local paper makes national headlines. *The Muse*, Feb 22, 1991.

Harrington, M.

1994. Danielle, Charles Henry. *Dictionary of Canadian Biography*, vol. 13. Toronto: University of Toronto Press.

Harrison, S. & E. Kirzner

1991. Friends plan memorial for Smith. *NOW Magazine*, Feb 21, 1991.

Hart, D.

1991. Hey! The Muse is ok! *The Muse*, Mar 01, 1991.

Hartery, L.

2001. The St. John's Rape Crisis Center & the women who made it happen.

Hebbard, G.

1992. Lawyer backs up commission critics. *The Evening Telegram*, Dec 11, 1992.

Hedderson, M. & A. Labonte

1999. Homophobia awareness campaign gets light response. *The Muse*, Jan 22, 1999.

Heritage Newfoundland and Labrador

2022. LSPU Hall. <heritage.nf.ca/articles/society/lspu-hall.php>.

Higgins, J.

2012. Mount Cashel Orphanage Abuse Scandal. Heritage Newfoundland and Labrador. <heritage.nf.ca/article/politics/wells-government-mt-cashel.php>.

Hill, K.

1991. Good manners more important than lives. *The Muse*, Feb 1991.

Hilliard, W.

1997. Gays, lesbians have waited too long for basic rights: groups. *The Evening Telegram*, Jun 17, 1997.

Hillier, D.

1988a. Newfoundland slow to help AIDS victims. *The Evening Telegram*, May 28, 1988.

1988b. World AIDS Day: emphasis on youth. *The Evening Telegram*, Dec 01, 1988.

Hoenig, J. & E. Duggan.

1974. Sexual and other abnormalities in the family of a transsexual. *Psychiatrica Clinica*, 7:334-346.

Jackman, M.

2018. The Gossip Miss: 25 years after the Village Mall affair. *The Independent*, Mar 04, 2018.

2016. Pride, visibility, and the blue uniform. *The Independent*, Jul 28, 2016.

Jackson, C.

1995. Rude cops biggest rap against RNC. *The Evening Telegram*, Mar 21, 1995.

1993. Settlement reached in HIV case. *The Evening Telegram*, Apr 03, 1993.

Jackson, P.

1991. Gays, lesbians cite Wells for blocking legislation. *The Evening Telegram*. Jun 27, 1991.

James, B.

1990. Email correspondence between James and other activists. QEII Archives and Special Collections, uncatalogued.

Kakutani, M.

1981. Theatre: 'Oscar Remembered'. *The New York Times*, Jun 24, 1981.

Kearney, W.

1991. We're your obsession. *The Muse*, Mar 01, 1991.

Keats, P.

1989. Sexuality: power and access are the keys to sexual abuse. *Waterlily*, 2.

Kelleherr, T.

1982. Letter from Terrence Kelleher, NLHRA Co-ordinator, to RGI Fairweather, Chief Commissioner of Canadian Human Rights. NLHRA Archive, Dec 22, 1982.

Kiefte, B.

1989. Difficult decisions, uneasy choices. *The Muse*, Mar 3, 1989.

Kinsman, G.

1993. Hughes Commission: making homosexuality the problem once again. *New Maritimes*, 9(3): 17.

1991. CBC Radio recording. CBC Internal Archives.

Knowling, R.

1991. Gay man upset. *The Muse*, Mar 01, 1991.

Lacey, B.

1989. Profile – Diane Duggan 1942-1989. *Women Speak*, 7(1): 10.

Leblanc, R.

1998. Poster contest, campaign missing. *The Express*, Dec 01, 1998.

Leonard, W.

1977a. CHAN narrowly escapes folding. *The Body Politic*, 30.

1977b. City's first gay bar opens. *The Body Politic*, 37.

Lewis, B. & R. Coates

1981. Moral lessons, fatal cancer. *The Body Politic*, 77.

Lockyer, W.

1924. Love – The greatest thing in the world. *The Evening Telegram*, Apr 19, 1924.

Loney, B.

1992. Police complaints process finalizes. *The Evening Telegram*, Nov 26, 1992.

Lynk, M.

1989. Being gay in Newfoundland: An activist's story. *The Sunday Express*, Mar 05, 1989.

Macafee, M.

1997. Gays, lesbians pursue human rights fight. *The Evening Telegram*, Nov 17, 1997.

Mackenzie, A.

1982. Lust with a very proper stranger. *The Body Politic*, 82.

Mandville, S.

1989. Opposition to homosexuality expressed. *The Muse*, Feb 24, 1989.

May, L.

1988. Gay athletics scrapped by Board of Governors. *The Muse*, Oct 07, 1988.

Mazumdar, M.

1981. *Invitation to the Dance*. Toronto: Personal Library, Publishers.

1977. *Oscar Remembered*, Toronto: Personal Library, Publishers.

McLeod, D.

1996. *Lesbian and Gay Liberation in Canada: A Selected Annotated Chronology, 1964-1975.* Toronto: ECW Press/Homewood Books.

Mitchell, D.

1990. Gay and lesbian support group formed. *The Muse*, Oct 05, 1990.

Muise, G.

1990. Friend beaten for being gay. *The Muse*, Mar 02, 1990.

Murphy, J.

1996. Gay issue over, says parish priest. *The Evening Telegram*, Nov 04, 1996.

Murphy, L.

1981. Frustration in Newfoundland. *The Body Politic*, Jul/Aug 1981.

Murphy, M.

1996. Homophobia taints day of awareness. *The Muse*, Feb 16, 1996.

Muzychka, M.

1982. Local feminist speaks to students. *The Muse*, Feb 26, 1982.

NAN

1995. NAN's News Newsletter. Jun.

1994. NAN's News Newsletter. Nov.

Newfoundland v. Newfoundland

1995. Newfoundland (Human Rights Commission) v. Newfoundland (Minister of Employment and Labour Relations), CanLII 6262 (NL SC), <https://canlii.ca/t/1p8w4>.

NLHRA

1984. COLL 111. MUNL Archives & Special Collections.

1973. Record of Meeting, Jun 11, 1973.

NSWC

1976. Au revoir, Mary Jane (The story *The Evening Telegram* refused to print by Sally Davis). Newsletter, Aug 1976.

1975. Newsletter, Mar 1975.

1974. Some thoughts on the future of NSWC. Newsletter, Jan-Feb 1974.

1973a. Newsletter, Apr 1973.

1973b. Communique, Dec 1973.

1973c. The women and film festival. Newsletter, Sep 1973.

1972. Newsletter, Oct-Nov 1972.

NGALE
1996. NGALE Queries Party Leaders on Homosexual Issues. NGALE Newsletter, 1(2).
Noftall, B.
1991. Deep Throat. *The Muse*, Feb 15, 1991.
Outlook
1996. NGALE Newsletter, 1(5).
Paddock, J.
1986. Newfoundland NDP favours gay rights. *The Body Politic*, August 1986.
Parsons, B.
1984. Why I won't join da Muse. *The Muse*, Oct 17, 1984.
Parsons, R.
1990. No no yick! Supplement again. *The Muse*, Feb 23, 1990.
Paterson, J.
2003. Changing genders, changing attitudes. *Times Colonist Monitor*, May 18, 2003.
Payne, L.
1991. Women elected in politics have nowhere to go but up. *Waterlily*, 3(2): 15.
Payne, M.
1972. Women's movement underway in St. John's. *The Muse*, Jul 24, 1972.
Peavy, D.
2012. "Miss Mabel Mary Baudains, Matron, Bishop Spencer Lodge (1923-1939)." *Bishop Jones Memorial Hostel Group Newsletter* Volume 4, Issue 3, October 2012.
Pope, S. & J. Burnham
1999. Change within and without: The modern women's movement in Newfoundland and Labrador. In Kealey, L. (ed.) *Pursuing Equality: Historical Perspectives on Women in Newfoundland & Labrador*. St. John's: ISER Books.
Popert, K.
1976. Gays find organization means better life. *The Body Politic*, Sep 1976.
Pride Toronto
2022. History. <pridetoronot.com/pride-toronto/history/>.
PACSW
1992. Out of the Closet and Into the Light: Improving the Status of Lesbians in Newfoundland and Labrador. December 1992.
R. v. Mercer
1993. CanLII 7755 (NL CA). <https://canlii.ca/t/2dx6x>.
Real Women Canada
1986. *Secretary of State* and Lesbianism. Jan 1986.
Reardon, G.
1979. Gay Lore: A Study of the Homosexual Movement in St. John's. Folklore and Language Archives, MUNL.
Riordan, M.
1996. *Out Our Way: Gay and Lesbian Life in the Country*. Toronto: Between the Lines.
RNC Public Complaints Commission
1994. Final decision rendered by Eaton. Aug 30, 1994.
Rodgers, G. & C. Rodgers
1991. Muse not a paper by fascists for fascists. *The Muse*, Feb 1991.
Rooney, F.
2017. *Working the Rock: Newfoundland and Labrador in the photographs of Edith S. Watson, 1890-1930*. Portugal Cove-St. Phillips: Boulder Publications.
Ryan, S.
1991. Engineers demand a real, unsubsidized newspaper. *The Muse*, Feb 22, 1991.
Sheehan, A. & M. Graven

1980. Murder suspect held after 12-hours siege. *The Daily Register*, Dec 17, 1980.

Smallwood, W.

1982. Mama probably didn't tell you. *The Muse*, Mar 26, 1982.

Smith, J.

1993. Province reviewing judicial appointments. *The Evening Telegram*, Oct 23, 1993.

Special Committee

1971. Report of the Special Committee concerned with the Report of the Royal Commission on the Status of Women in Canada.

Screenivasan, U.

1981. A study of effeminate behaviour in boys. Doctoral (PhD) thesis, MUNL.

St. Croix, C.

1991. The politics of protest: Activism – assimilation vs. confrontation. *The Muse*, Feb 15, 1991.

1990. Society won't accept reality. *The Muse*, Feb 16, 1990.

1989. Reader reacts to homophobic letter. *The Muse*, Mar 03, 1989.

SJSWC

n.d. Time for Action: A Brief Discussing the Needs of lesbian Feminists. PANL.

2002. History – Through Our Eyes. Newsletter, Summer 2002.

1992. Letter from Steering Committee to Membership. Jul 06, 1992.

1991. Women Centre Support Group. PANL.

1985. Women and Equality: A Presentation to the Federal Committee on Equality. Aug 26, 1985.

1972. Proposal for a women's centre in St. John's, Newfoundland. Submitted to the Secretary of State Office, Fall 1972.

Stacey, J.

1994a. Complainant wasn't drunk hearing told. *The Evening Telegram*, Jul 06, 1994.

1994b. Cop relates another version of Nolan case. *The Evening Telegram*, Jul 20, 1994.

1994c. Lockup officer testifies. *The Evening Telegram*, Jul 09, 1994.

1994d. Nolan says cops arrested him only because he is homosexual. *The Evening Telegram*, Jul 07, 1994.

1994e. Officers contradict each other at hearing. *The Evening Telegram*, Jul 19, 1994.

1994f. No grounds for arrest of gay man complains lawyer. *The Evening Telegram*, Jul 22, 1994.

Stagg, R.

1994. Gay Culture: Gay Immigration to St. John's from Other Parts of Newfoundland. Folklore and Language Archives, MUNL.

Stein, M.

2009. WMST 6128: Queer History [syllabus]. York University.

Stoodley, R.

1984a. Come out, come out wherever you are. *The Muse*, Mar 23, 1984.

1984b. Shedding some light. *The Muse*, Mar 23, 1984.

1983. Gays at MUN: A cramped closet. *The Muse*, Oct 28, 1983.

Stowbridge, L.

1988. Eight infected with AIDS virus at Memorial. *The Sunday Express*, Apr 17, 1988.

1987. Time to face gruesome facts. *The Sunday Express*, May 03, 1987.

Sullivan, D.

1995. Life lessons. *The Evening Telegram*, Mar 26, 1995.

Sweet, B.

1997. AIDS count dropping in C.B.N. *The Evening Telegram*, Oct 21, 1997.

Sweet, B.

2019. Was Charles Danielle out and proud in 1800s St. John's? *The Evening Telegram*. July

13 2019.

Taylor, J.

1974. 'What do you do at the women's centre?' A Study of Some Canadian Women's Centres. Secretary of State, Spring 1974.

Temple, J. & J. Taylor

1997. LBGT MUN target of homophobia. *The Muse*, Oct 31, 1997.

The Body Politic

1983. Lesbian & Gay Pride. *The Body Politic*, Sep 1983.

1982. Biking for custody across the country. *The Body Politic*, Sep 1982.

1974. Author halts Montreal production. *The Body Politic*, Jan 1974.

The Evening Telegram

1995. Gays, lesbians seek national link. *The Evening Telegram*, Apr 16, 1995.

1994. Roberts appoints four women to complaint panel. *The Evening Telegram*, Jan 05, 1994.

1991a. Checking on the police. *The Evening Telegram*, Mar 26, 1991.

1991b. Gay, Lesbian Pride Week proclaimed. *The Evening Telegram*, Jun 27, 1991.

1991c. MUN president apologizes for comments about gay articles in student newspaper. *The Evening Telegram*, Feb 20, 1991.

1991d. Wants gay rights entrenched. *The Evening Telegram*, May 16, 1991.

1990a. Letters of support pour in for women protesting budget cuts. *The Evening Telegram*, Apr 03, 1990.

1990b. MP wants women's centres to stay open. *The Evening Telegram*, Apr 06, 1990.

1990c. Federal minister agrees to meet with women over centre funding. *The Evening Telegram*, Apr 10, 1990.

1990d. Funding for women's centres must be reinstated, speakers say. *The Evening Telegram*, Apr 09, 1990.

1990e. In support of women's centres. *The Evening Telegram*, Apr 12, 1990.

1990f. Rally scheduled for this afternoon in support of city Women's Centre. *The Evening Telegram*, Apr 09, 1990.

1990g. Support for women's centres. *The Evening Telegram*, Apr 07, 1990.

1990h. Women come out for 'Weiner Roast'. *The Evening Telegram*, Apr 01, 1990.

1990i. Wrong decision reversed. *The Evening Telegram*, May 07, 1990.

1989. Community mourns loss of activist Diane Duggan. *The Evening Telegram*, Apr 28, 1989.

1988. Local AIDS association plans information hot-line. *The Evening Telegram*, Jan 27, 1988.

1987a. Gay group disappointed no action taken on code request. *The Evening Telegram*, Jun 16, 1987.

1987b. Lack of AIDS policy has school board concerned. *The Evening Telegram*, Mar 27, 1987.

1987c. Name of laest AIDS victim won't be released: Twomey. *The Evening Telegram*, Apr 10, 1987.

1987d. Province launches AIDS education campaign. *The Evening Telegram*, Oct 08, 1987.

1985. Gays make donation deal. *The Evening Telegram*, Dec 07, 1985.

1977. Women's Institute recognizes value of strong family unit. *The Evening Telegram*, Sep 23, 1977.

1953. Speaker at B.&P. Women's Club. *The Evening Telegram*, Oct 13, 1953.

1951. Present charter at meeting. *The Evening Telegram*, Oct 10, 1951.

The Express

1955. RNC watchdog files first report. *The Express*, Mar 22, 1995.

The Monitor

1972. Gander club holds workshop on status of women report. *The Monitor*, May 27, 1972.

The Muse

1991a. Are categories of identity even necessary? *The Muse*, Feb 15, 1991.

1991b. Gays and lesbians sick and perverted. *The Muse*, Feb 22, 1991.

1991c. Lettertorial. *The Muse*, Feb 22, 1991.

1991d. The gay and lesbian supplement and the importance of being... *The Muse*, Feb 15, 1991.

1991e. To be lesbian and to hear the heterosexual roar. *The Muse*, Feb 15, 1991.

1991f. Those disgusting Obsession ads. *The Muse*, Feb 22, 1991.

1991g. Gay, but not today. *The Muse*, Feb 02, 1991.

1989. Many and varied responses to Gay and Lesbian supplement. *The Muse*, Feb 24, 1989.

1974. Out of the closets, into the world. *The Muse*, Feb 01, 1974.

1965. Lutheran Pastor claims homosexual tie O.K. *The Muse*, Jan 22, 1965.

The Sunday Express

1990. Students support women's centres. *The Sunday Express*, Apr 08, 1990.

The Western Star

1952. Nfld. seaman convicted of manslaughter. *The Western Star*, Apr 04, 1952.

Thistle, W.W.

1992. Universities in the 1990s: Liability and litigation or prudence and prevention. MUNL.

Time Magazine

1975. The Sergeant v. the Air Force. *Time Magazine*, 106(10).

Vaughan, A.

1991. Board of Regents' rep has a go too. *The Muse*, Feb 22, 1991.

Vaughan-Jackson, M.

1996. Puppet masters. *The Evening Telegram*, Jun 28, 1996.

1994. Gay man wins against cops. *The Evening Telegram*, Sep 03, 1994.

Verge, L.

1990a. Human Rights. Newfoundland and Labrador House of Assembly Hansard 41st General Assembly Second Session 1990-1991, Nov 29.

1990b. Human rights. Newfoundland and Labrador House of Assembly Hansard 41st General Assembly Second Session 1990-1991, Nov 30.

Wadden, N.

2008. *Yesterday's News*. St. John's: DCR Publishing.

Warner, T.

2022. *Never Going Back: A History of Queer Activism in Canada*. Toronto: University of Toronto Press.

Waterhouse, J.

1980. Gays unfairly treated. *The Muse*, Nov 28, 1980.

Whelan, M.

1987a. Legal status of AIDS altered. *The Evening Telegram*, Nov 14 1987.

1987b. Public Health starts AIDS test. *The Evening Telegram*, Nov 03, 1987.

1987c. Schools develop AIDS guidelines. *The Evening Telegram*, Oct 15, 1987.

1987d. Social denial could prove deadly. *The Evening Telegram*, Nov 11, 1987.

Whiffen, G.

1994. Policewoman says Nolan arrested because he was too drunk to take care of himself. *The Evening Telegram*, Apr 30, 1994.

Whitaker, R.

1990. Gay Studies group conducts forum. *The Muse*, Feb 16, 1990.

1988a. Committee set up to examine AIDS issue. *The Muse*, Jan 15, 1988.

1988b. No gays on AIDS committee. *The Muse*, Jan 22, 1988.

Whitehead, K.

2010. Three accounts of a working life in Newfoundland: Violet Cherrington, 1922-1952. Women's History Review 19, 1.

Will, G.

1989. Condoms for students registering at university. *The Evening Telegram*, Sep 06, 1989.

Yaffe, B.

1987a. Confidentiality of AIDS victim will be protected. *The Sunday Express*, Oct 18, 1987.

1987b. Rise in AIDS cases causing panic in province. *The Sunday Express*, Apr 26, 1987.

YW Resource

1974. Resource, 4(7):3.

YWCA Canada

1974a. Extraordinatory Board Meeting Minutes, Apr 18, 1974.

1974b. Montreal raises some questions about Model 3. Resource, 4(7):1.

Zeidler, M.

2019. 25 years ago, this LGBT landmark in Vancouver took on 'big brother' and won. CBC News, October 20, 2019. <cbc.ca/news/british-columbia/little-sisters-cbsa-challenge-1.5325456>.

Cited Interviewees

Author's note: There were many interviews that were conducted over the course of the research for this book. I appreciate everyone that took the time to speak with me, and while not all of your information made it into the final copy, your words helped shape this history. To those who requested anonymity, thank you for your contribution and your courage.

Adams, Noah 2022

Atkinson, Marion 2021

Baggs, Roger 2022

Balka, Ellen 2021

Bandak, Patricia 2022

Barnholden, Patrick 2021

Bourgeois, Greg 2022

Brookes, Christopher 2022

Bishop, Derrick 2021. 2023

Boland, Rick 2021

Bragg, John 2021

Buchanan, Roberta 2021

Caines, Brian, 2022

Cairney, Steven 2022

Calcott, Michael 2021

Chaisson, Walt 2021

Crandall, Jennifer 2022, 2023

Dewling, Joan 2022

Dicks, Paul 2023

Dopler, Sharp 2021, 2022

Duff, Shannie 2022

Elder, Kris 2022

Escott, Ann 2021, 2022

Finlay, Aimee 2022

Golfman, Noreen 2021

Goundrey, Jane 2022

Gray, Sharon 2022, 2023

Hammond, Vicky 2023

Hartman, Dawn 2022

Hearn, Kayla 2022

Hickey, Gemma 2022

Hodder, Brian 2022

Jackman, Michael 2022

Johnson, Roger 2021

Kelly, Larry 2021

Kennedy, RM 2022

Kinsman, Gary 2021, 2023

ABOUT THE AUTHOR

Rhea Rollmann is an award-winning journalist, writer and audio producer based in St. John's, NL. She's a founding editor of The Independent NL and her journalism has appeared in *Briarpatch Magazine*, *CBC*, *Xtra Magazine*, *Chatelaine*, *PopMatters*, *Riddle Fence* and more. Her academic work has been published in the *Journal of Gender Studies*, *Labor Studies Journal*, *Canadian Woman Studies*, *Just Labour: A Journal of Work and Society*, *Canadian Theatre Review*, *Canadian Review of Sociology*, *Screen Bodies* and elsewhere. She also has a background in labour organizing and queer/trans activism, and is Program Director at CHMR-FM, a community radio station in St. John's, NL.

Photo credit: Tania Heath

Printed in the USA
CPSIA information can be obtained
at www.ICGtesting.com
LVHW040029050124
768234LV00008B/186